SENECA ON SOC

Seneca on Society

A Guide to *De Beneficiis*

MIRIAM T. GRIFFIN

OXFORD
UNIVERSITY PRESS

OXFORD

UNIVERSITY PRESS

Great Clarendon Street, Oxford, OX2 6DP,
United Kingdom

Oxford University Press is a department of the University of Oxford.
It furthers the University's objective of excellence in research, scholarship,
and education by publishing worldwide. Oxford is a registered trade mark of
Oxford University Press in the UK and in certain other countries.

Published in the United States of America by Oxford University Press
198 Madison Avenue, New York, NY 10016, United States of America

British Library Cataloguing in Publication Data

Data available

ISBN 978–0–19–924548–2 (Hbk)
ISBN 978–0–19–872331–8 (Pbk)

In Memoriam
Leighton Reynolds

Preface

This book has been many years in gestation. Over thirty years ago, when I was completing *Seneca: A Philosopher in Politics*, a general book on the relation of Seneca's life to his work, I was already aware that the seven books of *De beneficiis* had been seriously neglected and needed explication. There had been virtually nothing to help the reader of this complex and fascinating work since the comments in Latin of the learned scholar Justus Lipsius (1547–1606), whose profound understanding of Senecan argument and whose exceptional grasp of Roman law and history I had found, and have continued to find, invaluable, as have all students of Seneca. But the length and apparent disorganization of the work had clearly deterred scholars after him from analysing its arguments or its structure. Historians, of course, had made considerable use of its many anecdotes and examples, but without paying much attention to the arguments which they illustrate or elucidate, and without exploiting to the full the many clues which the work provides to social and political attitudes and norms.

After studies on the reign of Nero and on the place of philosophy in Roman intellectual and political life, I returned to *De beneficiis* and began considering how to make it more accessible and usable to students and colleagues. At that point I consulted Leighton Reynolds, who, having edited Seneca's letters and dialogues, was working on the text of *De beneficiis* and *De clementia*. I explained my feeling that, even were I capable of producing a full commentary, it would be so long as to deter even more the readers who already found the work daunting. I was also aware that quite a lot of continuous explanation was needed of its philosophical and historical background and of its complex structure, to make it more intelligible. What did he think of the idea of a series of essays, followed by annotated synopses of the books, to give the shape of the argument, so that readers could see how the bit that interested them was intended by Seneca to be understood? I asked in trepidation, for nothing could be further from the philological interests of Leighton who, as he said himself, liked 'boiling things down', not 'building them up'. In fact, he was highly encouraging about the project and read some of the sketches of the early chapters. Moreover, he was always there to be consulted about the text, even in his last illness. His death in December of 1999 was to me, as to so many others, a great personal and professional loss.

How great a loss, I only fully appreciated when I agreed, five years later, to translate the work, in collaboration with Brad Inwood, for the University of Chicago series of Seneca translations. Realizing that nothing could give me more help with the synopses and notes than discussing translation with an expert on Seneca's philosophy, I took time out from the book on *De beneficiis*, to wrestle with the language of the work itself in detail. By that time, largely thanks to some months of research at the Institute for Advanced Study at Princeton in 2000, I had drafts of all but Chapters 8 and 9 of the book and was completing the notes to the Synopses. Some of this work fed into the Introduction and the Notes in the joint translation volume, but the flow of knowledge was mainly the other way, and the *beneficia* I derived from discussions with Brad Inwood, who was always willing to explain difficult arguments to a non-philosopher, are immeasurable.

I owe also a great debt to Peter Brunt, once Camden Professor of Ancient History, who was working on Stoicism at Rome until he died in 2005. His knowledge of Stoicism, and his scepticism about its practical application by the Roman elite—soon to be more generally accessible in a collection of his papers to be called *Studies in Stoicism*—inspired both my books on Seneca. This one would have been much improved, had he and Leighton Reynolds still been alive when it was finally finished.

Many others have helped me at different times and in different ways. In 1997, I was fortunate to encounter a visiting student from Bonn, Michael Brinkmann, who was writing a thesis on the dialogue between Seneca and Nero composed by Tacitus in *Annals* 14. 53–6. His later doctoral thesis, published in 2002, is the best account of the two speeches as a pair. Jane F. Gardner I pestered, never in vain, with queries about Roman law; likewise Bruce Frier and my cousin Robert Natelson. At a late stage, I appealed to Boudewijn Sirks for help with the notes on the complicated discussion of |forms of ownership in Book 7. 4–13. I hope what I have written reflects, however inadequately, his valiant efforts to enlighten me on the relevant Roman legal concepts. Jonathan Barnes helped with logic. Peter Garnsey made me think more about patronage. Martin Degand alerted me to bibliography I had missed. Margaret Atkins, Andrew Lintott, Dirk Obbink, and Michael Winterbottom gave much needed help. Hilary O'Shea has been patient and supportive throughout. Leofranc Holford-Strevens has not only contributed his immense learning and publishing expertise, but also, through his sagacious comments, made the whole process of preparing copy for the Press feel like an enjoyable intellectual conversation. My husband Jasper, over the years, has read through yards of uncongenial material without complaint and never lost faith in the project.

M.T.G.

Somerville College, Oxford
February 2012

Contents

Abbreviations

AJP	*American Journal of Philology*
ANRW	*Aufstieg und Niedergang der römischen Welt*, ed. H. Temporini and W. Haase (Berlin 1972–)
BICS	*Bulletin of the Institute of Classical Studies*
BPhW	*Berliner Philologische Wochenschrift*
CAH²	*Cambridge Ancient History*, 2nd edn.
CQ	*Classical Quarterly*
EMC	*Échos du Monde Classique/Classical Views*
Hosius	C. Hosius (ed.), *L. Annaei Senecae* De beneficiis *Libri VII*, De Clementia *Libri II* (Leipzig, 1914)
I. Eph.	R. Merkelbach et al. (eds.), *Die Inschriften von Ephesus* (IK 11–17; Bonn, 1979–84)
IG	*Inscriptiones Graecae* (Berlin, 1873–)
ILS	H. Dessau, *Inscriptiones Latinae Selectae*, 3 vols. (Berlin, 1892–1916)
JRS	*Journal of Roman Studies*
Lipsius	Justus Lipsius (ed.), *L. Annaei Senecae Philosophi Opera Quae Exstant Omnia* (Antwerp, 1652)
L–S	A. A. Long and D. N. Sedley, *The Hellenistic Philosophers*, 2 vols. (Cambridge, 1987)
MW	M. McCrum and A. G. Woodhead, *Select Documents of the Principates of the Flavian Emperors* (Cambridge, 1971)
NGG	*Nachrichten von der Gesellschaft der Wissenschaften zu Göttingen*
OCD⁴	*Oxford Classical Dictionary*, 4th edn.
PBSR	*Papers of the British School at Rome*
PIR²	*Prosopographia Imperii Romani*, 2nd edn.
POxy.	*The Oxyrhynchus Papyri* (London, 1898–)
RAL	*Rendiconti della classe di scienze morali, storiche e filologiche dell'Accademia dei Lincei*
RE	A. Pauly, G. Wissowa, and W. Kroll, *Realencyclopädie der classischen Altertumswissenschaft* (Stuttgart, 1894–1980)
REL	*Revue des études latines*
Rh.Mus.	*Rheinisches Museum für Philologie*
Roman Statutes	M. H. Crawford, *Roman Statutes*, 2 vols. (Bulletin of the Institute of Classical Studies, Supplement 64; London, 1996)

SDHI	*Studia et Documenta Historiae et Iuris*
Sm. 1967	E. M. Smallwood, *Documents Illustrating the Principates of Gaius, Claudius and Nero* (Cambridge, 1967)
SVF	H. von Arnim, *Stoicorum Veterum Fragmenta*, 4 vols. (Stuttgart, 1903–5)
Vottero	D. Vottero (ed.), *Lucio Anneo Seneca: I frammenti* (Bologna, 1998)
ZPE	*Zeitschrift für Philologie und Epigraphik*

For further abbreviations relating to the manuscripts and editions, see Part III, p. 171.

Introduction

De beneficiis is the longest surviving work by Seneca on a single topic. It is also the only surviving example from a host of ancient works dealing with that same topic. The topic itself, the exchange of gifts and services, is of great importance in understanding how Greek and Roman society worked, and the social practice it describes at first hand has become, under the heading of 'gift exchange', one of the most fruitful for sociologists and anthropologists. The early manuscript tradition, by transmitting *De beneficiis* and *De clementia* separately from Seneca's other works, perhaps already marked the affinity of the two works, and both were crucial in the development of the image of the ideal ruler, the Mirror for Princes, in the Middle Ages and the Renaissance (see Ch. 9). Yet, despite these multiple claims on our attention, the treatise has received comparatively little scholarly notice in modern times. Even after the period when Latin philosophical works were studied merely as quasi-palimpsests through which one attempted to read earlier Greek works, most scholars have continued to regard it primarily as a source of parallels for Seneca's philosophical views expressed elsewhere or as a quarry from which isolated facts and anecdotes relevant to Roman social attitudes and practice can be extracted.

This is understandable because *De beneficiis*, when considered as a whole, is a baffling work. It is obviously a discussion of practical ethics; yet it has long disquisitions on divine providence and prolonged treatments of intractable Stoic paradoxes. The treatise concerns the highly practical mechanisms of social relations; yet it treats them in a curiously abstract way, giving, for its length, few concrete Roman examples. Seneca's own careful indications of the overall structure appear to be carried out to a greater extent than in some other dialogues;[1] but they only concern the first three books, while the last three are introduced by the author himself as a ragbag of inessential conundrums.

---

[1] That *De beneficiis*, *De clementia*, and the *Naturales quaestiones* are *dialogi*, like the twelve so named in the Codex Ambrosianus, is generally accepted. Of the four genres named by Quintilian 10. 1. 125, there is no other to which they can belong (Lausberg 1989, 1882–3). For Seneca's departures from his own structural indications in other dialogues, see Ch. 6.

Therefore, it is not clear what one can say about the form or content of the work as a whole. Sandbach's view of it, in 1975, might be said to be typical of the view that has largely prevailed:

> At times Seneca may have an eye on his relations with Nero, but for the most part he seems to be developing material provided by earlier writers. . . . The work lacks structure; even within a single paragraph Seneca leaps from one thought to another; indeed in search of epigrams he sometimes transcends thought. But there is much of interest: illustrative anecdotes drawn from his own lifetime, side-lights on contemporary society, and shrewd psychological observation.[2]

One thing is absolutely clear. The subject of beneficence was of great importance to Seneca. In one of the *Letters to Lucilius*, written somewhat later, Seneca actually says that philosophy teaches us 'above all else, to owe and to repay benefits well' (73. 9).[3] That this is not just rhetorical exaggeration is proclaimed, first, by the fact already mentioned, that he devotes a work of such length to what was already in the tradition a clearly defined and delimited philosophical topic (see Ch. 2A) within moral philosophy. The longest of his other extant works are not comparable: the *Natural Questions* ranges over a variety of natural phenomena, each assigned a different book; the *Letters* consider many different aspects of moral philosophy. The lost or unfinished *Libri Moralis Philosophiae* and the lost *De officiis* may well have been of at least comparable length, but the first presumably dealt with the whole of what was one of the three divisions of philosophy, and the second covered one of its three sub–divisions, namely, action or practical ethics, in which, according to the schema that Seneca himself adopted, the subject of *De beneficiis* would at most be included as a subordinate topic.[4] It is more appropriate to compare *De beneficiis* with *De ira* and *De clementia*, each of which treats an important topic under one of the two other subdivisions of moral philosophy: *De ira* belongs to the subdivison treating 'the passions', while *De clementia* belongs to the theoretical subdivision which included the virtues and vices.[5] But, even in their original unmutilated state, neither of these works probably ran to seven books.

Another indication of the importance of the subject matter to the author at all periods is the appearance of beneficence in his other works: which I shall discuss, as far as the extant works go, in Ch. 8. *De beneficiis* was

----

[2] Sandbach 1975, 157.

[3] For an explanation of the translation of *beneficium* as 'benefit', see pp. 171–2.

[4] On Seneca's adoption of Eudorus' scheme in *Ep.* 89, see Ch. 7A. For the place of *beneficia* in that scheme, see pp. 126–7 in that chapter, and Ch. 2A, p. 20.

[5] In Eudorus' scheme, the virtues and vices belong under the theoretical subdivision, while impulse, under which the passions fall, is a separate subdivision (Stob. 2. 43. 6–44. 6 W). The two dialogues mentioned range over these two subdivisions, and indeed treat the third, that of action, as well, where it falls within the area of anger and clemency. So these dialogues are less specialized than *De beneficiis*.

composed between 56 and mid-64 (Ch. 4). Seneca also treated the topic in
De clementia and *De vita beata* in the 50s, and he returned to it later in the 60s,
notably in the *Letters*, of which the lengthy Letter 81 is entirely and expressly
devoted to following up a problem already discussed in *De beneficiis*. Not only
De officiis, but the *Libri Moralis Philosophiae*, which Seneca was composing
about the time of the *Letters*, may well have included a discussion of the topic
in the larger context.[6]

Finally, not only did the topic of beneficence keep recurring in a variety of
philosophical contexts throughout his career: Seneca actually paid tribute
early on to its cardinal importance in maintaining social cohesion. Over a decade before he devoted a work specifically to the practice of giving and returning benefits, Seneca wrote in *De ira*, 'It is through benefits and harmony that
human life is maintained, and it is by reciprocal love, not by terror, that it is
bound to its obligations of mutual help' (1. 5. 3). In *De beneficiis* the same view
motivates him: 'Our task is to talk about benefits and to put in order a practice
that, more than anything else, holds human society together' (1. 4. 2), for 'What
alone equips us in life and fortifies us against sudden attack, but the exchange
of benefits?' (4. 18. 2).[7]

Recently, there has been an increase of interest in Seneca's treatise.
F.-R. Chaumartin's large volume of 1985, despite its sweeping title *Le De
beneficiis de Sénèque, sa signification philosophique, politique et sociale*, was
primarily concerned with establishing Hecato as the principal source, but it
also tried to relate the work to its political context (see p. 55). K. Abel's long
essay of 1987, 'Seneca's *lex vitae*', in addition to discussing the work's philosophical antecedents, provided a valuable analysis of the structure of the work,
which even the great Senecan commentator Justus Lipsius had declared
unfathomable (see Ch. 6).[8] In 1995 there appeared a volume devoted to Seneca
by J. M. Cooper and J. F. Procopé in the series Cambridge Texts in the History
of Political Thought; it includes a translation with notes to the first four books
of *De beneficiis*, as well as a helpful Introduction. In the same year Brad Inwood

---

[6] For the chronological relation of these works, see Ch. 4. Lausberg 1970, 182–6, like other
scholars before her, regards the concern with the *sapiens*, attested by fr. 124 = 96 Vottero of the
Libri Moralis Philosophiae, as a link between this work and *De beneficiis*: particularly significant
is *Ben.* 7. 5. 1, where Seneca postpones a general treatment of the paradox 'All things belong to the
Sage' (*omnia sapientis esse*) and 'meanwhile' (*interim*) turns to discuss only the more specific
question mentioned at 7. 4. 1, 'How can anyone make a gift to the Sage, if all things belong to the
Sage?' (*quemadmodum potest aliquis donare sapienti, si omnia sapientis sunt?*). The two works
may have been close in time of composition, *De beneficiis* datable to between 56 and spring–June
of 64 (*Ep.* 81. 3), the *Libri Moralis Philosophiae* to later summer or autumn of that year.

[7] *De ira* 1. 5. 3: *beneficiis enim humana vita constat et concordia, nec terrore sed mutuo amore
in foedus auxiliumque commune constringitur*; *Ben.* 1. 4. 2: *de beneficiis dicendum est et ordinanda
res, quae maxime humanam societatem alligat*; 4. 18. 1: *hoc uno instructior vita contraque
incursiones subitas munitior est, beneficiorum commercio*.

[8] It was reprinted in Abel 1995, 42–73.

produced an admirable analysis of the overall argumentative strategy of the work in 'Politics and Paradox in Seneca's *De beneficiis*'; in the decade that followed he provided further illumination of its philosophical arguments and its imagery in several essays, which can now be found, along with the first paper (ch. 3), in his *Reading Seneca* volume of 2005.[9] My own two papers '*De beneficiis* and Roman Society' (Griffin 2003c) and 'Seneca's Pedagogic Strategy' (Griffin 2007) are earlier versions of Chapters 3 and 7 respectively of the present study.[10] There is now an ongoing project to produce a collaborative commentary on the treatise by scholars at the universities of Palermo, Siena, and Verona. Preparatory seminars have been held, and the proceedings published, a volume of which I have been able to use in the later stages of this study.[11]

My aim here is to render *De beneficiis* more intelligible, to make it easier for readers to fathom and to use Seneca's treatise, in whole or in part, whether they are primarily historians, philosophers, or students of literature. All these readers need to understand, first, what phenomenon Seneca is treating, and why he thinks it is so important. That means knowing how the subject-matter fits into the philosophical tradition, and how it relates to Roman social practice and to Seneca's experience at the time. These matters will be discussed in Part I.

Readers also need to be aware of some more particular questions about this treatise, especially if they are to use sections of it with due regard to context. With what degree of precision can it be dated? Why does it have the title it does? What is its overall structure, and what purpose is served by that structure? How does it relate to Seneca's other works? Why was it so popular that it emerged among the first of Seneca's works from the 'Dark Ages' of textual transmission? These questions will be considered in Part II.

To judge from my own experience, readers will also find it helpful to have a map of *De beneficiis*. Therefore, in Part III, I have attempted synopses of the various books, accompanied by notes designed primarily to bring out clearly the structure of the argument. Throughout the work, these notes are referred to in the form **ad 3. 31**. The notes in no way aspire to the status of a commentary, which, even were I competent to produce one, could well prove as long and perplexing as the work itself and might deter, rather than encourage, readers to grapple with the treatise itself. Instead, my purpose has been to make it easier to comprehend *De beneficiis*, by providing the reader with a Guide. Only respect for Maimonides, and for my audience, has prevented me from borrowing the whole of his title.

---

[9] Ch. 7 is particularly important, but *De beneficiis* is treated as a central work throughout.

[10] The material in a paper on Seneca as a sociologist, presented at a conference in 1999 (Griffin 2003b), has also been included in Ch. 3.

[11] Picone, Beltrami, and Ricottilli 2009. A study related to the project is Raccanelli 2010.

Part I

The Subject-Matter of *De beneficiis*

1

Cicero and Seneca

In exploring the philosophical and historical aspects of Seneca's chosen topic, it will be instructive to start with an aerial view of the terrain. The salient features can be brought out by comparing, in broad terms, Seneca's essay with Cicero's *De officiis*, a work which was written a century earlier under different political circumstances, but with which Seneca's has obvious affinities.[1] It has indeed been suggested that Seneca emulated Cicero in his philosophical writings, producing like Cicero a *De officiis*, a work on friendship, consolations, oratory, and a series of letters to one friend:[2] the *Epistulae Morales* certainly make the emulation clear (*Epp.* 21. 4; 97. 1–3; 118. 1–2). But irrespective of whether Seneca knew *De officiis* in particular,[3] a comparison of Cicero's treatment of beneficence there with Seneca's will throw into high relief the key characteristics of *De beneficiis*, as it relates (1) to the earlier philosophical tradition inherited by Cicero and Seneca, (2) to the Roman social practices of Seneca's time, and (3) to the author's particular experience and place in Roman society. In what follows, these three aspects of the comparison between the two authors will be sketched in turn. This overview will serve as a prelude to the detailed treatment of these topics, with regard to Seneca's treatise, in Chapters 2 and 3.

PHILOSOPHICAL TRADITION

In *De officiis* Cicero organizes his teaching under the four cardinal virtues of wisdom, justice, courage, and temperance, as they are conventionally labelled.

---

[1] Fuhrmann 1997, 284. Cicero wrote *de Officiis* in the autumn of 44 BC.

[2] Ker 2006, 28–9. Seneca had certainly read *De re publica* (*Ep.* 108. 30–2, 34) and mentions Cicero's *libri ad philosophiam pertinentes* (100. 9). He also cites him for philosophical vocabulary (*Epp.* 58. 6; 111. 1). Allusions to other philosophical works of Cicero have been detected (see Setaioli 2003, 65–9), cf. S. Braund 2009, 21 on *De clementia*'s debt to Cicero's *Pro Marcello*.

[3] Chaumartin 1985, 48 denies that Seneca knew the work, but the sparsity of Seneca's references to Cicero's works, except for his letters, makes the argument from silence unconvincing.

Beneficence falls under the second. Although this subordination of beneficence to justice brings with it, as we shall see (pp. 21–4), certain differences
from treatments of beneficence on its own, like Seneca's, Cicero's conception
of a *beneficium* as an act without prior obligation fits with Seneca's, and much
of his detailed advice turns up in similar form in *De beneficiis*.

Here let us consider broader affinities of subject-matter. Cicero and Seneca
are both writing about social practices in a theoretical vein. They can be thought
of as writing, not only practical ethics, but political theory or political philosophy of a particular and similar kind. Saying this involves rejecting what
was until recently the prevailing view, that there was no systematic and theoretical political thought—nothing worthy of being called 'political theory'
or 'political science' or 'political philosophy'—after the period of Plato and
Aristotle. The philosopher Hegel may have been the first to proclaim that, in
the Hellenistic age, philosophy became apolitical, and morals became divorced
from politics: he was certainly not the last.[4] According to this conception of
political philosophy, the centre of concern must be the *polis*, elevated to an
abstract or ideal form, and the principal topics treated are constitutional form,
the working of political institutions, the definition of the citizenry and its
duties, and, to a lesser extent, the economic basis of society. In this vein Cooper
and Procopé, editors of a volume devoted to *Seneca: Moral and Political Essays*
in the series Cambridge Texts in the History of Political Thought, describe
Seneca's writing in general as having 'a markedly apolitical character, which it
shares with other Stoic literature'. They deny him the title 'political theorist',
saying, 'He has nothing to say about divisions of power, virtually nothing
about sources of authority or forms of government, and very little on social
regulation. He has no conclusions to draw for institutional reform. He is
simply not interested in institutions.'[5]

This view rests on caricatures both of 'classical' philosophy and of Hellenistic
philosophy. Plato's *Politeia* in fact embraced social customs and a general way
of life—marriage, education, *ēthē kai nomima*—as well as political arrangements.[6] Aristotle, who first defined *politikē* or political science, regarded it at
first as embracing the whole subject of human well-being and its achievement
(*NE* 1. 1. 1094ᵃ27–ᵇ11; 10. 9. 1179ᵃ33–1181ᵇ24). Even later when, in writing the
Politics, he narrowed the term to the study of what form of communal arrangements could best secure the mode of life that constitutes human happiness, he
included in its scope not only forms of government, but also economic factors
and social institutions, such as marriage and education. There was therefore no

    [4] Hegel 1979, xix. 254–5, 294 (ET ii. 234–5, 274); Zeller 1923, 13, 17, and on the Stoa in particu-
lar 302–6; Zeller 1879, 21, 25, 322–6 (Stoicism); Sinclair 1951, 261, 300; Winton and Garnsey
1981; I. Hadot 1969, 80–1; Schofield 1991, 102–3.
    [5] Cooper and Procopé 1995, Introduction, p. xxv.   [6] Walbank 1998, 46.

fundamental shift when the Hellenistic Schools included political and social relations under the subdivision of ethics called *peri kathēkontōn*, which embraced duties to the gods, to family, and to friends, but also duties to fellow-citizens.

This is not to deny, however, that there were new ideas that seem to have gained influence from the fourth century BC on: theories of natural law, the idea of the cosmic city, the notion of the individual's obligations to other men *qua* men, rather than to specific categories of men according to their relationship to him. But we need to think not so much in terms of a shift, but of an enlargement of the pool of concepts in which political thinking can be done. We can see the true scope of ancient political thought when we look at the authors of the Roman period. Polybius includes in his account of the Roman system, not only her formal political institutions, but her military organization, her funeral customs, and her religious habits. Cicero not only wrote a *Republic* (which in any case included a discussion of education) and a work *On the Laws*, but also the treatise *On Duties*. This sets out the code of conduct of the governing class at Rome, and it has just as much claim to be regarded as political theory as the two works inspired by Plato. Indeed, Long has said of this influential work, 'The *De officiis*, not the *De re publica*, is Cicero's Republic', that is, his serious work on the political system of the Roman Republic.[7] It would be perhaps nearer the mark to say that the *De re publica* and *De officiis* are in fact just two different ways of using philosophical tools to analyse the political traditions, the *mos maiorum*, of Rome.

Like Cicero, Seneca regarded moral philosophy, which traditionally included political theory, as the most important branch of philosophy, though, unlike Cicero, he wrote consistently from a committed Stoic point of view. Whereas Cicero had been inspired by the example of Plato and the Peripatetics to compose his *Republic* and *On the Laws*, Seneca did not write about the relative merits of different constitutions and showed little confidence in what could be achieved by legislation (*Clem.* 1. 23). Seneca's contribution can only be understood if political thought, and indeed political theory, are not conceived in too narrow a sense. For it is a substantial contribution and continuous with Cicero's, but its affinities are less with Cicero's earlier works of formal political philosophy and more with the *Pro Marcello* and with *De officiis*. In *De clementia*, addressed to Nero as Princeps, Seneca went further than Cicero when he addressed Caesar in the *Pro Marcello*, in exploiting the potential of political eulogy for theoretical exposition; in *De beneficiis*, Seneca provided, like Cicero, a code of social morality for the members of the Roman governing class, but he concentrated on social exchange relationships.[8]

---

[7] Long 1995, 240, on which see Griffin 1996a, 278–9, 282.
[8] These views are more fully discussed in Griffin 2000, 532–4; 2002, 325–8.

SOCIAL HISTORY

In the absence of Seneca's own *De officiis*, the comparison of Cicero's with Seneca's *De beneficiis* offers us our best insight into the effect that the transition from Republic to Principate had on the social practices and social attitudes of the Roman elite. For both works make close contact with the social scene, as we shall see (Ch. 3B), though Seneca offers less practical detail and at first appears to be less realistic. *De beneficiis* is also more restricted in the social practices it covers. For example, there is no equivalent to the lengthy discussions by Cicero of liberality in money and in services conferred by individuals on the community at large: what we call 'euergetism' (see Ch. 3C–D). Cicero's harsh criticism of the euergetism of his day shows how important a role it played in the political competition that finally put an end to the Republic. Under the Principate, political stability, as well as the supremacy of the Princeps, required that such ostentation in Rome be suppressed or rigidly controlled, as the historian Tacitus explicitly tells us (*Ann.* 3. 55). Pliny's *Letters*, and the massive evidence of inscriptions, show us the transfer of that kind of aristocratic liberality to the Italian and provincial towns, where members of the elite were born or otherwise had connections.[9] Seneca does not discuss this change, and communal benefits, when they are mentioned at all, almost all emanate from the Princeps (see Ch. 3C). Seneca largely restricts his discussion to the liberality towards individuals that continued to be practised by the elite as well as the Princeps.[10]

In these works both Cicero and Seneca not only reflected the attitudes and practices of their own day, but they gave their own literary responses to political and social change. Thus Cicero, writing during the civil war, saw that, with Caesar's Dictatorship, a new style of political discourse had become appropriate: one that exploited the potential of political eulogy, not only for theoretical reflection, but for serious admonition. His speech *Pro Marcello* mixes praise of the ruler with political proposals and reflections on the obligations of a man in Caesar's position. It owes much in inspiration to Hellenistic works on kingship, as does Seneca's *De clementia*, which offers an ideology for the Principate that accepts the fact of autocracy and stipulates moral training in place of the vanished constitutional constraints. Again, in *De officiis*, written after Caesar's assassination, Cicero tried to formulate in theoretical terms the ancestral code of behaviour of the Republican governing class, a code that he saw threatened by the apparently irreversible change in political conditions.[11] Only the traditional pursuit of glory through self-sacrifice and patriotism, he felt, not the

---

[9] Manning 1985 shows that the negative connotations that *liberalitas* acquired in the Late Republic, because of the competitive euergetism of the elite in Rome, ceased to operate under the Principate, because it was all in the hands of the Princeps. His view that the *de haut en bas* quality of the Princeps' liberality to individuals was accepted, however, is too simple (see 3C).

[10] For an ample demonstration of this continuity, see Saller 1982.

[11] I have considered Cicero's purpose in writing *De officiis* in Griffin 2011, 323–6.

new ruthless self-aggrandizement which had led to civil war, was compatible with the cohesion of the governing class and the maintenance of its political control. Like the laws against the political crimes of treason, extortion, and electoral malpractice, the social code, as he saw it, was designed to keep the overambitious in line and to preserve the virtual equality of the aristocracy against the ambitions of anyone who, like Pompey, could not bear an equal. Cicero was encouraging the young to preserve and live up to that social code.

There is a parallel here with Seneca, who, as I hope to show (Ch. 3C–D), reflects the tensions in the social position of the Roman governing class under the Principate. His teaching, with its emphasis on showing discrimination in giving, on maintaining an appearance of equality with the recipient, and on assuming that reciprocity is possible, is clearly directed both at his peers and at the Princeps, particularly as they interact. He tries, by incorporating the relations between the Princeps and his nominal peers in a description of exchange relationships, to reinforce the social side of being *civilis* and, through it, the theory of the Principate as a modification of the Republic.

THE AUTHORS IN ROMAN SOCIETY

It is already clear how similar are the social perspectives that we find in Cicero and in Seneca.[12] Both see the practice of liberality primarily from the point of view of the giver, because both were rich men with reputations to uphold and influence to maintain. Both are concerned with the maintenance of what they see as the traditional aristocratic code: patriotic, generous to the poor, protective of dependants—though Seneca's concern explicitly extends further down the social scale, to slaves and teachers.[13] Yet both are primarily interested in liberality and gratitude, as practised between social equals and those who are to be treated as social equals. Both address their works principally to senators or *equites*. Even if more of Seneca's addressees are *equites*, including the addressee of *De beneficiis* (see Ch. 4), the focus on the governing class remains the same as Cicero's, since under the Principate *equites* could perform government functions, and many of Seneca's equestrian addressees are in fact imperial officials.[14] The equestrian order was the social stratum from which both Cicero and Seneca rose to consular status, and they were both acutely conscious of their status as

---

[12] For an extended comparison, see Griffin 1988.

[13] The point is made by Fuhrmann 1997, 287.

[14] Notably, Pompeius Paulinus, Prefect of the Corn Supply (*PIR*² P 634); Annaeus Serenus, Prefect of the Watch (*PIR*² A 618); Lucilius Iunior, procurator in Sicily (*PIR*² L 288). One should also remember that Polybius, the addressee of a consolation, was one of Claudius' most influential freedmen secretaries, holding the post *a studiis* (Suet. *Cl.* 28) and possibly also *a libellis* at that time (*PIR*² P 558; see Griffin 1976, 21 n. 2).

'new men'. It is possible that their origins gave them a heightened conscious-ness of traditional practices and a deep commitment to their survival in the new political circumstances. For Seneca, of course, dealing with a *fait accompli*, adaptation to change, not resistance, was the order of the day.

If the perspective of Seneca on beneficence resembles Cicero's, because of his similar social status, economic position, and political standing, it is also significantly different, because his own career took a particularly 'imperial' form. At the time when *De beneficiis* was written, in the late 50s or early 60s, Seneca had for many years exercised far more political influence as an adviser to the Princeps than he did as a consular and senior senator, which had been the defining roles for Cicero. Indeed, the ancient historical sources for Seneca's life, notably Tacitus, Suetonius, and Cassius Dio, do not even mention his suf-fect consulship of 55 or 56, when he had an unusually long tenure of six months with three colleagues, one of them a patrician.[15] Nor do these authorities show Seneca active in the senate. It would be impossible to give a description of Cicero's activities with such omissions.

Cicero came from the municipal aristocracy of Italy, the *domi nobiles*, wealthy landowners who were the office-holders of their towns, in his case Arpinum, and who could afford to maintain houses in Rome and give their children an education both there and, in his case, abroad. Seneca came from a rich family of Corduba in modern Andalusia, the Roman province of Baetica.[16] The family wealth was essentially agricultural, though his father, L. Annaeus Seneca, who visited Rome in youth and returned to supervise the education of his sons there, may have owned at least one suburban villa near Rome. Cicero's exile had caused him financial embarrassment: temporary, for the most part. Though half of Seneca's property will have been confiscated in 41, when he was convicted for immoral relations with Julia Livilla and relegated to Corsica, he probably recovered it when he was recalled by Claudius in 49 in order to instruct the son of his new wife Agrippina in rhetoric. After his pupil Nero became Princeps in 54, Seneca's proximity to the Emperor meant a great increase in his wealth. Tacitus has his enemy Suillius Rufus attack him in 58 for having amassed 300 million HS, a fortune comparable to that of the great imperial freedmen, in four years of 'imperial friendship' (*regia amicitia*). He mentions in particular Seneca's testamentary inheritances and the interest from loans in Italy and the provinces.[17] Later, Tacitus has Seneca himself refer

---

[15] Camodeca 1986 and 1991 for the three colleagues, the patrician P. Cornelius Dolabella, M. Trebellius Maximus, and T. (or P.?) Palfurius. But for some doubts about his redating of Seneca's consulship to 55 and that of his elder brother Junius Gallio to 56, see Griffin 1992, 510–11. Ker 2009, 45 suggests that the pairing of Seneca, the teacher of rhetoric, and Burrus, the Praetorian Prefect, in Tacitus (*Ann.* 13. 2. 1, cf. 13. 14. 3; 14. 52. 1) 'is a telling substitute for the traditional annalistic language on consuls as paired leaders'.

[16] What follow recapitulates Griffin 1976, 287–94.

[17] Tac. *Ann.* 13. 42. 4, cf. Cassius Dio 62. 2.

to Nero's gifts of land, suburban villas, and money lent at interest.[18] His skill as a financier and practitioner of scientific agriculture will have enabled him to increase his fortune still further.[19] Seneca's detractors, according to the historian, alleged that the sumptuousness of his villas and gardens rivalled those of the Emperor. But Seneca was also renowned for his generosity: Martial and Juvenal celebrate him, among other consular patrons, for his generosity to his poorer *amici*, presumably those who attended his *salutationes*, and Tacitus shows him trying in his last moments to change his will in favour of his friends.[20]

Though Seneca offered to hand over his wealth to Nero in 62, the offer was refused, according to Tacitus (*Ann*. 14. 56. 3). But Seneca changed his lifestyle, in that he refused to entertain morning visitors any more and discouraged his numerous dependants from escorting him through the city, where he was now rarely seen. As Nero wished there to be no noticeable change, however, his protégés were continued in office; yet some will have noticed that Seneca was no longer so accessible as an intermediary with the Princeps.

Seneca's wealth was intact when *De beneficiis* was written, for, as we shall see (Ch. 4), the upper chronological limit for composition is the end of June 64, that is, before the great fire in Rome. It was after the fire of July 64 that Seneca, wishing to dissociate himself from the Emperor's sacrilegious appropriation of temple treasures, again requested permission to retire from Rome. Refused again, he was nonetheless allowed to contribute substantially to the rebuilding of the city: the fire gave him an opportunity to divest himself of part of a fortune that could now only increase his peril, as the Emperor's finances became more and more strained.[21] His brother Annaeus Mela, a year later, committed suicide under duress, after drawing attention to himself by attempting to recover the fortune of his son Lucan, who had died for his part in the Pisonian conspiracy on 30 April of 65.[22] Shortly before, Seneca too had committed suicide on imperial orders.[23] The will that Seneca had made before 64 must have left the bulk of his fortune to the Emperor, especially as the philosopher was

---

[18] *Ann*. 14. 53–6, cf. the gifts to powerful *amici* of houses and villas after the murder of Britannicus (13. 18).

[19] Plin. *HN* 14. 50–2; Colum. *RR* 3. 3. 3; Seneca describes himself at *NQ* 3. 7. 1 as a 'hard-working cultivator of vines' (*vinearum diligens fossor*).

[20] Tac. *Ann*. 14. 52, cf. Dio 61. 10. 3; Martial 12. 36, cf. 4. 40; Juv. 5. 109, cf. Tac. *Ann*. 14. 56. 3 on his *coetus salutantium* and *comites* before his semi-retirement in 62; Tac. *Ann*. 15. 62. 1.

[21] Tac. *Ann*. 15. 45; Dio 62. 25. 3, cf. Tac. *Ann*. 15. 64 of the will composed earlier when he was 'at the peak of his wealth and influence' (*praedives et praepotens*).

[22] Tac. *Ann*. 16. 17; 15. 70. The date for Lucan's death is given as 30 April 65 by the Vacca Life.

[23] Tac. *Ann*. 15. 61–4. He is shown in the later *Letters to Lucilius*, whose dramatic date is autumn 64, in Rome (104. 1), Nomentum (104, 110), and Alba (123), where he had villas. The retreat to his room that Tacitus mentions as coming after the Fire, when his request to retire to the country was refused (*Ann*. 15. 45), must come soon after that. But on the eve of the Pisonian conspiracy, in April of 65, he had come from Campania to his suburban villa near Rome (Tac. *Ann*. 15. 60. 4). See Griffin 1976, 93, 358 n. 1, 367, 400.

childless. In any case, it would have been taken by Nero, even had he succeeded in altering his will.[24]

For Cicero, *De officiis* was not an academic exercise. He had participated with remarkable success in the political and social life of the late Republic, and he speaks in the work of his own career and the prospects of his son; his passionate concern for the system he describes shows through, in the persistent justifications of Caesar's assassination and in the intimations of doom about the Republic.[25] Seneca in *De beneficiis* is more reticent. But that makes all the more striking the author's candid personal outbursts on the subject of imperial generosity to senators, which Tiberius made an instrument of humiliation (2. 7), and on the difficulties faced by imperial *amici* in advising a Princeps who is not as receptive to the truth as he pretends (6. 32).[26] How close the subject of the treatise was to Seneca's heart was clearly perceived by the historian Tacitus, who plays on the terminology of friendship and the exchange of benefits in constructing the dialogue between Seneca and Nero at *Annals* 14. 53–6. As we shall see (chap. 3E), both 'Seneca', in asking permission to give up his wealth and retire, and 'Nero', in refusing the favour, show themselves familiar with the arguments of *De beneficiis*. Tacitus presents us with 'two Senecas arguing'.[27] The philosopher's work gave the great historian added insight into the dilemmas faced by those who lived closest to the Princeps.

---

[24] Ibid. 293, 294, n. 1.
[25] Griffin and Atkins 1991, Introduction, pp. x f., xii–xvii, xxviii.
[26] These are discussed in chap. 3C and E.
[27] Alexander 1950–2*b*, 331–2. See now Ker 2009, 47–9.

2

De beneficiis and Philosophy

A. THE PHILOSOPHICAL TRADITION BEFORE SENECA

Seneca himself points us towards Stoic discussions of *charis* as the philosophical tradition to which *De beneficiis* belongs, when he mentions works by Chrysippus in the third century BC and Hecato in the first.[1] By then there was already a rich tradition of theoretical thinking about giving and returning favours, for from the fourth century onwards *euergesia* and *charis* had become subjects of moral discourse.

In the works of Plato we meet the idea of real and apparent benefits (*euergesiai*), often applied to teaching, and the notion that gratitude (*charis*) and honour are the appropriate recompense for the former.[2] It is, however, Xenophon and then Aristotle and his school, who, given their practical orientation, provide the fullest surviving early contributions to the subject, and those most relevant to Seneca. They anticipate much of what the Hellenistic schools were to elaborate. One of Aristotle's followers gave the first clear formulation we have of the idea that 'the giving and interchange of favours holds together the lives of men, some giving, some receiving, and some giving back in return' (χάριτος ἀμοιὴ καὶ δόσις συνέχει τοὺς τῶν ἀνθρώπων βίους, τῶν μὲν διδόντων, τῶν δὲ λαμβανόντων, τῶν δ' αὖ πάλιν ἀνταποδιδόντων).[3] This, as we have seen (p. 3), is a key idea for Seneca.

---

[1] For S.'s references to Chrysippus and Hecato, see **ad** 1. 3. 2–4. 5. The *liber* of Chrysippus referred to at *Ben.* 1. 3. 8 is probably the *Peri Charitōn* attested by Philodemus (*SVF* ii. 1081). However, the title of the work by Hecato in which he drew on this volume of Chrysippus (*Ben.* 1. 3. 9) is uncertain: a *Peri kathēkontos* is attested (Cic. *Off.* 3. 63 *de officio*, 89 *de officiis*) but some scholars, most notably Gomoll 1933, 72–83 and most recently Chaumartin 1985, 31–53, have argued for an unattested work *Peri charitos*. *Ben.* 2. 18. 2 is strong, but not incontrovertible, evidence that the work of Hecato Seneca used was about *kathēkonta*: it is adduced by Giusta 1964–7, ii. 449–50 n. 3, having been rejected by Gomoll 1933, 77–8 and again by Chaumartin 1985, 35.
[2] *Apol.* 36 C; *Meno* 91 C, 92 D; *Gorg.* 506 C, 520 E; also in the possibly Platonic *Seventh Epistle* 351 A.
[3] Pseudo-Aristotle fr. 3 in Plezia 1961, 44–5 = letter 4 in Plezia 1977, 21–2.

Xenophon

Xenophon might not strike us as representing the philosophical tradition proper, but rather a proto-philosophical tradition that surfaces also in the orators and the comic poets.[4] However, the sheer volume of his remarks about beneficence would make them difficult to ignore, even were it not the case that he rapidly acquired a reputation as a rival to Plato on his own philosophical ground.[5] Moreover, Xenophon treats the subject most fully in his Socratic works and in his *Cyropaideia*, a work which, as he suggests in the introductory chapters (1. 1–6), he regarded as a contribution to what we could call political theory, and which was much read in the Roman period. When the topic surfaces in the *Hiero*, the *Agesilaus*, and the *Anabasis*, it is again in discussions of how to govern properly.

In Xenophon *euergesia* (beneficence) and *charis* are normally correlatives, *charis* being used predominantly in the concrete sense of a favour returned, or in the abstract sense of gratitude.[6] In the *Agesilaus* 4. 2–4, however, it is also used in the sense of a favour gratuitously given. The ideas found in his contemporary Plato recur in Xenophon: that the teaching of virtue is a benefit,[7] and that honour is a fit return.[8] Other themes anticipate the concerns of Seneca. First is Xenophon's interest in motivation: only the person who gives benefits freely and according to merit wins true gratitude; gifts should be valued according to the donor's resources.[9] Xenophon is also aware that giving men what they really need to survive can move hatred rather than gratitude, and that, for those in power, receiving benefits can mean loss of face.[10] Ingratitude is deemed the most hated offence of all,[11] giving one a reputation one should take care to avoid.[12] Xenophon is more concerned with the feeling of gratitude than with the concrete return: only if one can make a return is it injustice not to do so.[13] The connection with justice, so manifest later in Panaetius, is already here, and Xenophon also considers the question of legal enforcement of gratitude with

---

[4] Hands 1968, 29–32 cites some passages from the orators and writers of comedy of similar date to Xenophon and later.

[5] Azoulay 2004, 9 notes that there are at least 300 occurrences of the term *charis* and its derivatives in Xenophon. Rivalry with Plato: D.L. 3. 34; Gell. *NA* 14. 3. His life is included in Diogenes Laertius' *Lives of the Philosophers* (2. 48–59), and [Plut.], *Lives of the Ten Orators* 845 E calls him *ho Sōkratikos*. Sellars 2003, 24–6 argues that Xenophon had a correct grasp of the Socratic conception of philosophy.

[6] For these senses, of which the concrete is primary and earlier, see Moussy 1966, 412–14.

[7] *Mem.* 1. 2. 8; *Apol.* 17.   [8] *Mem.* 2. 1. 28; 3. 12; *Anab.* 9. 9. 7.

[9] *Ages.* 4. 4; *Hiero* 7. 6; *Cyr.* 4. 4. 12, cf. Sen. *Ben.* 1. 1. 4–8: it is felt particularly when the benefit comes from someone one has wronged (*Cyr.* 3. 1. 29); gifts valued according to donor's resources: *Mem.* 1. 3. 3; cf. Sen. *Ben.* 2. 15. 3; 5. 2. 2–3.

[10] *Symp.* 4. 3; *Cyr.* 5. 5. 33; cf. Sen. *Ben.* 3. 5. 2; 6. 35. 3–4.

[11] *Cyr.* 1. 2. 7, cf. Sen. *Ben.* 1. 10. 4; 4. 18. 1.

[12] *Anab.* 7. 7. 22; cf. Sen. *Ben.* 4. 16. 2.

[13] *Mem.* 2. 2. 1; *Cyr.* 1. 2. 7; 3. 1. 34; *Ages.* 4. 2–4, cf. Sen. *Ben.* 4. 40. 1–2; 6. 41. 2.

which Seneca is to be so concerned.[14] Xenophon is interested in the practical advantages to be gained from beneficence: good will towards benefactors enables them to call on help in return,[15] and earns them loyalty and security, particularly important for rulers.[16] This is a theme later given prominence by Panaetius, whose work clearly inspired Cicero's treatment of beneficence from the point of view of the *utile* as well as the *honestum*.[17] Seneca is keen to condemn such motives, though well aware of the practical benefits to the individual giver; he does, however, stress the practical benefits for society at large.[18] Finally, Xenophon anticipates, the view so important in Seneca, that beneficence is a socially creative activity, and that we make friends by accepting or returning favours.[19]

The Aristotelian Corpus

It is, however, the Aristotelian corpus that provides the most important theoretical background for Seneca's treatment of the subject,[20] especially given the loss of the Stoic treatises on the subject. The definition in the *Rhetoric* 2. 7. 1385ª17–19, 'charis is a service to someone who needs it, not in return for anything, nor for the advantage of the person doing the service, but for the other person', marks out the importance of motive, and that work also adduces readiness to give favours, gratitude to benefactors, and the reverse types of conduct, as key examples of behaviour not regulated by the written ordinances of the law, but subject to praise and censure (1. 13. 1374ª23). The honour acquired through *euergesia* and the ability to practise it is also stressed (1. 5. 1361ª28-9), and the creation of *philia* through unasked and discreet beneficence noted

---

[14] *Mem.* 4. 4; *Cyr.* 1. 2. 7, cf. Sen. *Ben.* 3. 6–17, and see pp. 40, 42–3, 156.

[15] *Mem.* 2. 4. 7; 2. 6. 5–7; *Ages.* 4. 2–4.

[16] *Oec.* 12. 6; *Hiero* 7. 9–10; 11. 13–15; *Cyr.* 8. 2. 22. On the importance of this theme in later teaching concerning the proper conduct of rulers, see Kloft 1970, 23, 34. Azoulay 2004 is concerned to explore Xenophon's ideology of power through the concept of *charis*, which he thinks Xenophon sees primarily as an unbalanced reciprocity fundamental to all human association.

[17] Cicero attributes this division into the *honestum* and the *utile* of the whole treatment of *officia* to Panaetius at *Off.* 1. 9, and tells us at 3. 7 that Panaetius treated both these divisions in three books (though he failed to treat what he himself marked off as a third division, namely apparent conflicts between the *honestum* and the *utile*). Panaetius is actually cited during the discussion of liberality in Book 2 on the *utile* (2. 60; 76). At 2. 32 Cicero stresses that *benivolentia*, which he regards as the most potent way of attaining the support of men (2. 21, 23, 29), is secured most of all by actual *beneficia* but also by *voluntas benefica*, even without practical outcome. There is no reason to doubt that Panaetius subscribed to this view, which goes a step further in the Stoic direction of regarding intention as the heart of virtue than Aristotle's idea that not only those who have conferred benefits are honoured, but also those who can provide them (*Rhet.* 1. 5. 1361ª28).

[18] *Ben.* 4. 18. 16; 4. 22. 3; see below, pp. 27–9, 43–5.

[19] *Mem.* 1. 2. 7; 2. 9. 8; 3. 11. 11, cf. Sen. *Ben.* 2. 18. 5; 2. 21. 2, and also *Clem.* 1. 9. 11.

[20] As Inwood 1995*a*, 242 n. 10 = 2005, 67 n. 9 observes.

(2. 4. 1381ᵇ35). The most seminal treatments of the subject, however, belong to the discussions of *philia* in Books 8 and 9 of the *Nicomachean Ethics* and Book 7 of the *Eudemian Ethics*, and the analysis of the virtues of *eleutheriotēs* and *megalopsuchia* in Book 4 and Book 3 of the two works respectively.

Aristotle links beneficence to *philia*, the natural social instinct or virtue that relates men to each other as men, but that also holds particular communities together.[21] The conferring of benefits occurs within each of the three types into which *philia* is divided: relationships based on virtue, those based on pleasure, and those based on utility (*NE* 8. 13. 1162ᵇ31–1163ᵃ23). In fact, *philia* provides a necessary outlet for *euergesia* by the prosperous, and a necessary resource for the unfortunate (*NE* 8. 1. 1155ᵃ6–13). Just as the *philia* based on virtue is the highest, or indeed the only true, form, so the exchanges within that relationship are morally superior, their value being measured by the intention of the giver: he is satisfied with his action and not concerned about a return, but the receiver wishes to make return in proportion to the benefactor's intention, so far as it is in his power to do so (*NE* 8. 13. 1162ᵇ7–1163ᵃ21–3; 9. 1. 1164ᵃ33–1164ᵇ6). By contrast, the value of services within the friendship of utility is measured by the need of the recipient, and equivalent or greater repayment is expected (8. 13. 1162ᵇ31–1163ᵃ20; 9. 18. 1164ᵇ6–12). This is the type of exchange that comes closest to legally enforced transactions (8. 13. 1162ᵇ25–30), and that gives rise to recriminations precisely because, though motivated by self-interest, it cannot be regulated by the law (*EE* 7. 10. 1242ᵇ18–1243ᵃ14).

Aristotle has here anticipated some of the key themes in Seneca's treatise: the importance of motive in determining the value of a true benefit (1. 5–8); the demarcation of legally enforceable exchange from the exchange of benefits (3. 6–17). Aristotle, like Seneca (2. 18. 5; 2. 21. 2), stresses the importance of evaluating the donor, or the beneficiary, before entering into a relationship of (even utilitarian) *philia* (*NE* 8. 13. 1163ᵃ3–9); and, when treating the virtue of liberality, Aristotle too stresses that, like all virtuous action, it must be pursued for its own sake and with pleasure, or at least without reluctance, but with due calculation of the right persons and circumstances (*NE* 4. 1. 1120ᵃ24–26; *Ben.* 4. 9. 2–9). Other anticipations too have been noted.[22]

One major difference from Aristotle, however, shows the degree to which Seneca, and probably the Stoics who wrote before him, sought to reform the old aristocratic code of generosity in a more radical way than Aristotle. For him, *megalopsuchia*, that crowning ornament of the virtues, means conferring benefits but being ashamed to receive them, as well as trying to outdo one's benefactor in

---

[21] *NE* 8. 1155ᵃ 23–4, see also *Pol.* 3. 5. 1280ᵇ39. At *Pol.* 1. 3. 1253ᵃ1–6 Aristotle offers the simile of social interaction as a game, here of backgammon. Chrysippus was to use the analogy of a ball game for exchange of benefits in particular (below, p. 24).

[22] Cooper and Procopé 1995, 186 note the parallel drawn by Seneca (*Ben.* 2. 33. 2) and Aristotle (*NE* 9. 7. 1167ᵇ33–68ᵃ3) between the attitude of a benefactor towards the beneficiary and that of an artist towards his creations. See also *Ben.* 4. 15. 4.

return, in order to retain a position of superiority. Moreover, those possessed of greatness of soul remember their own benefits and forget what they have received, and, for that reason, they like being reminded of the former, but not of the latter (*NE* 4. 3. 1124^{b}10–16). For Seneca, however, it is right to receive gratefully and to publicize what one has received (*Ben.* 3. 22), and the recommended asymmetry of memory is just the reverse: one should not remember one's own benefit, nor forget what one has received (e.g. 2. 10. 4; 7. 22).[23]

Stoics

Outside the Stoic-oriented treatment in Cicero's *De officiis* and Seneca's own Stoic thinking, it is difficult to recover anything of the Stoic teaching about *charis*. It is clear that the canonical Stoic view saw *chrēstotēs* as a virtue, defined as the knowledge of doing good (*SVF* iii. 264) and a disposition to do it willingly (*SVF* iii. 273), while *eucharistia* consisted in knowing to whom, when, and how, to give, and to receive *charis* (*SVF* iii. 273). Except for the standard Stoic interpretation of the virtues as forms of knowledge, this is in keeping with Aristotle's treatment of the virtue of *eleutheriotēs* as behaviour that must be adopted for its own sake: without reluctance, but also with due calculation of the right persons and circumstances (above, p. 18).[24] Seneca himself in *De beneficiis* mentions various ideas of Chrysippus and of Panaetius' pupil Hecato (p. 24 below). But it is Plutarch who shows us that Chrysippus explicitly made the distinction between the act of giving a benefit, which is good, and the benefit given, which is indifferent, a distinction to be emphasized by Seneca (*Ben.* 1. 6. 1).[25] Moreover, Chrysippus apparently made use of this distinction, as

---

[23] Jaeger 1937 marks out the *megalopsuchos* as the prime instance of Aristotle's transformation of *Adelskultur* into a new ideal for humanity, as he renders in abstract philosophical vein the still living aristocratic tradition and makes virtue the basis of the claim to honour, which was formerly secured through descent and wealth. I am grateful to A. Dyck for pointing out the relevance of Jaeger's article. In real life, Aristotelian attitudes survived: Seneca, *Ben.* 5. 2. 1 (see **ad 5. 2–6**; Ch. 3, 34 and n. 69) shows the difficulty of countering such a notion in the leaders of society, as does Fronto, *Epist. Graec.* 5. 8 (van den Hout 247). (All references to Fronto are taken from van den Hout 1988.)

[24] Kloft 1970, 8, 23 (modified on 42) thinks it was the Stoics who introduced the idea of liberality as a matter of unselfish disinterested giving. However, Aristotle already mentioned that liberality is giving 'for the sake of the noble' (τοῦ καλοῦ ἕνεκα, *NE* 4. 1. 1120^{a}23–4) and stressed this also in treating exchanges of favours within *philia* based on virtue, a discussion that Kloft ignores. On the other hand, the Stoics were concerned with returning benefits as well as giving them, so that they were bound to treat forms of reciprocation. It is true, however, that after Xenophon it was difficult to approve so unreservedly the pursuit of good will and security as a motive for liberality, as Kloft 1970, 70 notes.

[25] *Mor.* 1038 A (*SVF* iii. 674), 1068 D (*SVF* iii. 672). Chrysippus must have analysed the two senses of *charis* in common usage (Moussy 1966, 412–14). Though Seneca says the fool can receive only *beneficiis similia* at *Ben.* 5. 12. 4, at 2. 34. 5 he points out that the term *beneficium* can mean both the action and the thing given through that action (*actio benefica* and *ipsum quod datur per illam actionem*).

Seneca was to do (*Ben.* 5. 12. 3–4), in answering the objection made by opponents of the Stoics that, on their assumptions, the fool cannot be ungrateful, since he is unable to receive anything beneficial. The solution is that the fool is able to receive the thing or service given (though not the benefit itself) and is obliged to reciprocate in kind.

Beneficence as Independent vs. Subordinate Topic

Aristotle's successor Theophrastus is credited with a work *Peri charitos*, the first we know of in a long line of works wholly and specifically devoted to the subject of gratitude.[26] These are attested for Demetrius of Phalerum, Epicurus, the Stoics Cleanthes and Chrysippus, the renegade Stoic Dionysius, and the Epicurean Philodemus.[27] The establishment of the subject as a discrete object of philosophical enquiry is confirmed by the schema for moral philosophy attributed to the mid-first-century-BC Academic philosopher Eudorus, where it features as a separate entity in the third division of the schema, the division devoted to practical ethics.

Eudorus' schema, however, also suggests that the subject could be treated as a subordinate topic in more general moral discussions. For the topic *Peri tōn charitōn* seems to exhaust, or at least to be the prime example of, that subset of *kathēkonta* ('proper functions') and *katorthōmata* ('correctly performed functions') that involve a relationship with our neighbours (see pp. 126–7).[28] Therefore it is not surprising to find that the subject was treated both independently and as a subordinate topic in more general treatises, sometimes by the same author. It was in fact in his work *Peri katorthōmatōn* (*SVF* iii. 674) that Chrysippus, as we saw, discussed the problem of whether the fool can receive benefits and owe gratitude, a subject covered by Seneca in *De beneficiis* 5. 12–14. Certainly, Panaetius treated beneficence in his treatise *Peri tou kathēkontos* and was followed in this by Cicero, who included the topic in *De officiis*, the only surviving example of this mode of treatment.[29] Panaetius' pupil Hecato wrote a *Peri kathēkontos*, which Cicero made use of in *De officiis*, but there is no way to determine whether or not Hecato followed his teacher in treating liberality in that work. Nor can we tell if he wrote in addition a

---

[26] D.L. 5. 48 (one book). For the meaning of *charis* here, see pp. 99–100). There are variant titles, the plural being used by Chrysippus (*SVF* ii. 1081), the combination with gifts (*Peri dōrōn kai charitos*) by Epicurus (D.L. 10. 28), and the combination with wealth and revenge (*Peri ploutou kai charitos kai timōrias*) by Dionysius (D.L. 7. 167).

[27] D.L. 5. 81 (Demetrius, one book); 7. 175 (Cleanthes). P. Herc. 4114 contains in fragmentary form a treatise Περὶ χάριτος by Philodemus (see Tepedino Guerra 1977). For the others, see note above.

[28] Stob. *Ecl.* 2. 44. 22–4 W. In the summary at the end (2. 45. 2–6 W) περὶ χαρίτων apparently stands for the whole subset.

[29] *Off.* 1. 42–60; 2. 52–85.

separate work *Peri charitos* or *Peri charitōn* and either reserved the topic for that work or treated it in both.[30] Treat it he did, for, as we have said, Seneca made use of an unnamed work by Hecato.

Seneca himself wrote both a *De beneficiis* and a *De officiis*, now lost.[31] Whether or not he included the topic of benefits in that lost work, cannot be discovered. If, however, as is often assumed, the *Formula honestae vitae*, written in the sixth century AD by Bishop Martin of Braga, was based exclusively, or at least substantially, on Seneca's *De officiis*, then we might have a clue.[32] For the topic of liberality is absent from the section of Martin's treatise devoted to the virtue of justice, the virtue under which Panaetius and Cicero treated it, and the virtue to which Seneca links gratitude in *Letter* 81. 7, 19. The omission might indicate that Seneca did not treat the subject in his *De officiis*, or at least only gave it a passing mention, saving his fire for *De beneficiis*. But it would only be piling one hypothesis on another to make the further inference that Hecato, whose *Peri kathēkontos* is assumed by some scholars to be the source of Seneca's *De officiis*, on which Martin's treatise is based,[33] must also have reserved the topic for his presumed work on *charis*.

In any case, Seneca's *De beneficiis* is the only surviving example of the category of works exclusively devoted to the subject of benefits. Therefore, we cannot tell if the length and detail of his work was unusual for this category.[34] Even more regrettable is our inability to determine whether it was characteristic of these works to treat beneficence in the way that Seneca does, especially as regards its relation to the virtue of justice. For Seneca differs from Cicero, who maintained the strong link between beneficence and justice that Aristotle, in his treatment of *philia* and of *eleutheriotēs*, had made (though he also

---

[30] See above, n. 1. For a summary of the scholarly debates on the subject, see Chaumartin 1985, 31–41.

[31] Fr. 25 Haase = 57 Vottero, on which see Lausberg 1989, 1925.

[32] The argument is based on the fact that Martin's *De ira* derives entirely from Seneca's extant *De ira*. The fullest treatment is by Bickel 1905. See also Barlow 1950; Trillitzsch 1971, i. 213–15; ii. 393–9 (Q. 19. 1). Colish 1985, ii. 297–302, while crediting the derivation from Seneca's *De officiis*, suggests that the discussion of justice owes something to Aristotle, Cicero, and Ambrose. There are certainly parts of the work very reminiscent of Cicero's *De officiis*, e.g. 'Do not wish the owner to be known for his house rather than the house for its owner' (*nec dominum notum velis esse a domo, sed domum a domino*, 4. 4), cf. *Off.* 1. 139: 'The master should not be made honourable by the house, but the house by the master' (*nec domo dominus, sed domino domus honestanda est*), unless Seneca had already appropriated the sentiment. For Gomoll (see n. 33 below), the explanation of such similarities to Cicero lies in the common source behind Cicero's *De officiis* and Seneca's *De officiis*, i.e. Hecato's *Peri kathēkontos*.

[33] Chaumartin 1985, 33, 37, following Gomoll 1933, 25–7; 55–6. The reservations of Abel 1987*b*, 105, accepted by Dyck 1996, 574, about alleged parallels between Martin's treatise and the fragments of Hecato, are strong: one cannot easily argue from Martin to the content of Hecato.

[34] Inwood 1995*a*, 243–4 = 2005, 68 believes that Seneca was not doing anything unusual in devoting seven books to the topic: 'It is only the accident of transmission which makes his lengthy treatise stand out.'

distinguished the spheres of liberality and justice at *NE* 4. 1. 1120ª19–21).[35] Was this characteristic of works treating beneficence in the context of *kathēkonta*, as opposed to works on *charis* on its own? We are told that the Stoics placed *chrestotēs* as a subordinate virtue under *dikaiosunē*, one of the four chief virtues (*SVF* iii. 264), and Cicero in *De officiis* was presumably following the Stoic Panaetius in treating *beneficentia* (= *liberalitas* = *benignitas*) as the positive part of that one of the four cardinal virtues that deals with our relations with others, and of which *iustitia* is the major part.[36] This mode of classification does seem linked to the fact that Panaetius' treatment of liberality formed part of his treatment of *kathēkonta* as organized under the four cardinal virtues.[37] The consequences are clear. For Cicero, liberality and beneficence must be exercised in accordance with the norms of justice,[38] whereas for Seneca, in *De beneficiis*, the relation of beneficence to justice does not seem to be closer than its relation to the other virtues (e.g. 3. 18. 4; 3. 31) or to virtue as a whole (1. 1. 12; 1. 15. 2; 3. 18. 4; 4. 1. 3; 4. 10. 2; 4. 21. 3). Indeed, it is only occasionally that injustice emerges as a relevant concern, as in the caution about harmful gifts (*Ben.* 2. 14), or in the discussion about the difficulty that legal enforcement would present (3. 6–17).[39] Cicero, however, not only stresses the hierarchy of obligations, according to his interpretation of the Stoic definition of justice, but places a lot of emphasis on cautioning against improper forms of generosity that transgress justice.[40]

As is appropriate in a discussion of justice, Cicero links beneficence to the obligations imposed by pre-existing social relationships, including those of kinship (*Off.* 1. 50–8), whereas Seneca likes to emphasize that a *beneficium* differs from an *officium* precisely in that it is given without prior obligation (*Ben.* 3. 18. 1), that it goes beyond the duties prescribed by any social role (3. 21, 34),

---

[35] Kloft 1970, 40 n. 20 adduces Plato *Resp.*10. 615 в for the long-standing place of this connection in the Greek tradition.

[36] *Off.* 1. 20, 42. The virtue is finally called *communitas* at 1. 152–3. Dyck 1996, 106 suggests *hē koinōnikē aretē* for the Panaetian designation.

[37] L–S i. 368 credit Panaetius with the idea of grounding *kathēkonta* ('proper functions') in the sphere of activity peculiar to each of the cardinal virtues, but he may not have been the first Stoic to do so.

[38] Atkins 1990, 261.

[39] *Ben.* 6. 41. 2 does say 'how much better and more just' (*quanto melius ac iustius*) and *Ep.* 81. 19–21 compares gratitude to justice as something which is vulgarly thought only to affect others, but then insists 'that the reward for all the virtues lies in the virtues themselves' (*quod virtutum omnium in ipsis pretium est*, 19).

[40] *Off.* 1. 42, of benevolence (*benignitas*) ('that it be bestowed upon each person according to his standing. Indeed that is fundamental to justice, to which all these things ought to be referred' (*ut pro dignitate cuique tribuatur; id enim est iustitiae fundamentum, ad quam haec referenda sunt omnia*)), worked out in 1. 50–8, cf. ἐπιστήμη ἀπονεμητικὴ τῆς ἀξίας (*SVF* iii. 262), and see pp. 36–7. Kloft 1970, 40–2 suggests that Cicero's concern with caveats (*cautiones*) shows the difficulty of getting the criterion right for generosity (*liberalitas*) as opposed to largesse (*largitio*), given Cicero's concern with the escalating use of competitive munificence in the politics of the Late Republic.

and that it creates bonds of friendship (2. 18. 5; 2. 21. 2, see below, pp. 36–7). A similar conception of beneficence may be suggested by the schema of Eudorus, in which *kathēkonta* and *katorthōmata* are subdivided in two different ways: the first division sets those that are self-contained against those involving a relation with our neighbours; the second division sets composite against incomposite. *Peri charitōn* belongs to the second subset of the first division; *peri biōn* to the first subset of the second division. According to Giusta, the proper functions and correctly performed functions prescribed by instruction *peri charitōn*, on the one hand, and by instruction *peri biōn*, on the other, both involve social rapport: the first emanate from a social rapport that is occasional and traceable to unilateral initiative, whereas the latter emanate from a social rapport that already exists through stable and durable relationships.[41] For Chaumartin, this difference of treatment coincides with the distinction between works on *charis* on its own, and works on *kathēkonta* which include a treatment of *charis*: the former regards beneficence as a matter of free initiative; the latter treats it in the context of specific social duties;. The fact that Seneca's statement of the distinction between a *beneficium* and an *officium* in *De beneficiis* 3. 18. 1 occurs immediately after a reference to Hecato is taken by Chaumartin to show that the work by Hecato that Seneca used was a separate work on *charis*.[42]

There is, however, a need for caution in adopting such a schematic view and assigning the view of beneficence as a matter of free initiative exclusively to works treating *charis* on its own, and the link with justice and the concern with pre-existing social relationships exclusively to works on *kathēkonta* treating beneficence as a subordinate topic. Cicero too regards conferring a *beneficium* as 'in our power', i.e. a free act not dictated by obligation (*Off.* 1. 48), whereas *officium* is an action dictated by obligations relating to social roles and relationships or obligations of gratitude for previous benefits.[43] And if he is not consistent in applying that distinction, neither is Seneca, as we shall see (p. 37). Hecato could, like Cicero, have mixed the two types of treatment in his *Peri kathēkontos*, and Seneca, while using this work, could have decided to place more emphasis than it did on the creative aspect of beneficence. Nor should we minimize the mixing of these approaches in *De beneficiis*, alluded to above

---

[41] Stob. 44. 20–6 with Giusta 1964–7, i. 169. It is notable that in Eudorus' schema *philia* is treated in a different section (under *theōria*, in the subdivision *peri agathōn kai kakōn*, Stob. 2. 43. 16–19 W), whereas in the Peripatetic doxography in Stobaeus, *charis* occurs alongside *philia* among the *pathē asteia* (2.142. 16–143. 24). This suggests that, for Peripatetics, the topic *peri charitōn* could still be linked to friendship, as in Aristotle.

[42] Chaumartin 1985, 35–7.

[43] Chaumartin 1985, 36 n. 35 ignores this passage when he says that Cicero, unlike Seneca, does not distinguish between *beneficium* and *officium*, though he cites the preceding sentence where *officia* is used when *beneficia* would be expected. See Dyck 1996, 162–3 ad *Off.* 1. 48 (with Ch. 5 n. 34) and Ch. 3 n. 32.

(p. 22). Seneca's way of treating the topic of returning benefits at the end of Book 2 and in Book 3 incorporates considerations of justice and particularly treats benefits within the relationships of master–slave and parent–child (p. 116 and notes **ad 2. 14–17.7** and **ad 3** (introduction)).

The Source Question

So far, in considering philosophical anticipations of Seneca and in noting important differences between earlier treatments and his own, we have made little mention of 'sources' as such. In the most recent thorough study of the question, Abel concluded that it was impossible to determine Seneca's debt to particular earlier Stoics, whereas, shortly before, Chaumartin, after an exhaustive investigation, had concluded that Hecato, whom Seneca cites five times, was his principal, indeed his exclusive, source.[44] Seneca himself once credits an opinion to multiple authors, but without naming them.[45] Otherwise, he mentions Chrysippus and Hecato, clearly claiming at 1. 3. 9 to have used Chrysippus—not only indirectly through Hecato, but directly. Though Seneca is by no means uncritical of them,[46] he appreciates Chrysippus' likening of social exchange to a ball game (2. 17. 3) and his comparison of the repayment of favours to a race that cannot start until the proper moment (2. 25. 3). He also seems to approve of his definition of a slave as a hireling for life (3. 22. 1). As for Hecato, he cites with approval his discussion of reciprocal duties (2. 18. 2) and appropriates one of his *exempla* (6. 37. 1).

Modern scholarship has little sympathy with traditional source criticism, which tended to deflect attention from the thought of the extant author actually under consideration.[47] However, it can be argued that a knowledge of Seneca's working methods would be illuminating,[48] from the perspective of literary form or of philosophical originality.[49] But the evidence is not there. What is clear is that *De beneficiis* had a long tradition of philosophical thought behind it, and that the subject, though by no means a Stoic preserve, was congenial to Stoic philosophers, concerned as they were with social bonding and with divine benevolence as an example for man. Indeed the notion that Seneca

---

[44] Abel 1987*a*, 17 = 1995, 58; Chaumartin 1985. Seneca mentions Hecato at 1. 3. 9; 2. 18. 2; 2. 21. 4; 3. 18. 1; 6. 37. 1.

[45] *Ben.* 2. 9. 1: 'all who teach wisdom' (*omnes auctores sapientiae*).

[46] Critical remarks about Chrysippus in 1. 3. 8–9, where 'over and above the material that Hecato copied out' (*praeter ista quae Hecato transcribit*) shows Seneca's direct use; about Hecato in 1. 3. 9; 2. 21. 4; 3. 18–19.

[47] Chaumartin 1985, 21–9 gives a balanced summing-up of the debates over its feasibility and value.

[48] Inwood 1995*a*, 246 n. 34 = 2005, 71 n. 33.

[49] Sonntag 1913 tried to separate Seneca's additions from the original of Hecato (see Ch. 6).

was following some particular Greek work slavishly, or even exclusively, is undermined by the fact of his long-standing interest in the subject.[50] Much of the thought in *De beneficiis* may predate its composition in the late 50s or 60s (Ch. 4). As we have seen (p. 3), the idea that it is through the exchange of benefits that the harmony of human life is secured is already found in the first book of *De ira* (1. 5. 3), probably written at least a decade earlier in the 40s,[51] while the notion of divine benevolence as an exemplar for human relations, particularly between ruler and ruled, is developed in *De clementia*, written in late 55–6, probably before *De beneficiis* (Ch. 4). Indeed, Bellincioni found the thematic connection so strong that she regarded these three treatises, *De ira, De clementia,* and *De beneficiis,* as steps on an ethical itinerary, during which Seneca developed a socio-ethical doctrine governing the exercise of power in its political and economic aspects.[52]

B. CHARACTERISTICS OF SENECA'S PHILOSOPHICAL APPROACH TO BENEFICENCE

Seneca's teaching derives, above all, from his belief that the exchange of benefits is vital to social cohesion. He states as his aim, 'Our task is to discuss benefits and to regulate a practice which, more than anything else, holds human society together' (*Ben.* 1. 4. 2). By teaching the correct way to give, receive, and return them—what he calls the *lex vitae* (1. 4. 2)—Seneca hopes to combat the vice of ingratitude. Cicero too had identified the exchange of benefits as that aspect of the cardinal virtue of *communitas* that holds together the fellowship of men and the communal life (*Off.* 1. 20, 22), and had said that no duty was greater than that of showing gratitude (*Off.* 1. 47). The social importance of such exchange and the damage done by ingratitude, already discussed in Xenophon and Aristotle, is a commonplace by Seneca's day. Valerius Maximus (5. 3 ext. 3f.) speaks of the 'interplay of giving and receiving, without which life would scarcely be that of human beings' (*dandi et accipiendi beneficii commercium sine quo vix vita hominum exstaret*) and gives a stinging diatribe against ingratitude. But Seneca goes further. Ingratitude, which is the most common of vices (1. 1. 2), is also the worst and the root of all others (1. 10. 4), because it disrupts the harmony of the human race and thus destroys security and the means divine providence has given us to survive and prosper (4. 18. 1–3; 7. 27. 3). Ingratitude thus violates the nature of man, in which the social instinct is innate, and rejects the gift of divine providence, which gave us that instinct.

---

[50] A similar misconception about Cicero was destroyed by the work of Boyancé 1936, who showed that Cicero was thinking about philosophy long before he wrote any.

[51] Griffin 1976, 398.   [52] See pp. 153–4.

Cicero, though an Academic sceptic, had chosen to follow the Stoics in his *De officiis* (1. 7). The philosophical foundations of his work and of Seneca's are therefore similar. For both, the provision of help to each other, through the exchange of goods and services, fulfils the intentions of divine providence and makes a practical reality of the social nature of man. The metaphysical aspect is, however, not the same in the two writers. Seneca's divine providence, as is often recognized, is more transcendent, more personalized. Though both he and Cicero speak sometimes in terms of nature and sometimes in terms of god or gods, when treating the source of man's innate social instincts, Cicero is more apt to speak in terms of natural law or the laws of nature, while Seneca prefers to speak in terms of god or gods.[53] Whereas Cicero alludes to the benefits of the gods (2. 11) and to our duty to maintain the social fellowship they have ordained (2. 11; 3. 28), for Seneca their beneficence is a model from which correct human conduct can be inferred (*Ben.* 1. 1. 9–11; 4. 25). Their example teaches us to give without thought of repayment; to include even the ungrateful when to exclude them would deprive the good as well (4. 28); to benefit the unworthy as an honour to their worthy ancestors (4. 30–3); to feel grateful for a share in communal benefits, provided they are not given self-interestedly (6. 20–3); to be grateful for benefits conferred at a time when we could not recognize or welcome them, as by our parents (6. 23. 7–24).

As regards the foundations of human society, Cicero and Seneca are on the same side in the debate as to whether it was natural sociability or practical necessity that directed man to live in communities. For Cicero it is the social instinct of *oikeiōsis*, a manifestation of the natural law implanted as reason in man, that directs us to form communities. In these we learn to receive help from our fellow-men (*Off.* 1. 12; 2. 14), and we then go on to form cities, in order to protect our possessions (2. 73), with the result that we meet all of our needs by exchanging goods and services (2. 15). Cicero explicitly denies that man embarked upon communal life with the purpose of providing for the necessities of life (1. 158). Cause and effect, he argues, are reversed by those who believe that men first formed societies in order to satisfy these needs: he has in mind Plato and Aristotle and the Epicureans, and, of authors well known at Rome, Polybius and Lucretius.[54] Seneca, like Cicero, takes the Stoic view: the

---

[53] Seneca speaks of nature in e.g. *Ben.* 4. 17; Cicero speaks of the gods in *Off.* 1. 160; 2. 11; 3. 28, and of god in the singular in *Off.* 3. 44, 102. He declares the equivalence at e.g. *Parad.* 14 and *Sen.* 40, in noting the gift of mind to men. As Brunt 2013, ch. 13, ¶ 50–51 notes, Seneca does speak more in terms of law than Epictetus and Marcus Aurelius, perhaps under the influence of Cicero, perhaps because he was writing in Latin for a Roman audience (Griffin 2013, 99–101).

[54] Plato, *Resp.* 2. 369 B; Aristotle, *Pol.* 1. 1. 1252^{b}16–31; Polyb. 6. 5. 4–7. When Cicero wrote, Epicurus' view had recently been eloquently described by Lucretius (5. 1019–60). Dyck 1996, 350 finds a contrast between the view in *Off.* 1. 11–12, 2. 73 and that in 1. 158 and traces the discrepancy to the sources: Panaetius vs. Posidonius. I do not see any inconsistency in what Cicero says, though he, and perhaps Panaetius before him, is trying to accommodate the utilitarian view within the Stoic view (see Griffin 1976, 203, n. 1).

social instinct and the conviction that we should behave virtuously towards our fellow-men were not devised by man to cope with his weakness, but are innate. This fundamental human tendency to social bonding is a part of Stoic teaching on *oikeiōsis*.[55] Seneca agrees with Cicero that the good effects, in terms of help and security, are a result, not a motive. However, Seneca's view is more complex and subtle, for the rejected motive is assigned to divine providence. 'God has given that vulnerable creature two things that make him the strongest of all: reason (*ratio*) and fellowship (*societas*). That is how, no match for anything if isolated, he comes to be the master of all' (4. 18. 2). In this way Seneca reconciles the two approaches to the origins of society. Probably inspired by the story in Plato's *Protagoras* 320 c 8–322 d 5 (see **ad 4. 18. 2**), where Zeus distributes conscience and justice to mankind to be the principle of organizing cities and a bond of friendship in a wide sense (*philia*), he attributes to the divine the aim of helping man in his weakness. But, for man, social virtue is pursued as an end in itself. So Seneca writes of ingratitude, 'This is the one thing that we have not covered by any law, in the belief that Nature had taken sufficient precautions against it. Just as there is no law that bids us love our parents or indulge our children (for it is useless to push us in the direction in which we are already going), just as no one needs to be urged to self-love (which he acquires at the moment of birth), so too he does not need urging to seek what is honourable for its own sake, for it attracts us by its very nature' (4. 17. 2, cf. 6. 23. 3–4). Some of the most stirring passages in Seneca convey his vision of divine concern for man. This glimpse of a personalized deity can be found in Cleanthes and the Old Stoa in general, as well as in the 'Late Stoa', and it has been explained as a mere rhetorical device deployed for greater pedagogic effect or as a 'mere metaphor'.[56] In Seneca, at least, it resolves an old dilemma by allowing for a two-tier solution and issues in a new conception of the origins of society.

Seneca is concerned to stress that, whereas the exchange of benefits generally helps society to cohere, the giving of benefits, in particular, actually helps to create social bonds. As we have said (above, pp. 18, 19), he regards conferring a benefit as an act of virtue which exhibits, like other virtuous acts, the characteristics of rationality and appropriateness to the giver, the recipient, the time, the place, and the circumstances (2. 16. 1; 4. 10), and which derives its value from the intention of the giver (4. 21. 3, cf. 1. 1. 8). Though these are the characteristics of *officium* in general, and conferring benefits is an 'proper function' or (less accurately) a duty of man *qua* man (4. 12. 5), there is a distinction, though it is an elusive one, between a *beneficium* and an *officium* in its narrower sense of a specific act within the social context. Seneca cites, and seems to accept, the view that a *beneficium* differs from an *officium* or a *ministerium* in being given by someone

[55] Inwood 1995a, 243 = 2005, 68.   [56] Edelstein 1966, 34.

'who could withhold it without incurring blame' (*qui potuit sine reprehensione cessare*), an *alienus*, not someone fulfilling the duties of an existing relationship (3. 18. 1).[57] The establishment of a network of *gratia* is set off by an act of beneficence which the giver is under no obligation to perform. The return of that *beneficium*, however, is a matter of *officium*, the fulfilment of an obligation (3. 18. 1). Receiving a benefit creates a relationship of friendship which is then consolidated by further interchanges of benefit (2. 18. 5; 2. 21. 1, cf. *Clem* 1. 9. 11).

While Cicero, too, distinguished a *beneficium* from an *officium*, in that it is a free act not dictated by obligation (above, p. 23), in Seneca this creative aspect of conferring *beneficia* is more strongly in evidence. Whereas family and other existing social relationships prescribe our *officia* towards each other, the essential way to bring into relationship with each other those not related by birth or marriage is through the exchange of benefits. In this way we create a network of *gratia*, which is essential for social cohesion (4. 18. 4). Cicero too had emphasized the need to extend our benefits to as wide a circle as possible of men capable of showing gratitude and even of passing that obligation down the generations, so that further liberality is encouraged (2. 63, cf. 2. 53). But, for him, the utility of beneficence that receives the most attention is the utility at the individual level. For Cicero, the pursuit of glory, influence, and power through liberality is legitimate, providing the utility is real: that is, providing it does not conflict with what is virtuous (2. 32, 65, 69–71). The central theme of *De officiis* is, precisely, showing how virtuous conduct need not conflict with the pursuit of advantage by individuals. In the case of liberality, the advantage it secures is the goodwill and support of others, but it is belief in a person's virtue, notably justice of which liberality forms a part, that procures the most secure and the most lasting influence and support, as opposed to the ephemeral and insincere support that can be purchased (*Off.* 2. 22–3, 53). But the only sure way to win a reputation for virtue is 'by being what we wish to seem' (2. 43–4). Thus Cicero seeks to harmonize the striving for influence and glory that seemed so natural to the political class with the demands of Stoic philosophy.[58]

---

[57] Though Seneca gives this as the view of others (and its proximity to the mention of Hecato may suggest that he is the immediate source), his terminology elsewhere appears to endorse it (e.g. his use of *officium* and *beneficium* in *Ben.* 6. 18–19. 1). Saller 1982, 18 thinks Seneca regards this view as mistaken: he certainly rejects Hecato's view of the capacities of slaves, but not the terminology given in 3. 18. 1, as he shows later in the discussion (3. 21. 1, see ad 3. 21. 1). (At p. 19, however, Saller is right to insist that such *beneficia* generate an obligation in the receiver.) Yet he does not consistently maintain the terminological distinction, see Ch. 3 n. 32.

[58] Cicero gives the straightforward prohibition on ulterior motives for liberality in *Amic.* 31, which Aulus Gellius cites as the standard philosophical view (*NA* 17. 5. 10). But he says something similar in *De officiis* 1. 44; 3. 118. Kloft 1970, 41–4 discusses the tension between this view and Roman values, and regards the emphasis on achieving glory through beneficence in *Off.* 2. 52 as 'in gewissem Widerspruch' with these high-minded utterances (41–2 n. 26). But Cicero is conscientiously trying to resolve that tension through philosophical argument. Even Panaetius must have been concerned with these issues, as he devised the idea of treating proper functions (*kathēkonta*) under the headings of virtue and expediency (*Off.* 3. 7–10).

For Seneca, however, 'So true is it that a benefit should not be given for reasons of self-interest (*utilitatis causa*), that often it should be given at our expense and peril' (4. 12. 2): it is the moral gain of conferring benefits and showing gratitude for them that is valuable for the individual (4. 1. 2–3; 4. 10. 2), and most of Book 4 is devoted to this theme.[59] For human society, however, it is the maintenance of the 'game', the social process, that is essential. The 'player' can help to make the game a success by giving his benefit to the right person, but ultimately the material return is unimportant to him. The recipient, however, regards himself as bound to repay, regardless of the benefactor's attitude (*Ben.* 1. 10. 4; 7. 16; 7. 22). This asymmetry in the moral code imposed on donor and recipient facilitates the maintenance of the social practice, for donors are not discouraged from giving by the ingratitude of recipients, while recipients are not afraid to receive merely because they lack the means for material repayment (2. 35. 2–5; 7. 16).[60] The process is therefore not vulnerable to fortune on the mental level, where intention is what counts, and, although it is vulnerable on the material level, where a physical repayment is made by the recipient in addition to the gratitude that already fulfils his obligation (2. 33–4), the attitude advocated maximizes its chance of survival. For donors continue to hand over tangible benefits, and recipients do their utmost to reciprocate tangibly. As in the dance of the Graces, the appearance of the whole is ruined if the sequence is anywhere broken, and it is at its most beautiful if it is continuous, and if the succession is uninterrupted (1. 3. 4).

How Seneca envisaged that 'game' or 'dance' being properly performed in his own social framework will be the subject of the next chapter.

---

[59] See also *Ep.* 81. 19–24.

[60] See also pp. 43–4. For an excellent account of the instrumental importance of the code in social terms, see Inwood 1995*a*, 259–64 = 2005, 86–92.

3

De beneficiis and Roman Society*

A. THE SOCIAL PHENOMENON TREATED BY SENECA

Why did Seneca and his philosophical forebears feel the need to give detailed instruction on the proper way to give and receive gifts and services? The modern reader may feel that the subject could be handled, as W. H. Alexander wrote, 'casually as the need arises, more by instinct than by reason, and more by certain loose ideas of "friendship" than by any agreed-upon philosophy of the same'.[1]

The usual explanation advanced for the prominence of the topic in the philosophical tradition lies in the area of social history. Scholars stress the existence and importance of a formal code that governs giving and returning in ancient society. Though philosophers continued to discuss the topic as part of other philosophical topics, the devotion of whole works to the subject in the fourth century BC and later (see p. 20) perhaps points to its heightened importance. Certainly, the reciprocal aspect of relationships with friends and associates seems to have been of great concern even at the lower social levels, to judge from their prominence in the gnomic school papyri.[2] While the analysis of Aristotle's *megalopsuchos* can be plausibly viewed as a self-conscious formulation and adaptation of aristocratic values to a more democratic society, the rejection by philosophers after him of the insistence on 'remaining top' included in that ideal can no doubt be connected with further social and political developments in the Hellenistic world, and with the new political ideas that gained influence at that time.[3]

---

* An earlier version of sections A, B, and C of this chapter appeared under the title 'De beneficiis and Roman Society' in *JRS* 93 (2003), 92–113. See also Introduction, n. 10.

[1] Alexander 1950–2a, 3. This is a reprint of two articles which appeared in *Classical Quarterly* 1934 and 1937.

[2] Morgan 1998, 127. The evidence she uses is Hellenistic and Roman.

[3] See pp. 18–19 and n. 23. I am grateful to A. Dyck for suggesting that the separation of the topic 'has to do with the adaptation of aristocratic to bourgeois value-systems. The aristocratic families of archaic Greece patterned themselves on (if they did not have a continuous tradition going back to) the Homeric heroes. The great aristocrats like Cimon presumably needed no instructions on the subject: it was bred into them.'

Unfortunately, we cannot tell, given the loss of their works, how Seneca's philosophical predecessors related their topic to contemporary social practices.[4] However, there are many signs that Seneca's own concern with the subject is no purely abstract interest but has its roots in Roman social history. In particular, as was suggested in Ch. 1, and as will be argued here, *De beneficiis* reflects the need to adapt the traditional Roman social code to the existence of a new phenomenon: the Princeps. For the part of the social code it treats was of particular importance in maintaining the aristocratic social patterns of the Republic. The new factor had to be assimilated without causing undue disruption.

However, before we can discuss the relevance of what Seneca says to the social practices he saw around him, we must be clear as to just what social phenomenon is here being analysed and translated into abstract terms. What is Seneca theorizing about, and to what purpose?

Is Patronage Theory the Key?

For Alexander, who approached the work primarily as a textual critic, *De beneficiis* was, in the eyes of a modern reader, about 'friendship': more precisely, about the Roman concept of *amicitia*, which, he said, laid greater stress than our 'friendship' on practical acts and less on emotion.[5] He likened the treatise to a course in business administration, in this case the formal exposition of the practical acts or *beneficia* in which *amicitia* manifests itself. The idea has good Aristotelian credentials, given the part that *euergesia*, or beneficence, plays in Aristotle's discussion of *philia* (a wider term than 'friendship', embracing as it does kinship).[6] Moreover, Aristotle attributed to *philia* the function of holding states together (*sunechein poleis*, *NE* 8. 1. 1155ª23), a notion of social cohesion similar to the function Cicero and Seneca ascribe to the exchange of benefits.

In the half-century and more since Alexander wrote, the work of sociologists and social anthropologists has made us more familiar and comfortable with the idea of analysing social habits and construing them as a social system. It has also made us see that to use terms for social relationships in a way that does not precisely match ancient usage can be illuminating in bringing out features that those immersed in the society do not notice: the application of these terms need not be misleading, if they are well defined and used explicitly and cautiously. However, it is not 'friendship' in the modern or the ancient sense, but 'patronage', that has been used by more sophisticated studies of Roman social relations to characterize what is discussed in *De beneficiis*.

---

[4] See now Inwood 1995*a* = 2005, 65–94, who points to the reflective awareness of this social phenomenon in political and social thinkers from the 4th c. BC on.

[5] See above, n. 1.   [6] See Ch. 2A.

'Patronage, defined as a voluntary, continuing exchange-relationship between men of unequal power or status, remained fundamental in Roman society: in the view of the Romans themselves exchange relationships were the glue that held human society together': Richard Saller's statement in the *Cambridge Ancient History*, xi², equipped with a footnote adducing *De bene- ficiis* 1. 4. 2, fairly represents the way the subject-matter of Seneca's treatise is generally regarded by Roman historians.[7] In his important study *Personal Patronage under the Early Empire* Saller actually subsumed much that is covered by the ancient notion of 'friendship' under 'patronage'. Basing his definition of 'patronage' on the work of anthropologists and sociologists, he gave as the distinguishing characteristics of the patronage relationship: (i) that it involves the *reciprocal* exchange of goods and services; (ii) that it is a per- sonal relationship of some duration; (iii) that it is asymmetrical, in the sense that the two parties are of unequal status and offer different kinds of goods and services in the exchange. To this he was subsequently persuaded to add that it is a 'voluntary' relationship.[8]

Saller is well aware that the word *patronus* itself is not used by any of the major prose writers of the late Republic or post-Augustan Principate, includ- ing Seneca, in the general sense of an influential protector, and that the cor- relative *cliens* was only used occasionally and then with reference to humble men.[9] That in itself does not rule out the idea that the modern concept of 'patronage', as he defines it, is the key to the phenomenon Seneca is analysing in his account of Roman social mores. For Saller argues, 'It is clear that amicus, beneficium, officium, meritum and gratia can be used as signs of reciprocal exchange relationships which, if the additional qualification of inequality of status is met, can be used as evidence of patronage'; and his whole discussion shows how often he thinks that additional qualification can be met.[10] He describes the Romans as 'living in a patronal society in which no pretense was made about equality'.[11] Saller has become aware of difficulties when it comes to exchanges within the aristocracy and prefers to speak of patron–protégé rela- tionships between young aristocrats dependent on their seniors for advance- ment, but he still preserves the emphasis on a vertical society.[12] Wallace-Hadrill too had spoken of 'the multifarious links which involved men of all social levels, rising to virtual social parity with the "patron"', and concluded, 'Of course there is a contrast between the friendship of social equals and the

---

[7] Saller 2000, 838: *Ben.* 1. 4. 2 'Our task is to discuss benefits and to set out systematically a practice that more than anything else binds together human society' (*de beneficiis dicendum est et ordinanda res, quae maxime humanam societatem alligat*).

[8] Saller 1982, 1; 2000, 838, a modification adumbrated in the introduction to Wallace-Hadrill 1989*a*, 3.

[9] Saller, 2000, 838.   [10] Saller 1982, 1, 11–15, 22.   [11] Saller 1982, 126.

[12] Saller 2000, 846–50. On these relationships, see below, p. 71.

dependent relationship of unequals; but what justifies describing the network as a whole as a patronage network is that it involves exchanges between those closer to the centre of power and those more distant from it, and has the effect of mediating state resources through personal relationships.'[13]

Chaumartin, in fact, tried to interpret *De beneficiis* as an exposé of the contemporary abuses current in the relations of patrons and clients and hence in the practice of beneficence, especially among favourites of emperors like Nero, notably the imperial freedmen, whose conduct set a bad example.[14] There are, however, fundamental objections to regarding patronage theory as the key to understanding the theoretical treatment of the exchange of *beneficia* by Seneca and by Cicero before him. In discussing liberality, Seneca and Cicero hardly mention relationships *de haut en bas*, not even the clearest example of 'patronage' in Roman linguistic usage: the relationship between freedmen and their patrons.[15] Catalogues of those to whom we have special obligations, when given by Seneca, as by Cicero and Horace before him, ignore the hierarchal relationships of *patroni* and *clientes*, while mentioning *amici*, even *hospites*.[16] Their exceedingly rare references to *clientes* concern a relationship created between persons that, because of the size of the *beneficium* given, runs counter to the usual social position of the recipient: he may not be able to repay such a *beneficium* and hence will be regarded, to his shame, as a client. Cicero writes, 'Those who think they are wealthy, honoured, and blessed, do not want even to be under obligation for a favour. For they think that they have conferred a favour themselves simply by accepting something, even if it is large; they suspect something will be demanded or expected of them in return, and they consider that accepting patronage or being labelled as a client is tantamount to death.'[17] As Seneca puts it, they refuse to acknowledge their debt of *vita aut*

---

[13] Wallace-Hadrill 1989*b*, 77. As regards the latter part of the statement, it is hard to see how the kind of financial assistance that Atticus gave his senatorial friends fits into this model.

[14] Chaumartin 1985, 290–310; Chaumartin 1989, 1718–19. He lays particular stress on imperial freedmen.

[15] Saller 1982, 9 notes that the word *patronus*, in the literature of the early Empire, is restricted to legal advocates, patrons of communities, and ex-masters of freedmen. Brunt 1988*c*, 408 points out that *cliens* is not the correlative term to *patronus* in this last relationship, nor is it in the case of *patronus* as advocate.

[16] Brunt 1988*c*, 416 adducing *Off.* 1. 53–8; *Ars Poetica* 312–16; Seneca, *Ep.* 95. 37 quotes a standard type of moral precept: 'You owe this to your father, this to your children, this to your friends, this to your guests' (*Hoc patri praestare debes, hoc liberis, hoc amicis, hoc hospitibus*) and adds 'wife' (*uxor*) in his discussion.

[17] *Off.* 2. 69: *Qui se locupletes honoratos beatos putant, ii ne obligari quidem beneficio volunt; quin etiam beneficium se dedisse arbitrantur cum ipsi quamvis magnum aliquod acceperint, atque etiam a se aut postulari aut exspectari aliquid suspicantur, patrocinio vero se usos aut clientes appellari mortis instar putant.* As Dyck 1996, 458 points out, Cicero here manages to present the feelings of the *locupletes, honorati, beati*, to whom most people prefer to give benefits, 'in a crescendo of suspicion and indignation'. He compares Caes. *BC* 3. 18. 4, where Pompey says that life and citizenship would not be worth having if he owed it to a *beneficium Caesaris*.

dignitas ('their life or their rank in society'), so that people will say that their success is owed to their own merits rather than to the help of others, 'and in dreading the reputation of being clients, they incur the more serious one of being ingrates'.[18] These are clearly people who are used to being on the giving end. Seneca, in fact, says that his addressee, characterized as a generous and considerate benefactor (5. 1. 3–5), regards the saying that it is shameful to be outdone in benefits as a glorious utterance (5. 2. 1) and suffers from a related anxiety about not returning a benefit immediately (6. 42), which Seneca views as wanting to be free of the obligation the benefit creates (6. 35. 3; 4. 40. 4).[19] In the words of Peter White, 'An exchange that was badly balanced over time might also work to clientize a friend.'[20] There is no question of an initial or continuing relationship of inferiority.

The usual way of meeting these objections is to emphasize the use in Roman social relations of polite language which represents as a horizontal relationship of equality (usually *amicitia*), what is really a vertical relationship of inequality (being a *cliens* or, even worse, a *scurra* to a *rex, maior,* or *princeps* in Horatian language). There is no doubt that such euphemisms were employed, and that in some cases the *inops, probus et modestus* on whom Cicero recommends that we focus our beneficence was in fact a hereditary client (*Off.* 2. 70). Indeed in his letters Cicero speaks in terms of *amicitia* to and of a man, who modestly describes himself as a *cliens* and Cicero as his *patronus*.[21] Even writers giving moral instruction on these matters, occasionally reveal the common, non-egalitarian, assumptions that they too accept. Thus Horace in *Epistle* 1. 18, giving advice on how to behave like an *amicus* rather than a *scurra* towards the *dives amicus,* nonetheless marks the latter's superior social standing by also referring to him as *potens amicus* (44, 86) and *venerandus amicus* (68). Again, as Saller points out,[22] Pliny disapproved of grading *amici* whom one invited to dinner and offering them different quality food and wine (*Ep.* 2. 6. 2), but elsewhere he speaks casually of 'friendships, both the grand ones and the modest ones' (*amicitiae tam superiores quam minores,* 7. 3. 2). Seneca himself in *De beneficiis* distinguishes between true friends and the *amici* who are ranked according to the ease of access accorded to them by great men at *salutationes*

---

[18] *Ben.* 2. 23. 3. The whole passage runs: *Verentur palam ferre, ut sua potius virtute quam alieno adiutorio consecuti dicantur; rariores in eorum officiis sunt quibus vitam aut dignitatem debent, et dum opinionem clientium timent, graviorem subeunt ingratorum.* Cf. *Ep.* 19. 11. Seneca would have approved the attitude of the Republican aristocrat Metellus Pius in Val. Max. 5. 2. 7 who gratefully calls the benefactor who carried a law restoring his exiled father 'the patronus of his house and of his household' (*patronus domus et familiae suae*).

[19] These attitudes had received their classic formulation in Aristotle's description of the *megalopsuchos* (*NE* 4. 3. 1124^{b}10–14).

[20] White 1993, 31.

[21] The most notable example is A. Caecina: with *Fam.* 6. 5. 4; 6. 6. 2; 6. 9. 1, compare 6. 7. 4; 7. 29. 2. See Brunt 1988*c*, 395.

[22] Saller 1982, 12.

(*Ben.* 6. 33. 3–34),[23] and in *Ep.* 19, the *salutantes* who are not true *amici* (11) are clearly those earlier called *clientes* (4). He shows no clear disapproval when alluding elsewhere to the necessity of offering different precepts to those pursuing 'friendships with kings', 'friendships with equals', and 'friendships with those beneath them' (*regum amicitiae, pares amicitiae*, and *inferiores amicitiae, Ep.* 94. 14).[24] In fact, Brunt has suggested that although clientship was decreasing in the late Republic, it started to flourish again in the circumstances of the Principate, when Seneca was writing.[25]

What Seneca is concerned with in *De beneficiis*, however, is not underlying social structures and mechanisms of power, but correct social practice and the theoretical formulation of it, that is, a social code of conduct: what has been called 'un'etica e un'etichetta', or a style of giving (Lentano 2009*b*, 19). Something more complex is being described and recommended here than the use of polite language to disguise harsh reality. Except for the occasional glimpse of the hierarchical structure of Roman society, Cicero and Seneca, when they are expounding moral philosophy and giving moral instruction, speak in terms of equality; and, in these general philosophical discussions, this cannot be explained in terms of politeness to individuals.[26] Specific relationships *de haut en bas*, like master–slave, parent–child, are mentioned by them, but, as we shall see, they are marginal, and indeed problematic, rather than central to the analysis. Horizontal relationships and behaviour towards equals are their prime concern.[27]

---

[23] Winterling 1999, 121 argues plausibly that Seneca does not refer to an overt classification and designation at the *salutatio* but to a *de facto* system of admission, possibly involving admission to different rooms, which the master of the house visited in sequence. The point Seneca is making at 6. 33. 4 is, however, misconstrued: Seneca does not mean that hierarchizing destroys true friendship, but that the courtesy term *amici*, used of the large numbers (illustrated by the ranking) at the *salutatio*, does not designate true *amici*, in the sense of people who speak frankly and are bound to one by true affection.

[24] The argument here is ascribed to Aristo, whose views about the value of precepts Seneca is opposing, but at *Ep.* 94. 35, when he comes to answer Aristo's point that precepts have to be numberless, he concedes that there are differences of 'times, places, persons' (*tempora, loca, personae*) that matter.

[25] Brunt 1988*c*, 439–42. 'Destitute of political rights, men were now in greater need of protection from those who had power and influence' (440).

[26] Yakobson 1999, 71 sees that explanations in terms of not needing to mention what is familiar, or of consideration for the feelings of individuals, 'would seem to apply to texts describing specific instances of social intercourse rather than to Cicero's general discussion of social norms and ties in *De Officiis*'.

[27] Roller 2001, 130–2, 173 observes that it is unsatisfactory to discuss the exchange of gifts in terms of 'patronage', because of the terminological misfit between ancient and modern usages; the obscuring of similarities with other forms of exchange, such as clemency; and the 'ideological importance of transactions that do *not* establish hierarchical relationships', but he still thinks that, in the Roman view, the relationship of gift-creditor to gift-debtor was a familiar type of authority relationship, parallel to father–son, slave–master, 'a means of establishing hierarchical social relationships' (12) and he sees the Romans as articulating 'how exchange is used to establish, buttress, or undermine power relations, not only between elites and nonelites, but also within the elite—especially between emperor and aristocracy' (133).

An even more important objection to regarding ancient theories about exchanges of benefit as theories of patronage is the fact that it means inverting cause and effect, as these philosophical authors see it. For them, as noted on pp. 17, 28, acts of beneficence are presented as *creating* a relationship of *amicitia*, rather than being generated by the obligations inherent in existing relationships. The idea is also explicit in Xenophon and Aristotle, and in Epicurus and Musonius Rufus, and it is not limited to philosophical writings: it is taken for granted by other authors, including Thucydides, Cicero the orator, and Seneca's younger contemporary Pliny.[28] Cicero separates off the strong bond created by the exchange of *beneficia* as a distinct type of relationship (*Off.* 1. 56 *fin.*).[29] It is true that he specifies, as the last of the caveats to be observed in conferring favours, that the degree of generosity we show should be proportionate to the closeness of the relationship (1. 50): clearly he means that if the recipient is someone already connected with us, these gradations must be observed. However, for the most part, he thinks in terms of benefits that look ahead, rather than those with a past, i.e. those that start a process and initiate a relationship, not those that we are obliged by past history to give (1. 45–6; 49 *fin.*; 2. 63).[30]

Seneca in fact adduces standard social relationships in order to pinpoint, by way of contrast, the nature of *beneficia* and gratitude. There are, as we have said (pp. 23, 27–8), terminological pointers to this contrast. Cicero regards conferring a *beneficium* as 'in our power', i.e. a free act not dictated by obligation, whereas we are bound to return one (*Off.* 1. 48). The Elder Seneca ascribes to the declaimer and senator L. Junius Gallio the distinction, 'It is no *beneficium* but an *officium* to do what you ought to do.' Seneca, as we saw, seems

---

[28] For Xenophon, see Ch. 2 n. 19; Musonius Rufus fr. 19, p. 109. 5–6 Hense: 'the possession of many friends, which happens to the willing benefactor' (τὸ κεκτῆσθαι φίλους πολλοὺς ὃ περιγίνεται τῷ προθύμως εὐεργετοῦντι); Epicurus: D.L. 10. 120; VS 23. Thucydides writes(2. 40. 4), 'It is not by having good done to us, but by doing good, that we acquire friends' (οὐ γὰρ πάσχοντες εὖ, ἀλλὰ δρῶντες κτώμεθα τοὺς φίλους); Cicero, *Mur.* 24 of the use of oratory (clearly in defending cases in the courts) as creating 'profound gratitude, very deep friendships, and substantial popularity' (*plurimas gratias, firmissimas amicitias, maxima studia*); Pliny 'You [who] have no connection with the province except the service you have rendered, and that a recent one; but I was born there and served as quaestor in that province' (*cui nulla cum provincia necessitudo nisi ex beneficio tuo et hoc recenti; ipse et natus ibi et quaestor in ea fui, Ep.* 7. 33. 5): the bond created by the *beneficium* is here less strong, but still there. At *Ep.* 19. 12, Seneca imagines an objector making what is clearly an obvious point, 'Do benefits not create friendships?' (*Beneficia non parant amicitias?*).

[29] This relationship is to be identified with Aristotle's utilitarian friendship, but Cicero does not call it friendship here, because he would then have to be critical of it in comparison with the friendship based on virtue that he has just described at 1. 55–6.

[30] Even in the case of country and parents, he gives, as the rationalization for placing them top of the list of those to whom we owe liberality, the fact that they have conferred *beneficia maxima* on us: that is, he does not think of the obligation to be generous simply as a consequence of the relationship itself, but explains the obligation as a requital for specific past benefits intrinsic to the relationship (*Off.* 1. 58).

to accept the view that a *beneficium* differs from an *officium* or *ministerium* in being given by someone (an *alienus*) 'who could withhold it without incurring blame' (3. 18. 1), and not by someone fulfilling the duties of an existing relationship.[31] Seneca then goes on to explain that conferring a *beneficium* lies beyond the duties prescribed by any social role, such as parent–child, teacher–pupil, doctor–patient, master–slave (3. 21, 34). It does not matter that the terminological distinction between *beneficium* and *officium* is not always observed in common usage, or even adhered to consistently by philosophers like Seneca, who subscribe to it in an effort to make language more systematic.[32] What matters here is the conception of beneficence as creative of relationships.

Given the first difficulty—the horizontal nature of the relationships depicted—Alexander's suggestion that 'friendship', along with the formal acts in which it manifests itself, was the phenomenon being described by Seneca, might seem more promising than 'patronage'. For one thing, 'friendship', like the Roman *amicitia*, avoids the hierarchical conception inherent in 'patronage': indeed the description by Latin authors of their own relationships of *amicitia*, often involving the exchange of gifts, has proved very elusive to scholars trying to pinpoint cases of patronage.[33] Friendship was compatible with a patron–client relationship, but was not reducible to it: the term indicated altruism, good will, and mutual respect in the relationship.[34] Another consideration is that *amicitia* is a more fluid relationship than the ones that Seneca regards as generating fixed duties. 'There is no fact of birth nor legally recognized or religiously sanctioned act, such as a wedding or purchase or manumission of a slave, to which one could point as definitively establishing that two

---

[31] Ch. 2, n. 57; *Contr.* 2. 5. 13: the whole passage runs: 'It is no benefit, but a duty, to do what you ought to do. On this basis, a son might say he conferred a benefit on a father' (*Non est beneficium sed officium facere quod debeas; sic filius patri se dicat beneficium dare*). The question raised by the final point is treated at length by Seneca, *Ben.* 3. 29–38.

[32] Saller 1982, 17–20 notes that the distinction between *officium* and *beneficium* did not govern common Latin usage. At *Ep.* 81. 6 in the phrase *officii meminisse* Seneca uses *officium* for what he has been calling, and will continue to call, a *beneficium*, while Cicero in *Off.* 1. 48, 'We do not hesitate to confer services on those who we hope will assist us in the future' (*in eos quos speramus nobis profuturos non dubitamus officia conferre*), contradicts his own notion in the next sentence, that the initiatory gesture is a *beneficium*. Sometimes the imprecision arises from the desire to refer elegantly and concisely to the two reciprocal actions by using the same Latin word (Greek *charis* is unproblematically reciprocal (see pp. 99–101), as in *ex duobus officiis* at *Ben.* 2. 18. 1 of reciprocal obligations of parent and child, husband and wife; *mutuis officiis, beneficiorum commercio* at *Ben.* 4. 18. 1 (the attempt to explain away the use of *officia* and *beneficia* as synonyms in these passages by Chaumartin 1985, 36–7 n. 35 is unconvincing), cf. Val. Max. 5. 3. ext. 3f. *dandi et accipiendi beneficii commercium*). Sometimes, in practical contexts, politeness may play a part, as in Cic. *Fam.* 2. 6. 1–2 where Cicero is at pains to minimize his own past favours and maximize his gratitude for what he is requesting: so his favours are called *officia*, as if reciprocating, and what he hopes to receive *beneficia*, which are not seen as an obligatory return.

[33] White 1993, 13, 27–8, 31–2; Spisak 1998; Kleijwegt 1998.

[34] See Konstan 1995.

people were friends. In social terms 'two people were *amici* if they called themselves *amici*', as Craig Williams puts it.[35] The idea has, as we have said, good
Aristotelian credentials, given the part beneficence plays in Aristotle's discussion of *philia*,[36] and his insistence that egalitarian friendship is primary: a point
picked up by Cicero and Seneca.[37] Finally, *amicitia* and *amici* figure copiously
in ancient discussions of *beneficia*.[38] But there is still the second difficulty, that,
for Seneca, *amicitia* is more often viewed as the result than as the cause of an
exchange of benefits (*Ben.* 2. 18. 5; 2. 21. 2, cf. *Clem.* 1. 9. 11). Indeed, Seneca
expressly regards the same benefit as more valuable when given to a stranger
(who thus becomes a friend) than when given to an existing friend (3. 12. 1).
Moreover, he had treated the subject of friendship elsewhere, and to judge from
the fragments of his treatise *Quomodo amicitia continenda sit*, *beneficia* were
only a small part of what he considered.[39] In *De beneficiis* itself Seneca gives no
special emphasis to reciprocity between friends, except when solving the
conundrum 'How can a friend be given anything by a friend, when friends have
all things in common?' (*Ben.* 7. 12–13).[40] Similarly, Cicero in *Laelius de amicitia*
says little about *liberalitas*,[41] and in *De officiis* he stresses the other aspects of the
friendships based on virtue, i.e. affection and shared activities (*Off.* 1. 55–6).
Recent scholarship has rightly accepted that, as Roman writers indicate,

---

[35] Williams 2008, 39–40.

[36] It is striking that, just as Aristotle uses *philikon* to mark the greater trust and flexibility
involved in long-term contracts such as loans, as compared to market exchange (p. 40 below), so
Seneca explains why, when a slave does more than is necessary, it is a *beneficium*, by saying 'When
the feeling involved becomes that of friendship, it ceases to be called a service' (*ubi in adfectum
amici transit, desinit vocari ministerium*, *Ben.* 3. 21). Clearly friendship is felt to be a less prescriptive relationship, in which trust and affection inspire the conferral of favours.

[37] Aristotle in fact raises the question what degree of inequality is still compatible with *philia*
(*NE* 8. 5. 1157ᵇ35–1158ᵃ1; 8. 7. 1158ᵇ28–1159ᵇ7; 8. 13. 1162ᵃ34–1162ᵇ5). The point is even clearer
in the *Eudemian Ethics* 7. 4. 1239ᵃ1–6, where Aristotle says that only when parties are equal can
they be friends: on which see Schofield 1999, 88. Cic. *Amic.* 69–71; Sen. *Ben.* 2. 15. 1.

[38] On friendship and exchange in Martial, see Spisak 1998. Dixon 1993, 451, 456 stresses that
exchange within the upper echelons of society based in the city of Rome 'is expressed by the participants in terms of friendship rather than the frankly unequal language of patronage characteristic of favours from the wealthy to the clearly subordinate'.

[39] Fr. 94 Haase (= 59. 6 Vottero); 19. 5 Trillitzsch 1971, ii. 418: 'In this way he used to confer
benefits willingly, and to bear with patience their not being appreciated; in this way his generosity
was quickly activated' (*sic solebat beneficia libenter dare, patienter perdere; sic properabat benignitas eius*). This is adduced as one example of the friend's virtues which should be rehearsed, in
order to keep his memory fresh. Fürst 1996, 187–93 discusses the treatise and shows its importance for the healing of rifts. Cf. *Ep.* 9. 8, 10.

[40] The point is made by Konstan 1995, 335. For the lacuna in the passage, see ad 7. 12–13.

[41] Kloft 1970 only lists §§11, about Scipio, and 31, which is a comparison of friendship and
liberality: 'Just as we are generous and liberal, not to extract gratitude (for we do not put beneficence out at interest but are naturally inclined to liberality), so we are not attracted to friendship
by the hope of gain' (*Ut enim benefici liberalesque sumus, non ut exigamus gratiam (neque enim
beneficium faeneramur, sed natura propensi ad liberalitatem sumus), sic amicitiam non spe mer-
cedis adducti . . . expetendam putamus*): a negative allusion to Aristotle's category of utilitarian
friendship. *Amic.* 71 and 73 treat the question of benefits appropriate to the recipient.

sentiment and the sharing of interests and activities were as inherent in Roman friendship as the exchange of favours.[42]

There are two problems to be solved here. One is to identify the social activity that Seneca picks out for analysis, and to characterize his theory of conduct in a way that does justice to its horizontal and creative aspects. The second (B. below) is to see just how relevant his teaching really was to the Roman society of his time: how close are his ideas to attitudes current in the early empire? how far do his exhortations reflect the concerns of his readers?

Seneca's Boundary Lines

One way of discovering what social phenomenon Seneca is elevating to the level of theory in this work is to consider his efforts to distinguish the exchange of *beneficia* from other social activities which it resembles.[43]

The most common contrast he makes is between two reciprocal processes: one is giving a *beneficium* and owing *gratia*; the other is making a loan and incurring a debt. Though Seneca often discusses the exchange of benefits in metaphorical terms drawn from credit and debt (*Ben.* 1. 1. 1; 1. 4. 6, cf. Cic. *Off.* 2. 69, 71), he is concerned throughout his treatise to distinguish sharply between the two kinds of exchange: indeed, in the later Letter 81 on the subject of *beneficia*, he makes a strong plea for avoiding language appropriate to debt when discussing benefits.[44] Unlike an ordinary creditor, the benefactor should only receive back what is voluntarily returned (1. 1. 3; 3. 15. 1); unlike an investor, he should not think of repayment when he makes the gift (1. 1. 9; 3. 15. 4; 4. 3. 3), nor keep a record of it and demand repayment at a set time (1. 2. 3; 3. 15. 2–3; 7. 14. 5); he should be satisfied with gratitude and the recipient's wish to return the benefit (7. 14. 4–5); he should be willing to give anonymously without witnesses (2. 10. 2). A recipient should be more careful in choosing benefactors than creditors because a permanent relationship is created by the acceptance (2. 18. 5, cf. 2. 21. 2); the recipient should not repay too soon like someone wanting to be clear of a debt (4. 40. 5; 6. 35. 3–4; 6. 40); unlike a debt,

---

[42] Brunt's classic 1965 paper, revised as Brunt 1988*b*, makes the point for the Republic; White 1993, 14–19, 28, 31 for the Augustan poets; Spisak 1998, for Martial in particular.

[43] Raccanelli 2010 adduces these activities, from which the exchange of benefits needs to be distinguished, in her analysis of Seneca's message in terms of 'communication theory', where he is seen trying to correct the confusing signals that often go with an exchange, and to replace them with clear indications of an intention of friendship.

[44] *Ep.* 81. 9, where he explains why common usage prefers *gratiam referre*, which means to repay voluntarily, to *gratiam reddere* which means to repay on demand. Moussy 1966, 253, 267–9 points out that Seneca himself does not always observe this distinction, for at *Ben.* 3. 2. 2; 5. 16. 4 he uses *gratiam reddere*, as he indeed just has at *Ep.* 81. 7, but that he is right to say that the first expression is more common than the second. It is observed in the maxim as quoted by Cicero in *Off.* 2. 69 (see Ch. 6 n. 20).

it is enough to have sought to repay a benefit (1. 1. 3; 7. 14. 5), for the transaction is in our minds (2. 34. 1).

The contrast with debt was already a common one. Cicero, rejecting self-interested liberality, says 'For we do not put our favours out at interest' (*neque enim beneficium faeneramur*, *Amic.* 31). He also cites a maxim, 'The person who has his money has not repaid it, and the person who has repaid it, does not have it, but the person who has requited gratitude still has it, and if he has it, he has requited it' (*pecuniam qui habeat, non reddidisse, qui reddiderit, non habere, gratiam autem et qui rettulerit habere et qui habeat rettulisse*, *Off.* 2. 69), and uses the enthymeme in *Pro Plancio* (68).[45] Seneca does not use this play on words: he prefers to use the Stoic paradox 'He who accepts a benefit willingly has repaid it' (*qui libenter beneficium accipit, reddidit*) to make the point about gratitude being in itself a form of return (2. 30–1).

Seneca also alludes to a contrast between giving and returning benefits as against buying and selling for profit, when he says that our own profit is sought when selling goods or services, hence invalidating the status of the exchange as a benefit to others (4. 13. 3).[46] He urges that *fides*, not legal enforcement, should remain the sanction for liberality as opposed to the legal sanctions that protect loans and leases (3. 7. 1) and buying and selling (3. 15. 1). Similarly, Aristotle had contrasted legal utilitarian friendship, i.e. market exchange or even more long-term contracts of credit (which involve trust and hence have more of the *philikon*) enforced by law, with moral utilitarian friendship, in which the gift or service is not made on specified terms enforceable by law, though an equivalent or greater return is expected (*NE* 8. 13. 1162^{b}22–34). Seneca is making a similar contrast, though he sets a higher standard for the moral type in specifying that no return should be expected by the giver. In Aristotelian terms, his view amounts to ignoring the moral (non-legal) friendship based on utility and concentrating on the friendship based on virtue where the value of the benefit depends on the donor's intention (*NE* 8. 13. 1163^{a}21–3).

Gift-Exchange or Reciprocity Theories

The fact that it is economic exchange that the ancient theorists hold must be carefully distinguished and marked off from the giving and returning of

---

[45] Dyck 1996, ad 2. 69 points out that the fact that Gellius *NA* 1. 4 reports the criticisms made by the rhetorician Antonius Julianus of the formulation in *Pro Plancio* alone, could mean that the maxim is an interpolation in *De officiis*. However, the passage in *De officiis* is not open to the particular criticism Julianus makes, as it does not use the metaphor *debitio gratiae*.

[46] He attributes this contrast of *beneficium* and *negotiatio* to Cleanthes at 6. 12. 2, but the contrast made there is not between the pure benefit to the recipient and the incidental benefit to the buyer in certain exchanges between seller and buyer, but between the pure benefit to the recipient and the incidental benefit to the animals and men sold, when the seller looks after them as a means of achieving more profit.

benefits points to an affinity with modern sociological theories of gift-exchange or reciprocity. Though the use of these modern theories has become perhaps too fashionable in classical studies of late, the *beneficiorum commercium* does seem an area that invites such analysis. It is here, rather than in the patronage theories that are usually adduced, that we find the same concern as we find in Seneca with such matters as variability of return, the creation of bonds between the partners to the transaction, and social disapproval as the sanction.[47]

Theorists commonly place the social phenomenon of gift-exchange on a continuum of exchange relationships between primitive forms of exchange, called total 'prestation' (a term adopted from the French), and economic exchange.[48] In the former relationship, made famous by the work of Marcel Mauss,[49] groups are locked into rigid ceremonial forms of obligatory giving and receiving, there is a permanent amical relationship between donors and recipients, and disgrace follows the failure to make sufficient repayment, though no amount is stipulated in advance. At the opposite extreme is market exchange between individuals where the terms of return are stipulated, requital is immediate and not voluntary but legally enforced, and the exchange is impersonal and involves no enduring relationship of any kind. Just above market exchange on the continuum comes the 'balanced reciprocity' of loans, where there are again stipulated and legally enforceable returns, but they are made not immediately but within a finite period. Again, no permanent relationship is forged.

Gift-exchange lies in between these two extremes of the continuum. It is like economic exchange in that it normally involves individuals, not groups, and there is no obligation to give, only to return. It is unlike economic exchange in that the type of reciprocation is generalized, being unspecified, indefinite as to time, quantity, and quality, and depending not so much on what gift the donor originally gave, as on what the original donor needs, and when he needs it, and also on what the original recipient can afford to give, and when. It is also unlike economic exchange in that there is at least a pretence of disinterested generosity, and a bond of solidarity is created between the partners. Finally, it is unlike economic exchange in that there is no legal sanction to enforce return. Trust is needed between the partners, because the only sanction is the social approval given to the recognition of past favours and the social disgrace conferred on failure to show sufficient gratitude.

Gift-exchange was described by Mauss himself as 'characteristic of societies which have passed the phase of "total prestation" (between clan and clan, family and family), but have not yet reached the stage of pure individual contract, the money market, sale proper, fixed price, and weighed and coined money'.[50]

---

[47] Gill 1998 traces this concept in Greek ethical thought, noting that the social ideal of shared life, or reciprocity, underlies the practical discussions of the ideal by Cicero and Seneca (326).

[48] Heath 1976, especially 50–60, provides a good survey and critique of such theories.

[49] Mauss 1954.   [50] Ibid. 45.

This clearly does not apply to Rome, though Mauss himself allowed for surviv-
als of earlier habits in more sophisticated societies. Clearly relevant to Rome,
however, is the explanation he offers for the relatively greater importance of
gift-exchange in pre-modern societies, namely, that in modern societies the
raison d'être of a gift-exchange system is challenged or replaced by impersonal
mechanisms such as commercial exchange, the law, and the whole apparatus
of the state.[51]

Therefore, the fact that Seneca is so keen to distinguish the exchange of
beneficia from transactions enforced by law helps to confirm that what he is
discussing is the phenomenon of gift-exchange. We have already pointed to the
fact that the involvement of the law is one of the contrasts he himself draws with
buying and selling, with lending and borrowing, and with renting and leasing
(3. 7. 1). However, just as he often uses the language of economic transactions
metaphorically in speaking of the exchange of benefits, so Seneca sometimes
borrows the language of law; particularly in *Ep.* 81, where the images of the
rigidus and *remissior iudex* are important in considering how we should assess
the balance of benefits and injuries conferred on us by the same person.[52] More
characteristic, however, is the way he draws a contrast in *De beneficiis* between
the way the law deals with men who first lend money and then injure the bor-
rower, and our freedom to balance out benefits and subsequent injuries (6. 5. 4;
6. 6. 1, cf. 3. 12. 4). Most important is his discussion of whether or not ingratitude should be made punishable by law (3. 6–17). Admitting that parents have
such protection,[53] he goes on to reject the idea that such sanctions should exist,
on three counts: that they would prove impractical, as the cases would be too
numerous and calculations of equivalent value too difficult; that both the benefit and the return of gratitude would suffer a loss of moral standing; and that
the acceptance of benefits would be discouraged, leading to a reduction in the
giving of benefits and in the discrimination we exercise in giving (3. 7. 4–14).
Seneca points out that social disapproval and fear of the gods (3. 17) already
provide a powerful sanction. As Paul Veyne says of post-Aristotelian philosophical writers, 'Whether they discuss the virtues of generosity or *beneficia*,
these texts unconsciously depict for us a society in which voluntary relations of
giving and benefaction fill the place held in our society by the market and by
regulations (even if these are protective and beneficent).'[54] Indeed, Suzanne

---

[51] Similar ideas are found in Hands 1968, 32–3; Saller 1982, 13–15; Seaford's introduction to
Gill, Postlethwaite, and Seaford 1998, 3–4; van Wees 1998, 47. This approach is branded as
'anthropological elementarism' by Cheal 1988, who prefers to see gift transmission as having an
emotional function in cementing relationships, rather than an economic or political one.

[52] The same comparison in *Ben.* 6. 4. 5. See pp. 155–63 for the treatment of this issue in the
treatise and in *Ep.* 81.

[53] This was true in Athens (Xen. *Mem.* 2. 2. 3). Seneca may have been thinking of the *patria
potestas* (see *ad* 3. 11).

[54] Veyne 1990, 7 (translation modified).

Dixon, who gives due recognition to the relevance of gift-exchange theories to Roman society, has argued that the favour of giving and the favour of lending were not easily distinguished; and though she underestimates the clear distinction between benefits and loans made in talking about them, she may be right to stress the similarity in practice as regards the forging of a long-term relationship, 'the public acknowledgement of a continuing debt relationship'.[55]

Social Purpose of the Exchange of Benefits

Sociologists suggest various ways in which gift-exchange contributes to the functioning of the society as a whole.[56] For example, it is suggested that in pre-state societies gift-exchange is a vital force for social cohesion and helps to keep the peace, where there is no centralized power to do so, by overcoming suspicion and hostility between individuals or groups.[57]

Seneca too, as we have seen, thinks that the exchange of benefits reinforces social cohesion. Though he believes that giving benefits and returning gratitude properly are intrinsically valuable, as are all virtuous acts,[58] this does not create a conflict with his socially instrumental view of morality. For what the arguments for intrinsic value are meant to rule out is the motivation and justification of acts of beneficence in terms of the narrow *self*-interest of the individual concerned, e.g. giving in the hope of return, or out of a desire for security (4. 22. 3); or, on the other hand, showing gratitude because of fear (4. 18. 4). The interests of the social system as a whole, or the public good as Seneca calls it (7. 16. 2), are different from the self-interest of individuals. In any case, the public good need not provide the motivation of individuals in order to be advanced by their actions.

Sometimes Seneca sees the instrumental nature of morality as affecting particular social groups. Thus it is in the interests of parents for there to be a general belief that children can confer benefits on parents, beyond what they have received, because children then have no excuse for not showing devotion to them and repaying their benefits with the hope of surpassing them (3. 36. 1–2). But usually it is the public good (7. 16. 2) that is adduced: cooperation serves to compensate for the physical weakness of the human animal (4. 17–18; 7. 27. 3). To this end divine providence has instilled in us the desire at least to appear beneficent and grateful, and to preserve social cohesion (4. 17. 1–2; 4. 17. 4; 4. 18. 2–3).[59]

---

[55] Dixon 1993, 451, 459.
[56] Heath 1976, 181–4 summarizes two approaches of macrosociology: functionalism and conflict theory. It is functionalism that is relevant to *De beneficiis*.
[57] Van Wees 1998, 25–9.
[58] This theme receives particular emphasis in Book 4. See also *Ep.* 81. 19–24.
[59] For more on the metaphysical basis, see pp. 26–7 and Griffin 2000, 545–8.

Seneca's approach is like that of the sociologists, in that he treats the phenomenon of exchange on two levels: that of individual motivation or 'rational choice', and that of social function—corresponding to microsociology and macrosociology. But whereas the sociologist claims to *describe* social processes and to explain them in terms of their social functions, Seneca aims to *improve* the process of exchange, by showing how it should best be practised. To ancient philosophers, of course, this distinction between the description of human conduct and moral exhortation does not appear so clear as it does to us, because they regard themselves as urging men to behave in accordance with what is in fact their nature.[60] For the Stoics in particular, it is divine providence that has devised human nature: we have only to live up to its design and not allow it to be corrupted.

In his efforts to improve individual conduct, in order that the social process should fulfil its function of social cohesion more effectively, Seneca often uses the image, taken over from Chrysippus, of a ball-game and players (2. 17. 3–5; 2. 32; 7. 18. 1). The maintenance of the game (*lusus*) requires both skill and cooperative spirit on the part of the players. The good player will adjust the way he throws to the position and skills of his partner, thereby maximizing the chances that the latter will be able to catch the ball and return it. If the return fails, the game, he admits, is damaged, even though the players are not necessarily at fault when this happens. Seneca's moral code is designed to protect the general process and the chances of other such games succeeding. By teaching us how to choose the recipient and how and what to give him, and by teaching us how to receive and return benefits, it maximizes the chance of the individual game succeeding. The code also aims to ensure that donors do not fail to give just because they have experienced on occasion no return or even ingratitude, while recipients are not afraid to receive just because they cannot make a material return. To this end Seneca insists that the value of the benefit to the donor does not consist in the return, while the recipient can repay by showing gratitude, if he is unable to do more, though he remains under obligation to help his benefactor, should the need arise.[61]

The Sophistication of Seneca's Theory

Seneca's theory is able to cope with one of the key problems of gift-exchange theory. How can the 'free gift', i.e. where nothing at all is given or required in

---

[60] Similarly Morgan 2007, 185–8, drawing on Foot 2001, suggests that the different genres purveying popular morality identify what is good for human beings with what holds society together, and that they tend to slip from statements of fact about the way the world is to the idea that it ought to be a certain way (cf. 203, 238).

[61] Inwood 1995*a*, 259–60, 263–4 = 2005, 87, 92 discusses the image of the game and shows how Seneca's high-minded advice actually has the practical aim of encouraging the process of exchange.

return, be fitted into a system of exchange?[62] Some time ago, a mathematical biologist set out to account for altruistic behaviour while accepting a competitive view of human society based on Darwin's principle of the survival of the fittest.[63] 'Indirect reciprocity' is the answer: the cost to the donor of the altruistic act is offset by the gain in goodwill that he secures from the community as a whole, which then increases the chance of his becoming the recipient of such an act later. For Seneca too, altruism on an individual occasion goes with an expectation of return over time, from the recipient, or from others because of the donor's reputation (7. 32, cf. Cic. *Off.* 2. 63).[64] Seneca often uses the image of benefit as sowing (1. 1. 2; 2. 11. 4; 4. 9. 2; 7. 32):[65] the harvest may be delayed but comes eventually through continual cultivation (2. 11. 4). Moreover, Seneca can accommodate the free gift through his advocacy of an asymmetrical set of obligations, whereby the benefactor does not demand or even expect a material return and forgets his good deed, whereas the recipient is bound to return gratitude and make a material return eventually if possible, and to broadcast the benefit (2. 10. 4; 2. 35. 1, cf. 1. 4. 3 *fin.*; 7. 22; 2.35. 1; 2. 11. 2–3). The gift is therefore 'free' from the donor's point of view but not, of course, from the recipient's, who feels obliged to repeat the exchange.

The appeal to social instinct explains how benefits can be free in another sense, i.e. that individually they result from a free choice by the donor (3. 18. 1, cf. Cic. *Off.* 1. 48), and yet, as a general practice, they are part of the human obligation. For there is a general human duty to give, but not on any particular occasion.[66] Thus the general obligation does not mean that each individual benefit is obligatory. Moreover, the general obligation to humanity can itself be discharged outside existing social roles, by either transcending the obligations inherent in those roles (3. 21–2), or by creating a new relationship by giving. Giving is thus a creative process that promotes flexibility and evolution within the social system.

---

[62] Heath 1976, 110.

[63] Nowak 1998. The problem has since been complicated by the recognition that chimpanzees also exhibit altruistic behaviour (Horner *et al.* 2011).

[64] In *Ep.* 81. 19 Seneca, urging that generosity is its own reward, nonetheless notes that 'An example of good conduct returns in a circle to the doer' (*bonum exemplum circuitu ad facientem revertitur*). *Ben.* 6. 3. 1 cites Rabirius' line 'Whatever I have given, that I still have' (*Hoc habeo, quodcumque dedi*), but not to suggest that delayed rewards will result, but that the deed of giving is intrinsically valuable. Martial, *Epig.* 5. 42 elaborates the theme in speaking of the fragility of good fortune.

[65] The image in this context goes back at least to Xenophon (*Mem.* 2. 1. 28; *Cyr.* 1. 6. 11). Cicero had already used it: *Off.* 1. 48, as had Horace: *Ep.* 1. 7. 21–2.

[66] Judson 1997 interprets Aristotle's explanation of the cult of the Charites (see pp. 101–2) in a similar sense. Aristotle says, 'this is characteristic of *charis*: one should repay a service done one, and should another time take the initiative in doing a service oneself'. Judson argues that there are two levels of benefit, not only the individual favour, which must be requited, but the initiation of the process that can only be requited by initiating some other mutually beneficial exchange. The giver in any individual transaction is both an initiator and a person acting under a general obligation to give at some time. Seneca seems to have the same idea in *Ben.* 4. 13. 3 and see **ad loc.**

B. THE RELEVANCE OF *DE BENEFICIIS* TO CONTEMPORARY ROMAN SOCIETY

De beneficiis frustrates the social historian. It is ostensibly a work of practical ethics, yet, as we have said (Introduction, p. 1), it is strangely abstract, more universal even than Cicero's *De officiis*. For that work exhibits many Roman examples, descriptions of specific legal cases, and justifications of Cicero's own political career and of his attitude to recent events.[67] Then again, Seneca presents us with a high-minded code of beneficence that might seem more suited to the Stoic Sage, who indeed often takes centre stage, than to his readers, who are presumably rich men like his equestrian addressee, Aebutius Liberalis: he stresses intention as opposed to performance; he expects the donor to be indifferent to material return; he insists on a human obligation to confer benefits, that goes beyond ordinary social obligations. It is therefore not surprising that Seneca's advice is sometimes criticized as unrealistic. As Ramsey MacMullen argued, the exchange of favours was a central mechanism of Roman society and, though there was an elaborate etiquette governing it, most Romans could not be expected to be more altruistic than other people.[68] Although Cicero has similarly been accused of giving unrealistic advice in *De officiis* because, in exhorting his son and, through him, youth in general, he deliberately chose the more uncompromising Stoic morality rather than the perfectly respectable Academic and Peripatetic perspective (3. 20), Cicero at least sought to harmonize with the rigorous demands of Stoic ethics the striving for influence and glory that seemed so natural to the Roman political class (p. 28).[69]

There are obvious points that can be made, and have been made, to lessen this apparent contrast between *De beneficiis* and the real world. Seneca does accommodate the Roman social expectations of repute and tangible return.[70] His solution is this: the first reward of a benefit is the consciousness of having performed a virtuous act; the secondary rewards are good repute and any material gain (*Ben.* 2. 33. 3). But, of course, the last two are just extras, additions to the principal reward, which is having performed the virtuous act (see

---

[67] Gabba 1979; Griffin and Atkins 1991, pp. xii–xv; Long 1995; Dyck 1996, 8–10, 29–36; Lefèvre 2001.

[68] MacMullen 1986, 522. The article treats the role of *beneficia* as 'instruments of control'.

[69] As Cicero says himself at 1. 65. Aristotle's *megalopsuchos* was a more natural ideal for the Roman governing class, as Polybius' account of the younger Scipio shows: a description that stresses reputation and conveys no hint of doing good by stealth, as Seneca recommends (Polybius 31. 25. 9; 28. 4, 7, 10, cf. *Ben.* 2. 9. 2–10).

[70] e.g. Publilius Syrus 515, 683, 631, 212 (the numbering here follows Duff and Duff 1935); Val. Max. 5. 3 ext. 3–4. But, as Morgan 2007, 167 points out, strict reciprocity is less prominent in popular morality than one might expect 'in a world where exchange and patronage permeated everyday life'. It features more, as in the authors just cited, in gnomic quotations and exempla, which originate in relatively high social strata (175), than in proverbs and fables (55).

ad 2. 33. 3). More important, Seneca's 'high-minded nonsense', as MacMullen called it,[71] is to a large extent created by our failure to understand the style of discourse and the pedagogic technique of hyperbole. Diogenes the Cynic had used the image of the chorus leader who deliberately sets the note a bit high in hopes of getting it just right (D.L. 6. 35). Cicero had described the Stoic method in his attack on Cato, 'Those teachers of yours and masters of virtue seem to me to have deliberately extended the bounds of moral duty a little further than nature intended, their purpose being that in our minds we should strive for perfection, and so at least make it to the point we ought to reach.'[72] Kierkegaard compared the severity of the Christian commandments to 'setting the clock ahead half an hour to make sure of not being late in the morning'.[73] Seneca himself, towards the end of *De beneficiis*, after three casuistical books that gradually modify the stark precepts of the early books in the direction of realism (see p. 123), tells us explicitly how to read moral exhortation:

> Certain things we teach in an exaggerated form so that they result in due meas-ure. When we say 'He (the donor) ought not to remember (giving a benefit),' we really mean 'He ought not to trumpet it, nor to boast, nor to give offence.' It is to quell excessive and reproachful memory of it that we have told the man who gives to forget, and, by way of ordering more than he is able to accomplish, we have urged silence (7. 22. 1–2).

In fact, though both Cicero and Seneca are concerned to present an ideal, the negative examples, and the descriptions of the way men can actually behave, in both writers, show their awareness of the more sordid realities of life.[74] As Tarrant points out, Seneca's pessimism is not confined to his tragedies: even in his philosophical prose, 'his imagination seems to respond more vigorously to vice than to virtue' (Tarrant 2006, 5–7). One of the contributions Seneca makes to social history is his provision of examples of the language used in giving and receiving favours. Particularly vivid are the ungracious ones:

> One man receives a benefit disdainfully, as if to say, 'I really do not need it, but since you so much wish it, I will let you prevail over me'; another accepts listlessly, so that he leaves the benefactor uncertain about his being conscious of the favour; someone else mumbles his thanks, scarcely moving his lips, and comes across as more ungrateful than if he had kept silent. (*Ben.* 2. 24. 2–3, cf. 2. 13. 3).

Cicero and Seneca make contact with social reality at another level: that of the ideals current in the society and voiced by less theoretical Roman writers.

---

[71] MacMullen 1986, 521.

[72] *Mur. 65: Etenim isti ipsi mihi videntur vestri praeceptores et virtutis magistri finis officiorum paulo longius quam natura vellet protulisse ut, cum ad ultimum animo contendissemus, ibi tamen ubi oporteret consisteremus.*

[73] Quoted by Auden 1970, 284.

[74] Examples are *Off.* 1. 43–4; 2. 54–5; *Ben.* 4. 20. 3; 5. 17. 4; 6. 38. 2–4.

Cornelius Nepos, a younger contemporary of Cicero, describes the liberality of his friend Atticus as being 'neither time-serving nor calculating', directed not at the flourishing but at the poor, while Atticus was more concerned to remember the *beneficia* he had received than those he had bestowed (*Att.* 11. 3–5).[75] Earlier still, Terence provides the *sententia*, 'But one thing grates on me: your recounting your favour (i.e. manumission) looks like a reproach to me for forgetting your *beneficium*.'[76] The late Republican mime writer Publilius Syrus, as popular in the first century AD as when he was alive,[77] shows us the proverbial wisdom of his day about liberality: 'He who boasts of a favour wants it back again' (71); 'he who has given to a worthy man has received a benefit in giving' (68); 'whatever you give to the good, you give partly to yourself' (582); 'giving gifts repeatedly teaches the recipient to return them' (73); 'a benefit is best bestowed on a recipient who remembers well'; (491); 'you have used up every insult when you call a man ungrateful' (149); 'unwelcome are the benefits that are accompanied by fear' (308); 'the gift that is needed is twice as welcome if offered unasked' (57); 'he gives a benefit to a poor man twice over, who gives it quickly' (274). The last sentiment occurs earlier, in Ennius.[78] All these *sententiae* contain the sort of lessons that Seneca inculcates.[79] Seneca in fact believed in the moral effect of such precepts (chap. 7A). His concern with the standards of popular morality marks his involvement with Roman social reality. As Pierre Bourdieu notes, 'official representations', in which he includes customary rules, sayings, proverbs, and other verbalizations, produce and

---

[75] Cf. 'Menander', *Sententiae* 827 Jäkel χάριν λαβὼν μέμνησο καὶ δοὺς ἐπιλαθοῦ.

[76] *Andria* 44–5: *istaec commemoratio quasi exprobratio est immemori beneficii.* The remark is uttered by a freedman to his patron.

[77] He is in fact one of the authors who supply Seneca with the maxims he uses to end his early *Letters to Lucilius.* Seneca pays tribute to the philosophical truths in poets ('How many poets say things that have been said, or ought to be said, by philosophers' (*Quam multi poetae dicunt, quae philosophis aut dicta sunt aut dicenda*)), including Publilius Syrus in *Ep.* 8. 8–10, cf. 94. 28; 108. 9. This supports Morgan 2007, 339–40 in regarding the formal philosophical influence on this purveyor of popular morality as minimal: clearly, Seneca likes the support from outside. She argues that popular morality in general had more influence on high philosophy than the other way round (14, 297–8).

[78] *Beneficium qui dedisse se dicit petit* (71); *beneficium dando accepit, qui digno dedit* (68); *quidquid bono concedas, des partem tibi* (582, cf. 541); *beneficium saepe dare docere est reddere* (73); *optime positum est beneficium <bene> ubi meminit qui accipit* (491); *dixeris male dicta cuncta, cum ingratum hominem dixeris* (149); *ingrata sunt beneficia, quibus comes est metus* (308); *bis fiet gratum quod opus est si ultro offeras* (57); *inopi beneficium bis dat qui dat celeriter* (274). Cf. Ennius: 'Provided that whatever you give, you give quickly' (*dum quidquid des, des celere,* Non. p. 510. 10). See also **ad 2. 1. 4**.

[79] For giving to the poor, see p. 52 below. Not reminding beneficiaries: *Ben.* 2. 11. 1–3; 7. 22. 1; on giving to the worthy as a reward in itself: *Ben.* 1. 10. 5; 2. 33. 1; 4. 9. 5; on encouraging gratitude by repeated giving: *Ben.* 1. 2. 5–3. 1; 2. 11. 2; 7. 32; on gratitude as the main quality to look for in a recipient: *Ben.* 4. 10. 4–11. 1; on ingratitude as the worst vice: *Ben.* 1. 10. 4, cf. 7. 27. 3; on coercion removing an obligation of gratitude: *Ben.* 2. 18. 6–7; 6. 7. 2; on spontaneous giving as more welcome: *Ben.* 2. 1–2; on giving quickly: *Ben.* 1. 1. 8; 1. 7. 3; 2. 1. 2–3; 2. 4. 2–5. It is likely that the maxim Cicero quotes several times, and which chimes with Seneca's teaching (above, p. 40), was proverbial.

reinforce the dispositions expressed in them. And, as he goes on to point out, this 'official definition of reality is part of a full definition of social reality'.[80]

De beneficiis and High Society

De beneficiis, like *De officiis*, is highly revealing about the social *mores* of the Roman elite in particular. The treatise is, as Brad Inwood has stressed, 'aimed primarily at the givers of benefits and favours, Seneca's social equals—and betters'.[81] It is because Seneca is also primarily interested in this, his own, class, that the emphasis in *De beneficiis* is on the donor, and the 'major message of the treatise' is indeed, as Inwood says, that 'man's ingratitude should never incite (and cannot justify) the abandonment of giving'.[82] Thus the treatise begins and ends with an account of the faults of donors and the giving of advice to them, as the people held principally responsible for ingratitude. Similarly, in *De officiis*, Cicero was concerned only with his (at least in theory) social equals. Though he says that liberality has two aspects, granting a benefit and returning it, both obligatory for a *vir bonus* (1. 48), it is the donor's obligations on which he concentrates.[83] Indeed, he is largely thinking of exchanges within the rich elite, for he says that we should enrich the person who needs it, but that people generally do the opposite (1. 49). Even Seneca's legacy hunters are probably high-ranking senators (*Ben.* 6. 38. 4). Veyne regards this type of gift-giving as an important part of social practice in the Roman Republic. 'The rich circulated wealth among themselves,' he writes, 'giving all the more lavishly because they were giving to the already rich.'[84] Pliny and Martial attest, and similarly condemn, for their own time, the giving of gifts as bait to the rich.[85]

The extent to which Seneca's ideas are in tune with the practices and ideals of his class is revealed most clearly by Pliny's correspondence.[86] The letters convey 'the professed ideals of a member of the governing elite in the age of Trajan'.[87] It was perhaps because he was setting an example for his actual, theoretical, or (in the case of younger *senatorii*) potential peers, of how to conduct themselves within the upper reaches of society, that Pliny does not

[80] Bourdieu 2000, 108, cf. 110.

[81] Inwood 1995*a*, 263 = 2005, 91; Bellincioni 1984*a*, 121, though her idea that Seneca is refusing to give practical guidance at the level of *kathēkonta* (118–19) fails to take account of *Ben.* 7. 22. 1–2 and of his many realistic examples (above, p. 47).

[82] Inwood, loc. cit.

[83] Unlike Seneca, Cicero does not even mention *receiving* a benefit as a distinct area of conduct; as Brunt 1988*c*, 389 says, he concerns himself with 'the duties of men of high station'.

[84] Veyne 1990, 6.

[85] Plin. *Ep.* 9. 30. 3 (see below, p. 52); Spisak 1998, discusses *Epig.* 4. 56 and 5. 18. 6–10 in particular.

[86] As Guillemin 1929, 8 n. 1 wrote, 'Le *De beneficiis* est à la fois un manuel des vertus sociales et un code de la civilité. Ses nombreuses coïncidences avec les lettres de Pline fournissent des points de repère pour la détermination des usages mondains de l'époque imperial.'

[87] Parker 1988, 6.

publish correspondence with his patently social inferiors.[88] Pliny, also a senator and *novus homo* from an equestrian background, is himself a teacher, but in a different vein from the philosophical discourses of Seneca. He is careful to distinguish his letters from *scholasticas et umbraticas litteras* (*Ep.* 9. 2. 3), like the letters of Epicurus or, what he must have had in mind, the letters of Seneca to Lucilius.[89] Although sometimes his own letters are straightforwardly didactic, he usually teaches by example, as he claimed to do in person (*Epp.* 8. 23. 2–4; 6. 6. 5–6). He represents himself as more realistic and more humane than the philosophers in his standards of behaviour, both for himself and others (*Epp.* 5. 1. 13; 5. 16. 9–10; 8. 16. 3–4). Pliny's letters have been described as 'a handbook for the perfect Roman senator. They are not only autobiographical testimony but are also intended to be didactic, exemplary.'[90]

How confidently can we use Pliny's *Letters* as an indication of shared ideals against which we can measure Seneca's? W. V. Harris has drawn attention to the problem of distinguishing texts that assert an accepted societal norm from texts that improve on the conventional rules. He tends to take Pliny's published letters as showing 'what was aspired to, in his circle at least' or advertising attitudes that were correct, 'but still needed to be asserted'.[91] Many of the letters Pliny published (Books 1–9) recount his gifts and favours or are letters of recommendation. They are clearly intended to exhibit the high standards he observed in discharging the 'duties to friends' which he mentions as a special area of obligation, lying between official duties and those of private life (*Epp.* 3. 5. 19; 7. 15. 1; 9. 37. 1). That Pliny expresses ideals which his readers shared is apparent, not only from his obvious desire for approval and from his determination to project an ideal image of himself,[92] but from the fact that he even published letters which failed to secure the requests made on behalf of his friends. His purpose here was clearly to celebrate his intentions and methods, not his material benefactions.[93] Book 10, comprising his correspondence with Trajan, which he probably did not intend to publish,[94] contains letters

---

[88] 'No letter to a doctor, a philosopher, a freedman', as Syme 1985, 343 = 1988, 460 remarks. Pliny must, of course, have written such letters.

[89] On Pliny's acquaintance with Seneca's *Letters to Lucilius*, see J. Henderson 2002*b*, 118–22, 196 n. 17; Whitton 2010, 130, n. 74: 'Seneca is named only once in the epistles (5.3.5), but that is no index of his allusive import'; Marchesi 2008, 15.

[90] Veyne 1990, 9. One may be less disposed to agree with the end of the statement: 'which falsely makes their author seem highly pleased with himself'.

[91] Harris 2001, 18, 312, 314.

[92] Riggsby 1998, 75–97 stresses his construction of an image that would win community approval.

[93] Syme 1960, 362–79 = 1979, 477–95.

[94] The view that Pliny published Book 10 himself, advanced by Woolf 1995, 139, presents difficulties, of which the principal ones are: (i) that the letters finish abruptly during the term of his governorship, (ii) that *Ep.* 1. 1 suggests that he only intended to publish letters by himself, a practice observed except in Book 10, and (iii) that *Ep.* 1. 10. 9 shows that he regarded letters written as part of professional duties as *inlitteratissimas*, whereas the letters Pliny published were *paulo curatius scriptae*.

requesting favours on behalf of himself and others, and also letters of gratitude. Clearly, Pliny is here not aiming for general approval; nor does he simply want the Emperor to approve his attitude. He has the more practical aim of succeeding in his requests and building up credit for future ones. Therefore he must be following the accepted etiquette punctiliously. Both the letters Pliny published and those he did not, then, show us the social code of approved practice, even if we may doubt whether it was as consistently observed as Pliny represents it, even in his own case.[95]

In *Ep.* 1. 8, Pliny spells out the rationale of his benefactions (*munificentiae ratio*) (8), in an example of teaching *vel praeceptis vel exemplis* (*Ep.* 4. 24. 7). Pliny is here considering whether or not to publish the speech he had delivered when he dedicated the library he built at Comum, a speech in which he had promised the further benefaction of an alimentary scheme for financial help with the rearing of children. The speech showed that his generosity sprang, not from impulse, but from the rational application of moral principles; and Pliny says that working over the speech helped him to avoid the regret that can follow impulsive generosity (8–9), as Seneca had pointed out (*Ben.* 4. 10. 2–3). Moreover it reinforced the freedom from avarice that goes with the love of generosity (cf. *Ben.* 4. 14. 4). Pliny next (10) discusses the excellence of what he chooses to give—not games and gladiatorial contests, but something less popular yet in the public interest, i.e. incentives to rear children (12). Cicero in *De officiis* 2. 55–6 had spoken against giving games as a form of liberality, and, in Pliny's own time, Plutarch (*Mor.* 821 F) and Dio Chrysostom (*Or.* 66) condemned such entertainments. But Pliny also touches on the general theme of giving necessary, useful, and enduring things, rather than agreeable things that offer pleasure (1. 8. 10), with which we can compare Seneca's extended treatment in *De beneficiis* 1. 11–12. 1. Finally, we find (14) a theme that concerns him also in *Letter* 5. 1, that glory should follow, not be the motive for, generosity. Here he adds that, if it does not follow, the deed is nonetheless a noble one. Cicero had stressed that liberality motivated by glory is more apparent than real (*Off.* 1. 44) and that enduring repute follows only just conduct (2. 71). It is one of Seneca's main themes in *De beneficiis*, that to confer *beneficia* is an *officium* for human beings, and that one should give as an act of virtue, not to secure gain (4. 11). Pliny closes his letter (15) with the reflection that one can be blamed for broadcasting one's own *beneficium*, or, as Seneca put it, 'Let the giver of a benefit hold his tongue' (*Ben.* 2. 11. 2).[96]

---

[95] Bourdieu 2000, 110 says of what he calls 'official truth' that it 'has a practical efficacy, for even if it were belied by the practice of everyone, like a grammatical rule to which every case proved an exception, it would still remain a true description of such practices as are intended to be acceptable. The ethic of honour bears down on each agent with the weight of all the other agents.'

[96] The letter incidentally reminds us where the euergetism of the upper classes was channelled under the Empire: if Rome was the preserve of the Princeps and the imperial house, others could supply amenities to their native towns. See below, pp. 61–2; 74–6.

Sometimes, as in *Letter* 1. 19, Pliny not only explains the rationale behind his own actions but indicates what is expected of the other party in the transaction, the admonition being part of the etiquette of conferring the benefaction.[97]

In *Letter* 9. 30, Pliny is even more overtly didactic and sets out some of his general criteria for true *liberalitas*. Everything he says can be easily paralleled in *De officiis*, or *De beneficiis*, or both.[98] Liberality should be shown to one's country, one's relatives, one's connections, and one's friends. Pliny's order here matches Cicero's in *De officiis* 1. 58, cf. 1. 50, where it is expressly an order of priority. Pliny then urges that liberality be directed to poor friends, not used as hooks in fishing for those who can give us most in return. This is also the advice of Cicero (*Off.* 1. 49; 2. 61, 69–71) and of Seneca, who even uses the same image, also common in poetic satire (*Ben.* 4. 20. 3, cf. 4. 3. 1; 4. 10. 5). The idea that one should fit one's generosity to one's resources (cf. *Ep.* 2. 4. 3–4), and not find the means of helping one person by taking from another, is also strenuously argued by Cicero (*Off.* 1. 42–3; 2. 54–5) and mentioned by Seneca (*Ben.* 2. 15. 3). The aim of all this, Pliny says, is, by helping those in need, to move in an 'unbroken circle of *socialitas*'—'friendly relationships' or 'fellowship'. The word may be a coinage by Pliny: the thought is thoroughly Stoic.[99] Like Cicero and Seneca, Pliny clearly connects liberality with social bonding, and his notion of the circle here hints at reciprocity, though he is not expressly describing the *exchange* of benefits, as they are.

The letter presents us with three levels of conduct: that of the general run of men, said to be governed by greed; that of the friend who practises liberality, but not perhaps to the highest standard; and that of Pliny's moral demands. Pliny clearly represents himself as advocating an elevated ideal on the level of the philosophers, but he presents it as a mere refinement of the presumed 'less than perfect generosity' (*imperfecta liberalitas*) praised by his correspondent, with Pliny's endorsement: 'if your friend can achieve all this, he is wholly to be praised; if any bit of it, he is still deserving of praise' (*quae cuncta si facit iste, usquequaque laudandus est; si unum aliquid, minus quidem, laudandus tamen*). Pliny thus maintains his rapport with his readers, represented by his correspondent, even while exhorting them to greater heights.

---

[97] 'I shall not even remind you, as I ought to, did I not know that you will do so of your own accord, that you should exercise your new status with due discretion, because it was received through me' (*Ego ne illud quidem admoneo, quod admonere deberem, nisi scirem sponte facturum, ut dignitate a me data quam modestissime ut a me data utare*). J. Henderson 2002a, 223, in approving Guillemin's point, adds that such an admonition is paraded for our instruction: 'this is how such things are best done'.

[98] Bütler 1970, 127 notes parallels with Cicero and Seneca; Manning 1985, 74–5 concentrates on the parallels, in this and other Pliny letters, with Cicero's arguments which 'had become part of the intellectual furniture of Rome's ruling classes'.

[99] Bütler 1970, 127 n. 32. The translation in the *Oxford Latin Dictionary*, 'sociable disposition, companionableness' suits the meaning in *Pan.* 49. 4, but not the meaning here. Lewis and Short's 'fellowship' is closer.

That Pliny is expounding the code professed by his readership shows too in the fact that he regularly parts company with the philosophers just where one would expect Roman values to do so: namely, over the question of glory. In *Letter* 5. 1. 13 he confesses that he is 'not enough of a philosophical Wise Man' (*tam sapiens*) to be indifferent to the recognition he has received for his generosity. This is also where his expectation of his readers' approval is most apparent, for they can hardly be expected to miss the point that the publication of the *Letters* performed just that self-praise before a wider audience that Pliny struggles, throughout *Letter* 1. 8, to eschew.[100]

Given what we have said about the reception Pliny expects from his readers, the fact that the ideal he presents closely resembles Seneca's must suggest that the code Seneca advocates is not remote from that widely accepted at Rome in the class conferring benefactions. Pliny teaches by example an ideal of social relationships that closely resembles Seneca's. Indeed, he runs no risk of being out of touch with his readers when he uses Senecan language, as he does, even while confessing his weakness for fame, in *Ep.* 5. 10. There he says that he has received 'a reward, not only in good conscience, but in reputation as well' (*fructus non modo conscientiae sed etiam famae*), in that the recipient of his generosity has left him a legacy and praised his conduct in his will, and at §13 his use of the verb *accedere*, for the addition of the reward of fame to that of conscience is reminiscent of Seneca's similar use of *accessio* at *Ben.* 2. 33. 1. Pliny's description of the code conforms very closely to the exhortations of Cicero and Seneca, for a generally educated man, even if he was not formally trained in philosophy, could appropriate and assimilate what philosophers said, much of which had become 'part of the intellectual furniture of Rome's ruling classes'.[101] What Seneca supplies, and what is totally lacking in Pliny, is the systematic analysis of the code and its grounding in a general theory about the nature of the universe and the nature of man.

What may seem to be lacking in all three authors is the perspective of those who feel that they are not involved in horizontal relationships, as they should be, but are permanently at a disadvantage: the view that we are given by the Augustan and Flavian poets, or, particularly as regards relations with the Emperor, by Epictetus.[102]

---

[100] Leach 1990, 28 shrewdly comments, 'We may suspect that he has no clear program for improving the speech in mind. Rather he raises the question of publication as an excuse to supplement the content of the speech by an exterior clarification of his intentions.' Cf. Hoffer 1999, 101, 109–10.

[101] Pliny may only have acquired what philosophy he knew through studying rhetoric with Quintilian (*Ep.* 2. 16; 6. 6), who recommended the reading of philosophers (12. 2. 8, 10. 1. 35, 10. 1. 123) and believed, like Cicero, that the deployment of philosophical themes was the province of the orator (1. proem. 10–17). But, for political reasons, Pliny was keen to stress his friendship with the Stoic philosophers who had been prosecuted by Domitian and cultivated by Nerva and Trajan (*Epp.* 1. 5. 10; 2. 18; 3. 11; 9. 13. 1). For the last quotation, see above, n. 98.

[102] Millar 1965, 147 points out that Epictetus is a good counterfoil to Pliny, in being critical of the values and aspirations of Roman society.

This does not mean that the theory presented in *De beneficiis* should be construed as a mode of euphemization in Bourdieu's terms, in which an objective reality of inequality, based on self-interested, economically based transactions and relationships, is being deliberately disguised as a set of disinterested moral transactions and relationships between equals, with the purpose of maintaining this inequality in the interests of those who benefit from it.[103] As we have seen (above, p. 47), Seneca frequently shows himself aware that people fall short of fulfilling the requirements of the social code. When the behaviour of the donor is arrogant and ungracious, recipients of beneficence feel in the power of their benefactors and struggle to free themselves of the burden (*Ben.* 1. 1. 4–8; 2. 1. 2–4; 2. 17. 6; 6. 35. 2–4);[104] then again, when the recipient is too proud and does not wish to give credit to another for his success, the donor does not receive the gratitude he deserves (*Ben.* 2. 23–4; 4. 40; 5. 20. 2; 6. 39. 2; 7. 26. 3).[105] Moreover, Seneca had his own idea of the underlying social function served by gift-exchange (above, pp. 43–4). Finally, such a view fails to do justice to the elaboration and subtlety of what is clearly designed as a serious guide to practice. Seneca is not setting out to misdescribe reality: he is urging his readers to realize an ideal they share. It is at the level of practice, not of theory, that euphemism may be necessary: but even the etiquette of personal interaction, as we shall see, is more subtle than Bourdieu suggests, requiring in fact a complex combination of egalitarianism and deference.

C. *DE BENEFICIIS* AS A REACTION TO SOCIAL CHANGE

It was suggested at the start of this chapter that the importance Seneca attributes to the topic of benefits stems from his own experience of the social practices he analyses; that, like Cicero, he was keen to preserve the position of the governing class and the aristocratic social code, challenged by changes in the political and social system; and that, in Seneca's case, this meant adapting it to include the Princeps. Before we expand on this notion, it will be well to review three other suggestions for what called forth Seneca's analysis of social exchange.

---

[103] So Bourdieu 2000, 105–7, 126–9, in post-Marxist vein, likes to represent the verbalizations of its own practice within a society: 'The official norm and the native theory reinforce the repression of the objective truth' (107).

[104] Marchese 2009 discusses ingratitude as a refusal of respect, when the donor makes public the position of inferiority a gift entails, and does not show respect to the recipient.

[105] Saller 1982, 127 notes the evidence for this concern in Seneca. At *Ben.* 2. 21. 5, however, Graecinus' reason for refusing the gift is not the fear of losing social status, but the immorality of the donors: for Seneca it is important not to accept a *beneficium* from someone with whom one does not wish to create a bond of friendship (2. 18. 5).

(i) F.-R. Chaumartin sees *De beneficiis* as a response to particular abuses that came in with the Principate. He describe it as a 'critique de la politique sociale des princes'.[106] On this view, Seneca, attacking earlier Principes by name and Nero by allusion, exposes the abuses current in the relations of patrons and clients and in the practice of beneficence, especially among the favourites of those Emperors whose conduct sets a bad example. Further, his attack on any move to make ingratitude actionable at law (*Ben*. 3. 6–17) is interpreted as a warning to the Emperor not to use such legal means to extract wealth from imperial freedmen.[107]

Aside from the difficulty of pinning down 'allusions' to contemporaries and contemporary events, this analysis means reading into Seneca's argument against legal sanctions for ingratitude a concern with freedmen, who are not even mentioned (see **ad 3. 6. 2**). Moreover, it means making the long-standing vertical relationships of patronage central to Seneca's analysis when, as we have seen, he is far more concerned with the forging and maintaining of, at least ostensibly, horizontal relationships through the exchange of benefits.

(ii) At the opposite extreme from Chaumartin, J. Michel has suggested that the background to *De beneficiis* is a far more general and gradual phenomenon: nothing less than an evolution in the place occupied by gift-exchange within Roman society. From an analysis of legal texts, he comes to the conclusion that *beneficia*, the services of friends, were gradually being replaced by commercial and legal institutions: Rome was moving further along the continuum between primitive forms of exchange and economic, legally enforced exchange.[108] He points out that Seneca is not just describing the Roman usages he knew from personal observation: his work is 'un travail d'élaboration morale de la pratique sociale' (529). But he argues that the practice whose moral level Seneca wishes to raise was already past its peak of social importance in the last century of the Roman Republic. The key evidence is of two kinds: first, the development of legal contracts for gratuitous services that provide, as an accessory to the existing social sanctions, legal sanction for the exchange of friendly services; second, the decline in the number of references to the services of friends found in the Theodosian and the Justinianic codes, as compared to those found in the opinions of the classical jurists preserved in the *Digest*. Michel detects a progressive decline of free services and an increase in paid ones.

---

[106] Chaumartin 1989, 1716.

[107] Ibid. 1718–19; at p. 1722 he is less certain that Seneca's liberal teaching about the ability of slaves to confer benefits on their masters is relevant to his own political aims or to the events of Nero's reign.

[108] Michel 1962. This is not true for him as the description of a historical process, for he thinks (528) that the place of gift-exchange in Roman society is not to be explained as a survival of primitive institutions, but by similar conditions producing similar results, namely, a restricted social group practising reciprocal exchange.

One might detect evidence that the jurist Ulpian was aware of such a change in the *Digest* 11. 6. 1–2, which concerns an action against a land surveyor. The service of a land surveyor was traditionally a *mandatum*, a contract described by the jurists as 'free and originating in duty and friendship', in contrast with *locatio* and *conductio*, the equivalent contracts where pay is involved.[109] Ulpian, feeling that the fact that only a very limited type of legal action can be brought against such a mandated person requires explanation, adduces the idea held by older legal authorities (*veteres*) that 'when one engages someone like a surveyor, one does not hire him, but rather he provides his services as a favour (*beneficii loco*), and the payment he receives is by way of requital; hence it is called an *honorarium*' (*Dig.* 11. 6. 1).[110]

Michel notes that the legal protection granted against misconduct by those providing gratuitous services starts, for the most part, at the end of the Republic and reaches its heyday in the second century AD. That is the case for *depositum*, *commodatum*, *mandatum*.[111] For Michel, the introduction of such legal sanctions for these essentially social practices is already a sign of decline.[112]

In his view, the services of friends were still preponderant in the Roman way of life in the last century of the Republic. The first century of the Empire saw a progressive decline in free services, because reciprocal exchange requires the social setting of a small, stable group with surplus wealth and little opportunity to conserve or invest it, like the senatorial aristocracy of the Republic; the Principate meant a larger, more diverse, and more socially mobile governing

---

[109] *Digest* 17. 1. 1. 4: 'There is no mandate unless it is gratuitous. The reason is that it derives its origin from duty and friendship, and the fact is that payment for services rendered is incompatible with this duty. For if money is involved, the matter rather pertains to letting and hiring' (*Mandatum nisi gratuitum nullum est. Nam originem ex officio atque amicitia trahit, contrarium ergo est officio merces: interveniente enim pecunia res ad locationem et conductionem potius respicit*).

[110] Cicero speaks of *mandatum* in *Pro Roscio Amerino* 111–12 in the terms in which he discusses *beneficia* in *De officiis*: 'Therefore an action for breach of trust was established, the result of which involved as much disgrace as an action for theft. This was because, in matters in which we cannot take part personally, the good faith of our friends is substituted for our own efforts; and anyone who violates this promise attacks the common safeguard of all and, as far as it is in his power, ruins the life of society. . . . That is why breach of trust is a disgraceful fault, because it violates two things of the utmost sanctity, friendship and good faith. For a person does not normally entrust a commission to anyone but a friend, and he only trusts one whom he believes to be faithful' (*Itaque mandati constitutum est iudicium non minus turpe quam furti, credo, propterea quod quibus in rebus ipsi interesse non possumus, in eis operae nostrae vicaria fides amicorum supponitur; quam qui laedit, oppugnat omnium commune praesidium et, quantum in ipso est, disturbat vitae societatem . . . Ergo idcirco turpis haec culpa est, quod duas res sanctissimas violat, amicitiam et fidem. Nam neque mandat quisquam fere nisi amico neque credit nisi ei quem fidelem putat*).

[111] Michel 1962, 437–43. *Mandatum* seems to have been actionable in the late 2nd c. BC to judge from *Rhet. ad Her.* 2. 19. Michel 439 believes, however, that the oldest of these gratuitous contracts and the most important, *mutuum*, had a legal sanction earlier (in the 4th or 3rd c. BC). Watson 1965, 15, n. 1 says that the first evidence for *mutuum*, a loan without interest, being actionable is in Cicero, *Pro Roscio Comoedo* 13–14.

[112] Michel 1962, 442: 'Mais pour une notion aussi typiquement sociale que la gratuité, peut-être est-ce déjà un signe de décadence que d'avoir besoin de la sanction du droit.'

elite, under the control of the Emperor, not characterized by durable alliances of friendship in which benefactors and beneficiaries remain socially linked.[113] As a result, the *honoraria* of doctors, teachers of the liberal arts, and lawyers, have to be legally protected, though Ulpian feels embarrassed about the idea of paid service and thinks that philosophers should be excluded—'not because the subject is not hallowed, but because they ought above all to claim to spurn mercenary activity'—and that teachers of civil law should be excluded because 'knowledge of civil law is indeed a most hallowed thing, but something which is not to be valued in terms of money.' He adds, 'For there are certain things that it is honourable to accept, but not honourable to seek.'[114] Eventually, fees of teachers and lawyers were included in Diocletian's price edict among the wages of artisans (*mercedes operariorum*).

Michel himself does not connect Seneca's concern with *beneficia* to this suggested decline. Rather, he regards him, like Cicero, as a moralist primarily concerned to purify the transactions between friends, and giving, in the process, a somewhat misleading picture of the usages around him, in that he minimizes their self-interested character.[115] However, it is open to us, on the basis of his analysis, to consider the possibility that Seneca, while having as his purpose the raising of moral standards, was in some cases identifying as moral decline, in characteristic Roman fashion, an institutional change in the social pattern he valued. Thus one could see in Seneca's insistence that very different attitudes should prevail in the exchange of benefits from those found in commercial legally enforceable transactions, and in his vigorous repudiation of the ideal of legal enforcement of gratitude, counter-attacks or moves to preserve the centrality of the institution of gift-exchange to Roman society. If, as Michel thinks, Cicero, Seneca, and Pliny reflect the same social practice of exchange that is mentioned by the classical jurists,[116] and the jurists provide evidence for a decline in that practice and the intrusion of impersonal institutions, then Seneca, too, could be reflecting such a change.

Certainly, there are striking similarities between the way that Seneca defends the exchange of benefits from commercial attitudes and the way that jurists distinguish the gratuitous type of contractual exchange from ordinary commercial exchange. We have already seen Ulpian explaining the difference between a *mandatum*, carried out by a land surveyor, and the ordinary hiring of services, by saying that such work was treated by older authorities as belonging in the category of a *beneficium*.[117] Paul speaks of *precarium* (a gift or service revocable when the donor wishes) being related 'more to grants and cases of benefit than to cases of business contracted'.[118] The fundamental difference

---

[113] Ibid. 554, 577–8, 584.

[114] *Dig.* 50. 13. 1. 4–5: *quaedam enim tametsi honeste accipiantur, inhoneste tamen petuntur.*

[115] Michel 1962, 528–30.   [116] Ibid., ch. 6.   [117] Above, nn. 109–10.

[118] *Dig.* 43. 26. 14 *magis enim ad donationes et beneficii causam, quam ad negotii contracti spectat precarii condicio.*

between the gratuitous and the commercial exchange, as *Digest* 17. 1. 1. 4 makes plain, is money: 'There is no mandate unless it is gratuitous. The reason is that it derives its origins from duty and friendship (*ex officio atque amicitia*), and the fact is that payment for services rendered is incompatible with this duty. For if money is involved, the matter rather pertains to hire.' Similarly, Seneca is quite clear that one owes no gratitude for what one buys (*Ben.* 6. 14. 3) and that a *beneficium* loses all its standing if it is reduced to *merces* (3. 14. 4). And just as Ulpian found some awkwardness in treating the *honoraria* of teachers and doctors as fees (*pretia*) and making their work mercenary (*Dig.* 50. 13. 1. 1–5), so Seneca takes, as one of the hard cases he explores, the question why we feel gratitude to teachers and doctors, despite paying for their services. The answer requires making a distinction between their time and skill, for which we pay, and their good will and friendly concern, for which we cannot pay in money but only in gratitude. Raising their remuneration would not, he argues, meet the case (*Ben.* 6. 15–17).

Was this gradual change perceptible enough to have inspired *De beneficiis*? The chronology is difficult, as Ulpian and Paul are writing over a century away from Pliny, a century and a half from Seneca, and more than two centuries from Cicero. Moreover, Michel sometimes sets the real decline even later, starting it at the end of the second century AD (442). Crook, however, who also believes that, in the period beginning with the Ciceronian age and extending to the age of Ulpian in the early third century, 'gratuitousness and *noblesse oblige* in contract were an old tradition less and less honoured in the observance, as services became more specialized and what had once been amateur became professional', suspects that 'the distinction between the gratuitous services of status-equals and the paid services of status-inferiors had partly ceased to be real even in Cicero's day and grew steadily more unreal'.[119] Thus the Lex Cincia of 204 BC already put legal restrictions on gifts, including a prohibition on those given to legal advocates, who no doubt were ceasing to regard them as optional. The restriction was reinforced by Augustus, but Claudius, more realistically, merely had a limit placed on the amount an advocate could receive, while Seneca himself was instrumental in reviving the law in 54. Some limit on payments continued in force, as Pliny attests. In this case, then, the law offers support to a category of free service, and then at least tries to prevent excessive abuse of the social institution over a long period of time.[120] It is clear that Seneca, who explicitly mentions defending someone accused of a capital offence as a *beneficium* (*Ben.* 3. 9. 2), would be responding to a very gradual process that started well before his time.[121]

---

[119] Crook 1967, 239–40.

[120] Cassius Dio 54. 18. 2; Tac. *Ann.* 11. 7; 13. 5, 42–3 (see Griffin 1976, 74–5); Suet. *Nero* 17; Plin. *Epp.* 5. 4. 2;. 5. 9. 4.

[121] Quintilian 12. 7. 12 suggests that receiving fees is more common, though he himself only approves of it in case of economic necessity.

Like Cicero, Seneca as a *novus homo* might be particularly aware of traditional customs under threat, yet one of the most striking contrasts between *De officiis* and *De beneficiis* is the lack of concern in the latter with *mos maiorum*. Seneca does not use traditional Roman conduct as a standard by which to condemn present immorality.[122] There are not many Republican *exempla*, and a number of those that appear are not admirable. Moreover, when, in Book 1. 9. 3–10. 5, Seneca castigates vice in a crescendo leading up to the arraignment of ingratitude as the worst of all, he specifically says that levels of vice change very little, though different vices are more prominent at different times, and every generation complains that morality is gone and things are getting worse. On the other hand, Seneca's insistence on delimiting the area subject to legal enforcement may show some awareness of encroachment;[123] his concern for the cohesiveness of society and its maintenance through the exchange of benefits could imply some perception of the consequences of the evolution described by Michel and Crook. But he betrays no sense that these friendly exchanges are giving way to greater individualism and freedom, combined with a reliance on government to regulate and hold society together. Similar changes in western societies now are much more rapid and hence more perceptible.

Seneca's examples, in fact, show that he saw the beneficence of the elite as still extending over a range similar to that treated by Cicero. There was clearly substantial continuity in this respect between the Republic and the Principate.[124] Both writers mention members of the Roman governing class rescuing friends from the pirates (*Off.* 2. 55, 63, *Ben.* 1. 5. 4; 7. 15. 1); defending men on capital charges (*Off.* 2. 66; *Ben.* 3. 9. 2; 4. 12); helping their peers with the expenses of advancement (*Off.* 2. 62, *Ben.* 2. 21. 5: giving *ludi*) or helping to pay off debts (*Off.* 2. 55; *Ben.* 3. 8. 2); exercising patronage with regard to magistracies, priesthoods and provinces (*Off.* 2. 67; *Ben.* 1. 11. 5, cf. 1. 5. 1; 4. 31. 3, 5).[125] Pliny's

---

[122] *Ben.* 2. 1. 4 and 2. 7. 1 show that having to request favours was felt to be as demeaning by the *maiores* as it is now. At *Ben.* 3. 6. 2 the practice of 'our ancestors, who were certainly great men' (*nostri maiores, maximi scilicet viri*), is adduced, not to lament a departure from their practice, but to strengthen Seneca's objection to change. At 2. 20. 2 Brutus should have realized that the loss of old-fashioned morality (*amissis pristinis moribus*) made the maintenance of the Republic impossible, but Seneca goes on to say that Brutus should also have learnt from the early history of Rome that monarchic ambition incites imitation. See also **ad 1.10.1–3**.

[123] Though, if so, it is remarkable that he does not mention, when discussing the question of legal checks on ingratitude, the introduction of an *accusatio ingrati liberti* in the time of Augustus (Treggiari 1969, 69, 73–5), to say nothing of the debate on the subject in 56 (on which see Griffin 1976, 279, 281–2).

[124] This is the main thesis, and the most convincing, in Saller's important book (Saller 1982).

[125] It is not clear in the latter passages if Seneca means the Princeps or some other supporter of the candidate. Saller 1982, 42 n. 6 thinks that in *Ben.* 1. 5. 1, it is the Princeps. In the list of activities in *Ep.* 8. 6, the supporter of a candidate in the senatorial elections is unambiguously a man like Seneca.

letters, too, show no sign of such a decline in beneficence to individuals, or any perception of a decline. Michel (583–4) explains away Pliny's evidence as, on the one hand, a fossilized survival of Republican practice and, on the other, a change of venue to the municipal scene. But, though euergetism—liberality to the public by individuals—moved to the municipalities, leaving Rome clear for the Princeps (see below, p. 75), Pliny's individual favours were by no means restricted to the municipalities with which he had connections, but included individuals in Rome and Roman officials. Moreover, as Michel himself rightly observes (533), Pliny was offering a model for imitation: had it been a hopelessly outdated model, he could not have hoped to be read and admired.

Saller, in fact, has pointed out that Michel's arguments for decline are by no means conclusive.[126] The contrast between the classical jurists and the later codes is questionable, given the difference in the subject-matter of the two bodies of material. The historical evidence suggests that the system of friendly services was still central to Roman life in the early Empire, and the changes Michel notes, e.g. the founding of public chairs for teachers of rhetoric and then of philosophy, are not sufficiently significant to cast doubt on that picture.

(iii) Matthew Roller in his book *Constructing Autocracy* has discussed *De beneficiis* as part of a general treatment of the relation of Seneca's ethical teaching to the political problems facing his peers under the Principate.[127] He regards Seneca as 'a Roman aristocrat in the first instance who presents Stoic ethics to his social peers (the implied audience) as a way out of contemporary ethical binds' (80 n. 27), helping the aristocracy to reasserts its traditional power and privileges against the power of the emperor (11). Symptomatic of Seneca's approach, for him, is his rejection in *De beneficiis*, 'a work utterly preoccupied with the protocols of social exchange', of traditional Roman ethics with its external modes of moral evaluation, and his insistence that the only criterion of moral value is the agent's state of mind. In general, Roller thinks that, though Seneca sometimes enlists traditional morality and examples as a way of winning over his readers, his ultimate aim is to unseat the traditional notions upheld by his interlocutor or addressee as representatives of those readers. There are many objections that can be made to the argument as it stands. First, it assumes that the Emperor would himself derive no benefit from such a work as *De beneficiis*, which is full of examples positive and negative of imperial conduct (pp. 62–3, 82 below; Ch. 9, p. 165). Yet Roller himself stresses the close relation of *clementia*, on which Seneca addressed a work to Nero, to exchange (132). Then, it assumes too readily that the interlocutor represents a single 'standard' view shared with his readers: all Seneca's addressees are represented as *imperfecti* (see **ad 2. 18. 4**), but not only are they not static—Lucilius being represented as becoming more sophisticated in the course of the *Letters*, and Aebutius Liberalis, I hope to show, in *De beneficiis* (7)—but each of them is

---

[126] Ibid. 119 n. 2.   [127] Roller 2001, 79–83.

represented as rather above the level of some of the readers (*Ep.* 47. 2; *Ben.* 5. 1). In construing Seneca's message as a radical challenge to traditional Roman values, it fails to take into account hyperbole as a traditional pedagogic strategy in Stoicism, and the warning that Seneca himself gives about how to read his more paradoxical utterances (above, p. 47). Most significantly, as regards *De beneficiis* in particular, Roller overlooks the resemblance between what Seneca teaches and the existing social ideals of Roman high society.[128] Some of these similarities we have already explored, but more will emerge when we turn to the interaction of the Princeps and his ostensible peers. Nonetheless, as Roller sees, it would be surprising if *De beneficiis* did not reflect and engage with the social changes that accompanied the great political upheaval that had taken place less than a century ago.

The Aristocratic Code and the Princeps

Seneca's treatise does in fact bear the marks of the significant social changes that accompanied the change from the Republic to the new political system. Epictetus puts it neatly in his picture of his rich successful man at Rome: 'What could anyone imagine you to need? You are rich, you have children, possibly also a wife, and many slaves. Caesar knows you, you have many friends, you perform the duties appropriate to you, you know how to reward benefits and return injuries' (2. 14. 18). In the last sentence, the other elements are familiar from the Republic; the first, 'Caesar knows you', sets us in a new world. Thus Seneca writes with two distinct types of men in mind, the ruler and the ruled. 'He has given me this (office) but gave more to So-and-so and gave sooner to someone else' (*Ben.* 2. 28. 1).

Most of the Roman examples of generosity concern the Emperors, who are shown giving money to individual senators (1. 15. 6; 2. 7–8; 2. 27. 1–2) or conferring magistracies (1. 5. 1; 2. 26. 2; 2. 27. 4–28. 2; 4. 28. 2 (nominally about a *rex*)) or pardoning individuals (3. 27; 2. 12. 1). Moreover, as we noted on p. 10, whereas Cicero's harsh criticism of the euergetism of his day shows how important a role it played in the political competition of the Late Republic, communal benefits, when Seneca mentions them at all, emanate from the Emperors, who are shown giving *congiaria* (4. 28. 2) or making grants of citizenship and immunity to whole peoples (6. 19. 2–5). Under the Principate, such ostentation *in Rome itself* was rigidly controlled or suppressed. Whereas Cicero's treatise reflects the fact that his peers were motivated by political ambition to adorn Rome with buildings, Seneca names only Agrippa as having contributed public buildings in the city (*Off.* 2. 60; *Ben.* 3. 32. 4). For when senators outside the imperial house lost the right to celebrate triumphs under

---

[128] He regards Seneca, mistakenly in my view, as more in the radical tradition of early Stoicism than does Brunt 1975 or Inwood 1995a, 260–5 = 2005, 87–92 or Veyne 2003.

Augustus, they also lost the ability to erect new public buildings in the capital. Again, whereas Cicero's treatise reflects the fact that his peers competed in popularity by the giving of lavish games, Seneca mentions only the refusal by L. Julius Graecinus of contributions to his *ludi* from immoral individuals (*Ben.* 2. 21. 5–6). For the Princeps' games now outclassed anything the magistrates could provide. In Nero's reign indeed, one of his favourites, the senator Fabricius Veiento, registered his protest at Nero's putting beyond the reach of magistrates the provision of chariot races by training dogs for racing rather than horses.[129] Nero responded by contributing prizes, and other generous Emperors provided help, but in such a way as to produce uniformity and reduce competition within the elite, so that the senate enjoyed a corporate eminence well below his own.[130] Large public dinners seem to be the only form of large-scale relatively impersonal entertainment envisaged by Seneca as being given by men in public life.[131]

How was the aristocratic code of beneficence to assimilate the phenomenon of the Princeps? It is notable that Seneca is often vague in his description of benefits. Of the examples above, those concerning magistracies are not explicitly attributed to the Princeps, though the parallel passage in *Ira* 3. 31. 2 makes that attribution difficult to contest. For Seneca does not merely reflect the realities of the new situation: he wants to make it clear that, in general, the advice he offers on conferring benefactions applies to the Princeps.

This is made unambiguous by the treatment of one of his principal themes, i.e. that a *beneficium*, to be a virtuous act, must be rational: though only the Sage can judge with infallible correctness when, where, why, how, and to whom benefits should be given (*Ep.* 81. 10), all others should use their reason to the best of their ability (2. 16. 1; 4. 9. 3).[132] To illustrate this point, Seneca adduces the practice of different Emperors. So, as the climax to Book 1, Augustus and Claudius are juxtaposed as good and bad examples. The senator Passienus Crispus made the telling comparison, 'From the deified Augustus I would rather have the judgement, from Claudius the benefit': that is, to receive from Augustus meant to be rationally judged as deserving; while Claudius, though generous, gave 'by chance and thoughtless impulse', like a gift of Fortune. Such random bounty, Seneca observes, is not only insecure, like all gifts of Fortune, but imposes no obligation of gratitude (1. 15. 3–6). Seneca makes it clear that, in general, it is a source of complaint when the Princeps

---

[129] Dio Cassius 61. 6; Suet. *Nero* 22.

[130] See on the whole question of the public prominence of senators Eck 1984; Griffin 1991, 42–5.

[131] *Ben.* 1. 14. 1; *Ep.* 19. 11: Lucilius, a procurator, is here being urged to retire from public life, which involves him in such activities. *Ben.* 4. 28. 6 may be another reference. Dunbabin and Slater 2011, 452–3 think that such banquets in Rome itself could only be given by the Emperor, but there is no indication in Seneca that these banquets are not in Rome.

[132] Cicero had also stressed the need for rational discrimination in *Off.* 1. 49, and we find it in Polybius' portrait of the younger Scipio (31. 28. 10–11).

does not give in accordance with virtue and dutifulness (2. 28. 2); but discrimination should not be censure. It is a matter of degree. Tiberius erred in the other direction from Claudius, who gave benefits without discrimination. He required impoverished senators to submit lists of their creditors, ordered the creditors to be paid, and then informed the beneficiaries that he had done so, adding an offensive admonition. This was, says Seneca, not really giving a benefit, but making them prove their desert as before a judge (2. 8. 2) and turning a favour into a moral assessment accompanied by rebuke (see ad 2. 8. 2).

The anecdote provokes an outburst from the philosopher and senator: 'It is not appropriate even for a Princeps to give, in order to humiliate.' How rigorous should his judgement be? What Seneca says here about Tiberius matches the practice of his own Emperor, but Tacitus regarded Tiberius' practice with more sympathy than Seneca and thought Nero too undiscriminating in his generosity to impoverished senators.[133] Seneca perhaps advised that, if a young Princeps could not achieve the mean between Tiberius and Claudius, as represented by Augustus, it was better for him to err on the side of generosity. Seneca and the other imperial writers in fact expect the Emperor to exercise judgement and to use the same criteria as they and their peers used, when conferring benefactions or securing them as intermediaries from each other.[134]

Seneca is, as usual, raising to the level of theory the concepts and standards of Roman society in his own time. Modern scholars, however, impressed by the lack of institutionalized systems of promotion in Rome, are often tempted to conclude that the Princeps and his 'brokers' dispensed offices and honours in return for loyalty and gratitude, not judging potential beneficiaries according to desert. In Saller's words, 'No attempt was made to transcend the particularistic criterion of patronage by the introduction of the universalistic and rational criteria of seniority and merit (in the modern sense)', or, as Cotton has put it 'gifts were not deserved but magnanimously bestowed'.[135] But Werner Eck has suggested that the needs of the imperial administration would require rational, if flexible, promotion procedures, rather than arbitrary ones, and that the Emperor would have to take into account not only loyalty, social and political status, and influential support, but also experience and competence: the experience would be general, but suited to the demands of the particular post.[136]

---

[133] *Ann.* 1. 75. 3–4: 'Through his wish to be strict, he was harsh even in those matters which he handled with propriety' (*cupidine severitatis in iis etiam quae rite faceret acerbus*); cf. 2. 48. 3 where he actually names Marius Nepos among those 'who were prodigal and whose need arose from their outrages' (*prodigos et ob flagitia egentes*); for Nero: *Ann.* 13. 34.

[134] For Tacitus, see n. 133 above, ad 1. 15. 1–6, and *Hist.* 1. 52, where Vitellius' generosity is criticized as 'without limit, without judgement' (*sine modo, sine iudicio*); cf. Fronto, *Ad M.Caes.* 5. 52 van den Hout 79–80; Dio Cass. 62. 19. 2–3; 71. 19. 1, cf. 52. 15. 3; 19. 1–2; *SHA Hadr.* 10. 3–6. For Pliny, see below.

[135] Saller 1982, 110; Cotton 1984, 165.

[136] Eck 2001; Eck 2002. He is principally concerned to establish the operation of rules, sociopolitical norms, in the promotion of officials at all levels.

Indeed, the ancient evidence suggests that appointments were made on the basis of qualities according to which men *can* be rationally assessed and compared, but the merits considered were not specific skills or experience, but industry, honesty, literacy, and general good character.[137]

Pliny's *Letters* provide a parallel. He confirms Seneca's idea that the Princeps, like other benefactors, is expected to exercise *iudicium*.[138] He had praised Trajan in the *Panegyricus* for liberality that showed *iudicium* and for encouraging industry, integrity, and thrift, in giving good men priesthoods and provinces and showing that they enjoyed his friendship and his approbation (44. 7–8). Just as Pliny, in noting the support he received from the senior senator Verginius Rufus, says that priests 'nominate men they judge highly worthy of priesthoods' (*Ep*. 2. 1. 8), so Pliny, in asking the Princeps for a priesthood, starts his request, 'Since I know, *domine*, that to be honoured by the *iudicium* of such a good Princeps lends approbation to my good character' (10. 13). Later, he writes to a well-wisher, 'You rightly congratulate me, first because it is glorious to win a mark of approbation [*iudicium* again] from so noble a Princeps' (*Ep*. 4. 8. 1). And again, just as Pliny persuaded a provincial governor that Suetonius *deserved* a military tribunate (3. 8), so, in the case of a young man for whom he had secured the *latus clavus* and the quaestorship from Trajan, he is anxious that the judgment of the whole senate should confirm the opinion that he himself had induced the Princeps to have of him, and he goes on to list the candidate's virtues (2. 9. 2–3). And just as he recommends Voconius Romanus to the governor of Lower Germany, giving reasons for his request in terms of his friend's 'interests, character, in sum his whole life' (*studia, mores, omnem denique vitam*, 2. 13. 10–11), so Pliny mentions in the same letter that he had secured Romanus the *ius trium liberorum* from the Princeps, who bestows these privileges 'sparingly and with discrimination' (*parce et cum delectu*, 2. 13. 8). Moreover, in requesting promotion for his friends, whether from provincial governors or from the Princeps, Pliny often casts his requests in such vague terms that we have to guess what precisely is being requested (e.g. *Epp*. 2. 13; 3. 2; 10. 26, 85–7). Pliny means to stress that the judgment implicit in a benefaction is more valuable than the benefit. As he says, after listing the good qualities of Voconius Romanus, 'Though you grant him the highest office in our power, you could give him nothing better than your friendship. It was in order to convince you that he is worthy of it, and

---

[137] Marcus Aurelius' letter of appointment to Domitius Marsianus as equestrian procurator (*AE* 1962, 183a) notes that continued imperial favour will require continued *innocentia, diligentia, experientia*.

[138] Guillemin 1929, 5–6, 10 shows that letters of recommendation must enumerate the virtues of the person recommended, to show that he is worthy of the favour. In Pliny's published letters, acquiring glory for the person praised with a wider public, and with posterity, is an additional motive.

even of your closest intimacy, that I have thus briefly sketched for you his interests, his character: in sum, his whole life' (2. 13. 10).[139]

The code being applied is not a new one. The Republican code of benefactions for the governing class was applied to the Princeps. He was to be judged by the same standards as they.[140] That was natural: in theory, the Princeps was one among equals, and it was in the interest of all parties concerned that the theory be respected. Thus, on this same subject of discrimination in giving, Cicero's letters attest the same expectations for the Republic. The letters prove that, when he insisted, in *De officiis* 1. 49, that judgement be exercised in conferring benefits, that was not just an unrealistic ideal. In *Ad Familiares* 13, he speaks of the enumeration of virtues as an intrinsic part of letters of recommendation (*Fam.* 13. 10. 3), and in many of these letters there is at least as much emphasis on the worthiness of the recipient, and the judgement of the potential benefactor, as there is on the weight of Cicero's advocacy and relationship with the benefactor, e.g. *Fam.* 13. 51; 13. 6 (especially para. 4); 13. 78: these are letters in which this emphasis is all the clearer because, as in some of Pliny's letters, what is actually being requested is itself left vague.

The Social Aspect of *Civilitas*

The extension of the Republican code of liberality to the Princeps meant not only that he was to be judged by the same standards as the 'giving' section of society, but that relations between members of the upper orders and the Princeps were to follow the same etiquette as obtained among themselves. It is the importance of this theme that probably explains why Seneca concentrated on generosity to individuals of similar status, and why he largely omitted the treatment of mass benefactions. If it were just a matter of making clear that, as a donor, the Princeps can be held to the same standards as his nominal peers, Seneca could have applied to imperial euergetism in Rome the same standards that had once applied to that practised by the governing class in the Republic, and that still applied to civic munificence under the Empire (see below, 3D). But Seneca prefers to concentrate on the area of generosity where the Princeps and his nominal peers were involved in exchanges with each other. Since the Romans saw these individual gift exchanges as part of a horizontal web, to

---

[139] *Nam licet tribuas ei quantum amplissimum potes, nihil tamen amplius potes amicitia tua; cuius esse eum usque ad intimam familiaritatem capacem quo magis scires, breviter tibi studia mores omnem denique vitam eius expressi.* See Cotton 1981. Eck 2002, 142 connects the vagueness with the existence of norms of promotion which guided expectations: both parties to the recommendation knew what was appropriate.

[140] Kloft 1970, 162, cf. 149 stresses that the ideal of liberality applied to the Princeps rested on the values of the Roman *nobiles* and on those contained in Hellenistic monarchical ideals, which were themselves based on Greek aristocratic culture.

include the Princeps in that network, and, in the code of behaviour that governed it, was to hold him to the exercise of *comitas*, the social side of *civilitas*.

Seneca in fact sketches the proper demeanour of the Princeps as benefactor, using Caligula as counter-example: 'the gifts that please are those that are bestowed with a look of human kindness, all gently and agreeably, by one who, although my superior when he gave them, did not exalt himself above me, but with all the generosity he could muster, put himself on terms of equality with me and banished all display from his giving'.[141] Seneca here touches on something of crucial importance. Pliny (*Pan.* 60. 6) points out that Trajan, in contrast with his predecessor, acknowledges obligations and confers benefits, 'seeing himself not as a mighty Princeps but as a not ungrateful friend' (*non tibi magnus princeps, sed non ingratus amicus videris*). *Amicitia* is a fundamentally equal relationship, and the use of the word *amicus* here points to the way in which the etiquette that had been developed in the Republic could be used to temper the realities of power and reinforce the requirements of imperial *civilitas*.[142] For that etiquette was still in use in the Principate. Thus Pliny tell us that the senior consular Corellius Rufus, who helped him in the early stages of his career, offered him, even when he was a mere *adulescentulus*, 'the respect he would show to an equal' (*ut aequali*, *Ep.* 4. 17. 6) and mentioned him on his deathbed as his particular *amicus*. Moreover, *amicus* had, as we noted before (above, p. 34), been used as a euphemism for *cliens*, and Pliny continued to use it of his own inferiors in rank or age when recommending them.[143]

The Etiquette of Equality and Deference

The Romans knew that they had a hierarchical society, and they defended it, but, in social relations between individuals, especially within the upper orders, a pretence of equality was supposed to be maintained by the superior party— whatever deference was actually shown, and indeed expected, from the inferior. Cicero had made Laelius explain in *De amicitia* 69–71 that, in relationships of friendship or kinship, superior and inferior should stand on terms of equality, that the superior in intellect, fortune, or position (*dignitas*) should make himself equal to the inferior and seek to raise him to his own level by his aid and support. Pliny may advise the provincial governor Calestrius Tiro to respect the 'distinctions of class and rank' (*discrimina ordinum dignitatumque*)

---

[141] *Iucunda sunt, quae humana fronte, certe leni placidaque tribuuntur, quae cum daret mihi superior, non exultavit supra me, sed quam potuit benignissimus fuit descenditque in aequum et detraxit muneri suo pompam* (*Ben.* 2. 12–13. 3).

[142] Note Juv. 5. 112: 'All we ask of you is that you dine with us as a fellow-citizen' (*solum poscimus ut cenes civiliter*).

[143] Of equestrians like Voconius Romanus (*Ep.* 2. 13); Arrianus Maturus (3. 2); Suetonius (3. 8); the elder Nymphidius Lupus (10. 87); or young men like Julius Naso (6. 6).

in governing his province (*Ep.* 9. 5), but he counsels the young Junius Avitus (*Ep.* 2. 6) not to insult people he invites to dinner by serving different food to *amici, minores amici,* and *liberti.* D'Arms has pointed to the ideals of the Roman *convivium*—equality, friendship-making, relaxation of social barriers—as 'a part of the cultural accoutrements of many Roman dignitaries' and shown how the literature of the Republic and early Principate celebrates them, while also providing evidence, as Pliny does here, for breaches of that code, resulting in 'snobbery, sycophancy, and humiliation'.[144] At his formal dinners, Augustus was apparently unwilling to entertain freedmen on equal terms with his other dinner guests, who were carefully chosen by rank and individual character, but—rather than behave like Trimalchio—he simply omitted them from the guest list.[145]

The complex efforts to soften through politeness inequalities that had long existed in Roman society undoubtedly made it easier for the Princeps to maintain the theory of his position as first among equals. As Wallace-Hadrill has noted, the kiss with which the Princeps greeted senators was a mark of equality already current in Cicero's day.[146] Pliny praises Trajan for dining on terms of equality with the guests, unlike his anonymous predecessor (*Pan.* 49. 4–8). But even Domitian's flatterers had similarly stressed his inclusion of all *ordines* and his personal participation (Martial 8. 50; Stat. *Silv.* 1. 6. 43–50).[147] The Emperor's *amici,* while enjoying his *beneficia* (*Pan.* 85. 8), could, if they chose, believe in the flattering implication of equality, just as Pliny's equestrian friend Atilius Crescens could boast of his *amicitia* with Pliny (*Ep.* 6. 8. 2). After Horace had refused the invitation to draft Augustus' personal letters, the Princeps wrote to his friend, 'Assume that you have some rights with me, as if you were sharing my table. Such behaviour would be right and proper.' One can compare the similarly encouraging remarks that Seneca recommends to the givers of large benefits: 'Next time you will demand by your own right whatever you need; this once I pardon your bashfulness.'[148]

The complement to this assumed equality is the courtesy of exaggerated deference which also characterized relationships within the elite. The complexity of behaviour and language shows up clearly in a letter of recommendation by Fronto on behalf of Gavius Clarus, an impoverished senator of praetorian rank: describing their relationship as *amicitia* and *familaritas,*

---

[144] D'Arms 1990, 308–19, to which add Epict. 4. 1. 45–8. See also Dunbabin and Slater 2011.

[145] Suet. *Aug.* 74, cf. Petr. *Sat.* 38. On less formal occasions, Augustus dined with *humiles* (Suet. *Aug.* 74; Macr. *Sat.* 2. 4. 28).

[146] Wallace-Hadrill 1996, 291. He remarks, 'In social life, early emperors behaved as members of their own social class, greeting, entertaining and on occasion reciprocating offices by accepting hospitality and attending functions.'

[147] On the reality under Domitian: D'Arms 1990, 309 and Zanker 2002.

[148] Suet. *Vit. Hor.: sume tibi aliquid iuris apud me, tamquam si convictor mihi fueris. Recte enim et non temere feceris;* Sen. *Ben.* 2. 3. 2: *postea, quidquid desiderabis, tuo iure exiges; semel rusticitati tuae ignoscetur.*

Fronto tells how his friend eventually performed the services of a *cliens* or *libertus* to him because of their great mutual affection, 'not from arrogance on my part or servility on his'.[149] Seneca, discussing the right manner in which to accept benefits, lays down that we should not display indifference and reluctance in taking the gift, nor, at the other extreme, be submissive and humble (*Ben*. 2. 24. 2) and, later on in Book 3, Seneca shows why it is so important to find just the right level. Petitioners may say 'The memory of your benefit will live always in my heart' or 'I will be yours to command and serve',[150] but later they think these compliments degrading and unworthy of a free man, banish the benefit from their memory and become ungrateful (*Ben*. 3. 5. 2). Yet even the examples of the language Seneca recommends may strike us as rather fulsome: 'You have laid more people under obligation than you think'; 'You do not know what it is that you have bestowed on me, but you ought to know how much more it is than you think'; 'I shall never be able to return gratitude for this, but at any rate I shall not cease to declare everywhere that I cannot return it'; 'The only injury that I have ever received from you is this—you have forced me to live and die an ingrate' (*Ben*. 2. 24. 4–25. 1).[151] His own warnings, and the high courtesy of Cicero's letters (e.g. *Fam*. 2. 6. 1–2; 13. 50. 1), suggest his advice is not unrealistic.

Unaccustomed as we are to elaborate courtesies, we find it hard to recognize them. The frequent use of the term *indulgentia* in Pliny's letters to Trajan has been studied by Hannah Cotton, who concludes that the word emphasizes a relation between unequals, such as father and son: 'The likening of the Emperor to a father and the insistence on his *indulgentia* conflicts with the image of a *princeps civilis*, the *princeps* as a fellow-citizen, a fellow-senator, an equal, a friend—*amicus*'.[152] It is certainly true that the primary use of *indulgentia* in the Republic to characterize the filial relationship still obtained in the early Empire,[153] and that the noun and its adjectival and verbal forms are often used of the Princeps.[154] However, Pliny uses the verb in requests to others. In

---

[149] *Ad Verum Imp*. 1. 6 van den Hout 110: *nulla hoc aut mea insolentia aut illius adulatione.*

[150] *Ben*. 3. 5. 2: *Nemo non victuram semper in animo suo memoriam dixit, nemo non deditum se et devotum professus est, et si quod aliud humilius verbum, quo se oppigneraret, invenit.*

[151] *Plures quam putas obligasti; nescis, quid mihi praestiteris, sed scire te oportet, quanto plus sit, quam existimas; numquam tibi referre gratiam potero; illud certe non desinam ubique confiteri me referre non posse; hanc unam, Caesar, habeo iniuriam tuam: effecisti, ut et viverem et morerer ingratus.* Though the last of these is addressed to Augustus Caesar, the way Seneca presents his suggestions up to that point indicates that his advice is general.

[152] Cotton 1984, 266.

[153] Cicero, *De Orat*. 2. 168, cf. the *SC de Pisone patre*, which, in l. 59, describes Tiberius in his relation to his adopted son Germanicus as 'excellent and most indulgent father' (*pater optimus et indulgentissimus*); Tiberius gave gifts 'out of his stepfather's indulgence' (*ex indulgentia vitrici*, Suet. *Tib*. 46), i.e. with the money his stepfather Augustus left to him.

[154] Plin. *Epp*. 2. 13. 8; 10. 2. 2; 10. 3A. 1; 10. 4. 1, 5; 10. 5. 1; 10. 6. 2; 10. 8. 4; 10. 10. 2; 10. 11. 1, 2; 10. 12. 2; 10. 13; 10. 21. 1; 10. 23. 1; 10. 24; 10. 26. 2; 10. 51. 2; 10. 86B; 10. 87. 3; 10. 92; 10. 94. 3; 10. 104; 10. 106; 10. 112. 1; 10. 120. 2.

Ep. 9. 24, having interceded successfully with a friend on behalf of the friend's freedman, he writes, 'You have paid me the tribute of bowing to my authority or granting my prayers' (*tantum mihi tribuis ut vel auctoritati meae pareas vel precibus indulgeas*)—either the friend or Pliny is showing deference, or both. Similarly, in *Ep.* 4. 15, when recommending a choice of quaestor to Minicius Fundanus, whom he expects to be elected consul, Pliny writes (11) 'Grant my prayers, take my advice' (*indulge precibus meis, obsequere consilio*). He then goes on to add (13) that the senate will show indulgence to his choice (*cuius et suffragio senatus libentissime indulgeat*).[155] And in the *Senatusconsultum de Pisone patre*, the inscribed senatorial decree giving the official version of the trial of Cn. Calpurnius Piso, the Princeps himself is the object of the senate's indulgence. By pardoning Piso's wife Plancina in accordance with the request of the Princeps' mother Livia, supported by Tiberius, the senate is represented as supporting and indulging Livia and the Princeps' devotion to his mother: 'the senate thinks that to Iulia Augusta ... and to the supreme piety of our Princeps towards his mother, support and indulgence should be accorded' (ll. 115, 118–19).[156]

In Pliny's correspondence, *indulgentia* is used by Pliny of Trajan, not by Trajan of himself, except in *Ep.* 10. 24, where Trajan says that he and Pliny together can indulge the desire of the people of Prusa to have a new bath (*possumus desiderio eorum indulgere*). Titus uses it of himself about generosity to a city; Nerva, of willingness to confirm in general past benefits to all.[157] But it would be heavy-handed, if used to an individual.

The use of the concept *indulgentia* shows up, not the explicit ascendancy of the Emperor, but the attempt by good Emperors and their ostensible peers to use the same language of liberality, the same elaborate mixture of egalitarianism and deference as characterized their social relations in general. The author of the *Laus Pisonis* in Seneca's own time gives a picture of *noblesse oblige* that shows the mixture clearly: he shows *indulgentia* to poor *cultores*, but he loves them *ex aequo*, having regard not to their fortune or their birth, but their character. Unlike those who subject a *tenuis amicus* or *cliens* to humiliations, in Piso's home 'a uniform tenor of friendship encompasses the highest and lowest' (*unus amicitiae summos tenor ambit et imos*): by including them among

---

[155] An imperial procurator under Hadrian received a dedication in Mauretania from a fellow citizen of his native town of Saldae as 'to his most indulgent *friend* for benefits which he had bestowed on him' (amico *indulgentissimo ob beneficia quae in se contulit*, CIL viii. 20684).

[156] Eck, Caballos, and Fernández 1996, 38–50 at 48. The whole passage (ll. 115–20) runs: *senatum arbitrari et* <u>Iuliae Aug(ustae)</u>, *optume de r(e) p(ublica) meritae non partu tantum modo principis nostri, sed etiam multis magnisq(ue) erga cuiusq(ue) ordinis homines beneficis, quae, cum iure meritoq(ue) plurumum poss<et> in eo, quod a senatu petere deberet, parcissume uteretur eo,* <u>et principis nostri summa<e> erga matrem suam pietati suffragandum indulgendumq(ue) esse</u> *remittiq(ue) poenam Plancinae placere.*

[157] *AE* 1962, no. 288; Plin. *Ep.* 10. 58. 7–9.

his *aequales amicos*, he teaches them *obsequium* and acquires affection by showing it (109–31). On the other hand, the alleged message of Seneca to this C. Calpurnius Piso, his real social equal (or superior), 'his own welfare depends on Piso's preservation' (*salutem suam incolumitate Pisonis inniti*), is interpreted by Seneca as a piece of flattery (*adulatio*), which others (though not he) might commit, and he explicitly draws a parallel between the freedom of expression he would use to Piso with that he has regularly used to Nero (Tac. *Ann.* 15. 60–1).

We find something similar with *domine*, Pliny's usual term of address to Trajan, which was once thought to derive from an assumed form of address from slave to master. In fact Eleanor Dickey has shown that Pliny is using the term as it was commonly used in Roman social relations, i.e. as a subliterary term of courtesy conveying respect but little in the way of deference.[158] In the early imperial period, it had spread from use within the family to more general use. Seneca already shows that people used it as a polite greeting to someone whose name one could not remember (*Ep.* 3. 1), and, in one letter, Marcus Aurelius, when already Emperor, addresses Fronto as *domine magister* (*Ad Ant. Imp.* 4. 1 van den Hout 105, ¶ 2). It is a very common address in the tablets from Vindolanda used 'in military circles both to equals and superiors'.[159] As Dickey says, 'Imperial Romans were not, after all, a servile lot who addressed their social superiors with the grovelling deference due to absolute masters; instead they tried to express affection for their superiors, addressing them like close relatives. In other words, Roman flattery exemplifies positive rather than negative politeness' (94). This generalized use is what we find in Pliny's letters to Trajan, where *domine* is a polite counterpart to Trajan's *Secunde carissime*: less formal than *imperator sanctissime* (*Ep.* 10. 1) or *optime imperator* (10. 14), used in some early letters, or the *Caesar* of the *Panegyricus*.

The Princeps and Reciprocation

Seneca raises the general question of what gratitude we owe for benefits from the Princeps that are received by us as members of a group, such as grants of citizenship or immunity to whole peoples (*Ben.* 6. 19). More difficult for his peers is the question of how one can repay individual benefactions. Thus Seneca speaks of '*principes* or *reges* whom fortune has placed in positions where they can give many gifts but can receive very few, and those very unequal to what has been given' (*Ben.* 5. 4. 2). In Pliny's praise of Trajan already mentioned, however, he not only speaks of him as 'a not ungrateful friend', but he then goes on to say, 'Everyone is made to feel that he has given as much as

---

[158] Dickey 2002, 77–99; cf. Adams 1995, 118–19.   [159] Bowman and Thomas 1983, 92.

he has received from you. Your generosity leaves me with nothing to ask, except that you will always create these mutual obligations, and so leave your citizens in doubt whether they do better as your debtors or your creditors'(*Pan.* 60. 7). The good Princeps is here shown fitting into the aristocratic pattern of *beneficia* and *gratia*, including the possibility of being repaid.[160] Yet Pliny's 'as much as he has received' touches on the key problem surrounding reciprocation.

Relationships within Pliny's social network may exhibit great *de facto* inequalities, but there is a chance of evening things out by taking turns.[161] Pliny writes to the Prefect of Egypt (*Ep.* 3. 2. 1), 'What I would have offered to my *amici* if the same *materia* were available to me, this I legitimately ask of you for mine': Pliny knew that he had possessed, or would possess, comparable *materia* to repay the compliment. Ultimately, reciprocation can occur within the class, even if not between particular individuals. The young dependant grows up and has his own dependants; the equestrian father has a senatorial son who can requite *beneficia*. Everyone is ultimately a beneficiary and a benefactor. With the Princeps, this role change is impossible, and problematic even with Emperors who were on the receiving end before accession. In a contrasting pair of examples, Seneca depicts Julius Caesar, when prompted, showing gratitude to a soldier who had saved his life in the civil war, and then Tiberius, who, even when prompted, refused to remember services received before he came to power: both have in common a frequent failing among beneficiaries, that they need to be reminded (*Ben.* 5. 25. 1–2).[162] With Tiberius, one had to be careful not to overdo the reminding. Tacitus, using the language of *beneficia* and *gratia*, explains Tiberius' hostile reaction to the boast of C. Silius that he had saved Tiberius' throne by keeping his German troops loyal at the time of the accession mutinies. The Princeps felt himself being trapped in a disadvantageous exchange. As Tacitus puts it, 'Services are welcome as long as it seems possible to repay them, but when they greatly exceed that point, they produce hatred instead of gratitude.' The Princeps here feels clientized (above, p. 34).[163] Once he becomes Princeps, the role change is irreversible. But he was expected to follow elite social practice and requite with gratitude benefits received. The well-conducted Emperor, as Lendon says, 'returned favours

---

[160] Saller 1982, 69: 'Emperor and subject alike believed that an imperial *beneficium*, like any other, created a debt which could be repaid in gratitude and in more concrete forms.'

[161] Brunt 1988*c*, 383 writes of young aristocrats who obtain the political support of respected figures of an older generation: 'subordination of this kind will naturally diminish or disappear, as the inferior himself advances, though he may continue to harbour sentiments of regard, affection, or gratitude'.

[162] Lendon 1997, 126 cites this among other favours given to emperors before their accession, and which they were expected to repay.

[163] *Ann.* 4. 18. See Flaig 1993, 289–305. He interprets (302) the reclaiming of gifts made by Augustus to Silius as a claim by Tiberius that it was Silius who was ungrateful, not himself. The parallel with *Ben.* 2. 23. 3 was noted by Lipsius ad loc.

done him because that is how he was brought up . . . he acted as any other Greek or Roman aristocrat would in similar circumstances, with an uncalculating and automatic regard for his own honour and that of others: he was no less a creature of his culture than they were'.[164] The general Cn. Domitius Corbulo, when summoned by Nero to Greece in a letter calling him 'father and benefactor', went unarmed, expecting to be treated with honour (Dio 63. 17. 5–6).

A Princeps who behaved as was expected also assumed the possibility of real reciprocation by others. Nerva, expressing his desire to confirm benefits conceded by his predecessors, speaks of people otherwise *owing* them to him—a kind of financial language often used, as we have seen, in these exchanges. In reporting the blanket extension by Trajan of an exemption from inheritance tax, Pliny speaks of his 'giving up so many occasions for conferring benefits, and so many opportunities for claiming credit and putting people in his debt'.[165] Even less generous Emperors, then, who, as Saller says,[166] 'manipulate *beneficia* in order to put people in their debt', subscribe to the theory that reciprocation is possible.

The assumption has to be maintained from the other side as well. Thus Pliny, writing to Trajan, speaks of 'not venturing to respond with equivalent gratitude, however much it may be in my power to do so', thus preserving the theory of reciprocation while flatteringly avowing his inability to match Trajan's liberality on this particular occasion.[167] More striking is the language used in the *Senatusconsultum de Pisone patre*. Recording its decision to pardon Plancina, the senate describes Livia as having earned this favour: 'who had served the commonwealth superlatively, not only in giving birth to our *princeps*, but also through her many great *beneficia* towards men of every rank, and who rightly and deservedly could have supreme influence in what she asked from the senate, but used that influence sparingly' (ll. 115–19).[168] In other words, the senate represents the senatorial pardon of Plancina, not as their response to an exercise of power by Livia (and the Princeps), but as an act of reciprocation for benefits received.

After Seneca's remarks about inequality (above p. 70), he goes on to say, 'I have spoken of *reges* and *principes* to whom, nevertheless, it is possible for us to tender assistance, and whose pre-eminent power rests upon the consent and service of their inferiors' (*minores*, *Ben.* 5. 4. 2–3). Seneca's own position had

---

[164] Lendon 1997, 128.

[165] Plin. *Ep.* 10. 58. 9; *Pan.* 39. 3: *ipsum sibi eripere tot beneficiorum occasiones, tam numerosam obligandi imputandique materiam.*

[166] Saller 1982, 69.

[167] Plin. *Ep.* 10. 51. This may seem grovelling to us, but it does not go beyond what Seneca advises recipients in general to say in answer to large favours at *Ben.* 2. 24. 4: 'I shall never be able to repay to you my gratitude, but, at any rate, I shall not cease from declaring everywhere that I am unable to repay it', or his emphatic approval of Furnius' response to Augustus' pardon at 2. 25. 1.

[168] See above, n. 156.

made him acutely conscious of the importance and the difficulties of that task (see 3E).

> I will show you what those at the summit of power are in need of, what the man who possesses everything lacks—someone, in fact, who will tell him the truth, who will deliver him from the constant cant and falsehood that so bewilder him with lies that the very habit of listening to flatteries instead of facts has brought him to the point of not knowing what the truth really is (*Ben.* 6. 30. 3).[169]

Yet Aristotle had made it a mark of unequal friendship that, when exchanges of benefits take place, they are different in kind: material advantage on one side; honour and service on the other (*NE* 8. 8. 1159^{b}12–15; 8. 14. 1163^{b}13–18). For Saller, this is a characteristic of a patronage relationship.[170] In the Republic, when Cicero had treated the theme of honest friendship compared with sycophancy, the emphasis was on men like himself being advised and flattered (*Off.* 1. 91; *Amic.* 89, 91), except when they chose to play the demagogue and flatter the people (*Amic.* 95–9).[171] Even Seneca does not envisage 'kings and rulers' as the only persons of power needing frank advice (*Ep.* 123. 9), any more than does Horace, who explains that to be an *amicus*, rather than a *scurra*, one must exercise *libertas* and speak the truth (*Ep.* 1. 18. 1–17). However, as the Horace example shows, it is hard for the adviser to maintain a pretence of equality in this role. Tacitus remarks that it is unusual for imperial *amici* to be able to contribute to the friendship with the Princeps something they have not received from him in the first place, and he points to the orators Vibius Crispus and Eprius Marcellus, whose sinister services constitute an exception since they 'contribute what no one could give them' (*Dial.* 8. 3).

The best way, in fact, to establish a convincing appearance of equality, is to be able on occasion to reciprocate in kind, rather than always offering in return the marks of an unequal friendship. Seneca in fact insists that not only loyalty and frank advice, but more ordinary gifts can be given to the Princeps himself, as to kings, in reciprocation: 'a house, a slave, money' (*Ben.* 7. 4. 2, cf. 3. 18. 3). If not in life, one could do this in death. Like many others, Seneca, who had been enriched by Nero, no doubt left a considerable amount of money to the Emperor in his will.[172] Augustus' behaviour showed full recognition of the significance of testamentary gifts, and the proper etiquette to be observed with regard to them. According to Suetonius (*Aug.* 66. 4), he made it clear that he desired a return of good will (*benivolentia mutua*) from his *amici*, when they were alive, and also when they were dead. He attached great importance to the

---

[169] *Ben.* 6. 32. 4 points out that that in reality they often did not listen (below, p. 82). Bellincioni 1984*a*, 63–5 emphasizes the link Seneca makes here with the security of the Princeps (cf. *Ira* 1. 1. 2): indulging the passions (which good advice should aim to restrain) leads to self-destruction.

[170] Saller 1982, 1.

[171] Griffin 1988, 148; Roller 2001, 109–10, noting this as characteristic of Republican writers generally.

[172] Griffin 1976, 294 n. 1; above, pp. 13–14.

wills of his friends and openly expressed pleasure or displeasure at what they wrote about him, and at the amount they left him. His attitude was made all the clearer, because he would not take under the wills of men unknown to him.

Being involved in such equivalent exchanges in kind enabled the Princeps to demonstrate his adherence to the aristocratic code, in receiving benefactions, not just in giving them. The fact that his friends were giving and returning in kind was confirmed by his own will, as they no doubt anticipated. For he was similarly generous, naming many friends, along with relatives, as heirs in the third degree, besides leaving many of his friends legacies. During his life he also showed the type of generosity celebrated by Cicero and Pliny as conceding your rights, in that he returned all or part of legacies and inheritances to the children of the deceased.[173]

The network of horizontal relationships created by favours that we see in *De beneficiis* is not a purely philosophical ideal, but a shared social ideal, an ideal to which behaviour often, if not always, conformed. Though more systematic and self-conscious in his thinking than most of his contemporaries, Seneca was not challenging and unmasking the standards that governed the activity of gift exchange in the upper orders. Rather, he was reinforcing the code at its most demanding level, grounding it in a metaphysical theory of man and the universe, and bringing out its contribution to social cohesion. To the modern eye, his theory has close affinities with the kind of analysis of social conduct, here gift-exchange, which is the province of sociologists or social anthropologists. Yet it is apparent from the testimony of less theoretical writers that Seneca reflects the language and the social etiquette characteristic of relations within the upper orders in the early Principate. This code was continuous with the Republic, and Seneca also reflects and supports the adaptation of that traditional aristocratic code to the existence of the new phenomenon of the Princeps. By making it clear that the Princeps was expected to practise beneficence according to that code, and to relate to his peers as they did to each other, he was endorsing the theory of the early Principate and strengthening the social side of *civilitas*.

D. LIMITATIONS OF SENECA'S PERSPECTIVE ON BENEFICENCE

The Omission of Mass Benefactions

We have noted that Seneca confines himself to teaching how individuals should exchange benefits. Communal benefits, when Seneca mentions them at

---

[173] Suet. *Aug.* 66. 4; 101. 2; cf. Plin. *Epp.* 7. 11; 7. 14; 5. 11; Cic. *Off.* 2. 64; cf. Arist. *NE* 4. 1. 1121ª4–7.

all, emanate from the Emperors (3C), reflecting the fact that, under the Principate, such ostentation *in Rome itself* had to be suppressed or rigidly controlled. Yet Seneca is also silent about the liberality of members of the Roman aristocracy to the Italian and provincial towns where they were born or with which they otherwise had connections. This transfer of corporate munificence by the Roman upper orders is well documented in the *Letters* of the younger Pliny and in the massive evidence of inscriptions, which show that the phenomenon is continuous from the Late Republic but gains momentum under the Principate. Senators and equestrians often maintained close ties with their own home towns, and, though senators enjoyed exemption from certain burdens in those towns, many willingly assumed burdensome office there and conferred benefactions.[174] Emperors encouraged the practice, and senators hoped to gain advancement by complying.[175] This important activity meant that the governing elite of Rome was not confined to the 'court' and limited to passing on favours from the Emperor to others.[176] Members of the governing class did not spend all their time in Rome: they had access not only to armies, but also to the grateful support of the municipalities they had helped.[177] Seneca's silence about this important activity is all the more surprising because his addressee, whose generosity he celebrates in the treatise (*Ben.* 5. 1. 2–4), was greatly attached to his home town of Lugdunum, as Seneca himself was to attest (*Ep.* 91): he may well have been a benefactor there (see p. 97).

Seneca does not even expatiate on the euergetism of the Princeps, though the *Res Gestae* alone shows how important it was to the first Princeps, while the current one was lavish in public subsidies, games, and buildings. In keeping with his inclusion of the Princeps in the aristocratic code, Seneca could have applied to imperial euergetism in Rome the same code that had once applied to that practised by the governing class in the Republic, and that still applied to civic munificence under the Empire. The way Pliny treats Trajan's *congiaria* and alimentary schemes in the *Panegyricus* (25–8), when set next to the way he describes his own generosity to his home town of Comum in *Ep.* 1. 8, shows how similar standards could have been applied to the Princeps and others,

---

[174] Eck, Drew-Bear, and Herrmann 1977; Eck 1980, 283–322 (many examples of benefactions in Italy by senators in the Julio-Claudian and Flavian periods are listed on pp. 295–6).

[175] Plin. *Ep.* 10. 8. 1. See Leach 1990, 29; Hoffer 1999, 94–7. In the period from Augustus to Trajan, senators adopted formally as *patroni* of communities—an honour usually conferred in recognition of benefactions, or in hopes of them, or both—were not natives of the towns, so their benefactions were spread even more widely than those of the *equites* (Nicols 1980, 365–85).

[176] As argued by Wallace-Hadrill 1996, 299–301.

[177] Though senators were required to attend meetings of the senate and handle the duties of their official posts, there were lengthy recesses of a month in spring, or two to two-and-a-half months in autumn, and some geographical areas were exempted from the need for permission (Dio 55. 26. 1–2; 60. 25. 6–7; Tac. *Ann.* 12. 23); and, even when in post, they could easily gain permission to leave Rome, for reasons connected with their estates or the duties of a municipal patron (Plin. *Ep.* 10. 8). See Talbert 1984, 138–45.

including some of the qualities that Seneca demands in individual giving, such as not basing generosity on wealth gained in dubious ways, and giving truly useful gifts.

Finally, Seneca's omission of euergetism is surprising, because the subject is likely to have figured prominently in Chrysippus' *Peri charitōn*, which Seneca clearly used (*Ben.* 1. 3. 8–4. 6). Chrysippus' use of the plural in his title, rather than the usual singular, was probably suggested by the association of the cult of the Charites with the honouring of civic benefactors in the Hellenistic period, especially as a precinct of this type was set up in Athens while he was head of the Stoa there (see pp. 101–2).

The explanation we have advanced is that Seneca's restriction of his discussion to individual benefactions is connected with his eagerness to concentrate on the area where the Princeps and his nominal peers were engaged in exchanges *with each other* (Ch. 1 and pp. 65–6). Also relevant, however, is the fact that Seneca's conception of a virtuous act involved a high level of discrimination and judgement, which he emphasized both as regards the upper orders and as regards the Princeps. For when he does allude to munificence of a corporate kind, it is to highlight, by way of contrast, the importance of discrimination in choosing individual recipients, and the role of such discrimination as a condition for gratitude: giving to groups is inevitably indiscriminate: 'A king gives offices to the worthy, but a *congiarium* even to the unworthy' (*Ben.* 4. 28. 2, cf. 6. 19. 2–5). There will, of course, be choices made between groups of potential recipients, the importance of which, as regards the Princeps, was widely recognized (Tac. *Ann.* 12. 61–2; *ILS* 206 = Sm. 1967, no. 368, ll. 30–3);[178] but, in selecting the groups, moral issues will be less relevant than political ones, while the moral worth of the individual recipients cannot be considered.

The Omission of Abuses in Exchanging Favours

Seneca leaves out the whole question of abuses in making and receiving gifts and in granting and accepting favours to individuals. It has often been remarked that in this area the line between legitimate practice and abuse is drawn at different points in different societies and is hard to draw unambiguously in any society. Yet every holder of public office must have been aware of the problem of distinguishing between what was legitimate and what was not, between giving a present and bribery, between receiving a present and extortion.[179] Cato

---

[178] Octavian, in refusing a request for freedom and immunity from taxation, tells the Samians, 'It is not appropriate for the greatest privilege of all to be granted at random and without cause' (J. Reynolds 1982, 104, document 13, l. 4).

[179] Roller 2001, 146, n. 24, in a discussion of Suet. *Cal.* 39. 2, says that there is no such thing as a 'bribe' in the context of a patrimonial administrative system. Yet the point of the story is that Caligula disguises a bribe as a purchase, so that it becomes respectable for him to receive it.

the Elder, hauled before the censors, argued that he was a man who did not exploit his positions of command to generate profits for himself or his friends at the expense of the *res publica*, to which he had given devoted service.[180] Cicero in *De officiis* mentions bribery of Roman officials and extortion by them (2. 75; 3. 36), but he does not treat the question under beneficence, aside from the insistence that the orator give his services without remuneration (*Off.* 2. 66).

In a similar way, Seneca mentions provincial extortion and judicial bribery in a digression on the prevalence of vice through the ages, but he treats them, with some irony, as ways of recouping the expenses of attaining office, 'since it is the law of nations that you can sell what you have bought' (*Ben.* 1. 9. 5): there is no suggestion that behaving like this can be regarded as an exchange of favours, however perverse and questionable. Yet Seneca himself was instrumental in reviving in 54 the Lex Cincia, which put legal restrictions on gifts, including a prohibition on those given to forensic orators in return for their services (Tac. *Ann.* 13. 5, 42–3).[181] Moreover, these legal questions turned on the very questions of definition and distinctions regarding the right person, the right occasion, etc., that so interested Seneca: 'for nothing in itself makes a becoming gift; it all depends upon who gives it, to whom, when, why, where, and all the other factors without which there can be no rational account of the deed'.[182] This shows up clearly in the formulation by the Severan emperors quoted by Ulpian in his work *de officio proconsulis et legati* (*Dig.* 1. 16. 6. 3):

> As for gifts, pay heed to what we think: there is an old proverb, οὔτε πάντα οὔτε πάντοτε οὔτε παρὰ πάντων ('not everything, not at all times, not from everyone'). For it is uncivilized to accept from no one, but to take from everyone is utterly contemptible, and to accept everything is sheer greed.

Ulpian goes on to distinguish token presents (*xeniola*) from the kind of gift (*donum*) or service (*munus*) that, according to the imperial *mandata*, go beyond the norm of hospitality and cannot be accepted by these officials, adding shrewdly, 'but neither may *xenia* be accumulated to the level of *munera*'.

Both Cicero and Seneca show some concern with the question of improper influence. In *De amicitia* Cicero returns often to the question of the obligations of friendship, including the giving of benefactions: he argues that we should neither ask nor grant, on grounds of friendship, favours that are dishonourable, and particularly those that are unpatriotic (35–7; 40;44, cf. *Off.* 3. 43–6). In *De officiis* he is particularly interested in the problem that faces the judge when it is a friend who is being judged (*Off.* 3. 43–5). But he does not mention here criminal corruption. The same is true of Seneca's brief reference, in the context of friendship, to not giving, or requesting, shameful favours (*Ben.* 2. 15. 2).

---

[180] *ORF*² pp. 70–1.   [181] Griffin 1976, 74–5; Griffin 1984, 251 n. 60.

[182] *Nihil enim per se quemquam decet; refert, qui det, cui, quando, quare, ubi, et cetera, sine quibus facti ratio non constabit* (*Ben.* 2. 16. 1, cf. 2. 18. 2–3).

There is an obvious explanation for Seneca's omission and Cicero's lack of interest, namely, that there were laws regulating the giving and taking of bribes to secure verdicts or positions. As philosophers, Cicero and Seneca are discussing morality, not law, and they are determined to promote standards more elevated than those enshrined in law. Cicero is willing to explore the interface between law and morality, when considering the pursuit of advantage in buying and selling, but he takes it for granted that all the alternative actions being considered, even the most hardheaded, are within the law, and he shows that the same assumption was made even by the philosophers whose standards he represents as not high enough (*Off.* 3. 51, 55, 63). He makes it clear that the demands of justice as a virtue, under which liberality is subsumed, are higher than what the law requires (3. 68, 73). Seneca, unlike Cicero, does not treat beneficence under justice (pp. 21–2), and he is particularly eager, as we saw (p. 42), to separate the area of *beneficia* from the area of activity covered by the law. This explanation is enough to account for Seneca's silence. But there may also be a secondary consideration: that the position of the Princeps in regard to such abuses is not parallel to that of his nominal peers. For he would not need to use bribery to exercise influence and, though many Emperors practised extortion in various forms, they were not in practice vulnerable to the law.

The Omission of Brokerage

Seneca's failure to discuss what is sometimes called 'second-order patronage' or 'brokerage'[183] is even more difficult to explain than the other two omissions. Cicero's letters of recommendation illustrate the practice, and Cicero specifically recommends indirect beneficence in *De officiis* for those who cannot themselves be legal advisers or advocates in court. 'It is still possible to assist many men by personal effort, by seeking *beneficia* for them, by recommending them to the jurors and magistrates, by watching over their interests, by soliciting for them those men that give advice or defend' (2. 67). Thus, already in the Republic, it was not only a recognized phenomenon, but a respectable way of exercising generosity. The best early imperial documentation of the practice comes in Pliny's *Letters*. Many of these concern his activities as a direct benefactor—giving money, advice, legal support; even more show him in the role of an intermediary in securing *beneficia* for others. That is natural, because being an intermediary often involves writing letters, and Pliny chose to publish many of his letters of recommendation. But however much using the *Letters* as evidence may lead us to exaggerate the importance of this type of beneficence, there is no denying that it accounted for a substantial part of the activities of

---

[183] Saller 1982, 75. He also uses the term 'mediator'.

Pliny. The ultimate benefactor is sometimes the Emperor, sometimes Pliny's peers. We have already mentioned some of his letters soliciting posts from Trajan and also from provincial governors (3C). Sometimes he is seeking, for a third party, financial benefits from the seller of a farm (*Ep.* 1. 24) or the estate of a debtor (*Ep.* 6. 8).

This kind of activity was found earlier under the Principate. In fact, we have a striking illustration of it in the Neronian period, when Quintus Veranius had some special role at *ludi* where he was the 'agent of the Emperor's (probably Nero's) generosity'.[184] His epitaph carrying this boast dates to 58, probably before Seneca wrote *De beneficiis*, while in 62, possibly at the time he was writing, a less reputable form of the practice is attested when Fabricius Veiento was convicted of selling his influence with the Princeps over appointments (Tac. *Ann.* 14. 50). It is also prominent in the discourses of Epictetus, which date from the reign of Trajan but draw on his experiences at Rome in the Flavian period, and perhaps under Nero.[185] Epictetus is, however, highly critical of this kind of soliciting of support. For the most part, he shows us the imperial slaves and freedmen being asked to intercede with the Emperor to secure appointments (4. 1. 148; 4. 7. 23) or money (1. 26. 11–12). But he also describes the consular candidate running around, kissing people's hands, hanging around people's doors, sending gifts to many and little tokens on a daily basis (4. 10. 20). The canvassing here, if that of a consular candidate, will relate to gaining the favour of those who have the ear of the Emperor, who directly controlled the election of consuls: so, probably, the imperial slaves and freedmen again. But it might relate to the lower offices which were necessary steps to the consulship, in which case it could include the soliciting of senatorial *suffragatores* that figures so prominently in Pliny's *Letters*.[186] Epictetus then confirms that this type of indirect beneficence is common to the experience of both the Emperor and his nominal peers, and can also involve interaction between them.

Given the prevalence of such networking in the Republic and the Empire, and Cicero's mention of it under beneficence, one might have expected Seneca in *De beneficiis* to evince some interest in it, especially as he was eager to portray the exchange of benefits as a socially creative activity (*Ben.* 2. 18. 5; 2. 21. 2). The use of intermediaries, in fact, enhances that creativity by multiplying the number of benefactors and beneficiaries in any transaction, and therefore multiplying the number of relationships of *amicitia* created or consolidated (above, 3A). Pliny certainly shows great enthusiasm for extended chains of

---

[184] Birley 1981, 50–4; Gordon 1983, no. 45: *ab Augusto principe, cuius liberalitatis erat minister.* The sepulchral inscription will have been erected soon after his death while governing Britain, probably in 58.

[185] Millar 1965.

[186] Millar 1977, 307. Plin. *Epp.* 3. 20. 4–5; 2. 9. 5. Pliny himself solicits support for his candidates at 2. 9; 6. 6. He does not explicitly tell us how he came to do so, but hints of the attentions he received from young aspirants emerge at 6. 6. 5–9 and 8. 23. 2–6.

benefaction. Having secured a military tribunate from the legate of Britain for the scholar and biographer Suetonius, who turned it down and suggested a relative of his own instead, Pliny was happy to make the substitution (*Ep.* 3. 8): 'I see that, since it is a distinction both to deserve *beneficia* and to give them, you will be praised on both counts, if what you yourself have earned, you give to another. Further, I see that it will add to my good repute if it is known through your action that my friends can not only hold tribunates but even confer them.' As Pliny indicates, the one appointment now involves three benefactors, all of whom deserve gratitude: the governor, Pliny, and Suetonius. It also involves three beneficiaries: Pliny, Suetonius, and his relative, all of whom owe gratitude. Moreover, Pliny—who was both benefactor and beneficiary—has now conferred two favours on Suetonius. The governor presumably deserves the gratitude of all three beneficiaries.

In fact, Seneca mentions the role of intermediaries only once in *De beneficiis*, and his view is quite different from Pliny's. At the start of Book 2, he is discussing the ways in which benefactors spoil their favours by the manner in which they give. He turns to 'immense benefits' and the donors who spoil them by being ungracious. His own advice to givers of large benefits is that they should add kind words to kind actions, issuing what he calls 'a friendly rebuke': 'I am angry with you because, when you wanted something, you were not willing to let me know long ago; because you went through such a formal rigmarole; because you involved an intermediary' (2. 3. 2). Other donors promise a benefit but delay it, so the recipient has to ask again, often involving a third party: 'You have to beg one man to remind the benefactor, another to make him complete the transaction. So one gift is eroded by passing through many hands, and, as a result, little gratitude stays with the promiser, since everyone who has to be asked subsequently takes away from the initiator. . . . Let no one intercept your benefits, let no one retard them; for in the case of an intended gift, no one can appropriate gratitude to himself without reducing yours' (2. 4. 2–3). As an explanation for such conduct, Seneca notes that

> for many it is a matter of perverted ambition to maintain the size of their crowd of petitioners. Such are the tools of royal power (*regiae potentiae ministri*) who delight in prolonging a display of arrogance and think they have too little power unless they show at length and in full measure, to one after another, what power they have. They do nothing quickly, nothing once and for all; their injuries are sudden, their benefits slow (2. 5. 1).

Seneca here seems to adopt a standpoint not very different from that of Epictetus, except that the rank of the 'tools of royal power' is not made clear, and they are represented as the primary benefactors, with 'Caesar' himself not appearing in the picture.

In trying to explain why Seneca plays down the practice of brokerage in *De beneficiis*, we can rule out one historical explanation at the outset. Given

Seneca's determination to teach conduct appropriate to both the Princeps and the upper orders, we might think that he omitted the type of beneficence that involves being an intermediary, because he could not include the Princeps in that process on the same terms as his nominal peers: though the Princeps could give, receive, and return gifts like them, we might think that he did not secure benefits for those he wished to favour through others. However, Pliny *Ep.* 10. 58. 6 is a letter of recommendation from Domitian to the governor of Asia, asking that he meet the demands of the philosopher Flavius Archippus, while Fronto, *Ad M. Caesarem* 5. 51 is a letter of recommendation from Marcus Aurelius, then heir apparent, to Fronto when he was preparing to be governor of Asia, asking him to befriend a Greek he had met.

Perhaps we can find a clue in the negative quality of his treatment of brokerage. The scandals about the influence of freedmen and wives under Gaius and Claudius, and which started to resurface *c.*61, may have discredited the practice, particularly as regards imperial favours, as the passage of Epictetus suggests.[187] However, that would not account for Seneca's particular emphasis on intermediates invoked when benefits are promised, but not delivered, by the primary benefactor. In any case, this explanation hardly seems adequate to explain the omission of such a central feature of ancient society, which was by no means confined to the imperial entourage.

The fact that Cicero's *De officiis* shows scarcely more interest suggests that philosophy, not history, must provide the primary explanation. Cicero's letters show that he practised brokerage and was also, when provincial governor, a target for the requests of intermediaries. So if he said little about it in *De officiis*, it may be because he thought the moral questions involved in beneficence were sufficiently explored without distinguishing primary and intermediate benefactors. Seneca may have shared this philosophical reason, being even less prone than Cicero to obscure the clear message of his teaching by a host of details drawn from real life. In addition, he may have been reluctant to dim the attention he paid to discrimination and judgement, which relate more to the directly chosen recipient, and he may not have wanted to complicate his picture of the exchange process, which is, on the moral plane, a transaction between minds: the goodwill of the donor and the gratitude of the recipient (*Ben.* 2. 31–34. 1).[188]

E. THE PERSPECTIVE OF THE *AMICUS PRINCIPIS* ON BENEFICENCE

Seneca was not just a generous benefactor, like the other consulars with whom Martial and Juvenal compare him (p. 13). He was also close to the Emperor

---

[187] Griffin 1984, 54–5; Saller 2000, 841.   [188] I owe this point to Brad Inwood.

Nero. As *amicus principis*, he will have played many roles connected with the beneficence of the Princeps: as intermediary, as adviser and benefactor, as beneficiary. As regards the first, Seneca must have had the opportunity many times to behave like the royal minions he describes, and his readers must have been well aware of his activities. It would probably be rating the importance of such possible embarrassment too high to adduce it as a reason for his avoiding discussion of brokerage in general, especially as Seneca generally avoids autobiography and tends to discuss issues in ways that do not correlate easily with his own career.[189] Nonetheless, he certainly gives nothing away about the many delicate transactions in which he must have been involved.

Seneca is somewhat less guarded when it comes to the second role, that of adviser. It is hard not to to connect his outburst over the humiliations imposed on senators by the stingy Tiberius with the more generous conduct of Seneca's own emperor, who in 58, when Seneca's influence was yet undimmed, gave generous annual grants to several impoverished *nobiles*, without distinguishing between the unfortunate and the extravagant, and without making them reapply (pp. 14, 63). More explicit is Seneca's other personal outburst in *De beneficiis*, which concerns the giving of advice itself, a function that he had described as the key repayment that can be made to *principes* and *reges* at the summit of power and wealth (pp. 72–3). Having explained, as we saw, that the most valuable way to return favours to men in such a position is to tell them the truth, thus counteracting the baneful influence of flatterers (*Ben.* 6. 30. 3), Seneca exposes, in a tone suggestive of firsthand experience, the difficulties confronting 'friends of the Princeps' who actually try to do this. Even the respectable Augustus, he says, who claimed to regret the loss of his advisers Agrippa and Maecenas, did not really value honest advice:

> Should I suppose that there were no more like them who could be enlisted, or that it was the fault of Augustus himself, in that he preferred to sulk than to search? There is no reason for us to suppose that Agrippa and Maecenas were accustomed to tell him the truth; had they lived, they would have been among the dissemblers. It is characteristic of the royal attitude to attribute the virtue of speaking the truth to those from whom there is no longer any danger of hearing it (6. 32. 4).

That is the voice of Nero's adviser in an unusually candid mood.

Seneca's position at court will have given him ample opportunity to observe and experience the issues surrounding the exchange of *beneficia* with the Emperor. He discusses in general terms the problem of returning a favour to a king or to a much richer person, 'since some men regard it as an injury to have their benefit returned and go on piling benefits upon benefits' (4. 40. 2): it is a display of arrogance to be unwilling to allow someone to free himself of his obligation, rather than accepting his return gratefully (2. 17. 6–7). On the other

---

[189] The exception is *De vita beata*. See Griffin 1976, ch. 1, 309–10, 391.

hand, Seneca is critical of the grudging way in which the impoverished aristocrat Cn. Cornelius Lentulus Augur had dealt with the wealth and prominence he owed to Augustus: 'He used to complain constantly that Augustus had enticed him away from his studies; that he had not heaped nearly as much on him as he had lost by giving up the study of oratory. And yet the divine Augustus had also freed him from ridicule and futile efforts' (2. 27. 2). Again, Seneca is aware of the difficulty for both the donor and the recipient, when they are distant in status and resources, for the benefit must be appropriate to both. In an example concerning Alexander, who wants to give a city as a gift, his sympathy lies with the recipient, who says it is excessive for him and shuns the *invidia*; in another concerning King Antigonus and a Cynic who asked for money, he sides with the king, who felt that his *persona* called for a larger gift than was appropriate to a scorner of wealth and so gave nothing (2. 15. 3–17. 2).

Seneca is also vividly aware of the distortion of beneficence by coercive power. Dealing with the need for discernment in choosing the donors from whom one is willing to accept a benefit, he turns to cases where the opportunity to choose a worthy benefactor does not arise, either because one is under duress in receiving a gift from a tyrant, a brigand, a pirate, or a king, or because the intention to benefit is missing in the benefactor, or because the power to help was unjustly acquired. He argues that, in these circumstances, one should accept, but that such gifts impose no obligation of gratitude and create no bond of friendship (2. 18. 6–7). The climax of the argument is the pardon of Brutus by Caesar, which, in Seneca's eyes, did not make of Brutus an ingrate when he later killed his benefactor (2. 20).[190] Yet it is a Greek example that probably comes closer to his own experience. In an extended treatment of Socrates' refusal to join the entourage of King Archelaus, Seneca refuses to accept as his real reason the reply attributed to him, 'that he might receive *beneficia* for which he could not make an equivalent return'. He points out that what Socrates could have taught the monarch would have been more valuable than any royal gifts or favours: his real reason was that he might have been forced to accept gifts that were unworthy of Socrates. 'Whether you are unwilling to give something to a king, or to accept something from a king, is all the same: both alike are in his eyes a rebuff . . . Would you like to know what Socrates really meant? He meant that a man like himself, whose freedom of speech even a free state could not endure, was unwilling to enter into voluntary servitude' (5. 6. 2–7).

The difficulties caused for Seneca by Nero's benefactions are brilliantly depicted by Tacitus in the debate in direct speech between the two in *Annals* 14. 53–6. 'Seneca and Nero compete in private with antiphonal orations', as Syme described them, commenting, 'No deception on the part of the historian,

---

[190] See ad 2. 18. 6–21. 2; 2. 20. 1; 2. 20. 3 and Griffin 2003*a*, 167–8.

but instruction as well as entertainment furnished by a master of parody.' Allowing his Seneca to speak for the first time, Tacitus shows us how a reader of the philosopher's works, admittedly a particularly perspicacious one, interpreted them in relation to Seneca's situation.[191] He also shows us indirectly that, half a century after Seneca's death, educated readers could be expected to pick up these allusions and thus enjoy the historian's *tour de force*.[192]

Many scholars have seen that the historian, in composing both Seneca's speech and that of his erstwhile pupil, drew on his knowledge of Seneca's works. Syme, regarding the dialogue as a means devised by the historian to convey the style and character of Seneca, found hints and echoes of authentic Senecan language and style; he noted that the thought was also reminiscent, adducing *De vita beata* 26 on the fragility of riches and *De clementia* 1. 9 on *nobilitas* and *novitas*.[193] The stylistic points have been contested (see p. 165), but the presence of Senecan ideas and themes is incontrovertible.[194] Pohlenz saw the dialogue as a Tacitean creation, showing a precise understanding of Seneca's situation, for which he drew on oral tradition about the period and also on Seneca's own works.[195] The theme of withdrawal from public life was meant to evoke Seneca's *De otio*, but the greatest debt, he thought, was to *De tranquillitate animi*, where the theme of reducing one's wealth to a moderate level short of poverty (8. 9) was picked up by Tacitus, when his Seneca asks, 'Where is that soul content with what is moderate?' and 'I will not consign myself to poverty.'[196] Fuhrmann notes a debt to *De vita beata* for the sentiments on wealth, but he also marks Tacitus' debt to the works generally, for the speech of Nero as well as Seneca's.[197] Bellincioni has remarked that *De beneficiis* reflects Seneca's bitter experience of gifts that enslave and the embarrassment he experienced in trying to return them to Nero, as depicted in the dialogue in the *Annals*.[198]

Though Tacitus could clearly draw on a broad knowledge of Senecan thought and expression, the situation dramatized in the dialogue particularly evokes three major themes prominent in his writings: how, when, and why to withdraw from public life; how to regard and make use of wealth; and how to manage benefits and the bond they create between donor and recipient. These

---

[191] Syme 1984, 23 = 1991, 179. As Pohlenz 1941, 96 = 425 says, 'Jedenfalls hat aber schon Tacitus Senecas Äußerungen als ein ganz persönliches Bekenntnis, als eine Frucht seines eigenen Erlebens angesehen.'

[192] Fronto's letter to Marcus Aurelius as Emperor, warning against the attractions of Seneca (*De orationibus* 1–4 van den Hout 153–4), shows us that he was still read half a century after Tacitus was writing (see Ch. 9).

[193] Syme 1958*a*, i. 334–6.

[194] For the importance of this distinction, see Brinkmann 2002, 23–4 n. 73; 26.

[195] Pohlenz 1941, 94–6 = 1965, 423–5.

[196] *Ann.* 14. 53. 5: *ubi animus ille modicis contentus?* and 14. 54. 3: *nec me in paupertatem ipse detrudam.*

[197] Fuhrmann 1997, 268–72.   [198] Bellincioni 1984*a*, 114 n. 5.

themes, besides their appearance in the *Letters to Lucilius* and in the tragedies, have specific works devoted to them. The first prompts one to look in Tacitus' dialogue for parallels in *De tranquillitate animi* and *De otio*; the second, to look in *De vita beata*. But it is the last, the subject of *De beneficiis*, that is at the heart of the dialogue, as has been well argued by Brinkmann.[199] The language of *munificentia* and *amicitia* features copiously in Seneca's plea and dominates the Emperor's speech of refusal, in which, as Syme put it, 'the pupil even surpassed his master'.[200]

The year is 62, the year Tacitus saw as the turning point of Nero's reign.[201] Seneca, his position at court weakened by the death of his ally, the praetorian prefect Afranius Burrus, tries to withdraw from his position of power, and to return most of his imperial gifts. Tacitus has Seneca start his interview with the Princeps by adducing the two *magna exempla*, Agrippa and Maecenas, whose role he had commented on so bitterly in Book 6 of *De beneficiis* (above, p. 82): Tacitus had clearly registered the personal feeling behind Seneca's account. His Seneca gives a false picture of the harmony between the Princeps and these *amici* as they go into happy retirement, which is betrayed by his allusion to the popular version of Agrippa's bitter withdrawal because of the advancement of Marcellus, and by Tacitus' previous remarks about Maecenas' retirement (*Ann.* 3. 30. 4). This not only shows up the weakness of Seneca's own present position: it also recalls what he had said in the treatise about Augustus' false picture of his relations with his supposedly candid advisers.[202] Seneca is then made to compare his rewards with those which Augustus had conferred on his two great *amici*. He speaks of the inadequacy of the return he could make in terms of teaching and advice for the influence, the money, and the properties that he had received: he is in the position Socrates claimed to avoid. But he has the excuse that he could not refuse: the position that Socrates really wanted to avoid. Nero's gifts, he says, have reached the limit one can fittingly give an *amicus*, or that an *amicus* can accept; even if the Princeps could go further, his acceptance would breed *invidia*: Alexander's invidious offer of the gift of a city comes to mind.[203] Seneca then asks the Emperor to take back the bulk of his fortune, freeing him of the responsibility and leaving him to enjoy the life of

---

[199] Brinkmann 2002, 25. I must acknowledge my debt to discussion with Michael Brinkmann and to his thesis on the subject of the dialogue, an earlier version of which I supervised while he was in Oxford in 1996–7.

[200] Syme 1958*a*, i. 335.   [201] Griffin 1984, 83–7.

[202] Bastomsky 1972, 177–8, stressing the pathetic quality of Seneca's request; Brinkmann 2002, 39–41.

[203] The language is similar: *Ben.* 2. 16. 1: 'The man to whom he was presenting it took the measure of himself and tried to avoid the envy such a grand gift would attract' (*cum ille, cui donabatur, se ipse mensus tanti muneris invidiam refugisset*); Tac. *Ann.* 14. 54. 1: 'Each of us has reached our full measure—you, as much as a *princeps* could give to a friend, and I, as much as a friend could accept from a *princeps*' (*uterque mensuram implevimus, et tu, quantum princeps tribuere amico posset, et ego, quantum amicus a principe accipere: cetera invidiam augent*).

the mind: he comes perilously close here to the grumbles of Lentulus Augur (*Ben.* 2. 27. 2), but Seneca does actually offer to surrender the encumbrances.

Nero starts by crediting his ability to reply *ex tempore* to what he has learned from Seneca, as a teacher of oratory. And he immediately shows up the fallacy in the parallel with Augustus' advisers: they did not return their gifts. (Later on he produces much less flattering parallels, with imperial freedmen, with the flatterer Vitellius under Claudius,[204] and with the inert Volusius.) He goes on to answer his teacher's arguments point by point, out of Seneca's own philosophical writing. What Seneca has given him in education and advice is of permanent value, worth more than the transitory gifts he has received, so that it is the Emperor who is embarrassed: exactly Seneca's argument about Socrates at *Ben.* 5. 6. 2–6.

Then comes the *coup de grâce*. Nero says that he still needs his mentor's help: if Seneca returns his gifts and deserts him now, people will attribute it, not to Seneca's moderation and desire for leisure, but to Nero's avarice and to Seneca's fear of his cruelty. 'But if praise of your self-denial does prevail, it is still not fitting for a wise man (*sapienti viro*) to burden his friend with ill repute, in order to acquire glory for himself.'[205] In Book 6 of *De beneficiis*, Seneca had carefully explained that it is ungrateful to make a return of favours to someone who does not wish it (40; 42. 2, cf. 4. 40. 4): to say 'Take it back' is insulting (cf. 1. 11. 1 *fin.*) and suggests regret at receiving the *beneficium* in the first place; the giver has a right to choose the time of return (6. 42. 1–2); the recipient should not be concerned with his own reputation; to be over-concerned with returning a benefit implies that the donor is too anxious to have it returned (6. 43. 3). So Nero is in fact accusing the philosopher of ingratitude: the vice that he had called the worst of all and had castigated through seven books of *De beneficiis*.

Nero is actually accusing his erstwhile mentor of a particularly heinous form of the vice: the case of returning after some time the *same gift* one has willingly received, and one the owner does not want returned. The situation is not one explicitly treated in *De beneficiis*.[206] Seneca's attempt to return some of his

---

[204] Tacitus' readers may well have seen the irony of Nero's point that Seneca should not rate him below Claudius in liberality, given the fact that Claudius' lack of discrimination in giving is placed prominently at the conclusion of the first book of *De beneficiis*, where Seneca takes the view that such gifts are to be accepted, but treated as windfalls which do not impose any obligation of gratitude.

[205] As Lendon 1997, 117 says, 'Nero refused to permit Seneca to retire lest his act be interpreted as a reproach.'

[206] The closest he comes is to say that a person may feel like rejecting a gift that he does not need. ' "Take it back. I do not want it. I am content with what I have"; sometimes he may feel like throwing it away, not just giving it back' ('*Recipe, non desidero; meo contentus sum.*' *Interim non reddere tantum libet, quod acceperis, sed abicere*, 1. 11. 1). But Seneca had not refused to accept Nero's gifts, and in the passage just mentioned there is no reference to ingratitude. At 6. 5. 2 he explains that repaying a benefit does not involve restoring the actual gift that we have received, but something in its place.

fortune in 62 may postdate *De beneficiis*, though scholars have differed in their attempts to relate his situation in 62 to the treatise (p. 95). Even if the treatise came later, however, Seneca, as we have said, rarely allows a close auto-biographical fit between his writings and his situation. Tacitus and his readers would not have needed allusions in the treatise to the author's experience of 62 to know how telling the philosopher would have found the argument that Tacitus ascribes to Nero. For, if it is ungrateful to make a return before it is wanted, how much worse to return the actual gift when the donor does not want it back?

Seneca, in the way that all conversations with a ruler end, said 'Thank you.' This is not just a cliché of Tacitus, already familiar from the *Agricola* and the *Histories*. Seneca himself had explained that one could only achieve old age at court 'by accepting injuries and giving thanks'.[207] Prevented from being ungrateful for what he had received in the past, the philosopher now had to declare his gratitude for what he was refused.

---

[207] *Ann.* 14. 56. 3: *Seneca, qui finis omnium cum dominante sermonum, grates agit; De Ira* 2. 33. 2: *iniurias accipiendo et gratias agendo.* Cf. also Sen. *Tranq.* 14. 4 *fin.*; Tac. *Agric.* 42. 3; *Hist.* 2. 71.

Part II

Seneca's Treatise

4

The Date and Addressee

THE DATE

There is general agreement among scholars on the chronological limits for the publication of Seneca's essay. First, the Emperor Claudius must have been dead when Seneca wrote of him at 1. 15. 6, 'Should what was offered by Claudius not have been accepted?' (*Non erat accipiendum a Claudio quod dabatur?*), since what Seneca goes on to say of that Emperor's judgement is so disparaging. In fact this *terminus post quem* of 54 can be advanced to 56 by what is said at 2. 21. 6 of the consular Caninius Rebilus, who committed suicide in that year (*Ann.* 13. 30. 2):[1] in a comparison with another dissolute senator, he is called 'a person of similarly bad reputation' (*homo eiusdem infamiae*). Seneca does not often refer to living contemporaries and never in such insulting terms.[2]

As for the latest possible date, we have the valuable evidence of *Ep.* 81. 3. Here Seneca, after answering a purported complaint from Lucilius about the ingratitude he has experienced, first offers some advice on the subject and then adds, 'But we have said enough about this topic in those books which are entitled *On Benefits*' (*sed de isto satis multa in iis libris locuti sumus, qui de beneficiis inscribuntur*). The points Seneca has just made about ingratitude can

---

[1] The name was restored by Lipsius from the 'C. Aminius rebius' of the Mediceus manuscript in Tacitus' description of the disreputable ex-consul: *ex primoribus peritia legum et pecuniae magnitudine cruciatus aegrae senectae misso per venas sanguine effugit, haud creditus sufficere ad constantiam sumendae mortis, ob libidines muliebriter infamis* ('among the leading men in his skill at law and the size of his wealth, he escaped the sufferings of an ailing old age by opening his veins, though he was believed incapable of the steadfastness to commit suicide, given his bad reputation for effeminate lusts.').

[2] Rebilus is there being likened to Fabius Persicus, who is insulted again later in Book 4 (see **ad 4. 30. 2**). Clearly, if his death was later than that of Caninius Rebilus, the *terminus post* for *De beneficiis* would need to be advanced. In fact, Persicus, who is not attested in the virtually complete *Acts of the Arval Brethren* after the winter of 57, probably died earlier (*PIR*[2] F 51): Syme 1986, 417 suggests that he died in the reign of Claudius.

indeed be found in *De beneficiis*, notably in Books 1 and 7, but also in Book 4.[3] That would suggest that he is referring, in the line quoted, to the whole work, allowing us to place its publication before the 'dramatic date' of the *Letter*, which is the late spring or early summer of 64, before the end of June.[4] However, Seneca goes on to discuss a question that he says has been explained, but not sufficiently explained, namely, whether a person who has benefited us, but and harmed us afterwards, thereby frees us from obligation. This question is touched on in Book 3. 12. 4 of the treatise, and more substantially discussed in Book 6. 4–6. Seneca is presumably referring to these discussions. Hence the idea often advanced by scholars, that it is only the first six books that can be confidently dated on the basis of *Letter* 81.[5] But since the *Letters* themselves were intended for publication, not just for the eyes of their addressee Lucilius (*Ep.* 21. 3–5), Seneca's reference to *De beneficiis* in the sentence before must be pointing his readers towards a work that was published and available at the dramatic date of the letter.[6] Now it is unlikely that Book 7 was published separately from Books 1–6, given the symmetry it displays with Book 1, as will be shown in Chapter 6. In fact, some of the differences that induced Préchac to believe that the last book was published later are precisely what makes it an integral part of the work, which it would be essential for the reader to have before him from the start. For, as will be argued in Chapter 7, this book is the culmination of the development of thought in the course of the treatise, a development that implements Seneca's pedagogic strategy.

The chronological limits of 56 and June 64 for the work as a whole allow us to supply only a broad context. As regards larger historical events, the work was written, certainly published, in the reign of Nero, after the death of Britannicus, and before the Great Fire of Rome that broke out on 19 July 64 and lasted nine days. The persecution of the Christians had not yet taken place, nor the Pisonian conspiracy. As for Seneca himself, he had not yet openly retired from public life, and he had not yet contributed a substantial portion of

---

[3] Parallels to the ideas in §1 of *Ep.* 81 down to *peribunt* can be found in *Ben.* 1. 1. 12–13 and 7. 29. 1; the agricultural metaphor recalled at the end of §1 is in *Ben.* 7. 32; the notion of trying again in §2 occurs in *Ben.* 1. 1. 9–10 and 7. 31. 5; the idea of life grinding to a halt comes in *Ben.* 4. 33. 3. For Mazzoli 2007, 586, n. 3, the clear allusion to *Ben.* 7. 32 (*sterilitatem soli*) at *Ep.* 81. 1 (*soli sterilitate*) is the conclusive argument that the whole treatise was finished before the letter.

[4] *Ep.* 67. 1 speaks of *ver . . . inclinatum in aestatem* ('spring . . . rounding into summer') while *Ep.* 86 places itself in the latter part of June: *Iunius mensis est, quo tibi scribo, iam proclivis in Iulium* ('it is the month of June as I write, well on the way towards July'). See Griffin 1976, 400.

[5] Préchac 1961, pp. xiv f., followed explicitly by Guglielmino 1968, p. x; Abel 1967, 165 and 1985, 708. Grimal 1978, 303 and Chaumartin 1989, 1702–3 think that at least the first six books, and probably the seventh, were composed before the letter; Cooper and Procopé 1995, 183 that 'the bulk of the work must have been completed before the composition, in summer AD 64, of *Letters* 81'.

[6] As was already seen by Münscher 1922, 64–5 and Albertini 1923, 33–4. They, however, thought that Books 1–4 were published earlier than 5–7, and that these last were issued singly as they were written: this is to take Seneca's openings of these books, where he claims to be induced by his addressee to go on adding trivial questions, at face value (against which see Ch. 6).

his wealth to the rebuilding of Rome, both of which he was to do after the Fire.[7]
His addressee Aebutius Liberalis had not yet seen his town of Lugdunum make
a contribution to those repairs, only to be laid waste by fire later that same
summer.[8] As for its relation to Seneca's other philosophical writings, the treatise can be placed after the *Apocolocyntosis*, the *Consolationes* to Marcia,
Helvia, and Polybius, *De ira*, *De brevitate vitae*, and probably *De clementia*,
though that work could just be contemporaneous with *De beneficiis*.[9] The
treatise belongs before the later *Letters to Lucilius* (at least those after *Ep.* 80),
but its relation to five of the *Dialogi*, to the *Natural Questions*, and to the early
Letters remains uncertain.[10]

Scholars have naturally found it frustrating not to have more precise knowledge of the background to the work.[11] Was the year 59, when Nero murdered
his mother Agrippina, already in the past? Had Tacitus' turning-point of 62,
marked by the death of Afranius Burrus, Praetorian Prefect and Seneca's political ally, and by the cruel murder of Nero's wife Octavia, already occurred?[12] As
for Seneca, had he already written the shameful letter explaining Agrippina's
death? Was he already semi-retired, refusing from 62 to hold the usual morning receptions and rarely going out when in Rome, pleading ill-health and
devotion to philosophy?[13] Was he in Rome or travelling in Campania and to
his villas, as we see him in the early *Letters*?

Given the reluctance of Seneca himself to mention current events or his current public position, or even to give many details of his private life, it is not
surprising that scholars have turned to a variety of indirect techniques, in an
effort to narrow the chronological limits of 56 and summer 64. The most common is the hunt for (i) allusions to historical events datable through outside
evidence and (ii) allusions to Seneca's circumstances known from the historical
sources. Both types are usually disputable, as to whether or not they really are

---

[7] Tac. *Ann.* 15. 45. 3 for the retirement in 64; Dio 62. 25. 3 on handing over money, confirmed
by Tac. *Ann.* 15. 64, where 'then at the peak of his wealth and influence' (*tum praedives et praepotens*) confirms Seneca's change of circumstances by his death.

[8] Tac. *Ann.* 16. 13. 3; *Ep.* 91 (dramatic date before the beginning of autumn 64, which is
marked in *Ep.* 122. 1). See also n. 26.

[9] *De clementia* dates itself to between 15 Dec. 55 and 14 Dec. 56 (Griffin 1976, App. A 3). We
do not know when in 56 Caninius Rebilus died.

[10] If it were certain that *Ben.* 7. 5. 1 (see Introduction, n. 6 and ad 7. 5. 1) was an allusion to the
Libri moralis philosophiae, which S. explicitly says he was working on at the time of the later
Letters, it would be reasonable to date the work to the 60s, close to the time of the *Letters*.

[11] See e.g. the remarks of Grimal 1949, 178.

[12] Ferri 2003, 251 suggests that the turning-point of 62, celebrated in the pseudo-Senecan tragedy *Octavia*, was taken over from a Flavian historian by Tacitus. However, the murder of Octavia
was already picked out as marking a stage in Nero's decline in Nero's lifetime by Subrius Flavus,
according to Tacitus *Ann.* 15. 67. In Griffin 1976, 226, I suggested that stressing the change of
advisers, Burrus being replaced by Tigellinus, was Tacitus' own idea: the praetorian prefect in
Octavia is unnamed and colourless.

[13] Tac. *Ann.* 14. 10–11 for the letter; 14. 56. 3 for his restricted activities from 62.

allusions or, if they are, as to what precisely they indicate in terms of chronology. More subtle is (iii) the negative argument that certain people or events could not have been mentioned, or certain things could not have been said, at a particular period of time.[14] Finally, (iv) similarities to, or contrasts with, what he says in other works have been used to argue for dates close or distant to them.

The general difficulties involved in dating Seneca's works have been discussed many times. I surveyed at length the speculative techniques just mentioned in the Introduction to Griffin 1976, where I decided to avoid them, because they would have introduced circularity into my investigation there of the relation of Seneca's life to his writings. My own attempt at narrowing the chronological limits for *De beneficiis* to before his semi-retirement in 62 (Appendix A1.G, 399) was based on the sheer volume of work that we know Seneca composed after that date: the *Natural Questions*, most of the *Letters*, and the lost *Moralis Philosophia*, mentioned in the *Letters*. Scepticism has been expressed, and rightly.[15] It can be objected that in the early 60s Seneca was busy composing some of the tragedies, but also, more fundamentally, that we understand little of Seneca's methods or rates of composition.

To review all of the suggestions advanced with a view to narrowing the chronological limits would be tedious, if not pointless. Instead, I give some examples, to illustrate the difficulties these techniques present, and to support the idea that it is better to rest content with the limits of 56 and summer 64.

(i) Alleged allusions to historical events. In 2. 7. 2–8 Seneca blames Tiberius for his censorious way of dealing with requests for cash by impoverished senators (see **ad 2. 7. 2–8. 2**). It is not unreasonable to connect what he gives explicitly as his own opinion, 'It is not really proper even for the emperor to give a gift in order to humiliate', with Nero's own generosity in 58, when he made annual grants to some noble senators (Tac. *Ann.* 13. 34). But how? Friedrich, followed by Münscher, regarded it as a flattering allusion to Nero's generosity;[16] but since Seneca was influential in 58 and Nero was probably following his advice then, Seneca could have expressed what is his own view, before or after Nero implemented it. Then again, Grimal, followed by Chaumartin,[17] thinks that Nero's generosity after Agrippina's death (Dio 61. 18. 1; Suet. *Nero* 11. 2) provided the occasion for a treatise on generosity. But Nero 's generosity was lavish on many occasions, as the Suetonian passage shows; and, in any case, *De beneficiis* is critical of such indiscriminate largesse (p. 76).

---

[14] This approach, applied to the tragedies by Nisbet 1990, has been well received, but there is evidence that, as regards tragedy, 'Roman audiences were quick to sense contemporary references' (97); one cannot assume that for Seneca's philosophical works (see Griffin 1976, 12–20).

[15] By Inwood 1995a, 244 = 2005, 69.

[16] Friedrich 1914, 1406; Münscher 1922, 66–7, followed by Pohlenz 1941, 80 n. 82.

[17] Grimal 1978, 304–5; Chaumartin 1989, 1703.

(ii) Alleged allusions to Seneca's personal circumstances. Many scholars have assumed that Seneca's offer in 62, to return some of the riches that he had received from the Emperor, is somehow reflected in *De beneficiis*.[18] But how? In 2. 19. 2 Seneca emphasizes that a benefit must be something one receives willingly: if a tyrant forces one to accept something, it is not a benefit, and one is under no obligation for it. Préchac assumed this was Seneca's answer to Nero's insulting refusal to accept the return of his wealth; Grimal felt that Seneca would not have said this after the refusal, because Nero would have seen it as an insult.[19]

(iii) This brings us to the negative approach to allusions, which has been widely applied to this work. Thus Abel 1985, 708 found a date before the Great Fire of July 64 confirmed by the praise of Agrippa's buildings in 3. 32. 4, because that shows that Rome was not yet damaged by the Fire. In fact, most of Agrippa's buildings (see **ad 3. 32. 4**) were on the Campus Martius, which was not damaged, and were used by Nero to provide relief housing for victims of the Fire (Tac. *Ann.* 15. 39. 2).

The difficulty of allusion-hunting in Seneca is in fact well illustrated by the Great Fire. Seneca did not mention this important event even in those *Letters* certainly written after that event, though it could have been used to demonstrate the fragility of human life and of tangible possessions,. Indeed in *Ep.* 91. 13, writing about the later fire at Lugdunum, Seneca allows himself only the most general reference to fires at Rome, saying that the historian Timagenes, who lived in the time of the Emperor Augustus, resented them because he knew that even better buildings would arise. It would be natural to believe that Seneca wrote this *Letter* before the July 64 fire, if we did not know for certain, from Tacitus *Ann.* 16. 13. 3, that the fire at Lugdunum postdated that at Rome (see below, p. 97). For teaching purposes, the philosopher apparently thought that a less notorious event, of personal significance to a friend, would be more effective.[20] We may safely disregard alleged allusions to the Great Fire in the later books of *De beneficiis* 6. 37. 3; 7. 19. 8; 7. 31. 5,[21] all of which are of even greater generality.

(iv) The relationship to Seneca's other works is hard to fathom. Many scholars have remarked the similarity of discussions in *De beneficiis* to the concerns in *De vita beata*, datable to 58, about wealth and its use; to the theological

---

[18] See the discussion in Gercke 1896, 307–11.

[19] Préchac 1961, p. xi; Grimal 1978, 304, followed by Chaumartin 1989, 1708.

[20] Fuhrmann 1997, 312–14 stresses that political caution was not the reason. He attributes it to philosophical detachment from the things of this world, since Seneca could easily have mentioned the Rome Fire safely in this letter. Ker 2009, 108 thinks the Roman reader would recognize Seneca's presentation of a 'much-needed perspective on their seemingly singular event', citing Bedon 1991, 53–7 for the idea that the Lyons fire is exaggerated by Seneca to the scale of the Rome fire, which he preferred not to mention, given the rumours surrounding it.

[21] The first two are adduced by Letta 1998, 231; the last by Préchac 1961, p. xxiii.

arguments in the undatable *De providentia*; and to the themes of the early *Letters* of 63–4, such as the treatment of slaves (*Epp*. 31. 11; 44. 4; 47; *Ben*. 3. 18–28) or the respect owed to teachers (*Epp*. 64. 9; 73. 4; *Ben*. 6. 16). Is any one of these affinities to be explained by chronological proximity? In fact, the chronological relation of this work to others by Seneca cannot be established through thematic comparison.[22] Since, as he says, philosophy teaches us most of all to be grateful for benefits and to return them (*Ep*. 73. 9), it is not surprising that the subject occurs in various works (see Ch. 8). Then again, negative remarks about Alexander the Great, common in the treatise (see **ad 1. 13. 1–3**), occur in many works from *De ira* on, and Phalaris is castigated in *De ira* and *De clementia*, as well as in *De beneficiis* and the *Letters*. Closest to Seneca's concerns in *De beneficiis* is *De vita beata*, datable to 58, but the attitude to wealth is different (see Ch. 8). It is important to remember that Seneca is not just producing a record of his own thoughts. Like all writers of works intended for publication, he has his readers in mind. What he writes to a particular addressee must strike them as appropriate to his circumstances, whether real or invented. Moreover, Seneca is addressing his readers as a teacher, so that events tend to be paradigms, and people *exempla*. It follows that, given similar subject-matter, similar opinions can occur in different contexts at different times, while contrasting opinions can emerge in different contexts close in time. Especially in a writer whose extant works belong to his maturity, we cannot make chronological schemes out of such repetitions and differences.

THE ADDRESSEE

We have noted that Seneca depicts his addressee Aebutius Liberalis as a rich and generous benefactor (Ch. 1), and we shall have more to say in Chapter 7 about Seneca's use of him as an *exemplum* at the start of Book 5.[23] Just after this presentation of Liberalis as an *exemplum*, Seneca draws attention to his name, at 5. 3, by inverting his *nomen* and *cognomen* and addressing him 'to you, Liberalis Aebutius, the best of men by nature and prone to benefits' (*homini natura optimo et ad beneficia propenso, Liberalis Aebuti*), whereas elsewhere he is just 'Liberalis', 'mi Liberalis' or 'Aebuti Liberalis' (**ad 5. 1. 3 Liberalis Aebuti**). Liberalis' name is certainly deliciously appropriate for the addressee of a work on generosity. Should we assume that Seneca chose Aebutius Liberalis from

---

[22] On the uselessness for dating purposes of Seneca's thematic repetitions, which occur geared to different questions, see Pohlenz 1941, 64 in particular (concerning the theme of providence), 66–8 in particular (concerning Seneca's attitude to Epicureanism): 'Die Haltung wird im Einzelnen durch das jeweilige Problem bestimmt. Das darf man auch sonst bei Seneca nicht vergessen' (68).

[23] On Aebutius Liberalis, see Griffin 1976, 455–6 (Appendix D. 8).

among his friends as addressee for the work because his cognomen was so appropriate and his lifestyle suitable,[24] or should we suppose that Seneca invented characteristics to go with his friend's *cognomen*?

One idea we can rule out is that Seneca invented him altogether. Against Liberalis' being a fiction stands the fact that Seneca mentions him again as a friend in *Letter* 91, where he acquires a more concrete identity as a citizen of Lugdunum, inconsolable at the destruction of his *patria* by fire.[25] Nor is there any reason to doubt that he actually had the suitable lifestyle attributed to him in *De beneficiis*, where Liberalis is assumed to be not only a rich man, but an educated man who can pick up literary references without identification, and who understands the working of the civil law (e.g. *Ben.* 6. 5. 4–5). He seems to be an *eques*, like so many of Seneca's correspondents—Lucilius, Annaeus Serenus, Pompeius Paulinus. That the real Aebutius Liberalis had these characteristics is perfectly credible. Lugdunum was a rich and prosperous Roman colony, presumably well supplied with *equites Romani*. Seneca describes it as a Roman city located in a province, rather than a provincial town (*Ep.* 91. 10). According to him, the fire, which he reports as a recent event, completely destroyed the city. Now Lugdunum is known from Tacitus to have made a substantial contribution to the rebuilding of Rome after the Great Fire there in mid-July 64, a gesture for which it was rewarded by the Emperor, who had its contribution repaid for use towards its own reconstruction in 65 (*Ann.* 16. 13. 3). The date for the fire of Lugdunum must therefore be after mid-July 64 and before the end of 65, and is probably before the autumn of 64, according to the dramatic date of Seneca's *Letters*.[26] As a wealthy man, Liberalis may have contributed to his city's benefaction to Rome.

Seneca offers the comforting thought that the city may rise from its ruins even better than before, and he predicts that its citizens will contribute to that result (*Ep.* 91. 14). In the end, the Emperor had to help, and Liberalis' grief, mentioned repeatedly (§§1, 3, 13), may have been compounded by financial loss.[27] Bedon 1991 argues that the lack of archaeological evidence for serious damage, and the lateness and small scale of Rome's help show that the fire was not as great as Seneca suggests, but Rome's own need for massive reconstruction counts against the last argument, and individuals could still be

[24] On the view of Sonntag 1913, 63, that he was chosen as addressee just because of his name, see p. 142.

[25] Compare the case of Annaeus Serenus, who is a real man known from Tacitus and other early imperial authors (*PIR*²A 618), and to whom Seneca addresses the appropriately titled *De tranquillitate animi*, among other works.

[26] See Griffin 1976, 400, where 'end of July—fire at Lyons' should read 'end of June—fire at Lyons'. Bedon 1991, 48 suggests a date for the Lyons fire of the first half of August, a time when fires are not uncommon in the Rhône valley.

[27] If the argument here is accepted, it must count against the otherwise attractive suggestion by Ker 2009, 107–8 that *Letter* 91's 'real purpose may be partly to present the disaster as an opportunity for Liberalis to live up to his name and contribute *beneficia* for the rebuilding of his native city'.

seriously affected, if their property was in the wrong place. Seneca could not have mentioned this mundane fact in a letter exploring, in elevated language, the themes common in consolation literature. But two inscriptions from Dalmatia, *ILS* 5953 and 5953a, may provide a clue. They reveal a Quintus Aebutius Liberalis serving as a centurion in the *primi ordines*, that is as one of the centurions of the first cohort, of the eleventh legion. He is in fact the most junior of these, the *hastatus posterior*. The legate of the province, under whom he is carrying out boundary rectification, is A. Ducenius Geminus, whose term as legate of Dalmatia can be fixed to between 62, when he served on a finance commission composed of consulars, and 19 January 69, when he is attested at Rome.[28] Centurions were recruited from the ranks of the legions or the praetorian guard, or they were directly commissioned from men of equestrian rank who had often held municipal office. The latter, described as *ex equite Romano* (e.g. *ILS* 2654–6) did not lose their equestrian status, and they had the best chance of promotion to the rank of *primuspilus*, which was highly lucrative. Promotion was via the *primi ordines*, and these centurions earned about twice what a praetorian soldier did, and about half of what a *primuspilus* earned. The primary reason why an *eques* would wish to become a centurion was money. Frontinus (*Strat.* 4. 6. 4) speaks of a young man, without military talent, becoming a centurion because of his poor family circumstances, and later Pertinax preferred it to entering the *militia equestris* (*SHA Pert.* 5–6), which did not guarantee the same lengthy period of lucrative employment.[29]

Various scholars have suggested that the centurion in Dalmatia, serving under Ducenius Geminus, is Seneca's addressee. There is no obstacle. If Aebutius Liberalis did indeed become a centurion because of financial losses in the fire at Lugdunum, that would have been no earlier than the latter part of 64 and before 69: in any case, some time after Seneca had written *De beneficiis*. We can assume that both addressee and author were rich men when that work was composed.

---

[28] Tac. *Ann.* 15. 18; *Hist.* 1. 14. That his consulship was in 61 or 62 is confirmed by the portoria law of Ephesus (see Eck 1981, 227–30).

[29] Dobson 1972; Dobson 1974, 405–12.

5

The Title

Only a few of the scholars who have studied *De beneficiis* have addressed the question of the title, at least explicitly. Sonntag and Gomoll, however, mention in passing that Seneca renders *charis* as *beneficium* in the absence of a Latin word that, like the Greek, could be used to cover both sides of the exchange: giving and returning.[1] As we shall see, this is a gross over-simplification.

GREEK WORKS ON THE SUBJECT

The philosophical tradition to which Seneca's treatise belongs is that established by Theophrastus and later Hellenistic philosophers who wrote works wholly and specifically devoted to the topic of *charis* (see Ch. 2A). Works *Peri charitos* are attested for Theophrastus, Demetrius of Phalerum, Epicurus, Dionysius the renegade Stoic, Philodemus, and the Stoic Cleanthes.[2] It is common to translate *Peri charitos* as 'On Gratitude', and the full title of Epicurus' work, *Peri dōrōn kai charitos*, like the title attested for Dionysius, *Peri ploutou kai charitos kai timōrias*, suggests that this is correct, for that would yield the sense 'On Gifts and Gratitude' (natural correlatives), for the first, and 'On Wealth and Gratitude and Revenge', for the second:[3] *timōria* would be revenge for an injury parallel to gratitude for a benefit, as in Seneca's 'Benefit and injury are the opposites of each other' and 'You conferred a benefit, and afterwards inflicted an injury; gratitude was owed for the benefit, and revenge for

---

[1] Sonntag 1913, 12; Gomoll 1933, 76. The same view is taken by Schwarzenberg 1966, 63 n. 2, writing about the Graces.

[2] See Ch. 2 nn. 26–7.

[3] At *SVF* i. 422 (D.L. 7. 166), von Arnim suggested separating Dionysius' into two works, the first on wealth, but *Ben.* 1. 3. 9 and *SVF* ii. 1083 show how closely the topics of wealth and beneficence were related for the Stoics, being worked together in these passages into the Stoic allegory of the Graces. See below, p. 103.

the injury'.[4] Moreover, as Moussy shows, of the abstract meanings of *charis*, gratitude for benefits is not only earlier, but remains more common, than the sense of favour or good will leading to their conferral.[5] The translation of the title *Peri charitos* as 'On Gratitude' is further supported by the emphasis in Seneca's work on ingratitude, especially as the Stoic paradoxes on the subject, which he discusses, suggest that this emphasis was already in the Greek Stoic authors he read (*Ben.* 5. 12. 3–17. 5).

The titles of works by Stoics and other philosophers on this subject are usually given, as we have seen, in the singular. But the first work that Seneca himself indicates as a forerunner was an exception. Early in *De beneficiis*, at 1. 3. 8, he alludes to a work by Chrysippus which is clearly that elsewhere attested as *Peri charitōn* (*SVF* ii. 1081). Chaumartin may be right to argue that there is philosophically no significant difference between singular and plural titles of this type.[6] Chrysippus may have used the plural because he wished to include in the work an elaborate allegory of the three Graces (*Charites*) representing three aspects of the exchange of benefits—giving, receiving, and returning (*Ben.* 1. 3. 8)—and thus to stress reciprocity (see below, p. 103). However, when used in the plural, the *charis* of the title now had, not the abstract sense of gratitude, but its original and concrete sense, in the context of beneficence, of objects or services given or, secondarily, returned: a sense already well established in Homer.[7] This could have aroused expectations that he would discuss the practicalities of exchange in more detail than philosophers usually did.[8]

---

[4] *Ben.* 3. 22. 3: *Inter se contraria sunt beneficium et iniuria*; 6. 5. 1: *Dedisti beneficium, iniuriam postea fecisti; et beneficio gratia debebatur et iniuriae ultio*, cf. *Ep.* 81. 7: '"But surely", you say, "it is the part of justice to render to each that which is his due—thanks in return for a benefit, and retribution, or at any rate ill-will, in return for an injury"' ('*Hoc certe', inquis, 'iustitiae convenit, suum cuique reddere, beneficio gratiam, iniuriae talionem aut certe malam gratiam'*), see Moussy 1966, 295. Compare the Epicurean idea in *KΔ* 1 (D.L. 10. 139) that the deity is affected οὔτε ὀργαῖς οὔτε χάρισι ('neither by feelings of anger nor of favour'), cf. Philodemus, *On Piety* 1148, being unaffected by human acts: Cicero translates this as *neque ira neque gratia* (*Nat. d.* 1. 45; otherwise Lucretius 2. 651).

[5] Moussy 1966, 412–14.

[6] In support Chaumartin 1985, 34 n. 26 notes the description by Diogenes Laertius of a work of Posidonius, once as *Peri kathēkontos* (D.L. 7. 129) and another time as *Peri kathēkontōn* (D.L. 7. 124); the singular without the article, and the indifference as to singular or plural, rather count against Dyck's attempt (1996, 7 n. 18) to explain Cicero's rendering of Panaetius' *Peri tou kathēkontos* as *De officiis* by the lack of a Latin definite article. Cooper and Procopé 1995, 187 clearly agree with Chaumartin, as they render both the singular and plural titles of such works as *On Favours*.

[7] Moussy 1966, 412–14.

[8] Similarly, Brunt 2013 argues in ch. 5, App. 1 §2 that the plural title of Posidonius' work, i.e. *Peri kathēkontōn*, is correct (see above, n. 6) and that, whereas Panaetius had concentrated on exposing the very nature of the *kathēkon* with illustrative examples, Posidonius was more concerned to catalogue the kinds of actions that should be performed. Cf. also §12 of the chapter: 'Cicero's title suggests that his work will register all the kinds of actions that are "appropriate" (*kathēkonta*) whereas that chosen by Panaetius indicates that his design was to show what is in its very nature appropriate.'

The allegory has usually been described as a Stoic invention.[9] This is plausible, because the Stoics regularly interpreted anthropomorphic gods as allegories for the benefits of divine providence, and also looked in the traditional poets for the seeds of their philosophical wisdom.[10] Moreover, this allegory is found in the Stoic philosopher Cornutus (*SVF* ii. 1083), and at least one of the two versions of it given by Seneca (*Ben.* 1. 3. 3), probably the first, should be assigned to the Stoic Chrysippus, as Seneca goes on at 1. 3. 8 to criticize him for including stories of this kind in his work, and thus for 'saying very little about the duty itself of doing, accepting, or returning a benefit'.[11] The implication seems to be that his allegory covered these principal aspects of the subject.

It has been argued that this Stoic invention sheds no light on the ordinary Greek use of the term *charis*.[12] However, the allegorical interpretation of the Graces involves understanding *charis*, as we have noted, not in the abstract sense of 'grace' or 'joy' in which it was originally applied to the Graces, but in its concrete sense of a gift causing joy, a benefit given or returned,[13] and this association of the *Charites* with the exchange of concrete benefits was anything but remote from ordinary Greek usage, at the time when Chrysippus was writing. The Hellenistic polis had shown the way here, while Aristotle had already provided this usage with philosophical credentials. In the course of his discussion of reciprocity in the *Nicomachean Ethics* 5. 5. 1133ª3–5, Aristotle remarks that shrines are set up to the *Charites* 'to promote the requital of services; for this is characteristic of *charis*: one should repay a service done one, and should another time take the initiative in doing a service oneself.'[14] The epigraphic evidence

---

[9] Moussy 1966, 442–3; Loew 1908, 82 n. 1.   [10] Cic. *Nat. d.* 1. 39–41.

[11] Cooper and Procopé 1995, 197 nn. 5–6 suggest that both versions are Stoic and both inadequate as 'the process of giving, accepting and returning a favour only needs two participants'. Yet another version of the allegory appears in the Peripatetic doxography, probably emanating from Arius Didymus in the late 1st c. BC and preserved by Stob. 2. 143. 18–20 W: 'That "*charis*" is used in three ways, the doing of a useful favour for its own sake, the return of the useful favour, the remembering of such a favour' (Χάριν δὲ λέγεσθαι τριχῶς, τὴν μὲν ὑπουργίαν ὠφελίμου αὐτοῦ ἐκείνου ἕνεκα, τὴν δ' ἄμειψιν ὑπουργίας ὠφελίμου, τὴν δὲ μνήμην ὑπουργίας τοιαύτης). The context is identifiably Peripatetic, so the allegory could be an independent development by the Peripatetics from Aristotle's reference to the cult of the Graces (*NE* 5. 5. 1133ª3–5), though the third element is different from his starting the process of giving again (see below). But it could be a development by the Peripatetics of the Stoic idea of allegorizing the Graces. It is notable that Chrysippus' version also included the idea of memory, symbolized by the youth of the goddesses (*Ben.* 1. 3. 5). For the connection with visual representations, see ad 1. 3. 2–4. 5.

[12] Loew 1908, 82 n. 1.

[13] Moussy 1966, 411–12, 437; Parker 1998, 108–9. The entry on *charis* in the Peripatetic doxography (see above, n. 11), just after giving an allegorical interpretation of the goddesses, notes the former sense of *charis* as 'grace' or 'joy': λέγεσθαι δὲ χάριν καὶ τὴν ἐν ὄψει ἢ ἐν λόγοις, καθ' ἣν τὸν μὲν εὔχαριν ὀνομάζεσθαι, τὸν δ' ἐπίχαριν ('grace in appearance or in discussion is said to be that in virtue of which one person is called "gracious", another "charming"', Stob. 2. 143. 21–3).

[14] For the significance of this way of defining the exchange obligation, see p. 45 with n. 66.

bears him out. Not only at Claros and Teos[15] were the Charites interpreted as symbols of gratitude and associated with the repayment of the favours of benefactors through decrees that conferred honours and privileges: at Athens itself, where the Charites had long had a special shrine at the entrance to the Acropolis, a new precinct, to Demos and the Charites, was built northwest of the Agora, probably in the 220s BC. In it, honorary decrees for foreign benefactors were displayed, to demonstrate the gratitude of the Athenian people. The precinct, it has been persuasively argued, had been set up to celebrate the liberation of the city in 229 BC.[16] Chrysippus would have been in Athens at that time, having become head of the Stoa *c*.232 BC. The precinct became the place where statues and inscriptions were erected, honouring benefactors to the city.[17] Whatever further significance the cult had for the Athenians, the sanctuary was the place where Athenians expressed their gratitude to foreigners.[18]

In such decrees the usual formulae use *euergetēs, euergetein, euergetēma* of the benefactor or his service to the city, and *charis* or *charites* of the return made by the city. A typical example in one of the municipal decrees reads: ὅπως φανερὸν ᾖ πᾶσιν, ὅτι τοῖς εὐεργέταις ἀποδιδῶι ἡ πόλις ἀξίας χάριτας τῶν εὐεργετημάτων ('that it may be clear to all that the city makes worthy returns to its benefactors').[19] However, the use of *charis* for a benefit given is also common in Hellenistic epigrams and funerary inscriptions, while Plutarch speaks of the *charites* of Flamininus, and imperial grants are called *hai tōn Sebastōn charites*.[20] Chrysippus was therefore following Greek usage familiar in his own day, both in using *charis* in its concrete sense of benefits given and benefits returned, and in developing his allegory of the Charites on the basis of this interpretation.

In employing *charis* in connection with taking the initiative in giving, as well as with showing gratitude in receiving, Chrysippus was also within the philosophical tradition. Aristotle in his *Rhetoric* (2. 7. 1385ª17–19) uses the word both in the concrete sense of objects or services given, and in the abstract sense of good will motivating such a gift, while his discussion of the cult of the Charites in the *Nicomachean Ethics* stresses its use on both sides of an exchange. The Peripatetics recognized *charis* as the ἀρχὴ τῆς εὐεργετικῆς φιλίας ('the source of beneficent friendship') (Stob. 143. 5–8 W). The Stoics clearly emphasized

[15] *SEG* 39 (1989), 1243 v 45; 41 (1991), 1003 C/D 29–44.

[16] Habicht 1982, 85–93; Parker 1996, 272–3.

[17] For the abundant evidence for public honouring of benefactors in this period, see Gauthier 1985.

[18] Mikalson 1998, 173–7 argues that for Athenians the cult had the traditional significance of agricultural prosperity and peace linked to democracy.

[19] *SEG* 43 (1993), 704, vv. 16–18, cf. e.g. *SEG* 41 (1991), 1003, C/D 40–1; cf. Ma 1999, no. 10. 17–18; 11. 10–12. Dio Chrysostom says: ὁ νόμος πᾶσιν ὧν ἂν εὐεργετήσωσιν ἑτέρους ἐκτίνει τὰς χάριτας ('the law renders thanks to all for the kindnesses they show to others', *Or.* 75. 6).

[20] Plut. *Flam.* 1; *OGI.* 669, 44; *P. Oxy* 273/14; *P.Grenf.* 2.70, 5; Ael. Arist. *Funeral Speech for Alexander* 15; Marcus Aurelius 5.6.1. uses it of a favour given. See MacMullen 1986, 523 n. 35.

the duty of giving, as is shown in the Eurynome part of the allegory, which is not only attributed to Chrysippus (*Ben.* 1. 3. 9), but found in Seneca's contemporary Cornutus (*SVF* ii. 1083): the name of the mother of the Graces—Eurynome—was explained by the wide distribution of benefits that is characteristic of an extensive fortune.[21] Chrysippus' use both of the plural of *charis* in his title and of the images of the Graces points to his desire to emphasize the element of reciprocity in beneficence, as is made clear by Philodemus, who says that he represented the Charites as 'our initiations and returns of favours'. Seneca writes of the 'most honourable rivalry in outdoing benefits by benefits, to which Chrysippus thus urges us'.[22]

WHY NOT *DE GRATIA*?

Seneca uses the Latin *Gratiae* to render Χάριτες, when discussing Chrysippus' allegory (though he also uses *Charites*). Though there was no etymological connection between these Greek and Latin terms, the connection in meaning had been made already in the time of Plautus.[23] The reinterpretation of the Charites as symbols of gratitude in Aristotle's time will have made the equation easier, for the primary meaning of *gratia* is 'gratitude', and all meanings of the term in the classical period develop easily from that fundamental meaning. The word is used in the active abstract sense of 'a feeling of gratitude', as in *gratiam habere*; it is also used in the active concrete sense of attesting one's gratitude: by verbal thanks, as in *gratias agere*, or by giving a service in return, as in *gratiam referre*.[24]

Gomoll, as we said, found the reason for Seneca's irritation with Chrysippus' allegory in his frustration at not being able to reproduce in Latin the Greek philosopher's title, inspired by that allegory: Latin, he said, cannot use the same word to cover both sides of an exchange of favours.[25] However, *gratia* can in fact be used of a benefit without a preceding favour. Both concrete senses, a

---

[21] Cornutus' formulation is οἱ δ' ἐξ Εὐρονόμης, καὶ τούτου παριστάντος ὅτι χαριστικώτεροί πώς εἰσιν ἢ ὀφείλουσιν εἶναι οἱ μεγάλους κλήρους νεμόμενοι ('some say they descend from Eurynome, and this represents that those who enjoy great possessions are more bounteous in some way than they are obliged to be'); Seneca's is *Eurynomen enim dictam, quia late patentis patrimonii sit beneficia dividere* ('she was called Eurynome because the sharing out of benefits requires an inheritance that spreads far and wide').

[22] *SVF* ii. 1081: φησὶν εἶναι καὶ τὰς Χάριτας τὰς ἡμετέ[ρ]ας καταρχὰς κα[ὶ] τὰς ἀνταπ[ο]δόσεις τῶν εὐε[ργ]εσιῶ[ν]; *Ben* 1. 4. 4: *ad hanc honestissimam contentionem beneficiis beneficia vincendi sic nos adhortatur Chrysippus.*

[23] Moussy 1966, 409.

[24] The best discussion of the various meanings of *gratia* and the expressions in which it occurs is still Moussy 1966, especially 249–302.

[25] Gomoll 1933, 75–6.

benefit given and a benefit returned, are found from the time of Plautus,[26] though *gratia* as a primary gift is not used as the object of verbs of giving: *gratiam dare* is not a classical Latin expression. The process tends to be seen from the receiving end, as in *gratiam accipere* ('to receive a favour'), or *gratiam remunerare* ('to repay a favour'), or *gratiam exigere* ('to demand a favour').[27] Nonetheless, the sense of a benefit given (not in reciprocation), though less common, leads to *gratia* sometimes being used in a doublet with *beneficium.*[28] Cicero even uses *gratia* in the plural in this concrete, non-reciprocating sense: *non excellentibus gratiis paucorum, sed universi populi iudicio, consulem ita factum* ('elected consul, not through the outstanding favours of a clique, but through the esteem of the whole people').[29] So what Sonntag and Gomoll and, still later, Schwarzenberg say, is not strictly true:[30] Latin does have a word which, like *charis*, can be used both of what is given and of what is returned. Indeed *gratia* also has, as its less common active abstract sense, that of the 'goodwill' or 'favour' initiating benefits, just like *charis*.

It is, of course, true that it is more common in Latin to use *beneficium* of what is given and *gratia* of what is returned, and that the most common verbal phrases with *gratia*, given above, are connected with the notions of recovery and gratitude. Nor is it difficult to find examples of *beneficium* and *gratia* used as correlatives of each other, like the Greek *euergetēma* and *charis*.[31] Seneca himself shows a clear preference for using *gratia* in its active sense, to mean (in the abstract) 'gratitude' and (in its concrete meaning) 'attestation of gratitude (by words or recompense)'.[32]

Nonetheless, it is clear that Seneca could have preserved the link with Chrysippus' allegory of the *Gratiae* by calling his work *De gratia*. He would

[26]   Moussy 1966, 286–7.

[27]   Cic. *Fam.* 2. 6. 2, which actually reads *nullam esse gratiam tuam quam non vel capere animus meus in accipiendo vel in remunerando cumulare atque illustrare posset* ('whatever favour you may bestow on me my mind would have the capacity to accept it and the ability to enhance and add lustre to it in repaying it'); *Amic.* 31.

[28]   e.g. *II Verr.* 3. 115: *benefici gratiaeque causa*, 189: *in benefici loco et gratiae.*

[29]   *Leg. ag.* 2. 7.   [30]   See n. 1.

[31]   e.g. Cic. *Sest.* 70: *ad amplissimi beneficii gratiam magis pertinere videret* ('he saw it would bring him greater gratitude for so generous a benefit'); *Fin.* 2. 117: *tollitur beneficium, tollitur gratia, quae sunt vincula concordiae* ('generosity is abolished, gratitude is abolished, which are the bonds of mutual harmony'); Seneca, *Ben.* 2. 33. 3: *cum benigne acceptum est beneficium, qui dedit, gratiam quidem iam recepit* ('when a benefit is received graciously, the giver has already received gratitude'); 5. 11. 1: *beneficium et relatio gratiae ultro citro ire debent* ('a benefit and the return of a favour ought to go reciprocally'); 4. 1. 1: *an beneficium dare et in vicem gratiam referre per se res expetendae sint* ('whether conferring a benefit and doing a favour in return are things worthy of choice in themselves'); 6. 11. 4: *beneficium dedero, non gratiam rettulero* ('I shall have given a benefit, not returned a favour'); *Ep.* 81. 7: *suum cuique reddere, beneficio gratia* ('to render to each his due, gratitude for a benefit').

[32]   Moussy 1966, 153 n. 1, 249–50: the active sense accounts for 75% of his uses (89% in *De beneficiis*; 65% in *Epistulae Morales*) vs. 45% of Cicero's and 48.75% of Livy's: these are the authors who show the most frequent use of *gratia*.

have had to raise the minority active meanings of the word—i.e. (concrete) benefit without a preceding favour and (abstract) goodwill leading to a gift—to equal status with the more common reciprocative meanings, but that is not a serious objection, for he had to stretch *beneficium* in a similar way, though in the opposite direction. He was in fact prepared to use *beneficium* of both sides of the exchange, e.g. at *Ben.* 1. 4. 4 where he renders Chrysippus' exhortation to gratitude with 'to this most honourable rivalry in outdoing benefits by benefits' (*ad hanc honestissimam contentionem beneficiis beneficia vincendi sic nos adhortatur Chrysippus*), or *Ben* 4. 18. 1, 'It is only through the interchange of benefits (*beneficiorum commercio*) that life becomes in some measure equipped and fortified against sudden disasters.'[33] In this he was not unique.[34] But why did he not instead stretch *gratia* to cover both sides of the exchange?

Seneca's choice appears even more curious when we consider that *gratia* should have had great advantages for him over *beneficium*. For one thing, Seneca shows great interest in the subject of ingratitude, in treating all three of his chosen topics given in 1. 4. 3: the discussion of giving benefits (1. 1. 1–3; 1. 10. 4–5; 2. 1–13) places a lot of emphasis on not incurring ingratitude, the advice on receiving benefits (2. 26–30) analyses the vice, while the discussion of returning benefits (3. 1–17. 4) largely takes the form of a discourse on ingratitude (see pp. 116–18).[35]

More important is the fact, unlike the case of *beneficium*, the abstract sense of *gratia* is the predominant one; or, as Saller puts it, *gratia*, unlike *beneficium* (and *officium* and *meritum*), primarily signified an attitude, rather than an action.[36] In the formulation by Hellegouarc'h, 'la *gratia* est d'abord une disposition de l'esprit créée par le *beneficium* et qui conduit à se comporter d'une certain manière'.[37] Seneca regards the real *beneficium* as a virtuous act, whose

---

[33] Chaumartin 1989, 36–7 n. 35 attempts, unconvincingly, to reinterpret 4. 18. 1 so as to avoid attributing to Seneca the reciprocal use of *beneficium*: the passages he adduces (*Ira* 1. 5. 3; *Ben*. 1. 4. 2) do not indeed imply that the word is being used of both sides of an exchange, but they are not true parallels.

[34] See Ch. 3 n. 32. The common use of *beneficium reddere* (e.g. Plaut. *Pers*. 762; Ter. *Phorm*. 336; Cic. *Sen*. 2; *Off*. 1. 48) as well as *beneficium referre*, *beneficium remunerari*, and *beneficia rependere* are not comparable (*pace* Dyck 1996, 162–3) because they do not strictly imply that the thing returned is also called a *beneficium*, any more than to 'repay a loan' implies that what we give the lender is itself a 'loan'. These expressions use the term appropriate to the original transaction, though what is returned is not a *beneficium*, any more than the actual thing returned is identical with the thing given, as Seneca indicates at *Ben*. 6. 5. 2: *Cum dicimus 'Beneficium illi reddidi', non hoc dicimus illud nos, quod acceperamus, reddidisse, sed aliud pro illo.* As the same discussion makes clear, *beneficium reddere* is just an alternative locution to *beneficio gratiam reddere*.

[35] As Armisen-Marchetti 2004, 7 remarks, 'De fait le *De beneficiis* est en grande partie un traité *De gratia*, la question du don étant considérée d'emblée dans la perspective de la reconnaissance, l'ingratitude du bénéficiaire tenant largement au fait qui la bienfaisance s'est mal exercée'.

[36] Saller 1982, 21. Schwarzenberg 1966, 63 n. 2 points out that neither Latin word conveys the sense of charm or grace in *charis*, but that *beneficium* conveys it less than *gratia*.

[37] Hellegouarc'h 1963, 205.

essence is its intention: 'A benefit is the actual goodwill of whoever bestows it' (*<beneficium est> ipsa tribuentis voluntas*, 1. 5. 2). It can only be repaid by a grateful attitude: 'If he (the donor) accomplishes what he sought, if his state of mind is conveyed to me and inspires me with a joy that we both share, he has gained what he wanted' (*si quod voluit effecit pervenitque ad me animus eius ac mutuo gaudio adfecit, tulit quod petit*) (2. 31. 2). He is at pains to explain that the true *beneficium* is incorporeal (6. 2), even for the Stoics.[38]

Thus Seneca's *beneficium* is a matter of the correct attitude, whereas he speaks of the things given (7. 13) as 'the means employed to give a benefit' (*ea per quae beneficium datur*), the true *beneficium* being here equivalent to *benevolentia*. Sometimes, it is true, he expresses the distinction as one between the *actio* and 'that which is given' (*ipsum quod datur*, *Ben*. 2. 34. 5): the latter can be a material gift or a service such as ransoming someone from the pirates (1. 5. 4). But it is an action that must be performed with the right intention. At 6. 10 he explains his meaning clearly: *voluntas* is a necessary (though not a sufficient) condition for a *beneficium*. One is only obliged to a person for giving or performing a service intentionally (*ex destinato*). Hence his definition: 'What then is a benefit? An act of benevolence bestowing joy and deriving joy from bestowing it, with an inclination and spontaneous readiness to do so' (*quid est beneficium? benevola actio tribuens gaudium capiensque tribuendo in id quod facit, prona et sponte sua parata*) (1. 6. 1, cf. 2. 34. 5 *actio benefica*).

It is important to realize that Seneca does not construe *beneficium* as an 'action' in the sense contrasted with attitude by Saller: Saller's 'action', which is inseparable from what is given, is that present in the etymology of the word *beneficium*, i.e. the giving of a material thing or a service.[39] Intrinsic to Saller's action, unlike Seneca's *benevola actio*, is the handling of things that are morally indifferent. Seneca's *beneficium* is construed as a *benevola actio*, which is a good in Stoic terms, and is contrasted with the thing given, which is an indifferent: it has attitude as its essential element. This is in fact a paradoxical use of *beneficium*, a term which in common usage clearly operated at the level of action in Saller's sense, i.e. the giving of tangible things, as the dedicatory inscriptions to benefactors show.[40] Seneca himself often uses the word of the favours and services bestowed (**ad 1. 5. 1–9. 1 fin.**), and he respects the etymology of the word in switching at 2. 34. 5 from the definition *benevola actio* (1. 6) to *actio benefica*. The common idiom *beneficio* with the genitive, as in the expression *beneficio legis*, shows the importance of the result of the action for the receiver. By contrast, the idiom *gratia* after the genitive, like *charin* after the

---

[38] See **ad 6. 2. 1–2**. Cf. 1. 5. 2 where the distinction is put as *non potest beneficium manu tangi* ('a benefit cannot be touched with the hand').

[39] As with *officium*, where, as Dyck 1996, 5 points out, 'the etymology from *facere/efficere* long continued to be felt'.

[40] This is the level of Phidias' *artificium* at *Ben*. 2. 33. 2 in which there is an expected return for something actually produced.

genitive, signifies intention. One might think that it would have been easier for Seneca to insist on the mental state as the essence of a favour if he had used *gratia* rather than *beneficium* for both sides of the transaction.

POSSIBLE REASONS FOR THE CHOICE OF TITLE

We must therefore conclude that Seneca had definite reasons for preferring *beneficium* despite its obvious disadvantages. Several reasons can be adduced:

(i) The influence of the similar title *De officiis*. Though there is no actual evidence that Seneca had read Cicero's work, which covered the topic of *beneficentia*, it is likely that he at least knew of it (see p. 7). Moreover, he himself had written a work with that title, which may or may not have handled the subject matter of beneficence.[41] He may also have thought that, like this plural title and Chrysippus' plural title in Greek, the plural *De beneficiis* would convey the nature of his treatise as a work of practical ethics (above, p. 100 and n. 8).

(ii) The fact that *gratia*, in the less common of its active abstract meanings, i.e. 'goodwill' or 'favour', can be pejorative in meaning, indicating partiality.[42] Even in the less common of its concrete active senses, it often means a favour done with a political end in view, as in the passage of *Leg. ag.* 2. 7 cited above (p. 104). In its passive sense, especially in the Ciceronian period and the early empire, it means political influence, often undue influence in legal contexts where it interferes with justice (*Ben.* 4. 12. 2), and it can be associated with *potentia* (Sen. *Vit. Beat.* 2. 4; *Epp.* 21. 6; 94. 72).[43] In Latin writers generally, it has been calculated that the use of *gratia* to mean political credit is 14.85% of the total.[44]

These reasons might not seem sufficient to outweigh the advantage of using *gratia*. We must look further.

(iii) *Beneficium* focuses attention mostly on the donor, whereas *gratia* focuses it on the receiver. Chrysippus could remedy this by using *charis* in the plural, but *gratia* was far less common in the plural, and its plural meaning is restricted to manifestations of gratitude, and its use to verbal phrases like *gratias agere*, *habere*, and *referre*.[45] Now, the subject traditionally was concerned with both giving and receiving, and Seneca, as we saw, spends a lot of time on the ingratitude of receivers. We think of the paradoxes at the end of book 2, and of his concern that recipients should not be oppressed by favours. Then again, in 6. 43 he says that receiving gifts can be more difficult than giving them. Nonetheless, the primary emphasis in *De beneficiis* is on the donor and,

---

[41] See Ch. 2A.
[42] Moussy 1966, 300; e.g. Cic. *QF* 1. 1. 20; Livy 3. 36. 7; Elder Seneca, *Controv.* 9. 2. 11.
[43] Moussy 1966, 376. [44] Ibid. 371. [45] Ibid. 273.

as Inwood says, the 'major message of the treatise' is, indeed, that 'man's ingratitude should never incite (and cannot justify) the abandonment of giving'.[46] Thus the work begins and ends with an account of the faults of donors, and the giving of advice to donors, as the people principally responsible for ingratitude (see **ad 1. 1–3. 1 *fin*.**).

In *De Officiis* Cicero devotes more space to giving than to receiving or returning benefits. It is natural to connect this with the fact that he is concerned only with his (at least in theory) social equals. Seneca too is primarily interested in this class.[47] Seneca, as we said, is more concerned than Cicero with the social relations existing between those who are not equals: not only masters and slaves, but also parents and children, and those in absolute power (including the Emperor) and their subjects.[48] The last two topics focus his attention on problems of receiving and returning benefits, because they affect his own class. But the primary emphasis is still overall on the donors, with the result that, as we have seen, there are remarkable continuities between Seneca's picture of the beneficence of the governing class in his day and Cicero's picture of this activity under the Republic (see Ch. 3C).

(iv) Finally, the apparent disadvantage of running counter to common usage and common conceptions could have been regarded by Seneca as an advantage for the philosophical task he has set himself. In the spirit of the Stoic paradoxes, Seneca may have wished to challenge directly the common conceptions of material exchange as the basis of friendship and society.

Beneficium was an important word for the members of the Roman governing class. It was widely used in connection with public life, where it could be synonymous with high office and privileges.[49] *Gratia* too merits substantial space in Hellegouarc'h's study of the vocabulary of Roman politics.[50] But *beneficium*, apart from the advantage that it lacks the pejorative meaning of *gratia* (above, ii), highlights by its very concreteness the misconceptions that Seneca wants to correct.[51] Thus there was a *liber beneficiorum* recording the Emperor's favours,[52] and, at least from the time of Trajan, epigraphic evidence for a post of *a commentariis beneficiorum*, terminology that fits Trajan's reference, in a letter to Pliny, to having entered in his *commentarii* the *beneficium* of the *ius trium liberorum* granted to Suetonius.[53] Moreover, the jurists regularly use *beneficium* with the genitive of the gerund to denote specific imperial

---

[46] See Ch. 3C. The quotation is from Inwood 1995a, 263 = 2005, 91.
[47] See Ch. 3C.   [48] See p. 11.   [49] *TLL* ii, cols. 1885–6, s.v. *beneficium* 2.C.a and b.
[50] Hellegouarc'h 1963, 202–8.
[51] Bellincioni 1984a, 122 regards the theme that holds the whole complex work together as the process of moving away from the usual meaning of *beneficium* to the meaning that captures its ethical content.
[52] Hyg. 2 *agrim*. 202 L = 158.31–2 Campbell.
[53] *CIL* vi. 1884: see *Diz. epig.* i. 998; Plin. *Ep.* 10. 95, cf. 10. 105 (a grant of *ius Quiritium*).

privileges.[54] Indeed, in the military sphere, soldiers who were released from routine duties to serve a senior officer were called *beneficarii*: they are attested in Caesar's *Bellum Civile* at the end of the Republic, and on inscriptions, from at least the mid-first century AD.[55] The connection of the term *beneficium* with imperial beneficence must also have appealed to Seneca, as one of his aims was to minimize the differences between the generosity to individuals shown by the Princeps and that shown by other members of the governing class, and to treat them as subject to the same code (Ch. 3C). In this respect, *beneficia* was the Latin equivalent of *charites*, used, as we have seen, of imperial privileges.

Seneca knows that he is trying to gain acceptance for the use of terms not in their usual sense, as is shown by his explicit discussion at 2. 34. 2–5 of the meaning of *beneficium* as primarily a beneficent act (rather than an object given) in the context of the Stoic paradox that feeling gratitude is a sufficient return of a benefit.[56] In fact, the revisionist direction of his theme is underlined by the important place accorded to paradox throughout the treatise.[57] But how far does Seneca's insistence on mental attitudes as the essence of the social exchange of favours amount to an attempt to 'change the currency'?[58] As we have seen (Ch. 3B), his advice is not really as unrealistic as it looks. Not only do we find such sentiments in the popular morality of Publilius Syrus, e.g. 'He who has given to a worthy man has received a benefit in giving' (*beneficium dando accepit qui digno dedit*, 68, cf. 683): Seneca makes it clear that his most high-minded teaching is actually a form of exhortation and not meant to be taken literally, as he explains towards the end of the work (7. 22. 1–23. 2). Thus, when discussing this very paradox, that 'He who receives a benefit gladly has returned it', he explains how his conception of the exchange of benefits as a transaction between minds (2. 34. 1) accords with the social bond that the Stoics take so seriously. Seneca solves the problem brilliantly, by his use of two powerful images: the first (2. 32) likens the exchange of benefits to a ball game and makes a distinction (*a*) between the morality of the 'players', for which throwing with the correct intention, and trying to return the ball, is enough, and (*b*) the success of the game, which requires that the throw actually be returned (see Ch. 3A). The second (2. 33) likens giving a benefit to the work of the artist, for whom the creative process is the reward from his art (*ars*); the returns he may receive in reputation and material advantage are the rewards of

---

[54] *Diz. epig.* i. 996: e.g. *beneficium respondendi; beneficium adsidendi; beneficium anulorum.*

[55] Caesar, *BC* 1. 75. 2, 3. 88. 5; Dise 1997, 274. According to the *Historia Augusta*, a *beneficiarius* serving Julius Servianus, governor of Upper Germany, was sent as a messenger to Rome to inform Trajan of Nerva's death in January 98 (*Hadr.* 2. 5–6).

[56] Compare also the discussions of paradoxical language at 7. 5. 1, and 5. 12.3–15. 2.

[57] As Inwood 1995a notes.

[58] A similar move by Seneca is pointed out by Moussy 1966, 264, that at 6. 43. 2 *fin.* and 2. 17. 6 Seneca tries to elide *gratias agere* (to give thanks verbally) and *gratiam referre* (to return a favour), but that this does not accord with ordinary usage, or indeed with his own usage elsewhere.

his work of art (*artificium*).[59] So the first fruit of a benefit is the awareness of having conferred the gift as he intended; glory, and what is received in exchange, are secondary rewards (Ch. 3B).

Returning to the paradox itself, he tells his readers how to read it: 'Although we say that he who receives a benefit gladly has repaid it, we, nevertheless, also bid him return some gift similar to the one he received. Some of the things we say seem abhorrent to our normal way of speaking, but then they come back round to it by an indirect path' (2. 35. 1–2). In the same spirit, he will later make a similar adjustment to the other side of the exchange, explaining that though intention is a necessary condition for a *beneficium*, it is not a sufficient condition: the *actio* that constitutes the *beneficium* actually comprises *res et animus*, so some favour or service is also required (**ad 6. 10. 2; 6. 11. 3**).

That is to say, Seneca's hyperbolic exhortation is here, as elsewhere, not to be taken literally. He is really stressing the importance of benevolence in the exercise of beneficence, and helping his readers to fulfil their own highest ideals of generosity. His adoption of the title *De beneficiis*, using a term whose most common conventional meaning he would go on to challenge, was itself a part of that exhortation.

---

[59] As Wilson Greatbatch, the inventor of the cardiac pacemaker said, during a ceremony to mark a Lifetime Achievement Award, 'the true reward is not in the results but in the doing' (*The Independent* for 30 Sept. 2011, p. 18 of 'Viewspaper'). The results here are both the thing invented and the honour received for it.

6

The Structure of *De beneficiis*

De beneficiis is the longest surviving treatise by Seneca on one subject. It is also the only treatment of that subject to come down to us from antiquity. An understanding of its structure is therefore of great potential importance, as a key to Seneca's literary and philosophical methods, and as a clue to the treatment of this important and once popular subject by earlier philosophers.

SCHOLARLY INTERPRETATIONS

The structure of *De beneficiis*, except in its broadest outlines, is hardly perspicuous. Like Erasmus before him, Justus Lipsius, despite his deep knowledge of the Senecan corpus and his detailed annotation of this work, pronounced himself baffled: 'The books are good but notably confused in order and treatment, which it is scarcely possible to unravel, even for one making an effort. Still, I am doing the best I can' (*Libri boni sunt sed mehercule in ordine et tractatu confusi: quem vix est vel adnitentem expedire. Tamen ut possumus*). Many commentators have followed his general condemnation. Thomas, for example, in 1918 regarded it as worse with regard to structure than Seneca's other works and gave up: 'Cet ouvrage est le plus mal composé, le plus décousu, de tous ceux de Sénèque: il serait aussi difficile que peu utile d'en donner une analyse.'[1] His view was deemed too extreme by Albertini in 1923, who described the treatise as lacking a methodical composition but did not regard it as unusual among Seneca's works, all of which, he aimed to show, were loosely composed.[2] As late as 1975, Sandbach wrote: 'The work lacks structure; even within a single paragraph Seneca leaps from one thought to another; indeed in search of epigrams he sometimes transcends thought.'[3] More recently and more

---

[1] Thomas 1918, 145.
[2] Albertini 1923, 92. The idea goes back to Caligula, who described Seneca's writing as 'sand without lime' (*harena sine calce*, Suet. *Calig.* 38).
[3] Sandbach 1975, 157.

sympathetically, Bellincioni traces its lack of a perceptible design, as well as its size and complexity, to the ambitious scope of its programme: she quotes with approval the dictum of Diderot, 'Le style de Sénèque est coupé mais les idées sont liées'.[4]

Not all scholars have been so ready to deny the work any methodological arrangement. Sonntag in 1913 discerned in the treatise a regular plan: but, in accordance with the view of philosophical works in Latin prevailing at the time, he ascribed the plan to Seneca's Greek source, which he identified as an unattested work *Peri charitos* by Hecato, who is frequently quoted in the treatise.[5] According to Sonntag, Seneca obscured Hecato's methodical arrangement, not only by reducing the scale of Hecato's work, while amplifying or adding purple passages on such topics as human wickedness and divine generosity, but, more drastically, by separating the main exposition of doctrine from the smaller casuistical arguments, with the result that the division of books no longer coincided with the division of subject-matter.[6] Sonntag took it for granted that any Greek philosophical treatise would be tightly organized, and that any Roman philosopher would take all his ideas from the Greek and then adorn them rhetorically, having diminished their philosophical value by a combination of poor comprehension and wilful oversimplification.

Later scholars have been more sympathetic to Seneca's organization, but their very lack of unanimity demonstrates how difficult it is to understand the structure of the treatise in detail. The most significant contribution has come from Karlhans Abel,[7] who applies to *De beneficiis* his experience of analysing the shorter *dialogi*, which he showed had an internal logic even when the structure, viewed from outside, was not obvious.[8] After all, *De beneficiis* was clearly assigned to the same category of Seneca's works by Quintilian.[9] In the case of *De beneficiis*, however, Abel also succeeds in showing that there is a clear overall structure which is carefully worked out, and that many of the repetitions, which have been seen as signs of artistic failure, are in fact either deliberate pedagogic ploys or thematic recapitulations, designed to modify and deepen

---

[4] Bellincioni 1984*a*, 122. She finds the unity of the work in its central theme of revising the utilitarian conception of *beneficium*.

[5] Sonntag 1913.

[6] Ibid. 38, 60–3. A notable example for him (19) is the placing of 2. 26–30 in Book 2, rather than in 3, although its subject-matter is ingratitude, the subject of Book 3. For another explanation, i.e. that Seneca intended the passage to function as a bridge from one book to another, see pp. 116–18 below.

[7] Abel 1987*a* = Abel 1995, 42–73. His analysis is accepted by Maurach 1996, 101–10.

[8] Abel 1967, where he treated five of the twelve *dialogi* listed in the Codex Ambrosianus. He discussed the structure of the rest of the twelve *dialogi*, plus *De beneficiis* and the *Quaestiones naturales*, in Abel 1991 = Abel 1995, 166–87.

[9] Introd. n. 1. The label may go back to Seneca himself. It presumably reflects the importance in all these works of interchange, sometimes with a generalized interlocutor, sometimes with the addressee (Griffin 1976, 412–15).

the original argument.[10] He also shows that the last three books are not just a ragbag of puzzles but are crucial to raising the level on which Seneca wishes the whole question of interchanges of benefit to be understood and discussed. Though, as will emerge in the following discussion, I do not find everything in his analysis convincing, he has certainly indicated a more fruitful line of approach to the treatise, and one truer to Seneca's own indications.

SENECA'S AWARENESS OF STRUCTURE

De beneficiis contains many signs of the author's self-consciousness about structure. He announces topics for the future (1. 4. 2–3, cf. 1. 1; 1. 11. 1; 4. 1), indicates when he has reached one of the divisions previously announced (2. 1; 2. 18. 1; 3. 1; 4. 3; 4. 16), and sometimes alludes back to previous topics he has treated (5. 1; 7. 14. 1). He is often careful to mark the end of a digression and its relevance to the subject in hand (1. 10. 1; 3. 29; 4. 3; 4. 9. 1; 6. 33), and to signal when he is re-using an argument (4. 22, cf. 4. 11. 4–6; 7. 14. 1, cf. 2. 34; 4. 40; 5. 2; 5. 4. 1; 6. 43. 2). He also compares his order of discussion with an order that might have been more popular with the reader (7. 1. 2) and comments on the appropriateness of his conclusion (7. 26. 1).

As we shall see, Seneca indicates, by an announcement of the main subjects to be covered, what is to be the general shape of the whole work. It must be remembered, however, that in other works, where he gives clues as to structure, they are often not reliable.[11] Thus, in *De clementia*, not all that is promised is treated, probably because the work is incomplete, possibly left unfinished by the author;[12] in the part of *De ira* dealing with therapy, Seneca indicates his programme of two topics at 2. 18 (the nature of anger and the remedies for anger, of which the first has already been treated and the second has two parts: not to become angry, and not to misbehave when angry). Of these two parts, he treats the first in Book 2 but only adumbrates the second at the end of Book 2 (2. 36. 4), and then says at the start of Book 3 that he will take this part up, only to proceed at 3. 5. 2 to announce three parts, the two parts of the topic of remedies for anger already given, and a new one: how to cure another person of anger; and he does not clearly follow that division either.[13] In *De vita beata*

---

[10] Abel 1987*a*, 19–23 = 1995, 59–65.

[11] As Erasmus also complained, Trillitzsch 1971, ii. 435.   [12] See S. Braund 2009, 45–7.

[13] Recently, attempts have been made to defend the overall coherence of *De ira*. Fillion-Lahille 1984, 283–94 stressed Seneca's concern with reviewing philosophical opinions in chronological order; Nussbaum 1994, 405–9 countered this with the idea that the structure of Seneca's therapeutic argument, addressed to a non-Stoic interlocutor, is dictated by the latter's resistance; and Ramondetti 1996, 9–10, 81–3 explained the apparent repetitions as re-elaborations of specific themes, rather as Abel 1987*a* stressed the development of themes within *De beneficiis*. The latter is an approach developed later in this chapter and in Ch. 7.

he announces two topics at the outset (1. 1), viz. what happiness is, and how to attain it; but when he reaches the second at 16. 3 he fails to mark it clearly and proceeds in the next chapter to handle the question of attainment so indirectly, via criticisms of the struggling *imperfectus*, that Fuhrmann thinks he never treated the second topic at all.[14] Finally, he appears to revert in 21 to the question of what happiness comprises.[15]

THE EXPLICIT PROGRAMME

In *De beneficiis*, however, despite its being a far longer work, Seneca does by and large fulfil his predictions.

The author's own indications divide *De beneficiis* into two sections. The first section comprises Books 1–4, which, to follow Seneca's own retrospective description at 5. 1. 1, treat the whole subject of giving and receiving benefits. Of the four books in this first section, Books 1–3, as Seneca indicates en route, cover the three topics of giving (1. 11. 1), receiving (2. 18. 1) and returning (3. 1) benefits: the topics announced in Book 1 (1. 4. 3) and already foreshadowed in the allegorical discussion of the Three Graces attributed to Chrysippus (1. 3. 2–3, 8). Book 4 is introduced as a treatment of the most essential question: whether conferring a benefit, and doing a favour in return, are things worthy of choice in themselves (4. 1. 1). The second section, Books 5–7, covers questions which Seneca repeatedly characterizes as an appendix on related but subsidiary topics,[16] unnecessary but possibly useful.[17] He excuses the

---

[14] Fuhrmann 1997, 236–7.

[15] For this analysis of the structure, see Griffin 1976, 306–9.

[16] 'In lingering further, I am not serving my subject, but indulging it, since it has to be followed where it leads, not where it entices me' (*Quidquid ultra moror, non servio materiae, sed indulgeo, quae quo ducit sequenda est, non quo invitat*, 5. 1. 1); 'Let us go on, now that we have completed what belonged to the subject, to study also what is, to tell the truth, connected to it, not integral to it' (*perseveremus peractis quae rem continebant, scrutari etiam ea quae, si vis verum, conexa sunt, non cohaerentia*', 5. 1. 2); 'This book collects the remnants; with the subject exhausted, I am looking around to see, not what I shall say, but what I have not said' (*reliqua hic liber cogit, et exhausta materia circumspicio, non quid dicam, sed quid non dixerim*, 7. 1. 1); 'Now that I am rounding up anything that has escaped me' (*nunc, si quid effugit, recolligo*, 7. 1. 2). No connection with the preceding books is claimed at the start of Book 6, which proclaims that some of the topics that will be treated 'are investigated only to exercise the intellect and lie invariably outside the scope of real life' (*exercendi tantum ingenii causa quaeruntur et semper extra vitam iacent*, 6. 1. 1).

[17] 'Non-superfluous rather than necessary' (*magis non supervacuum quam necessarium*, 5. 1. 1); 'Whoever inspects these things carefully is not repaid for his efforts, but does not waste them either' (*quae quisquis diligenter inspicit, non facit operae pretium nec tamen perdit operam*, 5. 1. 2); 'Other matters are both enjoyable while under scrutiny and, once investigated, useful' (*quaedam et, dum quaeruntur oblectamento sunt et quaesita usui*, 6. 1.); 'Instead, I piled up at the start all the most important themes' (*sed quidquid maxime necessarium erat, in primum congessi*, 7. 1. 2).

enterprise as undertaken at his addressee's request (5. 1. 2), or at least for his delectation (7. 1. 1), and subject to his consent (6. 1).

That is the bare outline of Seneca's conception as he reveals it, but the structure is not as clear as this suggests. To list only the most striking oddities: Book 3 treats the expected subject of returning benefits rather indirectly; the remaining books (4–7) have not been prepared for in the programme announced in Book 1; and the last three books (5–7) are each announced separately and, as we have just seen, characterized as a collection of rather trivial miscellaneous topics.

BOOKS 1 AND 2

Before addressing these oddities, it will be worth studying how the composition unfolds in the early books. After introductory remarks about ingratitude being the result of incorrect giving and receiving (with the emphasis on giving), and about the pointlessness of the allegorical mode of treatment adopted by Chrysippus, Seneca gives as his aim to provide a *lex vitae*, teaching 'to give gladly, to receive gladly, to return gladly' (*libenter dare, libenter accipere, libenter reddere*, 1. 4. 3). But first, he says (1. 5. 1), he must define what a *beneficium* really is, which he proceeds to do in 1. 5–9. 2. At 1. 11. 1 he announces that the next things to be discussed will be what *beneficia* should be given and how they should be given (a topic anticipated at 1. 7 and 1. 9. 2). These are clearly subdivisions of the first of the three topics promised at 1. 4. 3: namely, proper conduct in giving benefits. An apparent lacuna in the text prevents us from seeing how the earlier invective against vice, at 1. 9. 3–10. 4, fits into the plan; but 1. 9. 2 appears to relate to the question of who should give benefits, while the question to whom to give is at least mentioned in 1. 10. 5.[18] Half of the programme announced in 1. 11 is fulfilled in the rest of Book 1, which treats what should be given, with special emphasis being placed towards the end on the need for discrimination (1. 14–15); it is completed in the first seventeen chapters of Book 2, which discuss how benefits should be given.[19]

The second topic announced in 1. 4. 3, the receiving of benefits, is reached and clearly marked at 2. 18. 1, the discussion being divided into 'from whom' (2. 18. 3–21) and 'how to receive' (2. 22–35). A discussion of the Stoic paradox

---

[18] Sonntag 1913, 15 and Abel 1987a, 25 = 1995, 67 think that the first topic after the definition is 'to whom we should give' (*quibus demus*). See also **ad 1. 9. 2**.

[19] The four last chapters (2. 14–17) could be taken as reverting to the first topic, and indeed filling out the first division of the first topic by discussing what not to give. But the distinction of 'what' and 'how' is not always easy to make, and one can consider these chapters as treating how to give, with regard to the true interests of both benefactor and beneficiary, and how to make sure that gifts are appropriate to both (see the Synopsis of Book 2).

'the person who receives a benefit gladly has returned it' (*qui libenter bene-ficium accipit, reddidit*) in the last five chapters (31–end) forms a neat bridge to Book 3 which appears to announce the third topic of 1. 4. 3, the returning of benefits, in the opening phrase: 'it is shameful, and everyone knows it, not to return a favour for benefits conferred' (*non referre beneficiis gratiam et est turpe et apud omnes habetur*).[20]

THE PROBLEM OF BOOK 3

That Book 3 is regarded as discharging the third topic is suggested by the start of Book 4, which announces a new topic 'Whether conferring a benefit and doing a favour in return are things to be chosen for their own sake' (*an bene-ficium dare et in vicem gratiam referre per se res expetendae sint*). The inference is confirmed by the start of Book 5, where Seneca says that he has now covered the ground of the subject from end to end (5. 1. 1–2).[21] However, Book 3 itself, which was supposed to deal with returning benefits, immediately turns into a discussion of ingratitude. Indeed, this negative slant is maintained, even when the topic of returning reappears at the end of the book, in the closing discus-sion of whether or not children can give parents more than they received (29–end): for the emphasis is placed on the necessity of answering this in the affirmative, if children are not to have an excuse for ingratitude (3. 36. 2, cf. 3. 17. 4). The result is that one scholar does not recognize the presence of the third topic in Book 3;[22] and another thinks that the second topic, that of receiv-ing, is continued to chapter 17 of Book 3.[23]

---

[20] Seneca uses *beneficium reddere, beneficium referre, gratiam referre*, and less commonly *gra-tiam reddere* (but see his reservations about the last in *Ep.* 81. 9) as equivalents (Moussy 1966, 267–9). Shortly before the beginning of Book 3, in 2. 35. 1, the Stoic paradox itself, which had been given at 2. 31 as *eum qui libenter accipit beneficium reddidisse*, is rendered *rettulisse illum gratiam dicamus, qui beneficium libenter accipit*. Despite *Ep.* 81. 9, Seneca does not always eschew *gratiam reddere*. We find it at *Ben.* 3. 2. 2 and 5. 16. 4, and indeed at *Ep.* 81. 7 (in the mouth of an objector) *iustitiae convenit suum cuique reddere, beneficio gratiam, iniuriae talionem aut certe malam gratiam* ('It is in keeping with justice to render to each what is his due, a favour for a bene-fit, requital for an injury or, in any case, ill-will'). That the aversion was, however, common is suggested by Cicero's rendering of the familiar epigram, *pecuniam qui habeat, non reddidisse, qui reddiderit, non habere, gratiam autem et qui rettulerit habere et qui habeat rettulisse* ('that the person who has his money has not repaid it, and the person who has repaid it does not have it, but the person who has requited gratitude still has it, and if he has it, he has requited it'), where he uses *reddere* with *pecuniam*, but *referre* with *gratiam*, not only here in *De officiis* 2. 69, but in speeches: *Red. pop.* 23 (if that is the right reading) and *Planc.* 68.

[21] 'Now that we have completed what belonged to the subject' (*peractis quae rem continebant*, 5. 1. 2); cf. 'for these define the limits of this responsibility' (*hi enim sunt huius officii fines*, 5. 1. 1).

[22] Chaumartin 1985, 13.   [23] Fuhrmann 1997, 285–6.

In order to solve the problem of Book 3,[24] some attention must be given to the precise descriptions of Seneca's programme in the introductions to Books 4 and 5. The latter book actually starts: 'In the preceding books, I thought I had discharged my task, having treated how a benefit should be given and how it should be received; for these define the limits of this responsibility' (*In prioribus libris videbar consummasse propositum, cum tractassem quemadmodum dandum esset beneficium, quemadmodum accipiendum; hi enim sunt huius officii fines*). Neither the formulation of the subject to be treated in Book 4, nor the statement of accomplishment in Book 5, explicitly mentions the original three topics: rather, they elide receiving and returning, the former one mentioning only returning benefits, the latter only receiving them. In fact Abel, while identifying the subject of Book 3 as returning benefits, remarks that the opening of Book 5 appears to ignore Books 3, 4, 6, and 7,[25] all of which concern themselves with *beneficium reddere*. He rightly marks this as deliberate, and he comes close to solving the problem, when he notes that the original triadic division of the subject-matter is gradually shown to be superficial: to regard reception and reciprocation as separate operations belongs to the vulgar conception of *beneficium* as a material thing; in the sphere of the moral idea, the lasting relation of friendship is the outcome of giving and receiving and takes over the area of returning.[26]

In fact, there are important clues throughout the work to a solution. On the one hand, Seneca initially (1. 1. 1) points to our ignorance of how to give and how to receive benefits (*beneficia nec dare scimus nec accipere*) before announcing the threefold division of topics at 1. 4. 3; and, when he reverts to this original twofold division at 5. 1, he characterizes the two activities of giving and receiving as defining the limits of this responsibility (*huius officii fines*), i.e. as marking out the whole territory of handling benefits, from end to end. Moreover, at 2. 18 he mentions giving and receiving benefits as the two sides of an *ex duobus officium*, i.e. one that makes equal demands on two parties: father and son, husband and wife, or, here, giver and receiver; and the twofold division is reinforced by the symmetrical structure of Book 2, with how to give discussed at the beginning, and how to receive at the end; and by the corresponding treatment the two topics receive in Books 1 and 2 (see **ad 2. 22–5** and **2. 26–30**). On the other hand, at the beginning of Book 4, he frames what he says is the most essential question

---

[24] Sonntag 1913, 21–3, in trying to reconstruct how Hecato, whom he regards as Seneca's single source, would have dealt with *beneficium reddere*, points to a practical difficulty: it would be difficult to use the same divisions of the topic as for giving and receiving, because what we should give in return, and how we should give it, can be inferred from the discussion of *beneficium dare*, while there is no point in discussing to whom we should return a benefit, as it is obviously our benefactor. On the other hand, Sonntag thinks Hecato treated difficulties concerning the right opportunity, or a change in character of the benefactor elsewhere.

[25] Abel 1987*a*, 18, 22, 25 = 1995, 58, 63, 66–7. Book 5 itself is much concerned with the question of returning benefits.

[26] Abel 1987*a*, 31 = 1995, 73.

in terms of the twin obligations of giving and returning, instead of giving and receiving. The solution is clear: receiving and returning a benefit cannot really be separated, once it is understood that, just as a *beneficium* is the intentional act that confers the benefit willingly and rationally—not the material thing given or the practical service rendered—so the appropriate return to that act is the good will of grateful acceptance. As Seneca says at 2. 34. 1, the transaction occurs between our minds, and, at the end of Book 4, we are told that the only obligation that applies without qualification to every recipient of every *beneficium* is 'to offer a grateful heart' (*animum praestare gratum*).

The topic of how to return a *beneficium* collapses into that of how to receive one: if we receive it properly, we have returned it. The discussion of the paradox that begins at 2. 31 is not just a bridge to Book 3: it effectively removes the gulf in subject-matter between the two books. Therefore the simplest solution to the problem of Book 3 is to say that the book is not really treating a separate topic from the topic of receiving benefits, introduced in the second half of Book 2 (18–35); rather, Book 3 continues the diagnosis of ingratitude that began in 2. 26 as part of that discussion. Not that the argument fails to progress. For as Abel notes, the emphasis changes, from ingratitude as a failure to appraise rightly what we receive (2. 26–8) to ingratitude as a failure to remember what we have received (3. 1. 2–5), remembering being essential to the return of the benefit.[27] The difficulty of returning benefits appropriately is, in fact, highly complex, and most of the problems or *quaestiones* that occupy the remaining books explore it: the last problem of Book 4, all those of Books 5 and 6, and the last problem of Book 7. There is much justice in the idea that the main theme of the treatise is ingratitude.[28]

BOOKS 4–7 AND THE SYMMETRY OF THE TREATISE

That the last four books deal with topics not initially announced, does not necessarily point, as Albertini thought, to loose organization. For it is possible to uncover organizational principles not specifically avowed: notably, a large scale symmetry over all.

The symmetry is clear. Sonntag already pointed to the way the end of the work echoes the beginning, and Abel supports the idea.[29] Many of the points

---

[27] Abel 1987*a*, 22 = 1995, 63. For the importance of memory in the treatise, see Armisen-Marchetti 2004.

[28] Inwood 1995*a*, 250 = 2005, 76.

[29] See **ad 1. 1–3. 1**. Sonntag 1913, 11, 59 thought that 1. 1. 9–13 was echoed by 7. 26–32; Abel 1987*a*, 18 = 1995, 59 gives the parallel as with 1. 1–4, which I regard as preferable. Abel 1991, 186 finds similar symmetry in *De brevitate vitae* and the *Consolatio ad Helviam matrem*.

made in Book 1. 1–4, where Seneca is concerned with the mistakes of givers of *beneficia*, are taken up again in 7. 26–32, where he is considering how donors should deal with ingrates: the idea that benefits are already lost at the moment of giving (1. 1. 1, cf. 7. 29. 1; 7. 30. 1); the image of sowing on sterile soil (1. 1. 2, cf. 7. 32); the point that we make recipients ungrateful by harsh reproaches (1. 1. 4, cf. 7. 26. 2; 7. 28. 3; 7. 30. 1); the idea of imitating the gods in not letting ingratitude stop beneficence (1. 1. 9, cf. 7. 31. 2–5); the notion of imitating human optimism in trying again (1. 1. 10, cf. 7. 31. 5); the intrinsic value of giving (1. 1. 12; cf. 7. 32. 1); persistent kindness as a means of winning over the ungrateful (1. 2. 5; 1. 3. 1, cf. 7. 29. 2; 7. 30. 1; 7. 31. 1). But, as Abel points out (1987*a*, 19 = 1995, 59), there is more here than repetition: the level of discussion has also been raised, for in the meantime the nature of mutual human obligation has been developed. In keeping with the intervening discussion in Book 5. 17. 3–5, Seneca now reminds the giver that he too has probably been ungrateful when in receipt of benefits (7. 28), and whereas, in Book 1, he accused donors of sowing without discrimination on barren soil (1. 1. 2), now he says that the good farmer can overcome that barrenness by care and cultivation (7. 32).

Abel points to another symmetrical feature (1987*a*, 24–5 = 1995, 65–6). Book 4 stands in the middle of the work, between the first three books in which the basic topics indicated in Book 1 are covered, and the last three books in which particular conundrums are resolved. This book is marked out by Seneca as treating the most important issues: 'Of all the subjects we have treated, Aebutius Liberalis, none is as essential, or, to quote Sallust, more "in need of careful discussion", than the one we have in hand' (*ex omnibus quae tractavimus, Aebuti Liberalis, potest videri nihil tam necessarium, aut magis, ut ait Sallustius, cum cura dicendum, quam quod in manibus est*, 4. 1. 1). Here the discussion reaches a new level, treating the subject of benefits in the context of the fundamental tenets of Stoic ethics. Thus it is in Book 4 that the imitation of the gods is most pervasive, as a model both for giving benefits and for showing gratitude: 4. 25 on *imitatio dei* is picked out by Abel as the 'Gipfel des Gipfels' (1987*a*, 19 = 1995, 59–60).[30] In fact, three of the five passages which Abel points to, as showing that gratitude to the gods is the theological basis of the love and friendship manifested in the exchange of benefits (2. 29–30; 4. 4–8, 17–19, 31–2; 6. 20–4), occur in this book, and this is also where the Epicurean view of the gods as unconcerned with us is attacked. It is also in Book 4 that, partly again through contrast with Epicurean doctrine, the connection of giving benefits with the Stoic conception of virtue in general (4. 9. 2–11) and with the Stoic notion of true joy (4. 13–14) is developed.[31] Here too the relation of the

---

[30] The theme is also treated in 1. 1. 9 and 7. 31. 2–4, apart from the incidental mention at 3. 15.

[31] Even Albertini, so hostile to the idea of conscious design in Seneca, recognized (1923, 93–4) that 4. 1–25 is important and raises a fundamental issue of morality: the conflict of idealism and utilitarianism.

Stoic conception of the wicked man and the ordinary one are explored (4. 26–7), and the way in which the Stoic Sage adjusts to circumstances (35). But above all, it is in Book 4 (see **ad 4. 18**) that we are told that what enables the ultimate function of the exchange of *beneficia* in binding human society together to be fulfilled, is the work of providence in providing this social instinct, which. along with reason, compensates for human physical weakness (see Ch. 2, pp. 26–7). This idea is a conceptual advance on the praise of the general blessings the gods confer on man in 2. 29, and indeed in 4. 3–9. 1.[32] Seneca here indicates that the social phenomenon he describes in *De beneficiis* is actually the mechanism by which *oikeiōsis* extends beyond the family.

BOOKS 5–7

In addition to the role they play in the large-scale symmetry of the treatise, two important functions can be discerned for the last three books, which make it absolutely clear that the author's repeated description of them as unimportant and spontaneous (5. 1. 1–2; 6. 1; 7. 1. 1–2) is nothing but disingenuous coquetry, as has often been remarked.[33] Even the relatively trivial fact that Books 4–7 close with problems about returning benefits, as seen alternately from the perspective of the beneficiary (in Books 4 and 6) and the benefactor (in Books 5 and 7), suggests that their arrangement is not as casual as Seneca's introductions to the last three books might suggest.[34]

The last three books, in fact, consist of a series of dialectical exercises, answering hard questions and solving hard cases. This new style of argument had been anticipated in Book 3 and, particularly, in Book 4 which ends with a series of problematic cases that suggest refinements of the notion that one should always return a benefit (4. 40): these two books thus offer a glimpse in microcosm of the structure of the work as a whole.

Some scholars, not without reason, have called the final books of the work casuistical.[35] Strictly speaking, of course, the term casuistry is reserved for that part of ethics that resolves particular cases of conscience to which it is difficult to apply the general rules of religion or morality, because the circumstances are

---

[32] 6. 20–24 returns to the question of these benefits, exploring divine motivation.

[33] Chaumartin 1985, 12; Abel 1987a, 17 = 1995, 58.

[34] Abel 1987a, 23–4 = 1995, 65 regards all four books, 4–7, as being concerned at their close with the theme of repaying a benefit (*beneficium reddere*), the excessive sense of obligation by the beneficiary being damped down at the end of 4 and of 6; the insufficient sense of obligation being stimulated at the end of 5 and and of 7. But he does not note that the perspective alternates between recipient and donor.

[35] Albertini 1923, 93–4 notes that much of Book 3 is casuistical, as well as the last chapters of Book 4; Chaumartin 1985, 12; Fuhrmann 1997, 289.

abnormal, or because there appears to be a conflict of duties. The activity is taken to have appeared after AD 1000 in a Christian context; the term 'casuistry' is pejorative and is first attested in the eighteenth century, applied to the activity of the Jesuits, which had reached its peak in about 1550–1650. However, its roots can be found in antiquity.[36] For it was recognized by many ancient philosophers that the proof of moral doctrines is in their application, and that requires practice and imagination. As Cicero says at *De officiis* 1. 59, speaking of the different duties owed to different groups of people, 'precepts on observing duty certainly have been handed down, as I myself am handing them down, but a matter of such importance also demands experience and practice'.

It may not be mere coincidence that Cicero's *De officiis* also ended with a book of cases. If Sonntag were right, this arrangement would be due to Seneca himself, in contravention of his source (Hecato).[37] In that case, we might be tempted to adduce imitation of Cicero by Seneca. However, there is a notable difference in structural conception, for *De officiis* does not include anything equivalent to Seneca's Book 4. Indeed, in 1. 7 Cicero clearly distinguishes theoretical questions about the nature of *officium* from the *praecepta* that he intends to offer.[38]

It may be the case, however, that many ethical treatises ended with a section designed to give the reader practice in using the doctrines developed earlier, by presenting him with hard cases and moral dilemmas. One only needs to recall that the discussion of *philia* (what we inaccurately call 'friendship') in the *Nicomachean Ethics*, which contains a substantial discussion of reciprocation of benefits (notably 8. 13. 1162^{b}23–1163^{a}21), is divided into exposition in Book 8, and consideration of a series of conundrums (including one about benefactions at 9. 7. 1167^{b}17–1168^{a}27) at the end of Book 8 and in Book 9.[39] Moreover, Panaetius himself must have intended such a discussion as his third topic of his *Peri tou kathēkontos*, for it dealt with the question 'if that which has the appearance of honourableness conflicts with that which seems beneficial, how should one decide between them?' Cicero then gives an example of a particular hard case as typical of what Panaetius would have included.[40] He also cites in *De officiis* 3. 89–92 a series of hard cases from his disciple Hecato's book *Peri Kathēkontos*. Pohlenz plausibly deduced from the fact that they come from the sixth book that this portion of his treatise (fr. 11 Gomoll) comprised *zētēmata*

---

[36] Jonsen and Toulmin 1988, 8–13. They find the inspiration of casuistry in ancient philosophy and rhetoric, notably the writings of Aristotle and Cicero; in the judicial practice of Roman law; and in the traditions of Jewish rabbinical debate (47–87).

[37] Sonntag 1913, 60–1, 63.

[38] For the perspective of *De officiis* as practical ethics, and the omission of any treatment of the nature of ethics or of the first principles of morality, see Griffin and Atkins 1991*a*, pp. xxii f.

[39] Ross 1925 calls 8. 13 (1162^{a}34–1163^{a}23) 'Casuistry of Friendship'. Aristotle's word, to judge from 9. 2. 1164^{b}22, is *aporia*.

[40] *Off.* 3. 7 *tertio, si id quod speciem haberet honesti pugnaret cum eo quod utile videretur, quomodo ea discerni oporteret*; 3. 29–33 on Phalaris.

('questions') following upon the systematic presentation of the subject.[41] Seneca may have been following a well-established tradition. *De beneficiis* is not the only work in which he used this pattern. The *Letters to Lucilius* also exhibit a series of complex logical conundrums in the later books, often supposedly requested by Seneca's addressee, while in the earlier books there is more straightforward instruction, *Letters* 2–33 closing with maxims often drawn from Epicurus, that most dogmatic of teachers.[42]

A related function of the last three books of *De beneficiis* is to continue the work of Book 4 in raising the level of philosophical argument, so that detailed moral discussion becomes something more morally profound, and also more complex, than the rudimentary and straightforward instruction of Books 1–3. 17.[43] As to profundity, not only is the theme of divine providence maintained (6. 20–4; 7. 31. 2–4), but the *sapiens*, who is only mentioned in passing before Book 4 (e.g. 2. 18. 4; 2. 35. 2), now features prominently. Thus the Sage, who is shown acting subject to reservation in 4. 34. 3–5, and who then appears in the paradox 'There is no such thing as an ungrateful person' in 5. 12–14, becomes a major player in Book 7, where he receives a full-scale portrait (7. 1, 7; 7. 2. 4; 7. 3. 2–3), is the subject of the paradoxical question 'How can the Sage be given anything, since all things are his?' (7. 4–12), and features in a puzzle about benefactors who become unworthy (7. 17–19. 6).

As to complexity, many of the problems considered in these books probe the meaning of a benefit (e.g. 6. 2–5. 2; 6. 11. 3–4; 6. 19; 6. 26. 1) and of ingratitude (e.g. 4. 26–7; 5. 12. 3–14; 6. 27. 1–4) further than had been done in the earlier books, making important distinctions and continuing the process of refining and correcting vulgar notions that had started with the (re)definitions of *beneficium* in the first two books (1. 5. 1–6; 2. 19–21. 2; 2. 34. 5–35. 3). Mazzoli urges that the apparent contradictions, when Seneca returns to the earlier themes in these later books, are not explicable as the result of desultory composition, as earlier scholars thought (pp. 111–13), or of opportunistic pedagogy, as argued by Chaumartin (1985, 297–9), but that the casuistry of the later books modifies the definite assertions of the early books, adjusting good actions to particular circumstances.[44] Thus in 3. 37. 1–2 Aeneas and two Sicilian youths are given as examples of sons outdoing their father's benefit of giving them life by rescuing him; but in 6. 36. 1 Seneca adduces circumstances in which these rescues would no longer count as examples of *pietas*: if the sons had wished for the disasters that gave them the opportunity of rescue, that is,

---

[41] Pohlenz 1935, 107, apparently regarded as plausible by Dyck 1996, 612.

[42] See the discussion of the *Letters* in Ch. 7C and in Griffin 2007, 91–5. Cooper and Procopé 1995, 127 suggest that *De clementia* 'could well have gone into the casuistry of mercy' at the end of Book 2, which, as we have it, is incomplete.

[43] Mazzoli 2007, 589, 592–3 treats some examples of apparent repetitions in Book 5 of the same themes in the early books.

[44] Ibid. 589.

had wished to achieve good ends through evil means. Again, in 3. 1. 1–5 Seneca insists that forgetting a benefit is itself a form of ingratitude; but at 7. 28 he admits that not all forgetting is voluntary, and that we ourselves forget past benefits, so we should pardon others for doing so.[45] In 2. 18. 4 Sages are said always to be pleased to honour their obligations as recipients, whereas at 5. 25. 3 even Sages should be reminded, if their benefactors need returns. In Books 1 and 2 we are firmly told that the benefactor must not ask for a gift in exchange (1. 1. 3–4) or even remind the recipient of what he received: all we can do is repeat the benefit (2. 10. 4; 2. 11. 2, 5). But in Book 5 that opposition to reminding is assigned to a fictive interlocutor (5. 20. 6), while the author maintains that, if the benefactor needs repayment, he can ask for a return (5. 20. 7), provided he simply reminds the recipient without reproaching him (5. 21. 2–22). Seneca now distinguishes between the hardened ingrate and the recipient who is not a hardened ingrate (5. 21. 3) but a person who can benefit from such an act of friendship (5. 22. 1–23): in the latter case, preventing ingratitude is itself a second benefit (5. 22. 2). Then, in Book 7, the advice about a promising recipient is repeated (7. 25); but now even the hardened ingrate is said to be reformable through pardon and through patient and persistent goodness (7. 28), and we are told to imitate the gods in continuing to shower benefits on the ungrateful (7. 31. 2–5). Along with the process of refining the argument, there is also a tendency for Seneca's advice to become more and more humane, as we already saw, in the contrasting use of the agricultural image in the first and last chapters of the work (above, p. 119). The process of raising the level of argument, and the level of compassion, was to continue in Letter 81 (pp. 155–61)

These developments run parallel with Seneca's continuous insistence on decoding his Stoic discourse to reveal realistic and practical advice. Thus he unravels the Stoic paradoxes and shows that, by making the right verbal distinctions, what they say can be shown not to contradict common sense (2. 35. 1–2, on which see pp. 109–10; 5. 13. 1–14. 4; 7. 4. 2–6). Finally, in the last book, as we have seen (pp. 47, 110), we are given a strong hint that we must allow for the hyperbolic style of discourse in interpreting the high-minded message that is a dominant theme in the whole work, namely, the asymmetrical demand that the giver should demand no return while the receiver must forever feel his obligation (see **ad 1. 4. 5; 2. 10. 4 cum inter prima**).[46] Seneca spells out what this really means (7. 22. 2): 'We overstate some rules in order that in the end they may reach their true value. When we say, "He must not remember", we really mean, "He must not trumpet it, nor boast, nor give offence." '

---

[45] See Armisen-Marchetti 2004, 16.

[46] 'So that the donors forget, and the debtors retain a persistent memory' (*ut, qui praestiterunt obliviscantur, pertinax sit memoria debentium*, 1. 4. 5); 'The law that governs benefits between two people is this: one of them should immediately forget that the benefit was given; the other should never forget that it was received' (*Haec enim beneficii inter duos lex est: alter statim oblivisci debet dati, alter accepti numquam*, 2. 10. 4).

No reader of Seneca could claim that he is a completely systematic writer whose line of argument is always perspicuous and whose division of material is always systematic. Surprises in the form of unexpected points and ingenious examples, rhetorical *tours de force*, and changes of direction, are part of what makes his writing so absorbing. But *De beneficiis* is a long and complex work, and it has an intelligible structure. What the pedagogic rationale for that structure is, requires some further investigation. It will be treated in the next chapter.

7

The Pedagogic Strategy of *De beneficiis**

Whether or not the structure of *De beneficiis* fitted into a pre-existing tradition of composition for ethical treatises, there can be no doubt of its relation to Seneca's own conception of philosophical education. For the shape of the work as a whole reflects the way in which Seneca sees the relationship of the *praeceptiva pars* of philosophy—the translation he offers for the Greek *parainetikē*—to the dogmatic.

A. TEACHING BY *PRAECEPTA*

In *Letters* 94 and 95 Seneca discusses at length the question of the contribution made by *praecepta* and *decreta* to virtuous conduct and the development of virtue. In the first letter, he argues against the heterodox Stoic philosopher Aristo of Chios, who held that *praecepta*, i.e. specific recommendations and advice as to particular courses of action, are unnecessary.[1] Seneca defends the *pars praeceptiva* of philosophy on account of its educational and practical value; but in the second letter, he argues that this part is not sufficient, and that

---

* An earlier version of the material in this chapter appeared as ch. 3 in the first volume of R. Sorabji and R.W. Sharples (eds.), *Greek and Roman Philosophy 100 BC–200 AD* (BICS Supplement 94; London, 2007).

[1] Cicero at *Fin*. 2. 43; 3. 12; 3. 50 helps us to make sense of Aristo's position on *praecepta*, for he tells us that he recognized no distinctions within *adiaphora* or *indifferentia* and regarded the *katorthōma* or *perfectum officium*, as done by the Sage, as the only *officium*: *praecepta* help us to make the right choices among the indifferents, and hence to perform *kathēkonta* or *officia*. The Sage, of course, needs no guidance in behaving virtuously. Elsewhere, in *Ep.* 89. 13, Seneca tells us that Aristo also regarded the parts of philosophy other than ethics, that is, the *pars rationalis* and the *pars naturalis*, as unnecessary. See also D.L. 7. 160 and Sextus Empiricus, *Adv. Math.* 7. 12, who says that Aristo rejected the preceptive and hypothetical subject matter (*parainetikos topos* and *hypothetikos topos*) of ethics.

it is also necessary to have an adequate grasp of *decreta*, the basic doctrines of the system that alone can provide the rationale for the *praecepta*.[2]

Seneca explains in *Letter* 94 that *praecepta* have a role in preparing us for the understanding and adoption of *decreta*, but that they also give us practice, once we have that grasp, in applying that knowledge. For *praecepta*, as a form of exhortation, can prepare us for the full acceptance of *decreta* (*Ep.* 94. 18, 28–31, 34, 36, 49–52); then when our grasp of the *decreta* has removed the obstacles to natural behaviour, precepts can teach us the details of our duties (*Ep.* 94. 18–19, 22–3, 32, 50) and give us reminders (94. 21, 25–6) and practice in conducting ourselves virtuously (*Ep.* 94. 55).[3] It is clear that *praecepta* belong to what Seneca has described earlier, in *Letter* 89. 14–15, as the third division of the *moralis pars philosophiae*: the part concerned with actions (*de actionibus*) and their proper occasions (*in ipsa rerum actione tempora*), with the 'when, where, and how, each action should be carried out' (*quando quidque et ubi et quemadmodum agi debeat*). This is the aspect of philosophy that Seneca says elsewhere is particularly open to perpetual development: just as medical remedies constantly need adaptation to particular diseases, and to the particular stage of the disease at which they should be applied, so, in the case of the discoveries of philosophy, which are the remedies for the soul, work must be done on how and when they should be applied (*Ep.* 64. 8–9).

Seneca's tripartite division of the moral part of philosophy into theoretical (*inspectio*), hormetic (*de impetu*), and practical (*de actionibus*), is no more his own invention than the basic division of philosophy itself into moral, rational, and natural, which he discusses earlier on in *Letter* 89. 9–13. Stobaeus (*Ecl.* 2. 42. 7–45. 6 W) preserves a division of moral philosophy into the three parts Seneca uses, which was made by the late-first-century-BC Academic philosopher Eudorus.[4] The first is *theōrētikon*, concerned with ends and what

---

[2] Schafer 2009, 25–32, 80 suggests that Seneca, by choosing Aristo as his opponent in *Letter* 94 and supporting Cleanthes against him, is stressing that his own broad-minded practice is standard within the Stoic school. D.L. 7. 163 tells us that Aristo wrote four books of letters to Cleanthes.

[3] Nussbaum 1994, 338 points out that Seneca moves from the concrete to the general and back again. Inwood 1999, esp. 114–16, notes various uses of precepts at different stages. Sellars 2003, 77 concentrates on the role of precepts as a form of training after the doctrines have been learned, but his focus is on *askēsis*, which he admits is narrower than the notion of precepts (76). Schafer 2009 largely ignores the practical function Seneca attributes to *praecepta* after we have accepted *decreta* and says (56) that Seneca, in giving *praecepta* a role, has in mind only 'the moral beginner' and (63) that they are 'a ladder to be removed once they have been climbed', but at 57 n. 33 they are 'an educative and protreptic tool for beginners and backsliders' and at 94 'the rational component of the way *praecepta* work grows as the agent's rationality grows'. He has to admit (58) that at *Ep.* 94. 50 Seneca is clearly thinking of non-Sages, rather than of moral beginners.

[4] Giusta 1964–7, i. 151–3 regards Eudorus as the original source of the doxographic passages systematizing the teaching of various schools, and of the general schema for moral philosophy found in Seneca and Clement of Alexandria (*Strom.* 6. 8. 69). He reconstructs Eudorus' system at pp. 155–60. His attempt to date Eudorus before Cicero's philosophical works is contested: see Chaumartin 1985, 26 n. 13. I agree with Dobbin 1998, 94, that Seneca's division of ethical topics is not the same as

contributes to their attainment, including knowledge of virtue and vice, good and bad, and the indifferents; Seneca calls this 'the speculative part assigning to each thing its own function and assessing the worth of each' (*inspectio suum cuique distribuens et aestimans quanto quidque dignum sit, Ep.* 89. 14). Eudorus' second division is *hormētikon*, the way to deal with the passions and impulses to action; for Seneca this is the section *de impetu* and deals with 'curbing impulses and proceeding, instead of rushing, towards action' (*impetus refrenare et ad agenda ire, non ruere,* 89. 15). Eudorus' third division is *praktikon* and corresponds to Seneca's *de actionibus,* 'making your impulse and your action harmonize, so that under all these conditions you may be consistent with yourself' (89. 14), and knowing the correct circumstances of each action, as noted above. In Eudorus this section includes *hypothetikon, protreptikon,* and *paramuthētikon,* that is, presumably, *suasio, exhortatio,* and *consolatio* in Latin,[5] forms of teaching that Seneca says in *Letter* 95. 65 were advocated by Posidonius in addition to giving precepts (*praeceptio*).[6] In Eudorus this section deals with both 'correctly performed functions' (*katorthōmata*), *recte facta* in Latin, and more ordinary 'proper functions' (*kathēkonta*), *officia* in Latin, one category of which concerns our relations with our neighbours and gives rise to the topic *peri tōn charitōn,* Seneca's *De beneficiis.* Eudorus' division might have reached Seneca, as it was to reach Stobaeus, through Arius Didymus, but it is not in any case surprising to find Seneca's conception of moral philosophy in *Ep.* 89 in tune with Eudorus' scheme, since that may reflect the treatment of practical ethics by Posidonius indicated in *Ep.* 95. 65.[7]

As Inwood has emphasized, Seneca's *De beneficiis* is a 'treatise intensely concerned with the practicalities of ethical reasoning'. He cites it as a clear example of Stoic moral reasoning 'which mediates between the need for situational sensitivity and the demand for stable general principles'—what is now often called

---

that in Epictetus 1. 4. 11 or 3. 2. 1–5, despite L–S 1987–8, i. 346, who, however, were right to regard Epictetus' also as a division of ethics rather than of philosophy, the latter being the view of P. Hadot 1992, 98–115; P. Hadot 1995, 192–4, now followed by Long 2002, 117–18, 126.

[5] The identification of Posidonius' Greek terms behind Seneca's Latin rendering of them is very uncertain, given the fluidity of such Greek terms: see Kidd 1988, 647–51 ad F 176.

[6] In *Ep.* 95. 65 Seneca also mentions *aetiologia* which he renders as *causarum inquisitio* and *ethologia* (called by some *characterismos*) or the use of *exempla*. Giusta 1964–7, i. 165–8 equates the former with Eudorus' 'assigning of the causes that bring about certain states of movements' (ὁ δὲ τῶν αἰτιῶν ἀποδοτικὸς τῶν ἐπιτελούντων τινὰς σχέσεις ἢ κινήσεις) and takes it to refer to the practical consequences of virtue: that is, states and movements caused by virtue (or by vice).

[7] It is generally agreed that it was the through the work of the philosopher Arius Didymus that Eudorus' division reached Stobaeus, though scholars differ on which works of his were involved and whether the 'Epitome of Didymus', cited by Stobaeus at 4. 39. 28, is a work by Didymus or a work summarizing him. For a discussion of the question, see Hahm 1990. Eudorus' division might have reached Seneca through Arius Didymus (Dillon 1977, 121 n. 1; Brittain 2001, 277 n. 45, 279 n. 47). If he is identical with Augustus' friend (Suet. *Aug.* 89), Seneca knew at least one work by him (*Cons. Marc.* 4. 2–5. 6).

'situation ethics'.[8] What we have in the first three books is clearly a treatment of the subject in the manner characteristic, according to *Letter* 89, of the third section of moral philosophy, *de actionibus*. Seneca tells us *en route* that he is teaching 'what benefits should be given and how' (*quae beneficia danda sint et quemadmodum*, 1. 11. 1); 'how people should conduct themselves in receiving benefits' (*quemadmodum se gerere homines in accipiendis beneficiis debeant*, 2. 18. 1), and, at the start of Book 5, he says he has now treated 'how a benefit should be given and how it should be received, for these define the limits of this responsibility' (*quemadmodum dandum esset beneficium, quemadmodum accipiendum; hi enim sunt huius officii fines*). This clearly accords with the 'when, where, and how each action should be carried out' (*quando quidque et ubi et quemadmodum agi debeat*) of *Ep.* 89. 15, and with the link between *praecepta* and *officium* made in *Epp.* 94. 32–4 and 95. 45.[9]

In fact, the language of the teaching in these early books shows us that we are dealing with *praecepta*.[10] It is not only that Seneca uses the words *praecepta* and *praecipere*, as when he places the crucial instruction 'never to reproach, not even to remind anyone of a benefit' among the 'first and most essential precepts' (*inter prima praecepta ac maxime necessaria*, 2. 10. 4), and alludes to it later (7. 22. 1) in the phrase 'some things we teach in exaggerated form' (*quaedam praecipimus ultra modum*); or when he uses the phrase 'when we are teaching these things' (*cum ista praecipimus*, 1. 15. 2). It is not only that that he uses the words *moneo* and *admoneo*, which in *Letters* 94 and 95 characterize this style of teaching.[11] More significant is the fact that the grammatical forms in which he couches his advice in these books conform to those used to illustrate *praecepta* in these letters. There, it is clear that, whereas *decreta* are given in the form of statements, in direct or indirect speech, and answer questions of the form, 'what are' (*quid sint*) or 'what opinion we ought to hold concerning anything' (*qualem de quacumque habere debeamus opinionem*, 95. 54), *praecepta* answer questions of the form, 'how we should make use of things'

---

[8] Inwood 1999, 110. He adduces *Ben.* 4. 9–11 as an explicit statement of the connection between a general principle and the procedures of choice.

[9] e.g. *Ep.* 94. 33: 'Duties are set in order by precepts' (*officia praeceptis disponuntur*); *Ep.* 95. 45: 'Marcus Brutus in that book which he entitled *Concerning Proper Functions* gives many precepts to parents, children, and brothers' (*M. Brutus in eo libro, quem περὶ καθήκοντος inscripsit, dat multa praecepta et parentibus et liberis et fratribus*), cf. Priscian, *Inst. gramm.* 6.7.

[10] Mazzoli 2007, 590 remarks with some justice that *De beneficiis* is a conceptual laboratory where Seneca applies on a vast scale what he will theorize about in *Epp.* 94 and 95. But his idea that Books 1–4 teach dogmatically by *decreta*, whereas 5–7 more realistically use techniques of the *pars praeceptiva*, seems to reverse what is suggested by the linguistic forms that predominate in Books 1–3.

[11] *Ben.* 1. 15. 2: 'So, if anyone thinks that we, in laying down these precepts . . . he has misunderstood our advice' (*quare si quis existimat nos, cum ista praecipimus . . . ne perperam monitiones nostras exaudivit*); 1. 12. 3: 'No one is so foolish that he needs to be warned that . . .' (*Nemo tam stultus est ut monendus sit . . .*)—an example of *praeteritio*. In *Epp.* 94 and 95, *monitio* (94. 12, 21, 24, 39, 55; 95. 63) and *admonitio* (94. 25, 29, 31, 32, 33, 36, 44, 45; 95. 61) are used to characterize the work of *praecepta*.

(*quomodo rebus sit utendum*) and characteristically take the form of orders or prescriptive utterances in the imperative, or the gerund/gerundive, or the jussive subjunctive, or the future.[12] In fact in *Ep.* 95. 60 Seneca makes the difference in form explicit, when he argues that the proposition that *decreta* are unnecessary (for which he uses indirect statement) is itself a *decretum*, whereas instructions to avoid issuing *praecepta* (which he expresses with the gerund/gerundive) would themselves be *praecepta*.[13] An examination of *De beneficiis* Books 1–2 in particular turns up a number of such gerunds/gerundives,[14] many jussive subjunctives and futures,[15] 'one should' (*oportet*) and 'it is fitting' (*decet*) with the infinitive;[16] there are even imperatives.[17] Of course, Seneca is

---

[12] Imperative: 'walk in this way, eat in this way' (*sic incede, sic cena, Ep.* 94. 8), 'be good' (*bonus esto*, 95. 50); gerund/gerundive: 'one should never lose one's temper' (*irascendum non esse*, 94. 9), 'how we should make use of things' (*quomodo rebus sit utendum*, 95. 54), 'towards these things alone our study should be directed (*in haec sola studium conferendum*, 95. 60); jussive subjunctive: 'you must expect (*exspectes*, 94. 43), 'let us forbid' (*prohibeamus*, 95. 47); future: 'live thus with your father' (*sic vives cum patre*, 94. 5), 'avoid this, do that' (*hoc vitabis, hoc facies*, 94. 50), 'do that, if you would have self-control' (*illa facies, si voles temperans esse*, 95. 66). It is clear, however, from *Ep.* 94 that certain maxims in the indicative (in prose or in verse) perform the work of *admonitio* and count as *praecepta* (*Ep.* 94. 27–30, 43). Morgan 2007, 26–7, 84 n. 2, 261 concentrates on those *praecepta* and *sententiae* mentioned in *Ep.* 94 that are proverbs and gnomic quotations (note the reference to *Dicta Catonis* in 94. 27) and discusses the combination of commands and statements used in the teaching of popular morality (290–2).

[13] 'Moreover, those who reject doctrines do not realise that doctrines are established in the very act of rejection. What do they say? That life is sufficiently developed by precepts, that the doctrines of wisdom [that is dogmas] are superfluous. But the very thing they say is as much a doctrine, for heaven's sake, as if I were now to say that we must give up precepts as superfluous, must use doctrines, must pay attention to them alone; it would be a precept I uttered in the very act of denying that precepts were to be taken seriously' (*Praeterea non intellegunt hi qui decreta tollunt, eo ipso confirmari illa, quo tolluntur. Quid enim dicunt? Praeceptis vitam satis explicari, supervacua esse decreta sapientiae, [id est dogmata]. Atqui hoc ipsum, quod dicunt, decretum est tam me hercules quam si nunc ego dicerem recedendum a praeceptis velut supervacuis, utendum esse decretis, in haec sola studium conferendum; hoc ipso, quo negarem curanda esse praecepta, praeciperem*).

[14] *Ben.* 1. 9. 1: 'not the magnitude of each gift, but the quality of the giver, should be considered' (*non quanta quaeque sint, sed a quali profecta, prospiciendum*); 2. 4. 2: 'benefits should be bestowed' (*repraesentanda sunt beneficia*); 2. 9. 1: 'some benefits should be given openly, some in secret' (*quaedam beneficia palam danda, quaedam secreto*); 2. 11. 2: 'we should not mention . . . we should not press the point, we should not revive the memory' (*non est dicendum . . . non est instandum, non est memoria renovanda*).

[15] Jussive subjunctives at 2. 1. 1, 'let us give in the way we would wish to receive them' (*sic demus quomodo vellemus accipere*); 2. 4. 3, 'let no one intervene, let no one retard them' (*nemo illa intercipiat, nemo detineat*); 2. 11. 6, 'let us spare their ears' (*parcamus auribus*). Futures: 1. 11. 6, 'we shall be careful not to send gifts that are superfluous' (*cavebimus ne munera supervacua mittamus*); 2. 14. 1, 'so we shall consider the interests rather than the wishes of those making the request' (*aestimabimus itaque utilitatem potius quam voluntatem petentium*).

[16] *Ben.* 2. 10. 4: 'but if he should be helped' (*sin adiuvari illum oportet*); 2. 14. 2: 'it is appropriate to keep in view not merely the first effects of one's benefits but also the eventual outcome' (*initia beneficiorum suorum spectare tum etiam exitus decet*).

[17] *Ben.* 2. 6. 2, 'choose a different time' (*aliud tempus eligito*); 2. 15. 3, 'therefore compare the role of each and assess in that context the very gift you are going to give' (*utriusque itaque personam confer et ipsum inter illas quod donabis examina*).

much too skilful a writer to produce a straightforward list of precepts in their standard form. He uses all the other types of teaching that he lists in *Letters* 94 and 95 as 'kinds of advice' (*genera monitionum*), notably 'adjurations' (*adhortationes*), 'rebukes' (*obiurgationes*), 'encomia' (*laudationes*), and he dresses up the precept form in many guises.[18]

When Seneca says at the beginning of Book 5 that he has covered the territory of this *officium*, or when he says early in Book 7, 'I do not think there is much point in pursuing other points after the things that regulate our conduct have been said' (*nec ... nimis ad rem existimo pertinere, ubi dicta sunt, quae regunt mores, prosequi cetera*, 7. 1. 2), he means that Books 1–3, and to a lesser extent Book 4, have already provided the *praecepta* that one needs to perform the appropriate *officia* involving beneficence. That teaching is firmly at the level of *imperfecti*, as Seneca explains in *Letter* 94. 50–1.[19] In fact, throughout *De beneficiis* he frequently makes clear his paramount concern with them (e.g. 2. 18. 4; 5. 14. 5; 7. 2. 1; 7. 20. 5).[20] Indeed, in the latter part of the work he spells out the obligation of benefactors themselves, when faced with ingratitude, to advise and instruct those people who are imperfect but curable: 'the second-best form of virtue is to be willing and able to take advice . . . Few men follow reason as their best guide; next best are those who return to the right path when they are admonished; these must not be deprived of their guide' (5. 22–3, 25. 4–5). And near the end of the last book, he again explains, 'There is sometimes room for a reminder (*admonitio*), but a gentle one, one that does not demand

[18] *Epp.* 94. 39; 95. 34 and 65. Cancik 1967, 16–25 showed in her study of the *Letters to Lucilius* how the theoretical and doxographical style of teaching is characterized by descriptive grammatical forms, while the paraenetic passages use prescriptive ones. She points out that, in addition to sentences that have a prescriptive form, Seneca also uses for paraenetic purposes *exempla*, instances, and comparisons (23 n. 42). Codoñer 2000 rightly emphasizes that paraenetic teaching is not confined to certain grammatical forms, and that theoretical and paraenetic teaching are combined in single letters.

[19] Philo of Larissa, in his division of the ethical part of philosophy, justifies the hypothetical statement (*hypothetikos logos*) on the grounds that those who are not Sages need preceptive statements (*parainetikoi logoi*) to help them act correctly in particular situations (Stob. 2. 41. 18–25 W). Clearly, like Seneca's *Letters* 94 and 95, this reflects controversy over the usefulness of precepts (cf. also Musonius Rufus at Stob. 4. 50. 94). It also suggests that it is wrong to think *praecepta* are only for the moral beginner (see above, n. 3).

[20] Seneca switches from the level of 'correctly performed functions' (*katorthōmata*) to that of 'proper functions' (*kathēkonta*). At 1. 5. 3 he defines a *beneficium* as a *recte factum* in which the intention is everything, and Book 4 is much concerned with the *sapiens*. But since a *katorthōma* is, in fact, a *kathēkon* that has all its numbers, as done by the Sage (*Ben.* 7. 17. 1), Seneca naturally concentrates on the deliberations that make an action appropriate, providing it with a 'plausible defence' (*eulogos apologismos*, D.L. 7. 107), and giving it the quality of rationality required of virtue (*Ben.* 4. 9. 3), though, strictly speaking, the token actions of this type done by anyone but a Sage are 'errors' (*hamartēmata*). Similarly, Eudorus in the practical division of ethics is concerned both with *kathēkonta* and *katorthōmata*, including those concerned with *charis* and other activities, like marriage, that can be practised by the Sage and by others: there is no reason to think he treated the two levels of action separately, as Giusta 1964–7, ii. 455 suggests.

for trial or summon to court' (7. 23. 3), though he then goes on at 26–32 to explain what to do with those who are not receptive to subtle reminders.

Chaumartin has rightly pointed to the light shed on Seneca's teaching in *De beneficiis* by the two *Letters* that set out the theory of the paraenetic approach. He shows how this approach makes sense of the length of the treatise, for the function of refreshing the memory, mentioned in *Letter* 94. 21, clearly requires time.[21] He goes on to argue that the apparent inconsistencies in Seneca's views are to be explained by the paramount importance, in determining what he says, of the practical effect he is pursuing at any point—what Mazzoli termed opportunistic pedagogy (p. 122). Paul Veyne had already written of *De clementia*, 'Latin thinkers were not immune to self-contradiction, but Seneca had a philosopher's mind . . . and in his *De clementia*, as in the rest of his work, only the necessities and psychagogic *longueurs* of an exhortation to virtue (one needs time in order to convince) appear to drown the clarity of the concept.' However, Veyne went on to suggest that the striking differences between the concept of *clementia* in Book 1, where it is used as a synonym for *misericordia* and *venia*, and that in Book 2, where it is sharply distinguished from them, is to be explained by the need to woo the young Nero at first with the ordinary confused commonsensical concept of *clementia*, something he can be expected to understand.[22] This might suggest that Book 2 presupposes some progress on the part of the imperial addressee. Then again, Cancik, in her perceptive study of the *Letters to Lucilius*, noted that one can see an increasing complexity in Seneca's teaching during the correspondence.[23] The first doxographic letter is 58 and the longer letters start with Book 8 and *Ep.* 70 (p. 7). The series of dialectic letters in Book 5, *Epp.* 45, 48, 49, take dialectic less seriously than the later series, *Epp.* 82, 83, 85, 87 (pp. 36–42, 138–9), while with *Epp.* 89–95 we have a series handling the various aspects of philosophy itself (p. 42). She also realized that the situation of the addressee Lucilius, who is represented as a learner, determines the form of the epistolary message (pp. 42; 72). Though she rejected the idea that the literary presentation of Lucilius as making progress constituted a consistent spiritual development (pp. 42 n. 70; 72–5), Maurach rightly insisted that Seneca intends the reader to see the more theoretical and dialectical discussion in the later letters as the response of a skilful teacher to the different level of teaching required by a pupil ready for more demanding instruction; these later letters offer the pupil a fuller insight into the fundamentals of the Stoic system.[24]

---

[21] Chaumartin 1985, 292–3. At *Ep.* 27. 9 Seneca quotes with approval Epicurus' repetition of a valuable piece of advice: 'For some people, remedies need to be pointed out; for others, ground into them.'

[22] Veyne 1990, 351–2 (translation modified).   [23] Cancik 1967.

[24] Maurach 1970, 199–206. See also André 1970, 201–2, pointing to the way in which the evolution of Lucilius matches the spiritual maturation of the pedagogue.

These ideas, in combination, have implications for the structure of *De bene-ficiis*, which need to be explored. Whereas Chaumartin seems to think that the key to the whole work is *admonitio*, the preceptive style of instruction, it can be argued that, in the course of this long work, as in *De clementia* and the *Letters to Lucilius*, an evolution takes place in the type of teaching offered, as was already suggested at pp. 121–3. And whereas repetitions can be used to help the memory to retain precepts, and inconsistencies do find some explanation in the pedagogical needs of the context, it is also relevant that the recipients (the constructed addressee and readership) are envisaged as making some moral progress, the different stages of which require different levels and a greater refinement of argument on the same topics. Maurach has in fact pointed out that the later books serve the purposes of intellectual training and recreation.[25] In what follows, I propose to treat first the evolution of teaching style, then the evolution of the addressee.

B. THE EVOLUTION OF TEACHING STYLES

In defending the necessity for *decreta* as well as *praecepta* in *Letter* 95. 45, Seneca writes, 'It is not enough, when a person is arranging his existence as a whole, to give detailed advice. Marcus Brutus, in the book which he wrote *Peri kathēkontos*, gives many precepts to parents, children, and brothers; but no one will do his duty as he ought, unless he has some point of reference. We must set before our eyes the goal of the Supreme Good, towards which we may strive, and to which all our acts and words may have reference.' Similarly, in his *De officiis*, Cicero remarked that the *officiorum praecepta*, which he was about to treat, have relevance to the goal of good things, but that this is less obvious (than in theoretical works) because *praecepta* are more concerned with the instruction of ordinary life.[26]

It is in Book 4 of *De beneficiis* that the *praecepta* of the early books are clear-ly related to the *decreta* of Stoicism, as has already been shown (pp. 119–20). The question Seneca poses at the very start of Book 4, 'whether conferring a benefit and doing a favour in return are things worthy of choice in themselves' (*an beneficium dare et in vicem gratiam referre per se res expetendae sint*)

---

[25] Maurach 1996, 109 n. 115, arguing against Chaumartin 1985, 297–302.

[26] *Off.* 1. 7: 'The duties for which precepts are laid down are indeed relevant to the end of good things, though that is less obvious because they seem to apply rather to the instruction of ordinary life' (*Quorum autem officiorum praecepta traduntur, ea quamquam pertinent ad finem bonorum, tamen minus id apparet, quia magis ad institutionem vitae communis spectare videntur*). The *vita communis* is, as is made clear at 3. 14–15, that aspect of human activity which is shared between Sages and ordinary men. Precepts teach the type of conduct of which a 'reasonable defence' can be given, the *officia media* or *communia*, as Cicero calls them at 3.14. See Inwood 1999, 102.

requires an affirmative answer that is a *decretum*. For in *Letter* 94. 11 we are told that the proposition 'fairness is desirable in itself' (*aequitatem per se expetendam*) belongs to the 'topic of justice' (*de iustitia locus*), and that it is the notion of justice, and the *decreta* concerned with it, that provide the proofs for the particular precepts about how to treat a friend, a citizen, or an associate. In the same way, the proposition *beneficium dare et in vicem gratiam referre per se res expetendae* also follows from the notion of virtue, which has intrinsic value (4. 16. 2): for a true *beneficium* is a virtuous action, a *katorthōma* or *recte factum* (1. 5. 3.).[27] And it is the character of *beneficium* as a virtuous act defined by the intention and will of the actor that supports the particular precepts Seneca gives about how to give, receive, and return. The Sage begins to feature more prominently in Book 4 because his performance of the perfect right action, or correctly performed function, issues from his complete grasp of these *decreta*. He does not need *praecepta*, in order to turn into a reality that imitation of the gods that is here recommended.

In the three books that follow Book 4, the effects of that book are still felt, as we have seen, in the continued concern with the gods and the Sage. But, starting with the second half of Book 4, we are involved in a series of dialectical problems. Cancik in fact noted that dialectic is often the type of theoretical argument that Seneca opposes to paraenetic teaching and unflatteringly compares to *verba* vs. *res* (*Epp.* 83. 27; 87. 40).[28] So here the introductions to Books 5–7 deprecate what lies ahead, though, as we have seen in the previous chapter (pp. 114, 120), these remarks are clearly not to be taken literally.

Seneca's expressed attitude to logic is in fact quite complex. These belittling descriptions of the subject-matter that Seneca gives in *De beneficiis* are in keeping with the descriptions in the *Letters to Lucilius* of *cavillationes* (45. 5; 82. 8; 111. 1), *interrogationes, argutiae, quaestiunculae* (48. 5, 9; 85. 1; 87. 11; 111. 2), which are dismissed as 'sophistical argumentation' (*captiosae disputationes*, 45. 5) or 'Greek absurdities' (*Graecae ineptiae*, 82. 8), beloved of dialecticians (45. 13). In the *Letters to Lucilius*, as in *De beneficiis*, these puzzles are described as useless,[29] though entertaining and seductive: games fit only for exercising the intellect.[30] Erasmus complained bitterly about Seneca's inconsistency in

---

[27] It is defined at 1. 6. 1 as 'an act of benevolence bestowing joy and deriving joy from the action, performed from inclination and the spontaneous readiness to do so' (*benevola actio tribuens gaudium capiensque tribuendo in id quod facit prona et sponte sua parata*).

[28] Cancik 1967, 23 n. 41.

[29] *supervacua*: *Ben.* 5. 1. 1, cf. *Ep.* 45. 4; 49. 5. Uselessness decried in *Ep.* 45. 5; 48. 6–7; 113. 26; described as positively harmful in *Epp.* 48. 9–10; 49. 5–6; 82. 19.

[30] Enjoyment: *Ben.* 5. 1. 1; 5. 12. 2; 6. 1. 1, cf. *Ep.* 111. 5; games: *Ben.* 6. 1. 1, cf. *Epp.* 71. 6; 102. 20; 124. 21; refreshment to the soul: *Ben.* 5. 12. 2, cf. *Ep.* 65. 15. Fuhrmann 1997, 290 suggests: 'Wahrscheinlich gibt diese heitere ethische, der Lebenspraxis nicht eben nahestehende Rabulistik das Muster wieder, nach dem man in den Philosophenschulen Geschicklichkeit im Argumentieren zu erwerben suchte.'

practising what he condemned, naming among others two puzzles that resemble those in *De beneficiis*.[31]

Jonathan Barnes has inferred from Seneca's attacks on logic in the *Letters* that Roman youth were very interested in logic, and that Seneca was attacking 'the preferred practice of the bright young things'.[32] Should we therefore read as deeply ironic Seneca's avowal at 7. 1. 2, 'If I had wished to curry favour for myself, this work should have formed a gradual crescendo, with that part held back which any reader, however surfeited, would relish. But all that is most essential I have collected at the beginning; now I am merely recovering what escaped me'? Did Seneca know that, in fact, nothing could please at least his younger readers more than what he presents as mere 'remnants'? Such a consideration might well have weighed with Seneca, who was a popular author with the young and not one to deny his public, as Quintilian later remarked.[33]

But, in fact, Seneca's attitude to logical questions is not uniformly hostile nor incompatible with his having a serious purpose in treating them. Thus in *Letter* 89 he was to show that the *rationalis pars* of philosophy cannot altogether be dispensed with, even by schools like the Epicureans and Cyrenaics, who would like to do without it: in fact they have to reinstate some form of it, in order to be able to sort out ambiguities and to detect falseness hiding under the guise of truth (11–12, cf. 9). Though, as Barnes points out, the target of Seneca's attacks is narrower than the whole logical division of philosophy, which embraced the broad range of subjects that the ancients understood by rhetoric and dialectic,[34] Seneca also makes it clear that he thinks that even the dialectical puzzles he attacks have their uses, provided they are enlisted in the service of ethics; for he notes that certain logical questions are intertwined with ethical ones.[35] Barnes regards him as a 'logical utilitarian', prepared to allow that logic is an instrument to be used in ethical conduct. As Seneca himself says in Letter

---

[31] Trillitzsch 1971, ii. 436. Erasmus writes, ' "an sapiens sapienti possit prodesse"; "an sapienti dari possit beneficium a diis?" . . . Huiusmodi naenias quum frequenter inculcet usque ad tedium, tamen subinde damnat. Quid enim opus est facere quippiam, in hoc ipsum ut factum reprehendas?' The two examples resemble *Ben.* 7. 4. 1 'quemadmodum potest aliquis donare sapienti, si omnia sapientis sunt?' and 5. 4. 3 'quibus nihil potest praestare ipsa fortuna'. The first is treated in *Ep.* 109, which looks (17) to its appearance in the lost *libri moralis philosophiae*.

[32] Barnes 1997, 14.

[33] 'At that time he was almost the only author in the hands of the young' (*tum autem solus hic fere in manibus adulescentium fuit*, 10. 1. 126); 'if he had not been in love with his own ideas . . . he would have won the general approval of the learned rather than the adoration of boys' (*si non omnia sua amasset . . . consensu potius eruditorum quam puerorum amore comprobaretur*, 10. 1. 130).

[34] Barnes 1997, 8–10 points out that *dialektikē* included the study of sound and voice (which we would regard as a matter for psychology) and the study of sense impressions (which we would regard as epistemology).

[35] *Ep.* 102. 4. The examples concern the value of posthumous glory. Seneca gives examples of three questions concerned with *mores* (4), followed by three purely dialectical questions.

89. 18, 'I do not forbid you to read these things—provided that, whatever you read, you at once bring it to bear on conduct (*mores*).'[36]

What we find in the second half of Book 4 and in Books 5–7 are a series of questions (referred to as *interrogationes* or *quaestiones*), two paradoxes (5. 12–17),[37] and syllogisms that involve paradoxes as conclusions (5. 12; 5. 15. 1) or as premises (7. 4. 7–7. 4). Though the earlier books contain paradoxes, notably Book 2. 31–5, and the odd question, notably in Book 3 (3. 6, 18, 29), it is only in the last books that they form the principal subject-matter, and the introductions to Books 5–7, as we have seen, mark the change.

All of these conundrums feature in Aristotle's discussion in the *Topica* of *problēmata dialektika*, most of which, he says, were also called *theseis*. Their use, he explains, is to help with choice and avoidance (action) or with truth (knowledge).[38] Aristotle also divides the *problēmata* into universal and particular problems.[39] It was the rhetorician Hermagoras, in the mid-second century BC, who, appropriating this area for rhetoric, divided its sphere of investigation in the way we find it in Cicero and Quintilian: into the treatments of *theseis* (general or non-specific questions), rendered in Latin as *quaestiones infinitae* or as *proposita*,[40] and *hypotheseis* (specific questions), rendered as *quaestiones definitae* (or *finitae*) or as *causae*.[41] Their inclusion in discussions of rhetoric places these authors on the inclusive side of the rhetoric vs. philosophy debate.[42] It is true that Cicero, in his youth, disapproved of Hermagoras' claim that the general *quaestiones* belong to the province of the orator.[43] But, probably under the influence of the Academic Philo of Larissa, from whom his schematic analyses of the *thesis* probably derive,[44] he came to attach more importance than did most teachers of rhetoric in Republican Rome, to such philosophical exercises, which he describes as characteristic of Academic and

---

[36] Barnes 1997, 13–23 discusses Seneca's attitude to logic and logical puzzles. Cicero too recognized the value of dialectic to the orator and the jurist (Reinhardt 2003, 306–7).

[37] Another two paradoxes—all things belong to the Sage; friends have all things in common—give rise to questions at 7. 4–13.

[38] *Topica* 1. 11. 104[b]1–105[a]9.

[39] *Topica* 2. 1. 108[b]34–5. On Cicero's claim in *Or.* 46 that Aristotle used the *thesis* as a rhetorical device, see Brittain 2001, 335–6.

[40] Quintilian 3. 5. 5 tells us that, instead of Cicero's term *proposita* (*Top.* 79), others used *quaestiones universales civiles* or *quaestiones philosopho convenientis*. Cicero also uses *consultatio* (*De orat.* 3. 111; *Part. Or.* 4, 67). See Bonner 1969, 2.

[41] Cic. *Inv.* 1. 8. The principal discussions are in Cicero, *De oratore* 2. 78; 3. 111–18; *Or.* 44–6; *Topica* 79–86; *Part. Or.* 61–7, and Quintilian 3. 5. 5–18, but both authors discuss them elsewhere. All this is well analysed by Riposati 1947, 162–203.

[42] See the excellent discussion by Clarke 1951, who points out that Seneca's father wrongly regarded the *thesis* as confined to the period before Cicero. See also Bonner 1949, 10 and Fairweather 1981, 104–6, 117–19.

[43] *De inventione* 1. 8. Quintilian discusses Cicero's change of heart at 3. 5. 14–15.

[44] Brittain 2001, 339–43; Reinhardt 2000, 535–40; Reinhardt 2003, 14–17; 346–7. For the problem of relating Cicero's change of heart to Philo's teaching, see Reinhardt 2000, 535; 547 n. 57.

Peripatetic philosophers[45] and as part of Academic rhetorical theory.[46] Quintilian subscribed to his views.[47] Cicero had in fact given an oratorical treatment to the *theseis* that he claims presents the greatest challenge of all to the orator, the paradoxes of the Stoics.[48] Seneca is at home in this area, common to philosophy and rhetoric. He had been a successful orator and was able to deploy the tricks of that trade in the service of philosophy.

What we meet in *De beneficiis* are the *theseis* or *quaestiones infinitae*, problems that do not involve particular people, places, times, or incidents, either real or fictional. There is, however, as Quintilian demonstrates, a close connection between the universal and the particular, both in that the resolution of a particular question such as 'Should Cato marry?' involves the general question 'Should anyone marry?', and in that the general and the specific are often a matter of degree: 'Should one participate in politics?' is general; 'Should one participate under a tyranny?' is more specific, but not yet nailed to a particular time and place.[49] Some, he says, preferred to distinguish *theseis* from *causae*, not by their lack of particularity, but by their concern with establishing the truth, rather than with guiding conduct.[50] Seneca's discussion at times illustrates precisely the artificiality of this demarcation between the general and the particular. So at 4. 34. 3 Seneca considers, 'Must you keep a promise to give a benefit, if you discover later that the recipient is ungrateful?' The moral dilemma arises from the obligation to keep a promise, which here comes into conflict with the obligation not to give to the ungrateful.[51] Seneca goes on (4. 38) to give an *exemplum* involving Philip of Macedon, in which he puts Philip's dilemma in the form of a *quaestio finita*: 'Will Philip give to you (a soldier who has proved ungrateful to a third party) because he promised, even if he ought not to, even if it means inflicting an injury and committing a crime?' Another specific question, to be answered in the opposite sense, follows concerning Zeno (4. 39). Seneca here exploits his familiarity with declamation, for many of the *controversiae* and *suasoriae* recorded by his father have philosophical *theseis* implicit in them or were even inspired by them, and the study of *theseis* formed part of early rhetorical training.[52] In fact, the Elder

---

[45] *De orat.* 3. 107; *Or.* 46 (Aristotle himself).   [46] *Part. Or.* 139, cf. 61–7.

[47] On Quintilian's views, see Viano 1995.   [48] *Parad.* pref. 4–5.

[49] Cicero points out that *theseis* too, like *hypotheseis*, can be determinate with regard to one or more of the specifications (*peristaseis*), but not in the most important respects (*Top.* 80, on which see Reinhardt 2003, 351–2).

[50] Quint. 3. 5. 8–13.   [51] The sort of case envisaged by Aristotle at *Top.* 1. 11. 104^{b}31–5.

[52] According to Quintilian 2. 4. 25, *theseis* like the ones mentioned above, with the addition of named persons, become the *suasoriae* beloved of declaimers. Seneca's *Ep.* 14. 12–13 gives a good example of the *thesis* 'whether one ought to enter politics' (*an accedendum ad rem publicam*), adapted to the situation of Cato at the time of the civil war. As Bonner 1969, 8–9 points out, the series of rhetorical questions and arguments addressed to Cato in this letter suggests that this is an example of a *suasoria* formed by Seneca as a concrete case to illustrate and give practice in handling the general question.

Seneca's *controversiae* include two that are treatments, in the form of specific cases, of the question of ingratitude and the nature of benefit.[53]

Seneca's purpose in *De beneficiis*, however, is not rhetorical training, but rather exploration of the general question. His arguments here are hard to distinguish from the later practice of casuistry, in the proper sense of the resolution of particular hard cases of conscience, though the immediate point of posing the hard cases here is not the practical one of advising someone or deciding oneself what to do, but the more theoretical one of exploring the general question and explaining, for example, that promises involve unexpressed reservations (4. 39. 4). The effort of applying general principles to particular hard cases helps to refine those principles and our understanding of them.[54] As Sandbach (1975, 157) put it, 'There is a good deal of casuistry in an attempt to determine what does or does not constitute a service, and where the line is to be drawn between gratitude and ingratitude.'

The problems that Seneca treats illustrate the two types of *quaestiones infinitae* distinguished by Cicero and Quintilian in the wake of Philo of Larissa: one type concerned with knowledge, the other concerned with action. The first type has three subdivisions: *an sit* (questions of existence, cause), *quid sit* (questions of definition), and *quale sit* (questions of moral status).[55] They are not always easy to distinguish.[56] The second type, action, has two subdivisions, questions of how to behave (*officium*) and questions of how to control the emotions. In this work, Seneca is naturally concerned only with the first subdivision, *officium*.

The two questions explored in the early part of Book 4, 'whether conferring a benefit and doing a favour in return are things worthy of choice in themselves' (*an beneficium dare et in vicem gratiam referre per se res expetendae sint*) belong to the type of *quaestiones infinitae* concerned with *cognitio* and, within it, to the subdivision *quale sit*, to which Cicero assigns questions 'about the desirable and undesirable, the fair and the unfair, the honourable and the shameful' (*de expetendo fugiendoque, de aequo et iniquo, de honesto et turpi*, Cic. *Top.* 84). Other examples of *quale sit* are 'whether it is shameful to be outdone in benefits' (*an sit turpe beneficiis vinci, Ben.* 5. 7. 1), 'whether they are right in doing this (sc. praying that a misfortune may befall their benefactor so they can prove their gratitude) and act from a dutiful desire' (*an hoc recte faciant et pia voluntate*, 6. 25. 2).

---

[53] Sen. *Controv.* 2. 5 and 9. 1. See Bonner 1969, 6–11; 87. Sen. *Controv.* 1. pref. 12 identifies *controversiae* with what Cicero called *causae*.

[54] Reinhardt 2000, 540–1; Brittain 2001, 289–90.

[55] These subdivisions are *staseis* in Greek and *status* in Latin; their use in classifying lawsuits or political debates is associated with Hermagoras, Philo being credited with extending their application to the *theseis* (see references in n. 44).

[56] See Brittain, 2001 309, n. 25 and Reinhardt 2003, 348 n. 3 for the criticism of a certain Archedemos as reported by Quintilian 3. 6. 31, 33: he thought the third sub-division, *qualitas*, was already covered by the second, *definitio*.

Probably to be assigned to the subdivision *quid sit* are a series of questions that serve to define *beneficium* more precisely:

> already in Book 3. 18. 1, 'The question is raised . . . whether it is possible for a slave to give a benefit to his master' (*Quaeritur . . . an beneficium dare servus domino possit*)[57]
>
> in Book 5. 7. 2: 'Whether it is possible for someone to confer a benefit on himself' (*An possit aliquis sibi beneficium dare*)[58]
>
> 5. 20. 1: 'If two brothers are at variance, and I save the life of one, do I give a benefit to the other, who will probably regret that the brother he hated did not die?' (*Fratres duo dissident; si alterum servo an dem beneficium ei qui fratrem invisum non perisse moleste laturus est?*)[59]
>
> in Book 6. 2: 'Whether it is possible for a benefit to be taken away' (*an beneficium eripi posset*)[60]

Questions in Book 7 concern the different senses in which things can belong to, or be possessed by, people:

> 7. 4. 1: 'How can anyone give anything to a Sage if all things are his?' (*Quemadmodum potest aliquis donare sapienti, si omnia sapientis sunt?*)

and (implicitly)

> How can anyone give anything to his friend, if friends have all things in common? (*Quemadmodum potest aliquis donare amico, si omnia amicis communia sunt?*)

Or they concern the meaning of 'returning':

> 7. 14. 1: 'Whether someone who has done everything to return a benefit has in fact returned it' (*An qui omnia fecit ut beneficium redderet, reddiderit*).

The question about promises in Book 4. 34. 3, discussed above, clearly belongs to the category of *quaestiones infinitae* concerned with *actio* and, in particular, with *officium*, under the subheading *quomodo utamur*, as Quintilian puts it (3. 5. 6).[61] Others occur in Book 4:

> 4. 26. 1: 'Will the good man give a benefit to someone he knows to be an ungrateful person?' (*an vir bonus daturus sit beneficium ingrato sciens ingratum esse?*)

---

[57] The question turns on whether everything a slave does for his master is a *ministerium* (something he cannot choose not to do).

[58] The negative answer involves exploring the essentially social character of benefits (5. 8–11).

[59] The solution turns on whether doing good to a person against his will counts as a benefit.

[60] The solution turns on whether a benefit is the act of giving or the thing given.

[61] Quintilian divides the *quaestiones infinitae* relating to *actio* into two divisions, 'how to acquire; how to use' (*quomodo adipiscamur; quomodo utamur*). Cicero in *Part. or.* 63 gives (1) 'to pursue and to avoid something' (*ad persequendum aliquid aut declinandum*) and (2) 'what relates to some convenience or use' (*quod ad aliquam commoditatem usumque referatur*). Both divisions clearly belong to the *officium* half of *actio* (*De orat.* 3. 118).

4. 40. 1: 'Should a favour be returned in every circumstance and should a benefit in all cases be repaid?' (*an omni modo referenda sit gratia, et an beneficium utique reddendum sit?*)

in Book 5. 20. 6: 'Should one ever ask for the return of a benefit?' (*an repetendum est beneficium?*)

in Book 6. 5. 4: (of a benefactor who later injures us) 'Ought I to return to him the benefit and nonetheless avenge myself on him . . . or ought I to combine the two into one and take no action at all, leaving the benefit to be wiped out by the injury, and the injury by the benefit?' (*utrum et beneficium illi reddere debeam et me ab illo nihilo minus vindicare . . . an alterum alteri contribuere, et nihil negotii habere, ut beneficium iniuria tollatur, beneficio iniuria?*)

in Book 7. 16. 5: 'Ought a person to return the benefit that he has received from a Sage if he has ceased to be wise and has turned into a bad man?' (*quod beneficium quis a sapiente accepit, reddere debeat si ille desinit esse sapiens et in malum versus est?*)

7. 26. 1: 'How are we to deal with the ungrateful?' (*quemadmodum ingrati ferendi sint?*)

It was already remarked by Theon, a rhetorician contemporary with Seneca, that the *officium* subdivision of *quaestiones infinitae* relating to *actio*, is often hard to distinguish from questions dealing with *cognitio*.[62] It is not difficult to find examples of such ambiguity in Seneca's questions. So in Book 5. 18. 1, questions of conduct arise in determining to whom gratitude is owed, 'How far am I to pursue the list of relevant persons?' (*quousque personarum seriem sequar?*), and 'Should a benefit be reclaimed from the (recipient's) father?' (*repeti a patre beneficium debet?*, 5. 19. 8). But these questions of conduct are really designed to raise the question 'Where does a benefit stop?' and to make us distinguish between a benefit conferred knowingly and intentionally on someone, and the profit that person may derive from a benefit given to another. Again, in 6. 7. 1, 'Whether a person who has benefitted us without that intention, imposes any obligation on us' (*an ei debeatur aliquid, qui nobis invitus profuit*) turns into a discussion of the intention intrinsic to the notion of a benefit, for, as Seneca says, 'Both this question and any similar one that can be raised will be easily settled, if on every occasion we focus our attention on this idea: nothing is a benefit unless, first, some intention directs it at us; second, that intention is friendly and well-disposed' (6. 7. 2).[63]

---

[62] The *quale sit* subdivision of *cognitio* is the most obvious to be involved in such ambiguity. Theon in his *Progymnasmata* (p. 84 Patillon, 16–19 = ii. 121 Spengel, 14–17), notes 'It makes no difference whether someone says "Should one marry or not?" or again "Is marriage something to be sought or avoided", for it is one and the same thing that is indicated by all such questions'. Riposati 1947, 198 marks the difficulty particularly with reference to this subdivision, pointing out that e.g. *suscipiendine liberi* could belong with *de expetendo fugiendoque* under *quale sit*.

[63] *Et haec quaestio facile expedietur et si qua similis huic moveri potest, si totiens illo cogitationem nostram converterimus beneficium nullum esse, nisi quod ad nos primum aliqua cogitatio defert, deinde amica et benigna.*

The relation between these *quaestiones infinitae* about action and those about philosophical truth is somewhat analogous to the intimate connection which Seneca made in *Letter* 95, between *praecepta* and *decreta*. That is not surprising, given the close relationship between the action questions and *praecepta*, on the one hand, and between the truth questions and *decreta*, on the other. The problems raised by the action questions concerned with *officium*, are clearly a way of exploring the realm of the *praecepta* given earlier in the work, and of refining them: indeed, Cicero calls this category of question the *praecipiendi genus* (*Part. or.* 67).[64] For though Seneca can speak, in *Letter* 94, of *praecepta* as giving, not universal advice but instructions appropriate to each *persona*, the *personae* meant are social roles, such as those of husband, father, master (§1), and he soon makes it clear that they are not geared to individuals and specific occasions, i.e. to 'token actions' (§§14–15).[65] For they would have to be infinite in number. Precepts cover categories of action: they are *praecepta generalia*, in the formulation of §35. Thus *praecepta* give the answer to the non-specific questions (*quaestiones infinitae*) of action, but without the examination that they undergo, when posed as questions.

As for the *quaestiones infinitae* relating to *cognitio*, they explore the areas covered by *decreta*. This type of logical puzzle in the later part of the work brings out the issues that need to be explored, if we are to understand the rationale *behind* the precepts offered in the early part of the work. However, Seneca is eager to keep even this level of instruction on quite a practical level, the early part of Book 4 being the closest he gets to metaphysics and the highest level of theory, while many of the questions considered, as we have seen, are closely related to questions of conduct. Indeed, in the last book he endorses the argument of Demetrius the Cynic, that the basic principles to be learnt are few and simple. Seneca reduces them to a *regula* (7. 2. 2), a rule for deciding easily whether what he has done is right, as he defines it in *Letter* 95. 39. This rule, 'There is no evil except what is shameful, and no good except what is honourable' is similar to the rule of thumb that Cicero had offered in *De officiis* 3. 81, viz. 'Either the thing that seems beneficial must not be dishonourable, or if it is

---

[64] Giusta 1964–7, ii. 451 suggests that the questions in the later part of Book 4 introduced *peristaseis* ('complicating circumstances'), which lead us to qualify the positive answers to the two questions posed at the start of the book. However, his analysis of the *quaestiones* in the later books, purely in terms of Aristotle's *Categories* (453), ignores the substantial development of Aristotle's classifications by the Peripatos, the Stoa, and the rhetoricians, in the interval between Aristotle and Cicero.

[65] See Inwood 1999, 109 on *praecepta* as providing instructions for the kinds of actions that are normally appropriate and why. 'The distinction between normally and exceptionally appropriate actions operates at the level of types; it is a distinct point about token actions that the concrete particulars of each situation, including the character of the agent and the place of the action in his life as a whole, determine the final moral evaluation of that particular action.'

dishonourable, it must not seem beneficial.'[66] It is significant that Seneca puts the recital of basic essential principles there in the mouth of the Cynic Demetrius, who confines them to ethics and is made to refer to them as *praecepta sapientiae* (7. 1. 3). This looks like a kind of oxymoron in Stoic terms, for, in the language of *Letters* 94 and 95, what Demetrius gives is the substance of *decreta*, not *praecepta*: general statements of philosophical truth, not counsels to action (Billerbeck 1979, 34–5). However, even Seneca, speaking in his own voice in *Letter* 94. 31, where he is defending the effectiveness of instruction (*utraque res praecipit*) by precept, in comparison to that by doctrine, says that *decreta* are nothing but *generalia praecepta*, whereas *praecepta* are *specialia*, and goes on to blur the distinction by showing (§35) that even the *praecepta* are general, in not applying to specific situations.[67] Moreover, Demetrius' mode of teaching here is to sketch the mind of the *sapiens*, and Seneca says in *Ep.* 95. 66 that sketching the exemplar of a virtue, here the *sapiens* possessing *sapientia*, is equivalent to giving precepts for that virtue (see **ad 7. 1. 3**)

One is tempted to argue that, of the two basic functions that Seneca attributes to *praecepta* in this pair of *Letters* (p. 126), the first—that of awakening the natural inclination to virtue and preparing one to receive *decreta*—is covered by Books 1–3 of *De beneficiis*, which prepare one for Book 4. The logical puzzles, starting in the second half of that book, give us both the means to refine the precepts and the practice in applying them correctly in complex situations, thus enabling them to fulfil their second function.[68] Even a person who has the right *decreta*, he says in *Letter* 94. 32,

---

[66] Inwood 1999, 120 n. 74, 124 points out how slippery are the terms *formula, praecepta, lex, regula*. His own suggestion (126) that Stoic theory used general rules of thumb as a reference point in moral reasoning, enabling the moral reasoner to find the balance between abstract theory and the demands of a particular context, is helpful. He notes (120), as have others (e.g. Gomoll 1933, 48–52), the use by Cicero of the resources of Roman legal reasoning in his *formula* in *De officiis* 3. 19–20. But *regula* too has such credentials, as many jurists wrote books of *Regulae*, which seem to have been handbooks giving short statements of the basic principles of Roman law, without going into all the subtleties and qualifications.

[67] See Schafer 2009, 106, pointing out that the distinction between *praecepta* and *decreta* in *Letters* 94 and 95 belongs to Seneca's opponent, whereas Seneca is concerned to bring them together in his notion of philosophical training.

[68] It is worth noting that, in the functional ordering of ethical teaching, devised by the Academic Philo of Larissa in the 90s BC and paraphrased by Stobaeus (*Ecl.* 2. 7. 39–41 W), the third division concerned with safeguarding happiness puts in parallel the *parangelmata* of the doctor safeguarding health and the *theōrēmata peri biōn*, of which the examples given are *theseis*: should the sensible man participate in politics or consort with members of the ruling class; should the sage marry? In an appendix, it is said that men who are not Wise but 'in an intermediate condition' may need the *hypothetikos logos*, so that they will have in handbooks maxims for handling each matter securely and correctly. Thus bare precepts are pedagogically a step below the *theseis* and are said to be derivable from them by the Wise. This third *topos* then is operating at the level of *kathēkonta* in Eudorus' scheme (Brittain 2001, 288), but clearly at a more advanced and demanding level than particular *praecepta*, 'teaching the individual to cope with problematic situations by analysing them and generalizing his own situation' (Reinhardt 2000, 540). For the Stoics, of course, only the non-Wise would need either.

has indeed learnt to do things which he ought to do; but he does not see with sufficient clearness what these things are. For we are hindered from accomplishing praiseworthy deeds, not only by our emotions, but also by want of practice in discovering the demands of a particular situation. Our minds are often under good control, and yet at the same time they are inactive and untrained in finding the path of advice.

Precepts help, but they are not the whole solution; for, as Seneca had pointed out earlier in the correspondence (*Ep.* 22. 2), it is difficult to apply general rules of conduct, i.e. precepts, in particular circumstances. Cicero similarly had stressed that the precepts of any art need to be supplemented by experience and practice in fitting them to particular cases, so that we become 'good calculators of our duties', and he does this precisely in the context of beneficence, though he extends the relevance of what he says to all duties (*Off.* 1. 59–60). Accordingly, Seneca can often be seen, in these last books of *De beneficiis*, exploring the precise character of the obligations enshrined in familiar precepts (e.g. 5. 18; 6. 12). The last section of the treatise is comparable to a graduate level course in *officia* for the advanced *profectus*, and Demetrius' advice in the last book is aimed at the *proficiens* who is on the verge of becoming a Sage.[69]

C. THE PROGRESS OF AEBUTIUS LIBERALIS

Having considered the evolution of teaching style, we can now raise the question of its relevance to the level of progress made by the imagined recipient (above, pp. 131–2).

Long ago, Sonntag suggested that Aebutius Liberalis, attested in Seneca's *Letter* 91 as a real person, was selected as the addressee merely because of the appropriateness of his cognomen. He adduced in support the fact that Liberalis is not addressed at length (nor, we may add, characterized) until the *additamenta* in 5. 1 and 6. 41–2.[70] No doubt the cognomen did play an important part in Seneca's choice, as did his choice of Serenus as the dedicatee of *De Tranquillitate Animi*,[71] but that does not mean that the *persona* of the addressee is not developed. In fact, this emergence from the shadows in the

---

[69] In *Ben.* 7. 2. 1 Demetrius wants the *proficiens* to rehearse the necessary tenets, until they come to him spontaneously, and he can distinguish right and wrong without hesitation. At the end of his prescribed meditation, Seneca speaks of the pleasure experienced by the Sage. The slide from one to the other is clearly supposed to suggest the metamorphosis.

[70] Sonntag 1913, 63.

[71] Griffin 1976, 319 n. 5. Though there would be nothing unusual in Seneca's addressing Liberalis by his *cognomen* alone (as with Serenus), Seneca does use his *nomen* as well. The fact that he delays doing this until Book 3 suggests that it is the *cognomen* that he wants to emphasize. See Dickey 2002, 50, 53, 68–70.

later books, is precisely what suggests that Seneca wishes the reader to notice an increase in the role of the addressee, as he progresses in the course of the work towards parity with the author.

As is customary in Seneca, Aebutius Liberalis is addressed in the preface to each book.[72] He is just a name in Books 1 and 2, although he is also invoked in the body of Book 2 (2. 6. 1; 2. 30. 1). In 3. 1. 2 reference is made to a previous debate he has had with Seneca over forgetfulness and ingratitude, but the distance between Seneca and his addressee is made clear: 'You said such persons were ungrateful, but forgetful; just as if that which makes a man ungrateful could be any excuse for his being so, or as if the fact that a man had this misfortune meant that he is not ungrateful, when this misfortune only befalls the ingrate.' Seneca simply puts him right, without acknowledging any force in his argument.

The opening of Book 4—'Of all the question that we have discussed, Aebutius Liberalis'—is perhaps meant to give a hint of collaborative effort in the work so far, an idea reinforced in 4. 3. 1, where Seneca justifies a digression to Liberalis, and in 4. 31. 1, where Seneca appears to address his defence of the gods specifically to him. But it is really in Books 5–7 that Liberalis is depicted as becoming more active. With 5. 1. 2, 'Since, however, such is your wish' (*quia ita vis*), the fiction is that Liberalis wants the author to continue writing or, specifically, to elaborate particular puzzles. Then, at 5. 1. 3–5, the focus is clearly on Liberalis himself, whose *nomen* and *gentilicium* are reversed for emphasis (see **ad 5. 1. 3 Liberalis Aebuti**). We are shown Liberalis in action as a kind of *exemplum* of liberality, 'the best of men by nature and one prone to benefits' (*homo natura optimus et ad beneficia propensus*). He has 'goodness' (*bonitas*), he is an 'excellent man' (*optimus vir*), and 'a great soul' (*ingens animus*). The conduct Seneca ascribes to him fits very well with Seneca's teaching so far (especially, to give the earlier passages in the order of the points in the Book 5 portrait, 2. 11. 3; 2. 17. 6; 1. 7. 1; 2. 17. 7; 2. 11. 4–5; 1. 1. 10; 2. 9; 1. 2. 4–5). Yet at 5. 2. 1–2 one of the maxims Liberalis most admires, 'It is shameful to be outdone in benefits', is challenged.

At 5. 12. 1–2 Liberalis is first represented as finding the preceding discussion, about not being able to do oneself a benefit, useless and a waste of effort for Seneca; then Seneca imagines him becoming even more annoyed with the puzzles to come, and makes him say the kind of thing that Seneca himself says in some of the *Letters to Lucilius*, 'What is the good of laboriously untying knots which you yourself have made, in order that you might untie

---

[72] Mazzoli 2000, 251 marks this as a characteristic of the twelve *dialogi* in the Codex Ambrosianus, but it is true of *De clementia* and *De beneficiis* as well (see below, n. 75). The *Naturales Quaestiones* forms a partial exception, though Lucilius is addressed in the prefaces of those books that have them (1, 3, 4A), at the beginning and end of Book 6, and at the end of Books 2 and 5. Book 4B is incomplete at the start, so only Book 7 lacks any invocation of the addressee. But the incompleteness of parts of the work and the confused order of the books make it difficult to be clear about the pattern.

them?' (cf. *Ep.* 45. 4; 82. 19). But here Seneca defends the practice of dialectic in a way that makes clear the distance between an unskilled person, an *imperitus* (like Liberalis), who would find untying such knots difficult, and the person who has tied the knots and can untie them easily (clearly Seneca himself), for whom they provide pleasure and a mental challenge that drives away complacence and sloth.

However, at the start of Book 6 Liberalis is assigned the task of guiding Seneca, indicating by his facial expression how long he should dwell on certain topics and whether or not to dismiss some at once. The pleasure and profit to be derived from these puzzles now seem to be accessible to them both. At 6. 5. 3–7. 1, Liberalis is shown actually performing this task, and indeed going beyond it. He first steers Seneca away from a theoretical question ('whether a benefit has been removed, if we are not under obligation to repay') to a more practical one about our obligations to someone who first confers a benefit, then inflicts an injury (6. 5. 4), which he represents as a move from the kind of useless questions of definitions beloved of *iuris consulti* to real cases that are treated in the courts, whose practice Stoic philosophers should consider and either adopt or reject. Seneca accepts the challenge on his terms (6. 6). Then at 6. 7. 1 Liberalis ends the discussion altogether: 'Your face, by which I have agreed to be governed, is wrinkled and frowning, as though I were straying too far from the point.' At 6. 12. 1 Liberalis' rather plastic face suggests a question following on from whether we are obliged to an unwilling benefactor: that is, are we obliged to a self-interested one? Seneca addresses himself to this complaint, which he claims often to have heard Liberalis make about such people. At 6. 41. 1 Liberalis is told not to be anxious about returning benefits, and at 6. 42 Seneca says Liberalis is overanxious about requiting benefits and should not try to do it too soon. At the start of Book 7 Seneca again attributes to Liberalis his decision to continue writing. In 7. 17. 1, perhaps our last glimpse of the addressee, Seneca associates himself with Liberalis as *imperiti* in contrast to the Sage, and, in contrast with the perfect benefit, he speaks of 'the everyday common benefit, which *we* ignorant men exchange' (see **ad 7. 17. 1**).[73]

The degree to which Seneca characterizes his addressees (and himself), in building up an impression of dialogue in his prose works, varies considerably, as Mazzoli points out in a perceptive discussion.[74] In the consolations, characterization is at its most dense, because the advice is geared to the specific situation of the bereaved addressee. So Seneca continuously evokes Marcia's particular circumstances while consoling her on the death of her son; he supplies considerable biographical detail about his mother Helvia as he

---

[73] Seneca's 'we', 'I', and 'you' are often ambiguous as between the personal and impersonal. Here they appear to be specifically himself and Liberalis, whereas in 7. 28. 2 (mentioning senatorial office) and 30. 1 (*stulte*) we are clearly in the territory of the impersonal 'you'.

[74] Mazzoli 2000.

consoles her for his own exile (*Cons. Helv.* 2. 4–5; 14–16. 5; 17. 3–4; 18–19); and Polybius' relationship to his brother and the Emperor, along with his literary tastes, is sketched and exploited (*Cons. Polyb.* expecially, 2. 2–3; 6. 2–5; 8. 3–4; 18. 1–2). In *De brevitate vitae* Seneca narrows down his rather general advice in chapters 18–19 with a description of Paulinus' duties as prefect of the corn supply. Mazzoli thinks that the other treatises are to be sharply distinguished, in respect of their dialogic character, from the twelve works actually called *dialogi* in the index to the Codex Ambrosianus, and, in particular, that they are at the opposite extreme from the consolations, where the relationship of author and addressee is almost comparable to the *Letters*. But he seems to forget that Lucilius is quite fully characterized in the *Naturales quaestiones*, particularly in the preface to Book 4 (4. pref. 1, 3; 4. 14–18, cf. 3. 1. 1).[75] In *De beneficiis* Seneca has not provided his addressee with any concrete biographical details: we only learn that Aebutius Liberalis came from Lugdunum in *Letter* 91. But one thing Seneca has managed to do is to build up a consistent picture of Aebutius Liberalis as a benefactor. The advice in Book 6. 41–2 fits with the portrait in Book 5 of Liberalis as someone who is very generous, and who is perhaps too willing to overestimate what he has been given: Seneca has never seen anyone 'so generous in valuing even the most trivial services' (*tam benignum etiam levissimorum officiorum aestimatorem*, 5. 1. 3). In Book 5 Liberalis is anxious about being outdone as a benefactor; in Book 6 he worries about not repaying quickly enough.

Of greater importance to understanding the structure and strategy of *De beneficiis*, however, is the fact that Liberalis' role as addressee develops in parallel with the change in the style of teaching. He is a recipient of precepts in the first three books, and clearly in need of straightforward admonition at 3. 1. 2. But after the precepts have been succeeded by *decreta* in Book 4, and a new level of instruction has been reached, he becomes more active. He is now a more advanced *profectus*, but still not at the level of his mentor Seneca. In Book 6, he is guiding the enquiry, though still receiving advice, and by Book 7. 17, no distinction is drawn between mentor and addressee as *imperfecti*. The role of Liberalis as addressee in fact develops in parallel with the change in the style of teaching. The fact that mentor and addressee, like the readership of *De beneficiis*, are not Sages is underlined by the realistic advice that follows about tactful requests for repayment being acceptable, and even more by the characterization of Seneca's earlier and sterner teaching as hyperbole (7. 22–3), and by the indication that we are all ungrateful (7. 28).

The idea that Seneca's educational strategy involves matching the moral progress of his addressee to the evolution during *De beneficiis* of his teaching

---

[75] On the likelihood that the category of Senecan works that Quintilian termed *dialogi* includes these longer works, *Naturales quaestiones, De clementia,* and *De beneficiis,* see pp. 1, n. 1; 112, n. 9; Griffin 1976, App. B2. See also n. 72 for another similarity.

technique, can be supported by Seneca's practice in other works. Veyne's thesis (see above, pp. 131–2) about *De clementia* could be interpreted in this sense: the contrast in treatment between the two books could arise from the fact that the advice is geared to the addressee Nero, young and morally green in Book 1, but judged ready for more rigorous training in Book 2, where the necessary distinctions are made between clemency and the related terms. But *De clementia* is incomplete, perhaps unfinished, and its strategy is not unambiguous.[76] Then again, the three dialogues addressed to Annaeus Serenus, *De constantia sapientis*, *De tranquillitate animi*, and *De otio* (if we trust the entry *in rasura* in the index to the Codex Ambrosianus), certainly show the addressee undergoing a spiritual development, from an avowed Epicurean scoffing at the Stoics (*Const. sap.* 3. 2; 15. 4), to an *imperfectus* striving to follow Stoic doctrine (*Tranq. An.* 1. 10–12; 1. 17), to, finally, an orthodox Stoic championing those doctrines against the apparent heresy of the author (*Ot.* 1. 4; 7. 2).[77] But the fact that this happens across separate works makes it harder to discern a correlation between Serenus' development and changes in Seneca's teaching technique, though *De tranquillitate animi* is clearly more therapeutic and the others more polemical, with *De otio* advancing more complicated and subtler arguments. Easier to establish is the theory that the *Letters to Lucilius* attribute to the addressee a fictional spiritual development that parallels the change in the style and content of the Letters. I have sketched Lucilius' spiritual development elsewhere and need not repeat the details.[78] Here it is the parallel between the structure and content of the *Letters* and of *De beneficiis* that principally concerns us.

Foucault described Seneca's correspondence with Lucilius as a kind of adult education course, beneficial to the teacher as well. 'His correspondence with Lucilius deepens a preexisting relationship between the two men, who are not separated by a very great difference in age, and tends little by little to transform this spiritual guidance into a shared experience, from which each derives a benefit for himself.'[79] The method of teaching moves with the progress of Lucilius. In the early letters of Books 1–3 (1–29), Lucilius is given, at the ends of his mentor's letters, little moral tags to remember, in line with the advice in *Letter* 2 to pick out one precept every day from his reading and digest it. This practice is illustrated with a citation from Epicurus (2. 4–6), appropriate because Lucilius is depicted as having Epicurean sympathies when the correspondence opens (*Ep.* 23. 9, cf. 20. 9). At *Letter* 6. 5, Seneca makes it clear that

---

[76] Not incompatible with this analysis is the idea, adduced as an explanation of the contrast in Griffin 1976, 153–4, that the two books belong to different genres.

[77] Ibid. 316–17; 353–5.

[78] Ibid. 351–3. At 417 the wavering of the image of Lucilius resulting from Seneca's inconsistent tone of voice in addressing him, now from above, now as a fellow-learner, is discussed. See on the complexities, the discussion by Edwards 1997. See also Griffin 2007, 90–5.

[79] Foucault 1988, 49, 53. See also Nussbaum 1994, 337–8.

Lucilius is being taught through *praecepta* and *exempla*: he should come to visit Seneca in order to have first-hand experience of an *exemplum*, 'because the road is long via *praecepta*, short and effective through *exempla*'.[80] Then in *Letter* 13, Lucilius is said to be more in need of *admonitio* than of *exhortatio* (15) and to be training himself (1) in 'precepts that are health-giving and effective at overwhelming hardships' (*praeceptis salutaribus et dura vincentibus*), i.e. the more uncompromising Stoic precepts. Clearly, all the techniques associated with the preceptive part of philosophy are being used. After *Letter* 29, at the end of Book 3 of the correspondence, there is a change in the form of the letters, to which Seneca draws attention in *Letter* 33. He explains why he now refuses to give moral tags at the end of his letters, especially the Stoic tags that Lucilius is supposed to have requested. Lucilius, as a 'man of secure progress' (*certi profectus vir*), should read books as a whole and not rely on *chriae*, rendered in Latin as *sententiae* (7); he should become an active thinker and a teacher in his own right (8–9).[81] *Letters* 34 and 35 bring home the point about Lucilius' improvement: he is now making rapid progress and helping Seneca to improve in turn, as partners in an ideal friendship should. *Letter* 72 shows Lucilius asking a question, which Seneca cannot answer on the spot. Then, in *Letter* 75, Seneca describes the different levels of *imperfecti* and speaks of them both as struggling to improve.

Letter 85 inaugurates the series of late letters in which difficult dialectical questions are often discussed at considerable length. It is Lucilius who is said to have requested the syllogistic proofs for the Stoic tenet that virtue alone is sufficient for happiness, and Seneca is shown in *Letter* 87 sending him some more on that theme (11). Lucilius is shown requesting a difficult discussion of the parts of philosophy in *Letter* 89. 1, while Seneca warns him not to be too interested in logic for its own sake (18). At *Letter* 102. 3 Lucilius wants Seneca to finish a syllogistic discussion from which he had omitted the parts less relevant to conduct. Further difficult questions follow, in *Letters* 106. 1, 3–4; 108. 1–2; 109. 1, 17; 111; 113. 1; 117. 1; 120. 1, 3. By then, in 121. 1, it is Lucilius who is critical of questions that have no bearing on conduct, while Seneca defends the contribution of doctrines on human nature. Finally, in *Letter* 124, the last we have, Seneca says that Lucilius has the balance just right in practising and approving of highly subtle argumentation, so long as it contributes to moral progress (1). In *Letters* 106, 108, and 109, Seneca has mentioned that he is working on a comprehensive work on moral philosophy that will cover these difficult questions. Leeman suggests that it is really this outside project that explains the shift to more technical subject-matter in the later *Letters*; for, as he

---

[80] The order here is that described as standard in *Cons. Marc.* 2. 1.

[81] Wilson 2001, 183–5 suggests that *Letter* 33 redefines retrospectively Books 1–3 as preliminary protreptic and marks a turning-point in the collection and in the 'epistolary narrative' of moral and intellectual progress.

rightly points out, Lucilius's requests are only a fiction within a fictional correspondence.[82] Maurach, however, points out that the influence may work the other way and that, in any case, a deeper knowledge of Stoicism entails seeing the system more and more as a whole, so that Lucilius' progress would need to be matched by more systematic teaching.[83] In any case, Lucilius is clearly represented as ready for the systematic work on which Seneca is engaged.[84]

The fiction about Lucilius is central to the pedagogic purpose of the *Letters*. As Seneca says in *Letter* 34, just after his correspondent has been weaned off his mainly Epicurean tags: 'I claim you for myself: you are my handiwork. When I saw your talent, I laid my hand on you, I exhorted you, I used the goad and did not let you proceed slowly, but kept on rousing you; and now I am doing the same; but I am urging on someone who is already racing and encouraging me in turn.' For the fiction is not limited to Lucilius' requests and responses: Seneca has created a spiritual development for his addressee, to which these requests add verisimilitude. The parallel with *De beneficiis* should by now be clear: Lucilius, like Liberalis, becomes capable of a higher level of philosophical understanding, even as the philosophy offered becomes more difficult and technical. The parallel extends to the offering of reassuring remarks to the addressee about what standard is really being demanded. Thus, to Lucilius, Seneca praises the philosopher Sextius, who demonstrated the greatness of the happy life without instilling pessimism about its attainment (64. 5). For Lucilius, like Liberalis, remains an *imperfectus*. Nonetheless, the reader of the *Letters* or of *De beneficiis*, who identifies with the addressee, and indeed with Seneca, who is also presented as a learner, can feel that the extended course he has undergone has set him firmly on the path to virtue and happiness.

---

[82] Leeman 1953. Lana 1991, 285–6, 289 defends this view, pointing out that Seneca begins to label his theoretical problems *quaestiunculae* after his mention of the comprehensive work.
[83] Maurach 1970, 205.   [84] Schafer 2009, 75.

8

De beneficiis and Seneca's Other Philosophical Works

In *Letter* 73, as we have had occasion to notice before (pp. 2, 96), Seneca says that the pre-eminent task of philosophy is to teach us 'to owe and to repay benefits well' (9). Clearly, Seneca does not mean to exclude from philosophy's brief the important activity of giving benefits, but, as the letter concerns benefits received from rulers, he formulates philosophy's task in terms of the receiver. This sentence alone, then, prepares us for the flexible way in which Seneca treats the subject of benefits and gratitude elsewhere. In fact, this same careful tailoring of his teaching to the subject in hand, a general feature of Seneca's writing, can be further illustrated by considering the treatment in this same letter of certain topics, which are also found in *De beneficiis*.

CONTEXT AND ARGUMENT

Letter 73 aims to show that philosophers are unlikely to be rebellious trouble-makers, since they above all enjoy, and know how to use, the benefits of peace and leisure that governments provide for them. In the course of this discussion, Seneca touches on a number of issues found in the treatise, such as the role of envy in generating ingratitude (*Ep.* 73. 3, cf. *Ben.* 2. 28); the gratitude owed for communal benefits, including those conferred by the sun and moon (*Ep.* 73. 5–8, cf. *Ben.* 6. 19. 2–20); the way that different senses of possession make intelligible the Stoic idea that all things belong to the Sage (*Ep.* 73. 7, 14, cf. *Ben.* 7. 4–8. 2); and the fact that grateful receipt of a benefit is equivalent to its repayment (*Ep.* 73. 9 fin., cf. *Ben.* 2. 31–5).

The dramatic date of *Letter* 73 letter is early summer of 64, probably after the publication of *De beneficiis*, which certainly predates *Letter* 81 (p. 92, n. 4): in that case Seneca is revisiting topics already dealt with more thoroughly there. This may explain why he feels that he can say cryptically, after noting that philosophy teaches us *bene debere beneficia, bene solvere,* 'sometimes the repayment consists in the acknowledgement itself' (*interdum autem solutio est ipsa confessio*). He alludes briefly here to the Stoic paradox 'He who receives a benefit gladly has returned it', an idea that was fully discussed at the end of Book 2 of the treatise, where it served as an important bridge to Seneca's unorthodox treatment, in Book 3, of his next subject: how to return benefits (see Ch. 6). The other topics revisited in the letter, however, have been completely revamped to suit the author's current subject of concern. Thus, whereas in *De beneficiis* envy is part of the explanation why benefits are generally not properly received, here the point is the ingratitude towards rulers of those engaged in public life and competing for favours, as compared to the philosopher who has withdrawn from the public gaze to study. Then again, whereas in *De beneficiis* the treatment of benefits given to one as part of a group is an exploration of the kind of intention that enables a benefit to create obligation, in *Letter* 73 the point is the superiority over material things of the indivisible and communal goods made available by a divine or human ruler to everyone, such as peace and liberty. A consequence is that, in the *Letter*, this topic is closely connected to the topic of the Stoic Sage having everything: he alone knows how to use these communal things. In the treatise, however, the Stoic paradox 'all things belong to the Sage' (*omnia sapientis sunt*) is introduced in connection with a separate issue: namely, an apparent contradiction within Stoicism between the idea that the Sage is an expert in giving and receiving (as in everything else), and the idea that the Sage has everything (and therefore cannot be given anything), see **ad 7. 4–13**.[1]

We have had occasion to mention this habit of Seneca, whereby similar ideas are used in different contexts to very different effect, in discussing chronology; and we noted there that thematic parallels are useless for the comparative dating of Seneca's works (pp. 95–6). However, it will still be worth exploring the themes from *De beneficiis* that are anticipated or repeated most often in Seneca's other philosophical works, in order to see more clearly where the topic of benefits fits in his philosophical scheme of things.

DIVINE BENEFITS

The context in which beneficence appears most frequently in the other philosophical works, is that of divine providence and generosity to humankind. For example, a quick survey of the *Letters* shows that the *beneficia* referred to most often are the gifts of fortune (e.g. *Epp.* 8. 3; 18. 6; 63. 7; 72. 4–8), nature (90. 36; 119. 16), or the gods (15. 10; 74. 11), and in *De beneficiis*, where this theme is

---

[1] Only incidentally, in the treatise, does Seneca mention that the communal things are the only possessions the Sage would think worth having (*Ben.* 7. 7. 5).

also prominent (see pp. 26–7, 119–20, 122), Seneca explained that nature, fate, fortune, god are synonymous.[2]

Already in *De ira* (1. 5. 3; 3. 5. 6), written some years before *De beneficiis* handled the theme (*Ben.* 4. 18, cf. 1. 4. 2), Seneca noted that nature has designed man for mutual help, to confer benefits and live in harmony, and the idea is repeated in *De clementia* (1. 3. 2) and elsewhere (e.g. *Vit. beat* 24. 3; *Ot.* 3. 5). The advice in *De beneficiis* (4. 25–6; 7. 31. 2–5) that, as rational beings, we should imitate, in this as in other things, the gods who are generous to us, is already present as advice to rulers in *De clementia* (1. 5. 7; 1. 19. 9). Just as in *De beneficiis* Seneca defends the gods for bestowing favours on unworthy men (4. 31–2; 7. 31. 2–5), so in *De providentia* he insists on defending the gods for the apparent hardships they inflict on good men (1. 1). In *De beneficiis*, Seneca finds the root of ingratitude among men in their ingratitude toward the gods (2. 30. 1). This ingratitude, lamented already in *De ira* 3. 31. 1, is traced in *De providentia* and *Ep.* 74. 10–14 to a misconception of what things are really good and bad, as opposed to being positive or negative indifferents, and it can also involve, according to the *Natural Questions*, blaming the gods for our own misuse of their blessings (5. 18. 4–15).

Pohlenz therefore was right to stress Seneca's preoccupation with the problems of providence.[3] It is clear that the metaphysical basis of social exchange was always at the root of Seneca's belief that the theme of exchanging benefits was of central importance. It is only delayed in the treatise to Book 4, after the basic precepts have been rehearsed, as part of the author's teaching strategy (see Ch. 7B).

DIVERGENT VIEWS

Many more parallels between *De beneficiis* and Seneca's other prose works could be compiled, but it may be more illuminating to consider cases in which Seneca's views elsewhere diverge significantly from the treatise. One such case concerns the notion that conferring benefits is an investment or insurance policy. In *De clementia*, Seneca says that the good ruler is loved by his subjects, who are willing to defend him at the risk of their own lives (1.3. 4; 4. 1), and who make it unnecessary for him to have a bodyguard (1.13. 5); and that his generosity ensures that he is venerated like a god (1. 19. 8–9). In

---

[2] *Ben.* 4. 8. 3 (with notes ad loc.). 'Fortune' tends to be used when the gifts are being viewed negatively, to remind us that they are only positive indifferents.
[3] Pohlenz 1941, 104–7. However, his interpretation of *Ben.* 2. 26–30 on ingratitude, as an interruption of the plan of the work in order to accommodate this concern, is questionable: see pp. 115–18 for an explanation of this passage in terms of the difficulty of distinguishing receiving from returning, when *beneficium* is conceived as the act of giving, not the thing given.

De tranquillitate animi generosity, along with justice and kindness, provides safeguards against later bad fortune (10. 6), and in *De vita beata* benefits are compared to buried treasure that one can dig up when in need (24. 2). In *De beneficiis*, however, Seneca is far more guarded. Though, in praising his addressee, he allows that glory can follow beneficence (5. 1. 4), and he acknowledges that one can ask for repayment of benefits if the giver is in need (5. 20. 7), he is adamant that benefits are not investments: 'Let us give benefits rather than lend them' (*demus beneficia, non feneremus*),[4] thus imitating the gods (1. 1. 9; 1. 2. 3). Any advantage we derive from giving a benefit is an *accessio* (a bonus) of gratitude, not the true fruit of the benefit, which is the virtuous act itself (2. 33.1–2; 4. 1. 3). This we would perform even if it did not yield security and love (4. 22. 3); even if it involves risk and loss (4. 12. 2).

Accessio also features in *De vita beata*, but in relation to pleasure. The whole discussion there bears a close resemblance to *De beneficiis*, for in both works the Epicurean insistence on the link between *voluptas* and *virtus*, presented in *KΔ* 5, is challenged, and in very similar terms (*Vit. beat.* 7. 1–3; 11. 3; 13. 5; 14. 1; cf. *Ben.* 4. 2). Seneca argues that, in making virtue serve pleasure, the Epicureans reverse the proper order of things, for virtue must lead and bear the standard. But that is not to deny that virtue yields joy as an *accessio* (*Vit. beat.* 9. 2, cf. 22. 3): it is neither the cause nor the reward of virtue, which we do not practise in order to secure it. Here, in *De vita beata*, the idea of *gaudium* is associated with the happy life, which is attained through virtue alone; in the treatise, it is the virtuous act of giving that yields joy to the giver, and the virtuous act of offering gratitude that bestows joy on the recipient (1. 6. 1, cf. 4. 15. 2; 4. 29. 3; 2. 22. 1; 3. 17. 4).

De vita beata is, in fact, the work that is closest in subject matter to *De beneficiis*, for it shows the most interest in the proper use of wealth. Since the happy life consists in the exercise of virtue, the Sage would prefer to be rich rather than poor, for wealth enables him to be generous to others (21. 4–24). Seneca also allows that the imperfect person needs the indulgence of fortune for his happiness, though the Sage can be happy without it (16. 3). As in *De beneficiis*, wealth must be acquired honourably (*Vit. beat.* 23. 1–2, cf. *Ben.* 2. 17. 1–2; 6. 38. 4), and one must not be spiritually dependent on wealth (*Vit. beat.* 4. 2; 21. 2), being aware that it is not a good, but a positive indifferent, useful but not necessary to happiness (*Vit. beat.* 24. 5; 4. 3; 22. 4, cf. *Ben.* 1. 6. 2; 1. 11. 5; 5. 13). It is difficult to give properly, and discrimination in giving is vital.[5] Nonetheless, the attitude to wealth in *De vita beata* is different from the

---

[4] As Pohlenz 1941, 73–4 notes, the difference is all the more striking because the context in *De vita beata* is one where things very similar to Seneca's teaching in the treatise are said (*Vit. beat.* 24. 1 on difficulty of giving properly, cf. *Ben.* 2. 18. 2; *Vit. beat.* 24. 3 on need for discrimination in giving, cf. *Ben.* 1. 1. 2; 2. 15; 4. 10. 2–3).

[5] See references in n. 4 above.

austere view that prevails in *De beneficiis*; it is, in fact, unique among Seneca's works in its positive evaluation of wealth, the reason probably being its function as a defence against the charges of hypocrisy made against Seneca, notably by Suillius Rufus.[6] In *De beneficiis*, by contrast, Demetrius is made to say, with the author's approval, that the Sage would rather not have riches (7. 7. 5–11), and the negative view of wealth as a cause of evil prevails (6. 3. 2; 7. 10). Seneca even has Demetrius say that, if some god wished to commit all our wealth to his hands, 'I would not accept it, even if I were going to give it away, since I can see that there are many things which it would not be appropriate for me to give' (7. 9. 1). Throughout the treatise, Seneca is concerned to show that the things given and the services rendered are not goods and not benefits, but only positive indifferents at best (e.g. 1. 5. 6; 5. 13). The *beneficium* that give us *gaudium* is the *benevola actio* (1. 6. 1). Seneca in fact spends more time in defining precisely what state of mind is required, if a gift or service is to count as a benefit and create an obligation of gratitude, than in itemizing and celebrating the actual gifts and services conferred. Pohlenz may have been right when he suggested that the impulse to treat beneficence came from Seneca's having to defend himself, as he does in *De vita beata*, but that he only came to a deeper understanding of it when he worked more precisely with the question from a theoretical point of view.[7]

That deeper understanding of beneficence also guides Seneca's teaching in a more humane direction in *De beneficiis*. As we have already noted (p. 25), Bellincioni regarded the three treatises, *De ira*, *De clementia*, and *De beneficiis*, as steps on an ethical itinerary, during which Seneca developed a doctrine governing the exercise of power in its political and economic aspects: the first two concentrate on negative lessons about abstaining from anger and injury, while the last moves on to teach the necessity of benefitting humanity.[8] *De ira* treats the passion that most of all threatens the duty of mutual help that nature has ordained for man. *De clementia* advocates the virtue that is opposed to anger and cruelty (1. 5. 6; 2. 4. 1–3), cruelty being anger when associated with power (Sallust, *BC* 51. 14). But *clementia*, in addition to being a species of *temperantia* or self-control (Cic. *Inv.* 2. 164, cf. *Clem.* 2. 3. 1), also has an active aspect within a particular sphere of operation: namely, situations where there is provocation to revenge or occasion for punishment. In this work, especially in Book 2, Seneca concentrates on proper conduct in meting out judicial punishment for offences, a theme to which he gives even more attention than to overlooking personal injuries or sparing enemies in war. In doing so, he moves on, from insisting in *De ira* that judgement be free of anger but severe, concerned with enforcing the law and with inflicting the deserved punishment

---

[6] See Griffin 1976, 302–10.   [7] Pohlenz 1941, 74.
[8] Bellincioni 1984*a*, 10, 104–5. See also Maurach 1991, 110–11 and Griffin 2003*a*, 178–82.

(1. 16. 5; 1. 19. 5–6), to advocating punishment that stops short of what could deservedly be imposed (*Clem.* 2. 3. 2).

It is true that in *De ira* (1. 19. 5–7) Seneca already thinks of Plato's insistence that punishment should help to reform, and that he also urges making allowances for mistakes and weakness, as in *De clementia* (2. 7. 2); but Bellincioni points out the contrast between the image in *De ira* 1. 6, of straightening spear-shafts by fire and force, and the gentler image of punishment as reform, with which our text of *De clementia* breaks off. Here Seneca compares the way in which the Sage deals with wrongdoers to the way in which good farmers tend trees that need to be straightened, or trimmed, or nourished with fertilizer, or given more access to the sun (2. 7. 4–5). The same contrast appears between the medical simile in the same passage of *De ira*—where the physician treats patients by fasting or surgery, and no treatment seems harsh if it results in health—and the gentler medical analogy in *De clementia* 1. 17. 2, where gentle remedies, even placebos, are suggested, and the concern is with restoring health while avoiding shameful scars. Here Seneca is stressing the third ingredient of the Roman concept of *clementia*, which embraces the Greek *praotēs*, *epieikeia*, and *philanthrōpia*, and he is developing the Stoic notion that man is a social animal, born for the common good (above, p. 151).

De ira treats material belonging to the division of moral philosophy *de impetu*, *De clementia* is concerned both with that and with the division *de actionibus* (see pp. 126–8). *De beneficiis* concerns itself principally with the latter,[9] and it develops further the positive advice to benefit humanity in a political and economic sense, and thus to maintain the bonds of human society. Moreover, to the offence of ingratitude, which is not, and (according to Seneca) should not be, a punishable legal offence (*Ben.* 3. 6–17), but which he regards as the root of all crimes and vices (1. 10. 4), he now extends that degree of generosity and understanding offered to offenders against the law in the other two works. And, going further in that direction, he urges us to continue conferring benefits on the ungrateful. The image of the good farmer tending his trees in *De clementia* has its counterpart at the end of *De beneficiis*, where Seneca, after urging us at length to imitate the gods, who give benefits even to the malicious and ungrateful, advocates giving the ungrateful a second chance by persisting in conferring benefits on them, like the good farmer who overcomes the sterility of the soil by care and cultivation (7. 31–2).[10]

---

[9] All these works are also concerned with the first division, *inspectio*, assigning the right value to things: in *De beneficiis*, as we saw, there is a lot of discussion of the distinction between goods and indifferents.

[10] Cf. *Ben.* 1. 1. 9–11 for the sentiment, and 2. 11. 4–5 for the image.

BUILDING ON *DE BENEFICIIS*

After finishing the treatise, Seneca clearly went on thinking about the subject of benefits, as we have seen in the *Letters*. In fact, he thought further, not only about the subject itself, but about what he had said on it. For in *Letter* 81, ostensibly prompted by his addressee Lucilius, he returns to the subject of ingratitude, explicitly mentions *De beneficiis*, in which the subject is prominent, and takes up a question 'which has not, I think, been sufficiently clarified' (*quod non satis, ut existimo, explicatum est*). By this he means 'clarified by me', because it is a question he has mentioned in Book 3. 12. 4 of *De beneficiis* and discussed in Book 6. 4–6.

Letter 81, like so many of the *Epistulae Morales*, has a complicated structure, which I have tried to render intelligible in the synopsis that forms an Appendix to this chapter. It starts with Lucilius' complaint that he has encountered an ungrateful person. Seneca responds that Lucilius has been lucky not to meet such a person before—there are so many—and exhorts him in the same humane direction, and with the same image, that we have just noted as providing the conclusion to the treatise: 'Even after a poor crop one should sow again, for often what was lost through the stubborn barrenness of poor soil has been made up through one year's fertility' (*Ep.* 81. 1).[11] In this introductory section (1–3), Seneca goes on to repeat several points from the treatise, urging his correspondent not to give up conferring benefits, but to try again, as we do in other activities involving uncertainty and difficulty.[12] He then comes to the question that needs further clarification: 'Whether a benefactor who later injured us, has balanced things out and released us from our debt' (*an is qui profuit nobis, si postea nocuit, paria fecerit et nos debito solverit*). Seneca adds that we may suppose the harm to have greatly exceeded the earlier benefit (*Ep.* 81. 3).

This question about the subsequently injurious benefactor is brought in as a 'hard case' that will, as the introduction already suggests, lead us to explore the whole issue of showing proper gratitude for benefits and making an appropriate return.[13] The context thus guarantees a more ambitious analysis of the question than it had received in *De beneficiis*. Let us start, however, by reviewing the treatments of the question in the treatise, noting points that will be particularly relevant to its treatment in *Letter* 81.

---

[11] Though, in the *Letter*, the perseverance depicted in the image is directed at finding other people who are grateful, whereas in the treatise Seneca extends his perseverance to the conversion of the ingrates themselves.

[12] For the parallels, see Ch. 4 n. 3. My analysis of *Letter* 81 owes an incalculable debt to the two essays of Brad Inwood, Inwood 1995a, and Inwood 2004.

[13] On the *quaestiones* in the treatise that serve as 'hard cases' used to clarify philosophical points, see pp. 120–2, 135–42.

Seneca's previous responses to this question, in *De beneficiis*, have been given in contexts concerning the possible application of the law to cases of ingratitude—so it is not surprising that, in the *Letter*, we are going to hear a lot about judges and judgement.[14] First, in Book 3, where he has come to the third of his principal topics, that of returning benefits, Seneca considers whether or not ingratitude should be punishable by law (3. 6–17) and concludes that it should not. One reason is that the assessments involved in determining the value of benefits and injuries would be too complex (3. 7–12), and one difficult case he considers is this one:

> Aliquis dedit mihi beneficium, sed idem postea fecit iniuriam. Utrum uno munere ad patientiam iniuriarum omnium adstringor, an proinde erit ac si gratiam rettulerim, quia beneficium suum ipse insequenti iniuria rescidit? Quomodo deinde aestimabis, utrum plus sit, quod accepit, an quo laesus est? Dies me deficiet omnes difficultates persequi temptantem. (3. 12. 4)

> Someone gave me a benefit, but the same person later inflicted an injury on me. Am I committed by one gift to tolerate any and every injury? Or is it as though I had returned his favour because he cancelled his benefit by the subsequent injury? So how will you assess which is greater, the benefit received or the injury suffered? If I try to work through all the problems, there will not be enough hours in the day.

The unexpected shift in focus between the assessment of the case by the recipient (*mihi, adstringor, rettulerim, me*) and by a third party (*aestimabis*), who is neither the recipient nor the injurious benefactor, is something which we shall meet again in *Letter* 81. The substantive question posed by the recipient in the form of two alternative solutions is not resolved here. The first solution mentioned—total forgiveness of the injury—is not seriously pursued here, because the second solution—counting the injury suffered as a repayment of the benefit—suits the context better, in that it illustrates the problems that a legal settlement would involve, of calculating the relative weights of the benefit and the injury. It is worth noting that the argument given here in support of this second solution, that the subsequent injury has cancelled the benefit, is badly formulated, as Seneca will make clear in Book 6 of the treatise: there he will argue that one cannot cancel a benefit, because the benefit, properly understood, is the act of giving, and that subsequent behaviour can only spoil a benefit, removing the obligation to be grateful and to return the favour (6. 2. 2).[15] In *Letter* 81 that erroneous formulation of the balancing process will be avoided, and Seneca will ultimately come closer to the first solution.

---

[14] Inwood 2004 discusses Seneca's frequent use of the model of a judge in treating the moral agent, including the passages in *Letter* 81 (pp. 212–18). For a sketch of the use of legal terminology by Cicero and Seneca, see Griffin 2013.

[15] The verb here for undoing the benefit, *rescindere*, appears in 6. 2. 2, though the verb most often used in 6. 2–4 is *eripere*.

In Book 6, where the question is raised again of a benefactor who then injures one, the context is precisely this issue of whether a benefit can be cancelled. Seneca there explains:

> Non abstulit beneficium, sed opponendo illi parem iniuriam solvit me debito, et, si plus laesit, quam ante profuerat, non tantum gratia extinguitur, sed ulciscendi querendique libertas fit, ubi in comparatione beneficii praeponderavit iniuria. (6. 4. 1)

> He has not taken the benefit away but, by setting against it an equal injury, he has freed me from my debt; and, if he wronged me more than he previously benefited me, not only is any gratitude extinguished, but I am free to retaliate and remonstrate, when the injury has outweighed the benefit.

He adds at the end of the discussion:

> Dedisti beneficium, iniuriam postea fecisti; et beneficio gratia debebatur et iniuriae ultio; nec ego illi gratiam debeo nec ille mihi poenam: alter ab altero absolvitur. (6. 5. 1)

> You conferred a benefit, and afterwards, you inflicted an injury; gratitude was owed for the benefit and revenge for the injury; neither do I owe him gratitude nor does he owe me a penalty: one debt is cancelled by the other.

The similarity in language, especially of the first passage, to the formulation of this question in *Letter* 81. 3, 15,[16] supports the idea that it is this same question that is here answered in the affirmative, while the additional point made in the *Letter*, about the injury having greater weight, is here said to allow at least a grievance to remain. Next, Liberalis is represented as tired of the distinction between cancelling the benefit and removing the obligation it imposes, but eager to pursue the practical question of how to deal with the injurious benefactor: should I respond separately to the benefit and the injury, with gratitude and revenge, as one does in the courts,[17] 'or ought I to combine one with the other and do nothing, the benefit being removed by the injury and the injury by the benefit?' (*an alterum alteri contribuere et nihil negotii habere, ut beneficium iniuria tollatur, beneficio iniuria?*, 6. 5. 3–5). Seneca explains that, since benefits are not subject to the law, the recipient makes the decision: 'Rather, having compared the benefit and the injury, I shall ascertain whether anything further is owed to me' (*Potius comparatione facta inter se beneficii et iniuriae videbo, an mihi etiam ultro debeatur*, 6. 6. 2). So the same question that will be asked in the *Letter* is here again, as in *Ben.* 6. 4. 1, answered in the affirmative, but Seneca does not spell out this time what an imbalance licenses the recipient to do. He ends the discussion by correcting Liberalis, who has deliberately used

---

[16] *an is, qui profuit nobis, si postea nocuit, paria fecerit et nos debito solverit* (*Ep.* 81. 3); *in hac comparatione beneficii et iniuriae* (*Ep.* 81. 15).

[17] See **ad 6. 4. 4 debitori suo creditor** on the apparent contradiction with the legal cases adduced at 6. 4. 2 *fin.* and 6. 4. 5, where injury does seem to be weighed against a debt.

one of the expressions ruled out in that previous discussion, i.e. *beneficium tollere*.[18] Seneca insists that the benefit is not removed, only rendered invisible (6. 6. 3).

Letter 81 effectively takes up this question, of how to deal with an injurious benefactor, where *De beneficiis* left it. It is 'a kind of appendix to the treatise'.[19] Indeed, as we have seen, the context in which the discussion of the question arose in the treatise is still apparent in the concern with judges and judgement in the letter. It is not hard to see why Seneca was dissatisfied with his earlier treatments of this difficult question, when we consider the humane attitude to ingrates that he reached by the end of *De beneficiis* and advocated in its closing chapter, a chapter which he recalls in the opening of the letter. For those earlier treatments rested on the idea of repaying injury by injury, a view which Seneca had already disclaimed in previous works.[20]

In *Letter* 81, having posed the question 'whether a benefactor who later injured us, has balanced things out and released us from our debt' in §3, Seneca devotes to it a considerable portion of the letter: but he interrupts this discussion in order to consider the difference between the Sage and the Fool as far as returning benefits goes (8–14), and to defend the paradox 'only the Sage knows how to return a favour' (*Ep.* 81. 11). Then, marking the latter topic (15) as something already sufficiently examined (presumably in *De beneficiis* 5. 12–17), Seneca returns to finish the question of the injurious benefactor (15–17). After this, in the last sections of the *Letter*, he discusses the issue of gratitude more generally: returning a benefit, when rightly understood, as it is by the Sage, yields more joy than receiving one, because it is a virtuous act (17–23). But though the Sage alone has the wisdom to understand this (24–6)—for he alone knows the true value of things (27)—ordinary opinion, though it leads us to wrong valuations and hence to ingratitude (29), also regards gratitude as the most honourable of things (30). In fact, the shame this induces in the ungrateful can make it dangerous to confer great benefits on anyone, 'for, since he then knows it is shameful not to repay, he does not want there to be anyone whom he should repay' (32).[21]

---

[18] Cf. 6. 4. 2 *non beneficium tollitur, sed beneficii gratia, et efficitur, non ne habeam, sed ne debeam.*

[19] The phrase used by Inwood 1995a, 249 n. 44 = 2005, 75 n. 43.

[20] *Ira* 2. 32. 1–3; *Clem.* 1. 20. 2; 1. 7. 3 where *ignoscite* and *videtur* show that Seneca dissents from the idea that private citizens are right to feel they need to take revenge on wrongs to them.

[21] It is hard to resist the temptation to see in this curiously negative ending (a much stronger version of what is said in *De beneficiis* 3. 1. 1 *fin.*) Seneca's anticipation of Nero's ingratitude, which would cause his own death: he actually died about a year after the dramatic date of *Letter* 81, and near in time to its publication (on which see Griffin 1976, 349, 418 n. 4). There is perhaps an echo of the passage in the sentence Tacitus gives the philosopher, 'Who did not know that Nero was cruel? Nothing was left, after he killed his mother and father, than that he should add the killing of his teacher and instructor' (*educatoris praeceptorisque*, *Ann.* 15. 62. 2): the last leaves a strong hint of ingratitude, given *Ben.* 3. 17. 4 (*non educatoris non praeceptorum*); 6. 15. 2; 6. 16–17.

This pessimistic close, however, comes as a surprise, after the exhilarating depiction of the attitude of the Sage earlier on. Seneca perhaps wants to bring us back to the level of the *imperfectus*, with an echo of *De vita beata*, where the ill effects of public opinion on ordinary people were so vividly described (1. 2–2. 2).

In fact, in *Letter* 81 problems about moral level confront us already in the discussion of the question concerning the injurious benefactor. Thus we hear of the opinion of a 'strict judge' (*rigidus iudex*) and of a 'more lenient judge' (*remissior iudex*), but also of a *vir bonus* who appears in §6 and again in §15, after the interruption about the Sage. Is any of these identical with the Sage? The point is a vexed one,[22] not to be resolved lexicographically.[23] As will emerge in what follows, I do not think any of these is identical with the Sage.

The first thing to notice is that the *vir bonus*, on both his appearances, is the recipient himself, as is emphasized in both cases.[24] The *rigidus iudex* is brought in to adjudicate between the two parties, and he gives his just opinion (4) that benefits and injuries can balance out, because, 'although the injuries are greater, credit must be given to the benefits for what remains after the injury' (*quamquam iniuriae praeponderent, tamen beneficiis donetur, quod ex iniuria superest*). The grounds for this decision are, apparently, that the greater weight of the injury is balanced by the fact that the benefit came first.[25] In an aside (5–6), Seneca mentions that, of course, the state of mind of the benefactor (later injurer) must be considered, but, as this is hard to conjecture, he proceeds on the assumption that a true benefit and a true injury are involved, and that the injury is greater. The recipient, if he is a 'reasonable man of good

---

[22] Inwood appears to have changed his mind on this point between his earlier essay, where he thought none of them identical with the Sage 'who only comes into the discussion as sole possessor of relevant moral certainty first at 81. 8' (Inwood 1995a, 251 n. 54, cf. 252 nn. 55, 56 = 2005, 77 n. 53, 78 nn. 54, 55) and the later one, where he identifies the *vir bonus* (and apparently the *rigidus iudex*) with the Sage (Inwood 2004, 86 = 2005, 216).

[23] *Vir bonus*, which has a legal resonance from *formulae* containing clauses related to *bona fides* and from the provision in some contracts for arbitration by a *vir bonus*, is used by Cicero to denote 'good men' in common parlance, as opposed to Sages, and particularly men known for justice (*Off.* 1. 20; 3. 17; 1. 31; 2. 33; 2. 38). In *Ep.* 42. 1 Seneca points up the ambiguity of the phrase, as between the Sage (who occurs rarely if at all) and the *vir bonus secundae notae*, who is making progress. In *Ep.* 11. 8–10 we are told to adopt a *vir bonus* as a guardian: either one who is *rigidus* like Cato, or one who is *remissioris animi* like Laelius.

[24] 'The good man so makes his calculations of both (benefit and injury), that he himself limits himself (*utrosque calculos sic ponit, ut se ipse circumscribat*) in §6, and 'he will overlook it, that is if the injury exclusively affects himself (*remittet; id est, si ad ipsum tota pertinebit iniuria*) in §16.

[25] I agree here with the interpretation of Bellincioni 1984b, 174 (= Bellincioni 1986, 113). Inwood 1995a, 251 n. 52 = 2005, 77 n. 51 thinks a new point is introduced with *plus nocuit; sed prius profuit*, and suggests that the *ex iniuria superest* is literally something that is still enjoyed after the injury. But *Ben.* 6. 6. 1 (if Seneca is making a similar point) is against this: *ultra debeatur* here cannot be a part of the benefit still enjoyed, because the benefit is no longer visible beneath the injury. Again in *Ben.* 6. 4. 6 we are told that the endurance of the benefit does not guarantee that it imposes an obligation, if the giver spoils it by his subsequent grudging attitude.

moral intentions',[26] will now apply the assessment of the *rigidus iudex* to himself: he will set limits to his own calculations and add to the benefit and subtract from the injury, thus balancing them out (6). This gives an affirmative answer to the question posed in §3.[27]

Seneca, however, prefers a different solution. He now declares a preference for the opinion of the *remissior iudex*, who orders the injury to be forgotten, and only the service remembered. To Lucilius' objection (7) that this is against justice, which requires gratitude to be given for a benefit and requital for an injury, Seneca replies that this view is only true when separate agents are involved, not the same agent.[28] In the latter case, the force of the injury is extinguished by the benefit. As an illustration, he notes that, if someone deserves pardon for an offence without doing good deeds previously, he deserves more than pardon if he conferred prior benefits.[29] 'For I do not set an equal value on benefits and injuries. I give more weight to a benefit than to an injury'(8).

The passage on the Sage that follows (8–14) apparently explains this advice. 'The Sage will examine all the circumstances in his own mind: how much he has received, from whom, when, where, and how' (§10). By contrast, the ordinary man of good moral intentions does not know how to measure his debt of gratitude, and so he is better off not trying to calculate the relative weight of benefit and injury too exactly, but should incline towards the side of the benefit.

When the discussion of the question resumes (15), the *vir bonus* (the recipient again) favours the benefit, because it is a benefit. He will calculate the relative weight of benefit and injury, taking into consideration factors such as the persons affected (besides the recipient), but he will overlook a small overbalance on the side of the injury; in fact, he will ignore even a much greater injury, will incline to excuse it, and will be unwilling to regard the benefit as repaid by the injury, but will wish actually to repay it (16–17). He is thus following the assessment of the *remissior iudex*, given in §6, and answering the question initially posed in §3—whether he is released from his debt—in the negative.

Neither the first (affirmative) answer nor the second (negative) answer is that of the Sage, who, like the *vir bonus*, considers the question as a recipient of the benefit and of the subsequent injury, but comes up with a more precise answer. For the Sage dismisses the injury done to him and remains well disposed to his benefactor *unless the bad deeds far outdistance the good, and in an obvious way* (25). When they heavily preponderate, he goes as far as resuming the neutral attitude he had towards the person before he conferred the benefit

---

[26] The phrase used for *vir bonus* by Inwood 1995*a*, 251 n. 54 = 2005, 77 n. 53.

[27] I follow here the interpretation of Bellincioni 1984*b*, 173–5, as does Inwood 2004, 86 = 2005, 215.

[28] Bellincioni 1984*b*, 181 (= Bellincioni 1986, 122) rightly regards as a rhetorical strategy this concession to the stern Stoic view of justice as practical wisdom in distributing what is deserved (Griffin 1976, 158); see above, n. 20.

[29] On this passage, see Inwood 1995*a*, 252 n. 55 = 2005, 78 n. 54.

and the injury on him: he regards himself as owing the person nothing and resents nothing. That is, his assessment is less severe than that of the *rigidus iudex*, in that he agrees with his advice to balance out benefit and injury, but only when the injury heavily preponderates, and not when it is only somewhat greater. On the other hand, his assessment is more severe than that of the *remissior iudex*, in that he does not always dismiss the injury done to him, but does so only when the injury does not far outdistance the good. And it is only when benefit and injury are equal, that he will retain some benevolent feelings, and, while having no obligation, will go on wanting to have one, and will behave like someone who pays his debts even after they have been legally cancelled (25–6). The Sage, then, does not go as far in the direction of strictness as the *vir bonus* when he is following the *rigidus iudex*, or as far in the direction of laxity as the *vir bonus* when he is following the *remissior iudex*: the Sage can be just without being strict, like the former; he can be humane without being indiscriminately generous, like the latter. The reason is that he is capable of making an accurate calculation as to the weight of the benefit and of the injury, whereas the *vir bonus* is not. For ordinary people of good moral intention, the hyperbolic generosity advocated by the *remissior iudex* is the better course. As Seneca says, towards the end of *De beneficiis*, 'When you cannot quite trust the people to whom you are giving orders you must demand more of them than is necessary, so that the necessary level of compliance is achieved. The point of hyperbole is, in every case, to get to the truth by way of a falsehood' (7. 23. 1).

Letter 81 then continues the forward movement of *De beneficiis* itself, towards a more humane solution to the problem of ingratitude. In keeping with the generous attitude to ingratitude at the end of the treatise, where we are reminded that we too suffer from the vice and are *imperfecti*, Seneca here reconsiders the question of a benefit followed by an injury, to which he gave an unsatisfactory answer when he treated it as a subordinate topic in the treatise. Seneca's rethinking here shows that it was not just a rhetorical flourish, when he wrote that the primary job of philosophy is to teach us to owe and to repay benefits well. If we had the comprehensive work on ethics, the *Moralis Philosophia* that he was working on at the dramatic date of the later *Letters* (106, 108, 109), i.e. the autumn of 64, we might well have seen a further development of his humane attitudes. In any case, *Letter* 81 underlines Seneca's belief that the social instinct implanted in humans by providence, and the role of benefits in binding together human society, should take priority over cruder calculations of justice.

Appendix: Synopsis of *Letter* 81

1–3   Introduction

> 1 Lucilius has met an ingrate: he is advised not to become ungenerous.
>
> 1–2 Perseverance will bring success in finding gratitude.
>
> 3 These points were treated sufficiently in *De beneficiis*, but not the question that follows.

3–8   Has a benefactor who later injured us balanced things and released us from our debt?

> > 3 Let us assume that the later injury is much greater than the benefit.
>
> 4–6 The strict judge gives, as his just opinion, a positive answer: the priority of the benefit balances the greater weight of the injury.
>
> > 5 The question of the benefactor's attitude affects the weighting but is hard to assess: so we just assume the injury was greater.
> >
> > 6 The good man will restrict himself (to balancing the account) by adding to the benefit and subtracting from the injury.
>
> 6–8 The more lenient judge prescribes forgetting the injury, remembering the service. Seneca prefers this view, as benefits have more weight than injuries, when performed by the same person.

8–14   Only the sage knows how to return a benefit; the fool lacks the knowledge to gauge the amount, the time, the place, the manner, of its return.

> 9–10 The correct expression *referre gratiam* shows it must be voluntary.

15–17 The question about the benefactor who later injures receives a negative answer.

> 15–16 The good man, judging as the recipient, will ignore the discrepancy in weight, even if it is great.
>
> 17   He will not let the injury balance out the benefit but will want to make a return.

17–23 Returning a benefit brings greater joy than receiving.

    18 A benefit, like a loan, should be repaid with interest.

    19 Showing gratitude, a virtuous act, brings happiness, while ingratitude brings unhappiness.

24–6 The Sage gains eternal joy from remembering benefits received and deliberately forgets his injuries.

    25 When the subsequent injury is far greater than the benefit, he returns to his neutral attitude before the benefit.

    26 When the subsequent injury is equal to the benefit, he retains benevolence and ceases to owe, but not to want to owe, a return.

27–9 Gratitude requires knowing the true value of things.

    29 We are misled by public opinion.

30–2 Public opinion is right to advocate gratitude.

    32 Shame at an inadequate return leads to dangerous ingratitude.

9

The Afterlife of *De beneficiis* up to the Renaissance

In comparison with some works of Seneca, *De clementia* and the *Epistulae morales* in particular, *De beneficiis* is a self-effacing work. It has rarely been quoted or cited by name by authors who have made use of it, and its presence can be inferred more often than it is attested.

The anonymous author of the *Octavia*, and the poets Statius, Martial, and Juvenal, show that Seneca was highly regarded after his death, well into the first decades of the second century. Not even the satirists were interested in pursuing the criticisms of his lifestyle that had plagued Seneca in his last years, or in imitating the irony with which Petronius had treated his liberal views on slavery (*Ep.* 47, cf. *Sat.* 71).[1] Quintilian (10. 1. 125–31), Fronto (*De orationibus* 1–4), and Aulus Gellius (*NA* 12. 2), who were themselves critical of his style and literary tastes, felt it necessary to issue warnings aimed at discouraging the young from reading Seneca's prose. Despite the implication in Tacitus' *Annals* and in Suetonius' *Life of Caligula* that he was no longer in fashion in their day,[2] Seneca continued to be read 'down to the threshold of the Dark Ages', that is the seventh and eighth centuries. Nonetheless, we have no evidence that the poets and stylistic critics mentioned above were acquainted with *De beneficiis* in particular.[3] Even when Aulus Gellius quotes, as one of the few good remarks he can find in Seneca, an epigram about avarice, it is not in the form in which it is found in the treatise.[4]

---

[1] Trillitzsch 1971, i. 44–8, 53–4, 56–61. The historians Tacitus, at *Ann.* 13. 42, and later Cassius Dio, at 61. 10, do report Suillius Rufus' charges of hypocrisy.

[2] Tac. *Ann.* 13. 3. 1: Seneca's funeral speech for Claudius showed 'an attractive talent and one suited to contemporary ears' (*ingenium amoenum et temporis eius auribus accommodatum*); Suet. *Cal.* 53. 2: Caligula's criticisms of 'Seneca, then very much in fashion' (*Seneca tum maxime placentem*).

[3] Holford-Strevens 2003, 277 n. 75, however, suggests that Marcus Aurelius disobeyed Fronto and finds an echo of *Ben.* 5. 6. 2, 6 in *Med.* 11. 25. The praise of Seneca's generosity by Martial (*Epig.* 12. 36. 8–10) and Juvenal (5. 108–10) contains no hint of his literary celebration of generosity.

[4] 'What does it matter how much you have? There is far more that you don't have' (*quid enim refert quantum habeas? multo illud plus est, quod non habes*, *NA* 12. 2. 13), cf. 'Let him compare what he has with what he desires: he is still a poor man' (*quidquid habet, ei, quod cupit, comparet: pauper est*, *Ben.* 7. 10. 6), cited by Trillitzsch 1971, i. 74.

The historian Tacitus, however, as we have suggested (pp. 84–7), did make use of the treatise for the dialogue between Seneca and Nero that he included in the *Annals* under the year 62, and he clearly expected his readers to recognize the similarity of themes and ideas. Seneca is made to discuss the problems of receiving benefits; Nero is concerned with giving and returning benefits. Thus, between them, they cover the three topics the treatise aims to discuss (*Ben.* 1. 4. 3). The exchange of benefits that Tacitus treats here is the problematic one between those who are unequal in power, in this case, between ruler and ruled. It is well represented in *De beneficiis*, which deals with imperial gifts and favours in all but one book, and which shows mostly the negative side of imperial generosity and the difficulties experienced by recipients. All Nero's predecessors as Princeps provide concrete examples of doubtful gifts, and it is through such counter-examples that Seneca teaches how the ruler should give.[5] Tacitus does not, however, use Senecan vocabulary: he even eschews the term *beneficium*. He does not imitate Seneca's favourite prose rhythms either.[6] How far he alludes to Seneca's stylistic 'tics' has been actively debated. The presence of military imagery and the reference to *studia in umbra educata* are hardly peculiar to Seneca. More telling are the abrupt start and the personal address, features with which several of Seneca's dialogues begin, such as *De providentia* and *De brevitate vitae*: in *De beneficiis*, too, Seneca comes straight to the point. There is also the catalogue of questions that Seneca gives, and the use of *animus* as the subject of concrete activities which would be more suitably attributed to an actual person.[7]

The Latin church fathers knew Seneca's works well. In the early third century Tertullian, for whom he is 'Seneca, often one of our own' (*Seneca saepe noster, De anima* 20) actually quotes from *De beneficiis* (unnamed) from memory (*Ben.* 4.6.6); Lactantius, in the fourth century, provides many fragments from lost works; while Jerome's little biography of Seneca, written in 393, mentioning for the first time the correspondence with St Paul, ensured that Seneca's philosophy would be read by the Christian world. It is likely that the correspondence was forged precisely between Lactantius' assessment of Seneca as 'the most acute of all Stoics' (*Inst.* 2. 8. 23) in 325 and Jerome's mention of it.[8] St Augustine had doubts about the correspondence (*Ep.* 153. 14), and regarded Seneca as hypocritical in practising traditional pagan religion, while knowing it was false. However, Jerome's assessment of Seneca, as a man of virtuous life, he did not contest.

---

[5] Brinkmann 2002, 27–31. The preponderance in *De beneficiis* of *exempla* showing the way emperors confer gifts was noted by Mayer 1991, 159, 162 (= 2008, 307, 310).

[6] Woodman 2010.

[7] As pointed out by Grimal 1967. On the last, see **ad 7. 1. 7 si animum virtuti consecravit.** Syme 1958*a*, i. 335 found distinctive Senecan expressions and imagery in the dialogue.

[8] Momigliano 1955, 20–1.

Seneca was known to late antique pagan authors, but we have mostly scattered allusions, such as Sidonius Apollinaris' misunderstanding, in the fifth century, of Martial's celebration at *Epig.* 1. 61. 7–8 of two Senecas, father and son, as a reference to a tragedian Seneca and a philosopher Seneca (*Carm.* 9. 232–6): a division that was to linger on into the late seventeenth century.[9] Macrobius, however, in his *Saturnalia*, used, for a discussion of the humane treatment of slaves (1. 11. 23–4), not only Seneca's *Letter* 47 but the anecdote about the siege of Grumentum in *De beneficiis* 3. 23. This Senecan theme was to be picked up by writers in the Middle Ages.

In the sixth century Bishop Martin of Braga dedicated to King Miro a work entitled the *Formula vitae honestae*, which was very popular in the Middle Ages, when it passed for a genuine Senecan work (it was first unmasked by Petrarch, then again by Erasmus[10]). 'Spain rewarded its son by plagiarizing his work', in the words of Leighton Reynolds.[11] Since the Bishop had previously composed a work *De ira*, which is a mosaic of quoted and transmuted passages from Seneca's *De ira*, it is usually assumed that one particular Senecan work lies behind Martin's later work too (see Ch. 2, p. 21). The usual candidate is Seneca's lost treatise *De officiis*, attested by the grammarian Diomedes (fr. 57 Vottero; fr. 25 Haase), for Martin's *Formula* is organized around the four cardinal virtues, like Cicero's *De officiis*, and it would not be unreasonable to assume that Seneca's work of that title was similarly organized.[12]

The first of Seneca's works to emerge after the Dark Ages were *De beneficiis* and *De clementia*, which were copied in north Italy about the year 800. This manuscript is the archetype of the medieval tradition, and it still exists as the Codex Nazarianus, known as N, now in the Vatican library (Pal. lat. 1547). So does another ninth-century manuscript, known as R (Reg. lat. 1529): the Codex Reginensis, probably a direct copy of N incorporating corrections made in the hand called N^2.[13] It is from R that all the rest of our extant manuscripts descend. After a dormant period, copies begin to be made in the late eleventh century, spreading out from northern France, where R had ended up in one of the monasteries on the Loire.[14] The first quotation from *De beneficiis*, giving

---

[9] Trillitzsch 1971, i. 190; Ker 2009, 197–8. The implicit combining of the Elder Seneca, author of the declamations, with his son was to be repeated by Boccaccio in the 14th c. and only began to be sorted out at the end of the 15th, by Paolo Pompilio (Panizza 1984, 67–8, 70).

[10] Blüher 1969, 27.   [11] L. D. Reynolds 1983, 358.

[12] See Ch. 2 n. 32. Martin's four virtues are *prudentia*, *magnanimitas*, *continentia*, and *iustitia*. It is worth noting that when Seneca lists the four cardinal virtues, he uses *fortitudo*, not *magnanimitas*, and that he usually prefers *temperantia* to *continentia*.

[13] Busonero 2000. Gertz in his edition realized that N was the most authoritative evidence for the text of *De beneficiis* and *De clementia*, and he made it the basis of his edition of 1876. The Hosius text of 1914 that I generally follow, and on which the Loeb edition of 1935 by Basore and the translation by Cooper and Procopé 1995 are generally based, unfortunately rests on the idea that R is independent testimony, alongside N, to the lost archetype.

[14] L. D. Reynolds 1983, 363–4.

the name of the author, is in the *Chronicle* of Hugo of Flavigny in that region, written in the last decade of the eleventh century, and both works are listed in the catalogue, dated to 1093, of the abbey at Pomposa in northern Italy.[15] By the twelfth century, the text of the two works was available even in England and Germany; by the thirteenth century, in Spain as well.[16]

The Middle Ages inherited a picture of Seneca as a virtuous man whose philosophy had many overlaps with Christianity. The supposed friendship between Seneca and St Paul, widely accepted, may help to explain, not only the popularity of Seneca's writings in the Middle Ages, but the positive view taken of them. In transmission, the two treatises De *clementia and De beneficiis* may have been separated off from the other Senecan works and combined, because of their common theme of leniency and generosity;[17] but in any case their combination is symptomatic of the use to which they would be put after the renewed dissemination of Seneca's works. In Germany, in France, in Italy, and in Spain, both treatises were used to provide advice to rulers in the 'Mirror for Princes' tradition, *De clementia* actually furnishing the image of the mirror and giving political advice, *De beneficiis* offering exhortations to liberality and cautions against heeding flattery. The idea was to provide an ethical basis for rule, based on nature, not on religion, but compatible with Christianity. It drew on the ancient idea of the virtuous ruler, supported by willing subjects. Notdurft shows how, in the work *Moralium dogma philosophorum* written by William of Conches for the young Henry of Anjou, who in 1154 became Henry II of England, *De beneficiis* is used, along with Cicero's *De officiis*, to provide advice on how and what to give and on showing gratitude, including not complaining of ingratitude.[18] The humane view, in Seneca's treatise, of how to treat slaves is also applied to the serfs of his time. John of Salisbury followed Wilhelm, as did Giraldus Cambrensis, who, however, also brought in *De clementia*. In Italy, the roots of the Mirror of Princes tradition, which Machiavelli was to attack in the sixteenth century, can be traced back to the thirteenth century.[19] In Spain too, from the thirteenth century to the sixteenth, *De clementia* was read as a work of political ethics, a *Fürstenspiegel* geared to princely education, while *De beneficiis* was read as a tract about princely liberality, a subject central to that education.[20]

It would take another book-length study to collect and discuss allusions to *De beneficiis* in later centuries, and it is unlikely to be as illuminating for our present study of the work itself, as this sketch of the early history of its reception. For what is shown by the use to which *De beneficiis* was put immediately

---

[15] Mazzoli 1978, 92–7; L. D. Reynolds 1983, 364–5.
[16] Blüher 1969, 32–41.   [17] As suggested by Mazzoli 1978, 86.
[18] Nothdurft 1963, 93–122.   [19] Stacey 2007.
[20] Blüher 1969, 48, 75–78, 203. He points out (77) that, in the 13th and 14th centuries, *De beneficiis* was mostly known at second hand, particularly from William of Conches, whose *Moralium dogma philosophorum* was the source used by the author of the *Libro del Caballero Zifar*, and by Juan García de Castrojeriz, author of the *Glosa Castellana al* Regimiento de Príncipes *de Egidio Romano*.

after its re-emergence on the European cultural scene is that, even before Tacitus' work was rediscovered in the late fourteenth century, readers saw what the historian had seen: the theme of liberality between ruler and ruled was central to Seneca's concerns. This lends support, first, to Bellincioni's notion of *De beneficiis* and *De clementia* as related works, developing a doctrine governing the exercise of power (pp. 153–4). It also lends verisimilitude to the interpretation of *De beneficiis* given in Ch. 3 from the perspective of social history. For Seneca's essay has many aspects. It is a treatment, from the Stoic point of view, of an important topic in moral philosophy; it is a guide to ethical behaviour in relations of social exchange; and, finally, it is an analysis of the Roman aristocratic code of beneficence, which insists on the inclusion of the Princeps within aristocratic society, and which holds him to the same ideals in giving and receiving gifts as are appropriate for his nominal peers.

Part III

A Map of *De beneficiis*

Synopses with Accompanying Notes

The Notes are meant to be used with the Synopses and are primarily designed to help readers follow Seneca's argument. They make no claim to being a full commentary. In references to other chapters of the same book, the Notes give the book number in brackets, e.g. chapter 1. 3–5 of Book 5 appears as (5.) 1. 3–5 in the Notes to Book 5, but as 5. 1. 3–5 elsewhere.

For proper names, readers should check the Biographical Notes: names marked with an asterisk in the index are included in the Biographical Notes.

Textual problems are only mentioned where I have departed from the Teubner text of Hosius (2nd edn., 1914) on a matter of importance to the sense of the passage. N is the Codex Nazarianus, the medieval archetype; N^2 the hand that corrected it on the basis of conjecture; R the codex Reginensis, which incorporates the corrections by N^2 (see p. 166 and n. 13).

Finally, I shall explain the reason why I normally translate the key word *beneficium* as 'benefit'. Brad Inwood and I decided on this translation in Griffin and Inwood 2011, aware that there is no perfect English translation. Cooper and Procopé 1995 preferred 'favour', which they defended on p. 184. Their objection to 'benefit', the traditional translation, is that the meaning of 'benefit' in current English usage is too narrow: whereas in the days of Thomas Lodge's translation of 1614 it could mean also 'a good deed' or 'a kindly deed', its ordinary meaning now is 'advantage, profit, good', according to the *Oxford English Dictionary*. They argue that this focus on the result of an act of generosity, that is on the service or object received, ill represents the Latin *beneficium*, which means, strictly, 'benefaction' or 'kindly deed'.

They go on to quote, in support, *De beneficiis* 2. 34. 5, where Seneca says that the term *beneficium* covers both 'an action that does good (*actio benefica*) and an object bestowed by that action'. Seneca does indeed like to insist that the real *beneficium* is the intentional act: both in giving and returning, intention is the most important thing. At 1. 6. 1 he has defined *beneficium* as 'a well-intentioned action' (*benevola actio*), a phrase that lays even more emphasis on attitude than does *actio benefica*, which reflects the role of *facere* in the etymology of the word and implies that the intention leads to an action that actually does the recipient good.

However, this insistence of Seneca is necessary precisely because he is deliberately going against the normal connotations of the Latin word *beneficium*, which, as I argue at pp. 105–10, concern the service or material thing given. Seneca's usage here is, therefore, paradoxical, because it runs counter to the ordinary meaning of a concrete service or thing; in fact, the discussion in 2. 34. 5 occurs during a discussion of the Stoic paradox *eum, qui libenter accipit, beneficium reddidisse*, where intention is stressed on the other side of the transaction, the return of a benefit. Since, therefore, the implication of 'result' in the English word 'benefit' is not untrue to the ordinary Latin meaning of *beneficium*, and since Seneca's definitions, if they are to retain their paradoxical impact, need to be given against the background of that usage, I have persisted in using 'benefit' to translate the term *beneficium*. 'Benefit' also retains the etymological resonance of doing real good to someone, not just acceding to a request for a favour, and it connects with 'benefaction' and 'beneficence' which have the same resonance. Seneca shows himself conscious of the etymology at *Ben.* 5. 10. 3, and often develops the idea that real good must be done to the recipient (e.g. 2. 14; 5. 12. 3; 5. 20. 1–4; 6. 7. 3).

As for 'favour', Cooper and Procopé themselves (ad loc.) admit that it does not quite convey the idea they want of 'kind deed' or 'act of kindness' either. Again, as in Griffin and Inwood 2011, I have preferred to use it to render *gratia* in its active concrete sense, 'a favour given in return', in such expressions as *gratiam referre* and *gratiam reddere* (see pp. 103–4; p. 116 n. 20).

Synopsis of Book 1

---

*   The text is uncertain.   † There is a lacuna here.

10. 5 **To whom the benefit is given should matter, but we should not be too restrictive in helping the unworthy *qua* human beings.**

11–15 **What benefits should be given [‡and how they should be given].**

    11. 1–4   *Necessary Things*
        11. 2–3 Things indispensable to life
        11. 4   Things that make live worth living:
                liberty, chastity, good conscience
                Things that make life desirable:
                protection of family and home

    11. 5   *Useful Things*: money, public office

    11. 5–15 *Agreeable Things*
        12. 1–2 These should be enduring.
        12. 3   These should be suited to the time, place, and person.
        12.4–14 These should be rare and particular to the person:
                example of Alexander and the Corinthians.
        15   They should not be promiscuous but involve a judgement of worth: contrasting examples of Augustus and Claudius.

‡   This topic is in fact postponed to Book 2.

Notes to Synopsis of Book 1

Book 1 is by far the shortest of the seven books of *De beneficiis*, even allowing for the missing material between §§9. 1 and 9. 2.

Chapters 1–9 form an introduction to the whole work, in which Seneca:

(1–3. 1) explains the importance of giving and receiving benefits properly;

(3. 2–4) acknowledges and criticizes the approach of his Greek philosophical predecessors, urging the need for a law of life teaching us to give, to receive, and to return benefits gladly;

(5–9. 1) defines the true nature of a *beneficium*.

The remainder of the book (9. 2–15) begins the discussion of the first subject: giving benefits.

(1.) 1–3. 1. The opening and closing chapters of the work exhibit symmetry, as has been noted by Sonntag 1913, 11, 59 and Abel 1987*a*, 18 = 1995, 59 (see Ch. 6 n. 29). These chapters of Book 1 treat (in 1. 1–1. 8) the way in which giving incorrectly promotes ingratitude and (in 1. 9–3. 1) the correct response to ingratitude: perseverance in imitation of the gods (1. 9), giving for the sake of giving (1. 9–2. 3), realizing that multiple benefits can overcome ingratitude (2. 4–3. 1). In the closing chapters of Book 7 (26–32), Seneca treats these same themes but not in the same or the reverse order: 26. 2–28 treat the correct response to ingratitude, 29–30 the contribution to ingratitude made by incorrect giving, 31 deals with the need to persevere with persistent giving, like the gods, 32 with the intrinsic value of giving. The mood of the close of the work, however, is more humane and hopeful than the start. Thus the image of sowing is used in both ((1.) 1. 2; 7. 32) but differently. It is a common metaphor for giving benefits (e.g. Xen. *Mem*. 2. 1. 28; *Cyrop*. 1. 6. 11; Hor. *Ep*. 1. 7. 21–2) because the return in both cases is not normally immediate and depends both on sowing in appropriate soil = giving correctly to an appropriate beneficiary (*Ben*. 4. 9. 2), and tending the crop = following up the benefit (*Ben*. 2. 11. 4–5). Whereas in Book (1.) 1. 2 the metaphor is used to show that giving indiscriminately to the wrong people is responsible for ingratitude, in Book 7. 32 it is used to show that repeated cultivation of the most unpromising beneficiaries can at last overcome ingratitude. There is a corresponding change in what is said about the vice of ingratitude in the two books. In (1.) 1. 2 it is the most common vice, and in (1.) 10. 4 the worst vice and the origin of the others, and the donor is warned off committing it himself. In 7. 26. 4–28 ingratitude is one vice among others, and the donor who complains of it is probably not exempt from it himself.

These opening chapters already introduce the key themes that run through the whole work: that giving benefits is worthwhile in itself and that we should imitate the gods in this, is most fully developed in Book 4; that we should not remind beneficiaries to make a return or even remember our benefit ((1.) 2. 3), recurs at (1.) 4. 5; 2. 10. 4 and reaches its definitive treatment at 7. 22. 1. Also characteristic of the work as a whole is the heavy emphasis placed here (despite the opening coupling of mistakes in giving and receiving), as it will be at the end of the work, on the giver, the person similar in social position to Seneca himself and to his addressee as depicted at 5. 1. 3–5 (see Ch. 3B, 3E). As in his other works, Seneca, through heavy use of the second person plural, directs his castigation and exhortation to himself, as well as to his addressee and his readers.

(1.) 1. 1 errores (mistakes). For the Stoics, vice is a condition of mental sickness whose foundation is ignorance involving errors of judgement concerning values. The wicked man (*malus*) is a foolish man (*stultus*), Seneca says at 4. 26. 2; 5. 15. 1: one who rashly assents to propositions that misidentify as good and worth pursuing, or bad and to be avoided, things that are for the most part indifferent in value, since virtue and vice themselves are the only truly good and bad things. The vice of ingratitude in (1.) 1. 2 can therefore be traced to the errors mentioned here in receiving benefits (that is, in evaluating the benefits we receive). See L–S i. 385, Plut. *Mor.* 440 E–441 D; Marc. Aur. 8. 14.

nihil propemodum (almost nothing). The manuscript tradition has an apparent lacuna, since a neuter comparative adjective is clearly required to qualify this phrase, either before *dixerim* or after it. Most editors suggest a word signifying the degree of evil (*turpius, foedius*) implicit in the errors, or one signifying the prevalence of the errors in giving and receiving. But Seneca immediately after seems to be concentrating on the evil *consequences* of giving improperly, so that Lipsius' suggestion *nocentius* (more harmful), which he places after *dixerim*, would capture the meaning better. Concentrating on our ignorance of giving for the moment (overlooking *nec accipere*), Seneca explains that whatever we give improperly is received ungratefully.

male collocata (ill placed). The metaphor of debt is common throughout the work and is followed up immediately by *nomina facturi* (about to make a loan) and *vitam debitoris* (the way of life of the debtor) in (1.) 1. 2 and *genus huius crediti* (kind of loan) and *decoquere* (default) in (1.) 1. 3. For Seneca's use of the metaphor, despite his insistence on denying the similarity of a benefit to a loan, see Ch. 3A pp. 39–40.

(1.) 1. 2 non eligimus dignos quibus tribuamus (we do not select worthy recipients of our gifts). Since conferring a benefit is a virtuous act ((1.) 5. 3 *fin*), it must be a rational act based on judgement (see **ad (1.) 5. 3**); otherwise, it is just *inconsulta facilitas* (unreflective niceness). Seneca often lists the headings for our deliberations, as in (1.) 12. 3: occasion, place, people, and 2. 16. 1: who, to whom, when, why, where (in response to a critic who lists: to whom, where, how), or in 4. 10. 2: when, to whom, how, why. Aristotle (*NE* 4. 1. 1120ᵃ 25–6) had already said that the *eleutherios* would give rightly 'to the right people, the right amount, at the right time'. Seneca repeatedly stresses *dilectus*, as at (1.) 1. 2, and *iudicium*, as at (1.) 1. 15 (discrimination and judgement); and Valerius Maximus 4. 8 gives *verum iudicium* with *honesta benivolentia* as the two sources of rational *liberalitas*. Cicero in *De Officiis* 1. 45–50; 2. 61–3, 69–71 also discusses the choice of worthy recipients of generosity, linking it to the definition of justice as giving to each his due (1. 42). Seneca emphasizes the criterion of capacity to show gratitude. The brief discussion below ((1.) 10. 5) of 'to whom we should give' softens the view here, recommending giving, though to a lesser degree, to those who we know will be ungrateful.

(1.) 1. 8 *fin.* satis adversus illum gratus est, si quis beneficio eius ignoscit (The beneficiary shows such a person sufficient gratitude, if he forgives his benefit). The paradox makes an effective end to the subject in giving a powerful thrust to the fault of the donor. The fact of human nature, that injuries are remembered more than benefits, is a common sentiment (e.g Tac. *Hist.* 4. 3. 2; Dio 46. 34. 2).

(1.) 1. 9 tam effusa nec cessante benignitate (from their profuse and ceaseless generosity). Lipsius' correction of the mss. reading *effusa necessitate*.

(1.) 2. 1. The verses from an unknown author, 'When you set out to shower benefits on the multitude/ many must be lost to make one good gift' (Palliata fr. inc. 70 Ribb.) offer conventional wisdom about not expecting a return on each of many benefits. Seneca is critical of the first line on two counts: the multitude is not the proper recipient of generous giving, and there is no respectable way to make lavish gifts of anything, least of all benefits, if you eliminate judgement. *Largitio* has a pejorative sense in the Republic (see Kloft 1970, 40–1), as is clear in Sall. *Cat.* 3. 3; Cic. *De Or.* 2. 105; *Off.* 1. 43; 2. 53. It lost its pejorative colour in the Later Empire (Kloft 1970, 159). Cicero in *Off.* 2. 52 uses the term *largitio* of financial favours as opposed to favours in kind, which he esteems more because they do not exhaust their own means. But he goes on at 2. 55 to distinguish a good and a bad type of *largitio*.

(1.) 2. 4. Seneca's fivefold division of benefits here bears a certain resemblance to the fourfold one, attributed to Plato by D.L. 3. 95, into money (*chrēmasin*) = Seneca's *re*; personal services (*sōmasin*) = Seneca's *gratia* (influence); knowledge (*epistēmasin*) = Seneca's *consilio*; and speech (*tois logois*) = Seneca's *praeceptis salubribus*. Seneca's *fide* should probably be taken closely with *re* (in the sense of financial credit, as in 3. 15. 1, 7. 16. 3) or with *gratia*, in the sense of support. There is no sign in Seneca of the sharp division between financial benefits and other benefits that is so important for Cicero (*Off.* 2. 52).

(1.) 3. 2–4. 6. After the ringing end of the opening exhortation ('besiege him with your benefits'), Seneca glances ahead to his definition of a *beneficium* at (1.) 5 and then announces a digression on the Three Graces, the end of which is marked at (1.) 4. 5–6 where the material is branded as *ineptiae* (absurdities) and *anilia argumenta* (arguments fit only for old women). But in fact this section introduces the threefold division of the subject into giving, receiving, and returning, which will govern the first three books: first, at (1.) 3. 3, via Chrysippus' allegory; then at (1.) 4. 2–3, via the demand for a *lex vitae* (law of life). Chapters (1.) 3. 8–9 also serve to acknowledge the only previous philosophical treatments that Seneca mentions by author in *Ben.* (cf. the general acknowledgement to 'all philosophical writers' (*omnes auctores sapientiae*) at 2. 9. 1): the *Peri charitōn* of Chrysippus (attested by Philodemus, *SVF* ii. 1081), probably the work also mentioned at 2. 17. 3; 2. 25. 3; 3. 22. 1, and a work of Hecato which transcribed ((1.) 3. 9) some of Chrysippus' discussion of the Graces, probably the same as is mentioned at 2. 18. 2; 2. 21. 4; 3. 18. 1; 6. 37. 1. The latter could have been the attested *Peri kathēkontos* (mentioned in Cicero's *De Officiis* 3. 63; 89) or an unattested *Peri charitos*. According to Seneca, the Stoics were free to criticize their founders without becoming unorthodox (*Ot.* 3. 1; *Ep.* 33. 4, 8–11).

The allegorical interpretation of the Gratiae ((1.) 3. 3), which translates the Greek Charites, involves reinterpreting *charis*, which was originally applied to the Graces in the abstract sense of 'grace' or 'joy', in its concrete sense of a benefit given or returned. The allegory may be a Stoic speciality (see pp. 100–1). In Chrysippus' interpretation, the Graces symbolize the three stages of a benign process: giving a benefit, receiving (or accepting) it, and returning it; in the other interpretation, at (1.) 3. 3 (which may also be Stoic), they symbolize three kinds of benign activity: 'taking the initiative, returning the favour, accepting it with a graciousness that is tantamount to returning it'; so Cooper and Procopé 1995, 197, n. 6, who suggest (ibid. nn. 5–6) that both versions are Stoic and both inadequate, as 'the process of giving, accepting and returning a favour only needs two participants'. The allegory found in the Peripatetic doxography (see Ch. 5 n. 11) gives the three elements as giving, returning, and remembering, which avoids having one figure accept and another return, but which still presents a problem visually. The development of the allegory by Chrysippus also includes this element of memory, symbolized by the enduring youth of the maidens (1. 3. 5), as well as the idea of joy, which Epicurus connected with giving, and with the names of the Graces (fr. 544 Usener), but which Chrysippus connected with their facial expressions (**ad 2. 2. 2**). Cooper and Procopé are also critical of the allegory, because in the visual representations, the central figure 'the one who graciously gets and gives, is not returning the gift so much as passing it on'. However, the principal significance that Chrysippus' allegory derives from the position of the Graces, as opposed to their number and their individual appearance, is that they are indissolubly linked, as part of a continuous process. It is true that Seneca says 'benefit passing from hand to hand returns nevertheless to the giver', but that cannot be what he thought the Graces as depicted were doing, for their hands are interlocked (1. 3. 2, 4). Nor can Servius (ad *Aen.* 1. 720), who writes 'That one of them is pictured from the back while the two others face us is because for one benefit issuing from us two are supposed to return', apparently inspired by a nude representation such as is preserved from Pompeii, be thinking that his linked Graces are literally handing presents back and forth, because the single giver, with her back to us would have to be receiving from both those facing her, and either giving to one only or to both, both of which are absurd visually. The Peripatetic doxographer could not have imagined one of the Graces represented as remembering, while the other two exchanged gifts. On the visual representations inspired by the nude classical representation as interpreted to fit with Seneca, see Wind 1958.

(1.) 3. 6 **quae nomina Hesiodus imposuerit** (the names which Hesiod gave). In the *Theogony* 906–10, *Aglaië* means 'splendour', *Euphrosynē* 'joy', and *Thalia* 'flowering'. The mention of the Grace Pasithea occurs in Homer, *Iliad* 14. 275–6.

(1.) 3. 7 **Mercurius una stat, non quia beneficia ratio commendat vel oratio** (Mercury stands beside them too, not because it is reason or discourse that urges us to give benefits). Seneca is thinking of Hermes Logios, *ratio* and *oratio* being the two Latin words used in combination to capture the double meaning of the Greek word *logos* at least since Cicero (e.g. *Rep.* 2. 66; *Tusc.* 4. 38,. 60; *Off.* 1. 50), cf. *Ben.* 4. 8. 1. On the association of Hermes and the Charites, see Moussy 1966, 443–4.

(1.) 3. 8 **Chrysippus.** Seneca often criticizes Greek philosophers for displaying ingenuity and erudition irrelevant to practical moral teaching. So did Cicero before him, for example, in *De Orat.* 2. 18 where the same word *ineptiae* (1. 3. 8) is used of the inappropriateness of Greek displays of cleverness. Seneca adds to the effect by his Roman images: *nomenclator, in censum* ((1.) 3. 10); *novae tabulae* ((1.) 4. 6). Seneca sometimes targets dialectic; here, theological allegory and poetic analysis (cf. fr. 46 Haase = 24 Vottero).

(1.) 3. 10 **nomenclatori memoriae loco audacia est** (a nomenclator uses bravado in place of his memory). The *nomenclator* was a slave who accompanied his master in order to prompt him with the names of people he encountered. The rudeness of these slaves, who had the power to refuse entry to the *salutatio* or levée, is noted by Seneca in *Const.* 14. 1 and *Tranq.* 12. 6.

Thalia, de qua cum maxime agitur, apud Hesiodum Charis est, apud Homerum Musa (Thalia, with we are specially concerned, is a Grace in Hesiod, a Muse in Homer). In fact, Homer does not name the Muses, but Hesiod does, and lists a *Thaleia* among them (*Theog.* 77).

(1.) 4. 1. The remarks about oversharp *acumen* and pinpricks allude to the arid style that Seneca and Cicero criticized in Stoic philosophers (*Ira* 2. 1; *Epp.* 82. 8–9; 113. 1, cf. Cic. *Tusc* 3. 13; *Fin.* 4. 3, 52; *Parad. St.* pref. 2).

(1.) 4. 2 **danda lex vitae** (a law of life must be laid down). In *Ep.* 94. 39 philosophy itself is said to be the 'law of life'; in *Ep.* 90. 34 the 'law of life' means a set of general principles developed by the Sage. Closer to the usage here is the phrase 'laws of life as a whole' in *Ep.* 95. 57: these are apparently equivalent to the basic truths of Stoic doctrine (covering various areas), which must be learned before virtuous acts can be performed. *Ep.* 108. 6 speaks of philosophers giving to those who will listen 'a law of life, by which they may test their characters'.

liberalitatem quae nec deesse oportet nec superfluere (generosity which must neither fall short nor go to excess). The conception of virtue as a 'mean', invented by Aristotle, was still identified as Peripatetic by Cicero in the Stoic-inspired *De officiis* (Cic. *Off.* 1. 89), though he uses it at 2. 59 as Seneca does here and in *Ben.* 2. 16. 2; 2. 34. 4; *Ira* 2. 17. 2; *Clem* 1. 2. 2. That the notion is prominent in the *Formula honestae vitae* of Martin of Braga would not, therefore, count against Martin's reliance, in whole or in part, on Seneca's *De officiis* (Bickel 1905, 533): see Ch. 2 n. 32 and p. 166.

(1.) 4. 5 ut, qui praestiterunt, obliviscantur, pertinax sit memoria debentium (so that the donors forget, while those who owe retain a persistent memory). Seneca expects his readers to take for granted this piece of popular morality: see Nep. *Att.* 11. 5, 'He retained the kindnesses he had received in an unfading memory, while those he had himself bestowed he remembered for as long as the recipient was grateful.' Seneca, who regards not reminding someone of a benefit you have bestowed as one of the essential precepts, lays down the same asymmetrical rule at 2. 10. 4. He then modifies and refines the popular notion at 5. 20. 7–25, and, at the end of the work (7. 22. 2–25), he explains what this precept actually requires of the donor.

(1.) 4. 6 rem perniciosissimam, beneficiorum novas tabulas (the most destructive possible development, the introduction of fresh account ledgers for benefits). Seneca borrows the language of the frequent demands for cancellation of debts, so disliked by the Roman establishment. He implies that the elimination of the obligation to return benefits would be as big a moral disaster as the elimination of the obligation to return debts would be a financial disaster.

(1.) 5. 1–9. 1. Seneca, while eschewing further preliminaries, nonetheless feels obliged to define the subject of his enquiry, as Plato had insisted should be done (*Phdr.* 263 D) and as Cicero felt Panaetius should have done (*Off.* 1. 7). At 1. 5. 2, where he distinguishes the matter of a *beneficium* and the *beneficium* itself, and at 1. 5. 5, where he talks of the things and services given taking the false name of *beneficium*, Seneca assumes that to apply the term to what is given, rather than to the act of giving, is a mistake made by the ignorant. But at 2. 34. 5–35. 1, he reveals that the word *beneficium* is actually ambiguous, owing to the poverty of language, so that it has both meanings. Throughout the work Seneca himself often uses *beneficium* in the 'wrong' sense, though he sticks to his restricted definition until 1. 11, when he starts the discussion of what *beneficia* should be given. See pp. 105–7.

(1.) 5. 3. Seneca characterizes the 'act of benevolence' that is the true *beneficium*, as a *recte factum* (= *katorthōma*), a virtuous act done from a fully and permanently virtuous state of mind, such as only the Sage possesses. But Seneca's insistence on intention as the defining criterion (already implied in *libenter* at (1.) 1. 4. 3) would apply also to the wider category of *kathēkonta*, of which the *katorthōma* is a special case, for a *kathēkon* is a proper function dictated by reason and having a rational justification (D.L. 7. 107–8; *SVF* iii. 494). Agents who have not yet achieved perfection, those at whom his teaching is directed (2. 18. 4; 5. 14. 5; see Ch. 7 n. 20), can perform such acts.

(1.) **5. 5 ut aliubi sit species rei, aliubi ipsa res** (the appearance of something is one thing, the thing itself is another). The visible symbols of honour are taken from three categories: military decorations (the collar of twisted metal, the crown with turrets for being the first to scale a besieged city's wall, the civic crown of oak leaves for saving the life of a fellow citizen); paraphernalia of magisterial office (the purple-bordered toga, the bundles of rods carried before a magistrate by lictors, the platform on which the magistrate sat to give judgement); the chariot used in a triumphal procession.

(1.) **6. 2 id autem, quod fit aut datur, nec bonum nec malum est** (but what is done or given is neither good nor bad). Seneca alludes here, in non-technical language, to the Stoic doctrine of the 'indifferents', according to which nothing is good but virtue, nothing bad but vice, and everything else is strictly speaking 'indifferent', in that it makes no difference to happiness. Those things that tend to preservation of life are normally to be preferred or chosen, and those that are not appropriate to our constitution are normally not to be chosen. Virtue does not exist in a vacuum: its activities require choices to be made concerning how to use the indifferents: L–S i. 357–9.

(1.) **7. 1 qui 'regum aequavit opes animo'** (who matched the wealth of kings with his intention). Virgil *G.* 4. 132 has 'animis' and is speaking of the old man of Corycus, who was content with his little farm; Seneca may prefer the singular, to indicate the proper intention of the modest giver.

(1.) **8. 1 Itaque dono tibi, quod unum habeo, me ipsum** (And so I give you the only thing I have, myself). Seneca closes his discussion of the true nature of a *beneficium* with an anecdote about Socrates and his poor pupil, Aeschines, for whom see the unflattering account in D.L. 2. 60–4. The offer of Aeschines is quoted at D.L. 2. 34. Though elsewhere Socrates is himself the *exemplum*, and Seneca treats offerings from Socrates' pupils at 7. 24 as returns for his *beneficium* of teaching, here Aeschines is the *exemplum*, and what the pupils give are *beneficia*. See the illuminating discussion of the anecdote in Bellincioni 1986, 103–12.

(1.) **9. 1 vides, quomodo animus inveniat liberalitatis materiam etiam inter augustias** (you see how the spirit can discover the raw material for generosity, even amidst straitened circumstances). Aeschines illustrates the true nature of a benefit, not so much by the manner of his giving, but by the fact that he gives, not a material thing at all (an indifferent), but something truly good (*honestum*), that is, his moral being. Socrates realizes that he must reciprocate by effecting a moral improvement in his student, as a good teacher should (see 6. 16. 6; 6. 17. 2).

neque est, quod existimes illum vilem sibi fuisse: pretium se sui fecit (There is no reason for you to think that he set a low value on himself: he gave himself as payment for himself). As Bellincioni 1986, 106–9 explains, a thing that is *pretium sui*, 'its own reward', is a true good without price, sought for itself alone, like virtue in *Vit. Beat.* 9. 4.

(1.) **9. 2–10. 5.** Seneca starts the discussion proper, with the first of the subjects listed in (1.) 4. 2–3: to give gladly. There it was said that giving must not be 'unreflective niceness' (*inconsulta facilitas*). The headings under which the performer of a *beneficium* as a rational act must deliberate are variously given (see ad (1.) 1. 2), but the choice of donor (where it is included) and the choice of recipient are always at the top, or near the top, of the list. Seneca here follows the order: who ((1.) 9. 1–2), to whom (marked at (1.) 10. 5), what, and how (marked at (1.) 11. 1), though the last is actually postponed to Book 2, where it includes 'when' (2. 1. 2–2. 2. 2; 2. 4–2. 5. 4) and possibly 'where' (2. 10. 1). He follows the same order in discussing receiving benefits in Book 2 (see **ad 2. 18–35**).

(1.) 9. 2. As most editors think, there is probably a lacuna before *callidus* ('shrewd'), but the train of thought can be reconstructed. As Guglielmino 1968, 488 indicates, Seneca has just mentioned at (1.) 9. 1 the *ingeniosus adulescens* ('talented young man') whose behaviour shows that it is not how much or what is given, but the quality of the person from whom they come, that matters (*a quali prospiciendum*, the reading of N); the shrewd man is his negative counterpart, the man with a fortune who wants to avoid giving and deliberately creates false expectations. Therefore, what we are missing could be part of the treatment of the first topic under giving benefits, i.e. who should give (see Préchac 1961 *ad loc*). The whole discussion need not have been long (*pace* Cooper and Procopé 1995, 204 n. 27) because in Book 2. 18. 3–21 Seneca will treat the same subject matter under the topic 'from whom we should receive'.

(1.) 9. 3–5. This digression recalls Quintilian's description (10. 1. 129) of Seneca as an *egregius vitiorum insectator* (outstanding lambaster of vice). For Seneca and most Stoics, such rhetorical *exhortationes, obiurgationes, suasiones, dissuasiones*, were an important part of teaching. Seneca relates them closely to the giving of precepts, with which the early books of *De beneficiis* are largely concerned (Ch. 7A), and sees all of these techniques as forming part of the *praeceptiva pars* of the ethical division of philosophy, which he regarded as necessary, but not sufficient, to the attainment of virtue (*Ep.* 94. 39; 95. 1; 95. 65 = Posidonius fr. 176 E–K, with Kidd 1988, 646–81).

(1.) 9. 4 inde decentissimum sponsaliorum genus (as a result, adultery is the most respectable sort of betrothal). The text is disputed (Cooper and Procopé 1995 follow N in reading *certissimum*, not *decentissimum*: 'the most reliable route to betrothal'), but the general sense seems to be that, since adultery is now the normal prelude to matrimony, widowerhood and bachelorhood are common, since only those who are married can acquire wives by adultery.

(1.) 9. 5 quoniam, quae emeris, vendere gentium ius est (since it is the practice of nations to sell what you have bought). Seneca closes his recital of contemporary vice with avarice, especially destructive in those with authority. This ironic excuse for extortion and judicial corruption implies that provincial governors, and magistrates carrying judicial power, regularly bribe their way into office. Curiously, Seneca nowhere suggests that such conduct is regarded, or excused, as an exchange of *beneficia*, albeit of a questionable kind (see Ch. 3D). On *ius gentium* see **ad 3. 14. 3**.

(1.) 10. 1–3. On the incidence of vice in different ages Seneca, like Tacitus (*Ann.* 3. 55. 5), explicitly rejects the idea, so popular in the ancient world, of a progressive moral decline (see p. 59). Where Seneca uses the image of different vices advancing and receding like waves, Tacitus uses the image of a revolving globe with different moral climates coming round like the seasons. Tacitus leaves open the possibility of improvement; for Seneca there will always be human wickedness, cf. *Ira* 3. 27. 3; *Clem.* 1. 6. 3–4.

(1.) 10. 4 infra omnia ista ingratus est, nisi quod omnia ista ab ingrato sunt (lower than all of these is the ungrateful man—unless, of course, all those crimes actually stem from ingratitude). In describing ingratitude as the worst of vices, Seneca follows popular conceptions (e.g. Plaut. *Bacch.* 394), in defiance of the Stoic paradox that all wrong actions are equal (*SVF* i. 224, 450; iii. 527–33; Cic. *Parad. St.* 20–6). The qualification about all crimes stemming from ingratitude may be a bow in the direction of another paradox, 'He who has one vice has them all' (*SVF* iii. 560, discussed in *Ben.* 4. 27), which Seneca associates with this one at *Ben.* 5. 15. 1–2; but the same idea occurs in a non-philosophical context in Cic. *Att.* 8. 4. 2 ('there is no evil not included in this vice') and see p. 25. With the vice of ingratitude, the climax of the digression, Seneca moves the argument on from consideration of the right kind of donor to that of the right kind of recipient.

(1.) 10. 5 salutarem vocem homini non pigebit emittere (it will not bother me to utter the cry that will save a human being). See **ad 4. 29. 3.**

(1.) 11. 1–15. After the brief discussions of 'who' (1. 9. 2) and 'to whom' (1. 10. 5), Seneca ends with an extended discussion of 'what'. He uses the division into which jurists divide *impensa* (expenses) on dotal property, in order to calculate what deductions could be made when it was returned in the process of divorce (*Dig.*25.1): *necessariae, utiles, voluptariae* (necessary, useful, and agreeable), though Seneca avoids the term *voluptaria*, preferring *iucunda* for the last (cf. also *Ep.* 116. 1). In dealing with the first two divisions, he designates categories of services and gifts that people in general will find necessary to life (1. 11. 1–4) and useful (1. 11. 5). In dealing with the third (1. 11. 5–15), however, he gradually reveals that considering 'what', when deciding on a particular act of beneficence, involves considering 'when', 'where', 'to whom', 'from whom', and finally 'how', thus making a bridge to the treatment of 'how' in Book 2, where he explicitly says (2. 16. 1) that nothing in itself makes a fitting gift: everything depends on the particular circumstances, in assessing which the donor shows his good intentions, the essential element of a *beneficium* (1. 6. 1). In Book 2, qualifications in individual cases appear for *necessaria* (2. 9. 2) and *utilia* (2. 14. 1).

(1.) 11. 1 iucunda utique mansura (agreeable things, particularly those that will last). Seneca singles out, in his third division (agreeable gifts), the category of enduring things, which he discusses in 1. 12. 1–2. That is because other gifts in this division are agreeable only in relation to the particular circumstances at the time (see n. above).

(1.) 11. 2 sine quibus non possumus vivere (without which we cannot live). For the jurists, the category of *necessariae* are those needed to preserve the value of the property (*Dig.* 25. 1. 14). The analogue is preserving the life of the individual, which Seneca takes in the broad sense of preserving a life worth living.

(1.) 11. 5 nec enim utilius quicquam est quam sibi utilem fieri (nothing is more useful than to be made useful to oneself). The reading *sibi* of the archetype N has been questioned: suggestions include *civi* (Préchac 1961) and *ibi* (Alexander 1950–2a, 7, followed by Cooper and Procopé 1995; Griffin and Inwood 2011). Shackleton Bailey 1970, 361 suggests a lacuna before this clause. However, the jurists construe the category of useful expenses as those that improve, rather than merely preserve, the property. By analogy, Seneca's *utilia* enable the person to be independent of others' benefits, useful to himself and hence to others, cf. *Otio* 3. 5, *quisquis bene de se meretur hoc ipso aliis prodest quod illis profuturum parat* '(whoever deserves well of himself benefits others by the very fact that he prepares what will prove beneficial to them'), though there he is speaking of self-improvement through the life of contemplation.

(1.) 13. 1–3. Alexander is, in *De beneficiis* and in Seneca's works generally, as in Lucan (*BC* 10. 20–48), a bad example. Plutarch (*Mor.* 826 c–d) tells only the beginning of the story, with the variant that the donors are the Megarians, not the Corinthians, and Alexander is not negatively presented. In Seneca's version, Alexander as a recipient starts well, but the comparison with Hercules provokes the usual tirade (e.g. *Ben.* 7. 3): as a donor, he is worse (*Ben.* 2. 16. 1; 5. 6. 1). There is no need to posit an allusion to Nero, as does Picone 2009: Stoic writers, like Epictetus and Marcus Aurelius as well, were bound to disapprove of his arrogance (his alleged claim to be the son of Ammon, and his adoption of the style of the Persian king) and of his overweening ambition (Brunt 1977, 39–48). See **ad 7. 2. 5–3. 1.**

(1.) 13. 3 tam hostium pernicies quam amicorum (as dangerous to his enemies as he was to his friends). The killing of friends, notably Clitus, is noted by Seneca in the extended attack on the cruelty of Alexander in *De Clementia* 1. 25. 1. The logical inversion of the two halves of the comparison here, with the more surprising element coming second, not first, as we expect, is a characteristic Senecan trick (Gertz 1874, 62–3; 1876, 277). Other examples in *De beneficiis* with *tam . . . quam* can be found at 4. 28. 4; 5. 7. 4; 6. 32. 2; 6. 38. 5; and with other comparative constructions at 2. 17. 2; 3. 29. 7; 6. 40. 1; 7. 12. 2; 7. 19. 6. Translators often invert the elements or equalize them.

(1.) 14. 1 convivam dantis epulum (guest of the host of a public banquet). Seneca returns again to the question of individual gratitude for communal benefits at 4. 28. 2 and 6. 19. There, however, it is benefits of the gods to the human race, which cannot exclude unworthy individuals, or grants of grain or of citizenship given by the Emperor, where individual recipients cannot be selected. Here the gifts need not be given to many at once (at an inn), and even when they are (at a public banquet), the giver can make the gift personally and distinguish between recipients. Seneca clearly does not have euergetism in mind.

(1.) 15. The climax of the book is Seneca's insistence on judgement (**ad 1. 1. 2**), which he treats vividly in presenting the two contrary examples of Augustus and Claudius, and the comments of C. Sallustius Passienus Crispus, whose shrewdness in judging character Seneca praises at *NQ* 4, pref. 6. (On these people, see Biographical Notes.) With these comments Seneca agrees, though the philosopher goes further in denying the status of a *beneficium* altogether to gifts conferred indiscriminately. For judgement demanded of the Princeps, see Ch. 3C, and on Claudius' *facilitas*, **ad 6. 19. 2**. With Tac. *Ann.* 12. 61. 2 criticizing Claudius for giving the inhabitants of Cos immunity from Roman taxation, not in recognition of its many services to Rome but as a personal favour to his Coan doctor, cf. *ILS* 206, vv. 30–3, where the Emperor justifies his own mass *beneficium* of Roman citizenship to some Alpine tribes in terms of service to Rome.

(1.) 15. 1 ego vero beneficiis non obicio moras (I certainly place no obstacles in the way of benefits). Seneca introduces the recurrent theme of the work, already anticipated at 14. 1: his aim in teaching is to encourage the reciprocal process of exchanging benefits. Since this book is about how to give benefits, it is the encouragement of giving that he stresses at this point (see Ch. 3A and Inwood 1995*a*, 263–4 = 2005, 91–2).

(1.) 15. 3 nisi quam virtutem modus fecit (unless it is made into a virtue by the imposition of a limit). See **ad (1.) 4. 2 liberalitatem quae nec deesse oportet**.

(1.) 15. 6 quid ista inter se mixta dividimus? (why do we separate things that are thoroughly mixed together?). The worthless judgement of Claudius is intimately connected with the gift he gave. So one might think it odd to separate the thing given from the judgement which lay behind the gift. But they must be evaluated separately, since there is a reason to accept the gift (even though the bad judgement of the donor prevents it from being a true benefit) and to reject the reason why it was given.

Synopsis of Book 2

18–35 PROPER CONDUCT IN RECEIVING BENEFITS

18. 1–2   In cases where duties are reciprocal, the same rule should apply to both parties: a rule prescribed by reason.

18. 3–21   From whom: reason dictates that we should only receive benefits from those to whom we would give them.

18. 3–5   *For* imperfecti, *it is important to be even more discriminating in this than in giving, as obligation can irritate, especially as a permanent relationship of friendship is formed.*

18. 6–21. 2   *Givers from whom we should accept but whose gifts do not count as benefits and so impose no obligation of gratitude or bond of friendship:*

18. 6–20   Only what a willing giver affords a willing recipient is a benefit.

6–7   A gift from a tyrant, unwillingly received, should be accepted but without obligation.

18. 8–19   A gift, however beneficial, is not a benefit if given without intent to benefit. Cf. with a beast who cannot will to do one good.

20   Example of Brutus, who received his life without obligation because Caesar's ability to grant it rested on inflicted injury.

21. 1–2   Accept being saved from a disreputable man as a loan to be repaid, not as the foundation of friendship.

21. 3–6   *Givers whose gifts we should refuse.*

21. 3   Don't accept a benefit that will disadvantage and endanger a worthy giver.

21. 4   Hecato's example of a *filiusfamilias* is faulty, as he has no property to give.

21. 5   Graecinus was right to refuse contributions to his games from senators of ill-repute.

22–35   How benefits should be received.

22–5   *Receive a benefit with joy, acknowledge it publicly, declare your gratitude.*

23–4. 1   Do not evince shame by not speaking well of your benefactor.

24. 2–25 Show your gratitude by manner, language, and facial expression, especially for large benefits. Example of Augustus and Furnius.

25. 3 Begin immediately to think of repaying the benefit.

26–30 *What makes men ungrateful: conceit, greed, envy.*

26–27. 2 Conceit. Example of Lentulus Augur and Augustus.

27. 3–4 Greed and ambition bring discontent.

28 Envy makes us feel that benefits are insufficient.

29–30 Our ingratitude to the gods leads to these attitudes. Their benefits show there is no excuse for ingratitude, since gratitude is the only return we can make to them.

31–5 *Who receives a benefit gladly has repaid it: the most acceptable Stoic paradox.*

32 Comparison with a ball-game: failure to return the ball does not mean the player is not good, though the playing is imperfect.

33–4.1 What is received in return is extra to the requital of the benefit, for the real exchange of benefits is between minds.

34. 2–35 The two senses of benefit, action and object, explain the paradox: the act is requited by gratitude, the object requires an object in return. Point of the paradox is to remove fears of receiving benefits.

Notes to Synopsis of Book 2

Book 2 completes the discussion of proper conduct in giving benefits, which began in 1. 9. 2–1. 15, and goes on to cover, at (2.) 18. 1, the second subject listed in 1. 4. 3: proper conduct in receiving benefits. At the end, the chapters on ingratitude ((2.) 26–30) lead to an extended treatment of the Stoic paradox, 'He who receives a benefit gladly has already returned it' ((2.) 31–5), which in turn forms a bridge to Book 3 and to the third and last subject listed in 1. 4. 3: returning benefits.

(2.) 1–17. Having announced at 1. 11. 1 the topics of what benefits should be given and how, Seneca only completed the first of these in Book 1. 11–15 and deferred the second to Book 2. He marks the conclusion of the discussion of 'how to give' at (2.) 18. 1. The extended negative example of Caligula's arrogance, and the personification of Pride in (2.) 11. 6–13, separate the treatment in (2.) 1–11. 5 of 'how to give', in the obvious sense of the donor's manner and attitude, from the topics in (2.) 14–17. 3, that seem to fit uneasily under 'how' and could almost be presented as 'what gifts to give'—a supplement to the discussion in Book 1. 11–15. However, Seneca is actually insisting on the judgement and discrimination needed in particular acts of giving, as he had already indicated in discussing 'agreeable' gifts in Book 1 (**ad 1. 11. 1–1. 15**) and as he notes during the present discussion at (2.) 16. 1. 'How' here covers all the considerations listed in (2.) 16. 1 (except 'who' and 'to whom', already treated in Book 1), such as 'when', 'why', 'where': cf. the broad use of 'how' to cover all the headings under 'giving' and 'receiving' in Book 5. 1. 1.

(2.) 1. 1 quomodo vellemus accipere (in the way in which we should want to receive). By adducing the 'Golden Rule', Seneca recalls the connection of incorrect giving with ingratitude, made in *Ben.* 1. 1. 1–8, cf. (2.) 11. 6.

(2.) 1. 2 libenter (willingly). At 1. 4. 3 the three beneficent activities were each qualified by *libenter*: the requirement that benefits be conferred promptly and without hesitation is intimately connected with this demand, for such conduct is the outward demonstration of willingness ((2.) 2. 2; (2.) 5. 4).

(2.) 1. 2 multi autem sunt, quos liberales facit <in> fortes infirmitas (In fact, many people become generous only because they are feeble in the face of determined requests). The reading is Alexander's suggestion (Alexander 1937, 56), closer to the mss. consensus than Hosius' *facit frontis infirmitas*, which Cooper and Procopé 1995 translate 'there are many whose liberality is due simply to the lack of a firm frown'. Alexander does not repeat his suggestion in the 1950–2*a* publication.

(2.) **1. 3 os concurrat et suffundatur rubor** (his lips freeze together and he blushes all over). The same combination of signs of embarrassment occurs in *Ep.* 11. 2–3, in which Seneca discusses the involuntary physical reactions that accompany the involuntary emotional reactions that even the Sage experiences. Reason can prevent these *ictus animi* (or *propatheiai*) from becoming full-blown passions, by withholding assent. Seneca 's fullest discussion is in *Ira* 2. 1–4. It is disputed whether this doctrine originated in the early Stoa or was developed by later Stoics. The interest in the physical reactions is characteristic of Seneca, but also found in Epictetus (fr. 9 Schenkl, reported by Gell. *NA* 19. 1).

(2.) **1. 4 ut maioribus nostris gravissimis viris visum est** (as our ancestors, the weightiest authorities, thought). This looks ahead to the view of Fabius Verrucosus at (2.) 7. 1. For Seneca 's use of the *maiores*, see p. 59, n.122. Publilius Syrus, the first-century-BC mime writer, stresses not making people ask (57, 591 Duff and Duff).

vota homines parcius facerent (men would be more sparing with their vows to the gods). The comparison with the gods as donors is a persistent theme in *De beneficiis*, already appearing in 1. 1. 9, and again in (2.) 29 and 6. 20–3, and especially in Book 4 (4–9.1; 17–19; 25–32): see pp. 26, 119.

(2.) **2. 1 huius facienda est gratia amico et quemcumque amicum sis promerendo facturus** (you must spare from having to say it, a friend and anyone whom you intend to make a friend, by doing a service). The creation of friendship through conferring benefits is an important theme of the work (e.g. (2.) 4. 2–3; (2.) 18. 5; (2.) 21. 2), and Seneca regards benefits given to strangers, who are thus made friends, as more valuable than those given to existing friends (3. 12. 1). See pp. 27–8, 36–9.

(2.) **2. 2 itaque laetus facit et induit sibi animi sui vultum** (and so the donor gives happily and his facial expression displays his state of mind). The need to give gladly is in Aristotle (*NE* 4. 1. 1120ᵃ26–7). Seneca characteristically stresses facial expression in 1. 1. 5 (inappropriate), in 1. 3. 5, where the *vultus* (faces) of the Graces are said to be *hilari*, and in (2.) 13. 2 on the expression which a superior should wear.

(2.) **3. 2 adicias licet familiarem querellam** (you might add the friendly rebuke). On Seneca 's renditions of current polite (and impolite) language, see pp. 47, 67–8. The mention of an intermediary is surprisingly rare in Seneca, the treatment in (2.) 4. 2–3 being the only discussion, and a hostile one, of a practice common in Seneca's day (see pp. 78–81).

(2.) **4. 3 sine ulla, quod aiunt, deductione** (as they say, without any deduction). The metaphor is legal and financial. This expression *deductio* is used by the jurists of deductions for expenses, etc., when a dowry is being restored in divorce cases (*Dig.* 25. 1. 16; 31. 41. 1), or a *peculium* in inheritance cases (*Dig.* 12. 6. 38; 15. 1. 11. 2), or in the settlement of claims between sellers and buyers (Gai. *Inst.* 4. 65–8). It is found on inscriptions recording the fulfilment of testamentary requests without deduction for expenses (*CIL* ii. 1473–4) and, with *integra* as in Seneca here, of a testamentary benefaction handed over in full by the heirs (*CIL* ix. 449).

(2.) 5. 1 aequiore quidam animo ferunt praecidi spem suam quam trahi (some people can bear with more equanimity having their hopes dashed than having them stalled). Cf. Mart. 6. 20; 6.30; 7. 43. See p. 80.

(2.) 7. 2–8. 2. Tiberius is often an example of stinginess in Seneca, but this episode elicits a statement of policy from the *amicus principis* (see pp. 63, 82, 94). Marius Nepos is not named in the accounts of Tiberius' behaviour in Tac. *Ann.* 1. 75 and Suet. *Tib.* 47, but Tacitus names him in 2. 48.3 among those indebted profligates removed from the senate, or allowed to withdraw, by the Princeps. For this way of dealing with senators in debt, i.e. insisting that debtors make their case to the senate before helping them, Suetonius ascribes to Tiberius the same motive of discouraging requests for help as Seneca ((2.) 7. 3); Tacitus only mentions such discouragement as the result, not the motive, and he still applies the term *beneficium* to the emperor's assistance. The story in Macrob. *Sat.* 2. 4. 23, 'Without being asked, Augustus paid off the debt of a senator who was dear to him, 400 million sesterces in cash. The senator, by way of thanks, simply wrote to the Emperor, "And nothing for me!"' (*aes alienum Augustus cuiusdam senatoris cari sibi non rogatus exolverat numerato quadragies. At ille pro gratiarum actione hoc solum ei scripsi, 'Mihi nihil?'*) shows how a *civilis* Princeps might deal with a senator in debt, going on to toleration of his facetiousness (cf. *Sat.* 2. 4. 19).

(2.) 8. 2 non est illud liberalitas, censura est. Auxilium est, principale tributum est (that is not generosity, it is the behaviour of a censor. It is help, it is a contribution from the Princeps). In interrogating the senators about their debts, Tiberius acted like a censor who had power to remove members from the senate for misconduct or failure to meet the property qualification. That Nepos was removed by Tiberius (Tac. *Ann.* 2. 48.3) gives more point to the remark *censura est*, though no Princeps formally held the censorship until Claudius. Seneca thinks that generosity, including that of Emperors, should show judgement, but that Tiberius went too far (p. 63). *Tributum*, the word for tax and for compulsory contributions, emphasizes the unwilling nature of the Princeps' subsidy.

ad iudicem missus sum (I was summoned before a judge). The climax of the crescendo. The relief of debt is now likened to being sued for it.

(2.) 10. 1 Arcesilan aiunt (they say that Arcesilaus). See Biographical Notes. D. L. 4. 37 supplies the name of the friend as Ctesibius: Plut. *Mor.* 63 D (with the name Apelles of Chios) and Julian *Or.* 2. 1. 103 D tell the same story.

(2.) 10. 2 parum si fenerare cogitas (it is not enough if you are thinking of lending money at interest). See **ad 1. 1. 1 male collocata**.

(2.) 10. 4 in acta (into the gazette). Seneca probably means the *acta diurna*, a daily record recording official events, law suits (cf. 3. 16. 2: divorces are reported there, probably cases of recovery of dowry), and public speeches. It was published and read in Italy and the provinces.

cum inter prima praecepta ac maxime necessaria, ne umquam exprobrem, immo ne admoneam quidem (when one of the first and most essential lessons is never to reproach, not even to remind). Seneca does not often use the word *praecepta*, but the first three books of the work are giving that kind of instruction (see Ch. 7A). The asymmetrical rule (*lex*) that follows this remark is also stated at 1. 4. 5 and at 7. 22. 1, where Seneca, using the verb *praecipimus*, admits that the requirement to forget is an overstatement. The more reasonable prohibition on repeated *commemoratio* (recalling) of one's favours at 11. 1 is also given by Terence, *Andria* 43–4 and by Cicero, *Amic.* 71; that on *admonitio*, here, is modified at 5. 22–3 and 7. 23.

(2.) **11. 1 triumvirali proscriptione** (proscription by the triumvirate). The triumvirate was authorized by law in November of 43 BC, when a board of three, C. Julius Caesar (Julius Caesar's adoptive son Octavian), M. Antonius, and M. Aemilius Lepidus, were given dictatorial powers for five years. The proscriptions, in which hundreds were declared to be outside legal protection and could be killed and have their property confiscated without legal consequences, offered many moral examples, cf. *Ben.* 3. 25 on slaves rescuing their masters. For 'Hand me back to Caesar', cf. Seneca's father, in *Controv.* 3. 4.

istud, si meo arbitrio memini, vita est; si tuo, mors est (if I recall this rescue on my own initiative then it is life, but if I recall it on yours, then it is death). Cicero (*Off.* 2.69) says of a different kind of humiliation, that of the highly placed in society receiving a substantial favour, 'they consider that accepting patronage or being labelled as a client is tantamount to death (*mortis instar*)'.

(2.) **11. 3 quid alienum occupare officium?** (why are you doing another's job?). Cf. Mart. 5. 52. 6: 'if you want me to speak (of your generosity), you must hold your tongue'.

(2.) **11. 4.** For the image of sowing, see ad 1. 1–3. 1.

(2.) **12. 1–2.** The story of Pompeius Pennus may, or may not, be the sequel to the story in Dio 59. 26. 4 and Jos. *AJ* 19. 32–6, who call the senator 'Pomponius' and 'Pompedius' respectively and report his pardon after involvement in a conspiracy against Gaius. By *mores liberae civitatis* and *libertas* at (2.) 12. 2, Seneca marks the contrast between Rome (even under the Principate) and Oriental despotism. Proskynesis was the sign of subjection traditionally associated with Persia and abhorred by the Greeks (cf. *Ira* 3. 17. 1 for Alexander's alleged betrayal of Macedonian freedom). Gaius' footwear is luxurious and effeminate and not suited for public business like a trial (cf. *Ira* 3. 18. 3–4); the left was thought to be adverse, harmful, even immoral.

(2.) **12. 2 nisi in os senatoris ingessisset imperator epigros suos** (unless, as Emperor, he could jam his hobnailed boots into the face of a senator). This is a reference to Gaius' penchant for wearing military footwear (hence the nickname 'Caligula' or 'little boot' that he earned while in the army camp with his father Germanicus). 'Imperator' was originally a title acquired through military victory and became part of the titulature of the Princeps and one of the ways of referring to him. The allusion to hobnails also alludes to the pearls which studded the slippers Gaius was wearing.

[2.) **13. 2 iucunda sunt quae humana fronte, certe leni placidaque tribuuntur** (gifts that please are those that are given with a look of human kindness, or, at least, gently and calmly). Seneca here reminds us that giving *beneficia* is a human obligation which accords with our social instinct (4. 18), see pp. 43–5. Cf. *Clem.* 2. 6. 2, where Seneca also condemns arrogance in giving help and advocates giving as a man to his fellow man, out of the common store.

(2.) 14–17. 7. These sections, with their negative advice, are reminiscent of the *cautiones* in Cicero's *De officiis* 1. 42–9: one should not give what may harm the recipient (1. 42), exhaust one's own means (1. 44), or be inappropriate to the person (1. 45), and must exercise one's judgement (1. 49). For Cicero, unlike Seneca (see pp. 21–4), beneficence is treated under the virtue of justice, but Seneca here seems to include some material from that tradition.

(2.) 14. 4 quemadmodum pulcherrimum opus est etiam invitos nolentesque servare (just as it is a very fine service to save someone even without his consent and against his will). In passing Seneca touches on a question he will more fully explore in Book 5 (see **ad 5. 20. 1–5**). Here *invitus* appears to be distinguished from *nolens* (see **ad 6. 7. 1 qui nobis invitus profuit**).

(2.) **15. 1 numquam in turpitudinem nostram reditura tribuamus** (let us never give what will return to shame us). The combination with friendship here is reminiscent of Cicero in *Off.* 3. 43–6, where the risk of unjust behaviour is associated with improper demands in the name of friendship (see pp. 76–7).

cum summa amicitiae sit amicum sibi aequare (since the essence of friendship is to treat your friend as an equal). Aristotle had stressed the primacy of egalitarian friendship, as does Cicero, see Ch. 3A n. 37.

(2.) 15. 3–17. 7. The theme is the importance of matching the gift to the benefactor and beneficiary, so as to maximize the chance of reciprocation and continuation of the social game ((2.) 17. 3–7): a process that can also be spoilt by the reluctance of the benefactor to accept repayment ((2.) 17. 6–8). Cicero, in his discussion of *beneficentia* in *De officiis*, had noted that kindness (*benignitas*) should be bestowed upon each person according to his standing (*ut pro dignitate cuique tribuatur*), relating it to the definition of justice as giving each his due (1. 42), for justice and beneficence are part of the social virtue, in that work (1. 20). Seneca, for whom beneficence is an independent virtue (see pp. 20–2), adopts the term *persona* in this context (15. 3, 16. 2, 17. 2), a term taken from drama, where it refers to the role an actor plays, and which Cicero associates with *decorum* and places primarily under the virtue of *temperantia*, though he says (1. 94) that *decorum* is manifest in all the virtues. *De officiis* sets out an elaborate theory of the four *personae* that each person has (1. 107–21), a theory presumably found in Panaetius, Cicero's source for Books 1 and 2, and traceable in Seneca elsewhere (Griffin 1976, 341–3): the first is the *persona* given by universal human nature, the second that given by our individual character traits and talents, the third that imposed by what fortune has supplied in the way of position and resources, the fourth the one we choose ourselves. Seneca, considering the appropriateness of gifts to donor and recipient (note *decet* in 16. 1–2), seems to have the last in mind in the case of Alexander, who thinks of his own view of himself, not just his position as king ((2.) 16); in the case of the Cynic, who has chosen his role of hating money

((2.) 17. 2); and possibly in the case of the catcher, whose skill derives from effort ((2.) 17. 4). The third seems relevant to Alexander's recipient who mentions his fortune (*fortunae suae* at (2.) 16. 1). In *De officiis* 1. 124–5, at the end of the account of these four *personae*, mention is made of other *personae*, social roles to which certain *officia* are attached, for the Stoics gave precepts for performing the *officia* of e.g. husband, wife, father, child, master, slave (*Ep.* 94. 1). Seneca alludes to them at (2.) 18. 1, implying that giving and receiving benefits are roles distinct from these: beneficence primarily creates social relations rather than arising from them (3. 18. 1; 3. 21 and see **ad (2.) 2.1**).

(2.) 15. 3 **respiciendae sunt cuique facultates suae viresque** (each of us should consider his own means and resources). Already a concern for Aristotle (*NE* 4. 1. 1120^{b}3–4, 10–11), the question of limiting liberality to what we can afford is more a concern for Cicero than for Seneca: see *De officiis* 1. 42; 1. 44; 2. 54; 2. 64. Hecato was insistent on the preservation of wealth (*Off.* 3. 63).

(2.) 16. 1 **'non quaero', inquit, 'quid te accipere deceat, sed quid me dare.'** ('I am concerned', he said, 'not with what it is fitting for you to receive, but with what it is fitting for me to give.'). In Plut. *Mor.* 179 F no. 6, Alexander gives a large sum of money for a dowry to his friend Perillus, and makes this remark when Perillus suggests a smaller sum. For Seneca's hostility to Alexander, see **ad 1. 13. 1–3**.

(2.) 16. 2 **cum sit ubique virtus modus** (since virtue is always a mean). See **ad 1. 4. 2 liberalitem quae . . .**

ut congiaria tua urbes sint (that you can give cities as public largesse). *Congiaria* were distributions of food, oil or wine, given in the Republic by magistrates or private individuals, now by the Princeps to the *plebs*. With *in sinu*, Seneca is thinking of little presents scattered in the theatre, circus, or amphitheatre, which could be kept in the fold of the toga that served as a pocket. Both images emphasize the lack of discrimination as to recipient in Alexander's generosity.

(2.) 17. 1. The story is told by Plutarch (*Mor.* 182 E 15; 531 F) of Thrasyllus the Cynic and in reverse, for he asks first for a small sum. In *Gnom. Vat.* 104 the story is told of Alexander and Diogenes the Cynic.

(2.) 17. 2 **indixisti pecuniae odium** (you have declared your hatred of money). Seneca similarly disapproves of Cynics begging in *Vit. beat.* 18. 3, where he says his friend Demetrius did not beg. Cynics in particular were supposed to demonstrate their self-sufficiency by actual poverty, but Ulpian in *Dig.* 50. 13. 1. 4 thinks that philosophers in general should not be able to sue for teaching fees, because they should particularly demonstrate their contempt for paid work.

adspicienda ergo non minus sua cuique persona est quam eius de quo iuvando quis cogitat (everyone should take into account his own role in life, not less than that of the man he is thinking of assisting). The context shows that the terms of the comparison are reversed, as often in Seneca, see **ad 1. 13. 3**.

(2.) 17. 3. The image of exchange of *charis* as a ball game (also at (2.) 32. 1; 7. 18. 1, cf. 5. 8. 4) appears in Plut. *Mor.* 582 E–F, where it is the recipient's refusal to accept that can spoil the game, and in fr. 52 Sandbach, where the donor must choose a recipient who can make a return. In neither place is the metaphor attributed to Chrysippus, as here.

(2.) 17. 4 et in ipsam eius dirigentes manum remissae occurremus (and we will just meet it when it is volleyed back, guiding it right into his hand). *Remissae* is an emendation for N's *remisse*, suggested by Gertz 1876 and by Alexander 1937, 56; 1950–2*a*, 10–11, and accepted by Cooper and Procopé 1995; Griffin and Inwood 2011).

(2.) 17. 7 fenerator (moneylender). See **ad 1. 1. 1 male collocata**. The moneylender's motive for refusing repayment is presumably to secure more interest, just as one can today be penalized for early repayment of a mortgage (a parallel I owe to Leofranc Holford-Strevens).

(2.) 18–35. Seneca embarks on the second subject listed in 1. 4. 3, proper conduct in receiving benefits. He reminds us that the exchange of benefits involves two people in performing *kathēkonta* (*officia*) which must meet the same rational standard. The other examples of reciprocal obligations given are generated by fixed social roles, father–son and husband–wife; here the two, benefactor and beneficiary, become linked in friendship—a result of the initial *beneficium* (**ad (2.) 18. 3, ad (2.) 18. 5**). As with every *kathēkon* or *katorthōma* (**ad 1. 5. 3**), these rational acts require deliberation under headings (**ad 1. 1. 2**). In the case of reciprocal actions, the deliberations are related: this is stressed in 18. 3, where it is said that we should receive from those to whom we would have given. Appropriately, the order of headings for receiving is the same as for giving, but two of the four are omitted: 'who' is omitted, since the choice of proper recipient has been handled, albeit cursorily, in Book 1. 10. 5 (under 'to whom one should give'); 'what' is omitted, because of the inevitable overlap with the categories of gift treated in 1. 11–15, and because the preceding discussion has shown that this is an unsatisfactory heading, since what is given or received on any occasion needs to be fitted to the particular circumstances in which it is given (**ad (2.) 1–17**). This leaves 'from whom' to receive ((2.) 18. 3–21)—matching 'who' in giving—and 'how' to receive ((2.) 22–35). 'From whom', is broadly construed, so that Sonntag 1913, 19 thought that (2.) 21. 3–5 came under a heading of 'what' in Hecato's work, in his view, the unique source. The treatment of 'how to receive' has unusual features, so that Sonntag 1913, 19 thought that Seneca here again disturbed the rational order of Hecato's work, where the material of 3. 26–30 belonged to the topic of returning benefits, not, as here, under receiving benefits. But the treatment of 'how to receive' can be shown to correspond closely with 'how to give' (**ad (2.) 22–5; (2.) 26–30; (2.) 32**), while showing up the inseparability of receiving and returning, and preparing for the unexpected way in which Seneca handles the topic of returning benefits in Book 3 (see Ch. 6, pp. 116–18).

(2.) 18. 3 ubi amicitiam alioqui iucundam causa fecit et iustam (when a friendship that would anyway be agreeable is justified by having a good reason for it). Seneca stresses the permanent relationship created by giving a benefit (cf. Cic. *Off.* 1. 56). The reason why it can be more important to choose a benefactor than a beneficiary must be that to be obliged against one's will is worse than just becoming a friend to an unworthy person. On the connection of benefits with friendship in the philosophical tradition, see Chs. 2A, 3A.

(2.) 18. 4 totiens admoneam necesse est non loqui me de sapientibus (I must remind you again and again that I am not speaking of Sages). Despite having defined a *beneficium* as a *recte factum*, which only a Sage can perform (**ad 1. 5. 3**), Seneca is principally concerned with those trying to make moral progress (cf. *Ben.* 5. 14. 5; 7. 2. 1), and he always includes himself and his addressee in their ranks (e.g. Lucilius in *Ep.* 33. 6–7; himself in *Vit. beat.* 17. 3–4; *Epp.* 6. 1, 4; 75. 15–16; Liberalis, by implication, at *Ben.* 6. 42; Seneca in *Ben.* 7. 17. 1). His description of their difficulty ('whose passions often resist before submitting') is not technically accurate, for the Stoics believed the passions arose from reason's assent to intellectual error and did not originate in a separate part of the soul from reason.

(2.) 18. 5 at illi et plus solvendum est (but to the other creditor a larger amount must be paid). The comparison with the financial creditor has two elements: how much is due, and what follows repayment. The larger amount due to the 'other creditor' (the benefactor) is 'needing to start again', and the bond that survives repayment is friendship. For the obligation to start the process again, see Arist. *NE* 5. 5. 1133^{a}3–5 and Ch. 3A n. 66.

(2.) 18. 6–21. 2. Seneca here considers cases where the opportunity to choose a worthy benefactor does not arise, either because we are under duress, or because the intent to benefit was missing, or the power to help is unjustly acquired. Here no *beneficium*, and hence no obligation to be grateful, is generated. He ends with cases where we can accept from an unworthy giver without entering into a relationship of friendship ((2.) 21. 2).

(2.) 18. 6 aliquando beneficium accipiendum est et invito (sometimes one has to accept a benefit even against one's will). Reciprocity in the process requires that both donor and recipient be willing ((2.) 18. 8), though at 5. 20. 1–3 (hinted at in (2.) 14. 4) an unwilling recipient can be benefited under certain conditions. According to *Dig.* 50. 17. 3–4 jurists do not count someone commanded by a father or master as willing, for he has lost the power of refusal. For Tacitus' use of this argument in Seneca's speech at *Ann.* 14. 53. 3, see pp. 83, 85. At 5. 6. 6–7 Seneca says that Socrates' refusal of an invitation to court was motivated by fear of having to accept benefits against his will, thus being placed in 'voluntary slavery'.

parum dignus est cui debeam (he is unworthy of my being in his debt). Hosius, Préchac 1961, and Basore 1935, in the Loeb edition (and Cooper and Procopé 1995 in translation), punctuate with a question mark, but Lipsius rightly saw that it was a statement, not a question, which would require a negative answer implying that the coercive giver is morally acceptable as a benefactor.

(2.) 18. 7. For *vis maior*, see **ad 4. 39. 4.**

(2.) 18. 8. The tyrant is Jason of Pherae, and a similar story appears in Cic. *Nat. d.* 3. 70; Plin. *HN* 7. 166; Val. Max. 1. 8, ext. 6, and Plut. *Mor.* 89 c.

(2.) 19. 1 num ergo beneficium est ferae auxilium? (the savage animal's help cannot count as a benefit, can it?). The view here, that the lion did not act with intention, follows Stoic doctrine, taken over from Aristotle, that animals, being irrational, are not capable of moral action. Cf. the story in Aulus Gellius, *NA* 5. 14, for which he claims an eyewitness source, where Androclus publicly parades the fact that the lion who saved him in the arena was 'returning thanks for a benefit and for medical help' (*gratiam mihi nunc beneficii et medicinae referre*), and the stories told by Democritus and Demetrius *physicus* (perhaps another Presocratic philosopher), and recorded by the Elder Pliny (*HN.* 8. 58–61), of gratitude shown by animals. Pliny comments on the help given in return by a panther (60), 'so that it was quite clear that she was returning a favour and not reckoning on something in return, which is rare even in a human being' (*ut facile apparet gratiam referre et nihil in vicem imputare, quod etiam in homine rarum est*).

(2.) 19. 2 quo loco feram posui, tyrannum pone (replace the wild beast in my example with the tyrant). Seneca makes the comparison of the tyrant to a wild beast in *Clem* 1. 3. 3. It goes back at least to Plato (*Resp.* 8. 566 A, cf. 571 C on the beastly part of the soul not being under the control of the rational part).

(2.) 20. 1 disputari de M. Bruto solet an debuerit accipere ab divo Iulio vitam (it is commonly debated whether Marcus Brutus should have accepted the gift of his life from the divine Julius). Brutus, who fought for Pompey at Pharsalus in 48 BC (the battle referred to in 20. 2), was pardoned by Caesar and in 44 BC became one of his assassins. Seneca alludes to exercises in the rhetorical schools, which commonly dealt with dilemmas of the civil war. In *Ep.* 14. 13 he records one about Cato's participation in what was really a struggle for power between Caesar and Pompey (cf. 'which of two men they would serve' in (2.) 20. 2). Plutarch (*Comp. Dion and Brutus* 3. 3) tells us that the fact that Brutus had been honoured by Caesar (see Biographical Notes), and was spared along with others for whom he pleaded, added to the charge of ingratitude. For an interesting discussion of Seneca's treatment of Brutus here, see Lentano 2009*a*.

(2.) 20. 2 quam rationem in occidendo secutus sit, alias tractabimus (we shall deal elsewhere with the reasoning he employed in killing Caesar). If Seneca explained Brutus' reasons elsewhere, we have lost the account.

videtur vehementer errasse nec ex institutione Stoica (he seems to have gone badly astray on this issue and not to have comported himself in accordance with Stoic teaching). Seneca faults Brutus on three counts: one is that he departed from Stoic teaching about constitutional form; the other two are reasons why the political goals he adopted were futile. The constitutional charge is ill founded in two respects: (i) Stoics of the late Republic probably did not believe that the best government is under a good king (see Griffin 1976, 202–6). D. L. 7. 131 and Cic. *Rep.* 1. 34 suggest they favoured the mixed constitution, though they might have held that monarchy was the best of the simple constitutions. Moreover, they were less interested in the form of constitution than in the moral status of the ruler (strictly speaking, only the Sage had the requisite virtue, including that of justice, to be king). Accordingly, Seneca in *De clementia* does not describe monarchy as the best form of government, but teaches how it should be virtuously exercised. (ii) Brutus was not a Stoic, but an adherent of the Old Academy of Antiochus of Ascalon (Sedley 1997, 47–53 argues for the importance of this in Brutus' decision). Moreover, the constitutional charge rests on the assumption that Brutus thought Caesar a just king, but S's own account of Brutus' political aims presupposes that he thought Caesar a tyrant. As regards those political aims, Seneca maintains that both the precedents already set of excessive power, and the moral and political condition of Rome in his day, meant that the killing of Caesar could not achieve freedom or the restoration of the Republic. This looks like a valid criticism on Stoic grounds, since the Sage is not supposed to undertake action with little prospect of success (Cic. *Fam.* 9. 16. 5; 4. 92 with Griffin 1995, 335–7), but Brutus was not a Sage and did not think the venture was doomed to failure. (In fact, it can be argued that it might have succeeded; see Brunt 1988a, 85–7.) The king killed by a thunderbolt was Tullus Hostilius; Tarquinius Priscus and Servius Tullius were assassinated. Seneca clearly does not regard such ambition as confined to the end of the Republic, despite his remark 'abandonment of the ancient ways' (*amissis pristinis moribus*), on which see p. 59 and n. 122. Plutarch, in his assessment of Brutus' deed (*Comp. Dion and Brutus* 2. 3–5), defends Brutus for selflessly pursuing precisely the political aims that Seneca dismisses, i.e. defence of liberty against tyranny and restoration of republican government.

(2.) 20. 3 sed vitam accipere debuit, ob hoc tamen non habere illum parentis loco (But Brutus was right to accept the sparing of his life, yet not to regard Caesar on this account as a parent). The idea that saving someone's life entitles one to be revered by him as a parent is found in connection with the *corona civica* given for saving the life of a citizen (Polyb. 6. 39. 6–7; Cic. *Planc.* 72), and it is probably behind the branding of Caesar's assassins as *parricidae* and the Ides of March being called *Parricidium* (Suet. *Iul.* 88). Seneca similarly has Augustus call his would-be assassin Cornelius Cinna, whose life he had once saved, *parricida* (*Clem.* 1. 9. 11). On Cinna, see **ad 4.30.2 Cinnam**; on *parricidium*, see **ad 5. 16. 1**. It is unlikely that Seneca has in mind the improbable story that Brutus was Caesar's child (Plut. *Brut.* 5. 1–2). See Roller 2001, 188; 250.

in ius dandi beneficii iniuria venerat (Caesar had come by the right to confer a benefit, through inflicting injury). As Seneca says at 5. 16. 5, Caesar acquired the power to pardon, by ungratefully using the arms entrusted to him for the war in Gaul against his own country. (Later at 6. 27. 4 Seneca describes as hostile in intention the act of even an external enemy who conquers men in order to pardon them, since the kindness comes after cruelty.) Also at 5. 16. 5 Seneca includes in his charge of ingratitude to his country Caesar's retention of power by force, which comes closer to Cato's idea, according to Plut. *Cat. Min.* 66. 2, that Caesar had no right to assume tyrannical power and hence no right to use that power to pardon.

non enim servavit is qui non interfecit, nec beneficium dedit sed missionem (not killing is not the same as saving a life. What has been granted is not a benefit but reprieve). Seneca 's father reports in *Controv.* 2. 15. 2 the rhetorical point, 'It is not a benefit not to commit a crime.' *Missio* here is best construed as the pardon of defeated gladiators at the whim of the man giving the games (cf. Seneca *Ep.* 37. 2; Mart. *Spect.*

31 ShB), that is, as 'discharge from the authority of the *editor* who sponsored the spectacle, so that a gladiator who is *missus* will return to his barracks to train for future engagements; it does not mean discharge from service as a gladiator' (Coleman 2006, 221). The gladiator can still be killed in a later combat.

(2.) 21. 3–6. In the first two cases, the objection to the benefactor is not to his moral worth: in the first, receiving the service will be contrary to the relationship of friendship forged by giving a benefit, because it will mean endangering the benefactor without removing the risk for the recipient; in the second, the donor has no legal title to the property that he gives away. With the third, Seneca returns to the selection of worthy donors.

(2.) 21. 4 a filio familiae (from a man not yet legally independent). Seneca criticizes Hecato's example on the assumptions of Roman law, but the original story may just have been about conflict between a generous son and a miserly father. The Roman citizen whose father was alive had no independent property, though he might be allowed the management of a sum called his *peculium*. The gift then would be a theft, because the gift came from the property of his father. It would have to be restored as soon as the father found out. The legal arrangements at Rhodes, Hecato's city, are not known, but under Athenian law the father's control of his son's property ended when the son reached 18, and even when he was a minor the father's power did not approximate to the Roman *patria potestas* (MacDowall 1978, 85, 91).

(2.) 21. 5 ad impensam ludorum pecunias (contributions to meet the expense of public games). The *ludi* were games that magistrates gave in their official capacity, normally, under the Principate, as praetors. They received an official allowance which they could supplement up to a certain amount. Seneca admired the wit (*Ep.* 29. 6), as well as the virtue of L. Julius Graecinus, the father of Agricola, whom Tacitus also praises in his confrontation with Gaius (*Agric.* 4. 1).

(2.) 21. 6 Rebilus consularis, homo eiusdem infamiae (an ex-consul and of similarly bad reputation). This is probably the same man, C. Caninius Rebilus, as the sexually dissolute, rich legal expert whose suicide in 56 is reported by Tacitus (*Ann.* 13. 30. 2). This episode belongs in 37 or 38, when Gaius was Princeps, because Rebilus was consul in September 37 and Julius Graecinus died in 39 or 40. Paulus Fabius Persicus (similarly judged in Book 4: see **ad 4. 30. 2 nisi Verrucosi**) had been consul in 34, so both the would-be benefactors were senators of the highest rank.

an senatum legere? (or selecting a senate?). Seneca uses the technical term for the work of enrolling the senate, known as a *lectio senatus*. In implying that Graecinus' refusal showed that he thought neither of his would-be benefactors deserved to be senators, Seneca reminds us of Tiberius' quasi-censorship (**ad (2.) 8. 2**): but Tiberius there was refusing to give, and in a public and humiliating way.

(2.) 22–5. In keeping with the symmetry of giving and receiving ((2.) 1. 1; (2.) 18. 1–3; (2.) 23. 1), the discussion of how to receive resembles that of how to give, in its concern with gracious looks and speech, with promptness (here, in showing gratitude), and with publicizing the favour, which is the mirror image of giving secretly, just as the gratitude inspired by Augustus' favour ((2.) 25. 1) is the mirror image of the hatred generated by those of Tiberius ((2.) 7. 2–8) and Caligula ((2.) 12–13).

(2.) **22 primam eius pensionem solvit** (pays back the first instalment of it). The metaphor of the *beneficium* as a loan (**ad 1. 1. 1. male collocata**), which here contrasts with the mention just before of the relationship of friendship created by the benefit, is carried through in (2.) 23. 2.

(2.) **23. 2 non est ista verecundia, sed infitiandi genus** (but that is not diffidence, but a kind of denial). In Horace, *Ep.* 1. 7. 37–9, the client who is truly *verecundus* acknowledges his gratitude openly. On the legal terms used here, see **ad 3. 15. 1** and **ad 3. 15. 2**.

(2.) **23. 3 dum opinionem clientium timent** (while they fear to be thought dependents). Cicero (*Off.* 2. 69) describes in stronger terms this fear felt by rich men of standing, who prefer death to the name of *cliens*. Clientage is not central to the network of benefits, as Seneca sees it, and the people here are men of standing (*dignitas*), not permanent clients (see Ch. 3A, and, for the parallel with Tac. *Ann.* 4. 18, Ch. 3C n. 163). The obligations they fail to carry out must be open ones, like turning out for the *salutatio* in the morning or accompanying the benefactor to the forum.

(2.) **24. 2–25.** Seneca starts with ungracious ways of receiving: (i) silent but having the same effect as disobliging remarks; (ii) silent; (iii) verbal but inadequate. He goes on at 24. 4 to give examples of what one might actually say, ending with facial expressions that can substitute for gracious remarks (see **ad (2.) 2. 2 laetus** and **ad (2.) 3. 2 adicias licet**).

(2.) **24. 1 tutius est** (it is safer). In *Ep.* 81. 31–2 Seneca shows the beneficiary actually wishing his benefactor out of existence.

(2.) **24. 3 'non quidem mihi opus est, sed quia tam valde vis, faciam tibi mei potestatem'** ('I don't really need it, but since you wish it so much, I will put myself at your disposal'). Cf. Cic. *Off.* 2. 69 *beneficium dedisse arbitrantur*, of beneficiaries who think they have conferred a benefit by accepting.

(2.) **25. 1 quam ne ad spem quidem exaequandi umquam beneficii accedere** (than not even being able to hope to match the benefit one has received). On Augustus and Furnius, see Biographical Notes. Pliny's letter to Trajan 10. 51 has a similar elaborate formulation: 'not venturing to respond with equivalent gratitude, however it may be in my power to do so', see Ch. 3C, n. 167.

(2.) **25. 3 velut in certamen cursus compositum et carceribus inclusum** (like someone set for a race and waiting in the starting blocks). This is the third vivid metaphor Seneca owes to Chrysippus, the image of the dancing Graces and that of the ball-game (**ad (2.) 17. 3**) being the others. The comparison is probably to a foot race in the stadium, though for both a foot race and a chariot race in the circus, *carceres* is the term for the barred slots in which the contestants wait for the dropping of the napkin by the magistrate presiding at the games. Brad Inwood points out that Chrysippus was a long-distance runner before he took up philosophy (D. L. 7. 179).

(2.) 26–30. The correct assessment of the value of gifts, discussed here under 'how to receive', corresponds to the discrimination required to match a gift to benefactor and beneficiary, which was discussed under 'how to give' ((2.) 14–17. 7). Seneca proceeds here by counter-example, showing that conceit, greed and ambition, and envy, distort our judgement and make us ungrateful. The gifts of the gods represent the climax of our failures to evaluate benefits correctly and of our consequent ingratitude, but they also provide a transition to the last section of the book, devoted to the Stoic paradox that receiving a benefit gladly is tantamount to returning it, for the gods can only be repaid in gratitude.

(2.) 26. 2 inde est ut omnia meruisse se existimet et in solutum recipiat (the result is that each person thinks that he has earned all that he has, that it is merely repayment of what is owed). The metaphor equates the gift with repayment of a financial debt, which imposes no obligation but merely discharges one.

si illum aut illum aut me colere maluissem! (if I had rather chosen to cultivate this other fellow, or that one, or myself!). *aut me* is the manuscript consensus, rejected by Hosius for Feldmann's suggestion *ita me*, but adopted by Préchac 1961, who adduces *Brev. Vit.* 2. 4, where Seneca speaks of the time wasted on courting others instead of improving oneself.

honestius praeteriri fuit (it would have been more of an honour if he had passed me over). In political contexts, as here, the verb is used of the humiliation of not being adlected to the senate (by the Princeps) or not being commended for office, cf. Plin. *Pan.* 94. 3. The verb is also used of the disgrace of being passed over in a will (Val. Max. 7. 8. 4).

(2.) 27. 1 antequam illum libertini pauperem facerent (before the freedmen made him seem poor). Not his own freedmen, who would be called *liberti* (Treggiari 1969, 37, n.5; 53). Seneca compares Lentulus' wealth to that of the imperial freedmen who, particularly under Claudius and Nero, were resented by the governing class for the fabulous wealth they amassed through proximity to the Princeps. Seneca's own fortune is given by his detractors in Tac. *Ann.* 13. 42. 4 and Dio Cass. 61. 10. 3 as 300,000,000 HS, the same as the fortune of Pallas (*Ann.* 12. 53). The round figure of 400,000,000 here is also attributed both to him (Dio Cass. 62. 14. 3) and to Narcissus (60. 34. 4). Seneca alleges that Lentulus merely saw his wealth, because he made no good use of it. See Griffin 1976, 302 n. 1.

(2.) 27. 2 princeps iam civitatis (now a leading citizen). Tacitus uses a similar expression, including him among the *primores civitatis* (*Ann.* 4. 29). The Republican term *princeps*, even after being applied to the Emperor, continued to be used of other prominent men who had held high positions, cf. *in conspectu principum* ('in full view of the leading men', at (2.) 12. 2).

(2.) 27. 4 nemo agit de tribunatu gratias (no one gives thanks for a tribunate). Seneca here lists some of the posts in the *cursus honorum* in ascending order. The parallel with *Ira* 3. 31. 2 suggests that here too he is thinking of the Princeps, whose conduct of the elections ensured that he could secure the magistrates he wanted. Repeated consulships become more common under the Principate, starting with Claudius.

(2.) 29. 1 et quidem professi sapientiam (even men who lay claim to wisdom). *Sapientia* in this context strongly suggests philosophers: presumably Epicureans, who denied that the gods care for us. Lucretius 5. 218–34 uses the comparison with animals, who are said to be better equipped for survival and a menace to man. Seneca answers that argument by saying ((2.) 29. 3–4) that the intellectual gifts of the gods have given man power over the earth. Pliny, *HN* 7. 1–3 also has Nature creating all things for man but argues that she behaves like a stepmother, not a parent, in that she has made him weak and vicious, which makes things hard for him.

(2.) 29. 2 quod non bona valetudo etiam vitiis inexpugnabilis data sit, quod non futuri scientia (because we have not been given good health that is proof against our vices, along with knowledge of the future). For a lurid account by Seneca of the effect of vice on human health, see *Ep.* 95. 15–25. It is not clear if Seneca agrees that we do not have the ability to see the future (cf. the Stoic spokesman's confident assertion, against the Epicurean view, in Cicero's *Nat. d.* 2. 162–3). The Epicureans denied a rational predictable universe altogether; the Stoics thought there was a nexus of causation that was in principle intelligible, but they disagreed as to whether or not men could divine it.

(2.) 29. 3 quidquid nobis negatum est, dari non potuit (whatever has been denied to us could not possibly have been granted). The impossibility here seems to be a logical one: as men we cannot be given what would make us gods (29. 2 *fin.*; 29. 6). Cf. *Prov.* 5.8 on god constrained by fate.

(2.) 30. 2 eodem quidem momento, quo obligatus es, si vis, cum quolibet paria fecisti (at the very moment you incurred an obligation, you have already, if you wish it, squared accounts with whoever it might be). The legal term for settling accounts is here juxtaposed with the high-minded sentiment that equates grateful acceptance with repayment, which, as the perfect tense indicates, is then immediate.

(2.) 31–5. The paradoxes of the Stoics went with the role they inherited from the Cynics, of 'changing the currency' or challenging conventional moral views. Cicero in the *Paradoxa Stoicorum* had shown how they could be defended in oratorical fashion. The three other paradoxes mentioned by Seneca at (2.) 35. 2 are known from Greek sources (*SVF* iii. 567, 578–9; iii. 593; iii. 662–3). Seneca defends the paradox 'He who receives a benefit gladly has repaid it' in two ways: 1. by appealing to the primacy of intention in virtuous acts, so that the giving and receiving of benefits can be seen as in essence a transaction between minds ((2.) 31–4); 2. by demonstrating that the term *beneficium* is ambiguous, the Stoic paradox using it in the sense of the act of giving, not in its more ordinary sense of the object given. Though that common usage had been condemned as ignorant in 1. 5. 2, here Seneca makes clear that the Stoics respect it, to the extent that they impose on the recipient the obligation to try and make a return when possible ((2.) 35. 2–5).

(2.) **31. 2 non enim in vicem aliquid sibi reddi voluit; aut non fuit beneficium, sed negotiatio** (for he did not want to be given something in exchange; otherwise it was not a benefit, but a business deal). The antithesis is attributed to Cleanthes at 6. 12. 2, where the issue is discussed.

(2.) **32.** Just as the image of the ball-game was used to illustrate correct judgement in giving, so the same image is suggested here to illustrate correct judgement in receiving, and the relation of receiving to returning. For the distinction made here between the game (= the social network of exchange), in which actual material return is important, and the players (= the benefactor and recipient) to whose moral achievement it is irrelevant, see p. 44.

(2.) **33. 3 secundus est et famae et eorum quae praestari in vicem possunt** (both reputation and the things which can be provided in return are secondary rewards). To show that grateful acceptance is the benefactor's true return, while any increase of reputation or gift received in return is just an extra reward, Seneca has been using the analogy of the artist, whose real satisfaction is in the creation of a work of art, as opposed to any glory or profit the work of art brings him. Aristotle's parallel of the benefactor and the artist in *NE* 9. 7. 1167[b]31–1168[a]2 makes the different but related point that the benefactor loves the beneficiary as his handiwork, and not because of any return he may bring him. Some editors have supplied *tertius* instead of the second *et*, or *et tertius* after *secundus*; but, as is pointed out by Alexander 1950–2a, 13, Seneca did not necessarily develop the analogy in exact parallel. In fact, Seneca discusses the question in binary terms until *triplex* in 33. 2 and, at the end of 33. 3, has clearly reverted to that pattern with the opposition of *gratiam* and *mercedem*, and of *beneficium* and *quod extra beneficium est*. He thereby stresses the unimportance of any reward other than gratitude.

(2.) **34. 2–5.** On the ambiguities caused by the poverty of language, Seneca progresses from simple homonyms, to extensions of reference that reflect moral laxness (clearly inspired by Thucydides 3. 82), to the conceptually confusing use of the same term both for the beneficent act and for the object given. This last is related at (2.) 35. 2 to specifically Stoic uses of language.

(2.) **35. 2 a consuetudine quaedam quae dicimus abhorrent, deinde alia via ad consuetudinem redeunt** (some of the things we say avoid our customary way of speaking, and then they come back to it by a different route). In *Clem.* 2. 7. 4, *Const. sap.* 3, and *Ep.* 59. 1–4 Seneca makes the same point about their unusual use of language not leading to different conclusions from the ordinary usage. In *Clem.* 2. 7. 4 he speaks of disagreements *de verbo* rather than *de re*; in *Ep.* 59. 1, he speaks of words in their ordinary sense as *verba publica*. Cicero criticizes the Stoic habit, claiming Panaetius as an ally (*Fin.* 4. 79–80). Seneca here defends the Stoic habit of 'changing the names of things' while acting on ordinary assumptions, a habit that his addressee Serenus is made to attack in *De constantia sapientis* 3. 1–2, as an avowed Epicurean (15. 4). Seneca's point is that, by setting the importance of the recipient's attitude above his obligation to make a material return, he can diminish his fear of receiving benefits. At *Ben.* 7. 22 he will explain the Stoic use of hyperbole as a pedagogic strategy.

negamus iniuriam accipere sapientem, tamen, qui illum pugno percusserit, iniuriarum damnabitur (we deny that the Sage can receive an injury, yet the man who strikes him with his fist will be convicted of doing him an injury). The Stoic Sage cannot be injured, because only damage to his virtue would count as an evil and hence an injury, and his wisdom makes him invulnerable in that respect (e.g. *Const.* 5. 3–5, the whole dialogue being a defence of this paradox). Seneca uses for illustration the early praetorian *formula* called the *edictum generale*, which ran, 'That the cheek of Aulus Agerius was struck by a fist' (*Quod Auli Agerii pugno mala percussa est*), see Watson 1965, 248.

insanire omnes dicimus (we say that everyone is mad). As is explained by Stobaeus (*SVF* iii. 663) and by Cicero in the *Paradoxa Stoicorum* 27–34, not understanding yourself, or what is appropriate for you, is madness. Everyone but the Sage is therefore mad. Vice being an intellectual failing, these fools have all the vices as well (*Ben.* 4. 26–7; 5. 17. 3). Hellebore was regarded as a cure for madness, because it purged the body of black bile.

(2.) 35. 5 benigne accipe; rettulisti gratiam, non ut solvisse te putes, sed ut securior debeas (accept it with good will; you have returned the favour, not that you should think that you have paid off the debt, but that you may be indebted with a greater sense of confidence). Seneca is to reach the same conclusion in the last book, but in a different spirit. Here, the need to repay the favour by gift or service is a concession to ordinary language and custom, the main emphasis being on a grateful attitude as sufficient repayment, for Seneca's aim is to reduce the fear of accepting benefits. But In 7. 16 the demand that the recipient make every effort to repay materially is stronger, since the aim is to discourage ingratitude (see **ad 7. 14–16. 4**).

Synopsis of Book 3

* §§18.2 and 18.3 appear to be reversed.

Notes to Synopsis of Book 3

The opening sentence, 'Not to return gratitude for benefits is shameful and is held by all to be so', introduces the last of the three subjects proposed in 1. 4. 3, the returning of benefits; but it also indicates that the subject is to be treated in a negative fashion via a discussion of ingratitude.

Seneca needed to approach the third subject differently, for, as Sonntag 1913, 21 notes, to use any of the headings employed for the first two subjects, viz. who, to whom, what, and how, would have involved considerable repetition, since 'who' under returning benefits = 'to whom' under giving; 'to whom' under returning = 'who' under giving ; and 'what' and 'how' are going to be similar in returning and in giving. 'What' in any case has proved unsatisfactory and was dropped under receiving (see **ad 2. 1–17**). The negative treatment, as indicated **ad 2. 14–17. 7**, makes contact with the handling of beneficence by those authors who treat it under justice. So in the first section of the book (1–17.3) Seneca considers the possibility of legal enforcement of gratitude, and in the second (17. 4–38) the relationship of benefits to duties accompanying social roles, a subject treated by Cicero in *De officiis* 1. 34–41 and 45–59 under 'the social virtue', his equivalent of the cardinal virtue of justice. The legal character of the book would appeal to Seneca's Roman readers (as Book 3 of Cicero's *De officiis* must have done), while the detailed consideration of hard cases at the end prepares them for the problem-solving of the last three books.

(3.) 1. 1–5. This discussion of the causes of ingratitude effectively continues the one in 2. 26–30 under the heading of how to receive benefits, for the chapters in between (2. 31–5) have vindicated the paradox that diminishes the distinction between properly receiving and properly returning (pp. 115–18). Nonetheless, as Abel 1987, 22 = 1995, 63 points out, there is a difference in emphasis: under receiving, Seneca was concerned with our failure to value benefits we receive; here, he is concerned with why we lose the will to express gratitude. In stressing forgetfulness, Senseca is in line with Aristotle, who noted that beneficiaries have short memories (*NE* 9. 1167^{b}28–9), and with Cicero, who has gratitude (*gratia*) composed of memory and the will to repay (*Inv.* 2. 161). See also Stob. *Ecl.* 2. 143. 18–20 W on the Peripatetic definition of *charis* (p. 101 n. 11).

(3.) 2. 2 ad reddendam gratiam et virtute opus est et tempore et facultate et adspirante fortuna (actual repayment of a favour requires good character and time, resources, and good fortune). *Reddere* is rarely used with *gratia* (Moussy 1966,

267–9), and in the later *Ep.* 81. 9, Seneca argues for *referre* as the appropriate verb, even though just before (81. 7) he has his interlocutor speak of *beneficio gratiam* (*reddere*). He uses it again at 5. 16. 4. See Ch. 6 n. 20.

(3.) 3. 1–3. Seneca often refers to ambition for the future and envy of those ahead (*Ben.* 2. 27. 4; *Ira* 3. 31. 2; *Ep.* 73. 3) as effacing present contentment.

(3.) 4. 1 Epicuro. This passage = Usener fr. 435; cf. *SV* 17, 19, 55; Cic. *Fin.* 1. 57, 60, 62. Seneca, in arguing for the need to remember past benefits, develops this Epicurean idea that the memory of past goods gives us secure pleasure. He combines two themes that he treats elsewhere: 1. the past is secure from fortune, and so it is better to remember the past gifts of fortune than to concentrate on present and future ones (*Brev. Vit.* 10. 2); 2. it is ungrateful to forget what has given pleasure in the past and to concentrate on their loss, a theme much used in consolation (*Polyb.* 10. 3; *Epp.* 98. 11; 99. 4–5, cf. Plut. *De tranq. anim.* 473 C–D; 477 F). The celebration of 'pleasures' (*voluptates*) and of the gifts of fortune as 'goods' (*bona*) departs from Stoic orthodoxy and is attacked in *Vit. Beat.* 6, where the advice is to be happy with the present, and to value only the true good of virtue (4. 3–4), which gives true joy (*gaudium*). But Seneca in *Polyb.* 10. 3 and *Ep.* 99. 3–4 seems to regard enjoyment of past contingent goods as *gaudium* because they no longer are precarious or arouse passions (see Armisen-Marchetti 1986, 193–4 = 2008, 110–12).

(3.) 5. 2 ut ingratus sit, cui beneficium in mentem venit (that a person is ungrateful, if a benefit only 'comes to mind'). Some editors prefer to correct *ingratus* to *gratus* (and a later corrector of N inserted *non* before *ingratus* to the same effect) with the meaning 'that a person counts as grateful if the favour simply occurs to him'. However, Seneca often likes to end a subject with a striking epigram, and the paradoxical reading, that a benefit not continuously present to the mind is as good as forgotten, is stronger. It also follows better from the preceding discussion of the need to recall minor benefits repeatedly to mind, so as not to forget them, and serves as a climax to the description of forgetting as a process that starts with deliberately not recalling the benefit (*non subinde illa tractamus*), continues with regretting the promise to remember (*evitant*), and culminates in oblivion.

(3.) 6–17. 3. Seneca moves from the causes of ingratitude to the possibility of preventing and punishing it by law. He argues that the practice of most societies shows that they have judged human disapprobation and divine punishment more appropriate (6; 17. 1– 3); that such legislation would be too difficult to apply in practice (7–12); and that it would undermine beneficence and gratitude, rather than encourage them (13–16). Manning 1986 suggests that the discussion, though about the question of an action for ingratitude in general, may contain echoes of a running debate on how to deal with ingratitude in freedmen by legislation (cf. **ad (3.) 6. 2**) and also, less convincingly, of senatorial anxiety about use of the law by the Princeps against an 'ungrateful' testator.

(3.) 6. 1 haec lex quae in scholis exercetur (this law, which is applied in the (rhetorical) schools). Seneca's father includes two *controversiae* (rhetorical exercises debating

fictional legal cases) that presuppose that ingratitude is actionable: *Controv.* 2. 5 and
9. 1. The declaimer Cassius Severus played a joke on another declaimer by accusing him
before the praetor on this charge (*Controv.* 3 pref. 17: see Winterbottom 1974, i. 389
n. 5; 471 n. 1), and Juvenal 7. 169 mentions ungrateful husbands among fictional
rhetorical cases. Lentano 2009*b* notes (2) that this is the only explicit acknowledgement
in the treatise of Seneca's debt to declamation and suggests (2–16) that, by presenting
Roman norms as laws, declamation opens these norms up to casuistical discussion and
refinement, which resembles what Seneca does.

(**3.**) **6. 2 excepta Macedonum gente non est in ulla data adversus ingratum actio**
(among no other people but the Macedonian nation does a legal action lie against an
ungrateful person). In 4. 17. 1, Seneca admits no exception, and in 4. 38. 2, he implies
that the punishment Philip of Macedon imposed on a soldier guilty of ingratitude was
an act of military discipline, not 'a decree inscribed on bronze': so here he may just be
exaggerating this episode. Xenophon speaks of Persian boys accusing each other of
acharistia (*Cyr.* 1. 2. 7), but says that at Athens only ingratitude to parents was
punished (*Mem.* 2. 2. 13). This must count against Valerius Maximus' statement at 5. 3.
ext. 3f that it was possible to sue for ingratitude at Athens, even if that is read as a
rhetorical exaggeration of the fact that Athenian masters could strip their ex-slaves
of freedom for ingratitude, a practice he also attributes to Marseilles (2. 6. 6–7a):
the fact seems to be that a master whose liberated slave deserted to another patron
could bring a *dikē apostasiou*, and, if successful, return him, now a metic or resident
alien, to servile status (Bonner 1969, 87). In Lucian, *Abd.* 18–19 the context shows
that the law against ingratitude concerns the conduct of children towards parents; in
Dio Chrys. *Or.* 75. 6 it is not clear in what sense the law enforces gratitude, since
services to the city seem to be included. At Rome, Justinian was to treat *donatio* as a
contract and to make ingratitude towards a donor a juridical responsibility (*Cod. Just.*
8. 53. 35; *Inst.* 37. 2; *Cod. Just.* 8. 55. 10), but in Seneca's time the only person liable
to a legal charge of ingratitude was a freedman who failed to show gratitude to his
former master and patron. The procedure was instituted by the Lex Aelia Sentia of
AD 4, which allowed a patron to make a formal accusation against a freedman on his
grounds of ingratitude (Tac. *Ann.* 13. 26–7; Suet. *Claud.* 25; *Dig.* 37. 14. 1, 5; 40. 9. 30),
and the attitude of the law became progressively harsher (see Gardner 1993, 41–51).
Chaumartin 1985, 313–29; 1989, 1718–19, 1722 thinks (3.) 6–17 is a warning to the
Emperor not to use legal means to extract wealth from the imperial freedmen, but
Seneca hardly mentions freedmen in *De beneficiis*. There was concern about ungrateful
freedmen informing in his time, but the senatorial debate in AD 56 about ungrateful
freedmen, reported by Tacitus in *Ann.* 13. 26, concerned the rights of ordinary masters,
not the Emperor, and in any case did not issue in legal powers for the masters, who
could, however, take the case to the senate, which could order re-enslavement. In fact,
the institution of Junian Latinity had diminished the power of the ex-master in this
respect; for under the Republic those who informally manumitted their slaves could
change their mind, though the slave could appeal to a praetor (but see López Barja de
Quiroga 1998, 159–60).

(**3.**) **7. 1 si actio sicut certae pecuniae aut ex conducto et locato datur** (if the right to
sue is granted, as in the case of a fixed sum of money or of hiring and leasing). Seneca

chooses two common forms of action: the first, of which the full name is *actio certae creditae pecuniae* (an action for a fixed sum of money lent), is an action available in civil law for which the praetor merely provides the *formula*; the other is granted at the discretion of the praetor. The first may rest on a contract but need not, the second arises on a consensual contract.

si appello, si ad iudicem voco (if I summon him and call him before the judge). A fuller description of what is indicated here by *appello* is given at 4. 39. 2, where *appellare debitorem ad diem* (to summon a debtor on an appointed day) follows the calling in of the debt. Cf. also Cic. *Off.* 1. 89. The parties then came before the magistrate, who decided whether or not to grant the plaintiff the right to sue, and, if he agreed, issued a *formula* embodying instructions to the *iudex*, who would decide on the facts of the case (see **ad (3.) 7. 5**). So, in the first action mentioned at (3.) 7. 1, the *iudex* would be instructed: 'if it appear that the defendant owes the plaintiff ten thousand sesterces, condemn the defendant to pay the plaintiff ten thousand sesterces; if it does not appear, absolve him'.

(3.) 7. 4 fora (forums). Trials were usually held in the open-air meeting-places in cities. In *Ira* 2. 9. 4, Seneca mentions three forums: the Republican forum, the forum built by Julius Caesar, and the forum built by Augustus.

(3.) 7. 5 melior videtur condicio causae bonae, si ad iudicem quam si ad arbitrum mittitur (a good case is stronger when brought before a judge rather than an arbitrator). An *arbiter* in this period is normally only a special kind of *iudex*, similarly appointed by the praetor (in e.g. *Ep.* 65 *arbiter* in §2 and *iudex* in §10 are clearly synonyms, cf. Elder Seneca, *Controv.* 1. 1. 23; Armisen-Marchetti 1989, 156), though an *arbiter* could also be appointed by agreement (*compromissio*) between the parties, particularly to settle boundary disputes (Crook 1967, 78, 82). Cic. *Rosc. Com.* 10–13 makes the same point about good cases, showing that the praetor's *formula* binds the *iudex* to give or deny what is specified, whereas the praetor's *formula*, addressed to an *arbiter*, gives him scope to decide on an equitable amount. Seneca seems to imply that the *arbiter*'s freedom means not being bound by a *formula* at all, only by his own scruples (*religio*); but this is rhetorical exaggeration, as is shown by his going on in 7. 6 to imagine even a *iudex*, who would certainly operate under a *formula*, being given unlimited discretion in a case of ingratitude.

sententiam suam non prout lex aut iustitia suadet, sed prout humanitas aut misericordia impulit regere (to determine his opinion, not according to the promptings of law or justice, but by impulses of kindness and pity). On this passage, see Inwood 2004, 85–6 = 2005, 213–15. In 6. 6. 1, Seneca again approves of the question of gratitude not being subject to law, and he describes the recipient of a benefit and a subsequent injury acting as a kind of *arbiter* in weighing one against the other. In *Clem.* 2. 7. 3, Seneca similarly explains the operation of clemency by the metaphor of arbitration: it is not bound by *formula* but judges *ex aequo et bono* (according to what is fair and good). See Bellincioni 1984*b*. There, however, he makes it clear that the clement decision is in accordance with justice, clemency being opposed in that respect to pity (*misericordia*), which clouds the judgement by emotion (2. 6. 3–4); but Seneca reverts in *Ben.* to the ordinary use of the terms *misericordia*, *humanitas*, and *clementia* as synonyms (6. 29. 1).

(3.) 7. 6 quid sit enim beneficium non constat, deinde quantum sit; . . . quid sit ingratus, nulla lex monstrat (for what constitutes a benefit is not established, nor how big it is; . . . what constitutes an ingrate no law indicates). Seneca has given a definition himself (1. 5), but he means there is no agreed legal definition of a benefit or an ingrate that can feature in the *formula* that guides the judge, because not only does intention matter (which is true in defining many offences), but everything turns on the mental attitudes of donor and recipient respectively.

(3.) 7. 7 demittere tabellam (cast his vote). Seneca imports an image from the criminal law, where the members of the jury (*iudices*) voted by secret ballot placed in an urn (Cf. Elder Sen. *Controv.* 7. 8. 7).

ubi prolatis cautionibus controversia tollitur (when producing written guarantees settles the disagreement). These guarantees are written versions of the oral stipulations that constitute a very simple and common kind of contract (**ad (3.) 15. 1**).

iudex ex turba selectorum (a judge from the general crowd of *selecti*). *Iudices* selected from citizens of free birth and inherited equestrian census (400,000 sesterces) were on the official list (*album*) and divided into five decuries. *Selecti* was the title of one of the decuries, as Pliny *HN* 33. 30–3 explains, but inscriptions indicate that, though the three Augustan decuries were more prestigious, all five were, in common usage, called 'select'. See M. I. Henderson 1963, 67–9.

(3.) 8. 2 pro addicto (for a man bound over for a debt). Though the ancient institution of *nexum*—under which the debtor could be handed over by the praetor to the creditor who could imprison him and eventually, if no one paid his debt, as here, could sell him into slavery—was mitigated in some way by the Lex Poetilia of 326 BC, praetors and other magistrates continued to have the power to grant a creditor *addictio* (Quint. 5. 10. 60), and we hear of such bondsmen who had to work off their debts.

(3.) 9. 2 in quattuordecim deduxisse (to have escorted him to the fourteen rows). By the Lex Roscia of 67 BC *equites Romani* were given the privilege of sitting in the first fourteen rows at the theatre. The benefit here could be a gift from a friend of the requisite census (**ad (3.) 7. 7 iudex ex turba selectorum**), such as Pliny gave (*Ep.* 1. 19), or, if the Princeps is the imagined donor (as with the gift of citizenship), the conferral of the gold ring (cf. Suet. *DJ* 33), which also signified free birth (*Dig.* 38. 2. 3.1).

defendisse capitis reum (to have defended a person accused of a capital charge). Legal advocacy counts as a *beneficium*, because in Rome it was not regarded as a professional service, though gifts up to a certain limit were allowed in return (see p. 58 on the Lex Cincia). In fact, advocates garnered legacies and other forms of indirect payment.

cadentes venas vino refecisse (having revived his feeble pulse with wine). At *Ep.* 95. 22, this is listed among new medical remedies designed to deal with new ailments resulting from current luxurious habits.

(3.) 10. 3 intra pecuniam versabitur taxatio (the penalty will be limited to money). Having considered how the *iudex* would assess the benefit (7. 4–9) and how he would set the day for repayment (10. 1–2), Seneca turns to the specification of the appropriate penalty. A *taxatio* is a limit on the payment to be imposed on the defendant, as set in the *formula* given to the *iudex* in an *actio incertae creditae pecuniae* (Gaius, *Inst.* 4. 50–2). Here, the limit is the fact that nothing beyond money can be demanded, though only a capital penalty could be equal to the benefit of life.

(3.) 11.   Seneca here rebuts the counter-example of parents, who are, exceptionally, given legal protection against ingratitude. Xenophon attests to such protection at Athens (**ad (3.) 6. 2**), and Plutarch credits to Solon a measure freeing a son of the obligation to support his father, if the father did not teach him a trade (*Solon* 22). There was available what the *Ath. Pol.* 56. 6 calls a *graphē kakōseōs tōn goneōn* for those who used physical violence against a parent or failed to proved food and housing and proper funeral rites, but which may have been an *eisaggelia* (MacDowell 1978, 92; Todd 1993, 107, 117–18). In Rome under the Republic the law excluded the bringing of defamatory actions against parents by children, and parents could not be brought into court by their children without their consent (Schulz 1936, 201). Seneca does not explicitly refer to the Roman *patria potestas*, which technically gave fathers the power of life and death over their children without recourse to the public courts (Gardner 1993, 72–4, 83; 1998, 268–73; not an unsubstantiated Roman belief, *pace* Shaw 2001, 65–77) and which Dion. Hal. *Ant. Rom.* 2. 26. 3–5 credited with protecting the Romans against the many unseemly deeds committed among the Greeks by children against parents (cf. *CJ* 8. 46. 3 authorizing the use of *patria potestas* to enforce *pietas* of children towards the father), but the reference to parental *potestas* at the end of (3.) 11. 1, and the description of parents as 'domestic magistrates' at the end of (3.) 11. 2 suggest it. See Mommsen 1899, 16–17.

(3.) 11. 2 et quia utile est iuventuti regi, imposuimus illi quasi domesticos magistratos, sub quorum custodia contineretur (and because it is useful for the young to be controlled, we have placed over them a kind of domestic magistrate to keep them in protective custody).   Gertz 1876 suggested that this clause belonged at the close of (3.) 11. 1, where the idea of *potestas* leads naturally to the idea of magisterial *potestas* here. He is followed by Cooper and Procopé 1995, while Préchac 1961 removes the clause as a gloss. However, in (3.) 11. 1 the granting of *potestas* is explained as an incentive intended to offset the hazards of child-rearing, whereas here the idea belongs to the argument that, because parental benefits are continued after their original benefit, they are manifest and indubitable: part of that ongoing process is the socially useful regulation of the young, which requires parents to have authority over the young. Seneca shows this function in action in *Clem.* 1. 15. 3–7, where the father exercises *patria potestas* after a judicial procedure involving a *consilium*, voting, and imposition of the penalty of *relegatio*. See Jolowicz and Nicholas 1972, 119, 317, n. 1.

(3). 12. 1 si ei datur, quem nosse a beneficio tuo incipis (if it is given to a person whom you only begin to know when you confer the benefit).   On the priority Seneca gives to the role of benefits in creating relationships, pp. 27–8, 36–9.

(3.) 12. 1–2. To illustrate the difficulty of assessing the value of benefits, Seneca lists three categories, help, honours, consolation, and then describes the attitude to them in the order consolation, honours, help.

(3.) 12. 4 aliquis dedit mihi beneficium sed idem postea fecit iniuriam (someone gave me a benefit but the same person subsequently inflicted an injury on me). Seneca deals more fully with this difficulty in *Ben.* 6. 5–6, and then again in *Ep.* 81 (see pp. 155–63).

(3.) 14. 1 Hoc enim ipsum secuti sunt, qui nullam legem huic constituerunt (Why, this was the very aim of those who refused to pass a law on this matter). This answers the argument advanced in the previous sentence, by the fictive interlocutor, in support of legislation: 'Next point: there will be fewer benefits but more sincere ones; and what is wrong with discouraging the reckless giving of benefits?' So, rightly, Alexander 1950–2*a*, 16.

(3.) 14. 2 nulla lex te in integrum restituet (no law will restore you to your previous situation). The last of three legal remedies that, according to Seneca, legislation against ingratitude could make available: being granted the right to sue by the praetor; suing for restitution of property wrongly acquired; and finally, intervention by the praetor to rescind a transaction detrimental to the applicant, and to restore the *status quo*.

(3.) 14. 3 ius gentium (the law of nations). Here, combined with *aequissima vox* (a saying most just), the expression has its normative sense of a principle of justice universally recognized. Cf. *Ben.* 1. 9. 5, where *gentium ius* is merely descriptive of universal behaviour.

(3.) 14. 4 si beneficium mercem facimus (if we turn a favour into a commodity). If repayment can be demanded legally, then the favour is up for sale.

(3.) 15. 1 stipulatio (formal contract). A very old form of oral contract which imposed an obligation on a person who had answered in set terms (e.g. 'I pledge', 'I give') a formal question put to him by the promissee and containing the subject matter of the promise. It was *stricti iuris*, that is, it had to be honoured in strict adherence to its wording. There were also more modern forms of consensual contract, but Seneca deliberately chooses the most inflexible to make his point.

(3.) 15. 2 interpositis parariis (by making use of intermediaries). The creditor spreads the risk by having several people stand surety for part of the debt and enter it in their ledgers. Cf. 2. 23. 2, where Seneca condemns individual borrowers who fail to involve intermediaries and witnesses, in an effort to conceal their indebtedness. Here he condemns the whole system as based on distrust.

interrogatio (oral contract). The question and answer that make up the *stipulatio*. The written form of a *stipulatio* was a *cautio*, which is presumably what Seneca means was signed.

(3.) 15. 3 ornati viri (distinguished men). Seneca chooses this word because the literal sense is also appropriate, given the seal rings these witnesses wear, and suggests the superficiality of the trust placed in them: he goes on to say that we would demand witnesses of any loan we made to them.

(3.) 15. 4 sine sponsore (without a guarantor). The term is confined to those standing surety for a debt contracted by *stipulatio* (**ad** (3.) **15. 1**): such a guarantor also makes a promise by stipulation, by which he, as well as the principal debtor, becomes indebted to the creditor.

(3.) 16. Having discussed the bad effects on potential benefactors and beneficiaries of legislation against ingratitude, Seneca turns to the more general effect on society, using arguments already deployed in *Clem.* 1. 22–4, and which have some claim to be original with Seneca (Ducos 1993, 443, 451–5). Seneca argues, first, that to punish a crime of which a great many are guilty, as opposed to providing a deterrent, actually encourages others to commit the crime, because revealing how common the crime is makes it seem less shameful. Moreover, the malefactors, once they know their own number, become more influential. That the argument was recognizably Senecan is suggested by its evocation (in absurd form) by Tacitus, in the senatorial debate on the punishment of ungrateful freedmen at *Ann.* 13. 27, perhaps to suggest Seneca's participation (Griffin 1976, 282).

(3.) 16. 2 non consulum numero sed maritorum annos suos computant (they keep track of the years, not by the number of consuls, but of husbands). Seneca alludes to the Roman habit of dating by the two consuls of the year. Though in his day there was more than one pair in a year, and public and private documents were often dated by the *consules suffecti* actually in office at the time (Eck 1991*b*), the years were still often labelled, in the Republican manner, with the names of the *consules ordinarii* who opened the year.

(3.) 16. 2 acta (see **ad 2. 10. 4**).

(3.) 17. The chapter first (17. 1–3) identifies the loss of the pleasure in receiving and seeking to return a benefit, as the worst of the real punishments for ingratitude, and then goes on (17. 3–4) to identify its attainment as the real incentive to gratitude. It thus forms a transition between the first part of the book, dealing with the failure to return benefits, and the second, teaching us to be generous in recognizing and returning them.

   In (3.) 17. 3–4 Seneca sets out to encourage gratitude and the return of benefits by adducing the joy involved in receiving and seeking to return benefits, and by showing how many opportunities there are for such enjoyment, if we include certain marginal cases as appropriate objects of gratitude. Up to now he has conducted his discussion largely in terms of equal exchanges between people who become *amici* as a result of the initial benefit, and this is to remain for him the paradigm case. Here ((3.) 17. 4) he treats returning benefits to people with whom we have a pre-existing relationship that imposes obligations: parents and existing friends, but also persons of lower status, particularly the lowest category of person—a slave, whose benefit we must nonetheless not devalue.

(3.) 17. 4 educatoris (of a carer). *Educator* is the term for someone who brings you up, a family dependant responsible for early child-rearing (the male equivalent of a nursemaid), or, in the case of an exposed child, a foster-father. They were usually of servile origin. Such male child-minders, sometimes under the label *nutritor,* are well attested on inscriptions and in literary sources (Bradley 1985, esp. 499–500).

praeceptorum (of teachers). At 6. 16 Seneca discusses why we owe affection, in addition to fees, to those teachers who take trouble over us as individuals.

quomodo decoquat (how he may default). Etymologically, the term implies the running down of resources, resulting in inability to pay.

non solum parentibus et amicis, sed humilioribus personis (not only to parents and friends, but to persons of lower status). Seneca regards equality as the norm in friendship, cf. 2. 15. 1 **cum summa amicitiae** and Ch. 3A, p. 38 and n. 37. The last category mentioned includes, presumably, carers, teachers, and slaves, as the sequel shows. Slaves, in Roman law, were persons as well as items of property (*res*).

(3.) 18–28. Seneca raises the question as to whether it is in fact possible to confer a benefit on a person to whom one already has a defined relationship carrying obligations, and goes on to examine, in this light, the hardest case, i.e. where the benefactor is of lower social status, and in its most extreme form, i.e. where he is a slave. This is the best known passage of *De beneficiis*; but, according to Seneca himself ((3.) 29. 1), the lengthy proof that slaves can confer benefits on their masters is merely an *a fortiori* argument to establish that children can confer benefits on parents, which is the precondition for arguing that children can outdo parents in benefits ((3.) 29–38). Of the relationships of *necessitudo* indicated at (3.) 18. 1, he in fact goes on to consider at length only that of children and parents; but, in the text as we have it, Seneca does not spell out why the *ministerium* of a slave is particularly relevant to the *officium* of a child. The argument at 18. 3, about subordinate relationships in general, is clearly relevant to children, but the lengthy rebuttals of the alleged moral inferiority of slaves ((3.) 18. 2–20. 1; 28) do not seem to apply to children, though Seneca seems to think the arrogant attitude that accompanies this belief is also directed at children ((3.) 29. 1). But the heart of the argument is the conclusion reached in (3.) 21–2, that whatever one does beyond one's formal legal obligations, whatever is done not on command but voluntarily, is a benefit; and here, though Seneca applies the idea also to masters vis-à-vis their slaves ((3.) 21) and to hired labourers vis-à-vis their employers ((3.) 22), the parallel of slaves and children is clear. For Seneca does not need to spell out what every Roman knew: that the *patria potestas*, with its power of life and death and its power to inflict corporal punishment, made it hard to distinguish legally the subordinate position of children from that of slaves, vis-à-vis the head of the household or *paterfamilias*, even if fathers were not expected to use these powers normally against children

(Brutus in *Ad Brut.* 1. 17. 6: *dominum ne parentem quidem maiores nostri voluerunt* (our ancestors were not willing that even a parent should be a master); the episode in (3.) 37. 4) shows that undue harshness was condemned, even in the fourth century BC: Saller 1994, 105–14, 133–50; Roller 2001, 238). In fact, father and son, master and slave, were the favoured alternative paradigms for good and bad rulers respectively (*Clem.* 1. 14–16; Cic. *Rep.* 3. 37, cf. 1. 64; Plin. *Pan.* 2.3).

(3.) **18. 1 sicut ab Hecatone** (as by Hecato). See **ad 1. 3. 2–4. 5** and Ch. 2 pp. 20–1, 24.

sunt enim, qui ita distinguant, quaedam beneficia esse, quaedam officia, quaedam ministeria (there are those who make a distinction between benefits, duties, and services). Seneca does not say if Hecato himself employed this distinction in arguing against the possibility of slaves conferring benefits on their masters. In any case, Seneca apparently accepts the three-way distinction (see **ad (3.) 21. 1**). In the *Controversiae* written by the Elder Seneca, the *beneficium–officium* distinction, 'It is no benefit but a duty to do what you ought to do', illustrated by the relation of son to father (2. 5. 13), is ascribed to the declaimer L. Junius Gallio, who, by the time *De beneficiis* was written, had adopted Seneca's older brother. See Ch. 2 n. 57; Ch. 3 n. 32.

necessitudo suscitat (a bond rouses). The relationship can be one of kinship by blood or marriage, or of friendship (Cic. *Off.* 1. 59; Suet. *Nero* 35. 4; *Sest.* 39; Pliny *Ep.* 5. 7. 5). It is in keeping with the following discussion of services performed by slaves and children that Seneca names only the inferior partner (son, wife) in the two examples of *officia* specified, though at 2. 18. 2 he had treated parent–child, husband–wife as *ex duobus officia* (reciprocal obligations).

(3.) **18. 2.** The text involves a *non sequitur* as it stands. Lipsius already thought that something had dropped out at the end of 18. 1, and Sonntag 1913, 27 proposed inverting 18. 2 and 18. 3. Cooper and Procopé 1995, 255 n. 29 accept both and suggest that what is missing at the end of 18. 1 is 'perhaps the conclusion that favours cannot be done to the head of a family by his slaves since that would be a "menial service" (their translation of *ministerium*), nor even by subordinate members of the family, since that would be a "duty" '. That would prepare for the connection made retrospectively at (3.) 29. 1 between the two cases discussed, slaves and children. If we agree that paragraph 18. 3 precedes 18. 2, a brief discussion of subordinate relationships not preventing benefits follows 18.1 and precedes the argument for the capacity of slaves to perform virtuous acts in 18.2 and 18.4, introduced by *praeterea* (besides).

(3.) **18. 4 ut ipsos saepe beneficii sui fecerint** (that often what they have conferred by way of a benefit is the masters themselves). One of the more contorted of the *sententiae* with which Seneca likes to end a discussion: he means they have saved their masters' lives.

(3.) **19. 1 quare ergo non et domino suo possit?** (so why not also to his master?). The argument preceding, about a slave's capacity to perform a virtuous act, establishes that he can confer a benefit on someone, but not that he can benefit his own master. Seneca makes the objector point out that the slave cannot legally put his master in his debt by giving him money, because he cannot refuse to give it (see next n.). The point is argued more clearly at 7. 4. 4, where Seneca concedes that the slave and his *peculium* belong to the master, but argues that the slave still has something to give, even if the master has the power to take it. More generally, Seneca has not dealt with the fact that the slave has no power to refuse his services to his master, and he accepts the challenge at the start of (3.) 19. 2.

'Quia non potest,' inquit, 'creditor domini sui fieri, si pecuniam illi dederit' ('Because', it is said, 'he cannot become a creditor of his master if he gives him money'). At the end of the Republic, Servius Sulpicius Rufus ruled that a legacy left by a master in his will to a slave he was manumitting, in repayment of a debt, was invalid, *quia dominus servo nihil debere potuisset* ('because a master could not have owed anything to his slave', *Dig.* 35. 1. 40. 3). But even legal attitudes were changing, and the Flavian jurist Javolenus was to modify Servius' view: *ego puto secundum mentem testatoris naturale magis quam civile debitum spectandum esse, et eo iure utimur* ('I think that, in accordance with the wish of the testator, we should have regard to the natural, not the strictly legal, obligation, and that is the law we observe', ibid.). Mantello 1979 discusses the relation of Javolenus' opinion to Seneca's idea of *ius humanum* in (3.) 18–22, concluding that there is a similarity but not a direct link between the two (esp. 444–51).

(3.) 19. 2 ut in multa liber sit (that he is free in many respects). As Cooper and Procopé 1995, 256 n. 31 suggest, Seneca first shows ((3.) 20) that the slave is free in mind, if not in body, and then ((3.) 21–2) that he has freedom of action beyond the limits of his legal obligation to his master.

(3.) 19. 3 nullis cruciatibus victum (not overcome by any tortures). In cases in which the evidence of slaves was admissible, it was normally given under torture.

(3.) 19. 4 vide, ne eo maius sit, quo rarius est exemplum virtutis in servis (Consider whether the display of virtue by slaves is not the greater for its rarity). A glimpse of the grim reality: the corrupting influence of the institution of slavery on moral character and the slim chances of genuine affection for the master developing.

(3.) 20. 1 mens quidem sui iuris, quae adeo libera et vaga est, ut ne ab hoc quidem carcere, cui inclusa est, teneri queat, quominus impetu suo utatur et ingentia agat et in infinitum comes caelestibus exeat (the mind is autonomous, so free in its movement that not even this prison, in which it is confined, can hold it back from using its own powers and undertaking great things and escaping into the infinite as a companion of the celestial bodies). This passage uses Platonic imagery, particularly that of the *Phaedo*, notably the body as a prison from which the soul escapes to its celestial origins. With the last phrase, it is not clear if Seneca has in mind contemplation of natural phenomena, as in *Ep.* 65. 16–19, or suicide, though *Ben.* 6. 23. 6 'mente in alta data divina comitentur' favours the former (see **ad loc.**). However, he is really concerned with freedom of action on earth, as the sequel shows.

(3.) 20. 2 interior illa pars mancipio dari non potest (that inner part cannot be acquired by a formal transfer of property). *Mancipatio* was the old form of sale between citizens, involving witnesses and the weighing of purchase money in copper scales. Italian land, animals, and slaves were *res mancipii* because originally they required a formal and public conveyance, cf. *Ben.* 5. 19. 1.

nec enim aut nos omnia iubere possumus aut in omnia servi parere coguntur (for there are things that we cannot order our slaves to do, and they are not compelled to obey our every command). The lawyers agreed: see *Dig.* 47. 10. 17. 7 (Labeo): *nec in omnia servus domino parere debet* ('a slave is not obliged to obey his master in everything').

(3.) 21. 1 quaedam sunt, quae leges nec iubent nec vetant facere (there are certain acts that the laws neither command nor forbid us to do). See **ad 5. 20. 6 'praeterea lex, quod non iussit repeti, vetuit'** for the opposing view that Seneca contests at 5. 20. 6; 5. 21. 1.

quam diu praestatur, quod a servo exigi solet, ministerium est (so long as what is provided is what is customarily required of a slave, it is a 'service'). Seneca here employs the terminology mentioned in (3.) 18. 1. That he goes on to speak of *servile officium* in 21. 2 does not show that he rejected it: in drawing there a parallel between the benefits conferred by master and slave, he elides the difference between *officium* and *ministerium*, the respective contraries to *beneficium*.

ubi in adfectum amici transit (when it passes into the domain of friendly feeling). As Seneca says in 1. 6, the essence of a *beneficium* is in the attitude of the giver. In Xen. *Cyrop.* 4. 4. 12, Cyrus tells his war captives that any of them who shows himself well disposed in attitude and action will be regarded as a benefactor and friend, not a slave.

(3.) 21. 2 est aliquid quod dominus praestare servo debeat, ut cibaria, ut vestiarium (there is a certain amount which the master ought to give his slave, such as a food and clothing allowance). Cf. *Tranq.* 8.8. The master's obligations are spelled out more fully at (3.) 22. 3. Seneca only mentions benefits that masters confer while remaining masters: the greatest *beneficium* was manumission, alluded to in (3.) 22. 4 and (3.) 23. 3, cf. note **ad (3.) 23. 5**.

quod non ex imperio, sed ex voluntate praestatur, beneficium est (whatever is given, not on command, but voluntarily, that is a benefit). Cf. the jurist Ulpian in *Dig.* 50. 17. 3–4: *eius est nolle qui potest velle* ('the power of refusal belongs to someone who is in a position to be willing'); *velle non creditur qui obsequitur imperio patris vel domini* ('someone is not regarded as willing if he is obeying the command of a father or a master').

(3.) 22. 1 perpetuus mercennarius (a permanent hired labourer). The definition implies that there are no slaves by nature, as Aristotle maintained, but still acknowledges that the slave has no liberty of action and so cannot choose to terminate the employment. Cicero in *De officiis* 1. 41, where he is following the Stoics, approves the definition and glosses it, 'one should require work and grant just treatment', since a contract of hire would specify the obligations on both sides. The Roman Stoic Rutilius Rufus is said to have paid his slaves for fish they caught, like free men (Athenaeus 6.274d).

(3.) 22. 2 'Quid, si nollet?' (What if he were not to feel like it?). On Lipsius' interpretation, followed by Cooper and Procopé 1995, the master's question is a rhetorical one, implying a threat to compel the slave.

(3.) 22. 3 de iniuriis dominorum in servos qui audiat positus est (there is an official charged with hearing complaints of injuries done by masters to slaves). A proof is now offered for Seneca's claim at (3.) 21–22. 2, that the legal obligation of the slave is not unlimited. If a master can be considered to have injured his own slave, then the master's power is not unlimited, and there is an area of freedom within which the slave can act from choice. The official is clearly the Prefect of the City who, by the time of Septimius Severus in the late second century, is attested as hearing complaints of cruelty, harshness, hunger, and sexual compulsion: they were not formal accusations, and there was no punishment inflicted, but the slave could probably be sold (*Dig.* 1. 12. 1. 8). This passage of Seneca has been taken to prove that Nero instituted the procedure; but Augustus created the Prefect of the City, who was charged with keeping slaves under control and maintaining public order (Tac. *Ann.* 6. 11): he must have been concerned from the start with mistreatment that could lead to violence and revolt (Griffin 1976, 269–70, 460–1).

(3.) 22. 4 ne a servo acceperis, in tua potestate est (it is within your power not to receive it from a slave). As Lipsius saw, Seneca means that you can manumit the benefactor, so that the benefit comes from a free man.

(3.) 23. 1 multa iam beneficiorum exempla referam et dissimilia et quaedam inter se contraria (I shall now adduce several examples of benefits different from each other and some even contrary to each other). Seneca summarizes the types of benefit—life, death, saving by self-sacrifice, assisting suicide, preventing suicide—to be illustrated by the historical examples, which then follow in chronological order ((3.) 23. 2–25). The types, however, are not listed in that order, but relate in succession to 23. 2 (mistress at Grumentum); 23. 5 (Vettius Scato); 25 (proscriptions); 23. 5 (again); 24 (Domitius).

(3.) 23. 2–4. Claudius Quadrigarius. The story is *HRR* i, fr. 80, from the work of this annalistic historian of the Sullan period. The episode dates from the Social War in 90–88 BC. Grumentum is in Lucania in the south, where some of the toughest resistance was put up by the Italians who resented being refused the Roman citizenship.

(3.) 23. 3 aliter enim servata munus notae et vulgaris clementiae habuisset (if she had been saved in some other way she would have been the beneficiary of some familiar, rather ordinary, form of clemency). Dowling 2006, 207–9, cf. 200, adduces this incident as a case of clemency in the private sphere, here exercised by slaves, but Seneca avoids this interpretation of the incident by contrasting the clemency she might have received from the victors with the exemplary status she achieved by virtue of this *beneficium*. *Parricidium* implies that the victors had no right to kill her, hence no right to spare her either (**ad 2. 20. 3 in ius dandi beneficii**).

(3.) 23. 5 praetor Marsorum (the praetor of the Marsi). Another story from the Social War, this time about one of the generals of the Marsi. P. Vettius Scato is called *dux Marsorum* by his contemporary Cicero (*Phil.* 12. 27), so Seneca's *praetor* probably just means 'commander', though Scato may have become a magistrate in the new state of Italia founded by the rebel leaders at Corfinium: it had a senate, consuls, and praetors (Strabo 5. 4. 2). The general is Cn. Pompeius Strabo, father of Pompey the Great; the date 89 BC.

iam dominum manu misi (now that I have freed my master). The notion of death as freedom is developed by Seneca in *Ep*. 26. 10. The slave confers on his master a benefit equivalent to the highest his master could give him.

(3.) 24. This version of the story of Nero's Pompeian ancestor, L. Domitius Ahenobarbus, at Corfinium is more flattering than that found in Pliny *HN* 7. 186; Plut. *Caesar* 34; Suet. *Nero* 2. 2–3. Sonntag 1913, 6 suggests that Seneca here shows deference to the Emperor; Lucan depicts him in an even better light (2. 507–25, cf. 7. 219–20; 7. 597–616). But the later discreditable version may reflect posthumous hostility towards the Emperor.

(3.) 25 cervicem porrexit (he held out his neck for execution). The standard attitude for execution by the sword, cf. Plut. *Cic*. 48. 5; *Ira* 1. 18. 3, where again *speculatores* are the soldiers charged with carrying out the execution (Mommsen 1899, 924).

(3.) 26. 1 nostri saeculi exempla non praeteribo (I shall not omit examples from our own epoch). For Seneca's treatment of the four Emperors who had preceded Nero, see Griffin 1976, 210–17. Compared with Augustus and Gaius, Tiberius is not much treated. Here Seneca speaks of the *maiestas* charges that Tacitus regards as a bad feature even of the early part of his reign (*Ann*. 4. 6. 2). Neither Paulus nor Maro is otherwise known, but see Biographical Notes on Maro.

(3.) 26. 2 iam subscriptionem componeret (he was already composing his indictment). In *Apoc*. 14. 1, Seneca spells out the steps in a criminal prosecution in the statutory murder court: first *postulare*, demanding of the presiding magistrate permission to prosecute; then *nomen deferre*, naming the accused in a *subscriptio* or written indictment, so called because the accuser wrote his own name on the indictment so that he could be penalized if the prosecution was irresponsible (*Dig*. 48. 2. 3. 2; 48. 2. 7. 1; Mommsen 1899, 385 nn. 4–5). The treason trials of senators were held in the senate under Tiberius.

(3.) 27. 1 nondum hominibus verba sua periculosa erant, iam molesta (their words were not yet a source of danger to people, but already a cause of trouble). Seneca might seem here to contradict Tacitus (*Ann*. 1. 72. 3) who ascribes to Augustus the extension of the *maiestas* charge to cover not only actions, as under the Republic, but words. However, Tacitus only mentions defamation of 'illustrious men and women', so that it may not be until the reign of Tiberius that people were formally accused of insults to the Princeps himself, who is the target here of the joke, which turns on the fact that animals were sacrificed to thank the gods whenever the Princeps returned from a journey. Augustus, who is in the main favourably viewed by Seneca, here shows himself not only clement, but superior in wit: in *De ira* 3. 23. 4 Seneca had remarked that he did and said many things that showed he was not subject to anger. Nothing more is known of the senator Rufus.

(3.) 27. 4 quod liberalitatem clementiae adiecit (added a display of generosity to his clemency). For the close relationship of these two virtues, associated again at 5. 9. 2 and 6. 29. 1, see Val. Max. 5. 1. 1 pref. with Braund 2009, 321; Griffin 2003a, 177–82; see pp. 25, 153–4.

nec tamen gratis (not without payment). There was a tax to be paid on manumissions of slaves. Here the money is paid by the master from the gift that he induced Augustus to give him as a sign of pardon.

(3.) 28. 1 eadem omnibus principia eademque origo (we all have the same beginnings, the same source). In the Stoic view, all human beings have sparks of the divine cosmic reason and belong to a community of rational beings, cf. *Ep.* 44. 1–5; 47. 10. Roman lawyers agreed that all men were equal by natural law (*Dig.* 50. 17. 32).

(3.) 28. 2 qui imagines in atrio exponunt (Those who display masks in the reception room). The *imagines* were wax masks of his ancestors, housed in special cupboards in the part of the *atrium* of a distinguished Roman's house where visitors were received. Also displayed and mentioned here were painted family trees (the *stemmata* mentioned by Seneca) including portraits, also described by Pliny *HN* 35. 6. See Flower 1996, ch. 7.

(3.) 28. 5 ad hortos alicuius ne ordinarium quidem habentis officium (to a villa in the charge of some slave who does not even have regular duties). Seneca seems to envisage the master being carried in a litter to a rendezvous and having to gain access from the household slaves, including those who are only *vicarii*, that is, inferiors and stand-ins for other slaves (cf. *Ep.* 110. 1). The kiss must be on the hand, a sign of supplication (*Ep.* 118. 3).

(3.) 29–38. Seneca passes rapidly over the point for which he claims to have introduced the discussion of slaves, i.e. that children can give benefits to their parents. He presumably takes it for granted that, as with slaves, the duties they owe are not unlimited, for which one argument would be that fathers have obligations to their children, just as masters have legal obligations to their slaves (**ad (3.) 22. 3**). That Seneca thought this is clear from 2. 18. 1, where the reciprocal duties (*officia*) of fathers and sons are mentioned, and from (3.) 37. 4. Despite the theoretically unrestricted power of the Roman father (but see **ad (3.) 18–28**), even the law allowed children to contest the will if they were not provided for (e.g. *Dig.* 5. 2. 4), while public opinion, enforced in the Republic by the censors and then by the Princeps, expected reciprocal devotion or *pietas* e.g. *Ad Herennium* 2. 19; Sen. *Clem.* 1. 15. 1–2; *Dig.* 48. 5. 23. 4; Val. Max. 5. 7; Plin. *Ep.* 9. 12. As Hadrian put it, 'the power of the father ought to depend on compassion, not cruelty' (*patria potestas in pietate debet, non atrocitate, consistere, Dig.* 48. 9. 5).

The rest of Book 3 is devoted to showing that children can actually outdo the benefits they received from their parents, the importance of the proof being given at (3.) 36: the belief that they can surpass their parents encourages the generosity of children and leaves them no excuse for not returning the benefits their parents conferred on them.

(3.) 29. 1 quaeritur enim (in fact the question is raised). The *enim* is not explanatory here, but leads on to a new discussion.

(3.) 29. 3 ita numquam beneficio vincitur, cuius beneficium est ipsum quod vincitur (thus the father is never outdone as regards benefits, because the very fact that he is outdone is a benefit he bestowed). This point about the incommensurable gift of life was made by Aristotle in *EN* 8. 11. 1161^{a}13–15; 8. 14. 1163^{b}18–22, who suggests that it cannot be repaid, but that it can be acknowledged in honour. The point was in the repertoire of the declaimers, Elder Seneca *Controv.* 3. 4: 'qui vitam dat, si prior accepit, non obligat, sed reddit' (the person who gives life, after first receiving it, puts the other under no obligation—he is merely making a return). Lentano 2000, 365–8 argues that the attitude of the fictive interlocutor in Seneca is prevalent in declamation and represents the commensensical Roman view, Seneca's own position being highly original. However, he ignores the fact that the ps.-Quintilian declamations, important evidence for him, only preserve one side of the argument, and that the virtuosity of the declaimer is shown best in arguing a hard case (Bonner 1969, 83): in fact in *Controv.* 2. 5.10–11 denying a *beneficium* is shown to be particularly difficult. As with Seneca's position on slaves (Griffin 1976, 261–6), his views on relation of fathers and sons are not strikingly in advance of the more enlightened views of his time (**ad (3). 18–28**).

(3.) 29. 7 cum aeque sine patris beneficio quam sine nutricis non potuerim ad ulteriora procedere (since it is just as true that I could not have gone on to my later achievements without my father's benefit as without my nurse's). The terms of the comparison are reversed, as often in Seneca, see **ad 1. 13. 3**.

(3.) 30. 2 boni malique communem materiam (material with a potential for both good and evil). *Materia* is the practical means in terms of resources, opportunity, capacity, here life itself, which can be turned into good or bad acts according to our *animus* or intention (cf. 5. 2. 3; 6. 29. 1).

(3.) 31. 1 cum vitam tibi non voluptatis meae causa aut certe per voluptatem dederim (since when I gave you life, it was not for the sake of my own pleasure or at any rate by means of my pleasure). As it is with parents giving life to children.

(3.) 31. 2 ego tibi vitam dedi consummatam, perfectam, tu me expertum rationis genuisti, onus alienum (I gave you life that was complete and perfect, you sired me as a being without reason, a burden for someone else to bear). The Stoics held that reason only developed at a certain age (*SVF* ii. 83; Cic. *Fin.* 3. 20–1). That the mother, not the father, carries the child counts here against the magnitude of the father's benefit.

(3.) 31. 3 exposuisses; nempe iniuria erat genuisse (you might have exposed me, thereby doing me a wrong by having begotten me). The father by *patria potestas* had the power to acknowledge or to refuse to acknowledge a child born to him (see

ad (3.)11): in the latter case the child was exposed, usually in the countryside, where it would die or be found, and possibly reared, by others. So the benefit of life could be said to begin with the acknowledgement.

(3.) 32. 4 quae et priorem magnificentiam vincerent et nulla postea vincerentur (which would surpass all former grandeur and be surpassed by none in future). On Agrippa, see Biographical Notes. His building works included the Pantheon, public baths, a bridge, and two aqueducts, the Aqua Julia and Aqua Virgo. His generosity in paying for the adornment of Rome is celebrated in *Ep.* 94. 46. Abel 1967, 165 and 1985, 708, argues that this passage attests the survival of Agrippa's works and therefore helps to confirm the date of *De beneficiis* as before the Great Fire of 18–27 July 64 (but see p. 95). That date means that Seneca was not at risk of being thought to be making a comparison with Nero's great building works in Rome after the Fire.

(3.) 32. 5 illum umbra adoptivi patris abscondit (obscured as he was by the shadow of an adoptive father). Gaius Octavius, praetor in 61 BC, died without reaching the consulship; his son was adopted posthumously by Julius Caesar the Dictator, whose great-nephew he was through his mother Atia: hence his name Gaius Julius Caesar Octavianus, though he avoided using the adoptive cognomen. After 27 BC he became known as Imperator Caesar Augustus or Caesar Augustus (Syme 1958*b*).

(3.) 33. 1 praetextatus (still a boy). The *toga praetexta* with its purple border was worn by boys before they came of age and assumed the plain *toga virilis*. P. Cornelius Scipio Africanus is said by Livy 21. 46. 7–8 to have saved his father's life at the battle of the Ticinus River (218 BC), which Hannibal won. He would then have been *c*.17, somewhat late for the change in garb, by the standards of the late Republic and early Empire.

(3.) 33. 2 patrem reum defendat (he defended his father in court). A confusion with his brother Lucius Cornelius Scipio Asiaticus, who was accused of taking bribes from Antiochus, king of Syria, in 187 BC (Val. Max. 3. 7. 1).

(3.) 33. 4 legem, patria, praemia patrum (the law, his country, the rewards of father-hood). In an effort to raise the birthrate, Julius Caesar had granted privileges to fathers, and the Augustan marriage legislation added advantages in holding office and in receiving legacies. But, in speaking of rewards, Seneca is perhaps thinking more generally of the very powerful position of the father in Roman society, both legally and morally.

(3.) 34. 1 institutis liberalibus (in liberal studies). In *Ep.* 88. 23 Seneca explains that *liberalia studia* is the Latin term for the general education the Greeks had invented and called *enkuklios paideia* (hence 'encyclopedia'). The Latin term emphasizes the suitability of such studies, not vocational or useful, to a free man, though Aristotle *Pol.* 8. 1338^{a}30–2 had already characterized such education as free and noble. In the letter Seneca mentions grammar, music, astronomy, and geometry: the first along with rhetoric and dialectic was to make up the medieval *trivium*; the rest, along with arithmetic, the medieval *quadrivium*. He explains that they are a preparation for learning virtue through philosophy, just as the rudiments taught by elementary training (*litteratura*) prepare us for liberal studies: here he does not sharply distinguish elementary training from the liberal arts, nor spell out the more important thing for which they prepare us. Yet the Stoic proofs that follow in (3.) 35 show, by implication, that it is philosophical knowledge.

(3.) 35 quaedam ex nostra, ut ita dicam, moneta proferre (something coined, so to speak, in our mint). With 'so to speak' Seneca may mark a metaphor of his own invention (von Albrecht 2004, 35). As often, Seneca indicates by 'our' Stoic doctrines (e.g. *Ep.* 33. 3). Though he is elsewhere critical of the Stoic penchant for using dry syllogisms in teaching ethics (e.g. *Ep.* 82. 8, 19–20 and Ch. 7B), Seneca makes use of Stoic propositional logic, adducing five arguments that fit the first two of the five basic inference schemata for syllogisms attributed to Chrysippus (Sextus, *PH* 2. 157–8, cf. *Adv. Math.* 8. 224–7). As Cooper and Procopé 1995, 269 n. 58 suggest, all but the fourth argument ((3.) 35. 4) have the form of the first of these *anapodeiktoi tropoi* (indemonstrable or self-evident forms): 'if the first, then the second; but the first; therefore the second'. The fourth, they suggest, follows the form of the second: 'if the first, then the second; but not the second; therefore not the first', viz. if a person who has given life (which is necessary to giving benefits) cannot be outdone in benefits, then a doctor or sailor who has saved a person's life cannot be outdone in benefits; but these people can be outdone in benefits; therefore a father, like others who have given life, can be outdone.

(3.) 35. 1 est autem aliquid vita melius (but there is something better than life). For the Stoics, life is just one of the positive indifferents (D. L. 7. 106): virtue or the life of virtue, as the only good, is better, as Seneca says at (3.) 33. 5.

(3.) 35. 4 non potuissent enim referre gratiam, nisi vitam accepissent (for these could not have returned the favour unless they had been given their lives). Cooper and Procopé 1995 suggest emending the verbs to the singular, referring back to *alicui*, which makes the argument clear, but *nobis* two sentences down suggests that a looser logic obtains here.

ergo nec medico gratia in maius referri potest (therefore it is not possible to return a favour to a doctor beyond his desert). Seneca's appreciation of the services of at least some doctors, shown here and in 6. 15–16. 5, contrasts with the attacks on them by the Elder Cato, followed in his attitudes by the Elder Pliny (Nutton 1986). Seneca only considers here the case where a physician saves one's life; in the more substantial discussion in Book 6 he mentions the maintenance of the patient's health as well, and explains that we owe gratitude, not for the invaluable result itself, nor for the doctor's skill and time, for which we pay a fee, but for the concern and care with which he looks after one as a friend.

nec nautae, si naufragum sustulit (nor to a sailor, if he picked up a shipwrecked person). Paul (*Dig.* 39. 5. 34.1; *Sent.* 5. 11. 6) remarks, 'If one rescues someone from robbers or enemies and receives something from him in recognition of this service, this is an irrevocable gift: it should not be described as a reward for outstanding effort, since it is not accepted that regard for safety be valued at any particular amount.'

(3.) 37. In *Ep.* 95. 65–72 Seneca adds to the various forms of moral teaching recommended by Posidonius the use of historical examples, which Quintilian (12. 2. 30) marked as the distinctive Roman contribution to morality and moral instruction. The first two occur again at *Ben.* 6. 36. 1 to illustrate another point, which involves showing that their *pietas* would be compromised under certain conditions. The example of Aeneas and his father Anchises follows the version in Virgil's *Aeneid*, but it is here treated as an historical episode. The first three are in chronological order, but the last (37. 4) is earlier than the third but stands as a climax, since it illustrates piety towards a father despite mistreatment.

(3.) 37. 2 **Siculi iuvenes** (the Sicilian youths). The two Sicilians, Amphinomos and Anapias (Strabo 6. 2. 3 269C), performed their exploit at Catania. The incident, already a legend in the mid-fourth century BC (Lycurg. *Leoc.* 95) and dated to the mid-fifth century by Aelian (with different names), forms the climax of the hexameter poem *Aetna*, transmitted in the *Appendix Vergiliana* and usually dated to Seneca's time, though the attribution to his correspondent Lucilius, who was writing poetry about Sicily where he was a procurator *c.*62 (*NQ* 3. 1. 1 and *Ep.* 79. 4–7 where Seneca hopes he will describe Aetna) is speculative. Claudian, *Carm. Min.* 17 still celebrates the statues of them in Catania, and their heads appear on Sicilian and Roman coins.

(3.) 37. 3. Seneca confuses the Macedonian king Antigonus with his son Demetrius Poliorcetes, who in 306 BC won Cyprus from Ptolemy for his father. Seneca is careless with early history, probably relying on collections of *exempla* (Griffin 1976, 182–3).

(3.) 37. 4 **vicit patrem imperiosum quidem Manlius** (victory went to Manlius, and over a tyrannical father). Seneca plays on the name of the father, L. Manlius Capitolinus Imperiosus, as does Livy 7. 4. 5, but fails to note his dictatorship of 363 BC. Seneca also leaves out other details included in the other extant sources for the story (Cic. *Off.* 3. 112; Livy 7. 4–5; Val. Max. 5. 4. 3; 6. 9. 1): the name of the son, Titus Manlius, who later took the cognomen Torquatus and was consul in 347 BC; the name of the tribune of 362 BC, M. Pomponius; and the principal charges against the father, which were connected with his conduct as dictator. Cicero, who tells the story to illustrate the respect for oaths in early Rome, omits the reason for the son's relegation. Seneca cannot, then, have adapted the story entirely from Cicero's version. See **ad (3.) 18–28**; **(3.) 29–38** for the attitude to *patria potestas*.

Synopsis of Book 4

12. 2   A benefit is not self-interested: it should involve us in loss and risk.

12. 3–15   *The true rewards of giving benefits.*
12. 3–5   Good conscience is our reward, for giving benefits is one of our duties as human beings.
13–15   Contrary to the Epicurean view, we take pleasure in giving benefits without thought of return.

16–24   Doing a favour in return is worthy of choice in itself.

16   *Honourable acts are valuable in themselves, not for their expediency, and no one can deny that to be grateful is honourable. Therefore to be grateful is worthy of choice in itself.*

17   *Returning benefits is not motivated by profit, ambition, or fear (there is no legal sanction), but by the natural attractiveness of virtue which even the wicked feel.*

18   *That gratitude is to be chosen for itself is shown by ingratitude being something to be avoided in itself, because it destroys the harmony of human society, while reason and fellowship are the means to security furnished by god.*

19   *Even Epicureans recognize something intrinsically valuable when they worship god not from fear, gratitude, or expectation of reward: that something is what is honourable, and nothing is more honourable than gratitude.*

20–2   *Gratitude may be advantageous, but it is valuable even if it prove the reverse.*
21   The man who is grateful in the sense of feeling, not of action, receives no credit and may suffer from appearing ungrateful.
22   Testamentary gifts show that we regard the virtue of gratitude as its own reward.

23–4   *Virtue, especially gratitude, like the heavenly bodies, bestows advantage on us but should be valued for its majesty.*

25   THE GOAL OF LIVING ACCORDING TO NATURE AND IMITATING THE GODS MEANS GIVING WITHOUT ADVANTAGE TO OURSELVES.

Notes to Synopsis of Book 4

According to the retrospective description at 5. 1. 1, this is the last book devoted to the initial task Seneca set himself, although the three topics announced in Book 1. 4. 3 of giving, receiving and returning benefits, have in fact been covered in Books 1–3. At the start of Book 4, Seneca says that he has now reached the most important question: whether or not conferring benefits, and doing a favour in return, are things worthy of choice in themselves. Standing at the centre of the treatise, with three books of precepts preceding and three books of problematic cases and complex questions following, Book 4 serves to relate the three topics already treated in Books 1–3 to the fundamental doctrines of Stoicism: virtue as the *summum bonum* (2. 2–3); the nature of virtuous acts (9–11, 29. 3); the nature of true joy as opposed to the Epicurean concept of pleasure (13–15, 29. 3); the social instincts of human beings (18); and, forming the high point of the book (25), the nature of divine providence and its role as a model for human conduct (see **ad (4.) 3–9. 1**). In the second half of the book (26–40), the treatment of hard cases explores the concept and behaviour of the Stoic Sage (see pp. 120,122). In its deployment of syllogisms (1. 3, cf. 16. 2) and use of definitions (12. 1; 26–7), its appeal to the behaviour of providential nature (7–9. 1), and its discussion of human behaviour (e.g. 3. 1–2; 10. 3–11. 6), the book is a perfect illustration of the mixture of arguments from the logical, physical, and ethical branches of philosophy, mentioned as characteristic of some Stoics by Diogenes Laertius (7. 40).

(4.) 1–24. Seneca sets out at 1. 1 a double *quaestio infinita* or *thesis* (Cicero also used the term *propositum*). He then divides it into two, as he makes plain at 3. 1 and 16. 1: discussion of the first—whether giving a benefit is something worthy of choice in itself—occupies chs. 3–15 (see **ad (4.) 3. 1**); discussion of the second—whether doing a favour in return is something worthy of choice in itself—occupies 16–24.

On Seneca's use of *quaestiones infinitae* or general (as opposed to specific) questions, see Ch. 7B. They were divided into two types: theoretical (relating to *cognitio*) and practical (relating to *actio*), the theoretical being subdivided into three, of which the third, *qualitas*, included such questions as *expetendane sit gloria* ('whether glory is worthy of choice') and *si expetendae divitiae* ('whether riches are worthy of choice', Cic. *Top.* 84). *Qualitas* is clearly the subdivision of the theoretical to which Seneca's two questions here belong (cf. Cic. *De or.* 3.

112, where the general question, whether virtue is chosen for its own value or on account of some results, is given as an example of those relating to *cognitio*). Such questions were familiar to Seneca's readers from their rhetorical education: in *Top.* 69, Cicero gives as an example of the argument from comparison, used in oratory, putting what is chosen on its own account over what is chosen for the sake of something else.

(4.) 1. 1 aut magis, ut ait Sallustius, cum cura dicendum (or, to quote Sallust, more 'in need of careful discussion'). From Sallust's *Histories*, fr. 2. 72 Maurenbrecher = 2. 84 McGushin. The Sallustian phrase was *vir cum cura dicendus* and is used by Seneca, without indication of author, at *Prov.* 5. 9 and *Tranq.* 14. 10. Sallust was probably speaking of Mithridates (cf. Vell. Pat. 2. 18. 1).

(4.) 1. 2–15. The proofs that each of the two questions is to be answered in the affirmative rest on the common philosophical view that the honourable, or virtuous, is worth choosing for its own sake and, more specifically, on the Stoic view that virtue is the sole good, and that its achievement does not require the *acquisition* of anything, only the *selection* of things in accordance with nature (Cic. *Fin.* 3. 36; 5. 20). Seneca takes the Stoic view for granted ((4.) 1. 3 *fin.*) and opposes it to the Epicurean view that the highest good and aim of life is pleasure, virtue only being worth pursuing as a means to an end.

Most of Seneca's discussion of the first question consists of demonstrations that people are not in fact moved by the thought of return in giving benefits but, like nature (or the gods), give selflessly, combined with exhortations to this course of conduct. This mixture is not surprising, given that theoretical questions under *qualitas* are particularly hard to distinguish from those in the *officium* subdivision of the practical questions (Ch. 7 n. 62). Seneca starts with a syllogism in 1. 3, then contrasts the Stoic view of virtuous acts with the Epicureans' instrumental view of virtue (2), then tries to prove that people in fact do not give in hope of return (3.–9. 1) and answers objections to this view (9. 2–12. 2). Finally, he names the real rewards of generosity: a good conscience at fulfilling one's role as a human being (12. 3–5), and true delight in the action itself (13–15). The arguments he opposes are not all Epicurean, see below **ad (4.) 7–8**.

(4.) 1. 2 in ultro tributis sit (appears on our discretionary budget). A technical term of public finance, this is the only metaphorical use recorded. Contracts for public works were given by the censors and perhaps seemed more subject to the discretion of the senate (Mommsen, *Staatsrecht* ii. 446) in that they involved the handing over of public money once and for all, unlike the letting of contracts for tax collection which occurred at regular intervals and for limited periods (*Tabula Heracleensis* (*Roman Statutes* no. 24), v. 73; *Lex Irnitana* J, vv. 10–11 in González 1986, 212; Varro *LL* 6. 11; Livy 39. 44. 7; 43. 16. 2). At *Ep.* 113. 31 Seneca uses the less technical expression *ultro impendere* to indicate non-routine spending, perhaps with a suggestion of the public good.

(4.) 1. 3 Si quid commodi forte obvenerit, inter accessiones numerabis (if it happens that some advantage results, then you will count that a bonus). Following on the question *si hoc grate fecero?*, which suggests that, so far, we are still discussing both the reciprocal virtuous acts (giving benefits and doing a favour in return) that feature in the double question of 1. 1, the word *accessiones* in this sentence seems to mark the point at which the discussion of the first half of the question alone begins, for at 2. 33. 1 Seneca had developed the idea that any tangible reward for conferring a *beneficium* is a mere *accessio*, the real reward for a *beneficium* being good conscience. In *Ep.* 5. 1. 10–13 Pliny uses the verb *accedere* of the *fructus famae*, an addition to the *fructus conscientiae* of an act of generosity. Seneca waits to attach the term *bona conscientia* to the intrinsic reward of virtue until 12. 4.

beneficium autem honestum est (but a benefit is something honourable). Seneca here speaks of *beneficium*, rather than *beneficium dare* as in (4.)1. 1, because he has in mind the definition of *beneficium* given in Book 1 (1. 6. 1, cf. 2. 34. 5–35. 1) as *benevola actio*, the act of giving, not what is given (*materia beneficii*, 1. 5. 2): see **ad 1. 5–1. 9. 1**. Its status there (1. 5. 3) as *recte factum*, hence *honestum*, is assumed here.

per se autem expetendum esse honestum saepe et abunde probatum est (and that the honourable is worthy of choice in itself has been often and fully proved). The syllogism proving that *beneficium* (*dare*) *per se res expetenda est* appears to be set out as a Stoic hypothetical syllogism: if both *p* and also *q*, then *r*; *p* <and also *q*> ∴ *r*, where this proposition (in the form *beneficium per se expetendum est*, see n. above) is *r*, *p* is *honestum per se expetendum est*, and *q* is *beneficium* (*dare*) *honestum est*. But it also resembles the Aristotelian syllogism Barbara: all B are A; all C are B; ∴ all C are A, where B is *honesta*, A is *per se expetenda*, and C is *beneficia*. In saying that p (or, in Barbara, the major premise) has often been proved, Seneca has in mind defences such as Cicero gives in *Fin.* 3. 36, cf. *Leg.* 1. 48 where generosity is one of the virtues specifically mentioned. For his assumption that q (or, in Barbara, the minor premise) has been proved, see n. above *ad fin.*

(4.) 2. To clarify the Stoic position, Seneca—as elsewhere, notably in *De Vita Beata*—contrasts the Epicurean position in unflattering terms, though Seneca was not averse to borrowing arguments from Epicurus (**ad 3. 4. 1**), particularly in the early *Letters to Lucilius*, and knew that it was actually an austere doctrine (*Vit. beat.* 13.1–3). Here and later at 13–16. 1, Seneca confronts the Epicureans on the major question of the *summum bonum* (2. 3), which both schools agreed was the end of life and the source of happiness (*beata vita* at 2. 3) and rested on nature, but which the Epicureans identified with pleasure, the Stoics with virtue. In 4–6 (and later at 19) he will confront them on another key issue: the Stoics believed in divine providence, while the Epicureans thought the gods were indifferent to men. Seneca conducts the argument with the Epicureans like a philosophical debate (*disputationem* 2. 2; *disputatur* 2. 3).

(4.) 2. 1 virtus voluptatum ministra est (virtue is the servant of the pleasures). Seneca may have in mind Cleanthes' description of Voluptas decked out as a queen and seated on a throne, with the Virtues ministering to her as servile handmaidens (*Fin.* 2. 69).

This was a hostile representation of the Epicurean view that the virtues are desirable because they are productive of pleasure, properly understood: in *Fin.* 1. 52–3 the Epicurean Torquatus is made to argue that liberality wins affection and good will, and guarantees security, peace, and pleasure.

(4.) 2. 2 tu illam iubes signum petere (you are making it look elsewhere for orders). Having rejected the idea of virtue as slave to pleasure, Seneca now moves on to a military image. Virtue should be giving the orders, not waiting for a signal from a commander: an image used also in *Vit. beat.* 8. 1–2; 11. 2 (followed by virtue as a *praegustator*); 14. 1.

(4.) 2. 4 sed quod omnino cum voluptate (but that it is put in any relation with pleasure at all). The climax of the argument is that virtue should not even be the mistress or commander of pleasure, but should have no connection with it at all. The same point occurs at *Vit. beat.* 12. 3; 15. 1–3. Cicero uses similar arguments at *Fin.* 5. 21–2 and *Off.* 3. 119, to combat the views of the philosophers Callipho and Dinomachus, who made the *summum bonum* a combination of virtue and pleasure. However, this is hyperbole, since Seneca has admitted at 1. 3, and will again at 22. 3–4, that advantage of some sort, though not a cause or reward of virtue, can be a by-product (cf. *Vit. beat.* 9 on pleasure as an *accessio* of virtue).

virilibus incommodis (manly obstacles). The contrast of Epicureanism as effeminate and Stoicism as manly is common, e.g. *Vit. beat.* 13. 3.

(4.) 3–9. 1. Insisting that benefits are not in fact given in hope of recompense, Seneca first argues from the recipients we choose (3. 1), then from the donors (3. 2–3), the key example being the gods who need nothing from us. Seneca will have had in mind the classic discussion of whether we can give the gods benefits in Plato's *Euthyphro* 13 B–15 C. A lengthy defence of the Stoic notion of divine providence follows in 4–9. 1. This is the first of four extended treatments of Stoic theology in Book 4, the others being 17–19 and 31–32. 4, again on divine providence, and 25–26. 1 on the related subject of imitation of god. This is more than occur in any other book, though Book 2. 29–30 and Book 6. 20–3 are comparable in weight.

(4.) 3. 1 quia beneficium, de quo nunc agitur, dare (because conferring a benefit, our present topic). See **ad 4. 1. 3** for the question of where Seneca started this topic.

praeferam (I shall prefer). The reading *praeferimus*, preferred by Hosius, is rejected by Holmes 2004, 295, because it is the only instance of the present indicative plural form of *fero* or its compounds in Seneca: it was also avoided by Cicero. Holmes prefers either *praeferamus* or *praeferam*, one of which must have been the reading of N. Since the argument requires an indicative (for it is the fact of our giving by choice to the poor that is needed to refute the supposition that we give in hopes of a return), *praeferam*, favoured by Préchac 1961, is the better reading.

(4.) 3. 2 plenosque et tutos et inviolabiles (fully supplied and safe and inviolate). Seneca had explained at 2. 30. 2 that the gods can only be repaid by gratitude. At (4.) 19 he contrasts with the Stoic view the Epicurean way of making their gods safe, despite the removal of their power.

(4.) 3. 3 **istud non beneficium sed fenus est circumspicere, non ubi optime ponas, sed ubi quaestuosissime habeas, unde facillime tollas** (it does not count as a benefit but as an investment, if you are considering not where can you best place it, but where you can derive the most profit and secure the easiest returns). See Ch. 3A pp. 39–40 for the importance of the contrast with loans, and cf. Cic. *Amic.* 31. Seneca here looks forward to the argument, in 9. 2–11.5, that showing discrimination does not mean that we seek advantage.

(4.) **4–6.** Seneca starts his defence of the Stoic notion of divine providence by countering (4) the Epicurean conception of the gods as serene, untroubled beings, not concerning themselves with the world or with human beings. Spared distress of any kind, they are model Epicureans, enjoying true pleasure and happiness (D.L. 10. 76–7, 123–4; *KD* 1; Cic. *Nat. d.* 1. 45, 51–4, 85, 121–4). Stoic polemic against the Epicurean conception of the gods goes back at least to Aristo of Chios, pupil of Zeno (Kechagia 2010, 141–2). At 5–6 Seneca proceeds to list the divine benefits in a rhetorical crescendo, culminating in the idea that even what humans invent they owe to the gods.

(4.) 4. 2 **nec in hunc furorem omnes mortales consensissent adloquendi surda numina** (all mortals would not have agreed on the insane practice of addressing deities who are deaf). The argument from human consensus in general is favoured by Aristotle, e.g. *NE* 10. 2. 1172^{b}36–1173^{a}1. Xenophon (*Mem.* 1. 4. 14; *Apol.* 13) attributes to Socrates such an argument about the nature of gods, and such arguments were used by the Epicureans (e.g. Cic. *Nat. d.* 1. 43–4) and the Stoics (e.g. Cic. *Nat. d.* 2. 4–5; *Div.* 1.11–12, 84, 90–4). See Obbink 1992. Seneca mentions the consensus argument at *Ep.* 117. 6, giving universal belief in the gods as an example.

(4.) 5. 2 **ut omnis rerum naturae pars tributum aliquod nobis conferret** (so that every part of nature pays tribute of some kind to us). For the Stoics, plants and animals (here exhaustively listed as those of the earth, sea and sky) are there for the use of rational beings (e.g. Cic. *Nat. d.* 2. 133), a view that passed into Christian theology.

(4.) 5. 3 **quaedam aestatis diebus mirabile incrementum trahunt** (some of them miraculously increased in the days of summer). The Nile is the key example. At *NQ* 3. 26 Seneca gives four possible explanations of the phenomenon, not including the melting of snow.

medicatorum torrentium venae (sources of healing springs). Seneca has a lot to say about these in *NQ*, e.g. 3. 1. 2; 3. 2. 1; 3. 25. 11. The chapter closes with Virgil's praise of Lake Como and Lake Garda in *Georgics* 2. 159–60.

(4.) 6. 1 **cuius investigandi tibi facultatem dedit** (he has given you the skill to find). Elsewhere Seneca, like other Roman moralists, regards mining as a misuse of nature by man: *Ep.* 94. 57, where divine providence is said to have deliberately hidden corrupting metals, cf. 90. 45; *NQ* 5. 15. 1–4.

(4.) 6. 2 **domicilium sine ullo incendii aut ruinae metu** (mansion free of the threat of fire or collapse). Seneca ignores the Stoic idea, shortly to appear at 8. 1, of a periodic conflagration, in which the universe is consumed, only to reconstitute itself in the same form. The mansion is the universe, and the gleaming ceiling the stars at night.

(4.) 6. 4. Virgil, *Ecl.* 1. 6. The *deus* here is Octavian, to whom gratitude is expressed for restoration of land, confiscated in the proscriptions of 43 BC.

(4.) 6. 6 insita sunt nobis omnium aetatium, omnium artium semina, magisterque ex occulto deus producit ingenia (inborn in us are the seeds of all ages, and of all skills: and it is god who, as our teacher, draws forth from hidden depths our talents). When Seneca moves on at 6. 5 from the rustic song to the arts proper, he may be thinking of the distinction in Plato's *Gorgias* 465 A between a craft (*technē*), based on reason, and a knack (*empeiria*), based on experience or trial and error: the arts are harder to attribute to divine providence because of the input of human reason, but Seneca reminds us that our reason is an offshoot of the divine Logos. The sparks of the divine Logos are often described as seeds (*spermatikoi logoi*), cf. *Ep.* 120. 4 'seeds of the knowledge of the good and the honourable'; *Ep.* 108. 8 'seed of the virtues'. The Logos also oversees the development of the seeds, since it works by fate (L–S, p. 277), which is the necessary sequence of causes that controls all events. See D.L. 7. 148 for the way in which nature 'completes and sustains its products in accordance with seminal principles (*kata spermatikous logous*) at determinate times' (L–S 43A): a passage which leads to a discussion of fate, cf. L–S 46A and G, where the connection with fate is clear.

(4.) 7–8. Following on from the mention of human growth and development, which the Stoics ascribed to nature (*NQ* 2. 45. 2), Seneca turns to confront the objection that it is nature that offers these things. The objection is not a continuation of the confrontation with the Epicureans in 4–6 (which resumes in 13. 1), for the Epicurean nature is not providential. (Cf. Pliny in *HN* 2. 27, who, surveying conceptions of deity, settles on the power of nature as the most satisfactory: clearly not the Epicurean conception.) Seneca explains how the ordinary terms: nature, god, fate, Zeus, relate to Stoic conceptions of the divine. What he says accords with what D.L. 7. 136, 148–9 gives as Stoic doctrine, citing various authors. (*SVF* ii. 1024 treats (4.) 7–8. 2 as a fragment of Chrysippus.) Seneca goes on to explain the rationale for applying to the divine reason the names and epithets of the pagan gods: they are interpreted as allegorical descriptions of the divine powers and their consequences (7. 2 *fin.*; 8. 3), often with the aid of etymology (cf. Cic. *Nat. d.* 2. 60–9; 3. 62–4).

(4.) 7. 1 divina ratio toti mundo partibusque eius inserta (divine reason which permeates the whole world and its parts). D.L. 7. 134 explains that the Stoic divinity is not transcendent but immanent, the active principle of reason that makes things out of the qualityless substance that constitutes the passive principle (cf. *Ep.* 65. 2).

Stator (the Stayer). Livy 1. 12. 6 has Romulus promising Jupiter a temple to Jupiter Stator, if he stops the Roman flight in a battle against the Sabines (cf. Plut. *Rom.* 18. 7). Seneca's interpretation, already found in Cicero (*Cat.* 1. 11, 33) and Varro (*gram.* pp. 236–7, fr. 137), that Jupiter is called Stator as the stabilizing protector of the state, may be a later political one (Ogilvie 1965, 78). In *De matrimonio* Seneca ridicules

Chrysippus' argument that epithets of the gods can tell us how we should behave, by deducing from it that a person who willingly sat down would then be offending Jupiter Stator (fr. 46 Haase = 24 Vottero). He there interprets *stator* according to the opposition of *sto* and *sedeo*, in order to mock the etymological explanations so dear to the Stoics (cf. D.L. 7. 147, in which Zeus is falsely explained as Ζῆνα from ζῆν, to live). In *De beneficiis* 1. 3. 8–10 Seneca derisively characterizes Chrysippus' allegorical interpretation of the portrayal of the dance of the Graces, and the significance of their mother's name, as *fabulae* (see **ad 1. 3. 2–4. 5**).

(4.) **7. 2 hunc eum et fatum si dixeris** (if you call this entity 'fate' as well). D.L. 7. 135 names the *heimarmenē* as another name for god, reason, Zeus. The idea that god, divine reason, fate, nature, represent different aspects rather than a hierarchy of powers, is the orthodox Stoic view and is found in *NQ* 2. 45. Here Seneca identifies the different aspects as different gifts or benefits, because he is discussing the gifts of providence. In *Div.* 1. 125, Cicero, following principally Posidonius, shows how divination can be explained by adducing three of these aspects as sources: god, who sends signs to guide us; fate, which is the series of causes that allows us to predict an event from the preceding one; nature, which empowers the soul to divine in sleep or frenzy, and which gives natural signs that diviners can use (see Kidd 1988, pp. 426–8, 434–5).

prima omnium causa (the first cause of all), cf. *NQ* 2. 45. 2 *causa causarum*; *Ep.* 65. 12 *prima et generalis causa*.

(4.) **8. 1 Mercurius.** See **ad 1. 3. 7**, where Seneca rejects the interpretation of his standing with the Graces as showing that argument and speech commend benefits. The Greeks connected Hermes with *logos*. Seneca is here giving his own version of the allegory.

Liberum patrem. The Romans identified their god of fertility and wine with the Greek god Dionysus or Bacchus.

seminum vis est <vitae> consultura per voluptatem (the seminal power that provides <for life> through pleasure). Basore 1935, in the Loeb edition, supplies <*vitae*>; Préchac 1961 <*vitae perpetuitati*> in the Budé. The power symbolized by the fertility god is, according to Aetius (L–S 53H), one of the parts of the soul emanating from the *hegemonikon* and stretching out into the body.

(4.) **8. 3 sive praenomen eius sive nomen dixisses sive cognomen** (whether you used his *praenomen*, his *nomen*, or his *cognomen*). Seneca lists the parts of a Roman name in the reverse order from that in which he gave his own names.

sic nunc naturam voca, fatum, fortunam; omnia eiusdem dei nomina sunt varie utentis sua potestate (so now call him 'nature', 'fate', or 'fortune': all are names of the same god, using his power in different ways). The last term is now added to the previous equivalents. The Stoics defined *tuchē* (fortune) as 'a cause unintelligible to human reason' (*SVF* ii. 965–73), clearly the subjective form of fate, with which Seneca often identifies it, e.g. *Prov.* 5. 4 *non trahuntur a fortuna, sequuntur illam* ('they are not dragged by fortune, they follow her'). Seneca often uses it to represent the erroneous view of indifferents, good and bad, to which all but the Sage are liable, so that they set too much store by the 'goods' that fortune brings (see p. 150) and fail to see the providential nature of the 'evils' that she inflicts. See Stacey 2007, 14–15, 65–72, Asmis 2009 on fortune in Seneca, as something to be forcefully overcome, an externalized projection of the interior struggle to achieve a rational view of the world.

unius animi bona sunt (good qualities of one and the same mind). Seneca seems to offer, as a parallel to the idea of aspects of the divine reason, the doctrine of the unity of the virtues: whoever has one, has them all. He discusses later in this book (26. 2–27), and in 5. 15, the unity of the vices: the fool has them all; he argues that there is a sense in which they can be distinguished, as with fate and nature here. Cf. *Ep.* 113. 24: 'The same mind is both moderate and just and prudent and brave, being disposed in a certain way with respect to the individual virtues.' As L–S explain (p. 384), 'All the virtues have their theorems in common, but from differing perspectives. Each takes as a secondary perspective the theorems governing its own special area of conduct; and this is sufficient to differentiate it as a distinct virtue. But each takes as a secondary perspective the theorems governing other areas of conduct; and this is sufficient to guarantee that they have all their theorems in common, and hence are inseparable.'

(4.) 9. 2–12. 2. Seneca here counters objections based on turning his own views against him. In 9. 2–10. 2 he explains that carefully choosing the beneficiary does not mean looking for a donor who can afford to make a good return, but is part of the discrimination necessary for a rational and virtuous act, such as giving a benefit. He goes on to show that in practice our choice of beneficiaries shows that we are not concerned with reward (10. 3–11. 6). In 12. 1–2 he argues against the objection that calling a benefit an unpaid loan shows that we want a reward: he explains the metaphor and again adduces actual human behaviour. Schwarzenberg 1966, 60, n. 38 assumes that the objection is attributed by Seneca to Epicurus, but see ad (4.) 7–8.

(4.) 9. 2 quia ne agricolae quidem semina harenis committant (since even farmers do not sow their seed in sand). The objector uses Seneca's own image of sowing for selecting the right recipient (see ad **1. 1– 3. 1**), which has already occurred at 1. 1. 2 and 2. 11. 4–5. The issue of choosing the beneficiary returns at the end of the rebuttal of this objection (9. 3 *itaque, cum eligo, cui dem beneficium*), but, in the meantime, the objection is broadened to include other kinds of discrimination. The objection brings out the limitations of the metaphor, for sowing is not disinterested, and the return is everything, whereas Seneca does not regard the winning of gratitude as a reputable goal (*Ep.* 81. 19 spells this out). Cicero, however, who uses the same image of sowing at *Off.* 1. 48, does consider gratitude and good will earned from liberality as coming under the pursuit of the *utile*, which is justifiable when it coincides with the *honestum* (2. 21–2, 32, 85).

ubi et quomodo (where and how). These words were supplied by Gertz 1876 from *quocumque loco et quocumque modo* at the end of the sentence. In 9. 3 Seneca adds 'what' and 'when'. Similarly, in *Ep.* 89. 3, 'when', 'what', 'where', and 'how' are the headings. Gertz's suggested replacement of *quid* (what) in 9. 3 by *cui* (to whom), followed by Hosius, should be resisted, as Seneca only reverts to the issue of choosing a beneficiary at the end of the rebuttal, with *Itaque, cum eligo, cui dem* (9. 3), and only returns to it properly at 10. 3 (see **ad (4.) 9. 2–12. 2**). In the meantime, the discussion is broadened to include other kinds of discrimination.

(4.) 9. 3 id ago ut quandoque beneficium sit (I ensure that it is in fact a benefit). Cf. 1. 2. 1 where Seneca says a *beneficium* requires *iudicium*, and 1. 15. 3 where he says that it must be a rational act based on judgement (**ad 1. 1. 2**) to count as an act of virtue.

(4.) 10. 1. Seneca has in mind Plato, *Resp.* 1. 331 c, where the definition of justice as returning deposits is refuted by arguing that returning a weapon to the person who deposited it with one, but who has since become mad, cannot be just. Cicero in *Off.* 3. 95 uses the example in discussing apparent conflicts between justice and utility, showing that keeping promises and returning deposits does not always constitute justice.

utrum infitier an palam reddam (whether I deny the deposit or openly return it). Lipsius reversed *an* and *palam*, taking 'openly' with 'deny'. He is followed by Cooper and Procopé 1995, who translate *negabo* in the next sentence as 'I shall say "no" '—an open repudiation. Watt 1994, 227–8 suggests reading *an palam <non> reddam* ('or openly refuse to return it'), in support of which he invokes Cic. *Off.* 3. 95, *si gladium quis apud te sana mente deposuerit, repetat insaniens, reddere peccatum sit, officium non reddere* ('if someone has deposited a sword with you, when in his right mind, and asks for it back, when he is mentally ill, to return it is a fault, not to return it the proper action'). But Seneca's point here is that *infitiari* is, in some unusual circumstances, the proper return and so equivalent, paradoxically, to its diametric opposite, *palam reddere*, which is the correct return in normal circumstances (see 2. 23. 2, where furtive returning is deemed to be just another form of denial and not a true *beneficium*).

(4.) 10. 5 ad animum tendit aestimatio mea (my evaluation looks to character). Similarly Cicero *Off.* 1. 49; 2. 69–71 recommends giving to poor men who are good, because they are likely to be more grateful, while the rich may resent being beneficiaries and so not be very forthcoming.

(4.) 11. 1 non lucrum ex beneficio capto, non voluptatem, non gloriam (it is not profit, nor pleasure, nor glory, that I seek from a benefit). Seneca identifies the three motives of those donors who do not give for giving's sake. Cicero (**ad (4.) 9. 2**) regards *gloria* as a respectable result of the *benivolentia* earned by generosity (*Off.* 2. 31–2).

(4.) 11. 3 debitores nobis deos delegat (he designates the gods as our debtors). *Delegare* is a legal term, here for appointing someone to repay a debt or, as in 7. 19. 3, to receive payment. The verb is used similarly at *Ep.* 18. 14; the noun *delegatio* at *Ep.* 27. 4. *Symm. Rel.* 7. 3 and Ambrose, *Off.* 2. 126 use it of the poor delegating God to pay back what they cannot. See **ad 6. 5. 2 delegatione e verbis perfecta solutio sit**.

(4.) 11. 5 ubi mors . . . ad ferendam sententiam incorruptum iudicem misit, quaerimus dignissimos, quibus nostra tradamus (when death . . . has sent in an incorrupt judge to give his verdict, we seek out the most deserving to inherit our wealth). The *quaesitor* presiding over the court is death, which ensures that we as *iudices* are not swayed by self-interest. Seneca has in mind the practice among well-off Romans of leaving legacies to people outside the family, as a way of repaying favours (see **ad (4.) 22. 1**). Cicero at *Fin.* 3. 65 gives will-making as an example of our putting the common advantage over our own. A less altruistic motive, in practice, was the advertising of prestigious connections and the hope of being remembered (see Champlin 1991, chs. 7, 9).

(4.) 11. 6 **magna voluptas** (great pleasure). With this implied correction of the Epicurean idea of pleasure (mentioned in 11. 5) Seneca prepares the ground for another anti-Epicurean attack in 13.

(4.) 12. 1 **beneficium creditum insolubile ... imagine et translatione utimur** (a benefit is an unrepayable loan ... we are using a figure, a metaphor). As Seneca explains at 2. 18. 5, a benefit creates a bond of friendship which imposes further obligations and is thus unrepayable. On his use of the metaphor of debt, while distinguishing sharply between loans and benefits, see **ad 1. 1. 1 male collocata** and Ch. 3A pp. 39–40.

(4.) 12. 1 **sic enim et legem dicimus iusti iniustique regulam esse** (in the same way we call law a rule determining what is just and what is unjust). Cooper and Procopé 1995 suggest that Seneca is quoting Chrysippus, whose treatise *On Law* opened with a characterization of law as 'a rule or standard of things just and things unjust (*kanōn dikaiōn kai adikōn*, *SVF* iii. 314). As. Seneca implies that the law meant is something to be chosen for itself, he must be thinking of natural law emanating directly from the *logos* (Cic. *Rep.* 3. 33; *Leg.* 1. 18) and identical with the *orthos logos*, and with Zeus, and with virtue (D.L. 7. 88).

(4.) 12. 2 **quemadmodum dixi** (as I have said). At (4.) 1. 2.

ut tuto transire praemittatur (although I am allowed to go on in safety). The reading *at ... praemittitur* is preferred by Préchac 1961, retaining the indicative of the first hand's correction of N, but still with the meaning that I can be unaffected. Alexander (1950–2*a*, 22) retains Axelson's indicative, but prefers his *et* to N's *ut*, and interprets the sentence 'I defend him and [thus] it is allowed for him to pass safely on his way'. But consistency with the three further examples that follow requires that the cost and danger to the *benefactor* be spelt out (cf. especially *cum abire in partem alteram possim* (when I might take the other side)). Koch's conjecture of *cum* for *ut* would make the concessive idea even clearer.

quas illi detraxero sordes sub accusatoribus isdem fortasse sumpturus (ready to put on the garb of mourning that I have spared him at the hands of the same accusers). Seneca alludes to the conventional garb of mourning assumed by the defendant whose *caput* was at stake, letting his hair grow long, not washing, and wearing dark clothes to attract sympathy.

spondeo pro iudicato et suspensis amici bonis libellum deicio creditoribus eius me obligaturus (I stand surety for a man adjudged a debtor and, when the friend's property is put up for sale, I take down the notice, ready to make myself liable to his creditors). As soon as a man was adjudged a debtor or failed to appear in court (as in *Pro Quinctio* 25–7, 48), his creditors could apply for possession of the man's property, and notices were put up showing what goods were available for sale, in order to satisfy the creditors. The surety here tears down the notice, which signifies either that he offers to dispute the matter (as in *Pro Quinctio* 27), or, as here, to satisfy the creditors.

servare proscriptum (save someone who has been proscribed). Seneca is thinking of the actions by Sulla and the so-called triumvirs who put up lists of the names of their political enemies, citizens who were then denied the protection of the law, and might be killed without penalty and have their property confiscated.

(4.) 12. 3 Tusculanum aut Tiburtinum (a villa at Tusculum or Tibur). Tusculum, near Frascati, and Tibur, the modern Tivoli, were favourite places near Rome for the élite to have villas. Seneca compares buying a villa for enjoyment, so that one does not calculate how many years of profit will be needed to recoup its cost and actually incurs expense maintaining it, with giving *beneficia*, an activity which is intrinsically rewarding and which, as he will spell out at (4.) 15. 4, cf. 2. 11. 4, 7. 32, requires reiteration.

(4.) 12. 4 cum erit, tuendum est (when he has bought it, he must look after it). The simplest emendation, already accepted by Erasmus and Lipsius.

(4.) 12. 5 ita viri officium est inter alia et beneficium dare (so, among other things, it is the duty of a man also to confer benefits). Though conferring a *beneficium* is a free act, not an obligation (*officium*) in any particular instance (3. 18. 1; 3. 19. 1; Cic. *Off.* 1. 48), being a human being carries a general obligation of generosity to one's fellow men, though not on any particular occasion (see Ch. 3A, p. 45).

(4.) 13. 1 vobis voluptas est inertis oti facere corpusculum (your idea of pleasure is to give your contemptible body over to idle sloth). For discussion of the text, see Watt 1994, 228. The language of this chapter unmistakably identifies the 'you' as Epicureans, who are again under attack for teaching that generosity, like all virtues, is a means to pleasure. *Latitare* evokes the Epicurean *lathe biōsas*; *tranquillitas* is the Latin for *ataraxia*, and *intra hortorum latebram* evokes the garden attached to Epicurus' house in Athens, from which the school acquired its nickname, 'The Garden'. In 13. 2, for polemical purposes (cf. *Vit. beat.* 4. 2, *cui vera voluptas erit voluptatum contemptio* (for whom true pleasure will be the scorn of pleasures)), Seneca uses the terms *voluptas*, which is the usual Latin equivalent for *hēdonē* (the highest good to the Epicureans; a despised passion to the Stoics), to denote the true Stoic joy (*chara*, a good emotion), for which *gaudium* is the usual Latin equivalent, as in (4.) 29. 3 (cf. Cic. *Tusc.* 4. 13; Seneca, *Ep.* 59. 2–4, spelling out the problems of usage).

(4.) 13. 3 etiam cum recepero danda sint (even if I recover them, they must be given again). Seneca probably alludes to the general point made by Aristotle at *NE* 5. 1133ª3–5, that we have an obligation to keep the process of exchange going (see Ch. 3A n. 66). Or Seneca may allude to the bond of friendship formed by a *beneficium* and producing further obligations (2. 18. 5), or to the advice to enhance a benefit by renewing it (2. 11. 4–5 and **ad** (4.) 12. 3).

prodest . . . mango venalibus (a dealer is useful to the slaves he sells). This third example is not parallel to the other two, where the beneficiary pays for services. Here the slaves benefit by being fed, with a view to being sold at a profit (cf. 14. 2, on fruit trees and animals that we tend, in hopes of food or service). The point is treated with greater subtlety at 6. 12–17.

(4.) 14. 1. The law is the *Lex Julia de adulteriis coercendis*, which Augustus passed *c.*18 BC and which made adultery with a free respectable woman punishable by partial confiscation of property and relegation for both parties. Seneca has adapted Ovid *Amores* 3. 4. 4 'Who doesn't do it because she can't, does it', to fit his point about giving.

non immerito in numerum peccantium refertur quae pudicitiam timori praestitit, non sibi (she deserves to be reckoned among those who stray, if she owed her chastity to fear, not to herself). Intention is all: every individual action is either correct (*recte factum* = *katorthōma*) or wrong (*vitium* = *hamartēma*) even if the category of action is appropriate (*officium* = *kathēkon*). So being chaste is clearly in general the appropriate behaviour for a married woman; but if she acts from fear, and not from deliberate choice, her action is not correct but wrong. Compare Plato *Phaedo* 82 c on the fear of dishonour and bad repute as a motive for resisting bodily desires.

(4.) 14. 3 ex aequo et bono (out of a sense of justice). Seneca means: as an act of virtue, and thus done for its own sake.

(4.) 14. 4 iniecta manu trahit (drags us off). A favourite legal metaphor of Seneca, signifying asserting one's right to a person or property.

ipso bene faciendi opere laetissima (for the supreme delight of merely doing good). *Laetitia* is used as a synonym for *gaudium* at *Vit. beat.* 22. 3, but denotes a related, possibly subordinate, *eupatheia* at *Vit. beat.* 15. 2, possibly *terpsis* (*SVF* iii. 432): see Asmis 1990, 232 n. 46.

(4.) 15. 1 contraria sit beneficio iniuria (a benefit and an injury are contraries). The point is made and used differently at 3. 22. 3.

(4.) 15. 2 si dixero neminem non amare beneficia sua, neminem non ita compositum animo, ut libentius eum videat, in quem multa congessit (if I say that there is no one who does not love the benefits he confers, no one who is not disposed to take pleasure in seeing a person on whom he has heaped benefits). The latter point is made by Aristotle in *NE* 9. 7. 1167^{b}17–1168^{a}13, who compares the relation of benefactor to beneficiary to that of an artist to his handiwork. In 2. 33. 2–3, Seneca parallels the completion of the artist's handiwork and the completed conferring of the gift (see **ad 2. 33. 2**). Here he explicitly includes both the act of conferral and the recipient. He may be unfair here to the Epicureans, for Plut. *Mor.* 778 c and 1097 a = Us. 544 says that Epicurus held that conferring benefits was pleasanter (*hēdion*) than receiving them: Wind 1958, 37 plausibly ascribes the sentiment to Epicurus' *Peri dōrōn kai charitos*.

(4.) 15. 4 cui etiam infeliciter dato indulgere tam naturale est quam liberis pravis (treating it indulgently, even when it has been unhappily bestowed, is as natural as it is to treat our children so, when they turn out badly). Seneca turns to a comparison, used for a different purpose in *Ep.* 66. 26–7, with the love of parents for their offspring which is independent of their children's attributes, a fact brought out by our greater attachment, if anything, to the weaker (see Inwood 2007, 170–2).

(4.) 16–24. Seneca turns to the second general question posed at the beginning of the book: whether doing a favour in return is something worthy of choice in itself. He says (16. 1) he can use the same arguments as he used to answer the first question, and in fact he again attacks the Epicureans, who regard both giving benefits and returning favours as motivated by expediency, and again adduces arguments from human behaviour, including the law and the making of wills. But the argumentation also progresses in a continuous line from what preceded: Seneca starts with, and continues to stress (16. 3; 17. 2; 17. 4; 21. 6; 22. 3; 24. 1), the point about the intrinsic attractiveness of virtuous acts, with which he had ended the treatment of the first question (13–15). This is now shown to be the working of divine providence, which compensates our physical weaknesses by inclining us to the exchange of services that binds humanity together in fellowship and makes us strong (18). And, going beyond confronting them, he turns the tables on the Epicureans by using their own doctrines against them (19).

(4)16. 2–17. Treating the premise *si honestum per se expetendum est* as established, as in the syllogism at 1. 3, Seneca now argues that being grateful is *honestum*, in 16. 2, which enables him to conclude *gratum esse per se expetendum honestumque*; he then reinforces the intrinsic value of gratitude by rejecting, in 17, other motives for being grateful, and by showing its attraction even to the wicked.

(4.) 16. 2 nequam hominem existimas, cui poena, non cui curatore opus sit (you would count him a wicked man, in need of punishment rather than a keeper). Women, minors, and (as here) the insane, had *curatores* appointed by the praetor to administer their property. Seneca argues that, though his ingratitude in fact disadvantages him (*sibi ipsum inutilem* (useless even to himself); *tamquam rem utilem sibi et profuturam omiserit* (as if he has omitted to do something advantageous and likely to profit him)), in that he fails to attract more gifts or other benefactors (20. 2–3), we prefer to regard him as wicked rather than incompetent.

(4.) 16. 3 hoc expositum est pulchrius (this one is obvious and too beautiful). With *pulchrum*, Seneca recalls the Greek term *kalon* for morally good, using an aesthetic term, rather than *honestum*, to translate it, in order to make the point about its intrinsic attractiveness (see Cooper and Procopé 1995, 287 n. 34).

(4.) 17. 1 huic enim uni rei non posuimus legem (for this is the one thing for which we have provided no legal sanction). See **ad 3. 6–17. 3**, where Seneca defends the general practice, while noting one exception to it (**ad 3. 6. 2**) and ignoring, as here, the fact that Roman freedmen could be charged with ingratitude.

(4.) 17. 2 quomodo nulla lex amare parentes . . . iubet (just as there is no law that orders us to love our parents). See **ad 3. 11** where Seneca acknowledges the existence of laws to protect parents against ingratitude. *Oikeiōsis* (appropriation) saw to it that one proceeded from self-love (cf. Sen. *Ep.* 121. 6–15) to love of family members and beyond (Stob. 4. 671, 7–673, 11 = L–S 57G; Cic. *Fin.* 3. 62–8).

ut insitum sit etiam malis probare meliora (that even bad people instinctively approve what is better). Seneca may have in mind Ovid's Medea in *Met.* 7. 20–1: *video meliora proboque,/deteriora sequor* (I see the better and approve it; I follow the worse).

(4.) 17. 3 gratias itaque agi sibi quos adflixere patiuntur (And so they allow themselves to be thanked by those whom they have hurt). Seneca in *Ira* 2. 33. 2 and Tac.

Agric. 42. 4 remark on this habit of tyrannical emperors. Quint. 3. 8. 44 and Cic. *Off.* 1. 44 have a lot to say about wanting to appear good.

honesti et per se expetendi amor (love of what is honourable and worthy of choice for its own sake). Castiglioni is followed by Cooper and Procopé 1995 in replacing *et* (and) with *ut* (as); but Seneca has already used the combination *per se expetendum honestumque* at 16. 2 *fin.*, having stated at 1. 3 that both qualities have been shown to go together.

nec quisquam tantum . . . hominem exuit, ut animi causa malus sit (no one has . . . shed his humanity to the extent of being evil just for the fun of it). Pagan philosophy agreed that men pursued evil, either because they mistook it for the good, or because they could not resist sensual gratification. Augustine in the *Confessions* 2. 8 showed how evil can be attractive in itself.

(4.) 18. This chapter forms the climax of the argument about the intrinsic value of gratitude, fully illuminating the importance of the topic of *beneficia*, which Seneca said at 1. 4. 2 was the chief bond of human society. Here we learn that providence instils the impulse to give and acknowledge benefits in human beings in order to facilitate the creation of society, as compensation for their vulnerability. Seneca here reconciles the two approaches to the origins of society taken by philosophers since Plato: whether natural sociability (the Stoic view: Cic. *Off.* 1. 12; 2. 13; 2. 15; 1. 158) or practical necessity (Plato, *Resp.* 2. 369 B; Epicureans: Lucr. 5. 1019–27) directed man to live in communities. Sociability is an innate instinct which issues in the exchange of benefits and results in security, but it is implanted in humankind by providence, in order that it should be safe (see p. 27; Griffin 2000, 546).

(4.) 18. 1 nihil aeque concordiam humani generis dissociat ac distrahit quam hoc vitium (nothing so dissolves and disrupts the harmony of mankind as this vice). Seneca adds substance to the statement in Book 1 (see **ad 1. 10. 4**) that ingratitude is the worst vice.

(4.) 18. 2 nudum et infirmum societas munit (naked and weak as he is, it is fellowship that protects him). The ultimate inspiration for this idea is probably the story in Plato's *Protagoras* 320 C 8–322 D 5 of Epimetheus' gifts to the animals and the intervention of Zeus, who distributes a sense of justice and mutual respect to human beings, which is to be the principle of organizing cities and a bond of friendship in a wide sense (*philia*). Cf. the Elder Pliny (*HN* 7. 1–5) on nature as a severe stepmother, and evil as emanating from our fellow men (Beagon 2005, 108), though his ideal in 2. 18 is man helping man.

duas <deus> res dedit (god has granted two things). Hosius supplied *deus*, which fits with Plato's *Protagoras* (see n. above), but *natura*, added by hand N³, fits better with 17. 4 *maximum hoc habemus naturae meritum* (the greatest service we have from nature) and with *Ep.* 95. 53, discussing the gift of sociability. But see 7–8 on the interchangeability of the terms.

(4.) 19. 1 deos nemo sanus timet (no sane man fears the gods). Cf. *Ep.* 123. 16 where Seneca gives, as an important Stoic principle, that it is an error of superstition to fear those who ought to be loved, and an outrage against those it worships. This is because god is just and all-powerful and has a providential concern for his creation (Cleanthes' *Hymn to Zeus*, SVF. i. 537 and L–S, ch. 54).

deum inermem facis (you remove god's weapons). See **ad (4.) 4–6**. Since the Epicurean gods do not concern themselves with human doings, they have no power over them and are not feared by them.

(4.) 19. 2 in medio intervallo huius et alterius caeli (in the space between our heaven and another). Seneca locates the Epicurean gods in space between the worlds, of which there were an infinite number. This was the doctrine developed by later Epicureans (Cic. *ND* 1. 18; *Div.* 2. 40 ; Lucr. 3. 18–24; 5. 146–7; Quint. 7. 3. 5). This location was a way of explaining their imperishability, since they would not be buffeted by other matter; but this imperishability is still hard to reconcile with the Epicurean belief that the atoms composing entities eventually fall apart and destroy them. See L–S, ch. 23, especially p. 149.

(4.) 19. 3 hunc vis videri colere non aliter quam parentem grato, ut opinor, animo (you want to be seen to be venerating this being just like a parent, with, I suppose, the same grateful heart). On Epicurean piety, D.L. 10. 120, 123; Cic. *ND* 1. 45, 101, 123; Lucr. 6. 68–79. The Epicurean gods were models of conduct and deserving of veneration and worship, but without any element of fear. By putting in the comparison with veneration of parents, Seneca stresses the absurdity of this worship, since parents, unlike these gods, confer great benefits on their children (e.g. 2. 11. 5).

(4.) 19. 4. The Stoics, too, spoke of the the *maiestas* of the gods, but coupled it with their goodness (*Ep.* 95. 50).

(4.) 20. 3 secundum datum videt (envisages a second gift). See **ad 2. 18. 5** and **ad (4.) 13. 3.**

quia testamentum facturus est, cui de hereditate aut de legato vacat cogitare (because he is about to make his will and finds time to think about an inheritance or legacy). This second *ingratus* is a *captator* who is already a friend and has presumably benefited from the friendship. In fulfilling his obligation to visit the sick man, however, his motive is not gratitude but greed. Seneca has alluded to the practice before in 1. 14. 3 and will again in 6. 38. 4. In *Ep.* 95. 43 he uses the noun and the same comparison to birds of prey. The satirical term *captator* was coined by Horace (*Sat.* 2. 5. 57, cf. 23–4) and the metaphor is primarily from fishing, here evoked by the *hamus* (a fish-hook) used to carry bait (Mart. 4. 56; Plin. *Ep.* 9. 30. 2). Seneca speaks here of inheritance and legacy, but the word is usually used of capturing the whole inheritance. The *captator* is some-one who would not inherit automatically, if the target died intestate: so *captatio* connotes a denial of family claims. Seneca also writes of the wielding of power by the *testator* (*Brev. vit.* 7. 7; *Cons. Marc.* 19. 2). See Champlin 1991, 87–102, who finds little evidence for *captatio* being a common practice, though it clearly roused strong feelings.

(4.) 21. 1 Duo genera sunt grati hominis (there are two types of grateful people). With *dicitur* Seneca goes on to indicate that both senses of the word *gratus* are in common use. Similarly, Cicero (*Inv.* 2. 66) sees *gratia* 'in the remembering and repaying of obligations'. But Seneca has already given his view, in 2. 31–5 and in the chapter before this, that it is mental attitude that marks the true *gratus*, whether or not a return of the benefit is also made in material terms. Cf. his insistence that the thing given is not the real *beneficium* where *res animo geritur*, though he later admits in 2. 34. 5–35. 1 that the term is ambiguous (see **ad 1. 5. 1–9. 1**).

(4.) 21. 3 artifex (artist). See **ad (4.) 15. 2** for the rather different parallel drawn between the benefactor and the artist. Here there is no artefact produced, because circumstances prevent it; but the motivation and the skill entitle one to be called an artist or grateful person.

(4.) 22. 1. Cf. 16. 1 on using the same arguments to argue the second question as the first one in this book. At 11. 4–6 Seneca used wills as an example of altruism in giving; now of altruism in showing gratitude. See **ad (4.) 11. 5**. In Rome testators had great freedom in disposing of their property and in recognizing and rewarding favours, and friendship was a strong social pressure, though the great majority left family members as actual heirs: see Champlin 1991, 101; ch. 6.

(4.) 22. 3 ut multa hoc commoda oriuntur (but many advantages spring from it). See **ad (4.) 2. 1** for the Epicurean argument about virtue, there liberality, making men secure through love and esteem: here it is applied to the virtue of being grateful. Seneca turns the Epicurean argument against them, by crediting divine providence with the provision of advantages to accompany virtue.

(4.) 22. 8 ad istam virtutem, quae saepe tuta ac facili aditur via (to this same virtue, which often is reached by a safe and easy path). Seneca sometimes subscribes to the common view that the road to virtue is hard (*Vit. beat.* 20. 2; *Prov.* 5. 10), but at *Ira* 2. 13. 1 he opposes that view.

(4.) 23–4. In these two chapters, which complete discussion of the second question posed at the start of Book 4, Seneca adduces as a parallel to the reverence we feel for virtue (apart from its side benefits (22. 3–4)), the reverence we feel for the majesty of the heavenly bodies (apart from the many benefits they confer on us). The elevated style of the description of the heavens prepares the reader for the climax of the book—and indeed of the whole work—in ch. 25, on the goal of life according to the Stoa. Whereas, in discussing the majesty of god, Seneca could use the Epicureans' attitude of reverence against them (19. 3–4), Seneca's assumption of the providential care for mankind of these heavenly bodies (23. 1; 24. 1), and of their divine nature, evinced in their regular motion (23. 4), finds no common ground with the Epicureans, who saw the sun, moon, stars, and planets, as composed of atoms (D.L. 10. 90), and, who gave mechanical explanations of their movements (D.L. 10. 97, 112–15). In fact, the Stoics regularly used the argument about the glorious spectacle of the heavens to assert the divinity, rationality, and purposefulness of the universe, in opposition to the Epicurean view (Cic. *Nat. d.* 2. 93–7, 115).

(4.) 23. 2 quem non intentum in se tenet? (whose gaze does it not hold fixed on itself?). Seneca is unusual in separating the notion of providence from the glory of the spectacle and arguing that we would revere the spectacle of heaven, even without giving thought to the benefits (cf. *Cons. Marc.* 18. 2–3; Cic. *Nat. d.* 2. 49–56). He had already spoken of the pleasure in viewing the heavens as a consolation of exile, in *Cons. Helv.* 20. 2.

(4.) **23. 4 quantam fatorum seriem certus limes educit** (what a chain of destiny does that clear circuit define). Seneca refers to the signs of the Zodiac through which the 'wandering stars' move. They thus affect events on earth, according to astrology. Tacitus, *Ann.* 6. 22 distinguishes between astrology and the Stoic view of fate; but Cicero in *De Divinatione* makes Quintus, defending the Stoic theory of divination, name the stars as one kind of sign from which skilled interpreters can read future events, since all events are linked together by the nexus of fate (1. 118), while 'Cicero' is made to say that, of the Stoics, only Panaetius (who was sceptical of all forms of divination) denied the predictions of astrologers (2. 88). The idea that the stars provide signs is certainly reconcilable with the Stoic view of fate. At *NQ* 2. 32. 3–4 Seneca seems to regard the stars as doing that, yet at 2. 32. 7–8 they seem to have power to cause events, and in *Cons. Marc.* 18. 1–3 they seem actually to cause them. In *Ep.* 88. 15 he entertains both possibilities. Here the expression is ambiguous.

nec enim est, quod existimes septem sola discurrere, cetera haerere (there is no reason to think that there are only seven wandering stars, while the rest are fixed). The seven are the sun, the moon and the five planets, Mercury, Venus, Mars, Jupiter, and Saturn. The Stoics thought the 'fixed stars' were not fixed but moved around the polar axis (Cic. *Nat. d.* 2. 54); the planets shared that motion and also had a movement of their own, by which they revolved around the earth (*Nat. d.* 2. 49). These bodies are all divine, having rational intelligence that shows in the regularity of their movements (*Nat. d.* 2. 55; 2. 43; 3. 40).

(4.) **24. 2 gratus est, quia expedit? Ergo et quantum expedit?** (if a person is grateful because it is in his interest, is he then grateful only as far as it is in his interest?). Returning to confront the Epicurean view directly, Seneca ends his discussion of the second question posed at the start of the book, by showing that advantage is unreliable as a motive for showing gratitude because there will be times when it will lead to ingratitude instead. Being grateful, then, is a virtuous act that is done because it is right: that is, it is worthy of choice for its own sake.

(4.) **24. 2 soluto ad illam sinu veniendum est** (he must come to her with an open purse). For *sinus*, see **ad 2. 16. 2 ut congiaria.** Seneca returns here to his point about virtue in the opening chapter of this book (1. 2).

(4.) **25.** In this short but emphatic chapter, Seneca picks up the point made early in this book (3. 2), that if giving *beneficia* were motivated by expediency, the gods would not bestow gifts on us, as we cannot return them. Seneca drops his polemic against the Epicureans for good and affirms the fundamental doctrine underlying Stoic ethics: that the *telos* or aim of human life is τὸ ὁμολογουμένως τῇ φύσει ζῆν (to live in accordance with nature), a formulation that may go back to Zeno—certainly to Cleanthes and Chrysippus (D.L. 7. 87, see L–S, pp. 400–1)—and upon which all Stoics agreed, as Seneca often affirms, e.g. *Vit. beat.* 3. 2–3; *Ot.* 5. 1; *Ep.* 5. 4. The Stoics variously developed this to include life in accordance with universal nature, with human nature, and with our individual natures or human capacities. Here Seneca is concerned with the first, and, because of the identity of nature with god or Zeus for the Stoics (treated in 4. 7–8), he can consider living in accordance with the example of god as an alternative reading of the *telos* (as did other Stoics, e.g. Marc. Aur. 12. 31). This is the second of the three treatments of Stoic theology in this book (see **ad (4.) 3–9. 1**).

(4.) 25. 1 deorum exemplum sequi (to follow the example of the gods). The idea of 'following god' is by tradition assigned to Pythagoras, appears in Plato, and became important in later Platonism. It was construed in various ways. Seneca sometimes takes it, as here, to mean following the example of the gods (*Epp.* 95. 50), but elsewhere he takes it to mean obeying and accepting the command of god (*Vit. beat.* 18. 5; *Epp.* 107. 9; 16. 5), which accords with the Stoic identification of fate with god (see **ad (4.) 7. 2**) . There is a good discussion in Dobbin 1998, 140–1, apropos of Epict. 1. 12. 4–5.

(4.) 26–40. This pivotal book ends with three *quaestiones infinitae* or *theseis* of the practical kind, relating to *actio*, as opposed to the theoretical kind of general questions with which the book opened (**ad (4.) 1–24**). The brevity of their treatment marks a change from the extended exploration of the two earlier general questions, and it prepares us for the series of questions, paradoxes, and syllogisms, that constitute most of the content of the last three books (see Ch. 7B). However, chs. 31. 1–32. 4 also contain another extended treatment of Stoic theology (see **ad (4.) 3–9. 1**).

The three general questions belong to that division of practical questions that deals with how to behave, and that concerns *officium*, as opposed to the division that deals with how to control the emotions (Cic. *Top.* 86; *Part. or.* 67). They all concern apparent conflicts between familiar precepts governing our duty, conflicts that can be resolved if we draw the right distinctions and explore what exactly these precepts enjoin, and what are the morally relevant features of the circumstances to which they need to be applied. In the first two practical questions, Seneca explores problems in conferring benefits; in the third, problems in returning them, thus refining further his treatment of the two topics discussed, via the theoretical questions, in the first part of the book.

(4.) 26–34. 2. The conflict inherent in the first question—will a good man give a benefit to someone he knows to be ungrateful?—is between our duty to give with discrimination (cf. 4. 34. 3), in particular choosing a grateful beneficiary (e.g. 1. 1. 2; 1. 10. 5; 4. 9. 3), and our duty to imitate the gods, who appear to confer their blessings indiscriminately. Seneca resolves the dilemma by subtle redefinition of 'ungrateful' and of 'benefit' (26–9), by pointing (30–2) to unusual circumstances that require a *kathēkon kata peristasin* (*ex tempore officium*), and finally by refining the idea of 'knowing', so as to exclude most cases when men act: they must use verisimilitude and can give recipients the benefit of the doubt (33–34. 2).

(4.) 26–27. 5. On the Stoics' unusual use of language, see **ad 2. 34. 2–5.** This case resembles the paradox in 2. 35. 2 where all but the Wise, in strictly Stoic terms, are mad, but we do not treat them as such: here, all but the Wise are fools and bad and have all the vices, but we do not behave towards them as such but follow more ordinary ideas (so 'ungrateful in the ordinary sense' at (4.) 26. 2). Cf. Cic. *Off.* 2. 35 on the parallel point about the unity of the virtues and Panaetius' distinguishing them as in ordinary language.

(4.) 26. 2 stultus etiam malus est; quia malus est, nullo vitio caret (a fool is also a bad man, and, because he is bad, he lacks none of the vices). On the intellectualism of the Stoa, which equated vice with folly, see **ad 1. 1. 1.** The Stoic doctrine is that the vices are inseparable: a non-Sage = a fool = a bad man: he possesses them all, because every action that he performs falls short of being a right action (*katorthōma*) and is strictly speaking a vicious action, and only the Sage has the understanding that makes his actions reliably and consistently right. All others, even those advanced in progress (*Ep.* 75. 10), are always liable to get it wrong, which Seneca here calls having the potential for vice or a hidden propensity to it (26. 2).

(4.) 26. 3 huic ingrato, qui beneficiorum fraudator est et in hanc partem procubuit animo (on the latter kind of ingrate, who cheats you of benefits and has a natural inclination to do so). The donor will avoid giving to the ungrateful man (in the vulgar sense), who has already demonstrated this particular kind of viciousness, as the comparison with the bankrupt and the reneger show (cf. 27. 2 (*eminent*); 27. 5), or has a natural inclination towards that vice (26. 2: *in hoc vitium natura propensus*, cf. 27. 3 *si nondum deditus, ita formatus* etc.). Seneca does not explain how, in the latter case, the donor is to recognize whom to avoid: but this is not his last word on the subject, for at (4.) 33 he shows that we may be mistaken without attracting blame, and at 7. 32 he advises persevering in generosity, in hopes of inspiring gratitude in the beneficiary.

(4.) 27. 1 alius in avaritiam, alius in luxuriam, alius in petulantiam inclinatur (one person inclines to avarice, another to self-indulgence, another to insolence). On the inclination to particular vices, see Epict. 3. 12. 7–8.

(4.) 27. 2 itaque errant illi, qui interrogant Stoicos (and so it is a mistake to ask the Stoics). Seneca envisages an objector adducing men famous for particular virtues, who, not being Sages, could be accused of the corresponding vice. For the two Decii see 6. 36. 2; for Mucius **ad 7. 15. 2 Mucio manus**; for Fabius **ad (4)30. 2 nisi Verrucosi et Allobrogici.** Seneca quotes the characterization of him by Ennius in *Annales* 12. 363. On these persons, see Biographical Notes.

(4.) 27. 5 qui negotiorum gestorum damnato patrimonii sui curam mandaverit (if he hands over the care of his fortune to someone condemned for mismanagement). Gaius 4. 33 refers to *actiones negotiorum gestorum*, legal actions against those who manage the affairs and litigation of others in bad faith. The *negotiorum gestor* is responsible for the proper management of these affairs and can be sued for acting in bad faith. A *tutor* is a guardian who administers property for a person under age (*pupillus*) or a woman not in the *patria potestas*. He can be appointed, as here, by the will of the person in whose control the *pupillus* or woman would be, and the *tutor* can also be called to account for any loss his charge suffers through his fault.

(4.) 28. 2 rex honores dignis dat, congiarium et indignis (a king gives honours to the worthy, but largesse to the unworthy, too). *Honores* in a Roman context would mean official positions, as in 30. 1, where Seneca in fact shows that there are circumstances in which, justifiably, they are not given to *digni*. A *congiarium* was a distribution to the citizenry, originally of wine and oil; under the Principate, of money. The recipients were the same citizens as those inscribed on the register of recipients of *frumentum publicum*, the monthly ration of free corn, cf. Plin. *Pan.* 25. 2–3. That Seneca uses *rex* in the company of such Roman terms could suggest that he wishes it to include the Princeps, as it seems to later (see **ad (4.) 32. 2**): cf. such phrases as *regem aut principem decet* (1. 3. 3) or *principes regesque et quocumque alio nomine sunt tutores status publici* (1. 4. 3) in *De clementia*, though at *Ben.* 2. 16. 2 he uses *congiarium* with reference to Alexander.

(4.) 28. 4 tam bonis quam malis conduntur urbes (cities are founded as much for the good as for the bad). The terms of the comparison are reversed, as often in Seneca, see **ad 1. 13. 3**.

(4.) 28. 6 illud, quod iudicio meo ad aliquem pervenire debebit, ei, quem esse ingratum sciam, non dabo (that which should go to a person in accordance with my judgement, I shall not give to someone whom I know to be ungrateful). *Iudicium* is essential to a virtuous act, and to generosity in particular (1. 2. 1). Seneca has exempted mass benefits from the obligation to show judgement in choosing grateful recipients, by showing that there we are only failing to exclude people, not deliberately selecting them (28. 5 *utrum aliquem non excludas an eligas*). Seneca does not include, under *iudicium*, discrimination shown in selecting groups to benefit (reciprocation of such benefits is treated in 6. 19. 2–5), because the same problem would arise as with mass benefactions: the chosen group may include ingrates, who cannot be excluded.

(4.) 29. 1 'nec consilium deliberanti dabis ingrato nec aquam haurire permittes nec viam monstrabis erranti?' ('do you mean that you will not give advice to an ingrate in mental perplexity, nor allow him to have a drink of water, and show him the way when he is lost?'). See **ad (4.) 29.3**. As Alexander 1950–2*a*, 24 points out, there are two cases envisaged here: the person who has mentally lost his way and needs advice, and the person who has physically lost his way and needs a drink and directions.

(4.) 29. 2 beneficium est opera utilis (a benefit is a useful service). Seneca here uses *beneficium* in its ordinary sense, what he calls the *materia beneficii* at 1. 5 where *beneficium* itself is defined as a *benevola actio* (1. 6. 1). In the latter sense, but not the former, the size of the *beneficium* is unimportant (1. 6. 2; 1. 7. 1); the second criterion (being done for the sake of the recipient) applies in both senses.

(4.) 29. 3 et non homini damus, sed humanitati (we do not bestow them on a particular human being, but on humanity). In accordance with the social instinct implanted in man by nature (see **ad (4.) 18**), we have an obligation to provide basic services to each other (*Ep.* 95. 51), giving water, fire, advice, all things that do not diminish our own resources (Cic. *Off.* 1. 51–2; 3. 52), for it was understood that the size of a gift is relative and should be adjusted to our means (Val. Max. 4. 8. 1–2; Plut. *Mor.* 172 B; *Ben.* 2. 15. 3).

(4.) 30. 1–32. 4. Seneca now turns from cases that can be explained away by redefining terms and drawing distinctions to an actual exception, justified by the circumstances, to the rule against giving individual benefits to a known ingrate ((4.) 28 *fin.*). This is an *ex tempore officium* (Cic. *Off.* 3. 19), as is suggested by *aliquando* (sometimes), used at start (30. 1) and finish (32. 4 *fin.*). Though the discussion is carried on in terms of unworthy recipients in general, *ingrato ergo* at the end of 32. 4 brings us back to the question set out at 26. 1. Seneca justifies the giving of high position to unworthy descendants and even (by the gods) to unworthy progenitors of great men of virtue, as a way of showing gratitude for *beneficia* conferred by those great men, and thus of encouraging virtuous behaviour (elective office is also described as a *beneficium* by Cicero, *II Verr.* 5. 180; *Mur.* 2, 3, 86, 90 and by Sallust, *BJ* 85. 3 and 26). So what looks like indiscriminate generosity can be seen as discriminating gratitude.

(4.) 30. 1 in petendis honoribus quosdam turpissimos nobilitas industriis sed novis praetulit non sine ratione (in seeking office, nobility of birth has put some of the most disreputable men ahead of those who are hard-working newcomers, and not without reason). The expression *novi homines*, literally 'new men', refers most frequently to men of non-senatorial background who attained the consulship, like Cicero and Seneca himself. *Nobilitas*, literally 'renowned', indicates, in its political sense, those whose ancestors had reached high senatorial office, notably the consulship. See Badian in *OCD*[4], s.vv. *nobilitas* and *novus homo*. On the persons mentioned in 30–2, see Biographical Notes.

(4.) 30. 2 Ciceronem filium quae res consulem fecit nisi pater? (what made Cicero's son consul if not his father?). Cicero frequently mentions the legacy of political status and glory that, thanks to his own achievements, his son would enjoy, unlike himself, e.g. *Planc.* 59; *Fam.* 2. 16. 4; *Off.* 2. 44; 3. 6 and see van der Blom 2010, 316–21.

Cinnam nuper quae res ad consulatum recepit ex hostium castris? (what brought Cinna recently to the consulship from the camp of the enemy?). 'Recently', relative to the consulship of Cicero's son in 30 BC (cited in *Clem.* 1. 10. 1 as an act of clemency by Augustus parallel to his advancement of Cinna), suggests Cn. Cornelius Cinna (cos. AD 5), but that Cinna was too young to have fought with other followers of Pompey against Octavian in the civil war. Seneca should mean his father (or elder brother), L. Cornelius Cinna (cos. suff. 32 BC), but he may have conflated the two, as in *Clem.* 1. 9, where he uses the similar phrase *in hostium castris invenissem*, see Griffin 1976, 411 n. 2. This may be the sort of error which Quintilian 10. 1. 128, in his discussion of Seneca, attributes to 'those whom he employed to do research for him in some subjects'.

nisi unius viri magnitudo tanta (unless it was the greatness of one man). Sextus Pompeius Sex. f., consul in 35 BC, was the cousin of Pompeius Magnus, whose *cognomen* is alluded to by *magnitudo*, cf. *Cons. Marc.* 14. 3; *Ep.* 94. 64 and see Feeney 1986, 243 n. 15.

sacerdotem non in uno collegio (a priest in more than one college). Inscriptions show Fabius Persicus as *pontifex, sodalis Augustalis*, and *frater Arvalis* (*PIR*[2] F 51). In the first two centuries AD, only the Princeps and those destined for that office could be members of more than one major priesthood, i.e. the pontiffs, augurs, *XVviri*, and *VIIviri epulonum*, but others could hold minor priesthoods in addition to a major one. Syme 1986, 416 notes that, since he became consul in AD 34, he was probably about fifteen when he was co-opted into the place in the *Arvales* vacated by his father.

nisi Verrucosi et Allobrogici (except the Verrucosi and Allobrogici and those three hundred). The great patrician clan of the Fabii included both Hannibal's great enemy Q. Fabius Maximus Verrucosus and Q. Fabius Maximus Allobrogicus, who took the *agnomen* for subduing the tribe of the Allobroges in Transalpine Gaul in 121 BC. The Emperor Claudius mentions this agnomen in the Lyons Tablet (*ILS* 212, col. 2. 23–5), where he calls Fabius Persicus *nobilissimum virum, amicum meum*: 'the malice of Claudius Caesar furnishes the latest mention of Paullus Fabius Persicus', writes Syme 1986, 417. Roman tradition had it that in 477 BC, 306 members of the Fabian clan fell fighting against the Etruscans of Veii, only one young boy being left to continue the stock (Livy 2. 50).

(4.) 31. 1 excusare hoco loco tibi, mi Liberalis, deos volo (at this point, my Liberalis, I wish to offer you a defence of the gods). Up to now, Seneca has spoken in terms of election to consulships and priesthoods, effected by human beings (note *me* in 30. 1) out of gratitude to illustrious relatives. Now he turns to the defence of the gods and of providence for elevating wicked kings and Roman emperors, and the argument becomes an inversion of the doctrine about punishment being visited on later genera-tions, that was often used to explain how a provident and omniscient deity could allow the good to suffer and the wicked to prosper (Cic. *Nat. d.* 3. 90).

(4.) 31. 2 patri eius Germanico datum, avo proavoque (it was granted to his father Germanicus, to his grandfather, and to his great-grandfather). The father of Gaius Caesar (Caligula) is Nero Claudius Drusus Germanicus, called after his adoption by Tiberius in AD 4 Germanicus Iulius Caesar; as Seneca seems to be thinking of blood relatives (*dignos dedit* at 30. 3), the grandfather will be Germanicus' father by birth, the Emperor Tiberius' brother Nero Claudius Drusus; the great-grandfather meant could be Ti. Claudius Nero or, more probably, the Emperor Augustus, grandfather of Gaius' mother Agrippina.

(4.) 31. 3 quid? tu, cum Mamercum Scaurum consulem faceres (then again, when you yourself were making Mamercus Scaurus consul). Despite the change from the third to the second person, many commentators think this is a continuation of the criticism of divine providence (Cooper and Procopé 1995, 299 n. 64): Lipsius, in fact, suggested reading *tum* for *tu* and changing *faceres* to *faceret*, etc. But there are difficulties: (1) the preceding chapter was about terrestrial elections of the unworthy to the consulship (see **ad (4.) 31. 1**), so this appears to return to that point, giving a more extreme case as an argument against criticizing the gods in their choice of kings; (2) it is odd to attribute indignation (31. 5 *fin.*) to providence, which is purely rational; (3) the start of the next chapter (32), even without Madvig's supplement *idem facere* (apparently accepted by Cooper and Procopé), appears to compare the gods' behaviour with what has been described before. That the Principes in effect chose the consuls by this date (Tac. *Hist.* 1. 77) is not an objection, since the same was true of elections to the priesthoods of Fabius Persicus in 30. 2, which were probably even later than the consulship of Scaurus in AD 21, mentioned in 31. 3. Senatorial and popular elections were still held and, in theory, determined the results. *Tu* could be Liberalis, who could have been old enough to vote, about forty years before, for Scaurus, if he was roughly Seneca's age; but, given the fluidity of Seneca's pronouns, it could also be more general, just as in the *Consolation to Marcia* 9. 3; 17. 1; 18. 4, which is addressed to a woman, where *tu* becomes masculine.

(4.) 31. 5 dum veterem illum Scaurum senatus principem cogitas (while you were thinking of that ancient Scaurus who was leader of the senate). M. Aemilius Scaurus was chosen as *princeps senatus* by the censors in 115 BC and appointed as such five or six times in all. At that date it meant that he was entered first on the senate list, which the censors compiled, and had the privilege of speaking first on any motion in the senate. It was a position of great power, as he would move all routine senatorial decrees.

(4.) 32. 1 nota enim illis est operis sui series (for they know how their works unfold). Since fate is synonymous with god(s), such knowledge of the future can naturally be ascribed to them.

(4.) 32. 2 'sint hi reges, quia maiores eorum non fuerunt' ('let these men be kings, because their ancestors were not'). Here it is hard to deny that Seneca is using *reges* to refer to *principes* (ad (4.) 28. 2), given the allusion to the civil war and the victory of Augustus, and the apparent allusion to Claudius in 32. 3. The *reges* ought to be Gaius and his uncle Claudius, and what is said of their *maiores* is appropriate, since Germanicus, Gaius' father, and Drusus, Gaius' grandfather (ad (4.) 31. 2) and Claudius' father, were all reputed to have Republican views (Tac. *Ann.* 1. 33). The *proavus* could be T. Claudius Nero (as Cooper and Procopé 1995, 300 n. 68 suggest), Gaius' great-grandfather and Claudius' grandfather, who was defeated in the civil war by Augustus, to whom he ceded his wife Livia.

(4.) 32. 3 hic corpore deformis est, adspectu foedus (this man is ugly in body, hideous to look at). Seneca's readers will have recognized the Claudius of the *Apocolocyntosis*, particularly 5. 2–3.

(4.) 32. 4 apud me istae expensorum acceptorumque rationes dispunguntur, ego, quid cui debeam, scio (it is for me to compare the debits and credits on those accounts. I know what I owe to whom). Seneca here has god use a financial metaphor: he checks the debits and credits on his accounts and then repays his debts, at a time dictated by opportunity and the resources of his commonwealth, i.e. the larger *res publica* of the cosmos that Seneca discusses in *Ot.* 4. 2. On Seneca's frequent use of debt metaphor in speaking of *beneficia*, see **ad 1. 1. 1 male collocata**.

'ubi', inquis, 'iste aut quis est?' unde vos scitis ('where', you ask, 'is that man or who is he?' how are you to know?). Lipsius preferred the reading taken up by Wesenberg: *'ubi', inquis, 'iste aut quis est? unde'? vos nescitis* ('where', you ask, 'is that man, or who is he? what is his origin?' you do not know). In any case the ignorance of human beings is contrasted with the omniscience of god, who takes into account remote ancestors. The questions 'where?' 'who?' (also, 'of what origin?') are standard for identifying people we meet. The identity of the ancestor is here perhaps deliberately left imprecise, to reflect human ignorance; though Cooper and Procopé plausibly suggest Gaius

Claudius Nero (cos. 207 BC), who allowed his colleague credit for killing Hannibal's brother Hasdrubal: Val. Max. 4. 1. 9; Livy 28. 9, especially §§9. 11, 15: *Neronem . . . vel parta eo bello vel spreta eo triumpho gloria memorabilem fore* ('Nero . . . would be memorable, for the glory won in that war or despised in that triumph').

(4.) 33–34. 2. The last way of resolving the dilemma posed by the first question continues the theme of human ignorance broached in 4. 32 and applies only to action by humans. The Stoics believed that infallible knowledge of the world was possible, and that there is a type of impression on the mind from outside that gives its recipient a guarantee of its accuracy and commands assent. But human beings are precipitate in giving assent to false impressions; the Sage alone consents only to cognitive impressions and withholds assent from others (L–S, p. 258). Yet in practical life suspension of judgement may be impossible to maintain, so we should sometimes perform actions for which a reasonable defence can be produced. The story of the Stoic Sphaerus and the pomegranates (D.L. 7. 177) may show that the Sage would say that he sometimes gives assent to the reasonable, as opposed to the cognitive, impression: so here to the proposition that it is reasonable to think that the recipient would be grateful.

(4.) 33. 1 ut ait Platon (as Plato says). The passage of Plato cannot be definitely identified, but Charles Brittain suggests that *Phaedrus* 270 B–272 B may lie behind this. Seneca probably cites Plato from memory.

(4.) 33. 2 certissimam rerum comprehensionem (absolute certainty). *Compr(eh)ensio* is the Latin for *katalēpsis*, the scientific knowledge possessed by the Sage (Cic. *Luc.* 145).

(4.) 34. 2 nulla hic culpa tribuentis est, quia tamquam grato dedi (no guilt attaches to the giver here, because I gave it to him supposing him to be grateful). Intention is all in moral action, and success is not important.

(4.) 34. 3–39. The second of the general questions of the practical kind concerns the moral dilemma—this time spelt out explicitly at 34. 3 and 36. 2—between conferring a benefit on an unworthy person and failing to keep a promise to confer one. Essentially only one solution is offered this time: that the Sage always acts subject to the reservation that, if circumstances change, his purpose can change; though Seneca also makes use of the idea, applied to the first question in 29, that the smallness of what is promised can affect one's decision to honour the promise (36, cf. 39. 2). This second dilemma is also examined via *quaestiones finitae* or *causae*, particular cases concerning named individuals (37–9). This is not surprising, as there is a strong connection between the general and specific questions, as Quintilian pointed out (3. 5. 8–13 and see pp. 136–7).

(4.) 34. 3 constantia vestra hoc loco titubat (at this point your Stoic firmness falters). *Constantia*, in place of the MSS' *conscientia*, is Lipsius' suggestion, adopted by

Cooper and Procopé 1995. It certainly fits the context, and the verb *titubat*; *inconstantiae crimen* at 35. 2 strengthens the suggestion. *Vestra* points to the Stoic emphasis on firmness in the face of fortune as characteristic of the Sage. Cicero in *Pro Murena* 61 ridicules the doctrine as *sapientem nihil opinari, nullius rei paenitere, nulla in re falli, sententiam mutare numquam.* Seneca's treatise *De constantia sapientis* emphasizes the Sage's immunity to insult and injury; here his ability to remain true to his convictions shows in his making firm decisions in the face of circumstances not under his control, but building flexibility into those decisions (see n. below).

(4.) 34. 4 ceterum ad omnia cum exceptione venit: 'si nihil inciderit, quod impediat' (but he approaches everything with the reservation, 'if nothing occurs to impede'). *Cum exceptione* renders the Greek μεθ᾽ ὑπεξαιρέσεως (*SVF* iii. 564), on which see Inwood 1985, 119–24; Brennan 2000. Seneca chooses a Roman legal term (see Düll 1976, 377–80), and many of his examples are taken from the legal sphere (35. 1; 35. 2; 39. 4), on which see Griffin 2013, esp. 104–6. In law, an *exceptio* was a conditional clause, with a negative beginning ('if not' or 'unless'), added to the praetor's *formula*, in order to protect the defendant against condemnation (alluded to by Seneca in *Ep.* 48. 10), by recognizing special agreements between plaintiff and defendant, or by ruling out fraud or intimidation, or the contravention of a statute or senatorial decree (see Jolowicz and Nicholas 1972, 206–7). Seneca in fact applies the last type of *exceptio* to promises at 35. 1. The Stoic doctrine occurs in Epictetus (*Ench.* 2. 2; fr. 27) and Marcus Aurelius (4. 1; 5. 20; 6. 50; cf. 11. 37), often with a positive view of the altered action adopted.

Using a negative conditional clause to express the Sage's reservation fits with Seneca's use of the legal term *exceptio* (though in (4.) 39. 4 he uses the positive formulation 'if I can, if I ought, if things remain as they are'). A similar formulation *nisi si quid impedierit* (cf. Chrysippus' ἄν μή τι κωλύῃ, *SVF* iii.697) is used by Seneca to describe the creation of a *kathēkon kata peristasin* or *officium ex tempore* at *Ot.* 3. 2–3: when the condition is fulfilled, the injunction 'the Sage will enter politics unless something prevents him' can lead to the opposite duty. Cicero *Off.* 1. 31–2; 3. 92–5 treats breaking promises under particular circumstances as a case of *officium ex tempore*, and Seneca could have justified the breaking of promises in these terms; but he prefers to concentrate on the mental state of the Sage, here his state of mind when he made the promise.

(4.) 35. 1 promisi tibi in matrimonium filiam; postea peregrinus apparuisti; non est mihi cum externo conubium (I promised my daughter in marriage to you; afterwards you turned out to be a non-citizen; I have no right to contract a marriage with an alien). Seneca first canvasses various circumstances that cancel the obligation to confer a promised benefit, before returning to the one under discussion at 35. 3: the discovery that the recipient is an ungrateful person. First come legal obstacles (perhaps alluded to by the *si potero* of 39. 4): the political community requisitions the thing promised; a law is passed forbidding the action he promised to perform for his friend; and, finally, this one. *Conubium* or legal capacity to enter a Roman marriage only exists between Roman citizens, and between a Roman citizen and a non-citizen when the privilege has been granted.

(4.) 35. 2 promisi advocationem; postea apparuit per illam causam praeiudicium in patrem meum quaeri (I promised to plead in support; afterwards it became clear that through that case a precedent against my father was being devised). Seneca now moves to moral obstacles (the *si debeo* of 39. 4). A *praeiudicium* here is a previous legal judgement that could be taken to affect a later case involving his father.

in rem praesentem venturus fui: sed aeger filius, sed puerpera uxor tenet (I was about to come to the scene of action, but was detained because my son was ill or my wife about to give birth). The earlier example of promising advocacy may have called to Seneca's mind Cicero's example at *Off.* 1. 32 *si constitueris cuipiam te advocatum in rem praesentem esse venturum* (if you had made an appointment to appear for someone as advocate in the near future), where the illness of his son is a legitimate reason to go back on a promise. For Cicero this is an instance when the fulfilment of the promise would hurt the doer more than it would benefit the recipient; but Seneca does not mention any calculation here, since he is arguing that any change in circumstance can invalidate a promise. He imports further nuances in the next chapter and in 39. 3–4.

(4.) 36. 1 si exiguum est, dabo, non quia dignus es, sed quia promisi, nec tamquam munus dabo, sed verba mea redimam et aurem mihi pervellam (if it is trivial, I shall give it, not because you deserve it, but because I promised; nor shall I give it as a gift, but I shall make good on my words and fix it in my memory). As in (4.) 29, when discussing giving a benefit to an ungrateful person, Seneca has regard to the magnitude of the proposed *beneficium*: if it is trivial, and if it is not given to a person selected as worthy, it need not count as a *beneficium* (here called *munus*). *Aurem pervellere*, literally plucking the ear, which was thought of as the seat of memory, means to fix in one's memory, as here and in 5. 7. 6, or to jog one's memory, as in *Ep.* 94. 55.

(4.) 37–8. The first of the *quaestiones finitae*, explicitly formulated at the start of 38, concerns a promise made by King Philip of Macedon, granting a soldier's request for a certain property. Once the king learned that the property belonged to the very person who had saved the soldier's life, keeping the promise would have meant, not just conferring a benefit on someone unworthy, but committing an injustice against a third party (38. 1).

(4.) 37. 3 improbissimo militi, ingratissimo hospiti, avidissimo naufrago stigmata inscriberet ingratum hominem testantia (to mark that most shameless of soldiers, most ungrateful of guests, most greedy of castaways, with a tattoo proclaiming him an ungrateful person). The King inflicts a punishment used for criminals. This is probably tattooing, not, as it is usually taken, branding on his forehead or face (*frons, facies* at (4.) 38. 2), the word *ingratus* or *homo ingratus* or some abbreviation. Though the branding of humans may have been practised by the Romans, it was not a Greek practice, and the language of writing here (*inscribere, litterae*) points to tattooing by pricking the skin with a needle dipped in ink. This was a Greek practice, and a Roman one attested in Seneca's time (Petronius, *Sat.* 103. 1–4; 105. 11–106. 1), on which see Jones 1987. In 37. 4, *insculperentur* (carved into his flesh) seems to refer to incising and scarring the skin (Jones 1987, 142), whereas tattoos could be removed (Jones 1987, 143–4).

(4.) 38. 2 non omnibus miseris aqua et igni interdixerat? (would he not have made all unfortunates outlaws?). See **ad (4.) 29. 3** for the obligation to provide such basic services to a fellow human being. Seneca uses the legal formula *aqua et igni interdicere* to suggest that Philip, by depriving of his property the provider of such services and thus deterring others from providing them, would effectively have placed victims of misfortune outside the protection of human society.

(4.) 39. The second of the *quaestiones finitae* extends the issue being considered beyond a promise to benefit someone who turns out ungrateful. First, Seneca considers a promise to make a loan to an unsuitable person; then, in 39. 3–4, he promises to do things that turn out unexpectedly difficult or costly for the benefactor: the kind of calculation Cicero makes at *Off.* 1. 32, where he considers if fulfilment of the promise would do more harm to the doer than good to the recipient (see **ad (4.) 35. 2**).

(4.) 39. 2 pecuniae etiam male creditae exactio est; et appellare debitorem ad diem possum et, si foro cesserit, portionem feram; beneficium et totum perit et statim (one can call in even a bad loan. I can summon a debtor for a particular day and, if he has become bankrupt, I shall get my share, but a benefit is lost in total and at once). For the comparison and contrast of a benefit and a loan, see **ad 1. 1. 1 male collocata**, and, in this book, (4.) 12. 1. The *beneficium* that is totally lost (cf. 1. 1. 1; (4.) 10.4) is not the virtuous act (1. 5. 3), but the gift, which is the sense of *beneficium* that can be reasonably compared to a loan (cf. 2. 34. 1).

hoc mali viri est, illud mali patris familiae (the latter is the act of a bad man, the former of a bad head of household). The bad *pater familias* is the man who places a loan badly, it being his duty to look after the financial interests of his household and descendants (*Ep.* 64. 7). Alexander 1950–2a, 25–6 takes *malus* to mean, not morally bad, but practically unfortunate. But the man who confers a benefit on an unworthy person is morally bad, because a *beneficium*, as a moral act, must be done with reason and show discrimination, as Seneca says in (4.) 34. 3 *si facis sciens, peccas, das enim cui non debes dare* (if you do it, knowing what you do, you are wrong, because you are giving to a person to whom you ought not to give).

quingenti denarii sunt: illud quod dici solet, 'in morbo consumat' (it was 500 denarii—'a sum', the saying goes, 'one can fritter away'). This is the equivalent of two years' pay for a legionary soldier, but 400 denarii would have bought only an acre of cultivable land (Col. 3. 3. 8), and the property qualification for a Roman senator was 250,000 denarii.

(4.) 39. 3 sponsum descendam, quia promisi; sed non, si spondere me in incertum iubebis, si fisco obligabis (I shall go down (to the forum) to be your surety in a public contract, because I promised; but not if you demand that I stand surety for an unspecified sum, if you put me under obligation to the imperial treasury). The forum was where sureties for public contracts were declared. The imperial treasury enjoyed privileges under the law (see *Dig.* 49. 14), and the political realities could lead to legal process being ignored or interfered with (Millar 1963, 33–4); as Pliny says, the *fiscus* only loses a suit under a good Princeps like Trajan (*Pan.* 36. 4).

(4.) 39. 4 vadimonium promittimus, tamen deserti non in omnes datur actio: deserentem vis maior excusat (we promise bail, yet not all are liable to be sued for defaulting: *force majeure* excuses the defaulter). When a party to a suit took bail (mutual promises, on pain of a money penalty, for appearances in court on a due day) and then failed to appear, legal action would not be authorized if he was prevented by unavoidable circumstances for which he was not responsible: *vis maior* indicates a natural disaster (Plin. *HN* 18. 278; *Dig.* 19. 2. 25. 6) or human coercion (*Ben.* 2. 18. 7). Seneca's final example of reservation is an actual legal *exceptio*.

(4.) 40. Seneca finishes the book with a question about the other activity broached at the start of the book: showing gratitude and returning favours (**ad (4.) 26–40**). The conventional view, given in Xen. *Mem.* 2. 2. 1 and *Cyr.* 3. 1. 34, is that not to return a benefit, if one can, is unjust and ungrateful. Seneca imports nuances by distinguishing being grateful from making repayment (**ad (4.) 40. 1**); by differentiating two forms of inability to repay—lack of occasion and lack of means (40. 3); and by maintaining that sometimes one will not repay when one can (40. 5).

(4.) 40. 1 animum praestare gratum debeo (I have an obligation to show myself grateful). As earlier, notably in 1. 5–6, Seneca distinguishes between feeling gratitude and gestures of repayment: the former is always required, because the exchange of benefits is essentially a transaction between minds, as he says in 2. 34. 1; the former depends on having the occasion and the means. The book ends with a warning that undue haste in offering a return can cast doubt on whether one truly feels gratitude, or is in fact ungrateful. With this reaffirmation of the importance of the spirit in which we receive a benefit, Seneca prepares us for the description of the whole subject of the treatise as giving and *receiving* benefits at the start of Book 5 (see Ch. 6, pp. 116–18).

(4.) 40. 2 praebebo me amico meo exercendae bonitatis suae capacem materiam (I shall provide my friend with ample opportunity to practise his kindness). Préchac 1961 rightly points to Cicero's letter to Curio in 53 (*Fam.* 2. 6. 2), where he says of Curio's past *beneficia* to him, 'It is the mark of a liberal spirit to want to owe more to a person to whom you owe much'.

(4.) 40. 3 non per me mora, si aut occasio mihi deest aut facultas (the delay is not my fault, if I lack either the occasion or the means). *Occasio* is discussed in 40. 4; *facultas* in 40. 5. They correspond to *felicitas eius* and *mea infelicitas* respectively in 40. 1.

(4.) 40. 5 qui invitus debet, ingratus est (he who is unwilling to owe is ungrateful). Seneca makes a similar point at 6. 41–3 with an additional consideration (**ad 6. 41. 1**).

Synopsis of Book 5

9. 1–2   Generosity, like mercy and pity, must be a voluntary act affecting others; seeking what is beneficial for oneself is a natural drive.

10   *'Offering/giving a benefit', 'benefit' itself, and 'keeping faith' are terms implying the existence of others.*

11. 1–2   *One cannot return a favour to oneself, because returning a favour involves expending something.*

11. 2   Saying we give thanks to ourselves is an abuse of language: we cannot infer that we ought to return a favour to ourselves.

11. 3–5   *Conferring a benefit is a social act for the sake of the recipient.*

12–17   TWO STOIC PARADOXES TO EXERCISE THE MIND (IN DIALOGUE FORM).

12–14   No one is ungrateful.

12. 3–4   *Syllogistic Proof:*
A benefit is that which does good;
but nothing can do a bad man good;
therefore a bad man does not receive benefits and cannot be ungrateful.
A good man does everything right and therefore cannot be ungrateful.

12. 5–7   *Stoic explanation of why a bad man cannot receive or give a benefit.*

13. 1–14. 2   *Solution to the paradox: the bad man can receive 'goods' of the body and fortune. Since he regards them as real benefits, he is ungrateful if he does not return them.*

14. 3–4   *The bad man can also give quasi-benefits, and his recipient can be ungrateful, as he should reciprocate in kind.*

15–17   Everyone is ungrateful.

15. 1   *Syllogistic Proof:*
All fools are bad;
all men are fools;
therefore all men are bad.
But he who has one vice has them all;
therefore all men are ungrateful.

Notes to Synopsis of Book 5

This is the first of the books that is said to be treating merely auxiliary topics. Seneca claims to be doing so at the request of the addressee (cf. 6. 1. 2; 7. 1. 1), and in (5.) 1. 3–5 of the introduction he links the addressee's concerns closely to some of the issues raised later in the book. Seneca proceeds to treat five *quaestiones infinitae* or *theseis*—interrupted by two paradoxes—all dealing principally with questions of gratitude and returning benefits, the third of the topics promised at the start of the work (1. 4. 3). Yet at the opening of this book, he describes his completed task as comprising the giving and the receiving of benefits, omitting this third topic (see **ad (5).1. 1**).

Four of the *quaestiones infinitae* or general questions are of the theoretical type relating to *cognitio*, of which the first (treated in (5.) 2–6), like the two that occupied the bulk of Book 4 (see **ad 4. 1–24**), belongs to the third subdivision *qualitas*; while the other three (treated in (5.) 7–11, 18–19, 20. 1–5) belong to the subdivision *definitio* or *quid sit* (Cic. *Top.* 83) and explore the concept of a *beneficium*. The fifth and last general question is a practical one relating to *actio* ((5.) 20. 6–25), and it belongs to the subdivision concerning *officia*, like the three that end Book 4 (*Cic. Top.* 86; see **ad 4. 26–40**). The two paradoxes ((5.) 12–17) form a contradictory pair: no one is ungrateful; everyone is ungrateful. (Abel 1987, 27 = 1995, 69 regards the debates as a brilliant example of *in utramque partem disserere*.) The first is shown, logically, to be false; the second is shown, empirically, to be true.

(5.) 1. 1 quemadmodum dandum esset beneficium, quemadmodum accipiendum (how a benefit should be given, and how it should to be received). Whereas at 1. 4. 3 the topics to be dealt with are listed as three—giving, receiving, and returning—the pair of general questions raised at the start of Book 4 imply a twofold division of the subject, as here. But there it is giving and returning, while here it is giving and receiving. As argued on pp. 116–18, Seneca in this way reinforces the lesson of the preceding books that how to receive and how to return are really one question, once we understand that the true nature of a benefit is an intentional act, not a gift or service, and that the only proper way to return a benefit is to receive it gratefully.

nascetur, quo lacessat aliqua dulcedine animum, magis non supervacuum quam necessarium (something comes up that challenges the mind by a certain charm, a point non-superfluous rather than necessary). Cf. 1. 5. 1, where Seneca calls 'superfluous' the allegory of the Three Graces, developed by Chrysippus, and poetic treatments of the theme. However, in *Epp.* 45. 4 and 49. 5 it is logical puzzles (*cavillationes*), as here, that are deemed otiose; and the 'charm' at *Ep.* 111. 5 is attached to *sophismata* and *cavillationes*. The grudging defence here already hints at the condemnation attributed to

Liberalis at (5.) 12. 1–2, after the first general question. For Seneca's complex attitude to logical problems, see Ch. 7B.

(5.) 1. 3–5. The sketch of his addressee serves both to emphasize the more active role that he is shown taking, now that Seneca has moved on from elementary teaching by precept to more sophisticated questions (see Ch. 7C), and also to introduce some of the issues that are to be treated in the general questions that follow, ending in (5.) 2. 1 with an explicit link to the first of these. Liberalis is an *exemplum* of a man naturally inclined to the virtue of liberality. His attitudes fit with those recommended in the earlier books, but they are in need of the further refinement that practice in dealing with hard cases can supply. In particular, Liberalis accepts too readily the common idea that it is disgraceful to be outdone in benefits, just as at 6. 41–2 we learn that he is prone to return benefits too soon.

(5.) 1. 3 homini natura optimo et ad beneficia propenso (the best of men by nature and one prone to benefits). Seneca has already mentioned (4. 26. 2) that some individuals are naturally prone to particular vices more than others. The contrasting idea mentioned here was suggested in *Clem.* 2. 2. 1–2, where Nero's natural inclination to mercy is noted (cf. 1. 1. 6 *ista naturalis bonitas*; 1. 1. 3, where *clementia* and *misericordia* are stressed), and Seneca hopes that this *natura et impetus* will develop into a *iudicium*, i.e. that the merciful inclination will become the virtue of clemency, the right course of action being chosen rationally. Men with such inclinations have what Cicero calls 'images of virtue' (*simulacra virtutis*), and, though not *sapientes* but *boni viri*, can serve as exempla of particular virtues (*Off.* 1. 46, cf. 3. 13–14 and Sen. *Ep.* 95. 72); but true virtue must be learnt (*Ep.* 123. 16). Bonhöffer 1894, 10 thought that Panaetius' idea of one's particular nature (Cic. *Off.* 1. 107) was 'the physical and mental individuality of the human being, which entails that one person distinguishes himself more in this virtue, another more in that virtue', and Cicero does adduce there the virtues of *hilaritas* and *severitas* (*eucharistia* in *SVF* iii. 273; *austēria* in *SVF* iii. 272, cf. *Clem.*2. 4. 1). Stobaeus (*SVF* iii. 280) reports Panaetius' use of the simile of archers aiming at the same target by aiming at the different-coloured lines on it, to illustrate how humans aim at the single target of happiness by practising different virtues; though, if they achieve their goal, then they will have all the virtues, which are inseparable.

Liberalis Aebuti. This is the third time that Seneca uses two names for his addressee, not just the *cognomen* (a higher percentage than in his prose works generally, see Dickey 2002, 50), and the only case in which the order of *gentilicium* and *cognomen* is inverted. The use of the double name in *Ben.* seems to follow Cicero's usage in being more formal (Dickey 2002, 53), coming as it does at the beginning of books (3. 1. 1; 4. 1. 1; (5.) 1. 3: alternatively Seneca uses the qualified *cognomen* as in 1. 1. 1; 2. 1. 1; 6. 1. 1; 7. 1. 1). The inversion of the names here perhaps shows additional emphasis on the addressee, in keeping with the extended sketch of his personality.

benignum etiam levissimorum officiorum aestimatorem (generous in valuing even the most trivial services). At 2. 24. 4 Seneca approves of giving thanks for benefits in proportion to their value (adding complimentary remarks), but at 3. 5. 1 he disapproves of forgetting even small benefits.

ut tibi dari putes beneficium quod ulli datur (that you regard a benefit conferred on anyone as conferred on yourself). Cic. *Off.* 2. 63 points out that generosity, when exercised with judgement, wins gratitude from others too, because it is a potential refuge for everyone. At (5.) 17. 7 Seneca urges us to be grateful towards the gods, mankind, and those who have given to ourselves or to those who are dear to us, but he goes on to argue that one only owes gratitude for a benefit if one is the intended recipient, though one may feel moved to render a service out of a sense of justice ((5.) 18–19).

paratus es, ne quem beneficii paeniteat, pro ingratis dependere (to prevent anyone regretting a benefit, you are ready to repay debts for the ungrateful). As Lipsius points out, this goes with the preceding attitude: one repays for others because one feels generally grateful. But Seneca adds a further motive, i.e. to prevent the victim of ingratitude ceasing to be generous: he is concerned to keep the social process going (see pp. 43–4).

(5.) 1. 4 ipse usque eo abes ab omni iactatione (you yourself are so far from all boasting). Liberalis' conduct is in accord with Seneca's teaching at 2. 11. 2–3 and 2. 11. 6.

velis videri non praestare, sed reddere (you wish to appear to be repaying, not giving). The paradox here is similar to the teaching at 1. 7. 1, where the opportunity to give makes the donor feel he has received a benefit; but here it is appearance that is stressed, as at 2. 11. 3 where in public the donor denies giving.

fructus beneficiorum (return for their benefits). At 2. 33. 2 Seneca notes three auxiliary gains from giving a benefit: the awareness of it; the glory of it; what one gets in exchange. So the comparison with glory is particularly apt here, as Liberalis' conduct will win him glory.

(5.) 1. 5 nec recusabis conferre alia (nor will you refuse to confer others). Seneca has already advised repetition of benefits before return is made, because such nourishing of earlier gifts may ultimately elicit gratitude (1. 2. 4–5; 2. 11. 4–5). This lesson will form part of the climax of the work at 7. 32.

suppressis dissimulatisque (covert and undisclosed). The need sometimes to give in secret has been stressed at 2. 9–10.

succumbunt vitia virtutibus, si illa non cito odisse properaveris (vices give way to virtues, if you do not rush to hate them too soon). Though Seneca had already, in *De ira* 1. 16. 6–7; 2. 8. 1; 2. 10. 2–4, advocated an understanding view of human vices, he may have in mind here the well-known saying of the contemporary Stoic senator Thrasea Paetus, *qui vitia odit, homines odit* ('whoever hates vices, hates people'), later praised by Pliny, who admired his gentleness (*Ep.* 8. 22).

(5.) 2–6. The first general question (*infinita quaestio*), 'Is it shameful to be outdone in benefits?' is of the *cognitio–qualitas* type and might seem to be a natural counterpart of the second such question treated in Book 4. 16–24 (Is doing a favour in return for a benefit a thing worthy of choice in itself?), especially since at 1. 4. 3–4, the idea of an honourable contest in outdoing benefits is celebrated, and we are told that someone who owes a debt of gratitude never catches up unless he outstrips it. That it is shameful to be outdone in benefits is clearly an adage of popular morality, which is played on humorously by Martial 7. 42. 3 ('we are weak ... ready to be outdone' (*nos tenues ... sumus vincique parati*), cf. 10. 17. 2) but countered by Val. Max. 5. 2. 7 *fin*. Seneca, with a reproach to his addressee who, as a good man in the ordinary sense, subscribes to the adage (cf. (5.) 2. 1 and 4), is about to lift his treatment above this level by challenging it. Most of his critique relies on the idea that intention is all (see **ad 1. 5. 3**) and that, if one acknowledges or wishes to repay, one has either already repaid sufficiently, and so not been outdone ((5.) 2–4. 1), or one has done as much as practical circumstances allow, and so incurred no shame in being outdone ((5.) 4. 2–5. 4). In this way he counters the feeling that underlies the common attitude, i.e. the fear of being 'clientized', by putting oneself at a long-term social disadvantage when one cannot even the score, already described by Seneca at 2. 23. 2–3 (cf. *Epp.* 19. 11; 81. 32; Cic. *Off.* 2. 69). However, the two cases of Alexander and Socrates at the end are more ambiguous in their conclusions, raising the issues of being truly outdone by a superior person, and of using the adage as an excuse to avoid coercion.

(5.) 2. 1 quod an sit verum (whether this is true or not). Seneca is to show it is not, as he makes explicit at (5.) 2. 4.

(5.) 2. 2 non ut in certaminibus ad spectaculum editis meliorem palma declarat (nor, as in contests provided as public entertainment, does the palm declare the better competitor). The use of the palm as a reward of victory in the games is Hellenistic and was an addition to the traditional garlands: see Livy 10. 47. 3 with commentary in Oakley 2005, 462–3 for the introduction of the custom to Rome in 292 BC, and Plutarch, *Table-Talk* 8. 4. 5, 723 A–F for speculations on why it was used to signify victory. Seneca mentions it in *Ep*.30. 13 as a reward for chariot-racing.

(5.) 2. 4 in hac statione (in that post). The notion of our having been given a post (*taxis* in Greek) by god, a post we must not desert, is a military metaphor that goes back to Plato, as Marcus Aurelius expressly says (7. 45 quoting *Apol.* 28 D, cf. *Phaed.* 61–2; see Brunt 1975, 12, 21, 34–5). Cicero, probably following Panaetius, said that once a person has chosen a role in life, on the basis of his particular talents and circumstances, he should remain at that post with *constantia* (Cic. *Off.* 1. 119–20). So here the good man tries to fulfil his obligation to his benefactor, whatever the odds against him.

(5.) 3. 1 victi confessio (admission of defeat). Seneca carries on the idea of being unconquered in spirit. The Spartan prohibition of the pancration (a combination of wrestling and boxing), and of boxing with weights, was supposedly brought in by the legendary lawgiver Lycurgus (cf. Plut. *Mor.* 189 E; 228 D; Plut. *Lyc.* 19. 4) and was apparently still in force in the Roman period (cf. Phil. *VS* 6. 20; Prop. 3. 14): these contests involved such brutal fighting as to force admission of defeat.

cum invictos esse Lacedaemonii cives suos magno aestimarent (since the Spartans regard it as important that their citizens should be unconquered). Cic. *Off.* 1. 64, alluding to Plato, *Laches* 183 A, disapproves of the Spartan desire always to win.

vox cedentis et tradere iubentis (the voice of the loser as he admits defeat and surrenders the palm). With *tradere,* understand *palmam,* as in the preceding sentence. See **ad (5.) 2. 2** above. The gesture accompanying the vocal surrender is stretching out the hand (Plut. *Lyc.*19. 4).

(5.) 3. 2 ideo nemo trecentos Fabios victos dicit sed occisos; et Regulus captus est a Poenis, non victus (therefore no one describes the three hundred Fabii as conquered, but as cut down; and Regulus was captured by the Carthaginians, not conquered). On the Fabii see **ad 4. 30. 2 nisi Verrucosi et Allobrogici.** M. Atilius Regulus (cos. 267 BC), according to a legend unknown to Polybius (see Walbank 1957, 93–4), but already the material of a moral *exemplum* in Cicero (esp. *Off.* 3. 99–108, cf. Horace, *Carm.* 3. 5), was captured in the First Punic War and was sent by the Carthaginians to ask the Roman senate to exchange captives, under oath to return if he failed. He advised the senate against the proposal and returned to be tortured by the Carthaginians.

(5.) 3. 3 beneficia fortasse beneficiis victa sunt (perhaps one set of benefits has been conquered by another). Seneca counters with the distinction drawn in 1. 5. 1–2, between the true meaning of a *beneficium* as a virtuous act and the vulgar use of the word to denote the gifts or favours received, which are really only the *materia* or *signa* of a *beneficium.*

(5.) 4. 2–5. 4. Seneca here treats situations in which it is not shameful to be outdone because it is impossible to repay in equivalent measure. The principal discussion concerns cases where one's obligation is to someone in an exalted position, or to someone who has no wants or needs. The conjunction of both in the confrontation of Alexander and Diogenes is further developed in (5.) 5. 6, where the confrontation of Socrates, who is barely mentioned here, and Archelaus is also treated. Only then is the question of coercion by the powerful raised, as it was at 2. 18. 6–7. But here it is assumed that the recipient rightly feels an obligation to make a return.

(5.) 4. 2 a principibus dico, a regibus (I mean from rulers, from kings). The listing of *principes* and *reges* parallels the same combination in *De clementia* (1. 3. 3; 1. 4. 3; 2. 5. 2), where Seneca wishes to apply philosophical teaching about the behaviour of kings to the Roman Princeps (e.g. 1. 8. 7–9. 1 on *regia crudelitas*). Here the point is that those in a position to confer unrequitable gifts all pose the same problem for recipients of favours. Roller 2001, 195–6 thinks Seneca is here reassuring readers who fear receiving imperial benefactions as demeaning.

(5.) 4. 3 quibus tamen potest opera navari (to whom it is nonetheless possible to render services). Seneca thus qualifies the idea that we cannot make a suitable return, by stressing that even the powerful need support, in order to exercise their power, and acquiescence in their rule, in order to remain in power. Thus at (5.) 6. 1 he notes the role of the army in creating and supporting Alexander's power, and at 6. 31. 4–34 he argues that honest advice is a way of returning gratitude to the powerful.

a Diogene qui per medias Macedonum gazas nudus incessit calcatis regis opibus (by Diogenes who passed through the Macedonian treasures naked, trampling on the king's wealth). Cynics were not really naked but wore a cloak of coarse material without underwear (D.L. 6. 22); yet in the Roman period there is a statue of Diogenes nude, the nudity representing freedom from want and contempt for the body (Zanker 1995, 176–9). Anecdotes show Diogenes despising the gifts offered by Alexander (D.L. 6. 38; Plut. *Alex.* 14. 2; *Mor.* 605 D–E). Is Seneca here thinking of the story of Diogenes trampling on Plato's carpet (D.L. 6. 26)?

(5.) 5. 2 **a parentibus fere vincimur** (by our parents we are usually outdone). Parents here constitute another case where it may be impossible to repay favours, because, by the time we realize what they had done for us, they are dead. Earlier in 3. 29–38 Seneca rebutted the argument that we cannot repay parents, because the very power of giving comes from them, and insisted that children can actually outdo their parents in benefits, this counting as good fortune, not loss of dignity, for the parent (3. 38. 3).

(5.) 5. 4 **nos tamen nec vincemur animo nec turpiter his rebus superabimur quae non sunt in nostra potestate** (yet we shall not be outdone in intention nor shamed when overwhelmed by things not in our power). Seneca here brings together the arguments that answer the general question 'Is it shameful to be outdone in benefits?' in the negative: we are not in fact overcome with regard to intention, and we are not shamed by being overcome by circumstances not in our control.

(5.) 6. Though Seneca has just told us that it is not disgraceful to be outdone by men whose high position or exceptional virtue prevents any return of equivalent benefits, he now suggests that the powerful Alexander was actually outdone in benefits by his army and by Diogenes, and shamed by not acknowledging it. The story of Socrates that follows is a development of a story in Aristotle's *Rhetoric* 2. 23.8. 1398ª24 about Socrates refusing to visit Archelaus because it would be *hybris* (insult) to be unable to requite benefits as well as being unable to requite injuries. The story is taken up by Marcus Aurelius, who has Socrates give as an excuse for not visiting the court of Perdiccas (Archelaus' father: a slip by Marcus) 'that I may avoid coming to a most unfortunate end, that is, to be treated handsomely and not to have the power to reciprocate' (11. 25). Like Marcus, Seneca omits the idea of returning injury, since he disapproved of it (*Ira* 2. 32. 1: *non enim ut in beneficiis honestum est merita meritis repensare, ita iniurias iniuriis* ('whereas in the case of benefits it is honourable to reward services with service, it is not honourable to repay injuries with injuries'). Seneca also introduces the idea of coercion, which according to 2. 18. 6–7 would have removed the obligation to reciprocate. By going to court, Socrates would have voluntarily entered into a coercive relationship. For the relevance of this anecdote to Seneca's own position, see Ch. 3E, pp. 83–5.

(5.) 6. 1 **nec hoc sibi praestitisse regnum . . . iudicet** (nor regard this kingdom . . . as their gift to him). This is Seneca's rather opaque way of applying to Alexander the idea, already mentioned, of power resting on the service of others (see **ad** (5.) 4. 3): here the soldiers in his army, who had given him his empire—a benefit that he could hardly equal or surpass. The alternative way of translating the sentence, following Préchac

1961 ad loc., 'nor realize that it was his kingdom that had given him this advantage', fits less well with what precedes about Alexander's attitude to his soldiers.

eadem re gloriari Socrates potuit (Socrates could have made the same boast). Both Socrates and Diogenes could claim that no one had outdone them in benefits, because the knowledge they imparted (e.g. (5.) 6. 2–6; (5.) 7. 5) was so precious, and because they needed and wanted nothing in return.

quidni victus sit illo die (was he not in fact outdone on that day). Seneca may be thinking of the famous story of Alexander offering Diogenes any gift he requests, and Diogenes asking him to stand out of his light (D.L. 6. 38; Plut. *Alex.* 14. 2; *Mor.* 605 D–E). Plutarch has Alexander explicitly acknowledge Diogenes' spirit, by saying that he would wish to be Diogenes if he were not Alexander (cf. D.L. 6. 32).

(5.) 6. 2 in ipsius potestate non recipere (it was in his power not to accept). This is explicitly countered later on, at the start of (5.) 6. 7; but readers of Plato's *Gorgias* would remember the crimes of Archelaus there recounted (471), and would realize that what Seneca had already said at 2. 18. 6–7, about not being able to refuse a cruel and irritable tyrant, would apply, so that Socrates' fear of servitude ((5.) 6. 7) was plausible.

(5.) 6. 3 utriusque fines tenentem (and understanding the ends of each). *Finis* is the Latin for *telos*, used in philosophy for the proper purpose of life. Having started with Socrates' knowledge of ethics, Seneca moves on to physics, returning to ethics at (5.) 6. 6.

filium, quod in luctu ac rebus adversis moris est, tonderet (he shaved his son's head, as is customary in times of grief and disaster). Pliny *Ep.* 7. 27. 14 explains the superstition that long hair, which was worn by defendants, was a sign of coming disaster, which could be averted by cutting it. The king probably feared that the disappearance of the sun heralded some disaster to the royal house, though we are not told in what astrological sign the eclipse occurred. If the sign occurred in the sign of Leo, there was a threat to the king (Cic. *Div.* 1. 121); if in the royal trine of Aries, Leo, or Sagittarius, a threat to the royal court (John Lyd.*Ost.* 9 W). See Wardle 2006, 398.

(5.) 6. 4 non est ista solis defectio (this does not mark the disappearance of the sun). Socrates is here credited with a rational explanation of natural events, whereas sometimes (Cic. *Div.* 1. 122) he is depicted as superstitious and able to predict disasters, an idea going back to Plato (*Apol.* 39 C–42 A). Pericles (Plut. *Per.* 35), a pupil of Anaxagoras, knew the rational explanation, which is pre-Socratic.

(5.) 6. 5 dispositosque ac praedictos dies (appointed days known in advance). The Babylonians could predict solar eclipses with some accuracy (Wardle 2006, 377–9). Thales was credited with being able to predict eclipses, but this is now discounted. Hellenistic astronomers in the second century BC are thought to be the first Greeks to do so.

(5.) 6. 6 si illum regnare vetuisset (if he had forbidden him to rule). The text has been doubted. Lipsius read *docuisset* (had taught). If *vetuisset* (had forbidden) is correct, Seneca must mean, as Basore 1935 in the Loeb translation suggests, 'if he had taught him the true values of life', i.e. not to behave autocratically or even not to continue as ruler.

si ullum dare Socrati potuisset (had he been able to give one to Socrates). The king should see that being able to give a benefit to such a great man is in itself to receive a substantial benefit. Cf. (5.) 6. 2: 'He was about to confer a benefit first, since he was coming at his request'.

maluit ille nasute negare quam contumaciter aut superbe (he preferred to refuse him ironically, rather than defiantly or arrogantly). D.L. 2. 25 describes Socrates' refusal of presents and invitations to court from Scopas of Crannon and Eurylochus of Larissa as springing from his contempt of them and their wealth.

(5.) 6. 7 is, cuius libertatem civitas libera ferre non potuit (this man, whose freedom a free city could not bear). The paradox that Socrates successfully defied the Thirty Tyrants (Plato, *Apol.* 32 C; Sen. *Helv.* 13. 4), only to be put to death under the free democracy for exercising freedom of speech, is developed by Seneca in *Tranq.* 5. 2–3.

(5.) 7–11. The second of the *quaestiones infinitae* of the theoretical type is the first of three belonging to the subdivision of definition (*quid sit*). Seneca here considers if the concept of a *beneficium* allows for the exchanges involved to be reflexive, to and from oneself. The raising of this question is not as bizarre as it appears to us, because *oikeiōsis* (appropriation), the impulse to care for something as one's own, starts with care for oneself and one's own person and then extends to caring for other people, starting with one's offspring (Plut. *De Stoic repugn.* 1038 B; Cic. *Fin.* 3. 62): see **ad (5.) 9. 1**.

  The argument in support at (5.) 7 is predominantly verbal: many locutions involve speaking of ourselves as two parties to the transaction. But there are also arguments from common moral attitudes (**ad (5.) 7. 2–6**). The argument against ((5.) 8–11), is naturally more elaborate. First, Seneca addresses giving, receiving, and returning together, in (5.) 8–9; then giving, in (5.) 10; returning, in (5.) 11. 1–2; and then giving again, in (5.) 11. 3–5. This makes sense, because the question of giving benefits is fundamental: if giving under these conditions is impossible, so is returning ((5.) 9. 1). Seneca moves back and forth between his linguistic and logical arguments and the social rationale behind them: the giving of a benefit is a social act for the sake of another person; both giving and returning benefits mean benefiting someone else.

(5.) 7. 1 manifestum enim fuisset non esse turpe a se ipsum vinci (for it would have been clear that it is not shameful to be outdone by oneself). Seneca provides an elegant link with the previous general question ((5.) 2–6). The question of shame could not have been raised in the case of benefits, where giver and recipient are the same and so cannot outdo one another.

(5.) 7. 2–6. Just as Seneca uses arguments from common patterns of behaviour (**ad 4. 1. 2–15**), so he often uses arguments from common linguistic usage. 'The Stoics' belief in the providential arrangement of the cosmos, which accounts for god's gift of reason and language to humans, committed them to the basic reliability of the natural human capacity for apprehension of the world, including the fundamental correctness of language in both structure and vocabulary' (Atherton 1993, 92). But the Stoics were also aware that language was in a corrupt state and could mislead its users. The existence of ambiguity is one sign of this, so it was important to make distinctions and analyse the defects, so as not to obstruct the discovery of the truth (Atherton 1993, 94). At (5.) 7. 2–3 and (5.) 7. 5 *fin.*–6, customary language is invoked by an opponent to suggest that various reflexive expressions support the idea that we can give benefits and owe gratitude to ourselves. At (5.) 7. 4–5, however, it is common values that are appealed to, the condemnation or approval of actions directed toward others being lined up with similar attitudes to actions directed towards ourselves. But language and values are not always kept absolutely distinct: so Seneca reverts to a linguistic similarity at (5.) 7. 4: *ut ita dicam, adsentator suus* ('so to speak, his own flatterer').

(5.) 7. 4 **tam alieni corporis leno male audit quam sui** (a pimp acquires as bad a reputation for selling another's body as for selling his own). The terms of the comparison are reversed, as often in Seneca, see **ad 1. 13. 3.**

(5.) 7. 5 **M. Cato ait: 'Quod tibi deerit, a te ipso mutuare.'** (Marcus Cato says, 'What you lack, borrow from yourself.'). Here Seneca is interested in the form of words which (according to his opponent) suggests the possibility of dividing oneself into lender and debtor, but in *Ep.* 119. 2 the saying is employed in arguing that reducing need is equivalent to having wealth: *paratum tibi creditorem dabo Catonianum illum: a te mutuum sumes. Quantulumcumque est, satis erit si, quidquid deerit, id a nobis petierimus* ('I shall furnish you with a ready creditor, Cato's well-known one: "Borrow from yourself." No matter how small, it will be enough, if, whatever is lacking, we make up from our own resources').

(5.) 8–9. Seneca begins his refutation with an appeal to the real world: owing and returning are sequential acts in time and involve two participants. By (5.) 9. 4 he discerns three sequential events: receiving, owing, repaying, which require a span of time and two people. In between there is an explicitly linguistic argument: the expression 'to owe' implies the involvement of two people ((5.) 8. 3); a moral argument: looking after oneself is not a moral act and earns no praise ((5.) 9. 1–2); and curious comparisons of a man acting on himself to a sphere turning round ((5.) 8. 4), and then to physical nature itself, in which reciprocal processes ensure no loss anywhere ((5.) 8. 5–6).

(5.) 8. 1 **natura prius est, ut quid debeat, deinde, ut gratiam referat** (by nature a person owes first and returns the favour afterwards). Lipsius complained that the transition to the refutation was obscure and supplied *nemo sibi debet* (no one owes himself) before *natura*. Préchac 1961 supplies, before *natura* (but at the end of (5.) 7. 6), the *natura sibi dedit* of a late manuscript and translates, 'Il est conforme à l'ordre de la nature qu'il se soit fait du bien'. The idea fits with, and could derive from (5.) 9. 2, *sibi praestare natura est*. But either addition would detract from the force of *natura prius est*, for Seneca is not at this point appealing to human nature in particular, as in (5.) 9.

1–2 (where the key idea is *oikeiōsis*), but to the nature of things in its wider sense: how things really are, as opposed to the inferences drawn by his opponent in (5.) 7 from human language and behaviour.

(5.) **8. 2 quomodo nemo, quamvis pro se dixerit, adfuisse sibi dicitur nec statuam sibi tamquam patrono suo ponit** (just as no one, although he has spoken on his own behalf, is said to have appeared in his own defence, or erects a statue to himself as his advocate). This is the second of three examples, each marked off by *quomodo*, where a person does something for himself but creates no obligation: moving the body; appearing in his own defence; curing himself. In the early Empire the word *patronus* can mean a legal advocate, an ex-master of freedmen, a patron of a community (not of individuals). *Patronus* here has the sense of an advocate in court, as often in Seneca (*Ira* 2. 7. 3; *Brev.* 7. 8, cf. e.g. *Roman Statutes*, no. 1, ll. 9, 11; Ps.-Asc. 190, v.5 Stangl). Statues to honour advocates are known (*IG* xii/6. 351 = Eilers 2002, C51, 217, cf. 121; possibly *Inscr. Eph.* iii 630b = Eilers 2002, C87, 232–3). What limits should be put on financial rewards for advocacy was contested in Seneca's day (see p. 58), and, at all times, repayment in honour was appreciated (Tac. *Dial.* 36. 4–8).

(5.) **9. 1 naturae suae paret, a qua ad caritatem sui compositus est** (he obeys his own nature by which he is inclined to feel an affection for himself). Seneca alludes here to the doctrine of *oikeiōsis* (appropriation), according to which nature designs human beings so that they try to preserve themselves, and directs them towards choosing what is beneficial to themselves and avoiding what is harmful (see **ad 4. 17. 2**; *Ep.* 121. 6–15).

(5.) **9. 2 quod aliis praestare liberalitas est, clementia, misericordia** (what counts as generosity, clemency or pity, when given to another). On these virtues, see **ad 3. 27. 4** and **ad 6. 29. 1**.

(5.) **9. 4 accipere beneficium me oportet, deinde debere, deinde referre; debendi locus non est quia sine ulla mora recipimus** (it is proper to receive a benefit, then to be indebted, then to return it; but there is no opportunity to be indebted here, because, without any delay, we receive a return). Seneca here distinguishes three stages of receiving, owing, and returning, rather than the usual two of receiving and returning (1. 4. 3), in order to increase the objection to simultaneity.

(5.) **10.** Whereas his opponent concentrated on customary language and on inferences from such usage to the possibility of conferring a benefit on oneself, Seneca now points to the implication of the terms *praestitisse* and *dare* that two people are involved in the transaction, and of *beneficium* itself, etymologically related to the verbal expression *bene facere* ('to do good to'). Etymology was a favourite tool of the Stoics, going with their belief in the natural suitability of signifiers to significations (Blank and Atherton 2003, 316).

(5.) **10. 2 frater sum alterius, nemo est suus frater** (I am a brother, but of someone else, for no one is his own brother). Seneca could have used the argument from correlative relationships mentioned in (5.) 8. 1, but there he was concentrating on reality, not words, which, in the Stoic view, match when language is correct (Blank and Atherton 2003, ibid.).

(5.) 11. Seneca here gives the definitive negative answer to the *quaestio*, treating its two elements in the reverse order: (1) *versus* the possibility of returning a favour to oneself: there has to be some loss to the returner of a benefit, just as there should be gain when he accepts it; in giving a benefit, there needs to be the risk that it will not be returned. (2) *versus* the possibility of conferring a benefit on oneself: when only one person is involved, the transaction is selfish, whereas giving a benefit is a social act done for someone else's sake.

(5.) 11. 2 **cum hoc dicimus, laudamus nos et, ut factum nostrum comprobemus, gratias agentium verbis abutimur** (when we say this, we are congratulating ourselves and, in order to show approval of what we have done, we misuse the language of giving thanks). Seneca here finally challenges his opponent's opening move: that we are accustomed to say 'I am thankful to myself' ((5.) 7. 2). He does not deny that we say this, but points out that it is an abuse of language, because no gratitude is involved: it is just a way of showing approval of our own action.

(5.) 11. 5 **beneficium dare socialis res est, aliquem conciliat, aliquem obligat** (to give a benefit is a social act that wins someone over, that lays someone under an obligation). The bond between humans created by beneficence is the whole *raison d'être* for the practice. As Seneca explained in 4. 18, the fellowship thus created provides human beings with security, compensating for their physical weakness, in accordance with divine providence.

(5.) 12–17. This pair of paradoxical statements, like the one in Book 2. 31–5, are not listed among the common Stoic paradoxes, which concern the Sage (*SVF* iii. 599; 544). Plutarch treats such notions as the first one, that no one is ungrateful, as examples of self-contradiction by the Stoa (Plut. *Mor.* 1068 D–E = *SVF* iii. 672, cf. 1060 B) because such paradoxical statements rest on novel Stoic uses of language but are then unravelled by the Stoics themselves, to accommodate attitudes much closer to ordinary usage and conduct (**ad 2. 31–5**). The second paradox, that everyone is ungrateful, is presented ((5.) 15. 1), like the first, as the conclusion of a syllogistic argument, resting on the Stoic premises that all men are vicious, and that the vices are indivisible; Aristotle (*Rhet.* 2. 21. 4, 1394^{b}8–10) had maintained that, when maxims or *gnōmai* are paradoxical, they need *apodeixis*, and the most powerful kind of *apodeixis* is syllogistic. But Seneca has already modified this Stoic view at 4. 26–7, showing that the Stoics recognize a more ordinary sense of 'ungrateful', according to which not all vicious men are ungrateful in the ordinary sense. So here Seneca does not pursue the logical points but concentrates on empirical evidence and the support of ordinary opinion, not philosophical, that ingratitude is rife among human beings, even toward the gods. (Sonntag 1913 argues that the careful argumentation in Book 4 is from Hecato, whereas the treatment here is Seneca's own.) This second paradox, unlike the first, omits the Sage from consideration, as he is not ungrateful.

(5.) 12. 1. Seneca has Liberalis reproach him with his claim (at (5.) 1. 2) that he would be dealing with things that do not waste one's efforts. Seneca's defence, that such dialectical puzzles challenge the mind, picks up the *dulcedo* (charm) of (5.) 1. 1 (see **ad 5. 1. 1 nascetur**).

(5.) 12. 2 quid enim boni est, nodos operose solvere, quos ipse, ut solveres, feceris? (what is the good of laboriously untying knots which you have made yourself, in order that you might untie them?). In *Ep.* 45. 5 the same image of untying knots is used to condemn *cavillatio*, long puzzles and captious arguments; in *Ep.* 82. 19, to condemn dialectic altogether. See pp. 133–5.

securitatem ac segnitiam ingeniis auferunt (remove complacency and sluggishness from our minds). In *Ep.* 65. 15 intricate arguments about the classification of causes, provided too much subtlety is not applied, are justified as freeing the soul from more earthly concerns; but *Ep.* 48. 9–12 suggests that such puzzles actually interfere with the work of philosophy in leading us to higher concerns.

(5.) 12. 3–14. Seneca has his opponent attribute to the Stoics, as the supporting arguments for the view that no man is ungrateful, two syllogisms leading to the conclusion that no bad man can receive a benefit, and therefore no bad man can be obliged to return one, and so is not ungrateful; the opponent then completes the proof by adducing the doctrine that needs no argument, i.e. that a good man will always be grateful. Then, at (5.) 12. 5–7, Seneca gives, in his own voice, the rationale for the premise that no bad man can receive a benefit, adding at the end of §12 that he cannot give one, either. As Stobaeus explains at *SVF* iii. 94, μηδένα δὲ φαῦλον μήτε ὠφελεῖσθαι μήτε ὠφελεῖν· εἶναι γὰρ τὸ ὠφελεῖν ἴσχειν κατ' ἀρετὴν καὶ τὸ ὠφελεῖσθαι κινεῖσθαι κατ' ἀρετήν ('that no bad man can receive help or give help, for to give help is to act in accordance with virtue, and to receive help is to be affected in accordance with virtue'). As Seneca explains, since a benefit is a virtuous act (1. 5. 3), it cannot benefit the evil man, whose nature cannot accept anything good or virtuous. Nor can he perform a virtuous act, as he does not have the virtuous intention.

Then, at (5.) 13–14, comes the accommodation with ordinary language, as noted by Plut. *Mor.* 1068 E. A bad man can receive things that are not goods but positive indifferents, and, as he regards them as benefits, he is obliged to return them in kind, even if they come from a bad man (who also regards them as benefits).

(5.) 12. 3 ergo beneficium non accipit malus, * ingratus est (therefore a bad person does not receive a benefit; he is * ungrateful). The * marks a lacuna in N. The addition of *igitur non*, producing 'therefore he is not ungrateful' (Préchac 1961) or of *nullus itaque malus*, producing 'and so no bad man is ungrateful' (Haase 1893) restores the sense. The *homo malus* is here, according to strict Stoic usage, anyone but the Sage, the *vir bonus* of (5.) 12. 4 (see Ch. 8, n. 23).

(5.) 12. 6 quemadmodum stomachus morbo vitiatus et colligens bilem (just as the stomach when, impaired by disease and collecting bile). Seneca here alludes to the doctrine of the four humours: blood, phlegm, bile, and black bile. At *Ira* 3. 9. 4 Seneca recommends eating when afflicted with an excess of bile, which causes anger. See Migliorini 1997, 55.

(5.) 13. 1 quae beneficiis similia sint (that resemble benefits). A *beneficium* must do someone good (see *ad* 5. 10), but, according to Stoic usage, the only goods are those of the mind (namely virtue and virtuous acts), while those commonly called goods of the body and of good fortune are really 'positive indifferents': *commoda*, *expetenda* = the Greek *proēgmena*, as Seneca calls them just below at (5.) 13. 2 (cf. *Epp.* 74. 17; 87. 29; 92. 16), and as Plutarch does in his discussion of the paradox at *Mor.* 1068 E. But the Stoics often adopted common usage, which was followed by the Peripatetics (Cic. *Fin.* 3. 43).

Peripatetici quoque, qui felicitatis humanae longe lateque terminos ponunt (the Peripatetics as well, who extend the bounds of human happiness far and wide). The Peripatetics held that there were goods other than virtue, and that they enhanced happiness, though they were not essential to it: only virtue, the highest good, is essential (*Ep.* 92. 14). See Inwood 1995*b*, 71 = 2005, 17).

(5.) 13. 3 quaedam, etiam si vera non sunt, propter similitudinem eodem vocabulo comprehensa sunt (certain things, even if they are not genuine examples of something, are covered by the same term because of their similarity). As in 2. 34, Seneca has recourse to the imprecision of language to unravel a Stoic paradox. There the shortage of words led to ambiguity in language; here it is the desire to emphasize similarities that leads to imprecision: a metal box can be called *pyxis*, which originally denoted a wooden box (for the wood, *pyxacanthus*, see Plin. *HN* 12. 31), cf. the English 'iron' for an implement no longer made of iron; 'illiterate' and 'naked' can be used in an exaggerated sense. So here the term 'benefit' is extended to cover what appears to the giver and to the recipient to be a 'benefit', although, strictly speaking, it is not.

(5.) 13. 4 ita, qui veri beneficii speciem fefellit, tam ingratus est quam veneficus, qui soporem, cum venenum esse crederet, miscuit (And so the person who has failed to honour the semblance of a true benefit is just as much an ingrate, as that person is a poisoner, who has mixed a sleeping draught believing it was a poison). The Roman statute against murder, the *Lex Cornelia de sicariis et veneficis*, covered not just administering poison but *qui venenum necandi hominis causa fecerit vel vendiderit vel habuerit* ('who makes, sells, or possesses a drug for the purpose of homicide'), according to *Dig.* 48. 8. 3 pref. A senatorial decree under the Principate ruled that dealers in cosmetics were liable to the law if they thoughtlessly or recklessly handed over to anyone various poisons (*Dig.* 48. 8. 3. 3, see Mommsen 1899, 636). So here the person who intends to concoct a poison is liable to punishment. Hadrian was to rule explicitly that someone who intended to kill someone, but only injured him in the attempt, was to be regarded as a homicide (*Dig.* 48. 8. 1. 3). In the same spirit, Seneca regards the intention to be ungrateful as the crucial thing.

(5.) 14. 1 Cleanthes vehementius agit (Cleanthes argues the point more forcefully). The quotation spells out why the recipient's belief that he has received a benefit is what makes him ungrateful: his failure to make a return shows his bad intention, and it is bad intention that constitutes vicious behaviour. *SVF* i. 580 takes the quotation down to the end of (5.) 14. 2, but there is no reason to do so, and the coincidence with Roman law (**ad 5. 13. 4**) weakens the case for doing so.

(5.) 14. 2 **quia ad occidendum iam armatus est et habet spoliandi et interficiendi voluntatem** (because he is already armed to kill and has the intention of robbing and murdering). So under the *Lex Cornelia* (**ad 5. 13. 4**) a person is liable who goes about with a weapon for the purpose of homicide or theft (*Dig.* 48. 8. 1 pref.). The MSS agree in placing *ipsum, quod accepit, beneficium non erat, sed vocabatur*, after *incipit* in 5. 14. 2. It was moved by Gertz 1876 to (5.) 14. 3 (with the addition of *qui*), and Hosius is clearly right to follow Gertz, for the sentence interrupts the argument here, which is about intention being enough to make an action blameworthy.

(5.) 14. 2 **sacrilegi dant poenas, quamvis nemo usque ad deos manus porrigat** (those guilty of sacrilege are punished, even though no one can lay hands on the gods). The etymological meaning of *sacrilegium*, that is, 'the carrying off of sacred objects', lies behind the notion of not reaching as far as the gods; cf. *Ep.* 87. 22–4 for the association of sacrilege and theft.

(5.) 14. 3 **<qui> accipiet ab illo aliquid ex his, quae apud imperitos <in pretio> sunt, quorum et malis copia est** (<the person> who receives from him one of those things that are held <in esteem> by the ignorant, things of which bad men possess a good supply). The supplement *<qui>* is by Gertz 1876; *<in pretio>* is Madvig's, accepted by Préchac 1961. Lipsius supplied *bona* after *imperitos*, which would also serve. So far Seneca has considered the view of the beneficiary, and then of the benefactor, as to the status of the favour. Now with 'by the ignorant', this view is seen as the common one that regards preferable indifferents as goods.

(5.) 14. 5 **ad vos non pertinet; in alios quaeritur verum** (is of no concern to you; the truth is sought for cases other than yours). The text of the last clause is probably corrupt. Lipsius emended it to *ad alios spectat verum*, which he understood to mean that the truth should be reserved to others capable of understanding it, while the ignorant (you) are content with semblances of truth. Préchac 1961 translates the received text as, 'Cela ne vous regarde pas; c'est pour des cas différents du vôtre qu'on recherche le vrai', and I have followed him, taking the other cases to be those of Sages or of those further advanced in virtue. Basore in the Loeb edition, however ('your search for truth is to the detriment of others'), and Guglielmino 1968, take the *in* to mean 'against' here, and the sense to be that the insistence on the true sense of benefits is an excuse for not recognizing and returning ordinary favours. Gertz's suggestion of *<nec>* before *in alios* would, more plausibly, have Seneca warn against such a consequence of commitment to Stoic truth.

speciem veri (semblance of truth). Seneca subscribes to the view advanced in Cicero's *De officiis*, that the pursuit of what appears, in the common understanding, to be virtue (called *simulacra virtutis* at 1. 46) is important if the morally imperfect are to make moral progress (3. 17). To those who appear to be Sages in the common view, Cicero ascribes the *similitudo* or *species sapientium* (3. 16).

(5.) 15. 1 **omnes stulti mali sunt; qui unum autem habet vitium, omnia habet** (all fools are bad, and he who has one vice has them all). On the Stoic equation of ignorance and evil, see **ad 1. 1. 1**; and on the inseparability of the vices, **ad 4. 26. 2**.

(5.) 15. 2 pro pessimo pravoque numerantium, quidquid citra recti formulam cecidit (who regard as evil and wrong whatever falls short of the standard of right conduct). Seneca alludes back to the premise cited at 15. 1, that all men are foolish and bad. For the Stoics, every individual act is either virtuous or vicious and every person either a Sage or a bad man (*SVF* iii. 530–2, 536–9); and since no Sage is ever found, no truly virtuous acts are in practice ever performed.

(5.) 15. 2 ex medio conventu (from the midst of the crowd). As in *Ira* 2. 9. 2, Seneca uses Ovid, *Met.* 1. 144–6, a chronicle of vice in the Age of Iron, as a picture of contemporary wickedness: here the crimes committed are all treated as instances of ingratitude, in that those to whom benefits are owed by virtue of their relationship to others are instead plotted against by those same people. Cf. 1. 10. 1–3, where the prevalence of crime is noted and traced back to ingratitude.

(5.) 15. 4–16. Seneca's examples of ingratitude to one's fatherland start with an anonymous generalization about commanders who turn the armies assigned to them by Rome on the city itself. Of the examples that follow, only Marius (who reassembled his veterans along with new volunteers in 86 BC), Sulla, and Caesar fit this mould, and Caesar is questionable (see ad **(5.) 16. 5 castra**). The order of examples is chronological, except for Catiline, which suggests that Seneca intends a crescendo (see Mayer 1991, 156, who comments on the increasing length of sentences, through Pompey): Coriolanus and Catiline never actually invaded Rome; Marius, Sulla, and Caesar did; Antony wished to subject Rome to foreign rule. See Biographical Notes on those named.

(5.) 15. 4 hoc iam amplius est (this goes even further). This is the climax of Seneca's account of human ingratitude: worse than the vice that is simply, in the Stoic sense, a lapse from virtue, worse than Ovid's breakdown of trust in social relations, is the wickedness of attacking society itself out of ambition, and using her armies to do so.

imperatoria contio (the general's harangue). Such as Lucan gives Caesar at 1. 299–349.

(5.) 15. 5 qui ne triumphaturi quidem inire urbem iniussu senatus deberetis (you who were not supposed to enter the city without the senate's command, even to hold a triumph). In the Republic the senate was regularly approached by the magistrate or promagistrate wishing to triumph, and it would then instruct a tribune to bring a *rogatio* to the people, allowing the general to retain his *imperium* within the city boundaries. The senate would have to meet outside the city boundary (*pomerium*) on such an occasion, usually in the Temple of Bellona, so that the general could attend. There were, however, triumphs celebrated without senatorial permission (see Richardson 1975). Under the Empire, in Seneca's day, triumphs were restricted to members of the imperial house. To others, the Princeps recommended that the senate vote triumphal insignia and a triumphal statue instead.

urbem subrectis intrate vexillis (you enter the city with standards held high). These generals treat the city like a battlefield, so their soldiers have their standards flying.

(5.) 15. 6 aquilas suas (its own eagles). The people are frightened by the eagles on the standards of their own legions, now within the city of Rome.

(5.) 16. 1 in medio parricidio (in the midst of parricide). Etymologically, *parricidium* is the murder of a kinsman. In Early Rome it came to mean the murder of any free man, and then narrowed in the late Republic to mean murder of near relatives. Cicero spoke of *parricidium patriae* (*Sul.* 6; *Phil.*2. 17; *Off.* 3. 83), but he also uses *parricidium* alone to indicate civil parricide (*Rab. Perd.* 27). Of Coriolanus, Livy 28. 29. 1 writes: *revocavit (Coriolanum) … a publico parricidio privata pietas* ('family devotion called (Coriolanus) back from treason to the state'), i.e. his mother's plea.

diu debitas inferias Gallicis bustis (the sacrifices long overdue at the Gallic tombs). Seneca traces to the long-term hatred of the Gauls for Rome, going back to the Gallic siege of the fourth century BC, the adherence to Catiline's conspiracy in 63 BC of some envoys of the Allobroges, who were in fact motivated by the refusal by the senate to grant their tribe debt relief, as they had just requested (Sall. *Cat.* 40. 1–4). The *busta Gallica* was a place in Rome where tradition said that the Gauls in 390 BC, when they were besieging Rome, had interred the ashes of those of them who had succumbed to a pestilence on the spot, in a heap, without due ceremony (Livy. 5. 48. 3; 22. 14. 11, Ogilvie 1965, 737). They are now said to intend to offer Roman leaders (killed in Catiline's attack) as human sacrifices.

(5.) 16. 2 nisi civilis exitii et trucidationis non tantum dederit signum, sed ipse signum fuerit (unless he has not only given the signal for the death and slaughter of his citizens, but has become that living signal). When Marius returned to Rome in 86 BC with Cinna, after being exiled by Sulla, he engaged in the slaughter of his enemies. Seneca uses military language for his giving the command to his bodyguard to kill, and then alludes to his indicating that particular persons were to die, by refusing to greet them, or to acknowledge their greeting (Plut. *Mar.* 43; Florus 2. 9. 16).

(5.) 16. 3 impunitatem, pecuniam, tantum non civicam acciperet (impunity, money, all but a civic crown). Sulla invented the proscriptions, a list of people who could be killed with impunity, and rewarded the killers with immunity from prosecution and financial rewards. Seneca jokes that they were all but awarded the *corona civica*, a military honour for saving a citizen's life: as Lipsius comments 'ob cives non servatos sed necatos?' ('not on account of saving citizens but of killing them?'). Sulla is an important example of cruelty in *De ira* (2. 2. 3; 2. 34. 3; 3. 18. 1), and a counter-example in *De clementia* (1. 12. 1–3), where the slaughter of 7,000 mutineers may refer to the same episode as the slaughter of two legions mentioned here, and as the 4,000 killed in the Villa Publica in Florus 2. 9. 24.

(5.) 16. 4 hanc gratiam rei publicae reddidit, ut in possessionem eius alios quoque induceret quasi potentiae suae detracturus invidiam (repaid the commonwealth this favour by inciting others to join him in taking possession of her, as if he could reduce the odium attached to his power). Pompey is the only one of Seneca's examples here who did not contemplate turning his army on Rome, so Seneca blames him, instead, for dividing total political control of her between himself, Caesar, and Crassus: the so-called 'first triumvirate' of 60 BC. As Caesar became Pompey's father-in-law, Seneca can say that two-thirds of that control was in his family. Of the extraordinary commands mentioned, Caesar received Cisalpine Gaul and Illyricum, Crassus Syria, and Pompey Spain. On *gratiam reddere*, see **ad 3. 2. 2.**

beneficio servitutis (thanks to slavery). An ironic use of the common Latin idiom for an advantage secured by virtue of a law, or a grant by a person. Seneca represents slavery, i.e. Caesar's dictatorship and the Principate that finally ended the civil wars, as the means of securing Rome's survival, cf. Tacitus, *Ann.* 4. 33. 2. Seneca clearly subscribes to Cato's view (Plut. *Pomp.* 47. 2–3), that the formation of the triumvirate, rather than its breakdown, caused the destruction of the Roman Republic.

(5.) 16. 5 a Gallia Germaniaque bellum in urbem circumegit (from Gaul and Germany he whirled war into the city). See **ad 2. 20. 3 ius dandi beneficii iniuria venerat.**

castra in circo Flaminio posuit, propius quam Porsinae fuerant (pitched his camp in the Circus Flaminius, nearer to the city than Porsenna's had been). Porsenna, the Etruscan general, had camped on the Janiculum. Even the hostile Lucan at 3. 72 has Caesar bringing in some unarmed men to the city; Caesar himself (*BC* 1. 32. 1) says that, on his first visit to Rome after leaving his province, he came into the city, leaving his soldiers in nearby towns. Lipsius suggests that since the Circus Flaminius was near the temple of Apollo outside the city boundary, where Caesar held the senate, he could have brought in with him some soldiers, probably in civilian dress, to guard him.

arma ... satiata tamen aliquando abiecerunt (arms once sated, finally laid them down). Seneca compares Caesar with Sulla, who laid down his dictatorship, then his consulship, and retired into private life. Caesar's policy of clemency was adopted in conscious rejection of Sulla's cruelty (Cic. *Att.* 9. 7C.1), which Pompey was threatening to imitate (*Att.* 9. 10. 6). According to Suetonius *Iul.* 77, Caesar was reported to have said in public that Sulla had shown himself illiterate when he laid down the dictatorship. Caesar accepted appointment as *dictator perpetuus* by 15 February 44 BC, a move that helped to precipitate his murder (Dio 44. 8. 4).

(5.) 16. 6 ingratus Antonius in dictatorem suum quem iure caesum pronuntiavit (Antonius is ungrateful towards his dictator, whom he pronounced justly killed). Suet. *Iul.* 76. 1 gives *iure caesus* as the general verdict. For the legalistic overtones of the phrase, which goes back to the XII Tables, see Dyck 1996, 426 on Cic. *Off.* 2. 43. But there is no other evidence that Mark Antony justified Caesar's murder: Seneca is exaggerating Antony's failure to punish the assassins. In accordance with the amnesty of 18 March 44, which Antony as consul implemented, Brutus and Cassius were given curatorships of the corn supply and then the peaceful provinces of Crete and Cyrene respectively, though they moved on to Syria and Macedonia.

ne Romanis quidem regibus (to kings who were not even Roman). Cleopatra and her brother Ptolemy XIV are presumably meant. On Antony's betrayal of his Romanness, see Horace *Epod.* 9. 11–14. Actium was represented as a victory against a foreign queen (Hor. *Carm.* 1. 37).

(5.) 17. 2 Camillum in exilium misit, Scipionem dimisit (Camillus was sent into exile; Scipio was allowed to go). The two are paired by Valerius Maximus in his list of those treated ungratefully by the community (5. 3. 2a and 2b), no doubt a declamation theme. Furius Camillus, when faced with a large fine after being charged, probably with peculation, went into voluntary exile, probably in 391 BC (Livy 5. 32. 8–9 with Ogilvie 1965 ad loc.). Exile was not, in the early Republic, a formal penalty of the criminal law. P. Cornelius Scipio Africanus, the victor of the second Punic war against Hannibal, was accused in 184 BC of peculation before the people but avoided trial by withdrawing into voluntary exile at Liternum in Campania (cf. Sen. *Ep.* 51. 11). Seneca represents Scipio as being treated more mildly, either because Camillus, according to Livy, was fined in his absence, or, more probably, because he regards Scipio as having withdrawn simply in order to avoid his greatness endangering the Republic (as in *Ep.* 86. 1–3).

exsulavit post Catilinam Cicero (Cicero was exiled after Catiline). In *Tranq.* 16. 1 Cicero had also been placed in the company of Rutilius and Cato as victims of undeserved bad fortune. Seneca takes here, and in *Cons. Marc.* 20. 5, the view common in declamation, that Cicero's triumph over Catiline saved Rome (*Controv.* 7. 2. 7; *Suas.* 6. 21, 26; 7. 2), but was more guarded about his consulship in *Brev. vit.* 5. 1 (see Setaioli 2003). The losses mentioned here were inflicted by P. Clodius as tribune in 58: he was known as *felix Catilina*. Cicero was recalled after a year and a half in exile.

Rutilius innocentiae pretium tulit in Asia latere (Rutilius was rewarded for his innocence with a life of obscurity in Asia). An adherent of the Stoa, P. Rutilius Rufus, though widely believed to be innocent, was condemned in 92 BC for extortion by an equestrian jury, after serving as legate to the incorruptible Q. Mucius Scaevola, governor of Asia, who had curbed the abuses of the equestrian tax collectors. He went into exile at Smyrna among the people he was supposed to have despoiled. Seneca admired his uprightness in adversity (6. 37. 2; *Prov.* 3. 4): see Kaster 2005, 163 n. 20.

Catoni populus Romanus praeturam negavit, consulatum pernegavit (to Cato the Roman people denied the praetorship, the consulship it persisted in denying him). The Younger Cato was defeated for the praetorship of 55 but was elected for 54; he was defeated for the consulship of 51 and never stood for it again (cf. *Cons. Helv.* 13. 5).

(5.) 17. 3 atqui non potest fieri, ut omnes querantur, nisi querendum est de omnibus (but it cannot be the case that everyone has a complaint, unless everyone is an object of complaint). The argument requires that each person complaining about someone other than himself, complains about a different person.

<ingrati sunt> tantum? (<ungrateful> only?). The addition by Gertz 1876 is accepted by Basore in the Loeb edition and by Préchac 1961. Seneca elaborates on the theme of the inseparability of the vices (**ad 4. 26. 2**). Just as all are ignorant, they are all insane, because not under the control of reason.

(5)17. 4 quis non . . . ut moderatus sit, expectat? (who, however reasonable he is, does not look forward to it?). As Lipsius suggests, Seneca may have in mind the story in Rutilius Lupus 1. 5 and Quintilian 9. 3. 68 about Proculeius, who complained of his son *quod is mortem suam expectaret* ('that he was "waiting for" his death'), and when his son denied it, retorted *rogo expectes* ('please do wait'). Proculeius in fact eventually took his own life because of a painful illness (Plin. *HN* 36. 183).

ultra res proximas (longer than the most recent hearing). In this context *res* means *lites*.

(5.) 17. 5 vixi et quem dederat cursum fortuna peregi (I have lived and run the course that fortune gave me). Seneca cites Verg. *Aen.* 4. 653 (quoted also in *Vit. beat.* 19. 1 and *Ep.* 12. 9), spoken by Dido as she takes her own life, not intending the quotation to be read in context, where it hardly illustrates dying without complaint.

(5.) 17. 7 grati autem adversus eos, qui nostris praestiterunt (grateful to those who have done something for those dear to us). Seneca ends his exhortation to gratitude for the gods' gift of life, with a list of the proper objects of our gratitude in descending order: the gods, mankind, benefactors of ourselves and of those dear to us, the last being added to provide a bridge to the next *quaestio infinita* or *thesis.*

(5.) 18–19. This, the second of the three *quaestiones infinitae* belonging to the subdivision within *cognitio* of definition (*quid sit*), illustrates the difficulties (1) of distinguishing *theseis* from *causae* and (2) of distinguishing *theseis* concerned with *cognitio* from those concerned with *actio* (both discussed on pp. 131, 139). Thus, Seneca (1) first frames the question in (5.) 18.1 as one about father and son and other specified relatives, only at the end, with the question 'how far am I to pursue the list of relevant persons?', addressing the more general concern; and (2), with this same question, raises a question of conduct, as again at 19. 8, 'a benefit should not be reclaimed from the father'. However, (1) the crucial mark of a *thesis*, as against a *causa*, in one view, is its concern with establishing the truth, rather than solving a practical problem (Quint. 3. 5. 8–13), and (2) the conclusion of the discussion is to clarify the concept of a *beneficium* as a service that was intended by the donor to benefit the recipient ((5.) 19. 8). In (5.) 18. 1–19. 8 we have a dialogue between 'Seneca' and the fictive interlocutor. The latter's view is closer to the one upheld by Seneca at (5.) 19. 8–9 (see **ad (5.) 19. 8 si in patris honorem**). For other examples of such debates ending in compromise in *De beneficiis*, see Li Causi 2009.

(5.) 18. 1 numquid et uxori et socero? (then also to his wife and father-in-law?). The list of persons who might be thought to benefit from a favour to a son, in the way his father can be thought to benefit, omits the mother and her family, probably because in Roman law the wife, if not *in manu* (and most wives were not at this date) does not belong to her husband's family. In listing the son's wife and father-in-law, Seneca may be thinking of the Lex Cincia forbidding gifts above a certain maximum, from which they, along with the father, brother, paternal uncle, and grandfather mentioned (who are within the degrees of cognate relationship and so exempted), were also exempt (*Frag. Vat.* 302 in *FIRA* ii. 531), cf. **ad 5. 19. 9.**

(5.) 19. 1 idem de servo dicam: mei mancipii res est, mihi servatur (I would say the same of the slave: the act concerns my property, he is preserved for me). The interlocutor here emphasizes the legal position of the slave as property (on *mancipium*, see **ad 3. 20. 2**), though even Roman law recognized that the slave was also a person (Jolocwicz and Nicholson 1972, 133). At 3. 20 Seneca has emphasized that only the body of the slave is bought and sold, not his mind, and at 3. 21 he stressed that the master can give a benefit to a slave (as a man) by educating him: but Seneca does not contest the point here, because he is only interested in the benefit to the son. See **ad 3. 18–28** for the reasons why sons and slaves were natural terms of comparison to Romans.

(5.) 19. 8 ut dialogorum altercatione seposita tamquam iuris consultus respondeam (but to lay aside debating in dialogue mode and give an opinion like a legal expert). At *Ep.* 94. 27 Seneca compares the value of precepts without proofs to the validity of the *responsa* of jurisconsults, 'even if a reason is not given'. Cf. Cic. *De or.* 2. 68 contrasting rulings on law as delivered 'with no train of argument or barren verbal controversy', and the story in 1. 239–40; 198 showing that *responsa* were normally brief and did not give reasons (cf. also Hor. *Sat.* 2. 1. 4–6; 80–2). On the authoritarian nature of both cautelary and judicial opinions, see Schulz 1946, 61–2.

mens spectanda est dantis (it is the intention of the giver that must be scrutinized). The emphasis on *mens*, or intention, goes with Seneca's definition of *beneficium* as the act of giving, not the thing given (1. 6). As Düll 1976, 370 points out, it is particularly appropriate here, as the emphasis on *mens* was growing in Roman law of the late Republic and high classical period. Thus at *Dig.* 35. 1. 40. 5 Proculus, a contemporary of Seneca, is said to have approved the opinion of Trebatius and Labeo that the *mens* of the testator is decisive (cf. Labeo saying that the natural law bids us observe the *mens testatoris*, *Dig.* 35. 1. 40. 3). See also the case cited **ad 3. 19. 1 'Quia non potest'**.

si in patris honorem fecit (if he has acted out of regard for the father). Seneca's final view allows for the father being benefited by his son's rescue, if that was the intention of the benefactor, whereas the interlocutor so far has not considered anything but the ultimate effect of the son's rescue.

(5.) 19. 9 nam illud finiri non potest (for that kind of obligation can have no limit). Here, to reinforce the absurdity of the argument, Seneca allows a much wider circle of potential beneficiaries than in (5.) 18. 1, including the mother's family, relations by marriage, slaves, and country.

sorites (literally: heap). A logical term for the type of argument that, proceeding by small and seemingly harmless steps, leads to unacceptable conclusions (cf. Cic. *Luc.* 49).

(5.) 20. 1–5. This is the third and last of the *quaestiones infinitae* belonging to the subdivision of definition (*quid sit*) and, like the second (see **ad (5.) 18–19**), it starts with a case precise enough to make it a *causa* rather than a *thesis*; but Seneca soon makes it clear that he is concerned with the question whether benefiting someone against his will counts as a *beneficium*. The answer is yes, under two necessary conditions: if the favour actually benefits the recipient (20. 2–3), and if the donor intended to benefit the recipient, in particular (mainly treated in 20. 4–5). The first Seneca already discussed in 2. 14. 4 (see **ad 2. 14–17. 7**); the second was prepared for at (5.) 19. 7. Seneca clearly omits cases involving actual coercion, which have been disqualified as benefits (2. 18. 7–8).

(5.) 20. 1 non est dubium, quin beneficium sit etiam invito prodesse, sicut non dedit beneficium qui invitus profuit (there is no doubt that it counts as a benefit to be of use to someone even against his will, just as he has not given a benefit who has been of use against his own will). The first condition being fulfilled (**ad (5.) 20. 1–5**), the mental attitude of the donor alone matters, as a *beneficium*, in Seneca's view, is an intentional action. The first half of the statement is not so self-evident, as is shown by Plautus, *Tri.* 638, *nullum beneficium esse duco id quod quoi facias non placet* ('I do not regard as a favour something that does not please the recipient'). Moreover, the Severan jurist Paul, in *Dig.* 50. 17. 69, seems to state that what he calls the *beneficium* of allocating one's freedman to someone else (while alive or by will) cannot be conferred on someone who is unwilling.

(5.) 20. 3 non est beneficium quamvis ille dicat esse et gaudeat (that is not a benefit, although he says it is and is delighted). Since the first condition (**ad 5. 20. 1–5**), that real benefit should be conferred, is not fulfilled, Seneca does not even consider if the donor intended to harm or benefit the rejoicing brother.

(5.) 20. 4 quid enim illi per hoc commodi accessit? (what advantage came to him through this?). The interlocutor uses the technical Latin term *commodum* for a positive indifferent, to emphasize that the son has not secured any practical benefit, in the ordinary sense. Seneca then shows that he has benefited in the Stoic sense, because his moral obligation has been accomplished for him.

(5.) 20. 5 in publicum humanus (humane in the public interest). For the Stoics, human beings have obligations to the human race as a whole, as part of the community of gods and men (see **ad 4. 29. 3**).

(5.) 20. 6–25. The last general *quaestio* is concerned with *actio* and returns to an issue treated briefly at 2. 10. 4–11. 3 under the heading 'how to give', where Seneca adduced, as one of the most important precepts, that one should never reproach a person with a benefit, nor ever remind him of it. Here the stark advice is refined: the donor can ask for repayment if under pressure of necessity, or if acting for the moral improvement of the beneficiary ((5.) 25. 1 *fin.*). At the end of the whole work Seneca explicitly describes the precept as hyperbole for pedagogic purposes (7. 22. 1–24. 2) and advocates gentle reminders for the second purpose mentioned here (7. 25. 1 *fin.*). See Abel 1987*a*, 27 = 1995, 68–9.

(5.) 20. 6 'quid tanto opere quaeris, cui dederis beneficium, tamquam repetiturus aliquando?' (why do you study so carefully to whom you have given a benefit, as if you were going to reclaim it some day?). This objection serves as a bridge between the two previous *quaestiones* which explored problems, about whom I have actually helped, and the coming *quaestio* about if and when I can seek a return.

'praeterea lex, quod non iussit repeti, vetuit' ('besides, the law, by not laying down that it should be recovered, has forbidden it'). The objection is repeated at (5.) 21. 1, in different form: 'but the law, by not sanctioning the exaction of payment, has forbidden it'. This strange doctrine, that legal omission is prohibition, is given by Arist. *NE* 5. 11.

1138ᵃ8, to show that suicide is forbidden by the law. Seneca implicitly rejects the argument, by saying that many things have no legal sanction, but are enforced by the more powerful conventions of human life (see also **ad 3. 21. 1**). Seneca has already argued at length against the advisability of legal enforcement of gratitude (3. 6–17).

(5.) 20. 7 recipiendi beneficii necessitas repetendi verecundiam vincet (the need to recover my benefit will conquer my reluctance). Kaster 2005, 175 n. 127 draws a parallel with Cic. *Fam.* 2. 6. 1 where *verecundia*, a concern with showing respect for the other person in a social transaction (Kaster 2005, 13–27, 61–5), is, as here, associated with seeking repayment of benefits.

(5.) 21. 2 non enim exigo, sed repeto, et ne repeto quidem, sed admoneo (For I am not exacting, but requesting, and not even requesting, but reminding). Cicero at *Fam.* 2. 6. 1 associates *exigere* with treating a benefit requested as a *merces* (repayment); Seneca here, as often, with treating the benefit given as a *creditum* (loan), see **ad 1. 1. 1 male collocata** and Ch. 3A pp. 39–40.

(5.) 24. Seneca rounds off the argument with two *exempla*: this one positive, the one about Tiberius negative. This episode dates to Caesar's dictatorship, when he exercised jurisdiction by *cognitio*. The veteran is recalling an incident of the civil war in Spain against Pompey's sons, which ended with Caesar's victory at Munda in March of 45: it is not preserved in the *Bellum Hispaniense* as we have it. The river Sucro is the present Júcar and, in Seneca's day, was in the province of Hispania Tarraconensis.

(5.) 24. 3 agellos, in quibus vicinalis via causa rixae ac litium fuerat, militi suo donavit (the small plot of land—a local pathway through it had caused the quarrel and the lawsuit—he gave to his soldier). Seneca does not explain why the neighbours, in a dispute over a local pathway, should not have their own claim properly considered, because of Caesar's wish to pay a debt of gratitude. For such local pathways and the obligations of landowners to maintain them, see Sic. Fl. *agrim.* 110 T=112 Campbell.

(5.) 25. 2. Tiberius is also negatively presented at 2. 7. 2–3 and 3. 26. In fact, there is at least one notable example of his gratitude for pre-accession favours, which is recorded by Tacitus, *Ann.* 4. 15: the case of Lucilius Longus, who was the one senator who accompanied him when he withdrew to Rhodes.

(5.) 25. 2 Ti. Caesar inter initia dicenti cuidam (Tiberius Caesar, when someone said to him early in his reign). The translation of Lipsius, adopted by Préchac 1961, is preferable to Basore's in the Loeb edition, 'when a certain man started to say', since the story demands that Tiberius should just have become Princeps and was only pretending to forget a pre-accession friendship.

ab hoc quidni non esset repetendum beneficium? Optanda erat oblivio (why should he not have sought the return of a benefit from him? He should have wished he would forget). Again, the interpretation of Lipsius and Préchac 1961 is preferable to that of Basore's 'He (Tiberius) had a reason for desiring forgetfulness.' Seneca is thinking of the treason charges under Tiberius (*Ben.* 3. 26) that made it better not to attract the Princeps' attention. Cf. Plin. *Pan.* 90. 6 about people previously (notably under Domitian) wishing that they might slip from the Princeps' memory.

(5.) 25. 4 Homericus ille sacerdos (the priest in Homer), namely Chryses in *Iliad* 1. 39–42, who appeals to Apollo.

moneri velle ac posse secunda virtus est (the second level of virtue is to be willing and able to take advice). As Préchac 1961ad loc. points out, this is an ancient commonplace, cf. Hes. *Op.* 293–5; Livy 22. 29. 8. D.L. 7. 26 gives Zeno's reversal of Hesiod's priorities, putting the man who follows good advice first, the man who finds out everything for himself second, because the former translates wisdom into conduct. Strictly speaking, the Stoics acknowledged no levels of virtue (D.L. 7. 127); but Seneca has in mind the distinction between the Sage and those making moral progress (e.g. *Epp.* 71. 34–6; 75. 8–16).

(5.) 25. 6 sed ut magistri patienter ferre offensationes puerorum discentium memoriae labentis (but tolerate it as teachers patiently tolerate in the boys they are teaching mistakes that are due to lapses of memory). Having said in 3. 1–2 that the person who forgets a benefit is the most ungrateful of all (**ad 3. 1. 1–5**), and having stressed how a person can help himself to remember (3. 2. 3; 3. 5. 1), Seneca now shows how admonition by the benefactor can help to correct that fault.

Synopsis of Book 6

1   INTRODUCTION:

Aebutius will guide Seneca on pursuing or dropping
questions of purely theoretical interest, some of which will be
useful as well.

2–5.2   IS IT POSSIBLE FOR A BENEFIT TO BE
TAKEN AWAY?

2–3   Answer: No. The action in which the true benefit consists
cannot be undone; only the thing given can be removed.

3   *Saying of Antonius is true: the only way to keep
possessions is to give them as benefits.*

4–5.2   The fact that we sometimes cease to be under obligation for a
benefit does not mean that the benefit has been removed.

4.1–2   *The benefit can be spoiled by the giver doing the
recipient an injury.*

4.2–5.2 *As with debts or rents, the benefit must be weighed
against the injury: we repay, not the actual thing, but
an equivalent of the benefit or injury.*

5.3–6   LIBERALIS' PRACTICAL QUESTION: SHOULD
ONE RESPOND SEPARATELY TO A BENEFIT AND
TO THE INJURY THAT FOLLOWS IT?

6   Answer: A benefit is not subject to law; I can behave as an
arbiter and balance benefit against injury.

7–11   ARE WE UNDER AN OBLIGATION TO SOMEONE
WHO BENEFITS US WITHOUT THAT INTENTION?

7–8.1   The case of the person who benefits us in ignorance:

*No: intention, indeed friendly intention, is required
for a benefit: the result is irrelevant.*

8. 2–4   **The case of the person who benefits us, without wanting
             to, or even while wanting to harm us:**

      9. 1–3   *No: intention is essential to showing gratitude, doing
             an injury, or conferring a benefit.*

      10–11. 2   *No: intention is a necessary condition for a service
             that merits gratitude: good fortune should follow and
             is never sufficient.*

      11. 1–2   *Example used by Cleanthes.*

11. 3–4   **Intention is the necessary, but not the sufficient, condition
             for a benefit, though even the intention should be rewarded
             with friendliness.**

12–24 ARE WE UNDER AN OBLIGATION TO SOMEONE WHO DOES US GOOD FOR HIS OWN SAKE?

12   **If he acts only for his own interest, he is doing business,
             not conferring a benefit.**

13–14. 2   **If he intended to benefit me as well, even to a lesser extent,
             I owe him gratitude to the degree that I was chosen, or
             given the chance to be chosen, as a beneficiary.**

14. 3–17   **Payment for a service normally removes any obligation,
             as the transaction is self-interested.**

      15. 1   *Objection: that would mean we owe to doctors and
             teachers only their fee, though we receive priceless
             gifts of health and education.*

      15. 2   *First reply: the fee covers their time and service, not
             the value of the gift.*

      15. 3–8   *Truer reply: for most things the market, not their
             value, sets the price.*

      16. 1–17   *Solution: to doctors and teachers who show the
             devotion of a friend, we owe gratitude for their
             personal attention, not an extra fee for their skill.*

18–24   **Personal gratitude is only owed by a recipient, when the
             benefit is individually given for his sake (in dialogue form).**

      18–19   *Communal benefits deserve at most only communal
             gratitude.*

            19. 1   Example of the ferryman who charges no
             one: not a benefit to any individual passenger,
             as not done for his sake.

Notes to Synopsis of Book 6

In the second of the books treating auxiliary topics, Seneca, still assuming the interest of his addressee in them, as in 5. 1. 2, asks him for continued guidance in handling them ((6.) 1. 2). Seneca treats five *quaestiones infinitae*, concerned mostly, as in Book 5, with gratitude and the return of benefits. Two are of the theoretical type relating to *cognitio*: the first (2–5. 2), which belongs to the subdivision *quid sit* or *definitio* (Cic. *Top.* 83) and explores the concept of *beneficium*; and the last (25–43), which belongs to the subdivision *qualitas*. In between come three practical questions relating to *actio* in the subdivision *officium*, the switch to the practical being attributed to Liberalis' impatience with the impracticality of the first question. Though Seneca reverts to a theoretical question at the end, it is well to remember that questions *quale sit*, such as this one, can be hard to distinguish from the *actio* questions (Ch. 7B, p.139), and this one certainly issues in specific advice on how not to show gratitude.

(6.) 1 Liberalis, virorum optime (Liberalis, best of men). This is the same term of address as was used in the opening of Book 2, but the current book is unique in having a further three invocations of the addressee, at (6.) 6. 1; (6.) 12. 1; (6.) 41. 1.

quaedam et, dum quaeruntur, oblectamento sunt et quaesita usui (some matters are both enjoyable while under scrutiny, and, once investigated, useful). Cf. *Ep.* 124. 21 for the idea that exercising the mind in disputing general theoretical questions does the mind good, and see pp. 133–4. Here Seneca's defence is tied to selecting questions that Liberalis finds useful.

ex vultu igitur tuo pendebo (therefore I shall respond to your facial expression). Lipsius expresses irritation at this conceit, repeated at (6.) 7. 1 and (6.) 12. 1. He regards it as poetic, but it seems rather to be an epistolary trick, related to the idea of the letter as a substitute for a face-to-face conversation (cf. Seneca *Epp.* 38.1; 40. 1). See Trapp 2003, 238; *POxy.* XLII, 3067. For the parallelism between Seneca's treatment of his addressee in this work and in the *Letters*, see Ch. 7C.

(6.) 2–5. 2. The first question, a theoretical one, is answered in the negative. To show that a benefit once given cannot be taken away, Seneca clarifies the concept of benefit in two respects. (1) A benefit is not the gift or service given but the very act of giving (2–3). Seneca had made this point in 1. 5–6, where he defined the *beneficium* as a benevolent action giving and receiving joy from the act, which is a voluntary one (see **ad 1. 5–1. 9. 1**). There too he pointed out the ephemeral nature of the object and service given (1. 5. 3), which are subject to fortune, but here he adds the idea of the benefit being incorporeal and the gifts being made permanent by giving. (2) A benefit does not cease to be a benefit when it ceases to impose an obligation (4–5. 2). At 1. 7. 1–3, Seneca had tied the concept of a *beneficium* as action to the fact that the degree of obligation created does not depend on the size of the gift, but on the manner of giving; here he is concerned with the lessening or removal of obligation through subsequent injury (4. 1–2) and with clarifying the nature of return (4. 2–5. 2). The point about balancing benefit *versus* injury has already been raised at 3. 12. 4 as an example of the difficulty of calculating ingratitude precisely enough for it to be punishable by law. Here he adduces legal cases that ostensibly show such balancing (4. 2, 4, see **ad (6.) 4. 4 sic debitori suo**), but later, in §6, he will argue that the way in which the law deals separately with other reciprocal cases involving the same parties, such as deposit and subsequent theft, is inapplicable to benefit.

(6.) 2. 1–2 ita aliud est beneficium ipsum, aliud quod ad unumquemque nostrum beneficio pervenit. Illud incorporale est, irritum non fit; materia vero eius huc et illuc iactatur et dominum mutat (so the benefit itself is one thing, what has come into the possession of each one of us through a benefit is another. The first is incorporeal, it does not become invalid; but the material of it is passed from hand to hand and changes owner). The Stoics thought that many things that are intuitively incorporeal, like virtue and knowledge, were corporeal, but they did allow for incorporeals, notably *lekta* ('sayables'), void, place, and time (L–S, p. 163): these 'subsist' rather than 'exist'. Among the 'sayables' are predicates, something that is true of a body or belongs to it as an attribute, when another body acts on it. So, in the list given above, the actions 'being given' and 'is sailing', like the action *beneficium*, are 'sayables' and incorporeal, but the gift and the sailor, like the thing conferred, are bodies (L–S, pp.199, 340; Seneca, *Ep.* 117. 2–3). It is not clear how the third parallel of the sick man and his disease are to be construed (possibly, 'being sick' is the attribute, and the sick man the body), but Seneca had difficulties with the Stoic doctrine of *lekta*: see Inwood 2007, 264 on *Ep.* 106; 294 on *Ep.* 117.

(6.) 2. 2 cum eripis, <alicui quod dedisti beneficii materiam, non ipsum beneficium ei eripis> (when you snatch away <from someone the material of the benefit that you gave him, you do not also snatch away from him the benefit>). Gertz 1876 divined a hiatus in the text, and I have adopted his supplement (as in Griffin and Inwood 2011).

(6.) 2. 3 mancipium (a slave), a particularly appropriate term, since the slave is thought of as a possession here, cf. 7. 4. 2. See **ad 5. 19. 1.**

(6.) 3. 1 M. Antonius apud Rabirium poetam cum fortunam suam transeuntem alio videat (M. Antonius, in the poem by Rabirius, when he sees his good fortune passing to another). Rabirius was an Augustan–Tiberian poet, to whom is sometimes attributed a poem on the Battle of Actium (see Hollis 2007, pp. 384–6). The fragment (Blänsdorf 2; Hollis 231), 'Whatever I have given, that alone I still have' must relate to Antonius' defeat in that battle against Octavian, the later Augustus. The sentiment is echoed by Martial at 5. 42. 7–8. Antony was noted for his generosity (Cic. *Phil.* 2. 42–3; 1. 33; Plut. *Ant.* 67. 6–7). Préchac 1961 and others suggest that it echoes a *bon mot* of

Sardanapallus, *haec habeo quae edi,* as translated by Cicero in *Tusc.* 5. 101: 'the things I have eaten, these I still possess'.

(6.) 3. 2 procurator es (you are a steward). A *procurator* looked after the financial affairs of another person: here of Fortune, who has sway over material goods. In Seneca's day the Emperor had an extensive network of procurators: some looked after his private property, but others collected the taxes and even governed provinces under his control. Further on in this chapter, Seneca uses another financial metaphor: our worldly possessions have been deposited with you (and must be returned).

propter quae ruptis totiens adfinitatis, amicitiae, collegii foederibus inter contendentes duo terrarum orbis elisus est (for which the bonds of marriage, of friendship, and of collegiality, have been ruptured so many times, and the world crushed between two contenders). Seneca refers back to Antony and his struggle with Octavian, alluding to his marriage to Octavia and his link with Octavian as a fellow triumvir from 43 to 33 BC, and as his colleague in the consulship in 34 BC.

(6.) 4. 1 ita non aufertur beneficium, sed vincitur (thus the benefit is not withdrawn but outdone). This problem is the principal concern of *Ep.* 81, a letter that handles a number of conundrums about benefits similar to those discussed in Books 5–7 of the treatise (see Ch. 8, pp.155–63).

(6.) 4. 2 non tam duri quidam et tam scelerati patres sunt, ut illos aversari et eiurare ius fasque sit? (are there not some fathers so harsh and wicked that it is just and right to recoil from them and to disown them?). Seneca cannot refer to any kind of legal repudiation, for the *patria potestas* could not be undone by the child unilaterally, though it became free if its father sold it three times (*emancipatio*). He means that the child would stop showing his father the expected respect. (In *Cons. Marc.* 19. 2, where *eiurent* is a generally accepted emendation, fathers pretend to repudiate their sons in order to attract the attentions of legacy-hunters.)

(6.) 4. 4 colonum suum non tenet quamvis tabellis manentibus (a landlord has no claim on his tenant, though the lease is still in force). The agricultural tenant, having agreed to the payment of rent, has defaulted, and the creditor has attacked the products of his labour on the land: his crops, his trees. Marcus Aurelius ruled that a creditor must recover a debt through the courts and would lose his claim to payment if he seized anything of the debtor's (*Dig.* 48. 7. 7). Seneca gives, as the rationale for such a view, that the creditor has damaged the debtor's ability to pay.

sic debitori suo creditor saepe damnatur, ubi plus ex alia causa abstulit, quam ex crediti petit (thus a creditor is often condemned to pay his debtor when he has taken more from him, on some other account, than he claims on account of the original loan). On the apparent contradiction between the legal cases adduced here, at (6.) 4. 2 *fin* and (6.) 4. 5, where injury appears to be weighed against a debt, and Seneca's insistence at (6.) 5. 5 and (6.) 6. 1 that separate actions would be necessary, see Mantello 1979, 413–17. He points out that the obvious solution—that these are *iudicia bonae fidei* which allow for such compensation—would not work, since the cross-demand must arise *ex eadem causa* ('from the same transaction') according to Gaius 4. 61, whereas

Seneca carefully says *ex alia causa* ('from another transaction'), see **ad (6.) 5. 4**. He suggests instead that Seneca telescopes two legal actions into one, to give the final result.

(6.) 4. 6 manet beneficium, quamvis non debeatur, sicuti quaedam pecuniae, de quibus ius creditori non dicitur, debentur, sed non exiguntur (the benefit remains in place, though it is not owed, just as certain sums of money, to which the creditor has no legal right, may be owed to him, but cannot be claimed). Seneca is thinking of cases where the debt is not actionable at law because, for example, the debtor is a minor; or the rate of interest is illegal; or the debtor is protected by an *exceptio* in the praetor's *formula* respecting the particular terms of the original loan (see **ad 4. 34. 4**).

(6.) 5. 2 reddere est enim rem pro re dare; quidni? cum omnis solutio non idem reddat, sed tantundem (for to repay is to give one thing in return for another. This is obvious, because all payment consists in repaying, not the same item, but its equivalent in value). The etymology is typical of the Stoics, cf. that offered for *referre* in *Ep.* 81. 10. Seneca here is, of course, not indebted to any Greek source. It is important for him to establish that repaying a benefit does not mean returning the very thing received (as in returning a deposit), because, otherwise, sustaining a later injury from a benefactor could not be construed as repayment of his benefit, something he is going to prove at (6.) 6.

delegatione et verbis perfecta solutio sit (the payment is effected by the assignment of the debt, and orally). Seneca gives two examples to show that repayment of a debt is repayment of something equivalent in value to what was originally received: repaying with gold coins a loan originally made in silver coins, and repayment without coins at all, but by my transferring directly to my creditor (A), a debt which is already owed by (B) to me (C). This delegation (Gaius 3. 130) involved making a new contract, which, as a novation (the replacement of the old contract by the new), had to be by *stipulatio*, an oral procedure (Nicholas 1962, 200).

(6.) 5. 3–6. Liberalis is here shown fulfilling the task assigned him at the start of Book 6, by saying when a discussion should end. In fact, he goes further than what he was asked to do there, being represented by Seneca as suggesting a different, more practical, question for discussion: should one respond separately to a benefit and a subsequent injury, or allow one to balance out the other? This question is in fact related to the preceding one, for Seneca had argued at (6.) 4. 1–2 that a benefit is not cancelled by a later injury from the same person, only the obligation to show gratitude is; and he had adduced some legal examples, at (6.) 4. 4–5, as parallels to the procedure of balancing benefits against injuries, Liberalis' second alternative here. In these cases of Seneca's, creditors commit injuries while trying to collect debts, and the giving and injuring are treated by the law as connected. Liberalis at (6.) 5. 4–5 now confronts Seneca with a legal example concerning deposit, that points to his first alternative: depositing money with someone, and then stealing something from the same person, give rise to separate suits under Roman law—one for return of deposit, brought by one party; the second for theft, brought by the other. Seneca replies in (6.) 6. that benefits are not subject to the law, so that he can, as an *arbiter*, choose to weigh benefits against injury.

(6.) 5. 3 iuris consultorum istae acutae ineptiae sunt (these are the clever absurdities of legal experts). Liberalis compares the distinction Seneca has drawn at 4. 1, between removing a benefit and removing the obligation to repay a benefit, to the distinction drawn by jurists between an inheritance and the objects comprised by it. The point of the distinction is (Gaius 2. 14, 54–5; *Dig.* 37. 1. 3. 1; 50. 16. 24, 119) that one can acquire ownership by continued possession for a certain time (*usucapio*) of objects which are deemed corporeal things, but not of rights, such as the right of succession, which includes such duties as performing certain religious rites or paying creditors of the estate. Cf. *Ep.* 88. 12 for jurisconsults ruling that public property is exempt from *iuriscapio*. At *Ep.* 82. 8 *ineptiae* is applied by Seneca himself to philosophers' syllogisms.

(6.) 5. 4. illud enim video in hoc foro fieri; quid in vestra schola iuris sit, vos sciatis (the former is what I see happens in our courts. You are the ones who should know what the law is in your school). Liberalis here refers to the Stoic school as 'yours' in the plural, just as Lucilius in *Ep.* 8. 1 will refer to *illa praecepta vestra* (those teachings of yours): Seneca's addressee is not represented as a committed Stoic. What is said here of the requirement for separate actions under Roman law came to be modified by the time of Gaius (2nd c. AD) in the case of *bonae fidei actiones*, which included deposit. It became possible for the judge to take account of counterclaims, but only if they arose out of the same transaction (Gaius 4. 61; 63). See Jolowicz and Nicholas 1972, 212. This is not the case here, as shown by *postea* (afterwards) in Liberalis' framing of his question in (6.) 5. 4.

(6.) 6. 1 beneficium nulli legi subiectum est, me arbitro utitur (a benefit is subject to no law; it makes me the arbiter). See **ad 3. 7. 5** on an *arbiter* as a special kind of *iudex*: note in (6.) 6. 2 *ad eundem iudicem*. In 3. 12. 4 Seneca spoke of the difficulty that comparisons between benefits and subsequent injuries would cause a real judge (cf. 3. 8. 1), should ingratitude become actionable at law: he would have even more latitude than an *arbiter* (3. 7. 5), given the vagueness of the terms involved. Here Seneca stresses that such cases are not subject to law and imagines the receiver of benefit and injury exercising his moral judgement in weighing one against the other with the freedom of an *arbiter* (see Inwood 2005, 212).

(6.) 6. 2 comparatione facta inter se beneficii et iniuriae videbo, an mihi etiam ultro debeatur (having compared the benefit and the injury, I shall ascertain whether anything further is owed to me). As at the end of (6.) 6. 1, Seneca envisages that the injury may outweigh the benefit. When he returns to investigate the whole question of benefit and subsequent injury in *Ep.* 81. 3–8, he is inclined to recommend that the *vir bonus* remember the benefit and forget the injury, following the judgment of a *remissior iudex* ('more indulgent judge'), rather than a *rigidus iudex* ('strict judge'). See pp. 155–63.

(6.) 6. 3 si quis scriptis nostris alios superne imprimit versus (if someone inscribes other lines of writing over what I have written). Seneca is thinking of wax tablets, inscribed with a stylus, and used for school lessons and for informal correspondence. With this metaphor, he confirms the position adopted on the first *quaestio*: subsequent injury may obscure a benefit, but it does not erase it.

(6.) 7–11. Still exploring the subject of gratitude, Seneca turns to another general practical question. Though the grammatical form of *an ei debeatur aliquid* does not make clear that this question is concerned with *actio* rather than *cognitio*, the *nobis* in *qui nobis invitus profuit* and the *aliquid facere me vis* at (6.) 10. 1 show that the problem considered is how one should respond to a benefit that is given without intent to help. Yet, as suggested on p. 140, in order to answer the question Seneca has to clarify the concept of *beneficium*. At 2. 18. 6–20, in the course of considering from whom we should accept a benefit, Seneca noted cases when the opportunity to choose a worthy benefactor does not arise, because what is received is not a benefit and does not place us under obligation, on account of the circumstances: compulsion exerted by the giver; his lack of intention to help; or his unjust acquisition of the power to help. Here Seneca returns to the question of lack of intention to help on the part of the giver, and carefully distinguishes at (6.) 7. 1–2 between the giver acting under compulsion (who was mentioned in passing at 2. 18. 8), and two main categories: the giver who helps without wanting to do so, treated in (6.) 8. 1–4 (including the sub-category of those who intend to injure ((6.) 8. 2); and the giver who helps without knowing he is doing so, treated in (6.) 7–8. 1 (cf. 2. 19. 2, where the parallel of the tyrant as giver, and the wild beast as giver, suggests that these two are similar). Though at 2. 19. 1 he insisted that a benefit requires friendly intention, here he explores with greater subtlety the role of chance *versus* the intention necessary to occasion gratitude.

(6.) 7. 1 vultus tuus, cui regendum me tradidi, colligit rugas et trahit frontem, quasi longius exeam (your face, by which I have agreed to be governed, is wrinkled and frowning, as though I were straying too far from the point). As promised at (6.) 1. 1, Seneca claims to be using Liberalis' facial expression to tell him when he has pursued this question too far. Contracting the brow into furrows is regularly associated with disapproval and discontent (Juv. 9. 2, 9; Ovid *Am.* 2. 2. 33, cf. Quint. 11. 3. 79 on contracted eyebrows).

huc dirige cursum, litus ama (direct your course this way: hug the shore). The lines from Virgil (*Aen.* 5. 162–3) concern the boat race which is part of Anchises' funeral games. The captain of the *Chimaera* is urging the coxswain to grab the inside course, as they approach the turning-point. So Liberalis is seen urging Seneca to speed up his discussion, since the practical question Liberalis proposed at (6.) 5. 4. has been sufficiently discussed.

qui nobis invitus profuit (who has benefited us without intending to). Seneca's broad use of *invitus*, to cover not only being unwilling but also being unaware, is analogous to the definitions used in Roman law of those on the receiving end. At *Dig.* 3. 3. 8. 1, Ulpian says: *invitus procurator non solet dari. Invitum accipere debemus non eum tantum qui contradicit verum eum quoque qui consensisse non probatur* ('it is not customary to appoint an unwilling procurator. We should take the word "unwilling" to include not only the man who refuses, but also the one for whose consent there is no evidence'); cf. also *Dig.* 8. 2. 5.

(6.) 7. 3 ideo nec mutis animalibus quicquam debetur—et quam multos e periculo velocitas equi rapuit—nec arboribus (therefore we are neither indebted to dumb animals—despite the fact that the speed of a horse has rescued many from danger—nor to trees). See **ad 2. 19. 1** on the lion who protected a beast-fighter from other animals, because he recognized him. Here the horse is represented as having as little motive as a tree giving shade, in order to make the point that neither of them has the capacity to know it is doing someone good, as opposed to a human being who may not happen to know on this occasion.

(6.) 7. 4 qui aeque quam ista propositum bene faciendi nullum habuit, sed profuit casu (who had as little intention of conferring a benefit as they, but who helped me by chance). Whereas in 2. 19. 1 Seneca wrote, 'the benefit is the work of fortune, the injury of a human being' (*casus enim beneficium est, hominis iniuria*), here, more accurately, he does not attribute a benefit to fortune as also later on, at (6.) 8. 1: 'it was fortune that turned their evil designs to good' (*perniciosa illorum consilia fortuna deflexit in melius*).

(6.) 8. 1 quomodo multos fortuita sanant nec ideo remedia sunt (just as many are cured by accidents that are not, for that reason, remedies). Cf. 2. 18. 8, where poison is said to be *pro remedio* but not salubrious. Seneca introduces, as a parallel to people who help without knowing they are helping, things that help on one occasion, though they are not usually helpful and may actually be dangerous to health; but he goes on to set these unsalutary things in parallel with people who help without wishing to do so, or even while wishing not to do so (he is thinking primarily of the latter, which fit the parallel better). What links all these examples is the crucial role of chance in producing beneficial results.

et in flumen alicui cecidisse frigore magno causa sanitatis fuit (and falling into a river in very cold weather has restored a person to health). The medical fashion for cold-water bathing, which started at Rome with the success of Antonius Musa (Plin. *HN* 29. 6; Suet. *Aug.* 59; Cass. Dio 53. 30), seems to have reached a peak in Seneca's day, when Charmis of Marseilles persuaded people to bathe in cold water even during the winter frosts. Plin. *HN* 29. 10 cites the writings of Seneca for the enthusiasm this evoked even in aged consulars, and *Epp.* 53. 3 and 83. 5 record Seneca's habit of swimming in a canal or aqueduct, and then, when older, in the Tiber, and, finally in a tank warmed by the sun. The reason for choosing as an example the cure effected by the accident of falling into a river in cold weather may be that the person is not prepared for, or practised in, such exercises, and hence could drown or suffer hypothermia. Nero had became ill after swimming in the Marcian aqueduct in 60, but we do not know the time of year, and the illness was attributed to sacrilege, as the spot was sacred (*Ann.* 14. 22).

quorundam flagellis quartana discussa est (some have had a quartan fever dispelled by flogging). Fevers in the ancient world were often named after their regular period of recurrence, the pattern found in malaria (Nutton 2004, 32): here the period is three days, as in *plasmodium malariae*. Seneca frequently mentions fevers but only specifies quartan fever here and in *NQ* 3. 16. 2. Plin. *HN* 7. 169–70 regards fever, considered in antiquity a disease not a symptom, as a prime cause of human suffering, since no cure was known and, though the link with mosquitoes was made, its nature was not understood. Fevers were thought to be caused by an imbalance of the four bodily humours; so here the flogging presumably dispels the black bile, mentioned by Galen (see Beagon 2005, 379–80). Plin. *HN* 7. 166 reports that Q. Fabius Maximus was cured of the quartan fever while engaged in battle in 121 BC: a cure that coincided with, and hence was attributed to, a wound he received (see Beagon 2005, 375), cf. 2. 18. 8.

(6.) **8. 3 quosdam ipsa, quae premebat, potentia eripuit et iudices, quem damnaturi erant causae, damnare gratiae noluerunt** (certain people have been rescued by the very power that was crushing them, and judges who were prepared to condemn some-one for a crime, have refused to condemn him on account of undue influence). Seneca chooses his examples of unwilling help from war and law, his favourite sources for imagery, the latter distinctively Roman (Armisen-Marchetti 1989, 94, 232–3). For law, he mentions first the effect on the jurors of a perjured witness (8. 2); then he passes to the effect on them of attempts to use power and influence against the defendant (two of the triad of forces that can destroy the regular operation of law, according to Cicero, *Pro Caec.* 73), and ends with the accuser causing offence by his arrogance. For the prevalence of power and influence in Roman litigation in the late Republic and early Empire, and the resentment it could cause, see Kelly 1966, 42–84.

(6.) **8. 4 adversarius meus, dum contraria dicit et iudicem superbia offendit et in unum testem temere rem demittit, causam meam erexit** (my opponent, by contra-dicting himself and offending the judge with his arrogance, and rashly reducing his case to one witness, has revived my case). The idea that it is unjust to rely on one wit-ness to convict someone is credited to Q. Mucius Scaevola in the Republic (Val Max. 4. 1. 11, cf. 8. 5. 6) and finally became a rule of law: *Dig.* 48. 18. 20; *CT* 11. 39. 3 = *CJ*. 4. 20. 9 (Emperor Constantine in AD 334): 'and now we decree absolutely that the response [i.e. testimony] of a single witness in isolation should in no circumstances be admitted in court hearings, even if he should dazzle with his rank as a member of the most distinguished senate' (*et nunc manifeste sancimus, ut unius omnino testis responsio non audiatur, etiamsi praeclarae curiae honore praefulgeat*).

(6.) **9. 2 quam multos militiae morbus eripuit!** (how many men has illness rescued from military service!). In Seneca's day there was still conscription into the army, as well as voluntary recruitment, especially in the provinces (e.g. Tac. *Ann.* 13. 7 (AD 54); 13. 35 (58); 14. 18. 1 (59)), but also in Italy (Brunt 1974). Ill-health could excuse one from military service (*Dig.* 49. 16. 4. 12) and was ground for discharge before the term of service was completed, and this *causaria missio* (*Dig.* 49. 16. 13. 2–3) enjoyed the privileges of *honesta missio* or honourable discharge (*Dig.* 27. 1. 8. 2–5): see Campbell 1984, 312–13.

ne in piratarum manus pervenirent, quidam naufragio consecuti sunt (some have succeeded in not falling into the hands of pirates by undergoing shipwreck). At. 1. 5. 4 and 7. 15. 1 Seneca also mentions capture by pirates. Though the Augustan peace and the establishment of the imperial fleets reduced the problem of piracy, there remained small pockets of it, and the problem could always recur: it is not necessary to assume that Seneca is just repeating a literary theme. See Cic. *Off.* 2. 40 and 3. 107, written in 44 BC and mentioning pirates; Pompey had cleared the seas in 67, but *Att.* 16. 1. 3 mentions some in the east in that same year.

(6.) 9. 3 non est beneficium, nisi quod a bona voluntate proficiscitur, nisi illud adcognoscit, qui dedit (it does not rank as a benefit, unless it proceeds from a good intention, unless the giver acknowledges it as such). As Alexander 1950–2*a*, 35–6 points out, Seneca goes on to show that the second limitation on what counts as a benefit corresponds to *dum nescit*, the second category given in (6.) 7. 1; we would therefore expect to find, corresponding to the first limitation, *dum non vult*, but instead Seneca gives us the sub-category *cum vellet nocere* (**ad (6.) 10. 1**).

profuit, cum vellet nocere: imitabor ipsum (someone did me good when he wished to harm me: I will imitate him). But cf. **ad 5. 6**. Seneca will move away from the traditional requiting of injury with injury, at the end of Book 7 (*re* ingratitude) and in *Ep.* 81, **ad (6.) 6. 2** (*re* injury after benefit).

(6.) 10. 1 nam quid de tertio loquar, qui ab iniuria in beneficium delapsus est? (and what should I say about the third case, the person who, from inflicting an injury, has stumbled into conferring a benefit?). To the two categories distinguished at (6.) 7. 1, not knowing and not wanting to help, Seneca now adds a third, wanting *not* to help, previously a sub-category of the latter (**ad (6.) 7–11**). Though his final example at (6.) 11 fits the second category better than the third, Seneca has shown himself in (6.) 8. 2–4 increasingly interested in the paradoxical cases of those who help when intending the reverse, until in (6.) 9. 2–3 that sub-category is used to represent the whole category of those not wanting to help (*dum non vult*), and the two categories distinguished at (6.) 7. 1 become *dum nescit* and *cum vellet nocere*.

(6.) 10. 2 ut beneficium tibi debeam, parum est voluisse te dare; ut non debeam, satis est noluisse (for me to owe you a benefit, it is not enough that you wanted to give one; for me not to owe you one, it is enough that you did not want to give one). A new point; though the right *voluntas* is the necessary condition for a benefit, 'moral luck' is necessary too, for, as Seneca will explain at (6.) 11. 3, a benefit must actually be conferred as well as intended. There he will set out the requirements of intention and performance symmetrically, but here Seneca is interested in an asymmetry: the intention should be completed by a gift or service, but (as he will say at (6.) 11. 2, 4), credit is deserved even for the intention, whereas a gift or service has to be preceded by the intention, if it is to acquire any credit at all.

(6.) 11. 1–2 Cleanthes exemplo eiusmodi utitur (Cleanthes uses an example like this). Neither slave has conferred a benefit: one had the intention but did not succeed in conferring the favour; the other found Plato but only by accident, not by intention. But the first boy receives praise, the explanation being given at (6.) 11. 4.

(6.) 11. 3 parum est illi velle nisi profuit (it is not enough for a person to want to do me good, if he has not done it). See **ad (6.) 10. 2**. There is an apparent symmetry here: intention without performance is as inadequate as performance without intention; but it soon appears (§4) that merely wanting to help is not as useless as merely wanting to lend money. For the bond of friendship that a benefit creates (2. 18. 3, 5; 3. 12. 1, see **ad 2. 18. 3**; Chs. 2A, 3A) obtains in this case (*amicus quidem ero*), even though gratitude is not appropriate.

(6.) 12–24. Having established the conditions for a gift or service to count as a benefit, Seneca now explores more precisely what intention will fulfil the necessary condition. He considers three basic scenarios where the giver acts *sua causa*: (1) where the giver acts wholly in his own interest (but helps another incidentally), or partly in his own interest (12–14. 2); (2) where the giver is paid for his services (14. 3–17); (3) where the giver does not have a particular beneficiary in mind but gives to him as part of a group (18–24). The climax of this last discussion is the case of the heavenly bodies, who not only confer communal benefits but do not appear to have the intention to help, which was established as the necessary condition for a benefit at 7–11. Further exploration shows that they do in fact fulfil the conditions for a benefit.

(6.) 12. 1 vultus tuus loquitur (your face says it all). Seneca insists again on Liberalis' initiating role in the discussion, see ad **(6.) 5. 3–6.**

prius istam quaestiunculam dividam (first I shall divide up the little question). The diminutive is used here for the first time, though it is common in the letters, e.g. 49. 8, 111. 2, 117. 1, 120. 1, 121. 1. It does not seem to be seriously ironic here, but the 'smallness' of the question is perhaps emphasized, because Seneca's immediately splitting it into two shows that it is larger than it at first appears.

(6.) 12. 2 qui pecori suo hibernum et aestivum pabulum prospicit (the person who provides winter and summer fodder for his livestock). This herdsman, for his own benefit, provides feed even in the summer, when herds could normally feed themselves, for he hopes to get top prices for stall-fed beef. See Alexander 1950–2*a*, 34.

et <ut> opimos boves saginat ac defricat (and fattens (his captives) up like plump oxen and rubs them down). Rossbach's supplement is accepted as necessary by Hosius (hesitantly), Préchac 1961, and Alexander 1950–2, 34. The comparison looks back to the previous example.

lanista qui familiam summa cura exercet atque ornat (the gladiatorial trainer who takes enormous care in exercising and equipping his troupe). The word *familia* is appropriate, as the gladiators were mostly slaves.

multum, ut ait Cleanthes, a beneficio distat negotiatio (there is, as Cleanthes said, a great difference between beneficence and business). In the discussion of self-interested gifts at 2. 31. 2, Seneca used the same comparison (= *SVF* i. 576). At 4. 13. 3, he uses *auctio* (sale).

(6.) 14. 3–17. Seneca had dealt in passing, at 4. 13. 3, with services that do not count as benefits and do not deserve gratitude, because they are paid for, giving as two of his examples the trader in relation to the city, and the physician in relation to the sick. Here Seneca deals with the trader in grain in relation to an individual purchaser (14. 3). He then adds the example of the teacher to that of the doctor, and explores the relation between their fee and what we owe in addition, when they show us friendly good will (cf. Cic. *Planc.* 81 on this *grata recordatio*).

Throughout the passage (at 14. 2; 15. 6–8; 17. 1), Seneca is concerned to distinguish these professionals from workers who sell their services at market rates, such as retailers, artisans, and hired labourers: whereas further monetary reward is appropriate for exceptional service by the latter, something different in kind is expected for the former (17. 2). Similarly Cicero at *Off.* 1. 150–1 regards as sordid and illiberal those who sell their *operae* (physical labours), not their *artes* (skills), and regards medicine and the teaching of honourable things as respectable for all but the upper orders. Seneca's teacher instructs in the *studia liberalia*, the liberal arts: grammar, rhetoric, dialectic, arithmetic, geometry, and astronomy, most of which are discussed in *Ep.* 88. 1–20 (and dismissed as not inculcating virtue, like philosophy). Varro included medicine and architecture in his *Disciplinae*, but the tradition continued to exclude them from the liberal arts.

(6.) 15. 2 non rei pretium sed operae solvitur (it is not the price of the thing acquired that is paid, but the price of their work). In (6.) 16. 1 Seneca says that it is their *ars* they sell, but at 17. 2 it is their *opera* again (as opposed to mental attitude). Cf. Cicero, who at *Off.* 1. 150 belittles those who are paid for *operae*, rather than *artes*.

(6.) 16. 6 huic ego non tamquam medico sed tamquam amico obligatus sum (this man I am indebted to, not as a doctor, but as a friend). There are many references to doctors being friends as well (e.g. Cic. *De or.* 1. 62; Tac. *Ann.* 15. 64. 3; *ILS* 7788: *medico amico bene merenti*).

(6.) 17. 1 sordidissimorum quoque artificiorum institoribus supra constitutum aliquid adiecimus (to our shop managers selling even the meanest merchandise we pay more than was agreed). *Sordidum* is the regular word used for non-liberal occupations, i.e. not suitable for a free man, as in Cicero's *Off.* 1. 150–1, who points out the intellectual contents of the professions, like Seneca at 17. 2.

(6.) 18–24. The third category of gifts or services given by the provider for his own sake (**ad (6.) 12–24**) features three examples that involve difficult and varied conceptions of *sua causa*, the emphasis being on the negative idea that the giving is *not* for the recipient's sake. All three, the ferryman (19. 1), the Princeps (19. 2–5), and the sun and moon (20–4), confer communal favours, enjoyed by, but not directed at, a particular individual. Exploration of the third example will show that it is in fact very different from the others (**ad (6.) 20–4**), and that those favours in fact count as personal *beneficia*.

(6.) 19. 1 qui me gratuita nave per flumen Padum tulit (who has ferried me in a boat across the River Po for nothing). The Po (*Padus*) is the longest river in Italy, wide and with a strong current. 'There could be no bigger ferrying in Italy than that across the Po', remarks Alexander 1950–2*a*, 35. But however appropriate the example, the transition from the story of Plato is rather abrupt.

(6.) 19. 2 si princeps civitatem dederit omnibus Gallis, si immunitatem Hispanis (if the Princeps confers citizenship on all the Gauls, immunity from taxation on all the Spaniards). The Princeps often gave citizenship, and/or immunity from tribute, to communities or individuals, when they demonstrated particular loyalty or gave particular services to Rome. The extravagant offer here does not fit any particular Princeps to date: Nero's gift of freedom to the Greeks (actually the province of Achaea) came after Seneca's death. But it is hard not to think of Claudius, who is described in Seneca's *Apocolocyntosis* 3. 3 as having decided 'to see all the Greeks, Gauls, Spaniards and Britons wearing the toga'. There is, however, no evidence for citizenship being given to any ethnic group as such by Claudius, nor is immunity from taxation attested for any community in Spain (Eden 1984, Appendix, 152–5), though he was accused of indiscriminate grants of citizenship to individuals and groups (Dio 60. 17. 4–7). This is probably unfair, yet the charge of making grants to those who bribed his minions cannot be written off, in the light of Acts 22: 28. Seneca may well have had in mind, when writing the *Apocolocyntosis*, Claudius' speech justifying his admission to the senate of some Gallic notables (*ILS* 212), for Claudius there mentioned the extension of Roman citizenship over time (col. v. 41); he may also have the speech in mind here (see Griffin 1982, 404–4. 18, especially 416–17).

quidni debebunt? Debebunt autem non tamquam proprium beneficium, sed tamquam publici partem (Of course, they will owe something, but they will owe it, not for a personal benefit, but for a share in a public one). Even in official documents, grants of citizenship and other privileges, communal as well as individual, are described as being granted *beneficio principis* (e.g. *ILS* 206 = 1967 no. 368; *ILS* 1981 = MW no. 481; Plin. *Pan.* 37. 3). However, in Pliny's *Panegyricus*, Trajan's extension of exemption from the inheritance tax to new citizens, whose ties of kinship were disrupted by their new status, is, on the one hand, described in terms of taking the 'opportunity for benefiting' (*bene faciendi materia*) (38. 1) left to him by Nerva, and, on the other, as selflessly denying himself 'so many occasions for giving *beneficia*, so much material for obliging and putting people in his debt' (*tot beneficiorum occasiones, tam numerosam obligandi imputandique materiam*, 39. 3), because now individuals no longer had to petition for such exemption individually. Saller 1982, 69 n.169 notes the similarity to Seneca's distinction here.

(6.) 19. 5 si quis patriae meae pecuniam credat, non dicam me illius debitorem (if someone lends money to my country, I shall not say that I am in his debt). Seneca compares the communal gift to a communal loan, which a citizen might be expected to help pay off. The *patria* of Aebutius Liberalis, Lugdunum, gave money to Rome after the fire of July 64, which was repaid in 65 after it, too. suffered a devastating fire (Tac. *Ann.* 16. 13. 3; cf. Sen. *Ep.* 91); but it does not seem to have been a loan.

nec hoc aes alienum profitebor aut candidatus aut reus (nor shall I declare the debt, as a candidate for office or a defendant). This is the only evidence that a candidate for office at Rome, or a defendant in a lawsuit, was required to declare his personal debts, though the list of disqualifications for standing for municipal office in the *Tabula Heracleensis* (*Roman Statutes* no. 24), ll.108–36 includes forms of insolvency. Under the Principate, there was a property qualification, probably of 1,000,000 HS, for membership of the Roman senate, which election to a magistracy secured. This passage strengthens the idea of Mommsen 1887, i. 498 n. 2 that the law actually required the census qualification, not of senators, but of candidates for senatorial office. Lipsius suggested that a defendant might have to make such a declaration in cases involving financial penalties, such as extortion and peculation, for when the *litis aestimatio* (assessment of damages) was made, it would be important to know who the other claimants to the convicted man's assets were, and how encumbered his property was.

sic istius muneris, quod universis datur, debitorem me nego, quia mihi quidem dedit, sed non propter me, et mihi quidem, sed nesciens, an mihi daret (thus I deny that I am in debt for that service that is given to everyone, because he gave it to me but not for my sake, and because he gave it to me but was unaware that he was giving it to me). The sense in which the benefactor is unaware is different from that in (6.) 7–8. 1, where no benefit at all was intended. Here there is intention to help, but not to help a particular individual. Though *universis* looks forward to the benefits of the sun and moon, treated in the next chapters, *nesciens* marks off the limited vision of the human donor from the awareness of the heavenly bodies ((6.) 23. 4).

(6.) 20–4. As Abel 1987a, 21–2 =1995, 62 points out, this passage, the last and most profound of the five sections devoted in Books 2, 4, and 6 to the theme of divine providence, marks the climax of Seneca's treatment of the theme in this work (see Ch. 6, p.119). It is comparable to 4. 3–9. 1, and, as there, the discussion is carried on in terms of the heavenly bodies, notably the sun and the moon, the gods, and nature (the singular *deus* of 4. 9. 1, however, is missing here). The sun and moon are divine and are seen both as carrying out beneficial work assigned by the gods ((6.) 22, cf. 4. 26. 1) and as beneficent gods in their own right ((6.) 20. 2–21. 1, cf. 4. 23. 1). All this is orthodox Stoic doctrine (e.g. Cic. *Nat. d.* 1. 39). The notion that the sun, moon, and other stars are divine was not new with the Stoics, but the special place of fire among the four elements, as a permanent feature of the universe, coextensive with the designing activities of god or reason (L–S, p. 286), gave it a special significance. The sun and moon are composed of designing fire (L–S 46. D) and the sun activates the periodic conflagrations in which the world order ends (L–S 46. I and p. 278).

Seneca here explores the intention behind the divine benefits. Unlike human donors, the sun and the moon, if they act for their own sake, do not do so by making use of us, because there is nothing we can provide for them (20. 2); and, while we benefit incidentally from their greater purpose of governing the world, they are not unaware that we individually receive benefits, and they intend that we should (23. 4). Finally we learn that, in this case, ignorance and unwillingness are to be found in the beneficiaries, not as in (6.) 7–11 in the donors, whose gifts are in fact enhanced by the beneficiaries' failings ((6.) 22 *fin.* (6.) 24. 2). Like those of severe parents, these divine services are true *beneficia* deserving our gratitude.

(6.) 20. 1 sed cum in hoc moveantur, ut universa conservent, et pro me moventur; universorum enim pars sum (but when they are in motion, with the aim of conserving the universe, they are in motion also for me: for I am part of the universe). The argument follows the form of that about the Princeps and the Gauls in (6.) 19. 4, but Seneca is about to distinguish divine from human donors, and we ultimately learn ((6.) 23. 4) that the omission of anything parallel to 'he included me, if not in my own name, than in that of my nation' is significant (**ad (6.) 23. 4**).

(6.) 21. 1 'sciam', inquit, 'solem ac lunam nobis velle prodesse, si nolle potuerint; illis autem non licet non moveri' ('I might accept', he says, 'that the sun and the moon wish to do us a service, if they were able not to wish it; but they are not permitted not to be in motion'). The two objections—that they do not wish to help, and that they do not choose to perform the movement that conserves the universe—are answered in 21. 2–4 and 22–23. 2 respectively.

(6.) 21. 2 non ideo minus vult qui non potest nolle; immo maximum argumentum est firmae voluntatis ne mutari quidem posse (a person is not less willing because he cannot be unwilling; in fact, it is the greatest proof of a fixed intention, that it cannot be changed). The Stoic habit of comparing the gods to a *vir bonus* (good man) stems from their similar rational nature: they differ only in length of life (*Prov*. 1. 5). Seneca explains the fixed intention of the heavenly bodies in terms of the good man, whose character dictates his intention. This does not remove his moral responsibility: in fact, as he says at 21. 4, it explains it, since we are more to be praised or blamed for acts in character than for capricious ones. This kind of necessity is internal, not external, compulsion (see L–S, pp. 392–4).

(6.) 22 in tot saecula promissas vices (the sequence promised for so many centuries). The present world order is for the Stoics not immortal: it will end in a total conflagration, activated by the sun, but will then be reconstituted exactly as it was (L–S, pp. 278–9). However, the sudden conflagration Seneca goes on to describe is the result of the heavenly bodies deserting the tasks assigned to them, and is not the recurrent Stoic *ekpyrosis*: it is not part of the providential and rational order, and there is presumably no reconstitution.

opportunis libramentis mundum ex aequo temperantia (balancing the world and keeping it in equilibrium). The sun by day, the moon by night, balance heat and cool. Cf. 4. 23. 1 for other complementary benefits of the sun and moon.

prosunt tibi etiam invito euntque ista tua causa, etiam si maior illis alia ac prior causa est (they do you a service even against your will, and they move for your sake, even if they have another greater and more essential reason). The more essential reason is divine providence, which ordains the beneficial movements of heavenly bodies. But they act 'for your sake', because the creation and existence of man is part of the providential order.

(6.) 23. 1 non externa cogunt deos, sed sua illis in lege aeterna voluntas est (external factors do not force the gods, but their own eternal intention takes the place of law for them). Cf. *Prov*. 5. 8, where Seneca explains that the creator and ruler of the universe passed the decrees of fate and obeys them forever. The gods, then, are bound by the same necessity as man.

(6.) 23. 3 in prima autem illa constitutione, cum universa disponerent (in that original disposition, when they arranged everything). Cf. 23. 1 *primi consilii* ('their original decision'). It is not clear if Seneca means the arrangements when the first of the successive worlds was created, or what Zeus ordains for eternity, since god, as the rational commanding faculty of the universe, continues to exist during the conflagrations

(L–S, p. 279) and retires into his own thoughts (Seneca, *Ep.* 9. 16). See the questions raised in *NQ* 1 pref. 3.

(6.) **23. 4. ex destinato iuvant, ideoque obligati sumus, quia non in beneficium ignor-antium incidimus, sed haec, quae accipimus, accepturos scierunt** (they help us on purpose, and, for that reason, we are under obligation, because we do not stumble upon a benefit from those who know nothing about it; rather, they knew we would receive what we are receiving). Unlike our obligation to the Princeps as one Gaul among many (19. 2–4), we are indebted to the gods for a personal *beneficium*, because they knowingly create and sustain each one of us. That Seneca is thinking of their concern for us as individuals is shown by the comparison with parents, even though parents may not beget us intentionally (cf. 3. 31. 1).

(6.) **23. 6 non intra homines humani imperii condicio sit** (the terms of human domin-ion are not limited to the human race). Cf. 2. 29. 3–4 on man's dominion over animals; 2. 29. 5 on the speed and scope of the human mind; and 3. 20. 1 on its communion with the divine.

et mente in alta data divina comitentur (they (our minds) join the company of divine beings by sending their thoughts aloft). Like Axelson, Alexander, and Préchac, I fol-low the manuscripts in reading *data*, rather than *elata* with Haupt and Hosius here (see Alexander 1950–2*a*, 35).

(6.) **23. 7 quantus iste furor est controversia dis muneris sui** (what madness is this to dispute with gods over their gift). The dispute concerns whether or not we owe personal gratitude to the gods for their services to us. Cf. the defence of the gods against another accusation in 4. 31–2.

quomodo adversus eos hic erit gratus, quibus gratia referri sine impendio non potest? (how can this person be grateful to those to whom gratitude cannot be returned without cost?). An *a fortiori* argument, since, unlike humans, the gods are repaid without cost, there being nothing we can provide for them (cf. the longer discussion at 2. 30. 2). We repay them with our gratitude alone.

(6.) **24. 1 non vides quemadmodum teneram liberorum infantiam parentes ad salubrium rerum patientiam cogant?** (do you not see how parents constrain their children, during the tender years of infancy, into acceptance of wholesome things?). Cf. *Prov.* 1. 6 for the comparison of the gods to strict parents (in 2. 5–6, to fathers in particular).

ad ultimum audacem iuventam (finally, their reckless youth). Lipsius explains the apparent reversal of order, with *iuventa* coming before *adolescentia* and indeed marked as the last stage (*ultimum*), by noting that Seneca has moved from liberal education to moral training, and then backtracks at §2 to physical ailments and remedies.

(6.) **24. 2 adulescentibus quoque ac iam potentibus sui** (as they grow up and are now their own masters). Seneca is thinking of the assumption of the *toga virilis* when they are free of *paedagogi*. The youngsters are still under the *patria potestas* which can be used to coerce them.

dum aut nescimus aut nolumus (while we are either unaware or unwilling). Cf. 5. 5. 2 for the ingratitude of the young for parental severity, whose benefits they do not understand. Seneca here picks up the theme of our denial and rejection of the benefits of providence, through misunderstanding of the intention behind them ((6.) 22 *fin.*; (6.) 23. 8), thus preparing a transition to the next question, where we are to learn that apparent excess of gratitude is actually reluctance to be indebted and failure to understand how to repay benefits.

(6.) 25–43. The last question of the book (a theoretical one of the *qualitas* type) receives the lengthiest treatment, the length being principally attributable to the number of historical examples. The actual answer to the question does not occupy much of the discussion (25–6): to pray for misfortunes to befall the person to whom you owe gratitude is obviously ungrateful behaviour and wrong. But Seneca goes on to treat extensively the mistaken motivation of such a beneficiary. (1) The beneficiary's anxiety to show gratitude quickly, by manufacturing an opportunity to repay, is actually a desire to have power over his powerful benefactor and be quit of his obligation quickly (27–8). (2) The beneficiary thinks he needs to manufacture an opportunity, when, in fact there are ways to repay his benefactor while he remains powerful and prosperous (29–30, 35. 1). The second point is illustrated by the examples of Xerxes and Augustus; the first, in the conclusion to the book, becomes focused on Liberalis (35. 2–5; 40–42. 1), who is anxious about repaying on time, just as in Book 5. 2. 1 he was anxious about being outdone in benefits (see Ch. 7C, p. 145). (3) A third type of perverse motivation is now adduced: Liberalis is too concerned with preserving his reputation for gratitude (42. 2; 43. 3).

(6.) 25. 1 aliquid adversi, in quo adfectum memorem accepti beneficii approbent (something unfortunate which enables them to demonstrate an attitude mindful of having received a benefit). Remembering a benefit is the key to being grateful: as Seneca says at 3. 1. 4, the most ungrateful person is the one who has forgotten a benefit.

(6.) 26. 2 si hoc ei optares, cuius nullum beneficium haberes, inhumanum erat votum (if you wished this on someone from whom you had no benefit, it would be an inhuman wish). At 1. 11. 3 Seneca warned against delaying to help someone in dire straits, in order to enhance the person's fear and thereby the gratitude we receive from him.

(6.) 27. 1 non succurrere vis illi, sed solvere: qui sic properat, solvi vult, non solvere (you do not wish to help him, but to pay him: whoever is in such a hurry wants to be paid up, not to pay). There is a crescendo here: wanting to pay off a debt is not as good as wanting to help someone; wanting to be cleared of debt altogether is still worse. The unwillingness to remain under obligation is then shown to be a desire for power, a desire to humiliate the benefactor: cf. the pride involved in preferring to help someone in necessity, rather than on a suitable occasion (2. 13. 2).

(6.) 27. 3 iactura rerum suarum et status mutatione in id devocari, ut infra beneficia sua iaceat (by his loss of property and change of status, to be so reduced that he grovels to those he benefited). Seneca is keenly aware of the power relationships that can be involved in the exchange of benefits (see pp. 47, 53).

(6.) 27. 4 nec ideo non hostilia vota, in quibus, quod mitissimum est, post crudeli-tatem venit (these prayers still do not cease to be hostile when what is most merciful comes after cruelty). It is likely that Seneca is here condemning Caesarian clemency (**ad 2. 20. 3 ius dandi beneficii**): see Griffin 2003*a*, 167–8.

(6.) 27. 7 quidquid non efficis, dei munus est, iniuria vero quidquid optas (whatever you fail to achieve is a gift of god, but whatever you pray for is in truth an injury). The first part of the prayer (27. 1, 3) requires the gods to send misfortune on one's benefactor: if the gods do not answer that prayer, it is they who spare the benefactor, but the prayer itself is an injury, because it is the intention that counts (27.7). Seneca spells it out at. 28. 3: if what you pray for were in your power, you would yourself have brought it about.

(6.) 29. 1 naturam per se pronam ad misericordiam, humanitatem, clementiam (that his nature, so prone in itself to pity, kindness, and mercy). Seneca in *De clementia* 1. 1. 4, following ordinary usage, as here, regards *misericordia* as a virtue like the other two, but in the philosophically technical Book 2, he carefully distinguishes it from *clementia* as a passion, a distress of the mind, and explains why the Stoa disapproves of it, but countenances the other two qualities, which are virtues according with its rational concern for the common good of humankind (*Clem.* 2. 4. 4– 6. 4). For the link of these virtues with generosity, see **ad 3. 27. 4.**

(6.) 29. 2 quanto haec iustiora vota sunt, quae te in nullam occasionem differunt, sed gratum statim faciunt (how much more appropriate are these prayers which do not defer you to another occasion but show immediately that you are grateful). At 28. 3 Seneca urged the beneficiary to pray to be able to repay the benefit when the need arises: in 29 he has moved on, urging him to pray that no need arise, and to be grateful in attitude alone. He dilated on this at 5. 4–5, when discussing how not to be outdone in benefits by the powerful and prosperous. There too he went on to show that there were benefits that could be conferred on such people (**ad 5. 6.**): service and support (5. 4. 3); teaching true values (5. 6. 2–6).

neminem tam alte secunda posuerunt, ut non illi eo magis amicus desit, quia nihil absit (good fortune has raised no one so high that he does not feel the need of a friend, all the more because he lacks for nothing). Seneca goes on to explain, at (6.) 32. 3–34, what a true friend is, and he counts, among the benefits that can be given to the great and powerful, an understanding of this. As Roller 2001, 115 observes, 'What began as a generalized representation of a man favored by fortune (or more favored, at any rate, than Seneca's implied reader) slides over into a representation of a ruler or *princeps* in particular', soon to be exemplified by Xerxes and Augustus. Cf. 5. 4. 3, where the recipients of such benefits are called *reges et principes*. The vetoing of the idea of pray-ing for an opportunity provided by 'prison, chains, slavery, war, poverty' (30. 1), not realistic in the case of such benefactors, facilitates this shift.

(6.) 30. 1 si quis tecum contraxit, per ista dimittitur (if anyone has made a contract with you, it is through such means that he is released). Seneca uses the legal metaphor of a contract for debt (cf. *Ep.* 21. 11): the creditor is now being paid off, in the form of the relief of sufferings wished on him by his debtor.

(6.) 30. 2 ut dixi (as I said before). At (6.) 29. 2.

quid? tu nescis debitum etiam locupletibus solvi? (come now, you surely must know that there is such a thing as paying a debt to the rich?). This is the interpretation of Alexander 1950–2*a*, 35. Seneca draws a parallel between giving something in return to the benefactor who has everything, with repaying money to a rich creditor.

(6.) 30. 3 nec te invitum destringam (I shall not belabour you against your will). Seneca keeps up the fiction of Liberalis' guidance as to how long a problem should be discussed (**ad (6.) 5. 3–6**). He confessed at (6.) 30. 2 that he was repeating himself, and now he limits himself to giving one example of the kind of favour one can give to those at the height of prosperity and power.

(6.) 30. 4 extincta libertas et fides in obsequium servile submissa (the suppression of free speech and the transmutation of loyalty into servile sycophancy). *Libertas* in the sense of freedom of speech, and the connection with true friendship, is further developed at (6.) 34. 3. For *obsequium servile*, cf. Tacitus' *deforme obsequium* at *Ann.* 4. 20 and, for the danger of a diet of such flattery from so-called friends, see Tac. *Hist.* 3. 56 *fin.* Marcus Aurelius (albeit before his accession) thanks his tutor Fronto for his candour (3. 13, cf. 3. 17 van den Hout =1. 14, cf. 1. 106 Haines).

(6.) 30. 6 dum . . . perpetua credunt quae in summum perducta maxime nutant, ingentia super se ac suos regna fregerunt (while . . . they believe that what has reached its highest peak and is tottering to a fall will last for ever, they bring huge kingdoms crashing down on them and theirs). As Alexander 1950–2*a*, 35–6 points out, there is a causal relationship between 'has reached its highest peak' and 'tottering to a fall', since it was a cliché that being at the pinnacle of success leads to a fall (e.g. in Sen. *NQ* 3 pref. 9; *Brev. vit.* 4. 1; cf. in the mouth of 'Seneca', *Octavia*, 379–80). Alexander, however, proposes reading <*cum*> *maxime nutant* ('at this very moment tottering to ruin') as more dramatic. The causal connection of the MSS seems preferable, since failing to see that connection demonstrates the folly of the people concerned.

in illa scena vanis et cito diffluentibus bonis (on that stage, resplendent with empty and quickly passing goods). See **ad 5. 13. 1** for the non-technical sense of 'goods' here. These misapprehensions about the durability of good fortune are countered by the advice Seneca recommends at (6.) 33. 2. The metaphor of the theatre props emphasizes the unreality and transiency of fortune's gifts.

(6.) 31. The historical example of Xerxes' invasion of Greece illustrates what is said in (6.) 30. 5–6, about unprovoked wars being started by rulers mired in misapprehensions about the limits of their own power, about what is honourable and shameful, and about the value of honest advice—here disregarded, but ultimately appreciated and rewarded. The forces of Xerxes, king of Persia from 486–465 BC, were defeated by sea at the Battle of Salamis in 480 BC and by land at Plataea in 479 BC. The story of Demaratus' advice ultimately derives from Herodotus 7. 101–5, 234 (**ad (6.) 31. 4**). Seneca elsewhere shows his familiarity (direct or indirect) with Herodotus' account of the invasion, in recounting three of his stories about Xerxes: his cruelty to the son of Pythius the Lydian (*Ira* 3. 16. 4, cf. Hdt. 7. 38–9); his throwing fetters into the sea to punish it when a storm destroyed the bridge built for the army to cross (*Const. sap.* 4. 2, cf. Hdt. 7. 35), and his sadness at the thought that none of his many soldiers would be alive in 100 years' time (*Brev. vit.* 17. 1–2, cf. Hdt. 7. 45–6). He also alludes to the obscuring of the sun by the multitude of Persian arrows at *Const. sap.* 4. 2, cf. Hdt. 7. 226—perhaps also at *Ben.* 31. 3 *fin.* Seneca uses Xerxes similarly, as an example of *folie de grandeur*, in *NQ* 5. 18. 10 (where he is called *rex stolidissimus*, cf. *rex stolidus* in *Const. sap.* 4. 2) and *Brev. vit.* 17. 2 (*rex insolentissimus*), as he was used in the declamatory tradition (Elder Sen. *Suas.* 2. 17–18; Val. Max. 3. 2. ext. 3; 9. 5. ext. 2).

(6.) 31. 2 illa mole non vinci solum Graecia, sed obrui posset (with his mighty forces Greece could be, not merely conquered, but crushed). Whether or not the Spartans should stay and face certain defeat at Thermopylae against such odds was a natural subject for declamation. The Elder Seneca preserves such a debate in *Suasoria 2*, and the declaimer Claudius Marcellus is credited with advocating retreat in similar language: *non vincent nos sed obruent* ('they will not defeat us, they will crush us', §9).

(6.) 31. 4 Demaratus Lacedaemonius solus dixit ipsam illam, qua sibi placeret, multitudinem indigestam et gravem metuendam esse ducenti (Demaratus the Spartan alone told him that the very horde of which he was so proud, being disorganized and ponderous, should arouse fear in its leader). Demaratus, the Eurypontid Spartan king, reigned from *c*.515 to 491 BC but was deposed through the machinations of the Agiad King Cleomenes on a charge of illegitimacy and fled to the Persian King Darius (Hdt. 6. 61–70). He accompanied Xerxes on his expedition against Greece and did offer advice, according to Herodotus (**ad (6.) 31**), when asked, after the invading forces had reached Thrace, whether or not the Greeks would resist conquest. The advice Xerxes received before the invasion from his Persian advisers was not uniformly in favour of the invasion, and the king himself wavered (Hdt. 7. 8–18). So Demaratus was not alone in his view: the king's uncle Artabanus was both initially and later on negative about the venture (Hdt. 7. 10, 47, 49).

(6.) 31. 5 tot ista gentium milia trecenti morabuntur (three hundred will hold in check those thousands upon thousands of nations). 300 was the canonical number of the dead at Thermopylae, as given in the funeral inscription set up where they fell and were buried (Hdt. 7. 228). Demaratus cannot of course have predicted that number, as many soldiers only left the site when the treachery of Ephialtes, who told the Persians of a path that would enable the Persians to surround the men in the pass, became known. In Herodotus, Demaratus evades the question of the Greek numbers (7. 102), and his argument for the Greek chance of victory rests on their courage, not on the disadvantage of Persian numbers: but the declamatory tradition was strong on this argument (*Suas.* 2. 1, 7, 8 and see **ad (6.) 31. 11**).

(6.) 31. 6 cum te mutatis legibus suis natura transmiserit, in semita haerebis (when nature, altering her laws, has allowed you to cross the sea, you will be held up on a footpath). Cf. Elder Seneca, *Suas.* 2. 3, where the declaimer says of Xerxes *montes perforat, maria contegit* ('he tunnels mountains, bridges seas') ... *maria terrasque rerum naturam statione mutavit sua* ('he has moved seas, lands, nature itself, from their positions'). Xerxes had a canal dug across the isthmus of Mt. Athos (Hdt. 7. 22–4), thus making water of the land, and bridged the Hellespont, thus making land of the sea: in fact the bridge actually had earth heaped on it (Hdt. 7. 36). Demaratus is made to name Thermopylae, but he could not possibly have predicted that the Persians would be thwarted by this particular pass.

(6.) 31. 11 Xerxes pudore quam damno miserior Demarato gratias egit (Xerxes, more despondent because of his shame than because of his losses, thanked Demaratus). The king is moved by *pudor*, as Augustus is said to be moved by *verecundia* ((6.) 32. 2), here equivalent and meaning 'loss of face'. Demaratus, in fact, was rewarded by Xerxes, for going on the expedition, with two cities near Pergamum in western Asia Minor, Teuthrania and Halisarus (Xen. *Hell.* 3. 1. 6; *An.* 2. 1. 3; 7. 8. 17).

(6.) 31. 12 petit ille, ut Sardis, maximam Asiae civitatem, curru vectus intraret rectam capite tiaram gerens; id solis datum regibus (he asked to enter Sardis, the greatest city of Asia, in a chariot, wearing a tiara erect on his head, a privilege given only to kings). Sardis had been the capital of the Lydian Kingdom until the Persians defeated King Croesus *c.*546 BC; it then became the headquarters of the principal Persian satrapy. It was there that Xerxes had mustered his troops before crossing the Hellespont. In Seneca's day it was the capital of a *conventus* (centre for assizes) in the Roman province of Asia. That the king wore the Persian cap erect and the nobles wore it folded over is confirmed by Xenophon (*An.* 2. 5. 23) and the Suda s.v. *kurbasis* and, visually, by the Alexander mosaic in the Museo Nazionale in Naples, where Darius III wears the cap erect, and by the Achaemenid silver statuettes no. VA 4. 852 in the Vorderasiatisches Museum, Staatliche Museen, Berlin, where the Persian nobles wear it folded over. The story of Demaratus' reward is not in Herodotus but appears in Plutarch (*Them.* 29. 5–6), who has King Xerxes angered by his request but mollified by Themistocles. This may derive from the third-century-BC historian Phylarchus, for *FGrH* 81, fr. 22 of his *Histories* records the request of Demaratus and the significance of the upright tiara.

(6.) 31. 12 dignus fuerat praemio, ante quam peteret; sed quam miserabilis gens, in qua nemo fuit, qui verum diceret regi, nisi qui non dicebat sibi (he had deserved his reward up to the moment when he asked for it; but how pitiful was that people in which there was no one to tell the king the truth, except someone who was not used to telling it to himself). Demaratus' request shows that he does not have a true conception of what is valuable (no treasure is more than a 'positive indifferent' in the Stoic view). Persian kings furnish Seneca with examples of punishment being given to Persian purveyors of good advice, in *De ira* 3. 14–15: see Roller 2001, 116.

(6.) 32. Seneca's second example of the value of candid advice to those in power concerns a Roman Princeps rather than a Persian king, advice unavailable rather than neglected, and rash action in domestic affairs rather than foreign affairs. Yet, by the end of the anecdote, the first two differences have all but disappeared, as Seneca ascribes royal attitudes to Augustus, including an unwillingness to hear the truth, which makes his own subjects reluctant to proffer it.

(6.) 32. 1 divus Augustus filiam ultra impudicitiae maledictum impudicam relegavit et flagitia principalis domus in publicum emisit (the divine Augustus relegated his daughter, who was immoral beyond the reproach of immorality, and made public the scandals of the imperial house). In 2 BC Augustus sent his only child Julia, his daughter by Scribonia, to a villa owned by him on the island of Pandateria. Though *relegatio* to an island is later attested as the penalty for adultery (Paul, *Sent.* 2. 26. 14) (along with a loss of $\frac{1}{2}$ their dowry and $\frac{1}{3}$ of their property for women, and $\frac{1}{2}$ of their property for male adulterers), Julia may have been punished for it by a domestic tribunal, presided over by her father exercising his *patria potestas* and inventing a penalty, based on the Republican practice of fathers relegating unsatisfactory sons to particular properties. This personal *cognitio* may have been extended to her adulterers, at least one of whom, Iullus Antonius, was killed, while others were confined to islands (Tac. *Ann.* 3. 24; Suet. *Aug.* 65; Vell. 2. 100. 2–5; Cass. Dio 55. 10. 12–16; see Cohen 2008). In any case, he made public her misdemeanours by informing the senate of them through a letter read by his quaestor (Suet. *Aug.* 65. 2). On the possible political motives of all concerned, intimated by Seneca in *Brev. vit.* 4. 5, see Syme 1974, 18–31 = 1979, 923–34.

rostra, ex quibus pater legem de adulteriis tulerat, filiae in stupra placuisse (the platform from which her father had passed a law on adultery was her chosen venue for debauchery). Augustus' determination to support the institution of marriage, by legislating to regulate it, and by punishing adultery, met with considerable resistance, and the conduct of his own daughter, and later of his granddaughter Julia, he saw as undermining his stance. The *lex de adulteriis coercendis* was passed in or soon after 18 BC (Cass. Dio 54. 16) by Augustus, in virtue of his tribunician power. For the details of its content, see Treggiari 1991, 277–90.

cotidianum ad Marsyam concursum, cum ex adultera in quaestuariam versa ius omnis licentiae sub ignoto adultero peteret (that she visited the statue of Marsyas regularly when, turning from adultery to prostitution, she sought the right to every indulgence in the arms of an unknown adulterer). According to the Elder Pliny, Augustus' letter complained that a garland was placed on the statue of Marsyas at night, presumably one of those worn by her company of nocturnal revellers (*HN* 21. 9). Marsyas was a satyr, a servant in Rome of Father Liber, both of whom were associated with liberty and licence, so his statue would be a natural place to recruit clients. The fact that Marsyas had been punished by the god Apollo, Augustus' favourite deity, for daring to rival him as a musician, may have increased the Princeps' irritation, as did Julia's popularity with the people of Rome (Cass. Dio 55. 13): see Wiseman 2004, 68–9, 232, 235. It is unlikely that Julia really became a licensed prostitute who took strangers as clients, as the adultery law did not apply to registered prostitutes (Paul, *Sent.* 2. 26, 11), and it was only in AD 19 that the scandal of Vistilia, a woman of senatorial family who registered with the aediles as a prostitute to avoid prosecution under the law, led to the practice being legally forbidden to women of senatorial and equestrian family (Tac. *Ann.* 2. 85; Suet. *Tib.* 35. 2: see Levick 1983).

(6.) 32. 2 haec tam vindicanda quam tacenda (crimes that deserved to be punished as much as to be concealed). The terms of the comparison are reversed, as often in Seneca, see **ad 1. 13. 3.**

quae tam diu nescierat, donec loqui turpe esset (matters of which he had remained in ignorance until it was shameful to speak of them). Seneca means that by the time Augustus learnt of her conduct, it had reached a point where it was shameful even to mention it. Julia's adultery with Sempronius Gracchus is said by Tacitus to go back to her marriage with Agrippa (21 BC until his death in 12 BC) and continued, along with other liaisons, during her subsequent marriage to Tiberius (*Ann.* 1. 53; 6. 51. 2), who withdrew to Rhodes partly because of her infidelities (Cass. Dio 55. 10. 12–16; Suet. *Tib.* 10–11). The marriage ended in 2 BC through a divorce enforced by Augustus.

'horum mihi nihil accidisset, si aut Agrippa aut Maecenas vixisset!' ('none of this would have happened to me, if either Agrippa or Maecenas had been alive!'). Both had been close to Augustus from the period of the Triumvirate: Agrippa died in 12 BC; Maecenas in 8 BC. Had they been alive in 2 BC, they would both, in fact, have found it very difficult to advise in this situation: Agrippa, as Julia's husband, should, according to the *lex Julia de adulteriis*, have divorced and prosecuted her (*Dig.* 48. 5. 2. 2–7); Maecenas is said to have advised Augustus to make the marriage (Cass. Dio 54. 6. 5), which meant Agrippa's divorcing Augustus' niece, the elder Claudia Marcella.

(6.) 32. 3 caesae sunt legiones et protinus scriptae (legions were butchered and immediately enrolled). In fact the loss in AD 9 of three legions, owing to Quinctilius Varus' defeat in Germany, devastated Augustus. They were never reconstituted, and the number of legions remained at the reduced number of 25 under Augustus and for some time after.

tota vita Agrippae et Maecenatis vacavit locus (for the rest of his life, the place of Agrippa and Maecenas remained empty). Tacitus names Sallustius Crispus, the great-nephew and adopted son of the historian Sallust, as holding second place in Augustus' confidence while Maecenas lived, and then the first after his death (*Ann.* 3. 30); but Tacitus echoes Seneca's belief that no one really replaced Agrippa and Maecenas as close advisers to Augustus, in the retirement dialogue he composed for Seneca and Nero (*Ann.* 14. 53–5), where both think of these two as the precedents for Seneca's own position.

(6.) 33. 1 sed ut me ad propositum reducam, vides quam facile sit gratiam referre felicibus et in summo humanarum opum positis (but to return to my subject: you see how easy it is to return a favour to the fortunate and to those placed at the summit of human power). Seneca returns to the point he made at (6.) 29. 2–30 before giving examples of it in 31–2. Since his two examples were in fact counter-examples, showing the ill effects of rulers acting without sound advice, there is a need to mark the return of the argument. Sonntag 1913, 52 argued, however, that Seneca here marks the end of his own digression and his return to his source, Hecato.

(6.) 33. 3 amicum, rem non domibus tantum, sed saeculis rarum, quae non aliubi magis deest, quam ubi creditur abundare (a friend, something rare not only in palaces but in centuries, nowhere more lacking than where it is thought to abound). Various emendations have been proposed for the bold antithesis *non domibus tantum, sed sae-culis*. Alexander 1950–2a, 36 proposes *sacculis* (money bags) for *saeculis*. But Seneca wants to stress rarity in time as well as place, and in Latin *saeculis* fits the context better, as the following *aliubi* and *ubi* are ambiguous between time and place.

(6.) 33. 4 istos tu libros, quos vix nomenclatorum complectitur aut memoria aut manus, amicorum existimas esse? (do you think those lists, which neither the memory of the nomenclator nor his hands can easily retain, contain lists of friends?). The *nomenclator* (**ad 1. 3. 10**) was a slave who accompanied his master in order to prompt him with the name of persons he encountered. The situation here is the same as that described in *Ep.* 19. 11, where the *nomenclator* reminds the great man of the names of those who come to his morning *salutatio*, who are politely called *amici*, though many are really *clientes* or strangers. The true friend is someone bound to one by true affection, and who will give one candid advice ((6.) 34. 3, 5); and, as he explains at *Ep.* 19. 11–12, is someone whom we have carefully selected to receive favours, which then create true friendship. See **ad (6.) 34. 5** and p. 35, n. 23.

qui in primas et secundas admissiones digeruntur (who are divided into first and second audiences). This division, employed when large numbers attend a *salutatio*, is a *de facto* system of admission, according to which, as Seneca explains in (6.) 34. 1–2, some achieve entry into inner rooms, some not (Winterling 1999, 121). The institution was well enough established for the terms to be used metphorically (*Clem.* 1. 10. 1; *Ben.* 1. 14. 3).

(6.) 34. 2 apud nos primi omnium C. Gracchus et mox Livius Drusus instituerunt segregare turbam suam et alios in secretum recipere, alios cum pluribus, alios universos (Among us it was Gaius Gracchus and, a little later, Livius Drusus who were the first to separate into groups their own throng of visitors and receive some in private, some in a group, and others *en masse*). The indication *mox* suggests that Seneca means, not the elder M. Livius Drusus, who was contemporary with C. Gracchus and, as fellow tribune, opposed him in politics, but his son, the younger M. Livius Drusus; what is said of the numbers of followers attending the latter (Vell. Pat. 2. 14, App. *BC* 1. 36. *fin.*) rather confirms this. These two, tribunes of the plebs in 123–2 BC and 91 BC respectively, would be greeted and escorted to the form by crowds, as Cicero describes in the case of candidates for office (*Mur.* 70–1), probably in unusual numbers because their copious legislation could benefit so many people. The hierarchy of privilege and space assigns the *cubiculum* to intimate friends or confidential business; the *triclinium* to relatively favoured visitors; and the *vestibulum, peristylia, atria* to uninvited, possibly unknown, guests (see Vitruv. 6. 5: 'into which uninvited persons of the people can come by right' (*invocati suo iure de populo possunt venire*)). It is interesting that Seneca assumes a continuity of aristocratic custom from Republic to Principate, when the Princeps too adopted it (see Wallace-Hadrill 1996, 290). Trajan, according to Plin. *Pan.* 47. 5, somehow avoided the humiliations that went with grades of entry.

(6.) 34. 3 amicum vocas cuius disponitur salutatio? (do you call a 'friend' someone whose greeting is allotted a turn?). For the two qualities, *fides* (loyalty)and *libertas* (freedom of speech), that Seneca regards as characteristic of a true *amicus*, see **ad (6.) 30. 4.** For debasement of the vocabulary of friendship, see Konstan 1997, 140.

(6.) 34. 5 in pectore amicus, non in atrio quaeritur (it is in the heart that one seeks a friend, not in the vestibule). Cf. *Ep.* 19. 11: *errat autem qui amicum in atrio quaerat* ('he is mistaken who looks for a friend in the vestibule'). Here, and in 1. 34. 3, Seneca is thinking of what Aristotle called the friendship based on virtue, which is also in Cicero's mind at *Off.* 1. 55–6, where he stresses affection and shared activities.

(6.) 35. 4 'ista', inquit, festinatio nimia ingrati est?' ('that excessive haste', someone says, 'does it point to an ingrate?'). This is the reading adopted by Préchac 1961. The N text is *nimiam ingrati est*. Alexander 1950–2a, 37 prefers J. Mueller's *ista festinatio nimia, non ingrati* ('that haste is excessive, but does not point to an ingrate').

(6.) 36–7. To bring out the enormity of praying for ill fortune to befall a bene-factor, in order to provide an opportunity to show one's gratitude, Seneca adduces a series of historical examples, hypothetical (36) and actual (37). The hypothetical cases illustrate both features (as given at (6.) 39. 2 *fin.*) of the situ-ation being discussed: (1) that the ultimate aim of the prayer is good but the means invoked evil (cf. 37. 3); (2) that the person praying falls into the fault he was trying to avoid, that of ingratitude towards his benefactor. Thus the cases of Aeneas and of the Sicilian youths involve gratitude to benefactors, here parents, and their prayers invoke misfortune on the same benefactors, though only indirectly, by invoking it on their countries. The rescue of their city by Scipio and the Decii, after wishing misfortune on it, is presumably construed as repayment of benefits that citizens receive from their *patria*. The cases of Callistratus and Rutilius appear to illustrate only the first feature, since a well-wisher invokes misfortune on them indirectly through their city, but the aim is to put right an injustice to them (**ad (6.) 37. 3**), not to repay a benefactor, even indirectly (but see **ad (6.) 37. 2**). The two incidental comparisons, to the doctor (36. 4) and the arsonist (37. 3 *fin.*), look ahead to the motive of enhan-cing one's reputation, which is to be condemned later at (6.) 42. 2.

(6.) 36. 1 quis pium dicet Aenean, si patriam capi voluerit, ut captivitati patrem eripiat? (who will call Aeneas 'dutiful', if he wished his native land to be captured so that he might rescue his father from captivity?). Both Aeneas and the young Sicilians have featured, in 3. 37. 1–2, as examples of children outdoing the benefits received from parents. Seneca there remarks on Aeneas' *pietas* or filial duty, and here he is given his Virgilian epithet *pius*, while *pietas* is ascribed to the Sicilian youths (**ad 3. 37. 2**). Their supposed wish for bad means to their good ends, however, compromises that *pietas*.

(6.) 36. 2 nihil debet Scipioni Roma, si Punicum bellum ut finiret aluit (Rome owes nothing to Scipio, if he encouraged the Punic War in order to end it). This is presum-ably the elder P. Cornelius Scipio Africanus, victor of the Second Punic War against Hannibal.

gravissima infamia est medici opus quaerere (it is a highly disgraceful practice for a doc-tor to manufacture work). The point of the parallel with the Decii is to point out that the would-be repayer of benefits may not be able to rectify the calamity for which he prayed.

(6.) 37. 1 Callistratum aiunt (ita certe Hecato auctor est), cum in exilium iret . . . optante quodam, ut Atheniensibus necessitas restituendi exules esset, abominatum talem reditum (they say that when Callistratus (at least this is what Hecato writes), was going into exile . . . and someone prayed that some necessity might compel the Athenians to restore the exiles, he prayed that there should be no return of this kind). Callistratus, Athenian orator and statesman, went into exile in 361 BC. Athens was renowned for its ingratitude to those, like Cimon, Miltiades, Themistocles, and Alcibiades, who had done great services in the past (Plato, *Gorg.* 515 B–517 A; Cic. *Rep.* 1. 4–5). For Hecato as a source of *De beneficiis*, see **ad 1. 3. 2–4. 5** and Ch. 2, pp. 20-1, 24.

(6.) 37. 2 'quid tibi', inquit, 'mali feci, ut mihi peiorem reditum quam exitum optares?' ('what evil have I done you, that you should wish on me a return worse than my departure?'). For Rutilius Rufus, see **ad 5. 17. 2 Rutilius innocentiae pretium**. His condemnation for extortion in 92 BC was followed soon after by the Social War and the civil war between the followers of Sulla and Marius. The remark attributed to Rutilius may imply that the author of the wish was in his debt for a benefit, which would make the example more relevant: his wishing civil war on Rome, which would be indirectly a calamity for Rutilius, would then be aimed at repaying a benefit to him.

non est istud exilium cuius neminem non magis quam damnatum pudet (that is not exile of which no one is less ashamed than the condemned). Rutilius' punishment is not only a mere 'indifferent' and thus not bad in Stoic terms, but it is more a source of shame to the country that punished him unjustly than to him.

(6.) 37. 3 quia satius erat duos iniquo malo adfici quam omnes publico (because it was better for an unjust calamity to be visited on two people than a public calamity on all). Seneca seems to be glossing the last two examples as a contrast between the behaviour of a good citizen, who would not wish his country to suffer, even to undo an injustice to himself, with that of a would-be grateful man, who wishes ill on those to whom he owes benefits, so that he can repay them (cf. **ad (6.) 36–7**).

qui bene de se merentem <distringi> difficultatibus vult (who wants someone who has deserved well of him <to be beset> by difficulties). The supplement of Gertz 1876, accepted by Préchac 1961 and Alexander 1950–2*a*, 37, fills the gap in N and is preferable to the supplement of the later MSS, which give *opprimi* after *difficultatibus* and which are followed by Hosius.

ne in patrocinium quidem, nedum in gloriam cedet incendium extinxisse, quod feceris (there is no defence, let alone glory, in extinguishing a fire which you have caused). N has a second *quidem* after *gloriam* for which Gertz 1876 read *cedet*, which seems preferable to *est* in later MSS. Alexander, 1950–2*a*, 37 prefers *cuidam*; Préchac 1961 *cui dem*.

(6.) 38. Seneca here moves on to cases more remote from the prayers of perverse benefactors, cases of prayers that call down misfortune on others as a means to personal gain, usually financial. The prime case of Demades gave rise to a criminal prosecution, but Seneca insists that his wish for great gain was no worse than the prayers of most people, including ourselves, which involve profiting from the distress of others.

(6.) 38. 1 in quibusdam civitatibus impium votum sceleris vicem tenuit (in some states an impious prayer has been regarded as a crime). Lipsius rightly questioned why Seneca uses the Greek example of the prosecution by Demades, an important fourth-century-BC Athenian statesman and orator, when Claudia, an ancestress of the emperor Tiberius, was convicted for openly wishing that her brother might return from the dead in order to lose another fleet, as he had in 249 BC, and thus reduce the population of Rome (Suet. *Tib.* 2. 3; Val. Max. 8. 1 damn. 4; Gell. 10. 6; cf. Livy *Per.* 19).

(6.) 38. 3 miles bellum optat, si gloriam (if the soldier prays for glory, he prays for war). The one case set beside that of Demades' victim that concerns a wish for gain other than financial.

eloquentiae pretium excitat litium numerus (numerous lawsuits boost the price of eloquence). Cf. the juxtaposition of oratory and medicine in Tac. *Ann.* 11. 6. 2, an attack on accusers who do it for gain, *ut quomodo vis morborum pretia medentibus, sic fori tabes pecuniam advocatis ferat* ('so that, just as the virulence of disease brings rewards to doctors, so the rottenness of the forum brings money to advocates').

(6.) 38. 5 non est itaque dubium, quin hi magis, quod damnatum est in uno, optent, quibus, quisquis morte profuturus est, vita nocet ('there is therefore no doubt that these people pray more intensely for what was condemned in the case of that one man, since whoever will profit them by dying injures them by living). 'These people', as in the previous two sentences are the legacy-hunters (Seneca's named examples Arruntius and Haterius cannot be securely identified, see Biographical Notes) who actually spend money and effort making up to those they wish would die, whereas the funeral directors just want as many unknown people to die as possible. The 'one man' is of course Demades' victim, as at (6.) 38. 3.

omnium tamen istorum tam nota sunt vota quam impunita (yet the prayers of all men of this kind are as well known as they are unpunished). The terms of the comparison are reversed, as often in Seneca, see **ad 1. 13. 3**.

(6.) 39. 2 tam miser sit, ut illi beneficii loco sit, quidquid redditur (let him be so wretched that whatever is repaid to him counts as a benefit). The relief of the benefactor's misery would be so great as to make this return of a favour count as an independent benefit and earn the erstwhile beneficiary gratitude.

(6.) 40–3. Seneca returns to the theme of undue haste in repaying benefits, which, being in the interest of the beneficiary rather than the benefactor, counts as ingratitude. Like Book 4, this book ends with the problem of returning benefits, seen from the point of view of the beneficiary. See Ch. 6 n. 34.

(6.) 40. 1 quod aeque peccat, qui non sequitur, quam qui antecedit (because the person who fails to keep up with it is as much at fault as the person who anticipates it). The terms of the comparison are reversed, as often in Seneca, see **ad 1. 13. 3**.

(6.) 40. 2 quare quasi cum acerbo feneratore signare rationem parem properas? (why do you hurry to square your account, as if with a harsh money-lender?). When the amount borrowed and the amount repaid are equal, the account is marked *par ratio*, cf. *Ep.* 19. 10 and Tac. *Ann.* 13. 14. 1.

(6.) 41. 1 nemo enim libenter reddit, quod invitus debet (for no one repays freely what he owes against his will).   Seneca had said at the outset (1. 4. 3) that one of the things we need to learn is *libenter reddere* (to repay freely), for a virtuous action must spring from a good intention. Seneca here repeats that benefits create a bond between people, which he first said in the same context. But here he emphasizes the long-term relationship created between benefactor and recipient in particular, a bond that makes patience in repaying and accepting further favours in the meantime reasonable, a consideration he omits at 4. 40. 4–5, when making a similar point about undue haste in repaying.

(6.) 41. 2 'nulla mora in Turno est'.   Virgil, *Aen.* 12. 11 of Turnus meeting Aeneas in battle.

(6.) 42. 2 male agit qui famae, non conscientiae gratus est (the person who is grateful because of his reputation, not because of his conscience, behaves badly).   Lendon 1997, 68 n. 191 points to this as a case of replacing shame with conscience, and it is certainly hard not to translate *conscientia* here as 'conscience' in our sense. The question of concern about reputation has come up incidentally in this discussion before (36. 2 *fin.*; 37. 3 *fin.*; 38. 3 (the soldier)), but Seneca now directs this concern at his addressee and pointedly closes the book with this thought.

(6.) 43. 1 For *sinus* (pocket), see **ad 2. 16. 2 ut congiaria tua.**

non minoris est animi beneficium debere quam dare (it is not the mark of a lesser mind to owe rather than to confer a benefit).   Both are virtuous acts and hence equal in value (D.L. 7. 101). Seneca says *debere* ('to owe') rather than *referre* ('to return') or *reddere* ('to repay') because it is the grateful attitude towards a benefactor, not the return of the benefit, that he is praising as the virtuous act, parallel to giving with the right attitude (1. 6. 1). Seneca has already made it clear that receiving and returning a benefit cannot really be separated, since the appropriate return is the good will of grateful acceptance (pp. 116–18).

Synopsis of Book 7

5–6   Answer is to distinguish different senses in
         which a thing can belong to different
         people: owner vs. tenant; author vs.
         bookseller; and different senses in which
         one person can possess different things:
         everything belong to Caesar's authority, but
         his fiscus is his own; everything belongs to
         the Sage's mind, but he legally owns
         particular items and can receive gifts, owe,
         buy, and hire.

7. 1–4   *Bion's absurd syllogisms, using the premise 'all*
         things belong to the gods', lead to the
         contradictory conclusions that all men are
         sacrilegious and that none are.

         7. 3   Answer is to distinguish sacred things
                   that can be stolen from the gods, and
                   profane things that cannot.

         7. 4   Similarly, it is possible to steal from the
                   Sage only things that he owns individually,
                   not those under his universal control.

7. 5–11 *The Sage would rather not have possessions in*
         the ordinary sense.

         7. 5   Example of Curius Dentatus
         8. 2–11   Example of Demetrius the Cynic:
                   9–10   His speech against avarice and
                             luxury, and his claim to want to
                             possess only what belongs to all.
                   11   His confrontation with Gaius
                             Caesar.

12–13   **Solution to 2:**

12   *Things can be held in common in different senses,*
         yet distinct from the type of possession that
         allows one to sell or consume them.

13   (lacuna) *[?All of what is held in common*
         between friends is held by each, but each can
         possess and be given different amounts of it. For]
         though a benefit cannot be more or less, the
         means by which a benefit is conveyed can be.

14–16. 4 HAS SOMEONE WHO HAS DONE EVERYTHING TO RETURN A BENEFIT, RETURNED IT?

14. 2–5 **Repaying a benefit belongs to a category of duties that**
         are fulfilled by the effort, unlike repaying a debt.

14. 6–15   Intention is the most important thing: the man who has tried and failed is closer to the returner than to one who forgets to return.

> 15. 3–5   *If one makes an effort, one repays both the benefactor's intention and his gift. Intention is all we can give the gods.*

16. 1–4   Seneca's solution: The benefactor should regard intention as enough repayment; the beneficiary should not. This will deny the ungrateful this excuse.

16. 5–21 OUGHT ONE TO RETURN A BENEFIT FROM A SAGE IF HE HAS BECOME BAD?

17   We must distinguish between a true benefit and the ordinary type exchanged by the ignorant.

> 17. 2   *The latter should be returned whether the man is 'good' or bad.*
>
> 18–19. 4   *The former is problematic since only the Sage can accept a true benefit, as only he knows how to use it. (In dialogue)*
>> 18. 2   Though I will not *give* to someone what he cannot accept, I will *return* what he cannot receive, because to return is to give what one owes to a person willing to have it returned.
>> 19. 1–4   The responsibility for losing or changing the character of the benefit I return rests with the recipient.

19. 5–20. 4   **Suppose he has become, not just bad, but savage, like Phalaris.**

> 19. 5–6   *The Sage cannot fall into the depths of wickedness.*
>
> 19. 7–9   *If his wickedness affects only him, I will repay so he has no claim on me; if it affects the public good, then his destruction of human society has severed my bond with him.*
>
> 20   *But I will return to him what does not contribute to his power to harm; if he is beyond cure I will make him a return that will benefit mankind.*

20. 5–21   To an ordinary bad man, I will return a benefit, but not give one, for I must not profit from the benefactor's wickedness, or indeed from his death.

22–5   THE DUTIES OF BENEFACTOR AND BENEFICIARY ARE ASYMMETRICAL: THE FORMER MUST FORGET HIS BENEFIT, THE LATTER MUST REMEMBER IT.

This is hyperbole: we really mean that a benefactor should act as if he had forgotten and only remind the beneficiary of his obligation gently.

24   Example of Socrates.

25   One can remind a properly selected recipient as an act of friendship.

26–32   A FITTING LAST QUESTION: HOW ARE WE TO DEAL WITH THE UNGRATEFUL?

26. 2   Do not regret your benefit.

26. 2–27   Do not be surprised: ingratitude is only one common vice among many.

28   It is foolish to be angry at a universal failing, of which you yourself are guilty.

29–31   Though a bad choice of beneficiary is the cause, ingratitude can sometimes be corrected by patience and persistent goodness rather than reproaches and complaints, which breed hatred.

31. 2–5   *Imitate the gods who persistently give to the ungrateful who malign them.*

32   The ungrateful injure themselves; the benefactor triumphs, recovering his benefit from others, overcoming sterile soil, demonstrating greatness of soul.

Notes to Synopsis of Book 7

Like Books 5 and 6, this last book opens with an apology for adding to the essential books covering the subject of beneficence another book of unnecessary intellectual exercises desired by his addressee. However, Seneca here marks them as a final remedying of omissions, and he uses the apology as an occasion to give a summary of the basic philosophical doctrines that the man making moral progress must absorb, combined with a sketch of the mind of the Sage (1. 7, cf. 2. 4)—for such descriptions, as he says in *Ep.* 95. 66 and 72, have the same function as precepts. This concern with the imperfect person is picked up, at the end of the book, in his discussion of how to interpret philosophical hyperbole (22–5) and in the humane advice on how to deal with ungrateful beneficiaries: the last of his *theseis* or *quaestiones infinitae*, for which the opening apology was issued. In between, and in sharp contrast to the practical advice at the beginning and end of the book, come three more theoretical *quaestiones infinitae*, which are largely concerned with Stoic paradoxes and definitions, and one practical one concerning a rather remote possibility.

As he finishes his work, Seneca shows himself self-conscious about the structure of this book and of the work as a whole, both in the first chapter, where he mentions an alternative structure that might have been more attractive to readers, and at (7.) 26. 1, where he introduces the last chapters as a fitting conclusion to his whole discussion. In fact, this closing section (7.) 26–32 also exhibits a marked symmetry with Book 1. 1–4 (see p. 118 n. 29).

(7.) 1. 1 **in manibus terrae: non hic te carmine longo/atque per ambages et longa exorsa tenebo** (I shall not detain you with a lengthy song/winding its way through lengthy prologues). The quotation from Virgil (*Georgics* 2. 45–6) is altered, with *longo* ('lengthy') in line 45 substituted for *ficto* ('made up', 'artificial'), so as to reinforce the tedium already implied in 'lengthy prologues' in line 46.

(7.) 1. 2 **debuit paulatim opus crescere et ea pars in finem reservari, quam quilibet etiam satiatus appeteret. Sed quiquid maxime necessarium erat, in primum congessi** (this work should have formed a gradual crescendo, with that part held back which any reader, however surfeited, would relish. But all that is most essential I have collected at the beginning). Seneca is being coy and should not be taken seriously. It is for orators to build up to an emotional peroration, or for tragedians, like Seneca himself, to build up to a moving dénouement. Even a historian like Tacitus can be said to adopt an 'ascending structure' in the *Annals* (Hutchinson 1993, 157–9, who compares Seneca's 'more devious procedure', to which he defiantly draws attention in this passage). But, even if we allow that Seneca's 'necessary' material was attractively presented, teaching at precept level is elementary and inadequate on its own, as Seneca shows in *Ep.* 94–5. The practice of following such teaching with consideration of problem cases to provide practice in applying philosophical doctrines to particular actions, by refining our precepts, was probably common in ethical treatises (see pp.120–2)). Despite what Seneca says of the unattractiveness of this material, it is likely that the young relished these logical puzzles (see pp. 133–4).

(7.) 1. 3–2. 1. Seneca here reinforces his view that puzzles just exercise the intellect without curing our moral faults, by putting it in the mouth of Demetrius the Cynic, an appropriate ally, since the Cynics despised logic (D.L. 6. 103). In keeping with Seneca's admiration for Demetrius as an eloquent teacher who practised what he preached (*Ep.* 20. 9: *non praeceptor veri est sed testis* ('not so much a teacher of truth as a witness to it')), Seneca here presents him as a teacher and then, in 8.2–11, as a living example of contempt for wealth.

(7.) 1. 3 egregie enim hoc dicere Demetrius Cynicus, vir meo iudicio magnus, etiam si maximis comparetur (Demetrius the Cynic makes the point very well—he is in my judgement a great man, even when set beside the greatest). A living contemporary of Seneca, Demetrius is characterized as a Cynic again in *Vit. beat.* 18. 3, but sometimes just as *noster* ((7.) 2. 1; *Epp.* 67. 14; 91. 19) or with some complimentary description (*NQ* 4, pref. 7, *Prov.* 5. 5; *Ep.* 62. 3). Tacitus shows that he was an associate of the virtuous senators Thrasea Paetus and Barea Soranus (*Ann.* 16. 34–5). He was banished under Vespasian in 71 (Dio 66. 13. 1–3; Suet. *Vesp.*13). Demetrius is described as *seminudus* in *Ep.* 62. 3, cf. 20. 9, but he clearly fitted into his Roman environment, by eschewing Cynic immodesty and coarseness (of which there is, however, a hint at *Ep.* 91. 19), and by not begging (*Vit. beat.* 18. 3): see Billerbeck 1979; Griffin 1996*b*, 195, 200–1.

praecepta sapientiae (precepts of wisdom). See p. 141 for the apparent peculiarity of this description, given that the grammatical form (e.g. *scit non multum esse*; *ut illi liqueat*) of Demetrius' teaching in (7.) 1. 7 is appropriate to *decreta* (statements of philosophical truth), not to *praecepta* (prescriptive utterances and calls to action): it consists, in fact, of basic Stoic doctrines (see Billerbeck 1979, 34–5). However, in *Ep.* 94. 31 Seneca characterizes *decreta* as *generalia praecepta*, where he is bringing out the pedagogic power of both (*utraque res praecipit, sed altera in totum, particulatim altera* ('both teach, but the one through the universal, the other through the particular')). Moreover, one should not overlook the fact that Demetrius is describing the mind of the Sage, while at *Ep.* 95. 66 Seneca points out that sketching an exemplar of a virtue (*ethologia*) is equivalent to giving *praecepta* for that virtue: what we have in (7.) 1. 7 is an exemplar of the virtue of *sapientia*, the possession of *scientia*, albeit limited to the useful and necessary. Thus Seneca solved his problem of ascribing *decreta* to a Cynic by having Demetrius put the requisite beliefs in the mind of the Sage, which he describes. Though the content of the teaching is different, there is something in the idea of I. Hadot 1969, 56 n. 94 that the level of the teaching is reminiscent of Epicurus' *tetrapharmakon* (God presents no fears, death no worries, while good is readily attainable, evil is readily endurable).

(7.) 1. 4 sic in hoc studio multa delectant, pauca vincunt (similarly, in philosophical study there are many moves which entertain, but few which bring success). Seneca has

Demetrius put in parallel the wrestler—who does not need to know all the moves he might use, but just a few key ones that he is well trained to use skilfully—with the moral agent, who only needs a few key moral ideas to practise and have to hand (2. 1). Brad Inwood points out to me that the parallel with the more general knowledge that Demetrius thinks unnecessary for the moral agent (1. 5) would be, for the wrestler, the principles of physics, such as leverage, and of physiology, such as those that explain why certain moves work well.

(7.) 1. 5 non multum tibi nocebit transisse, quae nec licet scire nec prodest (it will not do you much harm to skip over such topics, which are neither possible nor useful to know). Demetrius' contempt for knowledge of natural history and human biology fits with the Cynic contempt for physics, as well as logic; their exclusive concern with practical ethics led to Cynicism sometimes being regarded as a way of life, rather than as a philosophy (D.L. 6. 103). However, Seneca himself, in *Prov.* 5. 5, depicts a Demetrius who believes in fate and providence, while Tacitus (*Ann.* 16. 34–5) has him discuss the nature of the soul. And here, in (7.) 1. 6–7, Demetrius is made to espouse views redolent of the Stoic belief in divine providence. *Ep.* 94. 1 shows that Seneca does not believe in ignoring the fundamentals of the other branches of philosophy; he wrote his own *Natural Questions*, which dealt with the first of the topics listed here, about the same time as he was writing *De beneficiis* (see pp. 93–4).

involuta veritas in alto latet (truth is concealed, hidden in the depths). An allusion to Democritus' remark (D–K 68 B 117), which expressed his scepticism about the evidence of the senses. At *NQ* 7. 32. 4 the remark forms part of a reproach against our failure to investigate enough what we can know about the world. Here the emphasis is on moral wisdom, which is accessible to us.

(7.) 1. 7 didicit a se petere divitias (has learned to seek riches from itself), i.e. not from fortune, as Seneca spells out at *Tranq.* 9. 2, cf. *Ep.* 119. 2.

et scit non multum esse ab homine timendum, a deo nihil (and knows that we have little to fear from humans and nothing to fear from god). The Sage's invulnerability to humans rests on his correct belief that nothing is bad but vice; his invulnerability to the gods rests on the fact that, in the Stoic view, the divine is benign and does not injure.

si animum virtuti consecravit (if he has consecrated his mind to virtue). In the course of this portrait of the mind of the Sage, Seneca appears to switch the subject from the mind of the Sage (*animus*) to the Sage himself, for here the object is *animum*, cf. *retracto animo* ('once the mind has withdrawn' at the end of the description). This prepares the reader for the portrait of the Sage's contentment in 2. 4; in fact, the Stoics often identify the person with the rational mind. Grimal 1967, 135 notes the Senecan habit of making *animus* the subject of activities belonging to the person (e.g. *Vit. beat.* 4. 2), a habit imitated by Tacitus in Seneca's address to Nero at *Ann.* 14. 53. 5; cf. also *NQ* 3, pref. 2 with Brinkmann 2002, 44, n. 148. Tarrant 2006, 11–13, noting the presence of this synecdoche in Seneca's tragedies and prose works, remarks that when the *animus* speaks, Seneca 'gives virtue a human voice'.

(7.) 2. 1 cotidiana meditatio (daily practice). The Stoics taught that learning the doctrines was not enough for moral improvement: daily practice was needed, to achieve the mindset that permits one to make the right decisions consistently and to put them into practice reliably, in accordance with virtue, like the Sage (I. Hadot 1969, 103–8; Newman 1989, 1484–93). See *Epp.* 16. 1–2; 82. 8; 94. 48; 95. 57 on the importance of achieving the right *habitus animi*, and Musonius Rufus 6 Hense *peri askēseōs*. Seneca gives various indications as to the content of such meditation: repeating striking sayings against misfortune (*Ep.* 2. 4); examining one's daily conduct at the end of the day, as Sextius did (*Ira* 3. 36): a practice Seneca claims to follow; reciting the basic doctrines until they become second nature, as here, cf. *Ep.* 94. 26. These doctrines include not only ethics, stressed in 2. 2–4, but, as he expressly indicates at 2. 4 ('expertise in divine and human law', cf. *Ep.* 74. 29), the other branches of philosophy as well. Since Stoic *meditatio* involved absorption in doctrine, its alleged advocacy by Demetrius here rests on a slide to Stoic from Cynic *askēsis*, which was a more practical training in endurance.

(7.) 2. 2–2. 4. Seneca, in his own persona, now illustrates the contents of the *meditatio* practised by the men making progress: first the most important items of knowledge that one must train to bring immediately to mind; then a rhetorical exhortation to himself about true and false pleasure (cf. the self-exhortation of the progressor in *Vit. beat.* 20. 3–5); then a sketch of the Sage's composure, leading up to the example of Alexander, the counter-example to the attitudes of the Sage (2.5). We are reminded of the rhetorical methods employed for self-improvement by Marcus Aurelius, which include positive and negative examples (Alexander among the latter) and sketches of the Sage (Rutherford 1989, 43–4, 165–6, 170).

(7.) 2. 2 nec malum esse ullum nisi turpe nec bonum nisi honestum. Hac regula vitae opera distribuat (that there is nothing bad except what is shameful, and nothing good except what is honourable. He should allot his activities in life in accordance with this guideline). At *Ep.* 95. 39 Seneca notes that, without a grasp of the doctrines, as opposed to the precepts, one has no *regula* to tell one if what one has done is right. The *regula* is clearly a rule of thumb, adherence to which will prevent one from choosing to pursue some indifferents as goods (here the pleasures of the table) and to avoid others as bad. It is interesting that Aristotle (*NE* 3. 4. 1113^{a}29–1113^{b}2), having identified *ho spoudaios* (the good man) with the *kanōn* (standard) of what is noble and pleasant, contrasts him with the mass of men who misjudge pleasure as a good. Cicero in *De officiis* adopts the same *regula* as Seneca here, though he speaks in terms of *utile*, rather than *bonum* (3. 81, cf. 3. 34, 78, 85 *fin.*). Seneca's reference to this *regula* as a *lex*, in the next clause, reminds us that Seneca and Cicero often draw on legal terminology (see Inwood 1999, 118–21; Griffin 2013).

(7.) 2. 4 hic, quem deformamus cum maxime (the person we have just now been sketching out). Seneca refers back to 1. 7, Demetrius' sketch of the mind of the Sage, and attributes to the Sage true *voluptas* (as opposed to the false pleasure just described), not using here his own technical term *gaudium* ('joy') as the equivalent of the Greek *chara*, see *ad* 4.13.1. That he has been speaking of the Sage is made clear by the application to this person, immediately after (2. 5), of the Stoic paradox that all things belong to the Sage (D.L. 7. 125; Cic. *Fin.* 3. 75).

(7.) **2. 5–3. 3.** As in 1. 13 (see **ad 1. 13. 1–2**), 2. 16 and 5. 6 and in Seneca's other works (*Ep.* 119. 7; *NQ* 5. 18. 10), Alexander is here an example of overweening pride, insatiable greed, and ambition for glory, which left him unsatisfied and hence poor. See Brunt 1977, 42–3. The Sage's contentment, having been compared with insatiable desire for pleasure (2. 2–4), is now compared to insatiable desire for territory: the result is a neat transition to the first conundrum arising from the Stoic paradox that all things belong to the Sage.

(7.) **2. 5 cum in oceano Onesicritus praemissus explorator erraret** (when Onesicritus, who had been sent ahead as an explorer, was roaming the ocean). Onesicritus was Alexander's head steersman, who served on the voyage in the Persian Gulf of 325–4 BC and later wrote a flattering account of Alexander. There is a lot to be said for the suggestion by Watt 1994, 230 that this clause be taken with what follows, not, as it usually is, with what precedes.

(7.) **2. 6 qui extra naturae terminos arma proferret** (he led his army beyond the bounds of nature). That the Ocean that surrounded the world was the end of the natural world, and the limit imposed on man by the gods, was a common idea in antiquity (Tac. *Germ.* 45. 1): it features in rhetorical exercises about Alexander (Elder Seneca, *Suas.* 1. 1; 1. 3). See D. Braund 1996, 20–2.

(7.) **3. 1 quem per Liberi Herculisque vestigia felix temeritas egit** (who was driven by his boldness and good fortune along the paths trodden by Dionysus and Hercules). At 1. 13 the comparison of Alexander with the great travellers Dionysus and Hercules is elaborated, to Alexander's disadvantage.

(7.) **3. 2 unus est sapiens, cuius omnia sunt nec ex difficili tuenda** (the Sage is the only one who possesses everything and can retain it without difficulty). Seneca thus contrasts the anxiety of conquerors like Alexander in acquiring and protecting their territory, with the serenity of the Sage, which is comparable to that of the gods.

(7.) **4–13.** Having explained the knowledge necessary for the making of moral progress, and exemplified the practice the progressor should undertake daily, Seneca effects a return to the intellectual exercises promised for this book. He imagines an objector pointing out a contradiction between the Stoic paradox under discussion (that all things belong to the Sage) and Stoic teaching about generosity, i.e. that only the Sage really knows how to confer a benefit or return a favour (*Ep.* 81. 10). He then adduces a further contradiction between the proverb adopted by the Stoics and other philosophers, 'friends have all things in common' (see Aristotle, *NE* 9. 8. 1168[b]7–8; Seneca *Ep.* 6. 2–3; 48. 2–3 makes it characteristic of true friendship), and Stoic teaching on friendship, i.e. that only a Sage is truly a friend (*Ep.* 81. 12) and practises friendship by doing things for his friends (*Ep.* 9. 8, 10). The two *quaestiones infinitae* posed here, *quemadmodum potest aliquis donare sapienti, si omnia sapientis sunt* ('how can anyone give anything to the Sage if all things belong to the Sage?') and

quemadmodum potest aliquis donare amico, si omnia illis sunt communia
('how can anyone give anything to his friend, if they have all things in
common?'), are concerned with *cognitio* and belong to the subdivision *quid
sit* (pp. 137–8). Seneca demonstrates the importance of such puzzles by
distinguishing different senses of ownership, entitlement, and belonging,
thereby clarifying the meaning, first of the Stoic paradox (4–11), and then of
the proverb (12–13). The use of some examples and concepts drawn from
Roman law will have appealed to his educated Roman readers (see Griffin
2013, 100–1; 114).

(7.) 4–11. Though the objector's scepticism really concerns the paradox *omnia
sapientis sunt* ('All things belong to the Sage': Seneca can hardly be expected, in a
work on benefits, to exclude the Sage from such exchanges), Seneca's answer
focuses on the erroneous inference drawn from it, i.e. 'whatever is given to him
comes from what is already his' and consists in distinguishing from individual
legal entitlement the sense in which everything belongs to the Sage. Professor
Sirks points out that the use of the genitive in formulating the paradox facilitates
this discussion, since the genitive means, in legal language, quiritary ownership,
but, in common language, it is less absolute and hints at all kind of entitlement,
legal, moral, and intellectual. Several explications of the paradox are canvassed by
Seneca, of which the third is given the fullest treatment: (1) The Sage has all things,
in the sense of not desiring or needing anything, the sense that best fits the contrast with Alexander (2. 4 *fin.*–6; 3. 3. *fin.*; 10. 6). (2) The Sage has all things, because
he alone knows how to make proper use of things; this interpretation, adopted by
Cicero *Fin.* 3. 75, seems to be endorsed by Seneca at 3. 2–3. (3) The Sage has all
things, in the sense of having power over things, in that his mind comprehends
their value (4. 2–3; 4. 6; 5. 1; 6. 2–3; 8. 1). Seneca uses several different techniques
to establish that the Sage can be given things, despite having all things. The
principal method throughout is to adduce other cases in which things can belong
to, or be possessed by, different owners in different senses (4. 2–6. 2), or in which
the same person can own different things in different senses (6. 3–11). But at 4.
7–8 Seneca turns to more negative forms of argument, showing what absurd
conclusions follow if the paradox, accepted as true and interpreted literally as
personal possession, is used as a premise in syllogistic arguments. Then at 7. 1–4
he uses absurd syllogisms, containing the same literal interpretation of the
premise that all things belong to the gods, as an *a fortiori* argument about the
Sage's style of possession. Finally, at 7. 5–11, he illustrates the meaning of
the paradox, by showing how truly great men (virtual Sages) view possessions in
the ordinary sense.

(7.) 4. 1 **atqui dicitis sapienti posse donari** (but you people say that the Sage can be
given things). The plural, here and in the next sentence but one, must indicate the
Stoics. There is no reason to think that the imaginary interlocutor here is meant to be
the addressee Liberalis.

(7.) **4. 2 iure civili omnia regis sunt** (according to civil law, all things belong to the king). As in 5. 1 and 6. 2, Seneca parallels the position of the Sage to that of a king, though in 6.3 where he wants to speak of specifically Roman institutions, he will speak of 'Caesar', that is, the Princeps. The discussion of the paradox tends to become more specifically Roman and technical (though not over technical, see n. below) as it progresses (at least, up to 8. 1): thus here Seneca speaks of the king's power as *potestas*; in 5.1 and 6.3 he speaks of *imperium*. The conjunction here of *iure civili*, which to his readers will signify Roman law, with *rex* reminds us of the attempt to universalize his teaching in *De Clementia* (especially 1. 4. 2, where he speaks of *principes regesque et quocumque alio nomine sunt tutores status publici*) and prepares us for the combination of Athens and Campania at 4. 3. The *potestas* of the king is a public power which, if necessary, can be used to expropriate or encumber private property; and, in inheritance law, if there is no heir, inheritances revert to the commonwealth, represented by the king.

in singulos dominos discripta sunt, et unaquaeque res habet possessorem suum (have been distributed to individual owners, and each and every thing is possessed by some one person). Hosius rightly accepts the correction by Gertz 1876 of N's *descripta* to *discripta* (see Dyck 1996, 298 ad 1. 124). In attempting to mark our different senses of belonging, Seneca does not observe the technical distinctions of Roman law: he does not distinguish between *dominus* and *possessor*, here or in 6. 3, or between *proprietas* and *possessio*, later in this chapter or in 6. 2.

(7.) **4. 3 fines Atheniensium at Campanorum vocamus, quos deinde inter se vicini privata terminatione distinguunt** (we speak of the territories of the Athenians and Campanians, which neighbours then divide among themselves, marking the boundaries by private agreement as an expression of their exclusive entitlement). The land belongs to the community as a whole in the sense that land that is left without an heir reverts to the community. But each occupier has exclusive entitlement to his land, as marked out by the agreed boundaries, and registers it as his with the censors.

et totus ager utique ullius rei publicae est (its entire territory certainly belongs to some commonwealth). *Utique* is Hosius' emendation for a corrupt text.

(7.) **4. 4 quin servus cum peculio domini sit** (that a slave along with his personal money belongs to his owner). According to Roman law, a slave, like a child still under the power of his father, could not legally own property, but the master could allow him to administer money and property, subject to his continuing consent, or even with full freedom of management (*libera administratio*), and use his gains (over what he was expected to turn over to his master), even to pay the master to free him. *Dig.* 15. 3. 7 envisages a slave making a gift to his master from his *peculium*: see **ad 3. 19. 1** and **3.19.2**.

(7.) **4. 5 quemadmodum probemus omnia? nunc enim omnia sapientis esse inter duos convenit** (how can we *prove* every last point? For we are now both agreed that all things belong to the Sage). Alexander 1950–2a, 39 follows Hosius in accepting the text as it is. Yet the placing of the remark seems curious, as Seneca has for some time been arguing on the assumption that the paradox is true, and as he goes on arguing in the same vein. The insistence that the paradox has been agreed makes more sense as an introduction to (7.) 4. 7, where the paradox is used as an agreed premise in syllogisms, whose absurd conclusions challenge that assumption.

omnia patris sunt, quae in liberorum manu sunt (all things that are in the hands of his children belong to the father). This is a reference to the Roman institution of *patria potestas*. Like a slave, a child still under the power of his father could not legally own property but could have a *peculium*. If a soldier, he could even have a *peculium castrense* containing his soldier's pay and his booty, over which his father had no authority. See **ad 3.18–28** for the powers conferred by the *patria potestas* and how fathers were actually expected to behave.

(7.) 4. 6 tamen et dis donum posuimus et stipem iecimus (and yet we have placed gifts on their altars and thrown them our coins). Varro *LL* 5. 182 explains that *stipes* is the traditional term for coins put in the treasury of a god. (Cf. fr. 120 Haase = 94 Vottero from the *liber moralis philosophiae: illis stipem iaciunt*; Tac. *Hist. 5. 5.* 1; Suet. *Aug.* 57. 1.)

(7.) 4. 8 innumerabilia sunt, per quae cavillantur, cum pulcherrime, quid a nobis dicatur, intellegant (they deploy countless sophistical quibbles of the kind, even though they understand perfectly what we are saying). On Seneca's sneers at hair-splitting logic, see pp. 133–4. At *Ep.* 111. 1 he explains that the noun *cavillatio* is Cicero's translation of the Greek *sophisma*.

(7.) 5. 1 quemadmodum sub optimo rege omnia rex imperio possidet, singuli dominio (just as under the best kind of king everything is in the possession of the king by virtue of his public authority, of individuals by virtue of their rights of ownership). See **ad (7.) 4. 2**. The qualification *optimus* reminds us that bad kings or tyrants often take possession of the private property of individuals without legal justification. Giliberti 1996, 6, 155–6 suggests that Seneca reflects contemporary concern about this tendency of monarchical rulers, such as the Princeps increasingly became, to use political power to encroach on private property.

tempus istius probandae rei veniet. Interim hoc huic quaestioni sat est (there will come a time for *proving* this point, but, meanwhile, this is enough for the question before us). In *Ep.* 87. 1 too Seneca puts off proving the truth of Stoic paradoxes, as he here postpones proving that 'all things belong to the Sage'. Various scholars (see Lausberg 1970, 185–6, cf. 175) have suggested that Seneca looks forward here to his systematic account of Stoic ethics in the *libri moralis philosophiae* which he mentions in the later letters (106. 2; 108. 1, 39; 109. 17): this work contained discussion of the Sage, including the question 'whether one Sage can help another' (*Ep.* 109. 1, 17), which is clearly related to the one that concerns Seneca here ('whether anyone can give the Sage anything'). Seneca goes on to adduce instances where a thing belongs to two different people in two different senses.

(7.) 5. 2 res tua est, usus rei tuae meus est (the thing itself belongs to you, but the use of your thing belong to me). Seneca considers various examples of the contract of hire (*locatio/conductio rei*), in which the *locator* places a thing, movable or immovable, at the disposal of the *conductor* for his use or enjoyment, thereby restricting his own entitlement to the thing to mere ownership and possession, but not enjoyment. He considers rental of a house, a farm (see next note), a slave, a carriage.

heu! frustra magnum alterius spectabis acervum (alas, you will see a great pile belong to another—to no avail (Virgil, *Georgics* 1. 158)). Seneca, quoting from memory, moves *frustra* from its central position in the line, after *alterius*. The *colonus* or tenant of agricultural land has the right, not only to the use of the land, but to the enjoyment of the fruits of the land.

(7.) **5. 3 nec servum tuum, mercennarium meum, abduces** (nor will you take away your slave, my hireling). For *mercennarius*, see **ad 3. 22. 1** where Seneca quoted Chrysippus' definition of the slave as *perpetuus mercennarius*, by way of urging slave-owners to treat their slaves in the same way as they would treat free hired labourers. Here, of course, he is a slave hired out to another. The hire or lease clearly implied that the lessor had no right, during the term of the lease, to take back what he had leased.

(7.) **6. 1 quia alter rei dominus est, alter usus** (because one is the owner of the thing, the other of the use of it). With this bold extension of *dominium* to cover *usus*, Seneca sums up the distinction he has been drawing between the ownership rights of the lessor and the lessee's rights to exclusive use for the duration of the lease.

(7.) **6. 3 Caesar omnia habet, fiscus eius privata tantum ac sua; et universa in imperio eius sunt, in patrimonio propria** (Caesar owns everything, but his treasury contains only his own private property; and all things are in his power, but only his personal possessions belong to his estate). The mention of buying and renting in the previous sentence, like buying and borrowing in 4. 8, prepares us for the idea that the Sage is not only given things, but acquires and owns things in the mundane sense: that not only can a thing belong to different people in different senses, but that one person can possess things in different senses. This sentence is one of the most important pieces of evidence for finance under the Principate. The contrast between the *imperium* of the Princeps, through which the whole world belongs to him, and his *patrimonium*, the things that are his legal property, is made in those terms by Pliny *Pan.* 50. 2. Seneca clearly sets up a parallel between the emperor's *fiscus*, holding *privata*, and his *patrimonium*, holding *propria*. *Fiscus* is the predominant technical term in speaking of the imperial wealth, especially in legal sources (Millar 1963, 29), and Seneca here uses it to mean the personal property of the Princeps.

nam id quoque, quod tamquam alienum abiudicatur, aliter illius est (for something that is adjudged to belong to someone else still belongs to him, in a different sense). See **ad 4. 39. 3** for Seneca's indication of the risks of being involved in litigation with the *fiscus*, given the political and legal realities. Tiberius is praised by Tacitus (*Ann.* 4. 6) because ordinary legal process was used for disputes between private citizens and the *fiscus*, and Pliny *Pan.* 36 praises Trajan for ensuring that justice was done, and that the *fiscus* sometimes lost a case. Claudius in 53 (Tac. *Ann.* 12. 60) seems to have made his financial procurators judges in cases concerning the *fiscus*, and there is no evidence that this was reversed under Nero (Griffin 1976, 105 n. 4 against Brunt 1966, 477 = 1990,

177–9). A special court was to be set up by Nerva, so that the private litigant could choose not to have an imperial procurator judge the case.

(7.) 7. 1 Bion modo omnes sacrilegos esse argumentis colligit, modo neminem (Bion uses arguments to infer, first, that everyone is impious, and then that no one is). As Kinderstrand 1976, 239–40 notes, Bion took a critical view of traditional religion, which shows in the flippant way in which sacrilege is treated in these paired syllogisms, the inspiration for which is probably the syllogism of Diogenes the Cynic that uses the premise that all things belong to the gods (D.L. 6. 37; 6. 72). Seneca imports Roman allusions to the Tarpeian rock (*de saxo*), a steep cliff on the side of the Capitoline Hill overlooking the Roman Forum, from which, during the Roman Republic, those condemned for murder, treason, and sacrilege were hurled to their death, and also to the Capitoline Hill, site of the great temple to Jupiter, Juno and Minerva (at 7. 2). Seneca has already paralleled the possession of everything by the gods with that by the Sage, at 3. 2 and 4. 6. He himself made use of paired syllogisms, albeit of a strictly Stoic character, in Book 5. 12–17.

(7.) 7. 3 sed non omnis dis dedicata; in iis observari sacrilegium (but not all things are dedicated to the gods; we note sacrilege in the case of things which religious observance has assigned to a divinity). *Res sacrae* are those things dedicated, under the authority of the Roman people, to the gods above. These legally belonged to the gods and were outside human ownership: theft of *res sacrae* was *sacrilegium*, not *furtum* (see Watson 1968, 1–5; Mommsen 1899, 760–2).

(7.) 7. 5–11. Seneca now rounds off his discussion of the paradox by reverting to the elementary teaching level of (7.) 1–3. Having established that the Sage can be given gifts though he has all things, Seneca says the Sage would repudiate such gifts. He gives *exempla*: first a Roman general, the opposite of the greedy Alexander of 2. 5–3. 1; then philosophers, among whom he singles out Demetrius, who is now shown, not only preaching against luxury and greed, but living up to what he says and repudiating a gift from the Emperor Caligula, even if he offered his empire (greater than Alexander's). What he was given by providence, however, his skill in preaching and his way of life, make him an example comparable to the Sage.

(7.) 7. 5 illam vocem quam Romanus imperator emisit (that famous statement, which the Roman commander uttered). The Roman general is M'. Curius Dentatus, a Roman general of the third century BC, renowned for incorruptibility in his dealing with the Samnites and King Pyrrhus, whom he defeated. Valerius Maximus 4. 3. 5b reports that he was offered 50 iugera of land but accepted only the 7 offered to each citizen. He and Pliny, *HN* 18. 18 attribute to him different versions of the remark here. Lipsius, to explain why Seneca says that the offer was of as much land as he could have covered in a day of ploughing, when two iugera was considered what a pair of oxen could plough daily, points out that he speaks of a day's circuit of the land (*quantum arando uno die circumire potuisset*).

(7). 8. 1 cum ad hoc ius cotidianum, si ita res tulerit, capite censebitur (when (we look to) the mundane legal situation, if he has to be assessed, it will be in the lowest census category). The *capite censi*, the largest class of Roman citizens enrolled by the censors, were registered as having no property, and all voted in one century of the 193 that made up the timocratic assembly, the *comitia centuriata*.

(7.) 8. 2 nec illum a nobis corrumpi nec nos ab illo corripi posse (that he could not be corrupted by us, any more than we could be castigated by him). Like Lipsius, Alexander 1950–2*a*, 40 rightly rejects Gruter's reading *corrigi* for *corripi*, which Préchac 1961 ad loc. adopts. The infinitives parallel the two providential functions in 8. 3: being an example of incorruptibility, and being a castigator of vice (however unheard).

virum exactae, licet neget ipse, sapientiae (a man of superb wisdom, though he might disclaim it). Cf. *Vit. beat*.18. 3: 'Demetrius claimed, not a knowledge of virtue, but (merely) of poverty' (see Griffin 1992, 516–17 and **ad 2. 17. 2**).

(7.) 9. 1 quoniam multa video, quae me donare non deceat (since I see many things that it would not befit me to give). In making Demetrius say he would not accept wealth from the gods, even if he could give it away, when he has just said himself (8. 3) that Demetrius would refuse it, if he could not give it away, Seneca highlights the hyperbole of the Cynic's kind of discourse.

(7.) 9. 2 ipsa illa, quae placet, varietas subditis medicamentis in similitudinem veri coloratur (the variegated colours which please the eye are themselves tinted with dyes applied to make them look real). Pliny, *HN* 16. 233 says that it was in Nero's reign that painting tortoiseshell so as to resemble fancy woods, such as citrus and maple, was devised.

mensas et aestimatum lignum senatorio censu (tables made of wood worth as much as the senatorial census qualification). The senatorial census was set by Augustus at 1,000,000 HS. Pliny, *HN* 13. 92 says that Asinius Gallus paid that for a citrus wood table, and that Cicero paid half that for one: he discusses the value of different markings at 13. 96–7.

(7.) 10. 3 diplomata et syngraphas et cautiones, vacua habendi simulacra (certificates of privilege, bonds, and written guarantees, vain images of ownership). These are all documents that are worth money to the possessor of them: *diplomata* are instructions given by the Emperor which allow the bearer to exact free transport and lodging; *syngraphae* are written IOUs, and *cautiones* are written versions of *stipulationes* (see **ad 3. 7. 7**). They are regarded as unnatural objects of desire since, like the paper records listed next and unlike the metals mentioned before, they have no physical attractiveness, visual or tactile (10. 4).

(7.) 10. 5 vasta spatia terrarum colenda per vinctos (the huge estates tilled by men in chains). Chained slaves were agricultural slaves; the large *familia* mentioned just below is composed of household slaves. It was normally criminal slaves who were kept chained and lived in *ergastula* (Col. *RR* 1. 6. 3.; 1. 9. 4; 1. 8. 16; Suet. *Aug.* 32). Like Seneca, Roman writers were critical of their use (Pliny, *HN* 18. 21, 36; Col. *RR* 1. 9. 5), and the younger Pliny claims that he never used chained slaves, and that they were not used in the neighbourhood of his estates in Tuscany (*Ep.* 3. 19. 7). They presented serious security problems.

(7.) 10. 6 ego sic omnia habeo ut omnium sunt (I have all things just in the sense that they belong to everyone). Since the contrast is with material possessions, Seneca probably means here what he means in *Ep.* 73. 7 where he says that the Sage regards as peculiarly his, those things that he shares with all mankind, things such as peace and liberty, which belong to all men, and to each without division. But at *Ep.* 62. 3 he says that Demetrius goes beyond wanting nothing (hence having everything): he lives as if he had handed everything over to others.

7. 11. 1 ridens reiecit ne dignam quidem summam iudicans, qua non accepta gloriaretur (laughing he refused it, thinking that it was not even worth boasting about rejecting that amount). Philosophers, especially Cynics, feature in anecdotes where they confront tyrants, like Diogenes *versus* Alexander (e.g. 5. 4. 4). Here we are not told what Demetrius actually said to Gaius, though the laughter hints at Cynic freedom of speech (cf. Epict. 1. 25. 22 on his retort to Nero). At 2. 17. 1–2 it is the rich ruler, not the Cynic, who comments on what size gift would be suitable.

(7.) 12–13. Seneca turns to the second contradiction adduced by the objector at 4. 1: that between the idea that friends have all things in common, and the possibility of giving a friend something. As with the first, the solution turns on distinguishing different senses of ownership, entitlement, and belonging: a thing can belong to both friends in one sense, and still be the private property of one of them, so as to be available as a gift to the other.

There is a lacuna of uncertain length at the start of 13, and Muretus already pointed out that a different question seemed to be broached here, i.e. whether one *beneficium* can be greater than another. Abel 1987*a*, 28 = 1995, 70, like Préchac 1961, 90 n., proposed reversing 12 and 13, so that this discussion would follow on from Demetrius' reference to a possible larger gift than the one he was actually offered, and would lead, through the comparison of benevolence shown through benefits with love shown through kisses, to a *tertium comparationis*: namely, friendship shown through exchange of gifts. However, at 14. 1 Seneca implies (*quoque*) that the question just discussed was treated in earlier books; but that is true only of the question raised in 13 (see **ad (7.) 14. 1**), not of the discourse about friends having all things in common in 12, despite Préchac's attempts to find parallels. Moreover, the discussion of the first contradiction in 4–11 was all closely relevant, whereas, on this view, 13 would move to something remote from it. Possibly Seneca is still discussing friends having everything in common equally, but answers an objection that they can have unequal amounts, and hence confer unequal *beneficia*, by saying that their beneficent acts are equal; only the means of carrying them out are not.

(7.) 12. 1 quomodo cum socio, ut pars mea sit, pars illius (in the way that they are shared with a business partner, one part being mine, one part being his). The *societas* was a consensual contract to contribute property or work to the prosecution of a common legal aim. Each had to contribute, but not necessarily in equal amounts, and profit and loss was allocated according to agreement between the *socii*. At dissolution, the communal property was divided among the *socii*. Its historical origins, in archaic common ownership of family property by the heirs, coloured the arrangement which retained a 'familial atmosphere' (Crook 1967, 229–32). So it is natural for Seneca to compare its rules with friendship and parenthood. In *Ep.* 73. 8 he draws a similar contrast between the common property of partners and that belonging to the Sage and the human race, which cannot be distributed.

(7.) 12. 2 qui me in societatem vocat, sciat se nihil mecum habere commune (I shall now proceed to make anyone who offers to go into a partnership with me know that he shares nothing with me). Pursuing what it means for friends to have everything in common, Seneca turns to the Stoic idea that only Sages can perform social duties properly, because those who do not possess virtue cannot really treat others as themselves in a true friendship (D.L. 7. 124), or rule others with wisdom, or, as here, form partnerships based on justice and good faith (Cic. *Fin.* 3. 71, cf. Sen. *Ep.* 81. 12 on good faith being found only in the Sage).

ceteri non magis amici sunt quam socii (the rest are no more friends than they are partners). As the context shows, the terms of the comparison are reversed, as often in Seneca, see **ad 1. 13. 3.**

(7.) 12. 3 equestria omnium equitum Romanorum sunt; in illis tamen meus fit proprius locus, quem occupavi (equestrian seating belongs to all Roman *equites*, but among those seats there is still one that is mine, the one that I have occupied). Cicero at *Fin.* 3. 67 apparently attributes to Chrysippus (credited with an opinion just above) a similar argument about communal property being compatible with private, using the comparison of the theatre (cf. Epict. 2. 4. 9–10 who uses the comparison in talking about marriage and adultery). But here the comparison is made, not via the public ownership of the theatre but via the rights of a particular group in the theatre: the Lex Roscia of 67 BC had reserved the first fourteen rows behind the orchestra to those assigned to the equestrian order by the censors, so these seats belonged to all of the *equites*. Seneca's point is that a friend can give a gift to a friend, even though their friendship gives them a claim on what belongs to each, just as it would count as generosity to give up one's seat to another *eques* (presumably because the equestrian rows in the theatre are full, 12.4) even though both hold that privilege in common. He may have changed the analogy from all seats in the theatre to seats reserved to *equites*, because the true friends who alone have all things in common are a restricted and limited élite, like the *equites* (Brunt 2013, ch. 2, §§ 28 with n. 37, 33 against Erskine 1990, 106–9), or because equestrian seating was a topical issue: in AD 63 Nero provided the *equites* with special seats in the Circus Maximus as well (Tac. *Ann.* 15. 32; Suet. *Nero* 11; Plin. *HN* 8. 21), and even if the change was later than the composition of *De beneficiis* (see Ch. 4), there will have been discussion of the issue shortly before.

(7.) 13 beneficium maius esse non potest (a benefit cannot be greater (than it is)). Since it is (1. 5. 3) a *recte factum (katorthōma)*, and the Stoics allowed no degrees of virtue and vice (*SVF* iii. 524–6, 528). At 1. 7. 1–3, distinguishing the things given from the generous act, which is the true *beneficium*, Seneca said that the latter does not become greater when the former increase, but he allows that the manner in which benefits are actually bestowed by *imperfecti* (cf. 17. 1) generates different degrees of gratitude.

(7.) 14–16. 4. Seneca's next *quaestio infinita*, 'whether someone who has made every effort to return a benefit has in fact returned it', is, like the two posed at

4. 1, concerned with *cognitio* and belongs to the subdivision *quid sit* about definition. The discussion clarifies the meaning of returning a benefit, by building
on the distinctions established earlier at 1. 5 and 2. 34. 4–35. 1 between *beneficium* as a well-intentioned act of generosity and *beneficium* as the actual gift or
service bestowed: in the first, its principal meaning, a *beneficium* is recipro-
cated by gratitude alone. But, as in the discussion in Book 2 of the Stoic paradox, 'Who receives a benefit gladly has returned it', Seneca admits that the
receiver should persevere in trying to make repayment eventually. There, this
was a concession to ordinary language and social habit (**ad 2. 35. 5**); here, the
demand is stronger, because the emphasis is on the public good, which requires
that ingratitude be discouraged (just as there, it was the paradox itself that was
to deter over-reluctance to accept favours). Seneca is always concerned to keep
the social process of exchange of benefits going, and he regards philosophical
teaching, like the law (16. 2–3), as one way of doing that.

(7)**14. 1 haec quoque, quae venit, quaestio profligata est in prioribus** (the next question too has largely been dealt with in previous books). The main discussion of the
previous question was in Book 1. 5–7; the question about to be discussed in 14–16 was
treated in 2. 31–5 (especially 2. 34. 1) and 4. 40. 1–3, with related topics in 5. 4–6 and 6.
27. 2, 29, 43. The remark points to a connection between the two questions, for in both,
the distinction between the act of giving, and what is given, is crucial (**ad 2. 31–5**).

(7.) **14. 3 quidam eius condicionis sunt ut effectum praestare debeant; quibusdam
pro effectu est omnia temptasse, ut efficerent** (some people are in a role that requires
them to achieve a successful outcome; for others, making every effort to succeed counts
as success). Alexander 1950–2*a*, 41 rightly prefers the suggestion *quidam* by Gertz
1876 to the MSS' *quaedam*, accepted by Hosius, because Seneca's examples are all
personal nouns. Indeed, in his earlier discussion in Book 2. 31–3 Seneca considered a
similar point about the donor's success in achieving what he intended, using a personal
subject, and at 2. 32. 2–3 he compared the receiver of a benefit to a player who is deemed
a good player even if circumstances prevented him from returning the ball, while the
game itself is considered to be damaged.

laus imperatoria etiam victo duci redditur (praise for his generalship is given, even if he
is defeated in battle). In *Ep.* 85. 31–2 Seneca admits that, although these practitioners of
the arts (there exemplified by a pilot) are deemed just as skilful, if circumstances beyond
their control cause them not to carry out their purpose, their work is still damaged.

(7.) **14. 5 debitoris exemplum dissimile est** (the case of the debtor is different). Seneca
answers the second objection raised at 14. 2. Seneca made the same point at 2. 34. 1. For
a benefit, repayment is in the intention; for a debt, it is the payment that counts. At 16.
3 he defends the legal position about debt on the grounds that the good of society
demands that *fides* must be preserved. The quotation is from Virgil, *Aen.* 6. 85.

(7.) **14. 6 iniquus es, si rem a me exigis, cum videas animum non defuisse** (you are
being unjust if you demand concrete repayment, when you can see that my intentions
have not been wanting). The declaimers too use the argument that it is the *animus* of

the receiver who fails to return that determines if he is ungrateful or not (Elder Sen. *Controv.* 2. 5. 10).

(7.) **15. 1 hieme tum saeva** (the winter then being harsh). Alexander 1950–2*a*, 41 rightly accepts Castiglioni's conjecture of *tum* for the MSS' *tam*. Seneca emphasizes the fact that the would-be rescuer does not delay, although the season is perilous for sailing.

(7.) **15. 2 at mehercules Athenienses Harmodium et Aristogitonem tyrannicidas vocant** (but, by god, the Athenians refer to Harmodius and Aristogiton as tyrannicides!). Seneca agrees with Thucydides 1. 20; 6. 53–9 that in 514 BC Harmodius and Aristogiton only killed Hipparchus, brother of the actual tyrant Hippias, who ruled for three more years.

Mucio manus in hostili ara relicta instar occisi Porsinae fuit (the hand which Mucius left behind on the altar of the enemy was as good as Porsenna's death). According to Livy 2. 12–13, when the Etruscan king Lars Porsenna was besieging Rome in the fifth century BC, Gaius Mucius sneaked into his camp and attempted to kill him. Porsenna ordered Mucius, when captured, to be cast into the flames, an act Mucius pre-empted by thrusting his hand into that same fire and giving no sign of pain. See Biographical Notes.

(7.) **15. 3 'duas', inquit, 'res ille tibi praestitit, voluntatem et rem; tu quoque illi duas debes'** (an objection is made, 'He provided you with two things, his willingness and the property. And so you owe him two things'). Cf. 2. 34. 5–35, where Seneca concedes this point, as he is to do at (7.) 16. 1–2.

(7.) **15. 5 quare non eo adversus hominem gratus sim, quo nihil amplius in deos confero?** (why should I not be considered grateful to a human being, when I do not offer anything more to the gods?). At (7.) 4. 6 Seneca admitted that we do offer gifts to the gods, but at 4. 32–3 he emphasized that the gods can derive no advantage from us, since they need nothing. So the gifts are tokens of gratitude, not real returns (4. 25. 1–2), or they are acknowledgements of the gods' existence and goodness (*Ep.* 95. 50).

(7.) **16. 1 si tamen quaeris, quid sentiam, et vis signare responsum** (but if you ask me what I think and want my opinion signed and sealed). As elsewhere, Seneca compares himself to a jurisconsult 'laying down the law' without argument and debate (**ad 5. 19. 8**). According to Pomponius (*Dig.* 1. 2. 2. 49), whereas previously anyone with confidence in his learning gave legal responses to judges or clients who requested them, and not under seal, Augustus laid down that *responsa* were to be given with his authority and under seal, to safeguard their authenticity (Jolowicz and Nicholas 1972, 359–60). According to Ducos 1991, 110, Seneca is the only writer to mention this practice of *responsa signata*.

(7.) **16. 3 nullam excusationem receperunt, ut homines scirent fidem utique praestandam** (they made no provision for excuses, so that people should know that one must always maintain good faith). Aulus Gellius (*NA* 20. 1) invents a dialogue between the sophist Favorinus of Arles and the Roman jurist Sextus Caecilius Africanus in the mid-second century, in which Favorinus attacks the XII Tables for, among other things, cruelty to debtors (20. 1. 19). Caecilius, perhaps giving the view of the earlier jurist Antistius Labeo (Holford-Strevens 2003, 127–9), justifies the obsolete punishment of cutting up and dividing a debtor's body among his creditors by the need to protect *fides*, particularly in borrowing money, because the necessary help would not be forthcoming if debtors broke faith and were lightly punished (20. 1. 39–49). He also claims that the deterrent to perfidy worked, as no one was actually punished in this way (20. 1. 50–2). Even after execution against the property of debtors and, later, *cessio bonorum*, a form of restricted bankruptcy, were introduced, Roman law only admitted any limitation of the debtor's liability in very exceptional cases (Poste and Whittuck 1904, 308–9). As for losses through accident, mentioned here, Ducos 1991, 116 points out that Seneca may have known of Claudius' decision to help corn merchants who suffered loss from winter storms (Suet. *Claud.* 18. 2).

(7.) 16. 5–21. Seneca's penultimate *quaestio infinita*, is, like the previous one, concerned with returning benefits, but is in form a practical one aimed at action and concerned with *officium*, i.e. whether one should make return to a Sage who has become a bad man. It is linked (*ideo*) to the previous discussion, where beneficiaries have been urged to go on trying to make a material return to a benefactor, even if he is bad, in the sense of not appreciating your unsuccessful but energetic efforts to repay. The consideration of the first case here (16. 5–19. 4), where the Sage has become a non-Sage and therefore a fool, is highly theoretical, involving definitions of *beneficium* and *reddere* and introducing the idea that our decisions on returning a benefit should be based on different criteria for assessing the recipient, from those used for determining to whom we should give in the first place (18. 2; 20. 5 *fin.*): Seneca's way of treating the return of *beneficia* in Book 3 left such questions undiscussed (see p. 116). The second case (19. 5–20. 4), where the change in the Sage has been more drastic, raises questions of obligations to society in practising beneficence. At the end Seneca returns to the second type of *beneficium* distinguished earlier in 17, the ordinary exchange by imperfect men; the emphasis is now on the ordinary moral obligation to return a benefit, which leads, in 22–5, to consideration of the contrasting obligations of benefactors and beneficiaries.

(7.) 16. 5 redderes enim et depositum quod a sapiente accepisses; etiam malo redderes creditum (for you would return a deposit that you had received from a Sage; even to a bad man, you would return a loan). The punctuation of Préchac 1961 and Alexander 1950–2a ad loc. rightly makes clear that the following *etiam malo* goes with *redderes creditum.* The comparison with the deposit is problematic, as it recalls Plato's famous example of not returning a deposited sword to a madman who might hurt himself (*Resp.* 1. 331 c–332 a), adopted by Seneca himself at 4. 10. 1–2, where, however, the comparison with conferring benefits is used to urge flexibility. In fact, repaying a benefit is different, since one does not return the same object one received and thus can find one that benefits the donor (20. 1–3).

(7.) 17. 1 duo sunt beneficia (there are two kinds of benefit). Seneca here makes a different distinction from his usual one, between *beneficium* as an act and *beneficium* as the thing given. Now he distinguishes between the act when performed by the Sage, and that performed by imperfect men. The first kind, the *katorthōma*, can only be performed by the Sage: hence the Stoic paradox that only the Sage really knows how to confer or return a benefit (*Ep.* 81. 10), or indeed how to receive it. The other is, strictly speaking, a *hamartēma*, because it is not done by the Sage, though both are, at the level of types, *kathēkonta*, types of action that have a rational justification (see Ch. 7 nn. 20, 65). Stoic redefinitions occur throughout the work, e.g. 1. 5–7; 4. 26–7; 5. 13–15, their rationale being explained at 2. 34. 2–35. 3: they ensure the teaching a greater impact, but ordinary usage is accommodated.

(7.) 18. 1 quid, si me remittere manco pilam iubeas? (what would happen if you urged me to return a ball to a man who had lost his hand?). Seneca returns to Chrysippus' metaphor of ball-playing for the exchange of benefits, which carries, at 2. 17, a lesson in giving, and at 2. 32, as here, a lesson for receiving and returning.

(7.) 18. 2 non dabo ulli, quod accipere non poterit; reddam, etiam si recipere non poterit (I will not *give* to anyone something that he cannot receive; I will, however, *return* it even if he cannot receive it). At 4. 26. 3 Seneca justifies giving benefits to ordinary imperfect people, because otherwise there would be no one to give to, whereas here he only seems to approve of returning benefits to such people (but see **ad (7.) 20. 5**), and his justification is that one should not profit from another's wickedness ((7.) 20. 5).

(7.) 19. 2 reddere est id, quod debeas, ei cuius est, volenti dare (to repay something is to give back what you owe to the person it belongs to, if that person wants it). Seneca refines the interlocutor's definition at 19. 1 in two respects: (*a*) he spells out that the thing is repaid to the person to whom it belongs, and (*b*) he replaces the idea that it goes to a person who will receive it, with the idea that it goes to a person who is willing to have it returned (though he may not in fact receive it).

(7.) 19. 2 non tutelam illi, sed fidem debeo (I owe him good faith, not the services of a guardian). *In fidem tutelamque* (or in the dative) is such a standard phrase that putting the two terms in antithesis has the force of a paradox (see Malaspina 2001, 241 ad *Clem.* 1. 1. 5).

(7.) 19. 3 si nummos quos accipiet, in sinum suum discinctus infundet (if he puts the coins he receives into the fold of his toga and then does not cinch his toga at the waist). Seneca expresses the returner's lack of responsibility for whether or not his creditor actually gains by the return, with three examples: the creditor who wastes it on gluttony; the creditor who has it given directly to his lover; the creditor who loses it through carelessness (see **ad 2. 16. 2 ut congiaria tua** for *sinus*).

beneficii accepti, non redditi, custodiam debeo (what I owe him is guardianship of the benefit that I received, not the one that I repaid). Seneca may be using a legal metaphor here, as so often. In contracts for loans, deposits, and pledges of security, the recipient had a duty of care which could make him liable for loss or damage. *Custodia* was liability, irrespective of fault, for loss not caused by superior force or 'acts of God' (Nicholas 1962, 170).

(7.) 19. 4 reddo illi quale nunc potest recipere (I return to him the sort of thing that he is now capable of receiving). The Sage who has become bad can no longer receive a true benefit, because he has lost the knowledge of how to use it (18. 1). In 5. 12. 3–13 Seneca explained why a bad man cannot receive a true benefit but can receive 'goods' of fortune that he regards as benefits.

(7.) 19. 5 sed ferus, sed immanis quidem, qualis Apollodorus aut Phalaris (but a veritable wild beast, a monster, like Apollodorus or Phalaris). Phalaris of Agrigentum in the sixth century BC is often cited as an example of cruelty; Apollodorus of Cassandrea in Macedonia in the third century is cited less often (e.g. *Ira* 2. 5; cf. *Clem.* 2. 4. 3; *Ep.* 66. 18).

numquam tantum virtus extinguitur ut non certiores animo notas imprimat quam ut illas eradat ulla mutatio (virtue is never so thoroughly snuffed out that it does not leave behind some marks on the mind which are too fixed to be erased by any change of character). Cleanthes maintained that virtue could not be lost, but Chrysippus said that it could, through madness, drunkenness, or the effects of drugs, which are outside even the Sage's control (*SVF* iii. 237–9; D.L. 7. 127, 128). But, according to Simplicius, though the 'whole rational disposition is lost', vice does not ensue: rather, the Sage reverts to an intermediate disposition which 'seems to be analogous to that state of the aspirant to virtue who has not quite made the grade' (Rist 1969, 16–17). Hence at 19. 4, Seneca envisages the possibility that he may be restored to wisdom. His contemplation of the Sage turned tyrannical monster is thus purely hypothetical.

(7.) 19. 6 tantumque a placidissimis absunt, quantum a veris feris (they are as far removed from the tamest beasts as they are from really wild beasts). As the context shows, the terms of the comparison are reversed, as often in Seneca, see **ad 1. 13. 3**.

(7.) 19. 7 Phalarim et \<alterum\> tyrannum (Phalaris and another tyrant). The addition is by Hosius. Phalaris being the archetypal tyrant, it would be odd to say, as the MSS do, 'Phalaris and a tyrant', but the more obscure Apollodorus (**ad (7.) 19. 5**) could well be described as just some other tyrant. The reference below to roasting (19. 8) will refer to Phalaris' burning his enemies in a brazen bull.

ne quid mihi cum illo iuris sit amplius (that there may be no further bond between him and me). Seneca makes more explicit what he has suggested before (17. 2 *fin.*; 18. 2), that repaying a benefit to a man who has become bad merely frees the beneficiary from obligation. At 2. 18. 5 Seneca said that, unlike repayment to a creditor, which simply frees one from further obligation, repayment of a benefit continues the bond of friendship and commits one to conferring other benefits on one's benefactor. He gives as exceptions compulsion from a tyrant (2. 18. 6–7), not applicable here as the tyrant's evil intentions have not yet issued in action, or having one's life saved by an immoral person, where the benefit counts merely as a loan (2. 21. 1–2). Presumably, the change of nature by the benefactor into an ex-Sage permits a similar interpretation of his benefit here, the rationale being that he cannot now receive in return the kind of *beneficium* that he gave (18. 1; 19. 4), only an inferior kind, so that the *beneficiorum sacratissimum ius* of 2. 18. 5 has been broken.

(7.) 19. 8 quidquid erat, quo mihi cohaereret, intercisa iuris humani societas abscidit (whatever there once was that connected him to me has been severed by the breaking of our bond of shared humanity). Cf. *Ira* 2. 5. 3 on anger expelling *omne foedus humanum* (every sense of human solidarity) from the mind of the tyrant. As Cicero points out (*Off.* 3. 19, 32), since the bonds of humanity do not exist with tyrants, it is, exceptionally, a duty to rob or kill them and amputate them from human society. Cicero is particularly concerned to justify Caesar's murder. Here Seneca spells out that, even if one's own country is not affected, the tyrant's behaviour in his own cancels any bond his benefit may have forged with me and justifies punishment.

(7.) 20. 3 **si ex toto desperata eius sanitas fuerit eadem manu beneficium omnibus dabo, illi reddam** (if there is no hope whatsoever for his sanity, then with the same hand I will return the favour to him and confer a benefit on everyone). Seneca clearly means tyrannicide, which frees the tyrant from wrongdoing with a stroke of the hand, as comparison with *De ira* 1. 6. 3; 1. 15–16 shows. Seneca no doubt has in mind Plato *Gorgias* 473–80, 525 B. The sentiment is ascribed by the ancient sources to a member of the Pisonian conspiracy to assassinate Nero in AD 65 (Tac. *Ann.* 15. 68. 1; Dio 62. 24. 2, cf. Suet. *Nero* 36. 2).

(7.) 20. 5 **diligenter istud excuterem, si non redderem, sed darem** (I would investigate that question with great care if I were giving a benefit to him, rather than returning one). Having previously approved only of returning benefits, not giving them, to such a man (18. 2, cf. 17. 2), Seneca is now not so categorical.

(7.) 21. 2 **misit poenas a se exigens improbae cupiditatis, ne alieno adsuesceret** (he punished himself for his unprincipled greed, so that he would not get used to being in debt). The example illustrates the point made in 20. 5 that it is not right to use the excuse of a benefactor's wickedness (or here death) to avoid repaying a benefit. The belief of the Pythagorean in metempsychosis only makes his action worse. The punishment he exacts from himself consists in repaying four denarii. This extreme case of the obligation to return a benefit, even when one cannot be asked for a return, leads on to the final discussions of how a benefactor is to deal with ingratitude.

(7.) 22–5. Having insisted at the end of the last two *quaestiones* (16. 1–4; 21. 2) on returning a benefit even in difficult and altered circumstances, Seneca now moves his focus to the benefactor and emphasizes his duty to forget his benefit, the first half of the maxim of popular morality that he has discussed before (**ad 1. 4. 5; 2. 10. 4 cum inter prima praecepta**) and modified at 5. 20. 7–25, a passage that exhibits considerable overlap with this discussion (**ad 5. 20. 6–25**). Seneca lays more stress here on the ingredient of candour in friendship, but what is particularly new is his interpretation of hyperbolic demands in general, as a pedagogic strategy that sets an impossibly high standard in order to achieve something sufficient and possible (cf. Cicero's explication of Stoic teaching in *Pro Murena* 65). By insisting on a light touch in reminding beneficiaries to repay, the hyperbole is being used to counter ingratitude and reluctance to return benefits (25. 2; 30. 1–2). The rationale behind Seneca's other favoured Stoic teaching instrument, the paradox (which also seems to offend our ordinary notions but ends up accommodating them) has already been explained in Book 2. 34. 2–35: to counter reluctance to receive benefits. As for countering reluctance to give, the conclusion to the work is devoted to that aim.

(7.) 22. 2 quidam enim beneficium, quod dederunt, omnibus circulis narrant (for there are some people who talk about the benefit they have given in every social gathering). See Lendon 1997, 71 on letters written to third parties accusing persons of ingratitude (e.g. Cic. *Fam.* 8. 12; *Att.* 8. 4).

(7.) 23. 1 quod non poterat fieri, dixit, ut crederetur, quantum plurimum posset (he described something that was impossible in order to communicate the notion 'as much as was possible'). Virgil, *Aen.* 12. 84 is describing Turnus' horses. Ovid, *Met.* 13. 801 gives Polyphemus this description of Galatea.

(7.) 23. 3 interveniat aliquando admonitio, sed verecunda, quae non poscat nec in ius vocet (there is sometimes room for a reminder, but a gentle one, one that does not demand or summon to court). As often, Seneca turns to legal terminology.

(7.) 24. 1 neminem poposcit, omnes admonuit (he demanded from no one, he reminded everyone). The example of Socrates illustrates tact in asking for repayment of benefits from friends, here presumably in return for teaching (cf. 5. 6. 3–6; 5. 7. 5 on Plato's gratitude): see **ad 1. 8. 1**. Von Albrecht 2004, 58 n. 3 cites this as an example of Socratic irony. Xenophon says he did not charge tuition fees (*Mem.* 1. 2. 60; 1. 6. 11–14).

(7.) 25. 1 Aristippus aliquando delectatus unguento (Aristippus once when savouring a perfume). A fuller version is given by D.L. 2. 76. The story is appropriate to Aristippus of Cyrene, founder of the hedonistic Cyrenaic school of philosophy.

beneficium ab eo repetam a quo petissem, qui alterius beneficii loco accepturus est potuisse reddere (I will seek repayment of a benefit from a person from whom I would have asked it in the first place, someone who will think of the opportunity to repay the first as being itself a second benefit). In 5. 22. 2 Seneca says that a gentle reminder to a friend is a second benefit, for it prevents him from being ungrateful. Here the ability to appreciate that point is a precondition for receiving such a reminder. Seneca has already explained that in choosing a benefactor we should apply even higher standards than in choosing a beneficiary (2. 18. 3), and that we should ideally choose a beneficiary who will be grateful. At (7.) 26 he turns to real ingrates.

(7.) 25. 2. Seneca finds in Dido's appeals to Aeneas in Virgil both a counter-example to (*Aen.* 4. 373–4) and a good example (*Aen.* 4. 317–18) of the correct way to give a reminder of benefits conferred, adding an imagined response by Aeneas to the latter appeal: a response that borrows from the former appeal and turns Dido's reproach into an admission of debt by Aeneas.

(7.) 26–32. The question with which Seneca chooses to conclude his work is a practical one dealing with *officium*, like the previous one (**ad (7.) 16. 5–21**), i.e. how we should deal with ingrates. Thus he returns to the opening concerns of the treatise: that improper giving leads to ingratitude, the worst of vices; that the proper attitude is that of the gods, who persist in giving to the ungrateful (on the symmetry of the beginning and end of the treatise, see pp. 118–19). But account is taken of the lessons learnt in beween: that ingratitude is the worst vice, because it disrupts social harmony (27. 3, cf. 4. 18), the important thing being the maintenance of the process of exchange (2. 17. 5; 2. 32. 3–4), which requires that the giver not be deterred by ingratitude, and that recipients not be deterred by the burden of repayment. The gentler and more realistic voice of Stoicism is heard in these chapters, in contrast to 3. 1. 1–5, as Seneca reminds benefactors that they too have been forgetful and ungrateful, and that memory loss is not all voluntary. Thus they should be more willing to pardon ingratitude in others and, more important, to try and overcome it by patience, gentle reminders, and kind treatment (28; 31. 1), whereas, in the early discussion of giving at 2. 10. 4–11. 3; 2. 17. 7, Seneca was urging forgetfulness on the donor and forbidding reminders (see **ad 5. 20. 6–25**). The form of the ending, 'a speech to deliver to oneself', regarded by Hutchinson 1993, 159 n. 23 as a 'less lofty but more search-ing form of ending' than 'the speeches by an august being that Seneca uses in *De Providentia, Ad Marciam*, and probably the *De Vita Beata*', suggests too that the reader is now ready to make these teachings his own.

(7.) 26. 2 semper illum paenitebit si te ne nunc quidem paenitet (it will always cause him regret, if it does not cause you regret even now). Seneca means that the ungrateful recipient will always feel regret for his ingratitude, if the donor refuses to regret his benefit even when it meets with ingratitude: see Kaster 2005, 179 n. 36.

(7.) 26. 3 alium turpis verecundia, ne, dum reddit, fateatur accepisse (another by a shameful sense of embarrassment that, by repaying a benefit, he will be admitting that he has received one). For being ashamed of accepting benefits, cf. 2. 23–4, 6. 40, and the famous remark of Cicero in *Off.* 2. 69 about fear of being labelled as a client.

(7.) 28. 2 sic factum est, ut praeceptoris tibi non esset ulla veneratio (that is how it has come about that you have no respect for your teacher). How terrible this is has been made clear in 6. 16–17, where Seneca discusses the veneration due to teachers for their devotion and friendship. Marcus Aurelius 1. 4–13 and Persius 5. 21–40 express grati-tude to their teachers, but the attachment of Epicurus' pupils show that the sentiment was not confined to Stoics.

sic evenit, ut circa consularia occupato comitia aut sacerdotiorum candidato quaes-turae suffragator excideret (this is how it has come about that when you campaign for election to the consulship or are a candidate for priesthoods you completely forget the man who supported you for the quaestorship). To illustrate the way that new benefits efface gratitude for older ones, Seneca uses the stages of the senatorial career. The quaestorship is the first office carrying membership of the senate. In 2. 27. 4 Seneca lists the tribunate and praetorship on the way to the consulship and second consulship. Here he mentions priesthoods after the consulship, a common progression, though not everyone had to wait that long. Though magistracies and priesthoods were effectively in the gift of the Princeps, whose recommendation counted in the senate's voting, formal election by the people, and cooptation by the members of the relevant priestly college, followed after. A *suffragator* who canvassed could act as an intermedi-ary with the Princeps or get out the senate vote. In *De ira* 3. 31. 2 Seneca also notes the expectation of more than one priesthood (and see **ad 4. 30. 2 sacerdotem non in uno collegio**). No one, except the Princeps, could hold more than one of the major priest-hoods: pontificate, augurate, quindecimvirate, epulones; but one of these could be combined with one of the newly created or revived priesthoods: *sodales Augustales, fetiales, fratres arvales* (Syme 1989).

(7.) 28. 3 nemo id esse, quod iam videtur, timet; deprenso pudor demitur (no one is afraid to be what he already seems to be. Once caught in the act, he loses his shame). Juvenal 6. 284–5 expresses the same idea, that being 'caught out' makes one feel less ashamed, in fact defiant. In this and the preceding two sentences Seneca uses *pudor* and *verecundia* as virtual synonyms, as often (Kaster 2005, 61).

(7.) 29. 1 inter consecrata beneficium est, etiam si male respondit, bene conlatum (but a benefit, if properly conferred, ranks among things offered up (to the gods), even if it turns out badly). Seneca compares benefits to offerings we make to the gods, who need no return (2. 30. 2; 4. 3. 2), ask for no return (4. 9. 1; 4. 25. 2), and confer benefits even on the ungrateful (4. 28. 1; (7.) 31. 2). Since we are supposed to imitate the gods (4. 25; (7.) 31. 2) conferring a benefit properly is a sacred thing, a kind of offering of gratitude to them.

(7.) 30. 1 saepe quod explicaris pertinacia, trahenti abruptum est (often what you will have unknotted by sticking to it gets broken off by you if you tug). Hosius gives *quod explicari pertinacia potuit, violentia trahentis abruptum est,* accepting two editorial additions: *potuit* and *violentia* (Haupt) between *pertinacia* and *trahentis.* Alexander 1950–2*a,* 44 prefers Buck's attempt to do without the additions, by reading *quod explicaris,* but he changes his punctuation and alters *trahentis* to *trahenti,* reading *explicaris pertinacia trahenti,* as followed here. Buck and Alexander suggest these are fragments of two iambic senarii from a drama.

(7.) 30. 2 nec desit <vox> (there will be no lack of <talk>). Hosius accepted Madvig's *dicere* for *desit,* the MS consensus. But either Rossbach's supplement (adopted here) or Alexander's *derit* (i.e. *deerit*) (1950–2*a,* 44) gives better sense.

(7.) 31. 3 alius illis obicit neclegentiam nostri, alius iniquitatem (one philosopher blames the gods for ignoring us, another blames them for their unfairness). Seneca speaks often in the treatise of the example of generosity provided by divine providence. At 1. 1. 9 he mentions neglect of the gods and sacrilege as forms of ingratitude, the latter including bad interpretations of their gifts. At 2. 29–30 he mentions human complaints about the plight of mankind, attributable to divine indifference and unfairness; at 4. 31–2, complaints about the gods' favours to the undeserving (unfairness); at 6. 20–4 complaints of their lack of intention to help us (indifference). At. 4. 4–8, 19. 1–3 he recounts the Epicureans' denial of providence and deems them ungrateful for not acknowledging their debt to the gods (1. 1. 9; 4. 6. 3; 4. 19. 3). For the benefits of the sun, also a god, see **ad 6. 20–4.** The view of the sun opposed here is that of Anaxagoras (D.L. 2. 8, 12).

(7.) 32. 2 perit mihi beneficium, iste hominibus (my benefit is being lost to me, but he is being lost to mankind). Seneca gives his reason for persevering in trying to convert the ungrateful by repeated generosity (a course he has recommended earlier, but not for this reason, see **ad 5. 1. 5**): he himself, at worst, is losing his benefit; but the ungrateful recipient is losing his place in human society, by not participating in the exchange process that cements it.

Biographical Notes on Persons
Mentioned in *De beneficiis*

Anonymous references are given in square brackets. References in bold are to the Notes to the Synopses.

ACHILLES, greatest of the Greek heroes, central character of Homer's *Iliad*: 4. 27. 2.

AEBUTIUS LIBERALIS, Roman *eques* from Lugdunum, the addressee of *De beneficiis* and mentioned in *Ep.* 91. 1, 3, 13 as grieved by the destruction of his city in the late summer of 64 (see Ch. 4): 1. 1. 1; 2. 1. 1; 2. 6. 1; 2. 30. 1; 3. 1. 1–2; 3. 5. 1; 4. 1. 1; 4. 3. 1; 4. 31. 1; [5. 1. 2]; 5. 1. 3–2. 1; [5. 12. 1]; 6. 1. 1; [6. 5. 3–5], 6. 6. 1; [6. 7. 1], 6. 12. 1; 6. 41. 1; 6. 42. 1; 7. 1. 1; [7. 17. 1].

AEMILIUS SCAURUS, MAMERCUS (COS. AD 21) was the last male member of that distinguished family. Despite his immoral habits, he was a renowned orator and advocate. He was twice prosecuted under Tiberius for treason, in 32 and 34, and committed suicide on the second occasion: 4. 31. 3.

AEMILIUS SCAURUS, MARCUS (COS. 115 BC) came from a patrician, but recently impoverished family. He worked his way up to becoming *princeps senatus* and married Caecilia Metella at a time when the Metelli were very prominent in politics. He was censor in 109 and was involved in many trials but was never convicted. Cicero said of him (*Font.* 24) that he 'almost ruled the world by his nod': 4. 31. 5.

AENEAS, son of Anchises and the goddess Venus, a Trojan hero, appearing in the *Iliad*, and the central character of Virgil's *Aeneid*. The episode of Aeneas carrying his father on the flight from Troy was often mentioned: 3. 37. 1; 6. 36.

AESCHINES, pupil of Socrates (see D.L. 2. 60–4), present at his trial and death, who wrote Socratic dialogues which survive only in fragments. His poverty led him to leave Athens for the court at Syracuse, from which he returned in 356 BC: 1. 8. 1–2.

AGRIPPA, see Vipsanius.

ALCIBIADES, son of Cleinias (451/0–404/3 BC), Athenian general and politician, rich and flamboyant aristocrat, who was a pupil and friend of Socrates, in which role he appears in Plato's *Symposium*: 1. 8. 2.

ALEXANDER III, THE GREAT (356–323 BC), king of Macedonia. His father Philip II had secured him Aristotle as his tutor. He conquered the Persian Empire and founded a great overseas empire including Egypt and areas of northwest India. He was a negative *exemplum* of pride and ambition for the Stoics: 1. 13; 2. 16. 1; 5. 4. 4; 5. 6. 1; 7. 2. 5–3. 1.

ALLOBROGICUS, see Fabius.

ANNAEUS SENECA, LUCIUS (*c*.4 BC–AD 65), author of *De beneficiis*. He was born in Corduba to Helvia and Lucius Annaeus Seneca, a wealthy equestrian of Italian stock and the later author of the *Controversiae* and *Suasoriae*. His elder brother was Annaeus Novatus (later L. Junius Gallio Annaeanus); his younger was Lucius Annaeus Mela, the father of the poet Lucan. In later life his wife was Pompeia Paulina, but he probably had an earlier wife by whom he had a son who died in AD 41. He entered the senate under Tiberius and was consul in 55 or 56, but his important political role under Nero was more informal, as *amicus principis*. He was ordered to commit suicide in AD 65, in the aftermath of the Pisonian conspiracy, having surrendered much of his wealth and retired to his chamber after the fire of July 64. For his background, see Ch. 1, and for his attempted retirement from court in AD 62, Ch. 3E: 4. 8. 3.

ANNIUS POLLIO, GAIUS (cos. suff. ann. inc., *PIR*² A 677). He was a consular when accused of treason in AD 32. The episode in *De beneficiis* should date to before the consulship of Mamercus Scaurus in AD 21: 4. 31. 4.

ANTIGONUS MONOPHTHALMOS (*c*.382–301 BC), Macedonian noble, general of Alexander the Great, for whom he governed Greater Phrygia. After Alexander's death he tried to reunite Alexander's kingdom. He and his son Demetrius Poliorcetes were welcomed in Athens and were proclaimed kings, but he was defeated and killed in the Battle of the Ipsus against rival generals including Cassander: 2. 17. 1; 3. 37. 3 with nn. **ad locc.**

ANTONIUS, MARCUS (Mark Antony) (cos. 44 BC, triumvir with Octavian and Lepidus 43), a partisan of Caesar against Pompey, he tried to restore harmony as consul after the dictator's death. He and his fellow triumvirs had leading Republicans killed in the proscriptions and then defeated Brutus and Cassius at Philippi in 42. With his consort Cleopatra, queen of Egypt, he was defeated by Octavian at the Battle of Actium in 31 BC: 2. 25. 1; 5. 16. 6; 6. 3. 1.

APOLLODORUS, tyrant of Cassandrea in Macedonia in the third century BC: 7. 19. 5; and see **ad 7. 19. 7.**

ARCESILAUS, of Pitane in Aeolia (316/15–242/1 BC), head of the Academy, known for introducing scepticism into Plato's school: 2. 10. 1; 2. 21. 4.

ARCHELAUS (413–399 BC), king of Macedonia, who gained the throne by murder and was eventually assassinated: 5. 6. 2, 6.

ARISTIDES, Athenian statesman of the fifth century BC, often called 'The Just' because of his reputation for honesty. He was a general at the Battle of Marathon in 490 BC and was archon in 489. A political enemy of Themistocles, he was ostracized in 482 but recalled on the eve of Xerxes' invasion and cooperated with Themistocles to win the Battle of Salamis in 480. He fixed the tribute for member states of the Delian League and died a poor man: 4. 27. 2.

ARISTIPPUS, traditionally the founder of the Cyrenaic school in the late fifth century BC, and a companion of Socrates. He taught that sensual pleasure was the proper aim of life and was known for his luxurious lifestyle. None of his writings survive: 7. 25. 1.

ARISTO, father of the philosopher Plato: 3. 32. 3.

ARISTOGITON. Plotted with his lover Harmodius to kill the Athenian tyrant Hippias at the Panathenaic festival in 514 BC. Thinking they were betrayed, they hastily killed his brother Hipparchus instead. Aristogiton was captured and tortured to identify his fellow conspirators. The tyranny of Hippias became harsher, and he was finally removed by the Spartans in 510. Despite the failure of their plot, both Aristogiton and Harmodius were celebrated as tyrannicides, and bronze statues of them were erected, and their tomb placed in the Ceramicus, where there were annual sacrifices to them: 7. 15. 2.

ARRHIDAEUS, see Philip.

ARRUNTIUS. Roman legacy-hunter, not otherwise identifiable. If *PIR*² is right to suggest that Haterius is a *nobilis*, then clearly Arruntius, who is paired with him, should also be one: 6. 38. 4.

ATILIUS REGULUS, MARCUS (cos. 267 BC). In his second consulship of 256 BC, he won victories in the First Punic War, but in spring 255 he was captured by the Carthaginians, and died in captivity, probably of natural causes. For the legend of his heroic return to captivity in Carthage, celebrated by Cicero in *De officiis* 3. 99–113 and by Horace in *Carm.* 3. 5, see **ad 5. 3. 2**.

AUGUSTUS (63 BC–AD 14), born C. Octavius, grand-nephew and heir of Julius Caesar. Victor of the battle of Actium against Antony, he became the first Princeps, who ruled Rome under the name Caesar Augustus 27 BC–AD 14. Seneca's assessment of him is generally favourable, but with reservations: 1. 15. 5; 2. 25. 1; 2. 27. 2; 3. 27. 1; 3. 32. 5; 6. 32. 1–4.

BION, of Borysthenes (Olbia) on the Black Sea (c. 335–c. 245 BC) is treated as an Academic by Diogenes Laertius (4. 46–58), since he studied in Athens at the Academy. He was also influenced by Crates the Cynic, Theodorus the Cyrenaic, and Theophrastus the Peripatetic. He was a popular itinerant teacher and writer but also used his debunking attitude in more technical types of argument. Fragments of his serio-comic writings are preserved in Teles and Diogenes Laertius: 7. 7. 1–2.

BRUTUS, see Junius.

CAESAR, see Julius.

CALLISTRATUS, Athenian orator and politician, noted for diplomatic offensives in the Peloponnese. After the loss of the battle of Mantinea in 362 BC and other Athenian mishaps, he was impeached and went into exile. Returning home and seeking sanctuary at the Altar of the Twelve Gods, he was executed: 6. 37. 1.

CAMBYSES, Persian king. The eldest son of Cyrus, he succeeded to the throne in 530 BC. He conquered Egypt, but died in 522, after leaving Egypt for Syria during the revolt of Smerdis: 7. 3. 1.

CAMILLUS, see Furius.

CANINIUS REBILUS, MARCUS (cos. suff. AD 37), possibly the great-grandson of the man whom Caesar the dictator made consul for a day in 45 BC. He is probably identical with the rich legal expert of dissolute sexual habits, who took his own life in AD 56 according to Tacitus *Ann.* 13 30, though the Codex Mediceus gives his name as 'G. Aminius Rebius'. On the death of C. Caninius Rebilus as the *terminus post quem* for *De beneficiis* see Ch. 4: 2. 21. 6.

CATILINA, see Sergius.

CATO, see Porcius.

CHRYSIPPUS (*c.*280–207 BC), Stoic philosopher from Soli in Cilicia who succeeded Cleanthes as third and greatest head of the Stoa. He came to Athens to study in the sceptical Academy, but then converted to Stoicism and defended it against the criticisms of the sceptic Arcesilaus. His voluminous writings made him the voice of orthodox Stoicism, but they have only survived in fragments, i.e. statements (often polemical) of his views and quotations from them. Seneca used his work *On the Emotions* for *De ira* and various of his works, critically, in *De beneficiis* (see Ch. 2A): 1. 3. 8–4. 5; 2. 17. 3; 2. 25. 3; 3. 22. 1; 7. 8. 2.

CINNA, see Cornelius.

CLAUDIUS (Tiberius Claudius Caesar Augustus), Emperor AD 41–54. The fourth Princeps at Rome, he was the first who was not directly descended by blood or adoption from Augustus, the founder of the Principate. When Caligula was assassinated, the Praetorian Guard produced him as the nearest relative, his mother Antonia having been the daughter of Augustus' sister Octavia, and his brother Germanicus the adopted grandson of Augustus. Because of his physical disabilities and his mental eccentricities, he had not had the military or political training normal for young male members of the imperial house, and his diligence and pedantic attention to detail were accompanied by political *naïveté* and susceptibility to manipulation by his wives (Messallina and then Agrippina) and freedmen secretaries, in appointments and jurisdiction. It was probably Agrippina who persuaded Claudius to ask that Seneca's life be spared when he was convicted by the senate on a charge of adultery in 41, and she was certainly instrumental in having him recalled from exile in Corsica in 49, after his transparent plea of 44 in the *Consolation to Polybius* (Claudius' freedman) was ignored. He had his revenge for the years of exile in the *Apocolocyntosis*: 1. 15. 5–6; [4. 32. 3], and see **ad 6. 19. 2**.

CLAUDIUS QUADRIGARIUS, QUINTUS, Roman annalist of the early first century BC who wrote a history of Rome in at least 23 books (now lost except for quotations by later writers), from the sack of Rome by the Gauls *c.*386 BC to his own times. The latest date preserved is 82 BC: 3. 23. 2.

CLEANTHES (331–232 BC), Stoic philosopher from Assos in the Troad, a student of Zeno, whom he succeeded as head of the Stoa. His religious spirit is shown in his *Hymn to Zeus*, which was often quoted. Seneca in *Ep.* 94. 4 reports his insistence that precepts are of little use, unless based on an understanding of basic principles: 5. 14. 1; 6. 11. 1; 6. 12. 2.

CORIOLANUS, see Marcius.

CORNELIUS CINNA, GNAEUS (cos. AD 5), grandson of Pompeius Magnus, said by Seneca (*Clem.* 1. 9, cf. Cass. Dio 55. 14–22) to have been pardoned by Augustus when detected as a conspirator: 4. 30. 2 with n. **ad loc.**

CORNELIUS LENTULUS, GNAEUS (cos. 14 BC), called 'augur' to distinguish him from Cn. Lentulus (cos. 18 BC). Rescued from poverty by Augustus, he governed a Balkan province, won a victory over the Getae, and became proconsul of Asia in 3–2 BC. He was a friend of Tiberius, whom he made his sole heir on his death in AD 25, after an abortive prosecution for treason: 2. 27. 1–2.

CORNELIUS SCIPIO AFRICANUS MAIOR, PUBLIUS (236–184/3 BC), hero of the Second Punic War. He fought under his father, who as consul in 218 BC was defeated at the Battle of Ticinus by Hannibal. After brilliant successes in Spain he was elected consul in 205, and finally invaded Africa, despite senatorial opposition. In 202 he defeated Hannibal at the Battle of Zama, for which he acquired the *cognomen* Africanus. Consul again in 194, he served under his brother Lucius, who was in command in the East, and was then implicated in his prosecution for misconduct in office and withdrew to Campania in 184, dying shortly after: 3. 33. 1–3; 5. 17. 2; 6. 36. 2.

CORNELIUS SULLA, LUCIUS (*c.*138–78 BC), dictator. When consul in 88 BC, he marched on Rome with his army in order to retain his command against Mithridates King of Pontus, with whom he concluded the Peace of Dardanus. He invaded Italy in 84, defeated his political enemy Marius, and became dictator in 82. He first carried out a proscription of his enemies, confiscating their property and denying them the protection of the law, then in 81 enacted a legislative programme designed to give an enlarged Senate political control. He gave up the dictatorship, held the consulship in 80, and then retired into private life in 79: 5. 16. 3.

CRISPUS PASSIENUS, see Sallustius.

[CURIUS DENTATUS, MANIUS (cos. 290, 284, 275, 274 BC), hero of the Third Samnite War and renowned for his frugality: 7. 7. 5.]

CYRUS (the Great), Persian king. Becoming king *c.*557 BC of a small kingdom in Persia, which was subject to the Median king, he proceeded to conquer Media, Lydia, Babylonia, and central Asia, where he died in 530. He thus established the very large Persian Empire and went on to provide an administrative system for it. Xenophon gave an idealized picture of him in the *Education of Cyrus*, a work well known at Rome: 7. 3. 1.

DECIUS MUS, PUBLIUS. The elder man of that name was consul in the Latin war of 340 BC, and the younger was consul in the Samnite War of 295 BC. They are both said to have vowed the sacrifice of the enemy and of themselves to the gods in return for Roman victory, and then plunged into the midst of battle to be killed (see Livy 8. 9. 1–10; 10. 28. 6–29. 5), an act of *devotio*: 4. 27. 2; 6. 36. 2.

DEMADES (*c.*380–319 BC), Athenian statesman and orator, who, after the battle of Chaeronea, took a realistic view of the power of Macedonia and tried to keep Athens out of trouble. On an embassy to Antipater he was executed by Cassander. He had received no formal training in rhetoric but had great natural talent: 6. 38. 1.

DEMARATUS, Eurypontid king of Sparta *c.*515–491 BC. He was dethroned on a false charge of illegitimacy, through the machinations of his Agiad fellow king Cleomenes, and fled to Darius. He accompanied Xerxes on his invasion of Greece in 480, warning in vain of the resistance the Greeks would put up and, after being proved right, was rewarded with three cities in the Troad: 6. 31. 4–12, with nn. **ad locc.**

DEMETRIUS, a Cynic philosopher admired by Seneca, who lived in Rome under Gaius, Nero, and Vespasian. Under Nero he is shown by Tacitus (*Ann.* 16. 34) discussing the nature of the soul with the Stoic senator Thrasea Paetus when the death order came in 66, and he was probably exiled to Greece. He returned in the reign of Vespasian, when he was criticized for defending the Stoic philosopher Egnatius Celer, who was accused of having given false testimony against his friend, the Stoic philosopher Barea Soranus. Vespasian subsequently deported Demetrius to an island for criticizing the regime: 7. 1. 3; 7. 2. 1; 7. 11; and see **ad 7. 1. 3–2. 1** and **7. 1. 3.**

DIOGENES (*c.*412/403?–*c.*324/321 BC), Cynic philosopher from Sinope on the Black Sea. A follower of Socrates' acolyte Antisthenes, he demonstrated his belief in living according to nature, his emphasis on self-sufficiency, and his rejection of social convention, education, and culture, by shocking behaviour, for which he was called a 'dog' (*kuōn*), from which the term Cynic derives. Anecdotes show him treating Alexander the Great with scorn: 5. 4. 3; 5. 6. 1, and see **ad 5. 4. 3 a Diogene.**

DOMITIUS AHENOBARBUS, LUCIUS (cos. 54 BC). Ancestor of Nero on the paternal side, he was an enemy of Caesar before and during the civil war with Pompey. After he and his son were pardoned by Caesar at Corfinium (Caesar, *BC* 1. 23), he fought again at Massilia and Pharsalus, where he was killed while trying to escape. For his behaviour at Corfinium, see **ad 3. 24.**

DORUS, probably a generic name for a bookseller: 7. 6. 1.

EPICURUS (341–270 BC), born on Samos to Athenian parents. He adopted the 'atomist' theory of Democritus. In 307/6 he moved to Athens, and his house with its garden became the headquarters of his school of philosophy, where he and his followers lived modestly, taking no part in politics. He taught that everything is composed of atoms and the void, that the gods exist but take no thought for us, and that the swerve of atoms somehow accounts for freedom of choice. His basic ethical tenet was that pleasure is the key to happiness, which was often misunderstood as a licence for self-indulgence, whereas in fact Epicurus approved natural and easily satisfied pleasures, particularly mental ones. Seneca eschewed his ethics and his theology but borrowed sayings from him, particularly in the *Letters to Lucilius*, acknowledging that some of these coincided with his own philosophy, though having a different doctrinal basis: 3. 4. 1; 4. 4. 1; 4. 19. 1.

EURYNOME, mother of the Graces: 1. 3. 9.

FABII, patrician clan. Kaeso Fabius Vibulanus (cos. 485 BC) is said to have led the clan to resist the soldiers of Veii at the Cremera in 477 BC: 306 men, of whom only one survived, according to the Roman annalistic tradition (Livy 2. 48–50; Diod. 11. 53. 6; DH *Ant.* 9. 20–2): 4. 30. 2; 5. 3. 2.

FABIUS MAXIMUS (ALLOBROGICUS), QUINTUS (cos. 121 BC). He subdued the tribe of the Allobroges in Transalpine Gaul, which became a Roman province, known under the Principate as Gallia Narbonensis: 4. 30. 2.

FABIUS MAXIMUS VERRUCOSUS, QUINTUS (cos. V 209; dict. 217 BC). After the Roman defeats by Hannibal at Trasimene (217 BC) and Cannae (216 BC), he brought about the

Carthaginian defeat in the Second Punic War by a campaign of attrition, attracting the nickname Cunctator ('Delayer'). At *De ira* 1. 11. 5 Seneca celebrates his achievement: 2. 7. 1; 4. 27. 2; 4. 30. 2.

FABIUS PERSICUS, PAULLUS (cos. AD 34), proconsul of Asia, probably between AD 51 and 54; called *amicus* by Claudius (**ad 4. 30. 2**). His cognomen may reflect descent from Aemilius Paullus who defeated Perseus, last king of Macedonia: 2. 21. 5; 4. 30. 2.

FURIUS CAMILLUS, MARCUS, consular tribune and dictator repeatedly in the fourth century BC. When faced with a large fine after being charged with peculation, he went into voluntary exile, probably in 391 BC (Livy 5. 32. 7–9 with Ogilvie 1965, 698–9). Seneca alludes to the story, probably fictional but preserved in Livy 5. 47–49. 7, that, when recalled as dictator the next year during the siege of Rome by the Gauls, he returned and prevented the Romans from paying a ransom to the Gauls, whom he then defeated in battle. For this he was hailed as 'Father of his Country' and 'Second Founder of Rome': 4. 27. 2; 5. 17. 2.

FURNIUS, GAIUS (cos. 17 BC). Having secured a pardon for his father, a partisan of Antonius, after the battle of Actium in 31 BC, he became a senator and fought the successful war against the Cantabrians for Augustus, as a commander in Spain *c*.22–19 BC: 2. 25. 1.

GAIUS CAESAR, the Emperor AD 37–41. He was the son of Germanicus whom the Emperor Tiberius had adopted, and was nicknamed Caligula or 'Little Boots' by the legionaries in Germany, where his father was proconsul. An anecdote in Cassius Dio (59. 19. 7) has Seneca in danger from Gaius, who envied his oratorical skill: certainly, Suetonius says Gaius criticized Seneca's written style as 'sand without lime' (Suet. *Calig.* 53. 2). As Emperor, he was renowned for arrogance and cruelty, which Seneca illustrates even more fully in *De ira* (1. 20. 7–9; 2. 33. 2–6; 3. 18. 3–19. 5) than in *De beneficiis*: 2. 12. 1; 2. 21. 5; 4. 31. 2; 7. 11. 1.

GERMANICUS, see Julius.

GRACCHUS, see Sempronius.

GRAECINUS, see Julius.

GRYLLUS, Athenian landowner, father of the historian Xenophon: 3. 32. 3.

HARMODIUS, the younger of the two Athenian 'tyrannicides', who was killed right after the assassination of Hipparchus (see under Aristogiton): 7. 15. 2.

HATERIUS, Roman legacy-hunter, not otherwise identifiable, though in *PIR*² H 23 it is suggested that he could be the son of Q. Haterius (cos. suff. 5 BC): 6.38. 4.

HECATO, Stoic philosopher from Rhodes, a pupil of Panaetius. Cicero attests a work *De officio* (*Peri kathēkontos*) in *De officiis* 3. 63 and 89, which is probably the work Seneca cites several times in *De beneficiis* (see pp. 15, 20–1): 1. 3. 9; 2. 18. 2; 2. 21. 4; 3. 18. 1; 6. 37. 1.

HERCULES, Italic pronunciation of the Greek name Heracles, the greatest of the Greek heroes. They were mortals who, after death, exercised power, not always benign, in a limited area. But Hercules was also regarded as a god. He had many adventures over a wide geographical area, including the 'twelve labours', and his cults were as widely dispersed: 1. 13; 4. 8. 1; 7. 3. 1.

HESIOD, Greek poet who lived in Boeotia, probably in the second half of the eighth century BC. His most notable works are the *Theogony*, on the relationships between the gods, and the *Works and Days*, on the farmer's life: 1. 3. 6, 10.

HOMER, the blind poet of the *Iliad* and the *Odyssey*, according to Greek tradition. The date of Homer, his birthplace, and the common authorship of both poems were disputed, even in ancient times. Their composition is usually dated to the eighth century BC: 1. 3. 7 and 10.

[JULIA (39 BC–AD 14), daughter of Augustus by Scribonia, married in 25 BC to Marcus Claudius Marcellus and in 21 BC to Marcus Vipsanius Agrippa (see below), to whom she bore Gaius and Lucius, both adopted by Augustus in 17 BC. When he died, she married Tiberius in 11 BC, but her infidelities continued and probably contributed to his withdrawal from Rome in 6 BC. Augustus had her divorced from Tiberius, punished her adulterers, and condemned her to banishment on the island of Pandateria (see **ad 6. 32. 1**) in 2 BC, sending a letter to the senate detailing her misdemeanours. In AD 4 she was allowed to move to Rhegium. In his will Augustus forbade her burial in his mausoleum. Tiberius stopped her allowance, and she died of malnutrition: 6. 32. 1.]

JULIUS CAESAR, GAIUS (100–44 BC), of a patrician family, he followed the *popularis ratio* in politics, opposing Sulla and the profiteers of the proscriptions, parading his family connection with Gaius Marius, voting against the execution without trial of the Catilinarian conspirators, and, in his consulship of 59 BC, collaborating with the tribune Vatinius to pass agrarian legislation. He also satisfied the needs of Pompey and Crassus, his partners in the coalition known as the 'first triumvirate', and secured for himself a five-year command in Gaul and Illyricum from the people. His command was extended in 55 by five years, and he completed the conquest of Gaul, but he was denied an extension of his command until he could legally stand for the consulship again, and, fearing a politically motivated prosecution, he marched on Rome in 49. He crossed the Rubicon, overran Italy, and forced Domitius Ahenobarbus (see above) to surrender at Corfinium. His old ally Pompey, who was leading the Republican forces, decided to leave Italy for Greece. Caesar defeated him at Pharsalus in Thessaly in 48, then conquered the Republican remnants in Africa at the battle of Thapsus in 46, and finally defeated the sons of Pompey in Spain at the battle of Munda in 45. He had been dictator briefly in 49 and then held repeated dictatorships and consulships until February 44, when he was made *dictator perpetuus*, i.e. without fixed term. He was planning to leave Rome for a campaign against the Parthians, when he was assassinated in the senate house, at the foot of Pompey's statue on 15 March 44. Whereas in *De ira* Seneca praised Caesar's clemency (2. 23. 4) and reproached those who repaid his generosity by killing him out of greed and envy (3. 30. 4), he omitted him in his later treatise *De clementia*, and in *De beneficiis* he is critical of his acquiring the power to pardon by ungratefully turning the armies entrusted to him against his own country: Brutus' part in the assassination, after Caesar had pardoned him, was not an act of ingratitude. He also blames him for not giving up power, like Sulla (see **ad 2. 20. 3 ius dandi** beneficii, and **ad 5. 16. 5 satiata tamen**). In the *Letters* Seneca follows up this charge of destroying the Republic (e.g. 94. 65; 104. 29–33): 2. 20; 3. 24. 1; [5. 16. 5]; 5. 24. 1–25. 1.

JULIUS CAESAR, GERMANICUS (15 BC–AD 19): He was the elder son of Nero Claudius Drusus, brother of the Emperor Tiberius, and of Antonia, and was the father of the Emperor Gaius, and eight other children, by his wife Agrippina. He was adopted by Tiberius in AD 4 before his own adoption by the Emperor Augustus, which placed him in the direct line of succession. He was a popular figure, whom Tiberius found hard to control. In his German command he tried to implement his dead father Drusus' original expansionist policy, which Augustus had put on hold after the Varus disaster. Tiberius sent him as proconsul with *maius imperium*, subordinate only to himself, to order affairs in the eastern provinces in AD 17, but he fell ill and died near Antioch, convinced that he had been poisoned by the legate of Syria, Cn. Calpurnius Piso. His death provoked demonstrations of grief: 4. 31. 2.

JULIUS GRAECINUS, LUCIUS, father of Cn. Julius Agricola, of whom Tacitus wrote a biography. As praetor under the Emperor Gaius, he refused to receive money to help with his games from disreputable senators. He died shortly after in AD 39 or 40, executed for refusing to prosecute Marcus Junius Silanus at the Emperor's behest (Tac. *Agric.* 4.1): 2. 21. 5.

JUNIUS BRUTUS, MARCUS (pr. 44 BC). Having fought for Pompey in the civil war, he was pardoned by Caesar after Pharsalus and received from the dictator the governorship of Cisalpine Gaul in 46–45 BC, the urban praetorship in 44 BC, and the promise of a consulship for 41. Unlike his father-in-law Cato, he was a follower of Antiochus of Ascalon, who founded the 'Old Academy'. He was one of the leaders of the conspiracy to kill the dictator: 2. 20.

JUPITER, king of the gods, identified with the Greek Zeus: 1. 3. 9; 1. 4. 4; 4. 7. 1.

LENTULUS, see Cornelius.

LIBER (PATER), Italian god of fertility, and of wine in particular; often identified, as by Seneca, with the Greek god Dionysus, adopted by the Romans as Bacchus, who was known for his travels: 1. 13. 2; 4. 8.1.

LIVIUS, TITUS (Livy) (*c.*59 BC–AD 17), from Patavium. He wrote a history of Rome from the foundation to 9 BC, in 142 books, of which we have only 1–10 and 21–45. He also wrote philosophical dialogues, which Seneca mentions in *Ep.* 100. 9: 7. 6. 1.

LIVIUS DRUSUS, MARCUS, tribune of the plebs 91 BC. Like his father, the tribune of 122 BC, who used *popularis* methods against C. Sempronius Gracchus, he defended the interests of the Senate by offering a programme that aimed to satisfy the grievances of various groups. He was murdered, and his legislation rescinded: 6. 34. 2.

LYNCEUS, one of the Argonauts who, in Greek legend, sailed with Jason, son of the King of Iolcus, to recover the Golden Fleece. Many of these heroes had supernatural powers, and Lynceus could see even beneath the earth: 4. 27. 3.

MAECENAS, GAIUS, one of the Emperor Augustus' earliest supporters. He remained an *eques*, his position resting on his friendship with the Emperor, for whom he went on diplomatic missions and served as an intermediary with poets like Virgil and Horace. With the neutral (Book 4) or sympathetic (Book 6) treatment Seneca gives him in *De beneficiis* we may compare the adverse criticism, in *De providentia* 3. 10–11 and *Epp.* 19. 9; 92. 35; 101. 10–11; 114. 4–8; 120. 19, of his literary style and the indulgent way of life that matched it, his good fortune undermining his ability: 4. 36. 2; 6. 32. 2–4 with nn. **ad loc.**

Manlius Capitolinus Imperiosus, Lucius, dictator in 363 BC. He was indicted for trial before the popular assembly by the tribune Marcus Pomponius in 362 BC on charges variously given in the sources, i.e. for prolonging his dictatorship beyond the legitimate time, for severity in conducting the levy, and for mistreating his son (which Seneca favours). His son (see below) forced the tribune to give up the prosecution: 3. 37. 4.

Manlius Torquatus Imperiosus, Titus (cos. 347, 344, 340 BC), son of the above, who saved his father from prosecution by threatening Pomponius and went on to acquire the name Torquatus by killing a Gaul in single combat and taking his torque as booty. In 340 BC he put his own son to death for disobeying his orders and engaging an enemy in single combat at Veseris: 3. 37. 4.

Marcius Coriolanus, Gnaeus, a successful Roman general of the fifth century BC who, when charged with tyrannical conduct, went into exile among the Volscians of Antium and became their leader against Rome. After capturing a number of Latin towns, he reached the gates of Rome but was persuaded by his wife and mother to turn back: 5. 16. 1.

Marius, Gaius (*c.*157–86 BC), seven times consul. Born in Arpinum of non-senatorial stock, he was related by marriage to Cicero's grandmother. He defeated Jugurtha and the Cimbri, but in his sixth consulship of 100 BC he joined with radical politicians, which led to a period of eclipse until, in 88, he tried to wrest the command against Mithridates from Sulla and became embroiled in civil war. He captured Rome in 86 and was ruthless to his enemies as consul with Cornelius Cinna, but died before he could take up the eastern command: 5. 16. 2.

Marius Nepos, Quintus, senator of praetorian rank in AD 15, when the Emperor Tiberius responded to his request for help with his debts by requiring him, along with others, to make his case for help to the senate. They all preferred to drop their requests, and in AD 17 Nepos was among the indebted and profligate senators ejected or allowed to withdraw from the senate (Tac. *Ann.* 2. 48. 3): 2. 7. 2.

Maro, one of the notorious informers under the Emperor Tiberius. It is suggested in *PIR*² M 409 that he may be identical with a C. Julius Maro of that period, known from inscriptions: 3. 26. 2.

Marsyas, a satyr who challenged Apollo to a competition of cithara-playing, lost, and was flayed alive. For his association in Rome with prostitution, see **ad 6. 32. 1 cotidianum ad Marsyam concursum.**

Mercury (Mercurius), identified with the Greek Hermes, the god of circulation of goods, people, and words: 1. 3. 7; 4. 8. 1.

Mucius Scaevola, Gaius. The story, preserved in Livy (2. 12–13. 5), is that, when the Etruscan king Lars Porsenna was besieging Rome in the fifth century BC, Gaius Mucius sneaked into the Etruscan camp and attempted to assassinate him, but mistook Porsenna's secretary for him. Mucius was captured and declared that he was one of three hundred other Romans willing to give their own lives to kill Porsenna. Porsenna ordered Mucius to be cast into the flames, an act Mucius pre-empted by thrusting his hand into that same fire and giving no sign of pain. Impressed by the youth's courage, Porsenna freed Mucius. Because of his maimed right hand, Mucius was for ever after known as *Scaevola* ('Lefty' or 'Left-Handed'). Since the burning of the right arm is the punishment for the breaking of an oath or pledge, the original story was probably about punishment for perjury and heroism in enduring it (see Ogilvie 1965, 262–3). According to Livy, he had informed the senate before going to the Etruscan camp, to avoid being taken for a deserter: 4. 27. 2; 7. 15. 2.

Octavian, see Augustus.

Octavius, Gaius, father of the Emperor Augustus. He came from a wealthy equestrian family of Velitrae, became praetor in 61 BC, and governed Macedonia the next year, with distinction. He died on his way home, before he could stand for the consulship. He fathered the later Emperor by his wife Atia: 3. 32. 5.

Onesicritus, Cynic philosopher and historian of Alexander, whose encomiastic approach provoked scepticism in antiquity. He was probably one of the sources of Arrian's *Anabasis*: 7. 2. 5.

Ovidius Naso, Publius (Ovid) (43 BC–AD 17), poet. Of an equestrian family, he refused the chance to become a senator. He was banished to Tomis on the Black Sea by Augustus in AD 8 because of the immorality of his poem *Ars Amatoria* and some involvement in a scandal concerning the imperial family. He was never recalled. His other works include the *Amores*, the *Heroides*, the *Metamorphoses*, and the *Fasti*. He expressed his misery in exile in the *Tristia* and the *Epistulae ex Ponto*. Seneca was clearly influenced by these works in writing the *Consolation to Polybius* from exile: 4. 14. 1.

Paulus, an ex-praetor, not otherwise identifiable, who narrowly escaped prosecution for *maiestas*, or treason, under the Emperor Tiberius: 3. 26. 1–2.

Pausanias, a nobleman from the westerly province of Orestis, who was one of Philip II's bodyguards and killed the king in 336 BC, at the wedding of his daughter Cleopatra to Alexander king of Epirus, allegedly out of revenge for bad treatment at the hands of Attalus, who was the uncle of Philip's new wife Eurydice. He was killed by the friends of Alexander the Great: 4. 37. 3.

Phalaris, tyrant of Agrigentum in the sixth century BC, renowned for his cruelty: 7. 19. 5, 7.

Phidias (active c.465–425 BC), Athenian sculptor, regarded as the greatest of Greek sculptors. He was best known for his ivory and gold statues of Athena Parthenos on the Acropolis and for the statue of Zeus at Olympia. A close friend of Pericles, Plutarch (*Per.* 31) reports that he was prosecuted for embezzlement and impiety: 2. 33. 2.

PHILIP II (382–336 BC), king of Macedonia, father by Olympias of Alexander the Great. He found the kingdom in low water, but through compromise and intrigue, as well as a newly trained citizen army, he greatly expanded his control to include Greece, winning a decisive battle at Chaeronea in 338 BC. Two years later he was murdered by Pausanias (see above): 4. 37–8.

PHILIP ARRHIDAEUS (357–317 BC), king of Macedonia, half-brother of Alexander the Great, who became king Philip III of Macedon in 323 BC, but was murdered in 317 by Alexander's mother Olympias who wanted his co-ruler, Alexander's posthumous son Alexander IV, to be sole ruler: 4. 31. 1.

PLATO (*c*.429–347 BC), pupil of Socrates and founder of the Academy in Athens. The most influential philosopher in western history, he raised in his dialogues fundamental questions of ethical and political theory, of epistemology, and of metaphysics. Seneca often cites him: 3. 32. 3; 4. 33. 1; 6. 11. 1–2; 6. 18. 1.

POMPEIUS, SEXTUS (cos. 35 BC), first cousin of Pompeius Magnus through his father Sextus Pompeius, the brother of Pompey's father. He was about sixty when he became consul, selected by the triumvirs Octavian, Antony, and Lepidus. His grandson of the same name was consul in AD 14, and helped on his way into exile the poet Ovid, who dedicated Book 4 of the *Epistulae ex Ponto* to him (Syme 1986, 414): 4. 30. 2.

POMPEIUS MAGNUS, GNAEUS (Pompey the Great) (106–48 BC), son of Gnaeus Pompeius Strabo (cos. 89), great Republican general. A military and political prodigy in youth, defeating Sulla's enemies in the 80s and fighting successfully in Spain in the 70s, he celebrated triumphs in 81 and in 71 BC and became consul with M. Licinius Crassus in 70, though under age and having held no previous magistracy. In 67 the Lex Gabinia entrusted him with an extraordinary command against the pirates all around the Mediterranean, and in 66 another tribunician measure, the Lex Manilia, gave him the command against Mithridates VI, king of Pontus, which resulted in an enormous increase in Rome's eastern empire. For that he held his third triumph in 62, but found that he faced opposition in trying to secure land on which to settle his veterans and to have his eastern arrangements ratified, so he supported Julius Caesar for the consulship of 59, taking his daughter Julia as his third wife. The third member of the coalition, known as 'the first triumvirate', that was to dominate politics for the next decade, was his old rival Crassus, with whom he held his second consulship in 55, while still retaining his curatorship of the corn supply. As consuls, they extended Caesar's command in Gaul for five years and secured for themselves five-year commands: in Spain for Pompey, and in Syria for Crassus, who was killed fighting the Parthians in 54. Pompey did not go to Spain but governed through legates. He became consul for the third time in 52, this time without a colleague, when his command in Spain was extended for another five years. Relations with Caesar had become strained, partly because of the death of Julia in 54. He now remarried and finally sided with the senatorial diehards, who refused to extend Caesar's command until he was eligible to hold the consulship again. He led the forces against Caesar, was defeated at Pharsalus, and was murdered as he attempted to land in Egypt: 5. 16. 4.

POMPEIUS PENNUS, senator maltreated by the Emperor Gaius: 2. 12. 1–2 with n. **ad loc**.

PORCIUS CATO, MARCUS (234–152 BC), known as the Elder Cato. He was the first in his family to hold a consulship (196 BC), and became known as 'Cato the Censor' for the energy with which he pursued moral reform as censor in 184. At the end of his life he was particularly associated with an uncompromising policy against Carthage. He was known for his vigorous defence of traditional Roman values and his lambasting style of oratory. He pioneered Latin prose literature, writing, among other works, letters of advice to his son; a history called the *Origines*, in which he omitted the names of generals and included some of his own speeches; and a treatise on agriculture, which alone survives. He was known for his pithy sayings, some of which were in the *carmen de moribus*: 5. 7. 5.

PORCIUS CATO, MARCUS (95–46 BC), known as the Younger Cato. Great-grandson of the above, he added Stoic convictions to the latter's moral rigour and sense of Roman tradition. As quaestor in 64 he put right the treasury records, and as tribune-elect in 63 he turned the senatorial debate against Caesar and helped Cicero secure a vote in favour of executing the Catilinarian conspirators. As tribune, he increased the numbers eligible to receive subsidized corn. He persistently opposed the actions of the 'first triumvirate', and in 58 he was appointed to carry out the annexation of Cyprus. Publius Vatinius defeated him for the praetorship of 54 through bribery, but he was elected to that office the next year. He stood for the consulship of 51 but was defeated. He joined Pompey's side in the civil war and, after his defeat, joined the Republicans in Africa. After Caesar's victory at Thapsus in 46 BC, as governor of Utica he organized the evacuation of the city, before committing suicide rather than recognize Caesar's right to pardon him. Seneca often mentions him with admiration for his Republican politics, as well as for his morals, notably in *De constantia Sapientis* 1. 3–2. 3, where the ingratitude of his contemporaries is again mentioned, and he is described as a better example of the Sage than the candidates of the Stoics, Ulysses and Hercules: 5. 17. 2.

PORSENNA, LARS, king of Clusium, one of the twelve cities of Etruria. The annalistic tradition has it that he besieged Rome, in an effort to restore Tarquinius Superbus to the throne, but, impressed by Roman acts of heroism (see above on Mucius Scaevola), he then withdrew and sent a force under his son Arruns to attack Aricia in Latium, where his son was killed. An alternative tradition (which Seneca clearly did not accept) has it that he captured Rome; in which case, the truth could be that he ended the monarchy: 5. 16. 5; 7. 15. 2.

PORSINA, see Porsenna.

RABIRIUS, GAIUS, an epic poet of the Augustan–Tiberian period, praised by Ovid, but not highly esteemed by Quintilian. His work is preserved only in fragments: 6. 3. 1.

REBILUS, see Caninius.

REGULUS, see Atilius.

RUTILIUS RUFUS, PUBLIUS (cos. 105 BC), Roman senator who studied with Panaetius and observed Stoic tenets, even in his austere style of oratory. He served as legate to Q. Mucius Scaevola (cos. 95 BC) when the latter was proconsul of Asia; he was unjustly condemned for extortion in 92 BC, after making an unemotional speech before a jury of *equites*: the jury was dominated by the *publicani* (tax-collectors), who resented the strict controls he and Scaevola had placed on their activities in Asia. He went into exile in Smyrna, and there he wrote a history of his own time: 5. 17. 2; 6. 37. 2.

SALLUSTIUS CRISPUS, GAIUS (*c*.86–35 BC), Roman historian. He came from Amiternum in the Sabine country and was the first of his family to enter the Roman senate. Tribune in 52, he was expelled from the senate by the censors in 50 for immorality and joined Caesar in the civil war. After serving as praetor in 46, he was appointed the first governor of the new province of Africa Nova, but was charged with financial malpractice on his return. He escaped trial, through the dictator's intervention, and retired from public life to write history. Two extant monographs, the *Bellum Catilinae* and the *Bellum Jugurthinum*, were followed by the *Histories*, covering events from 78 BC, possibly designed to continue the history by Cornelius Sisenna. Large fragments of that work survive. His style was highly influential, as is attested by Seneca himself, who speaks in *Ep.* 114. 17 of the resulting fashion for 'truncated epigrams, words finishing before expected, and obscure brevity': 4. 1. 1.

SALLUSTIUS CRISPUS PASSIENUS, GAIUS (cos. suff. AD 27; cos. II ord. 44), adopted son and heir of the wealthy Gaius Sallustius Crispus (great-nephew and adopted son of the above, and a confidante of Augustus). Born in the reign of Augustus, he entered the senate under Tiberius and, in the reign of Claudius, married and divorced Nero's aunt Domitia and then married Nero's mother, Iulia Agrippina. A gifted orator and wit, he was dead by the latter part of 47. *Epig.* 14 and 53, ascribed to Seneca, mention him as a loyal friend, and Seneca praises his shrewdness in judging character at *NQ* 4, pref. 6: 1. 15. 5.

SCAURUS, see Aemilius.

SCIPIO, see Cornelius.

SEMPRONIUS GRACCHUS, GAIUS, tribune of the plebs 123 and 122 BC. He and his brother Tiberius, sons of the famous general Tiberius Sempronius Gracchus (cos. 177 BC) and Cornelia, daughter of Scipio Africanus Maior, were both killed trying to implement radical reforms. Gaius not only renewed his brother's agrarian law redistributing some of the public land, but instituted corn subsidies and legislated for change in the collecting of provincial taxes, in the operations of the extortion court, and in the way the senate appointed provincial governors. This legislation survived his death. He died in a riot after failing to be elected to a third tribunate, when his proposal to enfranchise the Latins and give Latin status to the Italians was defeated by the elder M. Livius Drusus, tribune of 122 BC: 6. 34. 2.

SERGIUS CATILINA, LUCIUS, of a patrician family, had been a supporter of Sulla the dictator and was involved in carrying out the proscriptions. Praetor in 68 BC and then proconsul of Africa, he was prevented from standing for the consulship in 66, and in 65 was prosecuted for extortion in his province of Africa but acquitted, through having a collusive prosecutor. After being defeated for the consulship of 63, when Cicero and C. Antonius Hybrida were elected, and then again for the consulship of 62, he led a conspiracy of the indebted and dispossessed, which was foiled by Cicero as consul. See **ad 5. 16. 1 diu debitas inferias** for the role of the Allobroges: 5. 16. 1; 5. 17. 2.

SOCRATES (469–399 BC), son of Sophroniscus, citizen of Athens, philosopher known to us through the dialogues of Plato, the writings of Xenophon, and Aristophanes' *Clouds*, as he left no writings himself. Seneca, like Plato and Xenophon, depicts him as a poor man, but he at one time met the property qualification for a hoplite, as he served courageously in that capacity in the battles of Potidaea, Amphipolis, and Delium. Having shown great moral courage under the democracy and under the regime of the Thirty Tyrants, he was tried in 399 by a popular jury under the restored democracy and condemned to death for impiety and corruption of youth. See **ad 5. 6** and **ad 5. 6. 6 maluit ille** for his invitations from kings. Among his pupils were Plato, Xenophon, and Alcibiades. The Cynics, Plato's Academy, Aristotle's Peripatos, and the Stoa, all claimed descent from him in ethics. Seneca praises his self-control and calm in *De ira* 1.15.3; 3. 11. 2, 13. 3, and mentions his virtues frequently: 1. 8–9. 1; 3. 32. 3; 5. 4. 3; 5. 6. 1; 5. 6. 2–7; 5. 7. 5; 7. 24.

SOPHRONISCUS, Athenian citizen of the deme of Alopece, father of Socrates by his wife Phaenarete: 3. 32. 3.

SULLA, see Cornelius.

TARQUINIUS SUPERBUS (Tarquin the Proud), seventh and last of the kings of Rome, who traditionally reigned 534–510 BC. He reorganized the Latin League, giving Rome control of a strong military alliance, and completed the temple of Capitoline Jupiter. The traditional story has it that, after the rape of Lucretia by his son, her husband Lucius Tarquinius Collatinus and Lucius Junius Brutus, both related to the king, conspired to expel him from Rome. He fled to Caere and persuaded the Etruscan towns of Veii and Tarquinii to attack Rome, unsuccessfully. After the defeat of his Latin allies at Lake Regillus, he took refuge in Cumae, where he died in 495: 2. 20. 2.

TIBERIUS CAESAR, Emperor AD 14–37, the son of Tiberius Claudius Nero and Livia Drusilla, who divorced her husband to marry Octavian in 38 BC, shortly before his brother Drusus was born. In the reign of his stepfather Augustus, he held the consulship twice, in 13 and 7 BC, and had a distinguished military career. He retired to Rhodes in 2 BC, peeved at the advancement of Augustus' grandson and adopted son Gaius Julius Caesar, and was only allowed to return in AD 2. By AD 4 Gaius and his brother Lucius were dead, and he was adopted by Augustus, after himself adopting Germanicus, and was granted tribunician power for ten years, which was renewed in AD 13, when he was given proconsular *imperium* as well. When Augustus died, he thus had all the requisite powers to be Princeps, and the oath of allegiance was immediately taken; but he seems to have wanted the senate to consider the term of his power and his position as sole ruler. He was an intelligent man and a good speaker, but his dour and secretive personality irritated and baffled people, his meanness in providing public buildings and shows made him unpopular, and his long subordination to Augustus made him prone to paranoia, which eventually issued in a spate of trials before the senate for *maiestas* (diminishing the majesty of the Roman people, the emperor, his family, or other important people). His withdrawal to Campania and then to Capri, in AD 27, gave his praetorian prefect in Rome excessive power, until Tiberius finally realized that Sejanus' persecution of the house of Germanicus was self-seeking, and he destroyed him: 2. 7–8; 3. 26. 1; 5. 25. 2.

TULLIUS CICERO, MARCUS (106–43 BC) (cos. 63 BC), Rome's greatest Latin prose writer and orator. He came from the municipal aristocracy of Arpinum and was the first of his family to enter the Roman senate, which he did as quaestor in 75, by which time he had already scored his first forensic success in defending Roscius of Ameria on a charge of parricide. He held the praetorship in 66, at the earliest possible age, and was elected top of the poll for the consulship. In 'that very consulship of his, which he praised not without cause but without end', according to Seneca (*Brev. vit.* 5. 1), he unmasked the Catilinarian conspiracy and had the conspirators executed, a move of dubious legality, for which he went into exile in 58 when threatened with prosecution by the tribune Publius Clodius Pulcher. Recalled in 57, he opposed the activities of the 'first triumvirate', until brought to heel in 56 after their conference at Luca, and devoted his energies to writing *De oratore*, *De re publica*, and *De legibus*. In 51 he was sent to govern the province of Cilicia, where he won a military victory, for which he received the honour of a *supplicatio* at Rome, though his hopes for a triumph were scuppered by the civil war, in which he supported Pompey. Pardoned by Caesar, he retreated from politics to write the rest of his philosophical works. He returned to politics after the assassination of Caesar in 44, which he applauded, in order to attack Antony in the *Philippics*, for which he was to pay with his life, being placed on the proscription list by Antony with the consent of the other members of the Triumvirate. He met his death with courage. His philosophical works constitute an encyclopedia of Hellenistic philosophy. He remained true to the moderate scepticism of Philo of Larissa, of the New Academy, though in ethics he often exercised his right to adopt the most compelling position, which for him was Stoicism. Seneca was indebted to him for much of his Latin philosophical vocabulary but reacted against his periodic style: [4. 30. 2], 5. 17. 2; 7. 6. 1.

TULLIUS CICERO, MARCUS (cos. suff. 30 BC), son of the above and his wife Terentia. He was a successful cavalry officer in 49/8 with the Republican army and was pardoned by Caesar after Pharsalus, going on to hold office in his home town of Arpinum. His father wrote *De officiis* in the form of a letter to him, while he was in Athens studying philosophy, but he would have preferred to serve under Caesar in Spain, being unsuited to literary and intellectual pursuits. After Philippi and the defeat of Brutus, under whom he had served with distinction, he joined Sextus Pompeius, the son of Pompey the Great. Benefiting from the amnesty of 39, he was elected to a priesthood and became colleague to Octavian as consul in 30, after which he governed Syria and Asia. He had a weakness for drink: 4. 30. 2.

TURNUS, Italian hero, rival of Aeneas in love and war, even before Virgil's *Aeneid* gave him an important role as king of Ardea and the Rutulians. He was the unsuccessful suitor for the hand of Lavinia, daughter of King Latinus. As the Latin commander, he fought bravely but was eventually defeated and killed by Aeneas in single combat: 6. 41. 2.

VENUS, a goddess whose worship in Italy is attested early at Lavinium. She was later assimilated to the Greek Aphrodite, goddess of sexuality and reproduction, who was given the prize for beauty in the Judgment of Paris, a tale first recorded in the lost epic *Cypria*. She is already associated with the Graces in Homer (e.g. *Od.* 8. 364–6): 1. 3. 9.

VERRUCOSUS, see Fabius.

VETTIUS SCATO, PUBLIUS, commander of the Marsi, a prominent tribe in the rebellion against Rome, known as the Italic or Social War, of 90–89 BC. He won several victories and killed the consul of 90, Publius Rutilius Lupus. Marching south, he defeated the other consul and captured Aesernia, but was defeated by Cn. Pompeius Strabo and surrendered by his own army. Seneca recounts the loyalty of his slave: 3. 23. 5.

Vɪᴘsᴀɴɪᴜs Aɢʀɪᴘᴘᴀ, Mᴀʀᴄᴜs (cos. 37, 28, 27 ʙᴄ), Augustus' great general and associate He was born into a non-senatorial family and preferred not to use his family name (Elder Sen. *Controv.* 2. 4. 13). For his naval victory over Pompey's son Sex. Pompeius in 36 ʙᴄ, he won the naval crown (Plin. *NH* 16. 7), which was not quite unique, but was only won by one other: M. Terentius Varro. He was principally responsible for Augustus' victory at Actium in 31 ʙᴄ. For his munificence in building, see **ad 3. 32. 4**. He was married to Augustus' daughter Julia, and their two sons were adopted by Augustus: 3. 32. 4; 6. 32. 2–4.

Xᴇɴᴏᴘʜᴏɴ, son of Gryllus, Athenian historian, born *c.*430 ʙᴄ to a wealthy family. He was a supporter of the Thirty, and after the restoration of the democracy in 403, he left Athens to join the 10,000 Greek mercenaries involved in Cyrus' rebellion, about whose adventures he later wrote an account in the *Anabasis*. He then fought for Sparta, was exiled from Athens in 399, and was settled by the Spartans at Scillus, near Olympia. After the Spartan defeat at the battle of Leuctra in 371 ʙᴄ, he was expelled and settled in Corinth, where he remained, though he could have returned to Athens. His works include the *Hellenica*, a history of Greece that continued Thucydides' history down to the defeat of Athens by Sparta in 404 ʙᴄ; dialogues commemorating Socrates, with whom he had associated in youth; and the *Education of Cyrus*, an idealized picture of Cyrus the Great with a didactic purpose, which was very popular in Rome: 3. 32. 3.

Xᴇʀxᴇs I, son of Darius and Atossa, king of Persia (486–465 ʙᴄ). After crushing revolts in Egypt and Babylon, he followed up his father's attempt to invade Greece, which had ended in his defeat at Marathon in 490 ʙᴄ, by attacking by land and sea in 480 ʙᴄ with a much bigger force, though Herodotus' figure (7.60) of 1,700,000 for the army is generally regarded as exaggerated, and Seneca just says 'thousands' (6. 31. 5). Xerxes was defeated at the sea battle of Salamis, and his commander Mardonius, left behind with his army, was defeated at Plataea the next year. Seneca recounts elsewhere other stories about Xerxes' invasion, and he often uses him as an example of *folie de grandeur*: 6. 31 with n. **ad loc**.

Zᴇɴᴏ (335–263 ʙᴄ), founder of the Stoic school. He came from Citium in Cyprus and, on his arrival in Athens, began to lecture in the portico known as the *Stoa poikile* (Painted Stoa). His works survive only in quotations and discussions in later authors. He is credited with establishing the three parts of Stoic philosophy: logic, physics, and ethics. His successors as heads of the Stoa, Cleanthes and Chrysippus, were at pains to play down the more shocking views in his *Politeia*, a work said to be written in the Cynic vein: 4. 39. 1–2; 7. 8. 2.

Bibliography

Abel, K., 1967, *Bauformen in Senecas Dialogen* (Heidelberg).

—— 1985, 'Seneca, Leben und Leistung', *ANRW* II 32. 2.

—— 1987*a*, *Senecas* lex vitae (Pöner stoische Studien; Marburg); repr. with additions in Abel 1995, 42–73.

—— 1987*b*, '100 Jahre Hekaton-Forschung', *Würzburger Jahrbücher*, n.F. 13, 101–20.

—— 1991, 'Die "beweisende" Struktur des Senecanischen Dialogs' in Grimal 1991, 46–81 = Abel 1995, 166–87.

—— 1995, *Die Sinnfrage des Lebens* (Stuttgart).

Adams, J. N., 1995, 'The Language of the Vindolanda Writing Tablets', *JRS* 85, 86–134.

Albertini, E., 1923, *La Composition dans les ouvrages philosophiques de Sénèque* (Paris).

Albrecht, M. von, 2004, *Wort und Wandlung: Senecas Lebenskunst* (*Mnemosyne*, Suppl. 252; Leiden).

Alexander, W. H., 1937, 'Further Notes on the Text of Seneca's *De Beneficiis*', *CQ* 31, 55–60.

—— 1950-2*a*, 'Lucius Annaeus Seneca de Beneficiis Libri VII: The Text Emended and Explained', *University of California Publications in Classical Philology*, 14, 1–45.

—— 1950-2*b*, 'The Tacitean "non liquet" on Seneca', *University of California Publications in Classical Philology*, 14, 269–386.

André, J. M., 1970, review of Cancik 1967, *Latomus*, 29, 201–2.

Armisen-Marchetti, M., 1986, 'Imagination et méditation chez Sénèque: l'exemple de la "praemeditatio"', *REL* 64, 185–95 = 'Imagination and Meditation in Seneca', in Fitch 2008, 102–13.

—— 1989, *Sapientiae Facies: Étude sur les images de Sénèque* (Paris).

—— 2004, 'Mémoire et oubli dans la théorie des bienfaits selon Sénèque', *Paideia*, 59, 7–23.

Asmis, E., 1990, 'Seneca's *On the Happy Life* and Stoic Individualism', *Apeiron*, 23, 219–56.

—— 2009, 'Seneca on Fortune and the Kingdom of God', in S. Bartsch and D. Wray (eds.), *Seneca and the Self* (Cambridge, 2009), 115–38.

Atherton, C., 1993, *The Stoics on Ambiguity* (Cambridge).

Atkins, E. M., 1990, '"Domina et regina virtutum": Justice and *Societas* in *De Officiis*', *Phronesis*, 35, 258–89.

Auden, W. H., 2000, *A Certain World: A Commonplace Book* (London).

Azoulay, V., 2004, *Xénophon et les grâces du pouvoir: de la charis au charisme* (Paris).

Barlow, C. W., 1950, *Martini Episcopi Bracarensis opera omnia* (New Haven, Conn.).

Barnes, J., 1997, *Logic and the Imperial Stoa* (Leiden).

Basore, J. W., 1935, *Seneca: Moral Essays*, iii (The Loeb Classical Library; Cambridge, Mass.).

Bastomsky, S. J., 1972, 'Tacitus *Annals*, 14, 53, 2. The Pathos of the Tacitean Seneca's Request to Nero', *Latomus*, 31, 174–8.

Beagon, M., 2005, *The Elder Pliny on the Human Animal: Natural History Book 7* (Oxford).

Bedon, R., 1991, 'Sénèque, *ad Lucilium* 91: L'incendie de 64 à Lyon: exploitation littéraire et réalité', in Chevallier and Poignault 1991, 45–61.

Bellincioni, M., 1984*a*, *Potere ed etica in Seneca: clementia e voluntas amica* (Brescia).

—— 1984*b*, '"Clementia liberum arbitrium habet" (Clem. 2,7,3)', *Paideia*, 39, 173–82 = Bellincioni 1986, 113–25.

—— 1986, *Studi senecani e altri scritti* (Brescia).

Bickel, E., 1905, 'Die Schrift des Martinus von Bracara formula vitae honestae', *Rh. Mus.*, n.F. 60, 505–51.

Billerbeck, M., 1979, *Der Kyniker Demetrius* (Leiden).

Birley, A. R., 1981, *The Fasti of Roman Britain* (Oxford).

Blank, D., and Atherton, C., 2003, 'The Stoic Contribution to Traditional Grammar', in B. Inwood (ed.), *The Cambridge Companion to the Stoics* (Cambridge, 2003), 310–27.

Blom, H. van der, 2010, *Cicero's Role Models* (Oxford).

Blüher, K. D., 1969, *Seneca in Spanien: Untersuchungen zur Geschichte der Seneca-Rezeption in Spanien vom 13. bis 17. Jahrhundert* (Munich).

Bonhöffer, A., 1894, *Die Ethik des Stoikers Epiktet* (Stuttgart), translated by W. O. Stephens as *The Ethics of the Stoic Epictetus* (New York, 1996).

Bonner, S. F., 1949, *Roman Declamation in the Late Republic and Early Empire* (Liverpool).

Bourdieu, P., 2000, *The Logic of Practice*, trans. R. Nice (Cambridge); orig. *Le Sens pratique* (Paris, 1980).

Bowman, A. K., and Thomas, J. D. (with contributions by J. N. Adams and R. Tapper), 1983, *Vindolanda: The Latin Writing Tablets* (Roman Society Monograph, 4; London).

—— Cotton, H., Goodman, M., and Price, S. (eds.), 2002, *Representations of Empire: Rome and the Mediterranean World* (Proceedings of the British Academy, 114; Oxford).

Boyancé, P., 1936, 'Les méthodes de l'histoire littéraire: Cicéron et son œuvre philosophique', *REL* 288–309 = *Études sur l'humanisme cicéronien* (Collection Latomus, 121; Brussels, 1960), 199–221.

Bradley, K., 1985, 'Child Care at Rome: The Role of Men', *Historical Reflections/ Réflexions historiques*, 12, 485–523.

Braund, D., 1996, *Ruling Roman Britain* (London and New York).

Braund, S., 2009, *Seneca, De Clementia* (Oxford).

Brennan, T., 2000, 'Reservation in Stoic Ethics', *Archiv für Geschichte der Philosophie*, 82, 149–77.

Brinkmann, M., 2002, *Seneca in den Annalen des Tacitus* (Diss. Bonn).

Brittain, C., 2001, *Philo of Larissa: The Last of the Academic Sceptics* (Oxford).

Brunt, P. A., 1966, 'Procuratorial Jurisdiction', *Latomus*, 25, 461–87, revised in Brunt 1990, 163–87.

—— 1974, 'Conscription and Volunteering in the Roman Imperial Army', *Scripta Classica Israelica*, 1, 90–115, revised in Brunt 1990, 188–214.

—— 1975, 'Stoicism and the Principate', *PBSR* 43, 7–35, reprinted as ch. 7 in Brunt 2013.

Brunt, P. A., 1977, 'From Epictetus to Arrian', *Athenaeum*, 55, 19–48 = ch. 9 in Brunt 2013.

—— 1988*a*, *The Fall of the Roman Republic* (Oxford).

—— 1988*b*, 'Amicitia in the Late Roman Republic', in Brunt 1988*a*, 350–81; revised from 'Amicitia in the Late Republic', *Proceedings of the Cambridge Philological Society*, 11 (1965), 1–20.

—— 1988*c*, 'Clientela', *The Fall of the Roman Republic and Related Essays* (Oxford), 382–442.

—— 1988*d*, 'The Fall of the Roman Republic', in Brunt 1988*a*, 1–92.

—— 1990, *Roman Imperial Themes* (Oxford).

—— 2013, *Studies in Stoicism* (Oxford).

Busonero, P., 2000, 'Un caso esemplare di antigrafo e apografo nella tradizione di Seneca: il Pal. Lat. 1547 e il Reg. Lat. 1529' in Parroni 2000, 295–337.

Bütler, H.-P., 1970, *Die geistige Welt des jüngeren Plinius* (Heidelberg).

Camodeca, G., 1986, 'I consoli del 55–56 e un nuovo collega di Seneca nel consolato: P. Cornelius Dolabella (*TP* 75–140+135)', *ZPE* 63, 201–12.

—— 1991, 'Novità sui fasti consulari delle tavolette cerate della Campania', in Eck 1991*a*, 45–74.

Campbell, J. B., 1984, *The Emperor and the Roman Army 31 BC–AD 235* (Oxford).

Cancik, H., 1967, *Untersuchungen zu Senecas Epistulae morales* (Spudasmata, 18; Hildesheim).

Champlin, E., 1991, *Final Judgments* (Berkeley, Los Angeles, and Oxford).

Chaumartin, F.-R., 1985, *Le De beneficiis de Sénèque: sa signification philosophique, politique et sociale* (Lille and Paris).

—— 1989, 'Les désillusions de Sénèque devant l'évolution de la politique néronienne et l'aspiration à la retraite: le "De vita beata" et le "De beneficiis"', *ANRW* II 36. 3, 1686–723.

Cheal, D., 1988, *The Gift Economy* (London and New York).

Chevallier, R., and Poignault, R. (eds.), 1991, *Présence de Sénèque* (Paris).

Clarke, M. L., 1951, 'The *Thesis* in Roman Rhetorical Schools', *CQ*² 1, 159–66.

Codoñer, C., 2000, 'Los recursos literarios en la obra en prosa de Séneca' in Parroni 2000, 377–93.

Cohen, S.T., 2008, 'Augustus, Julia and the Development of Exile *ad insulam*', *CQ*² 58, 206–17.

Coleman, K. M., 2006, *Martial: Liber Spectaculorum* (Oxford).

Colish, M. L., 1985, *The Stoic Tradition from Antiquity to the Early Middle Ages*, 2 vols. (Leiden).

Cooper, J. M., and Procopé, J .F., 1995, *Seneca: Moral and Political Essays* (Cambridge).

Cotton, H., 1981, 'Military Tribunates and the Exercise of Patronage', *Chiron*, 11, 237–8.

—— 1984, 'The Concept of *Indulgentia* under Trajan', *Chiron*, 14, 245–66.

Crook, J. A., 1967, *Law and Life of Rome* (London).

D'Arms, J. D., 1990, 'The Roman *Convivium* and the Idea of Equality', in O. Murray (ed.), *Sympotica: A Symposium on the Symposion* (Oxford, 1990), 308–20.

Dickey, E., 2002, *Latin Forms of Address* (Oxford).

Dillon, J., 1977, *The Middle Platonists* (London and Ithaca, N.Y.).

Dise, R. L., Jr., 1997, 'Trajan, the Antonines and the Governor's Staff', *ZPE* 116, 273–83.

Dixon, S., 1993, 'Gift and Debt in the Roman Élite', *EMC*, n.s. 12, 451–64.

Dobbin, R., 1998, *Epictetus Discourses Book 1* (Oxford).

Dobson, B., 1972, 'Legionary Centurion or Equestrian Officer? A Comparison of Pay and Prospects', *Ancient Society*, 3 (1972), 193–207.

—— 1974, 'The Significance of the Centurion and "Primipilaris" in the Roman Army and Administration', *ANRW* II 1. 392–434.

Dowling, M. B. (2006), *Clemency and Cruelty in the Roman World* (Ann Arbor).

Ducos, M., 1991, 'Sénèque et le monde du droit', in Chevallier and Poignault 1991, 109–26.

—— 1993, 'La réflexion sur le droit pénal dans l'œuvre de Sénèque', *Helmantica*, 44, 443–56.

Duff, J. W., and Duff, A. M. (eds.), 1935, *Minor Latin Poets* (Cambridge, Mass.).

Düll, R., 1976, 'Seneca Iurisconsultus', *ANRW* II.15. 364–80.

Dunbabin, K., and Slater, W. F., 2011, 'Roman Dining', in M. Peachin (ed.), *The Oxford Handbook of Social Relations in the Roman World* (Oxford, 2011), 438–46.

Dyck, A. R., 1996, *A Commentary on Cicero*, De Officiis (Ann Arbor, Mich.).

Eck, W., 1980, 'Die Präsenz senatorischer Familien in den Städten des Imperium Romanum bis zum späten 3. Jahrhundert', in W. Eck, H. Galsterer, and H. Wolff (eds.), *Studien zur antiken Sozialgeschichte* (Cologne and Vienna, 1980), 283–322.

—— 1981, 'Miscellanea prosopographica', *ZPE* 42, 227–56.

—— 1984, 'Senatorial Self-Representation: Developments in the Augustan Period', in F. Millar and E. Segal (eds.), *Caesar Augustus* (Oxford, 1984), 129–67.

—— 1991*a* (ed.), *Epigrafia: Actes du Colloque international d'épigraphie latine en mémoire de Attilio Degrassi pour le centenaire de sa naissance* (Rome).

—— 1991*b*, 'Consules ordinarii und consules suffecti als eponyme Amtsträger', in Eck 1991*a*, 15–44.

—— 2001, 'Spezialisierung in der staatlichen Administration des römischen Reiches in der hohen Kaiserzeit', in L. de Blois (ed.), *Administration, Prosopography and Appointment Policies in the Roman Empire: Proceedings of the First Workshop of the International Network Impact of Empire* (Amsterdam, 2001), 1–23.

—— 2002, 'Imperial Administration and Epigraphy', in Bowman *et al.* 2002, 131–52.

—— Caballos, A., and Fernández, F., 1996, *Das senatus consultum de Cn. Pisone patre* (Munich).

—— Drew-Bear, T., and Herrmann, P., 1977, 'Sacrae Litterae', *Chiron*, 7, 355–83.

Edelstein, L., 1966, *The Meaning of Stoicism* (Cambridge).

Eden, P. T., 1984, *Seneca:* Apocolocyntosis (Cambridge).

Edwards, C., 1997, 'Self-Scrutiny and Self-Transformation in Seneca's Letters', *Greece & Rome*, 44, 23–38, reprinted in revised form in Fitch (ed.), 84–101.

Eilers, C., 2002, *Roman Patrons of Greek Cities* (Oxford).

Erskine, A., 1990, *The Hellenistic Stoa* (London).

Fairweather, J., 1981, *Seneca the Elder* (Cambridge).

Feeney, D. C., 1987, ' "Stat magni nominis umbra" ', *CQ*[2] 36, 234–43.

Ferri, R. (ed.), 2003, *Octavia: A Play Attributed to Seneca* (Cambridge).

Fillion-Lahille, J., 1984, *Le De Ira de Sénèque et la philosophie stoïcienne des passions* (Paris).

Fitch, J. G. (ed.) (2008), *Oxford Readings in Seneca* (Oxford).

Flaig, E., 1993, 'Loyalität ist keine Gefälligkeit: Zum Majestätsprozeß gegen C. Silius 24 n. Chr.', *Klio*, 75, 289–305.

Flower, H., 1996, *Ancestor Masks and Aristocratic Power in Roman Culture* (Oxford).

Foot, P., 2001, *Natural Goodness* (Oxford).

Foucault, M., 1988, *The Care of the Self*, trans. R. Hurley (London); orig. *Le Souci de soi* (Paris, 1984).

Friedrich, W., 1914, 'Zur Abfassungszeit vom Senecas Werk De beneficiis', *BPhW* 34, 1406–8, 1501–3, 1533–6.

Fuhrmann, M., 1997, *Seneca und Kaiser Nero* (Berlin).

Fürst, A., 1996, *Streit unter Freunden: Ideal und Realität in der Freundschaftslehre der Antike* (Stuttgart and Leipzig).

Gabba, E., 1979, 'Per un'interpretazione politica del *de officiis* di Cicerone', *RAL*, 8th ser., 34, 117–41.

Gardner, J. F., 1993, *Being a Roman Citizen* (London).

—— 1998, *Family and Familia in Roman Law and Life* (Oxford).

Gauthier, P., 1985, *Les Cités grecques et leurs bienfaiteurs (IVᵉ–Iᵉʳ siècle avant J.-C.)* (*Bulletin de Correspondance Hellénique*, Supplément 12; Paris).

Gercke, A., 1896, 'Seneca-Studien', *Jahrbücher für Classische Philologie*, Suppl. 22, 1–334.

Gertz, M. C., 1874, *Studia critica in L. Annaei Senecae Dialogos* (Copenhagen).

—— 1876, *L. Annaei Senecae Libri De clementia et De beneficiis* (Berlin).

Giliberti, G. 1996, *Studi sulla massima 'Caesar omnia habet'* (Turin).

Gill, C., 1998, 'Altruism or Reciprocity in Greek Philosophy', in Gill, Postlethwaite, and Seaford 1998, 303–28.

—— Postlethwaite, N., and Seaford, R. (eds.), 1998, *Reciprocity in Ancient Athens* (Oxford).

Giusta, M., 1964–7, *I dossografi di etica*, 2 vols. (Turin)

Gomoll, H., 1933, *Der stoische Philosoph Hekaton: Seine Begriffswelt und Nachwirkung, unter Beigabe seiner Fragmente* (Bonn).

González, J., 1986, 'The Lex Irnitana: A New Copy of the Flavian Municipal Law', *JRS* 76, 147–243.

Gordon, A. E., 1983, *Illustrated Introduction to Latin Epigraphy* (Berkeley).

Grewing, F. (ed.), 1998, *Toto Notus in Orbe, Perspektiven der Martial-Interpretation* (Stuttgart),

Griffin, M. T., 1976, *Seneca: A Philosopher in Politics* (Oxford; pbk. repr. 1992).

—— 1982, 'The Lyons Tablet and Tacitean Hindsight', *CQ²* 32, 404–18.

—— 1984, *Nero: The End of a Dynasty* (London).

—— 1988, 'Philosophy for Statesmen: Cicero and Seneca', *Antikes Denken — Moderne Schule* (Gymnasium Beiheft, 9), 133–50.

—— 1991, '*Urbs Roma, Plebs* and *Princeps*', in L. Alexander (ed.), *Images of Empire* (Sheffield, 1991), 19–46.

—— 1992, 'Postscript', in repr. of Griffin 1976, 505–20.

—— 1995, 'Philosophical Badinage in Cicero's Letters to his Friends', in J. G. F. Powell (ed.), *Cicero the Philosopher* (Oxford, 1995), .325–46

—— 1996a, 'When is Thought Political?', *Apeiron*, 29, 229–82.

—— 1996b, 'Cynicism and the Romans', in R. B. Branham and M.-O. Goulet-Cazé (eds.), *The Cynics* (Berkeley and Los Angeles, 1996), 190–204.

—— 2000, 'Seneca and Pliny', *The Cambridge History of Greek and Roman Political Thought* (Cambridge), 532–58.

—— 2002, 'Political Thought in the Age of Nero', in J. M. Croisille and Y. Perrin (eds.), *Neronia VI: Rome à l'époque néronienne* (Collection Latomus, 268; Brussels, 2002), 325–37.

—— 2003a, 'Clementia after Caesar: From Politics to Philosophy', in F. Cairns and E. Fantham (eds.), *Caesar against Liberty? Perspectives on his Autocracy* (Papers of the Langford Latin Seminar, 11; Cambridge, 2003), 157–82.

—— 2003b, 'Seneca as a Sociologist: *De beneficiis*', in A. De Vivo and E. Lo Cascio (eds.), *Seneca uomo politico e l'età di Claudio e di Nerone: Atti del Convegno internazionale (Capri 25–27 marzo 1999)* (Santo Spirito (Bari), 2003), 89–122.

—— 2003c, '*De beneficiis* and Roman Society', *JRS* 93, 92–113.

—— 2007, 'Seneca's Pedagogic Strategy', in R. Sorabji and R.W. Sharples (eds.), *Greek and Roman Philosophy 100 BC to 200 AD*, i (*BICS* Supplement 94; London, 2007), 89–113.

—— 2011, 'The Politics of Virtue: Three Puzzles in *De officiis*', in B. Morison and K. Ierodiakonou (eds.), *Episteme: Essays in Honour of Jonathan Barnes* (Oxford, 2011), 310–27.

—— 2013, 'Latin Philosophy and Roman Law', in V. Harte and M. Lane (eds.), *Politeia: Essays in Honour of Malcolm Schofield* (Cambridge, 2013), 96–115.

—— and Atkins, E. M. (eds.), 1991, *Cicero* On Duties (Cambridge).

—— and Inwood, B., 2011, *Lucius Annaeus Seneca* On Benefits (translated with notes) (Chicago).

Grimal, P., 1949, "Est-il possible de dater un traité de Sénèque?', *REL* 27, 178–88.

—— 1967, 'Le discours de Sénèque à Néron dans les "Annales" de Tacite', *Giornale italiano di filologia*, 20, 131–8 = *Rome: La littérature et l'histoire* (Collection de l'École française de Rome; Rome, 1986), 575–83.

—— 1978, *Sénèque ou la conscience de l'Empire* (Paris).

—— (ed.), 1991, *Sénèque et la prose latine* (Entretiens Fondation Hardt, 36; Vandœuvres-Geneva).

Guglielmino, S., 1968, *Lucio Anneo Seneca: I benefici* (Bologna).

Guillemin, A.-M., 1929, *Pline et la vie littéraire de son temps* (Paris).

Habicht, C., 1982, *Studien zur Geschichte Athens in hellenistischer Zeit* (Hypomnemata, 73; Göttingen).

Hadot, I., 1969, *Seneca und die griechisch-römische Tradition der Seelenleitung* (Berlin).

Hadot, P., 1992, *La Citadelle intérieure: Introduction aux 'Pensées' de Marc Aurèle* (Paris).

—— 1995, *Philosophy as a Way of Life*, translated by M. Chase (Oxford).

Hahm, D. E., 1990, 'The Ethical Doxography of Arius Didymus', *ANRW* II 36. 4, 2935–3055.

Hands, A. R., 1968, *Charities and Social Aid in Greece and Rome* (London).

Harris, W. V., 2001, *Restraining Rage* (Cambridge, Mass.).

Heath, A., 1976, *Rational Choice and Social Exchange* (Cambridge).

Hegel, G. W. F., 1979, *Werke in zwanzig Bänden*, xviii–xx: *Vorlesungen über die Geschichte der Philosophie* (Frankfurt am Main); English translation by E. S. Haldane and F. H. Simson, *Lectures on the History of Philosophy*, 3 vols. (London, 1894).

Hellegouarc'h, J., 1963, *Le Vocabulaire latin des relations et des partis politiques sous la République* (Paris).

Henderson, J., 2002*a*, 'Finding Homegrown Talent—Pliny *Letters* 1.19', *Greece & Rome*, 49, 212–26.

—— 2002*b*, *Pliny's Statue: The Letters, Self-Portraiture & Classical Art* (Exeter).

Henderson, M. I., 1963, 'The Establishment of the *Equester Ordo*', *JRS* 53, 61–72.

Hoffer, S. E., 1999, *The Anxieties of Pliny the Younger* (Atlanta, Ga.).

Holford-Strevens, L. A., 2003, *Aulus Gellius: An Antonine Scholar and his Achievement* (Oxford).

Hollis, A., 2007, *Fragments of Roman Poetry c.60 BC–AD 20* (Oxford).

Holmes, N., 2004, 'Ferimus', *CQ*[2] 54, 296–7.

Horner, V., Carter, J. D., Suchak, M., and Waal, F. B. M. de, 2011, 'Spontaneous Prosocial Choice by Chimpanzees', doi: 10.1073/pnas.1111088108.

Hout, M. P. J. van den (ed.), 1988, *M. Cornelius Fronto: Epistulae* (Leipzig).

Hutchinson, G. O., 1993, *Latin Literature from Seneca to Juvenal* (Oxford).

Inwood, B., 1985, *Ethics and Human Action in Early Stoicism* (Oxford).

—— 1995*a*, 'Politics and Paradox in Seneca's *De beneficiis*', in Laks and Schofield 1995, 241–65 = Inwood 2005, 65–94.

—— 1995*b*, 'Seneca in his Philosophical Milieu', *Harvard Studies in Classical Philology*, 97, 63–76 = Inwood 2005, 7–22.

—— 1999, 'Rules and Reasoning in Stoic Ethics', in K. Ierodiakonou, *Topics in Stoic Philosophy* (Oxford, 1999), 95–127 = Inwood 2005, 95–131.

—— 2004, 'Moral Judgement in Seneca', in J. Zupko and S. Strange (eds.), *Stoicism: Traditions and Transformations* (Cambridge, 2004), 76–94 = Inwood 2005, 201–23.

—— 2005, *Reading Seneca* (Oxford).

—— 2007, *Seneca: Selected Philosophical Letters* (Oxford).

Jaeger, W., 1937, 'Der Großgesinnte', *Humanistische Reden und Vorträge*, 199–208.

Jolowicz, H. F., and Nicholas, B., 1972, *Historical Introduction to the Study of Roman Law* (Cambridge).

Jones, C. P., 1987, '*Stigma*: Tattooing and Branding', *JRS* 77, 139–55.

Jonsen, A. R., and Toulmin, S., 1988, *The Abuse of Casuistry: A History of Moral Reasoning* (Berkeley).

Judson, R. L., 1997, 'Aristotle on Fair Exchange', *Oxford Studies in Ancient Philosophy*, 15, 147–75.

Kaster, R. A., 2005, *Emotion, Restraint, and Community in Ancient Rome* (Oxford).

Kechagia, E., 2010, 'Early Epicureans against the Stoa', *CQ*[2] 60, 132–55.

Kelly, J. M., 1966, *Roman Litigation* (Oxford).

Ker, J., 2006, 'Seneca, Man of Many Genres', in Volk and Williams 2006, 19–41.

—— 2009, *The Deaths of Seneca* (Oxford).

Kidd, I. G., 1988, *Posidonius*, ii: *The Commentary*, 2 vols. (Cambridge).

Kinderstrand, J. F., 1976, *Bion of Borysthenes: A Collection of the Fragments with Introduction and Commentary* (Uppsala).

Kleijwegt, M., 1998, 'Extra fortunam est quidquid donatur amicis', in Grewing 1998, 256–77.

Kloft, H., 1970, *Liberalitas Principis: Herkunft und Bedeutung* (Cologne and Vienna).

Konstan, D., 1995, 'Patrons and Friends', *Classical Philology*, 90, 328–42.

—— 1997, *Friendship in the Classical World* (Cambridge).

Laks, A., and Schofield, M. (eds.), 1995, *Justice and Generosity* (Cambridge).

Lana, I., 1991, 'Le "Lettere a Lucilio" nella letteratura epistolare', in Grimal 1991, 253–305.

Lausberg, M., 1970, *Untersuchungen zu Senecas Fragmenten* (Berlin, 1970).

—— 1989, 'Senecae operum fragmenta: Überblick und Forschungsbericht', *ANRW* II 36. 3, 1879–961.

Leach, E. W., 1990, 'Politics of Self-Presentation in Pliny's *Letters* and Roman Portrait Sculpture', *Classical Antiquity*, 9, 14–39.

Leeman, A. D., 1953, 'Seneca's Plans for a Work "Moralis Philosophia" and their Influence on his Later Epistles', *Mnemosyne*[4], 6, 307–13.

Lefèvre, E., 2001, *Panaitios' und Ciceros Pflichtenlehre: Vom philosophischen Traktat zum politischen Lehrbuch* (Historia Einzelschriften, 150; Stuttgart).

Lendon, J. E., 1997, *Empire of Honour* (Oxford).

Lentano, M., 2000, '*An beneficium patri reddi possit*: note a Seneca, *De beneficiis* 3, 29–38', *Euphrosyne*, 28, 355–68.

—— 2009a, 'Come uccidere un padre (della patria): Seneca e l'ingratitudine di Bruto', in Picone, Beltrami, and Ricottilli 2009, 185–209.

—— 2009 b, 'La gratitudine e la memoria: una lettura del *De beneficiis*', *Bollettino di studi latini*, 39, 1–28.

Letta, C., 1998, 'Allusioni politiche e riflessioni sul principato nel *De Beneficiis* di Seneca', *Limes*, 9–10, 228–43.

Levick, B., 1983, 'The *Senatus Consultum* from Larinum', *JRS* 73, 97–115.

Li Causi, P., 2009, 'Una mediazione conflittuale per una practica della teoria: dinamiche e funzioni dell'interlocutore immaginario in alcuni *loci* del *de beneficiis* di Seneca' in Picone, Beltrami, and Ricottilli (eds.), 211–32.

Loew, O., 1908, Χάρις (diss. Marburg).

Long, A. A., 1995, 'Cicero's Politics in *De officiis*', in Laks and Schofield 1995, 213–40.

—— 2002, *Epictetus: A Stoic and Socratic Guide to Life* (Oxford).

López Barja de Quiroga, P., 1998, 'Junian Latins: Status and Number', *Athenaeum*, 86, 133–63.

Ma, J., 1999, *Antiochus III and the Cities of Western Asia Minor* (Oxford).

MacDowell, D. M., 1978, *The Law in Classical Athens* (London).

MacMullen, R., 1986, 'Personal Power in the Roman Empire', *AJPh* 107, 512–24.

Malaspina, E., 2001, *L. Annaei Senecae De* Clementia *libri duo* (Turin).

Manning, C. E., 1985, '*Liberalitas*—The Decline and Rehabilitation of a Virtue', *Greece & Rome*, 32, 73–83.

—— 1986, '*Actio ingrati* (Seneca *De Benef.* 3.6–17); A Contribution to Contemporary Debate?', *SDHI* 52, 61–72.

Mantello, A., 1979, '*Beneficium*' *servile* — '*debitum*' *naturale: SEN.*, de ben. *3.18.1 ss.* — *D. 35.1.40.3 (Iav., 2* ex post. Lab.*)*, i (Milan).

Marchese, R. R., 2009, 'Dignità e diseguaglianza. Il rispetto nella relazione fra benefattori e beneficati', in Picone, Beltrami, and Ricottilli (2009), 245–71.

Marchesi, I., 2008, *The Art of Pliny's Letters: A Poetics of Allusion in the Private Correspondence* (Cambridge).

Maurach, G., 1970, *Der Bau von Senecas Epistulae Morales* (Heidelberg).

—— 1996, *Seneca, Leben und Werk*, 2nd edn. (Darmstadt).

Mauss, M., 1954, *The Gift: Forms and Functions of Exchange in Archaic Societies* (London, rev. 1966) = translation by I. Cunnison of 'Essai sur le don, forme et raison de l'échange dans les sociétés archaïques', *Année Sociologique*, n.s. 1 (1902–3), 30–186.

Mayer, R., 1991, 'Roman Historical Exempla in Seneca', in Grimal 1991, 141–69; reprinted in revised and abbreviated form in Fitch 2008, 298–315.

Mazzoli, G., 1978, 'Ricerche sulla tradizione medievale del *De beneficiis* e del *De clementia* di Seneca I', *Bollettino dei classici*, 26, 85–109.

—— 2000, 'Le "voci" dei dialoghi di Seneca', in Parroni 2000, 249–60.

—— 2007, '"Simplex ratio" e "admonitio": teoria e relativismo morale nel "De beneficiis" di Seneca', in G. Hinojo Andrés and C. Fernández Corte (eds.), *Munus quaesitum meritis: Homenaje a Carmen Codoñer* (Salamanca, 2007), 585–94.

Michel, J., 1962, *Gratuité en droit romain* (Brussels).

Migliorini, P., 1997, *Scienza e terminologia medica nella letteratura latina di età neroniana: Seneca, Lucano, Persio, Petronio* (Frankfurt).

Mikalson, J. D., 1998, *Religion in Hellenistic Athens* (California).

Millar, F., 1963, 'The Fiscus in the First Two Centuries', *JRS* 53, 29–42.

—— 1965, 'Epictetus and the Imperial Court', *JRS* 55, 141–8.

—— 1977, *The Emperor in the Roman World* (London).

Momigliano, A., 1955, 'Note sulla legenda del cristianesimo di Seneca', in *Contributo alla storia degli studi classici* (Rome), 13–32.

Mommsen, T., 1887, *Römisches Staatsrecht*[3] (Leipzig).

—— 1899, *Römisches Strafrecht* (Leipzig).

Morgan, T., 1998, *Literate Education in the Hellenistic and Roman Worlds* (Cambridge).

—— 2007, *Popular Morality in the Early Roman Empire* (Cambridge).

Moussy, Cl., 1966, *Gratia et sa famille* (Paris).

Münscher, K., 1922, 'Senecas Werke: Untersuchungen zur Abfassungszeit und Echtheit', *Philologus* Supp. 16/1, 1–146.

Newman, R. J., 1989, '*Cotidie meditare*. Theory and Practice of the *meditatio* in Imperial Stoicism', *ANRW* II 36. 3, 1473–517.

Nicholas, B., 1962, *An Introduction to Roman Law* (Oxford).

Nicols, J., 1980, 'Pliny and the Patronage of Communities', *Hermes*, 108, 365–85.

Nisbet, R. G. M., 1990, 'The Dating of Seneca's Tragedies, with Special Reference to *Thyestes*', *Proceedings of the Leeds International Latin Seminar*, 6: 95–114; repr. in id., *Collected Papers on Latin Literature*, ed. S. J. Harrison (Oxford, 1995), 294–311.

Nothdurft, K.-D., 1963, *Studien zum Einfluß Senecas auf die Philosophie und Theologie des zwölften Jahrhunderts* (Leiden).

Nowak, M., 1998, 'Maths Used to Explain Benefits of Co-Operation', *Oxford University Gazette*, 16 July, 1472.

Nussbaum, M., 1994, *The Therapy of Desire* (Princeton).

Nutton, V., 1986, 'The Perils of Patriotism: Pliny and Roman Medicine', in R. K. French and F. Greenaway (eds.), *Science in the Early Roman Empire: Pliny the Elder, his Sources and Influence* (London, 1986), 30–58.

—— 2004, *Ancient Medicine* (London).

Oakley, S. P., 2005, *A Commentary on Livy Books VI–X*, iv: *Book X* (Oxford).

Obbink, D., 1992, 'What All Men Believe Must be True: Common Conceptions and Consensus Omnium in Aristotle and Hellenistic Philosophy', *OSAP* 10, 193–231.

Ogilvie, R. M., 1965, *A Commentary on Livy Books 1–5* (Oxford).

Panizza, L., 1984, 'Biography in Italy from the Middle Ages to the Renaissance: Seneca, Pagan or Christian?', *Nouvelles de la République des Lettres*, 2, 47–98.

Parker, R., 1988, 'The Values of Pliny', *Omnibus*, 15, 6–8.

—— 1996, *Athenian Religion* (Oxford)

—— 1998, 'Pleasing Thighs: Reciprocity in Greek Religion', in Gill, Postlethwaite, and Seaford 1998, 105–25.

Parroni, P. (ed.), *Seneca e il suo tempo: Atti del Convegno internazionale di Roma-Cassino, 11–14 novembre 1998* (Rome),

Picone, G., 2009, 'Ercole e il serpente: figure di ricordo, modelli mitici, modelli etici nel *de beneficiis* di Seneca', in Picone, Beltrami, and Ricotilli 2009, 289–302.

—— Beltrami, L., and Ricottilli, L., 2009, *Benefattori e beneficati* (Palermo), 289–302.

Plezia, M. (ed.), 1961, *Aristotelis Epistularum Fragmenta cum Testamento* (Warsaw).

—— 1977, *Aristotelis privatorum scriptorum fragmenta* (Leipzig).

Pohlenz, M., 1935, review of Gomoll 1933, *Göttingische gelehrte Anzeigen*, 197, 104–11.

—— 1941, *Philosophie und Erlebnis in Senecas Dialogen*, *NGG* 4, 55–118 = *Kleine Schriften*, ed. H. Dörrie (Hildesheim, 1965), i. 384–447.

Poste, E., rev. Whittuck, E. A., 1904, *Institutes of Roman Law by Gaius with Translation and Commentary*[4] (Oxford).

Préchac, F., 1961, *Sénèque: Des bienfaits* (Paris).

Raccanelli, R., 2010, *Esercizi di dono* (Palermo).

Ramondetti, P., 1996, *Struttura di Seneca, De Ira, II–III* (Bologna).

Reinhardt, T., 2000, 'Rhetoric in the Fourth Academy', *CQ*[2] 50, 531–47.

—— 2003, *Cicero's* Topica (Oxford).

Reynolds, J., 1982, *Aphrodisias and Rome* (London).

Reynolds, L. D., 1983, *Texts and Transmission* (Oxford).

Richardson, J. S., 1975, 'The Triumph, the Praetors and the Senate in the Early Second Century B.C.', *JRS* 65, 50–63.

Riggsby, A., 1998, 'Self and Community in the Younger Pliny', *Arethusa*, 31, 75–97.

Riposati, B., 1947, *Studi sui 'Topica' di Cicerone* (Milan).

Rist, J. M., 1969, *Stoic Philosophy* (Cambridge).

Roller, M., 2001, *Constructing Autocracy: Aristocrats and Emperors in Julio-Claudian Rome* (Princeton).

Ross, D., 1925, *Aristotle: The Nicomachean Ethics* (Oxford).

Rutherford, R. B., 1989, *The* Meditations *of Marcus Aurelius: A Study* (Oxford).

Saller, R. P., 1982, *Personal Patronage under the Early Empire* (Cambridge).

—— 1994, *Patriarchy, Property, and Death in the Roman Family* (Cambridge).

—— 2000, 'Status and Patronage', *CAH*[2] xi. 817–54.

Sandbach, F. H., 1975, *The Stoics* (London).

Schafer, J., 2009, *Ars Didactica: Seneca's 94th and 95th Letters* (Göttingen).

Schofield, M., 1991, *The Stoic Idea of the City* (Cambridge).

—— 1999, 'Political Friendship and Reciprocity', *Saving the City* (Cambridge), 82–99.

Schulz, F., 1936, *Principles of Roman Law* (Oxford).

—— 1946, *History of Roman Legal Science* (Oxford; repr. 1963).

Schwarzenberg, E., 1966, *Die Grazien* (Bonn).

Sedley, D., 1997, 'The Ethics of Brutus and Cassius', *JRS* 87, 41–53.

Sellars, J., 2003, *The Art of Living* (Aldershot).

Setaioli, A., 2003, 'Seneca e Cicerone', in E. Narducci (ed.), *Aspetti della fortuna di Cicerone nella cultura latina* (Florence), 55–77.

Shackleton Bailey, D. R., 1970, 'Emendations of Seneca', *CQ*² 20, 350–63.

Sinclair, T. A., 1951, *A History of Greek Political Thought* (London).

Shaw, B. D., 2001, 'Raising and Killing Children: Two Roman Myths', *Mnemosyne*⁴, 54, 31–77.

Sonntag, M., 1913, *L. Annaei Senecae de beneficiis libri explanantur* (Leipzig).

Spisak, A. L., 1998, 'Gift-Giving in Martial', in Grewing 1998, 243–55.

Syme, R., 1958*a*, *Tacitus*, 2 vols. (Oxford).

—— 1958*b*, 'Imperator Caesar: A Study in Nomenclature', *Historia*, 7, 172–88 = *Roman Papers*, i (Oxford, 1979), 361–77.

—— 1960, 'Pliny's Less Successful Friends', *Historia*, 9, 362–79 = *Roman Papers*, ii (Oxford, 1979), 477–95.

—— 1974, 'The Crisis of 2 B.C.', *Bayerische Akademie der Wissenschaften, Philosophisch-historische Klasse. Sitzungsberichte.* 7, 3–34 = *Roman Papers*, iii (Oxford, 1984), 912–36.

—— 1984, 'Fictional History Old and New: Hadrian', James Bryce Memorial Lecture, 10 May 1984 = *Roman Papers*, vi (Oxford, 1991), 157–81.

—— 1985, 'Correspondents of Pliny', *Historia*, 34, 324–59 = *Roman Papers*, v (Oxford, 1988), 440–77.

—— 1986, *The Augustan Aristocracy* (Oxford).

—— 1989, 'A Dozen Early Priesthoods', *ZPE* 77, 241–59 = *Roman Papers*, v (Oxford, 1991), 421–34.

Talbert, R., 1984, *The Senate of Imperial Rome* (Princeton).

Tarrant, R., 2006, 'Seeing Seneca Whole?', in Volk and Williams 2006, 1–17.

Tepedino Guerra, A., 1977, 'Filodemo sulla gratitudine', *Cronache ercolanesi*, 7, 96–113.

Thomas, P., 1918, *Morceaux choisis de Sénèque* (Paris).

Todd, S. C., 1993, *The Shape of Athenian Law* (Oxford).

Trapp, M., 2003, *Greek and Latin Letters* (Cambridge).

Treggiari, S., 1969, *Roman Freedmen under the Late Republic* (Oxford).

—— 1991, *Roman Marriage* (Oxford).

Trillitzsch, W., 1971, *Seneca im literarischen Urteil der Antike: Darstellung und Sammlung der Zeugnisse*, 2 vols. (Amsterdam).

Veyne, P., 1990, *Bread and Circuses* (London), an abridgement and translation of *Le Pain et le cirque* (Paris, 1976).

—— 2003, *Seneca: The Life of a Stoic*, trans. D. Sullivan (New York/London).

Viano, C., 1995, 'Quintiliano e la storia della filosofia: l'uso delle *quaestiones philosopho convenientes*', *Rhetorica*, 13, 193–207.

Volk, K., and Williams, G. D. (eds.), 2006, *Seeing Seneca Whole* (Leiden and Boston).

Walbank, F., 1957, *A Historical Commentary on Polybius*, i (Oxford).

—— 1998, 'A Greek Looks at Rome: Polybius VI Revisited', *Scripta Classica Israelica*, 17, 45–59.

Wallace-Hadrill, A., 1989a (ed.), *Patronage in Ancient Society* (London).

—— 1989b, 'Patronage in Roman Society: From Republic to Empire', in Wallace-Hadrill 1989a, 63–85.

—— 1996, 'The Imperial Court', *CAH* x^2, 282–308.

Wardle, D., 2006, *Cicero: On Divination Book I* (Oxford).

Watson, A., 1965, *The Law of Obligations in the Later Roman Republic* (Oxford).

—— 1968, *The Law of Property in the Later Roman Republic* (Oxford).

Watt, W. S., 1994, 'Notes on Seneca, *De beneficiis*, *De clementia*, and *Dialogi*', *Harvard Studies in Classical Philology*, 96, 225–39.

Wees, H. van, 1998, 'Reciprocity in Anthropological Theory', in Gill, Postlethwaite, and Seaford 1998, 13–49.

White, P., 1993, *Promised Verse: Poets in the Society of Augustan Rome* (Cambridge, Mass.).

Whitton, C. I., 2010, 'Pliny, *Epistles* 8.14: Senate, Slavery and the *Agricola*', *JRS* 100, 118–39.

Williams, C., 2008, 'Friends of the Roman People: Some Remarks on the Language of *amicitia*', in A. Coşkun (ed.), *Freundschaft und Gefolgschaft in den auswärtigen Beziehungen der Römer* (Frankfurt am Main, 2008), 29–44.

Wilson, M., 2001, 'Seneca's *Epistles* reclassified', in S. J. Harrison (ed.), *Texts, Ideas, and the Classics* (Oxford, 2001), 164–87.

Wind, E., 1958, 'Seneca's Graces', *Pagan Mysteries in the Renaissance* (Oxford), 26–36.

Winterbottom, M., 1974, *The Elder Seneca Declamations*, 2 vols. (Cambridge, Mass.).

Winterling, A., 1999, *Aula Caesaris: Studien zur Institutionalisierung des römischen Kaiserhofes in der Zeit von Augustus bis Commodus (31 v.Chr.–192 n.Chr.* (Munich).

Winton, R. I., and Garnsey, P., 1981, 'Political Theory', in M. I. Finley (ed.), *The Legacy of Greece: A New Appraisal* (Oxford, 1981), 37–64.

Wiseman, T. P., 2004, *Myths of Rome* (Exeter).

Woodman, A. J., 2010, '*Aliena Facundia*: Seneca in Tacitus', in D. Berry and A. Erskine (eds.), *Form and Function in Roman Oratory* (Cambridge, 2010), 294–308.

Woolf, G., 1995, 'Becoming Roman, Staying Greek', *Proceedings of the Cambridge Philological Society*, 40, 116–43.

Yakobson, A., 1999, *Elections and Electioneering in Rome* (Historia Einzelschriften, 128; Stuttgart).

Zanker, P., 1995, *The Mask of Socrates* (Berkeley).

—— 2002, 'Domitian's Palace on the Palatine and the Imperial Image', in Bowman *et al.* 2002, 105–30.

Zeller, E., 1879, *Stoics, Epicureans and Sceptics*, trans. O. J. Reichel (New York).

—— 1923, *Die Philosophie der Griechen*, iii/1 (Leipzig).

Index Locorum

(excluding passages from *De Beneficiis*)

General Index

See also the Synopses and Biographical Notes not included here. Persons marked with an * are also listed in the Biographical Notes, where the references to them in *De beneficiis* are given. Authors other than Cicero and Seneca are given under their commonly used names. [Anonymous references are given in square brackets.]

Printed and bound by CPI Group (UK) Ltd, Croydon, CR0 4YY